Third Edition

WRITING and REPORTING the NEWS

Jerry Lanson
Emerson College

Mitchell Stephens
New York University

New York   Oxford
OXFORD UNIVERSITY PRESS
2008

Oxford University Press, Inc., publishes works that further Oxford University's
objective of excellence in research, scholarship, and education.

Oxford New York
Auckland   Cape Town   Dar es Salaam   Hong Kong   Karachi
Kuala Lumpur   Madrid   Melbourne   Mexico City   Nairobi
New Delhi   Shanghai   Taipei   Toronto

With offices in
Argentina   Austria   Brazil   Chile   Czech Republic   France   Greece
Guatemala   Hungary   Italy   Japan   Poland   Portugal   Singapore
South Korea   Switzerland   Thailand   Turkey   Ukraine   Vietnam

Published by Oxford University Press, Inc.
198 Madison Avenue, New York, New York 10016
http://www.oup.com

Library of Congress Cataloging-in-Publication Data

Lanson, Jerry.
    Writing and reporting the news / by Jerry Lanson and Mitchell Stephens.—3rd ed.
        p. cm.
    Includes index.
    ISBN 978–0–19–530666–8 (pbk.)
    1. Reporters and reporting. 2. Journalism—Authorship. I. Stephens, Mitchell.
    II. Title.
    PN4781.S775 2008
    070.4'3—dc22

                                                                2007001082

Printing number: 9 8 7 6 5 4 3 2 1

Printed in the United States of America
on acid-free paper

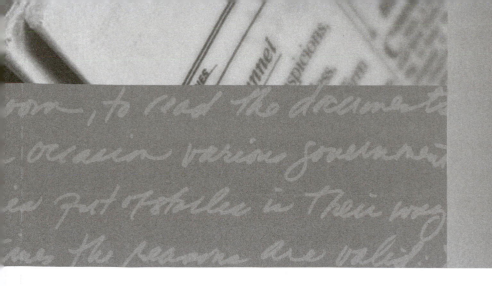

Contents

THE BASICS

Exercises

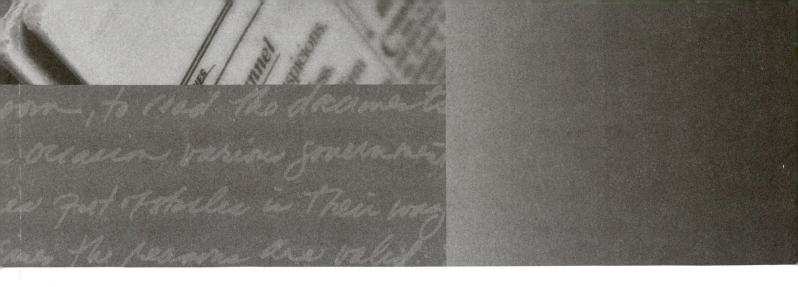

Preface

This is a book about the reporter's craft; its title makes that clear. While the delivery systems of news have changed and continue to change rapidly, and while new formats for news from blogs to podcasts crop up with regularity, we believe it is the high standards held by the best news organizations that in the end matter most. Whatever the delivery system, with news, content counts. Clarity counts. Good writing counts. Perhaps all count more than ever in a 24–7 environment of endless news updates. And so, we believe, this book continues to be a strong starting point for anyone entering the rapidly evolving world of news.

This book is unusual in that it combines thorough instruction in writing and reporting with extensive opportunities to apply that instruction. It is both a textbook and a workbook. Those who read its discussions and tackle its variety of exercises, whether to improve their writing or to prepare for careers in professional newsrooms, should come away with a clearer sense of language and how it can be used most effectively. They should also gain an understanding of what goes on in the offices, meeting rooms, courtrooms and board rooms where society's decisions are made.

We have made substantial changes in this third edition. First, we have updated the book's numerous examples and photographs. Second, we have added summaries to the end of each chapter. Third, we have interviewed a dozen additional reporters, from those in their first year or two in the field to those with Pulitzer Prizes, and asked them to offer tips on such things as developing stories and sources, covering meetings and covering medicine. Fourth, we have extended the book into an age of multimedia. We have added a chapter on writing news for the Internet, revamped the chapter on research to reflect the enormous resources and sizable risks of surfing for ideas, sources and information online, and incorporated references to important websites throughout. And finally, we have updated both pictures and recommended readings to reflect current trends in news and the news industry.

The style and philosophy of the book, however, have not changed. As the debate grows among news executives over how to bring readers and revenues from newspapers onto newspaper websites and perhaps even whether, in the coming decades, newspapers on paper will survive, we remain focused on the skills we believe audiences will always demand: intelligent information gathering and clear, compelling prose, whether in the succinct, summary approach most effective in short reports online or in the longer, story-telling forms still widely popular in newspapers.

In writing and organizing this book, we continue to try to use the techniques we are trying to teach students to use.

- The writing is designed to engage as it informs. We hope the book is, among other things, a good read.
- Each chapter attempts to break sometimes difficult procedures into their component parts. By explaining step by step how reporters go about their business, we have tried to take the mystery out of their transformations of two-month-long trials into two-column-long stories.
- The discussions are illustrated by hundreds of examples selected from scores of large and small newspapers (and their websites) around the country. We have tried to demonstrate our points, not just expound on them.
- The chapters are organized in what we believe is a logical order: building from the basics—news judgment, leads, paragraphs—to the complexities of writing and reporting longer stories.
- Our writing is based on thorough reporting, updated again for this edition. Rather than rely exclusively on our own experience, we've interviewed, and quoted, dozens of first-rate reporters. And we have tried to pass on not only their advice but a sense of the challenges, pressures and rewards of their jobs.
- Finally, this book, like a good news story, is designed to have some depth. The text emphasizes the basic stories and traditional beats—such as police and city government—on which most reporters cut their teeth. But we've also devoted substantial coverage to specialized areas—business; education; science, education and the environment—that today are just as frequently found on Page 1.

Journalism cannot be taught without a set of good assignments. The exercises in this book are intended both for beginning and somewhat more advanced reporters. Those who are just starting out might concentrate on the exercises in Parts 1–5 and initial exercises in Part 6. Those who have some experience in journalism might use the early chapters for review and concentrate on the later chapters.

We set four goals for ourselves in preparing the hundreds of assignments included here.

- First, we wanted the exercises to reflect our concern with introducing complex skills one step at a time. Readers will find plenty of fact sheets for writing leads (in Chapters 4 and 5) and stories (in Chapter 9 and all succeeding chapters). However, we have also included separate exercises on such skills as paragraphing, using transitions and quotations, translating jargon, selecting information, supporting the lead, organizing the story, and using analogies and attribution.
- Second, we wanted the exercises to be as realistic as possible. There is no Mayor Jones from Hometown, U.S.A., here; there *are* speech transcripts, police reports, announcements, interviews, press releases and masses of facts and quotes similar to those reporters must actually unscramble when the time comes to write a story. Our belief is that realistic exercises are both more meaningful and more fun.
- Third, we wanted the exercises to encourage readers to think like reporters. For example, rather than asking only that they write stories on city council meetings, we present readers with sets of questions about local government that direct them to look through government records and find and talk to sources in government. It's important to know how to write up a city council meeting, but it's also important to begin to think about where and how information on the workings of government can be found. (Though more and more is available online, many states, cities and towns do not organize it in readily accessible ways. Reporters still must know what's available and how it can be used.)

- Finally, we wanted to offer readers exercises that do more than provide opportunities to practice journalism. We wanted, simultaneously, to offer them chances to think about words and how they are used, and we wanted to encourage visits to unfamiliar but important corners of the community—the board of adjustment, civil court, the local unemployment office, community and civic leaders who hold no elected position and may occupy no office other than a neighborhood storefront. We hope our exercises are of some use in training better writers and better citizens, as well as better journalists.

We asked for help at many stages on the production of all three editions of this book. We are particularly grateful to all the thoughtful journalists—from most of the major newspapers in the United States and many of the smaller ones, as well as selected websites and academic institutions—who took the time to discuss their work with us. They include Karen Arenson, Fred Barbash, Tim Belnap, Tracy Breton, Joel Brinkley, Doreen Carvajal, Mike Cox, Jim Detjen, Stuart Diamond, Jack Encarnacao, David Espo, Maureen Fan, Thomas Farragher, Walter Fee, Jim Flagg, Tom French, Michele Fuetsch, Andrea Gabbidon-Levène, Bob Greene, Michelle Guido, Kathryn Harris, Ron Harris, Ken Herman, the late Molly Ivins, Rachel Jones, Michelle Johnson, Ric Kahn, Saundra Keyes, Jim Killackey, Paula LaRocque, Jessie Mangaliman, Brendan McCarthy, Bruce Maxwell, Don Melvin, Katie Oliveri, the late James Reston, Dale Rice, Ted Rohrlich, Doug Rainey, Louis Rose, Chris Schmidt, William Serrin, Sree Sreenivasan, Chris Welles, Leon Wynter and David Yarnold.

Although many of these reporters and editors have moved on to other jobs since we interviewed them, they are, for the most part, identified by the news organizations they worked for and the positions they held when we interviewed them.

Our special thanks in the preparation of this third edition go to Julie Polovina, our primary research assistant, who worked tirelessly in identifying and gathering the photographs that illustrate its pages, sought out several of the reporters featured in its "Lessons from the Pros" boxes, and suggested elements of the design of these boxes. Two Emerson College graduate students, Diana Schoberg and Amanda Patterson, played a significant role in seeking out pertinent and contemporary examples from newspapers around the country of the points the book seeks to make.

We are also appreciative of the thoughtful reading and useful suggestions for this edition furnished by Ira Chinoy, University of Maryland; Timothy J. Connolly, Clark University; Jean Stow Cotton, Texarkana College; Reggie Ecarma, North Greenville College; Arnold Karr, Fashion Institute of Technology; Scott McNabb, Grand Rapids Community College; Nikhil Moro, Kennesaw State University; and Richard J. Roth, Northwestern University.

Joshua Mills of Baruch College originally helped draft two of these chapters. Carey Lovelace and Hyman Bender pitched in with research on earlier editions. Drafts of chapters were read and improved by Mary Benedict, the late Richard Cunningham, Junetta Davis, Jo Ann Dickerson, Arthur Engoron, the late Herb Jackson, Eleanor Lang, Alan Neckowitz, Cecil Neth, Robert Odom, Cynthia Rawitch, Ted Rohrlich, David Rubin and Laurie Ruskin.

We have been delighted to work with a strong group of editors at Oxford University Press. The book was significantly improved by their dedication, energy and thoughtfulness. Thanks to John Carey, Chelsea Gilmore, Lisa Grzan, Josh Hawkins, Peter Labella and Sean Mahoney.

Our wives, Kathy Lanson and Esther Davidowitz, one an educator, the other a journalist, have read copy, saved us from errors and helped keep us smiling through it all. The book is dedicated to them, with love.

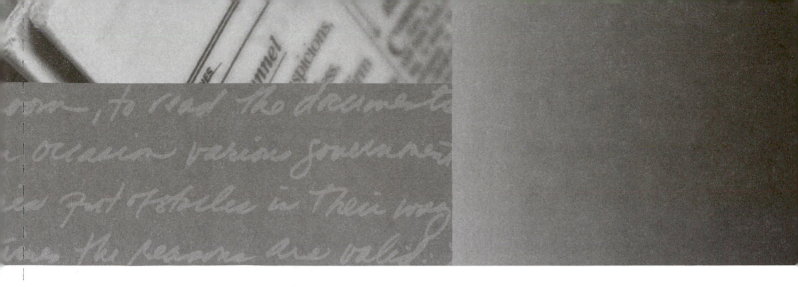

Newspapers and Wire Services

The discussions in this book are illustrated by examples drawn from the stories and comments of the staffs of the following newspapers (we have occasionally made minor changes in the printed examples so that they conform with the style used in the text):

Wire Services

Associated Press
Knight-Ridder News Service
New York Times News Service
Newsday Service
Reuters
United Press International
Washington Post News Service

Newspapers (by state)

Alabama
   The Birmingham News
Arizona
   The Arizona Republic
Arkansas
   Arkansas Gazette
California
   Los Angeles Times
   Sacramento Bee
   San Diego Union
   San Diego Union-Tribune
   San Francisco Chronicle
   San Jose Mercury News
Colorado
   Rocky Mountain News
   The Denver Post

Connecticut
   Hartford Courant
D.C.
   The Washington Post
   The Washington Times
Florida
   St. Petersburg Times
   The Miami Herald
   The Orlando Sentinel
   Sun-Sentinel
Georgia
   The Atlanta Constitution
Illinois
   Sun-Times
   Chicago Tribune
Indiana
   The Indianapolis Star
Iowa
   The Des Moines Register
Kansas
   The Hutchinson News
   The Wichita Eagle
Kentucky
   The Courier-Journal
Louisiana
   The Daily Advertiser
   The Times-Picayune

Maine
Bangor Daily News
Massachusetts
The Boston Globe
Quincy Patriot Ledger
Maryland
The Sun
Michigan
Battle Creek Enquirer
Detroit Free Press
Minnesota
Rochester Post-Bulletin
The Minneapolis Star and Tribune
St. Paul Pioneer Press
Missouri
St. Louis Post-Dispatch
Nebraska
Omaha World-Herald
Nevada
Las Vegas Review-Journal
Reno Gazette-Journal
New Jersey
Asbury Park Press
The New Jersey Herald
The Record
The News
Trenton Times
New Mexico
Albuquerque Journal
New York
Times Union
Newsday
Daily News
New York Post
The New York Times
Post Standard
The Public Employee Press
Saratogian-Tri-County News
The Register
The Rockland Journal-News
The Westsider
North Carolina
The News & Observer
The Charlotte Observer
Ohio
The Columbus Dispatch
The Plain Dealer
The Toledo Blade

Oklahoma
The Daily Oklahoman
Tulsa World
Oregon
The Oregonian
Pennsylvania
The Express
The Philadelphia Inquirer
The Philadelphia Daily News
Rhode Island
The Providence Bulletin
The Providence Journal
South Carolina
The Post and Courier
The State
Tennessee
The Commercial Appeal
The Tennessean
Texas
Austin American-Statesman
Dallas Times Herald
Houston Chronicle
Lufkin News
The Dallas Morning News
Vermont
The Burlington Free Press
Washington
The Seattle Times
Spokane Spokesman-Review
Virginia
Richmond Times-Dispatch
Roanoke Times & World-News
West Virginia
Bluefield Daily Telegraph
Charleston Gazette
Wisconsin
La Crosse Tribune
The Milwaukee Journal
Milwaukee Journal-Sentinel
National
The Christian Science Monitor
The Wall Street Journal
USA Today
Canada
The Toronto Sun

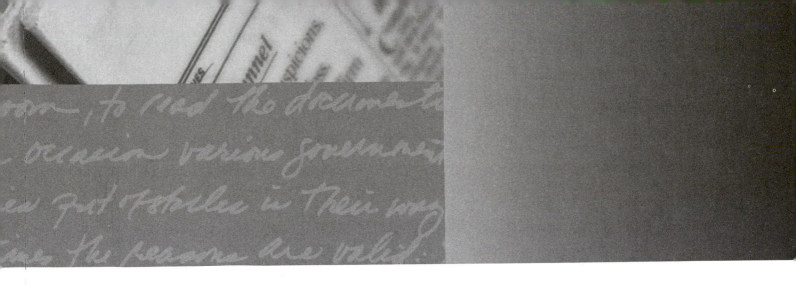

Introduction

> With county health insurance bills topping $5 million this year, the Bergen County freeholders say they can't afford to let Diane Belka, a widow with a 15-year-old daughter, work an extra hour a week to qualify for medical benefits.
>
> Mrs. Belka, a part-time clerk from Lyndhurst, is among 22 county employees kept on a 19-hour work week, one short of the 20 needed for insurance coverage under state regulations.
>
> Yet the freeholders provide health benefits to some of their political friends at public expense, even though these friends work fewer than 20 hours a week—if they work at all. . . .

These paragraphs began a three-part series in *The* (Bergen County, N.J.) *Record* exposing a scam Republican county officials apparently used to reward political appointees.

The series, by reporter Michele Fuetsch, had some impact: Five political appointees were dropped from the county payroll; some changes were contemplated in the county's hiring policy; and the county prosecutor launched an investigation. But the fuss soon faded. The Democrats had unseated the Republican majority in an election just before the story ran. And as the prosecutor's investigation dragged on, the Democrats continued some of the same questionable practices. Fuetsch, who covered county government for *The Record*, found herself facing the chore of investigating the Democrats, too.

Fuetsch's series won second place in a state journalism contest. But she was offered no book contracts. She made no television appearances. Hollywood never called. After all, first-rate reporters have been exposing similar scams almost as long as second-rate politicians have been devising them. Certainly, there was nothing glamorous about Fuetsch's reporting. She spent most of her time reading computer printouts and talking with county workers. Her articles, in other words, were nothing more and nothing less than good, solid journalism—the type of journalism this book is seeking to encourage.

The first clue to Fuetsch's story emerged at a meeting in which she overheard the county personnel director mention that part-time workers were being kept on a 19-hour week because they would qualify for medical benefits if they worked 20 hours or more. Interesting.

Fuetsch went to interview the personnel director. He noted, off-handedly, that despite this policy of holding down the cost of benefits, some part-time political appointees *were* allowed to receive medical coverage. Very interesting.

Fuetsch contacted someone she knew and trusted in county government, one of her *sources*. He mentioned the name of a part-time political appointee who, sure enough, was getting medical benefits—benefits worth more than his salary.

"I felt like a detective who had found a body but who had absolutely no idea who the person was or how the person died," Fuetsch recalls. She believed she was onto a story, but getting the story and pinning it down would take hundreds of hours of work, done in the rare free moments she could find between covering meetings, speeches, fund-raising dinners and campaign appearances.

First, she waded though a four-inch-thick computer printout listing about 3,000 county employees. Fuetsch was looking for people with low salaries—part-time employees. There were hundreds of them. Then she had to find out whether these employees qualified as political appointees. Did they have any regular responsibilities? Did they even bother to show at some county office? Political appointees, she was learning, often did not. It took Fuetsch five weeks to get through all the names on the printout. Tracking down a single part-timer sometimes took dozens of phone calls. When she was finished, Fuetsch had a pile of blue index cards as thick as a healthy Sunday newspaper, with the name of a county employee on each.

The next question was what benefits, if any, the people on her cards were taking advantage of and how much they were costing the county. To calculate the value of medical benefits, she needed the age of each of the employees plus details of their family situations. This required a search of county personnel records and many more dozens of phone calls. The blue cards were filling up.

Fuetsch interviewed all the suspect employees and the people who had hired them to give them a chance to comment on her findings. And she talked with numerous other people at all levels of government—from guards she had befriended at the county office building (many county workers were anxious to help expose this patronage scheme) to the state's pension director. She spent so much time at the county office building interviewing and digging through personnel records that one of the janitors assumed she worked there.

"By the end of my investigation," Fuetsch says, picking up the analogy to a detective on a murder case, "I had the entire life history of that murder victim, and I knew who murdered him."

Her blue cards were covered with facts, but molding those facts into a lively series of stories would take additional weeks. Fuetsch would have to guide readers through the intricacies of health plans. She would have to pare down the information she had worked so hard to gather so that it could be conveyed in three articles, each filled with about 2,000 well-chosen words. "Readability was uppermost in my mind," Fuetsch says. "Each impropriety had to be explained with concrete examples."

In working on this series, Michele Fuetsch demonstrated a number of the qualities that good reporters must have: curiosity, a healthy skepticism, attention to detail, and the ability to work with sources and use public records. She also showed the ability to write clearly and accurately about what she had found.

These are crucial qualities for anyone who gathers and communicates information for the public about the public's business, qualities that will be referred to many times in this book. But we choose this example primarily for another reason: because it shows how hard reporting is.

Often moving the news is exciting. Occasionally, reporters even have the satisfaction, as Michele Fuetsch did, of exposing one of the little tricks people in power play when the public's back is turned. But journalism, if it's being done well, is *always* difficult. It requires long hours tracking down sources, talking with people whose reputation you may be about to assault, reading through often tedious records, checking and rechecking facts. "You do your homework," is how James Reston, the legendary *New York Times* columnist, bureau chief, and editor used to put it.

"I've been able to reach the position I'm in simply by working harder than other reporters," asserts Stuart Diamond, an English major in college who became a well-respected environment writer for *Newsday* on Long Island, N.Y. and then for *The New York Times.*

Good reporters study the fields they are covering. They spend whatever spare time they can muster reading relevant records, documents and journals. They are always looking for one more knowledgeable source. "You have to be willing to make the extra phone calls," advises David Espo, who has worked his way from the Associated Press's Cheyenne, Wyo., bureau to the AP's bureau in Washington. "If you make a perfunctory effort, you're going to get a perfunctory story."

Good reporters also take great pains with the writing of their stories. They strain for slightly more exact, slightly more graceful wordings. They are brutal, unforgiving editors ... of their own work. "I think the people who really make it in journalism are the ones who try to make every story special, who don't kiss off anything," says Joel Brinkley, who won a Pulitzer Prize for *The Courier-Journal* in Louisville, Ky., well before he turned 30.

To say that Michele Fuetsch, in uncovering that medical benefits scam, was both a good reporter and a hard-working reporter is redundant. Tenacity, thoroughness and tirelessness are a large part of what good reporting is all about.

An essay on the value of hard work might not seem the most inspiring introduction for a journalism textbook. Why not begin by recalling the glories of the press's investigation of Watergate or by quoting Thomas Jefferson on the importance of a free press? But then we believe there *is* something inspiring in the notion that in newspaper journalism industriousness pays off, that effort—more than wealth, looks, connections, maybe even more than talent—is the key to success.

This discussion of the difficulties of journalism should also be reassuring. If beginning reporters find themselves struggling, under deadline pressure, to pin down a fact or find the right word, it is not a sign that they aren't cut out for a career in journalism. Rather it is an indication that they have joined the struggle for precision in perception and expression that *is* the practice of journalism at its best. If the writing and reporting assignments in the chapters that follow seem too easy, *that* may be cause for worry.

WRITING and REPORTING the NEWS

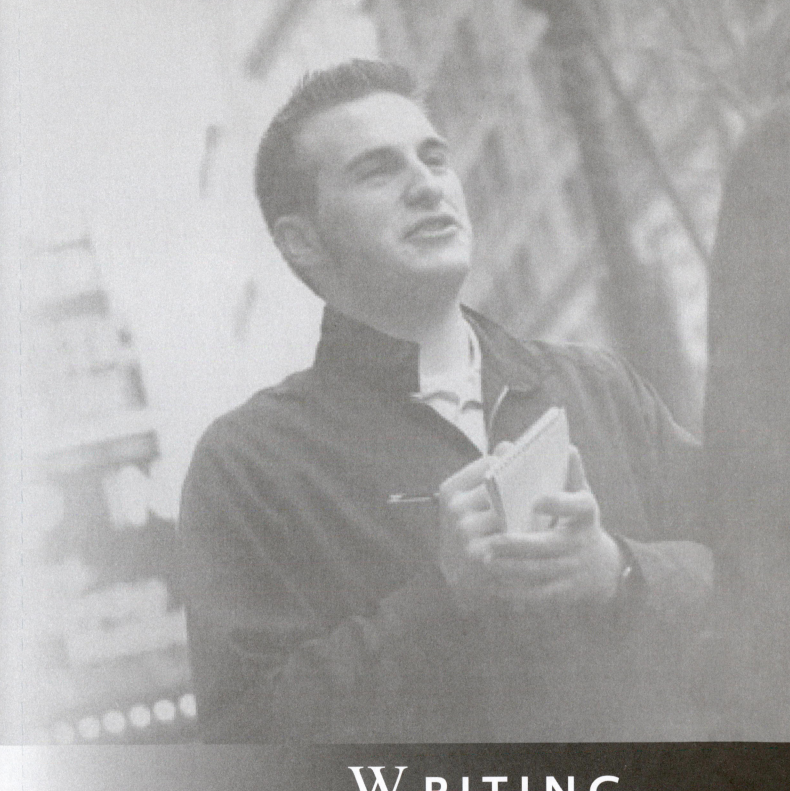

WRITING

PART 1 THE NEWS

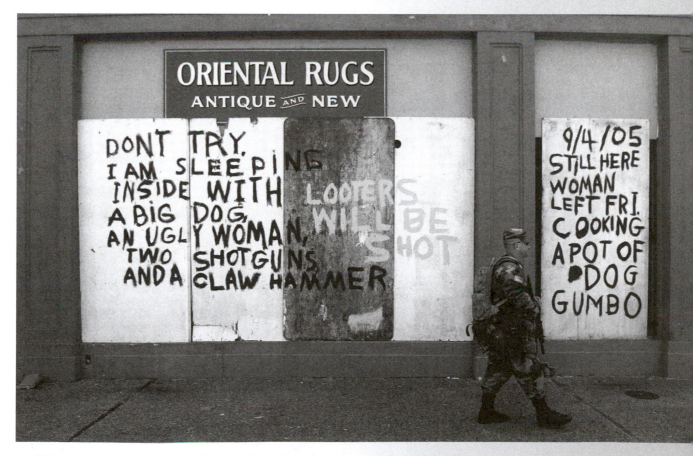

An Oklahoma National Guardsman walks past a New Orleans business with a message for looters.
(*Photo by Ellis Lucia © 2005 The Times-Picayune Publishing Co., all rights reserved. Used with permission of* The
[*New Orleans*] Times-Picayune.)

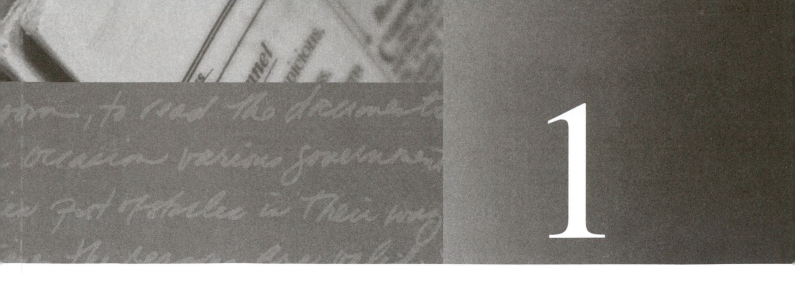

News Judgment

As sleepy Sundays go, Oct. 20, 1991, looked as if it would be a decent local news day at the *San Jose* (Calif.) *Mercury News*. KFAT, an old rock-and-roll station in South Santa Clara County, was throwing an anniversary party. Mention of an aborted landing at San Jose International Airport crackled over police radio. And it was hot, hot enough for a story on new temperature records for the day.

Not big news, but news enough to merit coverage by the three local reporters who were on duty—until flames leapt from the Oakland hills and began devouring some of the most stately houses in the Bay area.

Firefighters survey devastation caused by the Oakland hills fire.
(*Courtesy of the* San Jose Mercury News. *Photo by Eugene Louie.*)

Reporter Mary Anne Ostrom was on her way to report on KFAT's birthday when she heard a radio report about the fire. Ostrom and a staff photographer immediately turned around and headed for a helicopter. (The reporter would later file a story about watching the fire's horrific advance from the air.) Ernie Torriero, a reporter who was still in the newsroom, quickly began studying maps and monitoring radio and television.

Editor Jerry Lanson, one of the authors of this book, stopped three paragraphs into a weather story ("The Bay area sizzled Sunday....") and started calling reporter after reporter at home, directing them to hospitals, shelters, fire-command posts and the fire's rapidly spreading flanks.

By morning, news of the Oakland hills firestorm—a frenzied explosion of flames that killed 25 people and incinerated thousands of homes—would fill six full pages of the *Mercury News*.

Nothing appeared in the paper that Monday about the KFAT reunion, not one word about why a plane had aborted a landing in San Jose. There was no story about the late-fall heat wave. The fire, as everyone in the newsroom had immediately realized, was simply more *newsworthy*.

This was an easy call. Every day, journalists must make similar, often more difficult, choices about what readers want or need to know. In fact, *news judgment* is an indispensable skill at all levels of journalism. Editors need this skill to decide which of the flood of press releases and tips they get every day are worth pursuing, and which stories in each day's paper deserve the most prominence. Reporters need it to help find stories and to determine which aspects of these stories they should focus on. Writers need it to decide which of the facts they have collected they should *lead* with—use in their first paragraph.

Most journalists take their *news sense* for granted. Many maintain that news judgment comes only through experience. We disagree. We believe there are two things beginning reporters can do to improve their sense of what's news.

First, reporters can study the news. A familiarity with the news is necessary to understand its habits and special preferences. Anyone considering a job in journalism should read, and read

Firefighters from several Michigan-area departments battle a house fire in Emmett Township. (*Photo by John Grap*, Battle Creek Enquirer)

critically, at least one newspaper (in print or online) every day. As often as possible, that paper should be one of the country's best—such as *The New York Times*, *The Washington Post*, the *Los Angeles Times* or *The Wall Street Journal*. It's also necessary to follow national and local broadcast newscasts and to read at least one of the weekly news magazines.

A second technique for learning news judgment is to analyze in detail the qualities that make something newsworthy. That is what this chapter does. It breaks down that abstract attribute—newsworthiness—into eleven somewhat less mystical qualities: impact, weight, controversy, emotion, the unusual, prominence, proximity, timeliness, currency, usefulness, and educational value.

IMPACT

On a routine day, the Milwaukee Common Council's decision to approve the sale of an old junior high school for conversion to a shelter for the homeless might have begun, or *led*, a local reporter's story. But at the same meeting, the council also approved a plan to change winter parking rules throughout the city. The parking change affected more readers' lives. It had greater *impact* on the community. And it is the news the reporter began with:

> The Milwaukee Common Council has approved permanent one-side-only parking for much of the city from Dec. 1 to March 1.
>
> *The Milwaukee Journal*

The school sale was mentioned, but lower in the story.

Reporters are constantly measuring what effect events have on their readers. A tiny fly can be more newsworthy than a space-shuttle landing if that fly and its offspring have a taste for fruit and you are writing for a newspaper in a fruit-producing region.

Political and economic stories receive so much attention because they frequently have a profound impact on our lives. A vote on Social Security benefits can swell or shrink the monthly check received by many readers. A slight fluctuation in the prime lending rate may ultimately make it more difficult for readers to buy a home or find a job.

All other things being equal—and they rarely are—facts and events with the greatest impact on the most readers have the greatest news value.

WEIGHT

Fourteen persons in Nassau County, N.Y., were charged with welfare fraud. But two of them, a husband and wife, were accused of defrauding the county out of more money than the other 12 combined. Their alleged crime had more weight; it deserved more emphasis than the charges against the other suspects.

> A Freeport husband and wife who Nassau County officials say cheated the county out of more than $133,000 in welfare payments over an 11-year period were among 14 persons charged yesterday with welfare fraud.
>
> (Long Island, N.Y.) *Newsday*

Loss of life has more weight than injury, and injuries generally are more newsworthy than loss of property:

> A taxi driver was shot and wounded during a holdup early yesterday morning in North Philadelphia.
>
> *The Philadelphia Inquirer*

The taxi driver in this story was robbed of $30, a fact that is clearly outweighed by his injury. (Without the injury, this story would not have made the newspaper.)

A murder has more weight than a robbery, a robbery more weight than a burglary. The weight required for a story to make the newspaper will vary depending on the size of the city or town in which that paper circulates. *Austin American-Statesman* reporter Mike Cox notes that murders are definitely news in Austin, Texas. But Cox remembers a Houston reporter joking that there were so many homicides in his city that "if it doesn't have to do with voodoo, I'm not interested."

Some stories are newsworthy because they have historical weight. The gradual erosion of the Parthenon in Athens because of air pollution has little direct impact on American readers. But it has historical significance, and many papers have printed reports about it.

While flying over the Oakland hills fire, *San Jose Mercury News* reporter Mary Anne Ostrom spotted "the unmistakable profile of the Claremont Hotel" standing "defiantly against the blackened sky." She mentioned the hotel in her story, but Ostrom's story began by describing a "ridge-top neighborhood reduced to nothing." That had much more weight.

CONTROVERSY

The news loves arguments, debates, charges, countercharges and all-out fights. Newspapers rarely pay much attention to the pace at which governmental organizations spend their money, but if a congresswoman attacks that pace, it becomes controversial; it becomes news.

> The Cuyahoga Metropolitan Housing Authority has been awarded $1.7 million in federal grants to upgrade properties, but it isn't spending the money fast enough to suit one critic.
>
> The (Cleveland) *Plain Dealer*

By the same token, a city official praising members of the Board of Selectmen likely won't make news. But if city officials attack members of that board, that's news.

> The Board of Selectmen came under fire last week, as 12 town department heads issued a "vote of no confidence" letter against two members, accusing them of airing personal conflicts in public.
>
> The Boston Globe

EMOTION

Some news appeals directly to our emotions. Deaths of young children are treated as especially newsworthy because they are especially moving. A New Jersey fire in which five people died might not ordinarily have made the front page of the second section of *The New York Times*. But it became a bigger story because all five victims were children:

> Five children, including a 4-month-old boy lost when his mother stumbled during a desperate escape attempt, were killed in a house fire early today.
>
> Associated Press in *The New York Times*

Heroic exploits—a passerby capturing an alleged mugger, balloonists crossing the Pacific— also touch our emotions. So, too, do stories about tragedy and survival.

These stories often have much more resonance with readers if they key on one life, one individual's experience, rather than overwhelming with statistics. When the Spokane, Wash., city council decided to close a transient boarding house in that city, reporters for the *Spokane*

Spokesman-Review gave the story emotion, and humanity, by profiling some of those who would be displaced. Here is how one such story, no more than 350 words, began.

> Katherine Williams* crouches on the seventh stair of the Merlin Apartments, thin legs pulled against her 16-year-old stomach, insides cramping.
>
> She's dope sick. Not from withdrawal, but from injecting cocaine she suspects was cut with lidocaine, a local anesthetic.

"The stories that survive are usually short, precisely limited, and clearly focused," notes author and former writing coach Donald Murray in *Writing for Your Readers*. He means "survive" in our memories, get talked about. "Most good stories say one thing. They tell not of a battle but of a soldier; they talk not about governance, but a deal: they discuss not a socio-economic group, but reveal a person and a life."

Finally, while no major American daily will print smut, stories with a hint of sex have their appeal, too. This murder trial was widely covered, in part, no doubt, because it was steamy:

> One of Anna Arlington's* alleged lovers testified about a sexual interlude with her as prosecutors pressed forward yesterday at the murder trial of the Orange County woman accused of poisoning her wealthy husband with painkillers.
>
> *Richmond (Va.) Times-Dispatch*

Readers are not always concerned only with what is most important. Reporters must take into account these human interests.

THE UNUSUAL

Ron Dowdy's 50th birthday would not normally have been mentioned in *The Orlando* (Fla.) *Sentinel*. Scores of people turn 50 every day in central Florida. But Ron's wife and his secretary chose to advertise the event. That is unusual. That is news:

> A billboard on Interstate 4 near the Fairbanks Avenue exit proclaims, "Ain't it nifty? Ron Dowdy is 50!"
>
> *The Orlando Sentinel*

Firsts, largests and leasts make news: the first derailment in the 30-year history of a passenger railroad line, the highest highway death toll ever on a Labor Day weekend, the least rain ever to fall here in April. And, once a year:

> Shortly after midnight Friday, Kathy Bigoni of West Linn gave birth to Portland's first babies of the year.
>
> *The (Portland) Oregonian*

That the first babies born in Portland that year were twins made it even more unusual, bigger news. The Bigoni babies were featured in the lead story in the paper's Metro section.

The unusual is the news judgment standard that explains the old journalism cliché: "When a dog bites a man, it's not news. But when a man bites a dog, it is news." The cliché still holds:

> When Los Angeles County sheriff's deputies sent their dog sniffing into the bushes

---

* *The name in this story has been changed.*

for the driver of an apparently stolen van in Carson early Monday, neither they nor he realized the incident would meet the criteria for news.

Chris, an 8-year-old Rottweiler, quickly located Jose Martinez,* 26, and grabbed him by the leg.

Martinez, deputies reported, bit back.

Los Angeles Times

PROMINENCE

The birth of your average zoo animal doesn't warrant a story, let alone one on the front page. But news in the animal world is no more democratic than news among people. The *prominent* get more attention:

Hua Mei, San Diego's beloved first panda baby, is now a mom.

San Diego Union-Tribune

Events in the lives of particularly well-known people also are given particular attention by the press. Newspapers in the United States would have no interest in the story of a man who snuck into the bedroom of an ordinary woman and chatted for ten minutes. But when that woman is the Queen of England, the story becomes front-page news in major newspapers around the world.

Relatively minor arrests don't make Page 6 of a big-city newspaper unless the person arrested is prominent:

White Sox outfielder Biff Henderson was arrested yesterday at his North Side apartment on narcotics and weapons violations charges.*

(Chicago) *Sun-Times*

PROXIMITY

The Nuclear Regulatory Commission had released a list of nuclear plants with a special problem and had ranked them in order of the seriousness of the problem. The problem was most severe, the NRC said, at a plant in Hartsville, S.C. But when a New York newspaper reported the story, it concentrated instead on the 7th and 15th plants on that list:

The reactor walls of some nuclear power plants—including Indian Point 3 in Westchester and the Ginna plant near Rochester—are becoming dangerously brittle and may rupture unless "modifications" are made, the Nuclear Regulatory Commission staff warned in a report yesterday.

(New York) *Daily News*

Why Westchester and Rochester rather than Hartsville? They are in New York state. The problems of plants there are of more local interest than the potentially more serious troubles of a reactor in Hartsville, S.C.

Readers are interested in the problems of people and places they know. All other things being equal, the closer the news is, the bigger it is.

---

* The name in this story has been changed.

The defeat of a councilman in San Francisco warrants a significant story in local papers, but it may not be mentioned in the *Los Angeles Times*. One death in the newspaper's readership area often will command more attention than half-a-dozen deaths in another state. And the closing of one small soda plant in town may be more newsworthy than the closing of a major automotive plant in Detroit.

TIMELINESS

The news is impatient. Yesterday's headlines fade fast. Monday's dramatic murder may not even be newsworthy enough to mention in the paper again Thursday.

Most news that appears in daily newspapers happened either yesterday or today. Even in major stories, such as natural disasters, the news each succeeding day must emphasize what is new; the reporter must search for a fresh, more timely aspect of the story—a *second-day angle*.

Here is a first-day story on what would become one of the biggest American news stories in the early twenty-first century:

> Whirling ashore like a destructive pinwheel, Hurricane Katrina delivered a hard but glancing blow Monday to New Orleans, then spent its full fury on the Mississippi Gulf Coast, swamping beach resorts and inland towns. At least 58 deaths were reported, most in Mississippi.
> Public officials feared that deaths from Katrina would rise.
>
> *Los Angeles Times*

Notice how the *Times* continued to advance the story on the second and third days as more information became available.

Day 2

> Across the storm-devastated Gulf Coast, overwhelmed rescue teams and public officials struggled Tuesday to cope with the enormity of Hurricane Katrina's rising toll of chaos and death. New Orleans sank into crisis as floodwaters rushing through breached levees endangered hundreds of storm victims, while searchers in Mississippi's ravaged shore towns recovered 100 bodies and pressed to find scores of missing.
>
> *Los Angeles Times*

Day 3

> The city's police and emergency officials worked desperately Wednesday to prevent complete social disintegration as widespread looting continued for a second day and cresting floodwaters hid untold numbers of dead.
>
> *Los Angeles Times*

The news keeps changing.

CURRENCY

The news must also take into account what's on people's minds. When Thanksgiving is approaching, a story about a new technique for breeding turkeys becomes more newsworthy. As April 15 gets nearer, we're a bit more likely to hear about proposals to change the tax laws.

The New York *Daily News* might have found room on another day for a story on a man from Colorado who became seriously ill after swallowing three apparently contaminated headache

Downtown New Orleans lies underwater after Hurricane Katrina breached the city's levees.
(*Photo by P. C. Piazza of* The [*Lafayette, La.*] Daily Advertiser.)

tablets. But the story made Page 3 because five people had recently died from contaminated Tylenol capsules:

> A Denver-area man who took three Extra Strength Excedrin capsules apparently contaminated with toxic mercuric chloride was in critical condition today in a Denver-area hospital.

Readers were worried about contaminated medicines. Therefore, the importance of anything relating to that subject was magnified.

Reporters and editors sometimes look for a current event or trend that will enable them to investigate ordinarily less newsworthy subjects. The Tylenol deaths, for example, provided such a *news peg* for discussions of the problem of packaging over-the-counter drugs in such a way that they cannot be tampered with. Similarly, the death from starvation of an elderly man might provide a news peg for a discussion of the problem of poverty among the elderly.

USEFULNESS

- How do produce prices compare at local supermarkets?
- Who do doctors go to when they get sick?
- What is the best way to invest your money with interest rates falling?
- When and where will the school board be holding its meeting on that new grading system?

Readers regularly turn to their local newspaper to help them solve problems and answer basic questions about their daily lives. They find these answers in weather maps showing them whether that storm front has arrived at their vacation destination. They find answers in *information boxes* telling them where to donate to holiday food banks. They find answers in weekend entertainment listings, which tell them, as one *St. Paul* (Minnesota) *Pioneer Press* headline promised, "ten great things to do."

Providing the practical may not be the most stimulating assignment a reporter will work on. But there's little, if anything, that readers want more than "news you can use."

Worried about your kid's fever?

> Experts say that undue attention to a child's temperature and mishandling of fevers generate a great deal of unwarranted parental anxiety, avoidable medical complications and countless calls and costly visits to doctors, clinics and emergency rooms....
>
> A child's temperature would have to soar to over 106.5 degrees Fahrenheit before there is danger of brain damage or death.
>
> *The New York Times*

Your curiosity piqued on promises of get-rich-quick opportunities?

> Be careful! Clever people have designed ways to cash in on the millions who are in your situation. Some job-finding offers are almost sure rip-offs, such as "900" number job lists....
>
> "Beware of employment ads directing applicants to call '900' numbers," warns the Federal Trade Commissioner. "You will be charged either a flat fee or a per-minute charge."
>
> *The (Bergen County, N.J.) Record*

EDUCATIONAL VALUE

As journalists attempt to reflect on, as well as react to, an often puzzling world, more and more stories are being written that are designed to make us more knowledgeable rather than merely better informed.

"You want to make some sense out of the things that are in the news," is how *Philadelphia Inquirer* science writer Jim Detjen puts it. "If the weather is all screwed up, I might do a piece on El Niño and other ocean currents, and consider what effect they might have on the weather."

The better newspapers today aren't merely telling readers that more severe hurricanes are reaching landfall. They are discussing why and to what extent the increase can be tied to global warming. They aren't merely reporting the ebb and flow of gasoline prices. They're looking at issues of supply and increasing global demand. And they increasingly are explaining how such seemingly arcane institutions as the Federal Reserve Board influence the direction of the American economy.

Perhaps newspapers are becoming less hesitant about telling us what they think we should know rather than just what they think we want to know. Or perhaps we as readers are demanding to be told more. Whichever is the case, newspapers have gone into the business of educating:

> LUANDA, Angola—For those who view Africa as a chessboard of opposed forces, Angola is a critical piece.
>
> It is not, perhaps, the dominant piece in the region—in economic and military terms, that would be South Africa—but it is certainly a principal warrior in black Africa's campaign in South Africa....

This piece, which devoted some 30 paragraphs to discussing Angola's place in Africa, appeared in *The New York Times* during a time in which there was no compelling reason for writing about Angola. The country was relatively peaceful; no event had thrust it into the news. Yet the paper considered it a good time to reflect on the balance of power in that part of the world.

An understanding of these eleven qualities will not answer all questions of news judgment. It is unlikely that you could program them into a computer and get the computer to select the correct angle for a story. For one thing, these qualities will often have to be weighed against one another.

A legislature may have voted to provide a scholarship fund for the children of a policeman killed on duty (emotional appeal) on the same day that it approved a new welfare office in your town (proximity) and voted to raise the sales tax by a percentage point statewide (impact). Which angle should be emphasized in a story about the legislature's actions? It takes common sense to balance these different considerations. Here common sense says lead with the sales tax increase. Its widespread impact on the price of most purchases in the state outweighs the emotional appeal and local interest of the other two actions. (The welfare office might warrant its own, smaller, story.)

CHAPTER 1 SUMMARY: NEWS JUDGMENT

Reporters need to develop good *news judgment* to determine the *newsworthy* elements of a story. Establishing the best angle for a story means understanding what makes the story relevant to readers. Without news judgment, a reporter can report thoroughly, write diligently and still miss the story's main point.

Here are some tips for honing your news judgment:

- Death is more newsworthy than injury, and injuries generally carry more weight than monetary loss.
- Firsts, largests and leasts often make news.
- Today's story might not be news tomorrow. The news must be timely.
- A fatal accident close to home typically will trump a bigger accident far away.
- The unusual, seasonal and controversial all make news.
- News stories that help readers solve problems are important.
- Journalists are placing increasing emphasis on explaining the how and why of events rather than just the what.

ADDITIONAL READING

Newsthinking: The Secret of Making Your Facts Fall into Place, Bob Baker, Allyn & Bacon, 2001.

Beyond the Inverted Pyramid, George Kennedy, Daryl R. Moen and Don Ranly, St. Martin's Press, 2002.

News in a New Century, Jerry Lanson and Barbara Croll Fought, Pine Forge Press, 1999.

Writing for Your Readers, 2nd ed., Donald Murray, Globe Pequot Press; 1992.

EXERCISE A

Check the item with greater news value, all other things being equal, in each of the following pairs.

1 _____ City Council met from 8 to 10 p.m. tonight.

   _____ City Council increases fine for illegal parking $10.

2 _____ Hurricane headed toward this city.

   _____ Two die as hurricane hits Caribbean island.

3 _____ New flyweight boxing champion.

   _____ New heavyweight boxing champion.

4 _____ Drugstore robbed, $10,000 stolen.

   _____ Shoe store robbed, $50 stolen, owner killed.

5 _____ "Decent business people are the backbone of this town's economy," said president of local Chamber of Commerce.

   _____ "Greedy business people are ruining this town's economy," said president of local Chamber of Commerce.

6 _____ Car kills woman hurrying home for Christmas dinner.

   _____ Car kills woman hurrying to dentist's appointment.

7 _____ Police still investigating death of two infants two days ago.

   _____ Teen-ager dies today, police to investigate.

8 _____ Mayor's limousine sideswipes woman's car causing $100 in damages.

   _____ Two cars collide downtown causing $2,000 in damages.

9 _____ Fifteen-year-old boy criticizes governor's politics.

   _____ Governor criticizes 15-year-old boy's politics.

10 _____ Five cases of malaria reported here, no deaths.

   _____ Five die from malaria in India.

11 _____ Lunar eclipse can be seen in town tonight.

   _____ New movie can be seen in town tonight.

12 _____ Two people found starved to death on Dec. 1.

   _____ Two people found starved to death on Dec. 25.

13 _____ Seventy-eight-year-old woman raped.

   _____ Twenty-eight-year-old woman raped.

14 ____ Eight-year-old found dead in collapsed building.

____ Uncle of 8-year-old found dead in collapsed building.

15 ____ New progress on cancer treatment.

____ New progress on bird flu treatment.

16 ____ Legislature passes new tax.

____ Legislature designates Monday "Househusbands Day."

17 ____ Policewoman sues for sex discrimination.

____ Policeman sues for sex discrimination.

18 ____ Mayor fires fire commissioner.

____ Mayor hires new fire commissioner.

19 ____ Federal Reserve says it will lower interest rates.

____ Dow Jones Index up seven points.

20 ____ City's baseball team wins fourth straight.

____ State college basketball team makes final round of national basketball playoffs—"the final four."

21 ____ Long lines at unemployment office the day stock market suffers record loses.

____ Long lines at unemployment office the day after local team loses the World Series.

22 ____ Local professor comes up with new explanation for formation of the solar system.

____ Local teen-ager wins award for magazine sales.

23 ____ City Council votes to increase department heads' salaries.

____ City Council votes to increase its members' own salaries.

24 ____ Widely used painkiller found ineffective.

____ Experimental glaucoma treatment found ineffective.

25 ____ Alleged robber shot by policeman.

____ Policeman shot by alleged robber.

EXERCISE B

Indicate by writing an *M* which item in each of these sets has the *most* news value; indicate by writing an *L* which has the *least* news value. (Again assume that all other considerations are equal.)

1 _____ Jury selection.

_____ Testimony of key witness.

_____ Verdict.

2 _____ Local football team's coach fired.

_____ Local football team wins preseason game.

_____ Local football team wins regular season game.

_____ Local football team wins Super Bowl.

3 _____ "We made a mistake," mayor says.

_____ "We were right," mayor says.

_____ "They made a mistake," mayor says.

4 At a board of education meeting:

_____ Disciplinary action taken against a principal.

_____ Disciplinary action taken against a teacher.

_____ Disciplinary action taken against a student.

5 In raid on allegedly illegal gambling club:

_____ Minister arrested.

_____ Teacher arrested.

_____ Businessman arrested.

2

Fairness

When whole city blocks are burned to the ground, as they were in the Oakland hills fire, the people charged with protecting them come under a lot of criticism. It's incumbent on reporters not only to air the criticism but to give officials a chance to respond. That's exactly what the *San Jose Mercury News* did the day after the fire:

> Oakland fire officials requested help at an almost leisurely pace during the critical first hours of the fierce wildfire that charred the East Bay hills, neighboring fire departments and state agencies said....
> Oakland fire officials denied that they were slow to call for help.
> "When you look at a situation from afar it's easy to second-guess what should have been done," said Lt. Mark Garcia of the Oakland Fire Department.

Reporters at American newspapers are expected to strive to be fair. That means giving a fair hearing to the different sides on an issue, no matter what the reporter's personal opinion.

Opinions *are* voiced in newspapers. Editorial writers are allowed to take swings at politicians. Columnists are invited to sound off on pressing issues. The Ann Landers column is free to offer advice on dealing with a brooding spouse or an oppressive father-in-law. But, even in this era of blogs and all-talk-all-the-time television, almost all American newspapers strive to keep opinion out of their *news* columns and, therefore, out of the writing with which this book is concerned. *The New York Times* may rail against domestic surveillance on its editorial pages. But it is expected to capture the arguments of those for and against it in the paper's news coverage. That's fairness as defined at most American newspapers.

This strict line between news and opinion was not always honored or even drawn. In the days when news organizations were small enough to reflect the personalities of individual printers and when there were enough papers to ensure that most points of view would be represented, newspapers were not shy about mixing their news and their politics.

Readers who bought Horace Greeley's *New York Tribune* in the 19th century knew they would get the news from a liberal, abolitionist perspective. If they wanted the news with a different tint, they could buy James Gordon Bennett's *New York Herald*, Henry Raymond's *New York Times*, or any of the dozen or so papers being published in New York City at the time.

Likewise, those who spend hours trolling the Internet today know that they'll get a liberal perspective on such sites as www.commondreams.org and a conservative one at such places as www.weeklystandard.com. But today's traditional news organizations have grown too large and too few to be personal vehicles. Few cities now have more than one daily newspaper, and though sharp divisions in national politics tug at news outlets to take sides, most American newspapers have, appropriately, continued to try to play it straight.

True *objectivity*, most journalists now realize, is impossible. It doesn't take a philosophy major to realize that there are innumerable possible perspectives on every event and that a choice of one of them represents a subjective decision of a sort. Three thousand people enjoyed a concert. Is it fair in some ultimate sense to concentrate on the one person who was stabbed? Journalists have to accept the fact that they can never be free of this sort of philosophical bias. Subjective or not, they're going to write about the stabbing. But they must be on their guard against the danger of a cruder, more pernicious bias seeping into their stories.

Journalists today have also become sensitive to the need for another kind of fairness, an effort to avoid stereotyping or overlooking the different types of people who live in their communities.

Here are some of the ways in which journalists fail in their quest for fairness.

ROOTING

Journalists have feelings, too. They like some of the people they write about. They dislike others. They agree with some of the statements they report. They are offended by others. They have their own political leanings.

Some people go into journalism to right wrongs. That's fine. Sometimes a fair and accurate marshaling of the facts can jolt the establishment, if not rearrange the world. The trick is to make sure the facts are doing the talking, not the reporter's own preconceived notions. It's fine to report malfeasance on the part of local Democrats, as long as the evidence is solid (see Chapter 12, Facts) and as long as the reporter would be as interested in similar misbehavior by Republicans.

The *New York Post* has violated this rule more than once in recent decades. When Rupert Murdoch first ran the paper, its rooting interests often colored its news coverage. Murdoch's *Post* would, for example, run stories alleging that Israel feared that a Democrat might win an election in the United States, without including any quotes from Israelis to lend support to this charge, or it would run a feature on the political preferences of Hollywood stars that included only interviews with stars supporting the Republican candidate.

The publisher's political interests colored the news. More recently, the press seemed all too eager to write off Howard Dean, who faltered in the Iowa caucuses after weeks of leading the pack of Democratic hopefuls for the 2004 presidential nomination. This report of *The Washington Post,* offered as news, read somewhat like a self-fulfilling prophecy of Dean's collapse after his concession speech to supporters gathered at the Iowa caucuses came to be known as "the Dean scream":

> LEBANON, N.H.—The reporters are all talking about the implosion.
> As Howard Dean campaigned across New Hampshire on Thursday, the journalists trailing him were conscious of watching history unfold.
> When a candidate loses his footing, even fleeting moments seem to feed the larger narrative....The commentators who once saw Dean flying so high wasted no time in declaring a new conventional wisdom.

"Howard Dean is done," Fox News's Fred Barnes told viewers on Wednesday. "He's finished.... He's gone."

Rooting in times of war can be subtler, particularly in the post-Sept. 11 era when the United States is engaged in a "war on terror" with no clearly defined enemy or battlefield. When the U.S. bombs killed Abu Musab al-Zarqawi, the leader of al Qaeda in Iraq, a front-page sentence in *The Boston Globe*, referring to a story on an inside page, read "the killing is likely to raise hopes for a victorious exit and give the president a short-term lift." There was no attribution.

Less subtle forms of rooting were evident on at least two cable television stations in the weeks after the United States invaded Iraq, as newscasters were shown reading their reports with computer-generated, waving U.S. flags behind them.

IGNORING

One candidate is loud and aggressive, another seeks out the press less frequently, a third seems likely to receive the smallest fraction of the vote. Do they deserve equal coverage?

Apportioning space in a story, or in stories, during a campaign is one of the trickiest tasks journalists face.

During the early months of the 1992 presidential campaign, political reporters pretty much wrote off former California Gov. Jerry Brown. Brown ended up being Bill Clinton's last remaining challenger for the Democratic nomination. A look at history shows that it is not uncommon for candidates to be slighted. In the 1976 Democratic primary in New Hampshire, Jimmy Carter won 28 percent of the vote to Morris Udall's 24 percent, a victory most might consider comfortable but modest. *Time* and *Newsweek*, two of the country's most influential sources of news, saw it otherwise. According to David L. Paletz and Robert M. Entman, authors of *Media Power Politics*, the two magazines combined to give Carter *26 times* as much coverage as Udall in the issue that followed the primary. Carter was on the cover of both magazines. Is that fair? Is that reporting the political climate or creating the political climate?

Fairness requires a balancing act, but the balance will never please everyone. Aggressive candidates are going to claim more space than cautious candidates; major-party candidates are usually a bigger story than minor-party candidates. Still, reporters have to be sure cautious candidates and minor-party candidates are not ignored. Too much time spent tracking front-runners and predicting their victories can make those predictions self-fulfilling.

Issues, even more than elections, are likely to have more than two sides. Fairness requires more than just some quotes from the "pros" and "cons." The "yeah, buts" and "maybes" may make blander copy but better sense. They deserve space, too. It's also better to bend a bit to make room for the views of so-called extremists and splinter groups than to condemn them to silence because their views seem extreme.

AGREEING

Sometimes it's the easy issues that cause trouble. Most of us probably agree that taxes are unpleasant, dictators objectionable, and China's treatment of dissidents distasteful. It would be easy to write:

The city council did us a favor today, lowering the property tax by one percent.

In a long-overdue development, Attila the Hun has been ousted in a coup.

> The Communist regime in China took a well-deserved slap in the face today when a leading poet spoke out in favor of human rights.

All these wordings, however, are unacceptable. Even widely shared opinion has no place in the news. The widely held opinions of one generation may later prove to be its bigotry.

During the 1950s, for example, *The New York Times* ran a story reporting hysterical charges that there were "sex perverts" (homosexuals) working in federal agencies. This story, which would offend many people today, apparently sneaked by without notice because so many people then shared the belief that homosexuals were both perverted and dangerous. Each age tends to equate its most cherished beliefs with truth.

The work of good reporters can generally be read without embarrassment decades later precisely because they struggle to avoid confusing beliefs with truth.

CONCLUDING

It is possible to add a touch of subjectivity to a story with just one, seemingly innocuous word:

> The council voted to raise real estate taxes *only* 2 percent.

Yes, that 2 percent hike is less than the 6 percent increase that had been considered. But there are some who believe any tax increase is too high. The reporter's job is to present the facts and leave it to readers to draw conclusions about those facts.

This is not a call for know-nothing journalism. The reporter must communicate enough facts for the reader to understand the meaning of the story. Those needed to place developments in context must be included. (See Chapter 10, Background and Context.) Tell the reader the council had been considering a much higher tax increase. Include quotes from council members commenting on the reason for their decision. Compare the tax increase with that of past years and increases in comparable communities. But don't take that extra step of concluding that the tax went up *only* 2 percent.

Writing fairly means writing so that your reader has a chance to agree or disagree with the action or comments on the newsmakers in the story, not with you.

STEREOTYPING

Although they are constantly struggling to say a lot in limited space, reporters must be careful not to fall into the use of stereotypes. Some reporters who covered Hurricane Katrina picked up on an unfortunate example of stereotyping manifested in photo captions of that tragedy.

> In one photo, taken by the Associated Press, a dark-skinned young man is shown in New Orleans flood waters, a 12-pack of Pepsi under his right arm, holding a garbage bag with his left hand. A caption reads: "A young man walks out through chest deep flood water after *looting* a grocery store in New Orleans."
>
> In the second photo, taken by the news organization AFP [Agence France Presse], a light-skinned woman, packages floating in tow, also navigates through New Orleans waters, a man trailing her. The caption: "Two residents wade through chest-deep water after *finding* bread and soda at a local grocery store." ... (emphasis added)
>
> *Houston Chronicle*

Robert Steele, leader of the ethics group at Poynter Institute for Media Studies in St. Petersburg, Fla., addressing students at Emerson College's class of 2006 award ceremony.
(*Photo by David Rosen*)

Just as one person's "looter" is another's "finder," one person's "fanatical sect" is another person's orthodox congregation of committed believers. And the word "fanatical," while applied with some regularity to Islamic organizations, somehow rarely gets tagged onto Christian or Jewish groups. Even the designation "sect" seems loaded. The Methodists are never called a Christian "sect." It is sufficient, in the following case, to note the charge the Egyptian government is making against the organization named. Readers can decide for themselves what they find fanatical and what they find devout.

Acceptable:

The Society for Repentance and Flight from Sin, the Muslim group accused by the Egyptian government in the assassination....

Similar difficulties arise when reporters label fighters who blow up bridges for a popular cause as "resistance fighters," while labeling fighters who blow up bridges for more questionable causes "terrorists." The solution again is simply to detail the damage done and avoid the name-calling entirely.

Stereotyping often is found closer to home as well. In 1992, a group of gay and lesbian reporters at the *San Jose Mercury News* circulated a memo about coverage of their community. Among other things, they noted their frustration that coverage of San Francisco's gay pride parade unerringly homed in on the most outrageous marchers instead of reflecting the diversity of participants within the gay community.

Most newspapers now instruct their reporters to use the term "firefighter" instead of "fireman." But gender stereotyping by job still can sneak onto the pages of newspapers when the person who fulfills the role of a homemaker or teacher, for example, is referred to as "she." One easy solution is to recast the sentence in the plural.

Unacceptable:

The new thermometer will help a nurse when she needs to take a patient's temperature quickly.

Acceptable:

The new thermometer will help nurses when they need to take patients' temperatures quickly.

The NAACP struggled a few decades ago to keep news organizations from routinely mentioning the race of the suspect when a black person was arrested. A white suspect's race, of course, was not specified. The race or religion of a person should be mentioned only rarely, for example, when that information is relevant to the story or when it would be useful in helping to arrest a suspected criminal. When an Arab leader meets with leaders of local Jewish organizations, religious identification becomes important. When police issue a bulletin for a suspected robber described as "a tall white man with a blond beard and a large scar on his forehead," the description should be printed. But if the best the police can do is to say the man was "white, about 6 feet tall and of average weight," leave out his race.

This description of a suspect in a car theft, which appeared in a newspaper on Tuesday about a crime that occurred Sunday, should not have been printed:

Police are looking for a black male about 6-foot-3, 190 pounds, and wearing dark clothes and a black ski cap.

The (Bergen County, N.J.) *Record*

Presumably, the suspect had changed his "dark clothes and ski cap" after two days. Even if he hadn't, a few dozen people a day might fit his description on an average city street.

EXCLUDING

Newspaper editors can argue with some justification that they've been more vigilant about keeping stereotyping out of their pages in recent decades. Yet an equally pernicious, though less obvious, form of bias continues unchecked in too many publications: Whole segments of the community are barely being covered at all.

What's not covered is often more difficult to measure than what is, but the disproportionately white complexion of U.S. newsrooms offers a clue. The Knight Foundation found that in

Rachel Jones, former feature writer and columnist at the *Detroit Free Press*.
(*Courtesy of the* Detroit Free Press, *photo by Hugh Grannum*.)

2005, only 13 percent of newsrooms reflected the diversity of the communities they covered, and 37 percent of newsrooms had staffs that were entirely white. Furthermore, the foundation found the diversity of staffs was decreasing at 73 percent of the top 200 daily newspapers.

Reporters and editors of color argue that such choices in hiring often are reflected in what's covered as well. "The easy way to correct the problem," argues Rachel Jones, a former feature writer and columnist at the *Detroit Free Press*, "is to have people of color and diverse backgrounds well represented on reporting staffs and in decision-making positions."

But another, perhaps more difficult, step also must be taken: "Individual journalists each have to go out of their way to come up with stories that reflect the diverse lives of the people in their communities," Jones suggests. "They have to make it part of their mission." Jones, an African-American woman, believes she has had some success in doing this. So, she reports, did another reporter on her staff who was particularly sensitive to this question of fairness—a white male.

CHAPTER 2 SUMMARY: FAIRNESS

American reporters are expected to give a fair hearing to all sides of an issue, without letting their personal opinions color their coverage. Most journalists accept that true *objectivity* is impossible, but that *fairness* is an attainable goal. Reporters should take care to:

- Rely on verifiable facts and not personal perceptions to tell stories.
- Talk to a wide range of sources, representing varied points of view.
- Avoid stereotypes, in part by building sources among all ethnic, racial, socioeconomic and generational groups.

ADDITIONAL READING

"Clout: Murdoch's Political *Post*," Mitchell Stephens, *Columbia Journalism Review*, July/August 1982.

The Elements of Journalism: What Newspeople Should Know and the Public Should Expect, Bill Kovach and Tom Rosenstiel, Three Rivers Press, 2001.

A History of News, Mitchell Stephens, Oxford University Press, 2006.

"Listen Up, Bias Mongers! The Audience Doesn't Agree," Andrew Kohut, *Columbia Journalism Review*, March/April 2002.

The Press, Geneva Overholser and Kathleen Hall Jamieson, editors, Oxford University Press, 2005.

The Press Effect: Politicians, Journalists, and the Stories That Shape the Political World, Kathleen Hall Jamieson and Paul Waldman, Oxford University Press, 2001.

"A Reporter's Legacy: Five Decades of Fairness," Patrick J. Sloyan, *Columbia Journalism Review*, January/February 2001.

"We're all Postmodern Now," Mitchell Stephens, *Columbia Journalism Review*, July/August 2005.

EXERCISE A

Edit the following sentences to remove any potentially unfair wordings.

1. Fortunately, the rabidly pro-choice judge was defeated.

2. The big-spending Democrats have dominated the city council for 20 years.

3. The African-American militants blocked the auditorium's entranceway, making it impossible for the candidate to address the audience.

4. The convicted child molester got what he deserved: a nine-year sentence.

5. The company's owners, Rod Kanchl and his cute, blonde wife, Jennifer, attended the meeting.

6. With luck, the drought will end on Wednesday when heavy rains are expected.

7. The union had received a whopping 9 percent salary increase two years ago.

8. The heroic teenager jumped into the pool but sadly was unable to reach the baby.

9. She was able to destroy that argument by pointing out that abortion is a form of murder.

10. The protesters shouted obscenities at police.

11. With their usual insensitivity to the problems of the poor, the Republicans voted to cut taxes and spending.

12. He rashly accused his opponent of lying and cheating.

13. The governor and her staff struggled heroically to keep the budget under $600 million.

14. Government troops liberated a southern town that had been seized by extremist rebels last week.

15. The economy has been helped by the fiscally sound policies used by business to keep down wages.

16. Only Alderman Harry Kanes was willing to come forward and call the decision to raise the council's own salary "a rip-off."

17. Welfare freeloaders receive $97 million each year.

18. Members of the extremist homosexual-rights group ACT UP shrieked and pranced in protest outside the hall as the dedicated doctor outlined his AIDS research.

19. He refused to be interviewed about the accounting mess that had put his agency $100,000 over budget.

20. On the reviewing stand, smiling and waving to the marchers, stood Republican candidate Stella Shapiro, a tall, good-looking woman. Democratic candidate David Jerome seemed filled with pride at performances of the city's high school students as he stood next to her. Citizen's Party candidate George Ikels was also on the reviewing stand.

21. The two speakers at the Chamber of Commerce dinner were Victoria Alvarez, a Mexican American who owns the local 7-Eleven franchise, and Jason Coleman, a white male who is president of Coleman Industries.

22. The stars of the old-timers game were Larry Bird, who was known for his intelligent play, and Julius Erving, the marvelous leaper.

EXERCISE B

Edit the following story to remove any potentially unfair wordings.

The state Assembly, after wasting eight hours debating what obviously would be the proper procedure to employ, voted last night to expel Assemblywoman Alice Tallyrand of North Amboy, who has been arrested for viciously abusing and neglecting her 5-year-old son.

The Assembly voted 136–1 in favor of the toughly worded motion by Assemblyman Theodore Wolinski of Saddle Brook that removed Tallyrand from her seat immediately for "inhuman behavior." The only negative vote was cast by Assemblyman Mark Adler, a bleeding-heart liberal from New Falls, who not coincidentally shares an office with Tallyrand. Predictably, the left-leaning Democrat said that the Assembly should not act until Tallyrand "has had her day in court."

Tallyrand was finally arrested Friday night on charges of child abuse. Police said they had received reports over a number of months from Tallyrand's neighbors accusing her of actually forcing her son, William, to stand at attention for hours at a time in their backyard.

Tallyrand, who won custody of the boy in a bitter divorce trial two years ago, still claims she is innocent of the charges. She, of course, refused to present a defense or give an opinion about the Assembly's decision last night.

The Assembly's debate on how to handle the awful charges against one of its members began at noon and stretched on into the evening as one nervous Democrat after another expressed concern about the propriety of acting on a case that has not yet come to trial.

Three weak Democrat-supported motions that would have merely expressed the Assembly's "concern" about the charges were defeated, with the honor-bound Republican majority standing firm behind efforts to invoke sterner punishment.

When it appeared certain that no watered-down action would sneak through, all the Democrats except the eccentric Adler voted with the Republicans in support of expulsion. Said one: "We don't want to be accused of condoning child abuse." Hardly a heroic stance for an elected official to take.

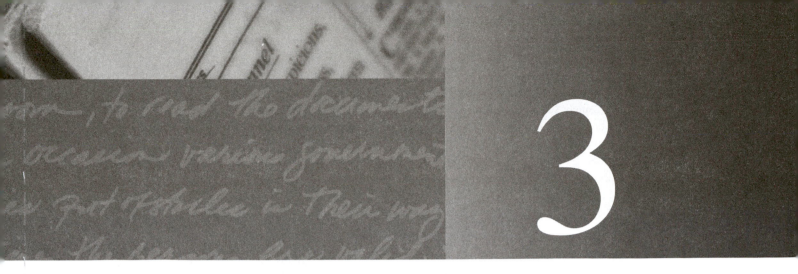

The Language of News

Jimmy Snipes thought he heard the car's radio.

Then he realized the sounds were children's voices. And they were calling from inside the trunk.

Snipes freed two sisters, ages 2 and 4, from the trunk of their mother's Chevrolet Monte Carlo.

The Charlotte (N.C.) Observer

These four sentences are short and direct. They don't dally. The words they use are unvarnished and precise.

There's good reason for this. With thousands of news outlets a mouse click away, hundreds of magazines and alternate weeklies already available, and 24-7 broadcast news clamoring for attention, readers don't have time to waste. They want their information crisp, clear and accurate.

That is the language of today's news.

PRECISION

A *blackout* of undetermined origin cut off power last night.... Lights *flickered* off throughout the city at 7:26.

The writer of these sentences, which appeared in *The Dallas Morning News*, wanted to inform readers that power had failed at 7:26, plunging the area into darkness. The words he chose to convey that, however, didn't work, as the paper's writing coach, Paula LaRocque, noted in *F.Y.I.*, her in-house newsletter. A *blackout* cannot cut off power; a *blackout* is what happens when power *is* cut off. What's more, power that is cut off precisely at 7:26 presumably does not *flicker*—blink on and off.

Just as the first thing a musician must worry about is hitting the right notes, the first thing a writer must worry about is choosing the right words. Reporters must choose words that are not only grammatically correct (see The Basics, following Chapter 27: Section C, Spelling and Grammar) but *semantically* precise—words should say what authors mean. This is a more exacting challenge than it might seem to be, as the reporter for *The Dallas Morning News* learned.

The curse and gift of the English language is the richness of its vocabulary. English offers us countless opportunities to err in our choice of words. But it also offers us, through its super-abundance of words, the capability of describing the world with remarkable exactness. Consider, for example, all the different terms for situations in which someone has illegally taken someone else's property:

steal	extort	burglary
rob	blackmail	stickup
pilfer	lift	larceny
sack	swipe	ripoff
pinch	shoplift	holdup
mug	plunder	piracy
embezzle	filch	heist
swindle	knock off	second-story job
poach	purloin	theft

Faced with such a wealth of possibilities, the writer must choose well. It would be wrong, for example, to describe an incident in which a store has been robbed at gunpoint as a *theft*. Theft, by definition, does not involve the use or threat of violence. The right word here is *robbery*. Similarly, it would be wrong to report that someone has been stopped and *burglarized* on the way home. Burglaries are defined as acts of stealing after entering a building. The right term here would be *held up*.

Good writers possess two basic skills: They sense when they are using a word incorrectly and they know how to find an acceptable substitute. For many beginning reporters, mastering the first skill presents more problems than mastering the second. Some of us have been getting away with poorly chosen words all our lives; it may not have mattered much—our friends seem to have gotten the point. But newspaper readers won't be as tolerant.

Sometimes the use of an ambiguous wording simply causes an unintended chuckle...at the writer's expense. The following sentence appeared in the (Little Rock) *Arkansas Gazette*:

> Four years ago, the 91 residents of McCaskill (Hempstead County) lived in fear of being *burned out* and faced rising insurance rates.

Burned out is an expression commonly used to describe a person who is exhausted from having worked too much on something. A better phrase here would have been *losing their homes to fire*.

Sometimes use of the wrong word will leave readers perplexed. How did readers of *The News* in Paterson, N.J., react to this sentence, which appeared on Dec. 31?

> While most people were preparing to ring out the old, someone rung out the new this week, depositing an infant in a cold parked car outside Riverside Hospital in Boonton Township.

Aside from the reporter's bad taste here in joking about an abandoned baby, the word *rung* is misused. *Rung* is the past participle of *ring*; there is, fortunately, no way to *ring out* a baby. The only way to save this sentence would be to cross it out and start again.

Some errors are more subtle. Is it correct to write, as one (New Orleans) *Times-Picayune* reporter did, that the conditions at the ceremony did not "dampen the jailhouse marriage" of a prisoner? No. *Spirits* can be dampened but not *marriages* (unless the couple spends time in the rain); and the story would be clearer if the reporter had used the more precise word *wedding* instead of *marriage*.

Sometimes use of the wrong word can cause legal trouble. You could be sued for libel for writing that a man has been *indicted* when he has only been *charged*. (See The Basics, Section F, Law.)

If there is some doubt about the correct meaning of a word, look it up. Dictionaries are full of information about meanings, and they can answer many usage questions too, as can style books. (see The Basics, Section B, Style.) It's also no sin to keep a usage book on your desk.

If reference books are unable to relieve your doubt about a word, leave it out, even if that requires recasting the entire sentence.

Reporters should be particularly wary in their choice of verbs of attribution. (see Chapter 6, Attribution.) It's quite easy to distort the news by mixing up these common verbs. This story, from the *San Francisco Chronicle*, misuses either *announced* or *emerged*:

> The Interior Department *announced* yesterday that it was delaying its plans to lease sites off the Northern California coast for oil and gas drilling.
> News of the postponement of the sale...*emerged* in testimony presented at a San Francisco congressional hearing....

Information that only *emerges* during a hearing has not been *announced*.

There are dozens of words like *announced* that can be used in specific circumstances to describe what someone said. Among the most common are:

told	maintained	suggested
stated	exclaimed	added
revealed	shouted	declared
indicated	recalled	charged
argued	noted	insisted
claimed	retorted	pointed out

All these words must be used with care because they have narrower meanings than the blander—and thus more versatile—word *said*. For example, *indicate* tends to be vague. To say someone *claimed* something implies that there is reason to doubt the person's statement. *State* is for formal pronouncements, and something can be *pointed out* only if it's a fact.

Said, probably the most used verb in journalism, is still the best option in most cases. It solves the problem in that story from the *Chronicle*:

> The Interior Department *said* yesterday that it was delaying its plan to lease sites off the Northern California coast for oil and gas drilling....

There is a place for alternatives to *said*. Reporters do not want to use the same word in every paragraph. But in a profession whose goal is accurate communication, the simple, familiar word is often the best choice.

Most errors of meaning are caused by reporters straining to use colorful words and expressions they are not quite able to control. Too many beginning reporters fancy themselves artists. They would be better off seeing themselves as artisans working with precision tools—the words of the English language.

CLARITY

In 1984, according to *The New York Times*, the U.S. Department of State removed the word "killing" from its reports on human rights violations in favor of the phrase "unlawful or arbitrary deprivation of human life."

This is an exaggerated example of the sort of language reporters must avoid. There's no reason to use seven words when one will do. Nor is there any excuse for substituting an obscure,

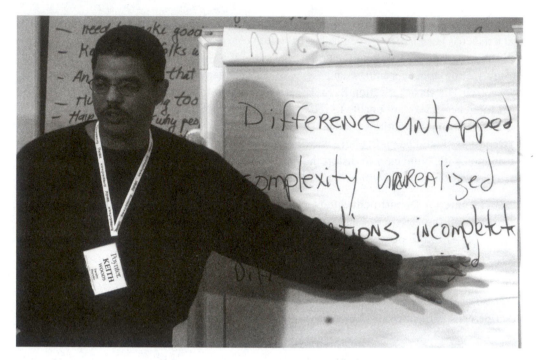

Keith Woods, Dean of Faculty at the Poynter Institute, which offers a variety of journalism seminars. (*Photo courtesy of the Poynter Institute*)

though presumably less upsetting, phrase for a blunt, direct word like *killing*. Unlike some government officials, reporters are paid to tell it simply and tell it straight.

A newsroom is not the place for bad poets. The emphasis on style over content, on meaningful obscurity, found in some poetry and in some creative writing classes, has no place in journalism.

Unacceptable:

In a bloodbath of Homeric proportions, 289 of our brethren saw the hooded specter of death on the city's main thoroughfares last year.

Journalists tell news. They want to engage; they want to entertain; but their primary goal is always to communicate. Literary flourishes, obscure terms and jargon may impress; slang may amuse; but to communicate clearly, journalists must rely on a vocabulary that is more easily understood.

Acceptable:

As of yesterday afternoon, 289 people had died on Dallas roads this year.

Dallas Times Herald

There are times when a writer can show a little style, particularly in feature stories, but style, too, can best be conveyed in simple, unvarnished language. Notice how simple the words are in this sentence from a war report by Ernest Hemingway, printed in *The New York Times* in 1937:

On the corner, twenty yards away, is a heap of rubble, smashed cement, and thrown up dirt, a single dead man, his torn clothes dusty, and a great hole in the sidewalk from which the gas from a broken main is rising, looking like a heat mirage in the cold morning air.*

---

* Louis L. Snyder and Richard B. Morris, editors, *A Treasury of Great Reporting,* Simon and Schuster; 2nd edition, 1962, p. 525.

Difficult Words and Slang

Those three-dollar words some people strain to fit in their sentences should be left in the dictionary. There is no sense in using a word that significant numbers of readers won't understand.

Ron Harris of the *Los Angeles Times* recalls being criticized by an editor once for a sentence that used the word "indigent." "I wasn't thinking about the reader," Harris, now an editor himself, says. "You have to say, 'Wait a minute. Let's explain this.' What does indigent mean? It means poor."

Unacceptable:

A court edict has temporarily interdicted the dismissal of James Redburn, Brookhaven Town's environmental protection director, who has been the subject of considerable contention.

Slang, too, is out. Expressions that may be current on the street may still be unfamiliar in many of the homes in which a newspaper will be read. Slang also intrudes on the telling of the news; it forces the writer's personality on the reader in an unwanted way. And, adds Harris, it's just not "classy."

Unacceptable:

A court order has knocked down plans to can James Redburn....

Journalists seek a more common language.

Acceptable:

A court order has temporarily blocked the firing of James Redburn, Brookhaven Town's embattled environmental protection director.*

(Long Island, N.Y.) *Newsday*

Here are more examples of potentially obscure words and clearer alternatives:

Difficult	Slang	Common
apprehend	bust	arrest
officer of the law	cop	policeman or policewoman
cannabis	weed	marijuana
exemplary	bad	good
gentleman	dude	man
relieve oneself of stress	chill	calm down

Jargon

Jargon is another enemy of clear writing. Many specialties have developed their own languages. When writing about these jargon-infested professions and hobbies, the journalist must take responsibility for translating their specialized languages so they can be understood by a general audience. A failure to translate jargon will leave many readers confused.

Who but a sailing buff would be able to understand this sentence from *The New York Times*:

The 96-year-old square-rigger Wavertree is getting a new main deck to go with her new bowsprit...

---

* The name in this story has been changed.

If the reporter had been doing her job, the sentence might have read:

> The 96-year-old Wavertree is getting a new main deck to go with her new "bowsprit"—the pole that projects from the front of the ship. Since all its sails face forward, the Wavertree is known as a "square-rigger."

One solution to the problem of jargon is to include both the unfamiliar term and its definition in the article.

Unacceptable:

The galaxy is more than 100 *light years* away.

Acceptable:

The galaxy is more than 100 light years away; in other words, it would take light more than 100 years to reach it.

But if the unfamiliar term is *not* important enough to force on the reader, it is wise to replace it completely with a translation.

Unacceptable:

Two years of declining *apartment occupancy rates* have hurt landlords.

Acceptable:

Landlords have been hurt by two years in which the percentage of apartments they have been able to rent has declined.

Beginning reporters will become entangled in thickets of jargon. Jargon is found in government—"the Iowa Civil Rights Commission *closed* [completed] a record 174 cases in September." It is found in legal proceedings—"the defense asked for a *change of venue* [a change in the site of the trial]." It is found in economics—"the drop in the *prime rate* [the interest rate at which favored customers can borrow] has increased the availability of mortgages." And it is found in science—"scientists did not agree on whether the chemical was a *teratogen* [agent that causes birth defects]."

Even local undertakers have their own jargon: People don't die, they *pass away*, at which point they are referred to as "loved ones." These undertakers, like the Department of State with its "unlawful deprivation of human life," are trying to take the sting out of bad news. Such attempts to put a kinder face on events are called *euphemisms*. Euphemisms are also used to inflate: Garbage collectors become *sanitary engineers*, police become *law enforcement officers*. Though euphemisms are rampant in daily usage—there are no longer old people, just *senior citizens*—they have no place in clear writing. At best they confuse; at worst they distort reality.

Using simple language is not always easy, but it is not impossible, even on the most difficult stories. "If you really work at it," says *Philadelphia Inquirer* science writer Jim Detjen, "you can explain almost any scientific theory in words the average reader can understand."

Some jargon can be translated with the help of the dictionary. More often the solution is thorough reporting: asking a member of the commission to explain exactly what it means to "close a case," asking the court clerk to review the legal meaning of "changing the venue." Reporting is not complete until reporters understand every important term in their notes, and writing is not finished until writers have expressed every thought in their stories in plain English.

CONCISENESS

Every word in an article must not only be understood, it must have a purpose. A reader's time and a newspaper's space are too valuable to squander.

Unacceptable:

An agency of our federal government has stated its objection to the planned construction of a 15-story-high building designed to be used for offices, which would be located in the heart of Arlington. The agency said its primary concern was that the structure's penthouse roof "would mimic the Washington Monument."

Acceptable:

A federal agency has objected to construction of a 15-story office building in the heart of Arlington, arguing that the structure's penthouse roof "would mimic the Washington Monument."

The Washington Post

Redundancy

One way to waste words is to say things twice. A *15-story-high building* is the same size as a *15-story building*. Here is an example of redundancy that appeared in the *Los Angeles Times*:

…whenever the Redskins are ahead on points…

Is there any other way the Redskins, a football team, could be ahead? "Whenever the Redskins are ahead" is sufficient.

One trick for smoking out redundant modifiers is to replace them with their opposites. If the resulting phrase makes no sense, then the original modifier may have been unnecessary. Since you cannot *partially* destroy something, it is redundant to say something has been *completely* destroyed.

Some other redundant or potentially redundant word combinations:

overexaggerate	two twins
future plans	quick second
controversial issue	very first
general consensus	true fact
sad frown	past history
personal feelings	assembled crowd
loud scream	dead corpse
little baby	definite proof
young freshman	an approximate estimate
close down	jewish rabbi
new record	7 a.m. in the morning

Wasteful Phrases

Words also are wasted when a phrase is used where a single word would do. *Located in* can be replaced with no loss of meaning by *in*, for example. Here are some other potentially wasteful phrases:

Phrase	Word
at this point in time	now

as a result of	because
strike a tune	play
venture a suggestion	suggest
take action	act
with the exception of	except
was the recipient of	received
is of the opinion that	believes
in the event that	if
along the lines of	like
due to the fact that	because
with reference to	about
having to do with	about
in the near future	soon
at the present time	now
for the purpose of	to
in an effort to	to
in order to	to

Detour Words

Because of their vagueness, some words seem inevitably to lead to wordy sentences. *Involved* is perhaps the most common of these "detour words": The relationship it describes is too weak to be meaningful. Sentences frequently can be improved by substituting more specific words.

Unacceptable:

A 13-year-old student at Severn River Junior High School died yesterday after she was *involved* in an accident in the school's gymnasium, where she was performing some basic maneuvers on the parallel bars.

Acceptable:

A 13-year-old student at Severn River Junior High School died yesterday after a freak accident in the school's gymnasium, where she was performing some basic maneuvers on the parallel bars.

The (Baltimore) *Sun*

Unacceptable:

Night and weekend service on the trolleys that use the tunnel routes will be *experiencing* interruptions.

Acceptable:

Night and weekend service on the trolleys that use the tunnel routes will be interrupted.

The Philadelphia Inquirer

One thing good journalists and good poets should have in common is an obsession with making each word they use count.

DIRECTNESS

Editors see the problem all too often: Reporters are so full of information about an event, so tuned in to its complexities, that they seem incapable of writing an account clear and straightforward enough for readers to understand. Their sentences appear hopelessly tangled.

If the fog fails to lift after a rewrite or two, veteran editors have been known to resort to this strategy: They simply ask reporters to *tell* them the story. "Forget what you wrote. Forget how complex it all is. Just *tell* me what it's all about." More often than not, after a moment's thought, frustrated reporters will recite a version of their story that is significantly simpler and more intelligible than anything they have been able to come up with at their keyboards. And instinctively, the sentence structure in the oral version will arrange itself in the most direct sequence: subject, verb, object—in that order.

There's a lesson here. The same basic, direct sentences that help keep things clear when we speak can also do the job when we write:

> RICHMOND (AP)—A fire destroyed a block-square warehouse containing fertilizer yesterday.
>
> *Roanoke* (Va.) *Times & World-News*

Subject: *fire*; verb: *destroyed*; object: *warehouse*.

Reporters who find their ideas disappearing in a tangle of adjectives, adverbs, interjections and clauses might step back and see whether they can find a few sharp and direct sentences to cut through the confusion. "It's nice to have things real simple," says Ron Harris of the *Los Angeles Times*.

Verbs

Editors or writing coaches, trying to diagnose a sentence's problems, frequently begin by examining its verb.

Action

The verb's job is to describe an action. Journalism is predominantly about actions, so its sentences generally work best when they are powered by strong verbs:

> Government officials routinely *broke* or *skirted* Indiana's open records law during a statewide test by eight newspapers.
>
> *The Indianapolis Star*

When adjectives and adverbs begin stealing the action, writing loses some of its power.

Weak:

The United States said *threateningly* yesterday....
The *fast-moving* bullets went through the wall *quickly*....

Better:

The bullets *tore* through the wall.

Stories about dynamic events should have dynamic verbs:

> OJIYA, Japan—A series of powerful earthquakes and aftershocks *struck* northern Japan yesterday, killing at least 16 people and reportedly injuring more than 900 as buildings *crumbled*, a bullet train *derailed*, and roadways *were torn* apart.
>
> Associated Press in *The Boston Globe*

Weak:

...the camper in which they were riding was *involved* in an accident on a Staten Island highway.

> (Long Island, N.Y.) *Newsday*

Better:

…the camper in which they were riding *flipped* on its side and *burst* into flames on a Staten Island highway.

One sign that the verbs are not carrying their load in sentences is overuse of forms of the verb *to be*.

Weak:

The corner of 165th Street and Broadway *was* the most frequent destination on the route for passengers.

Better:

More passengers *took* the bus to 165th Street and Broadway than to any other stop.

To be, a relatively sedentary verb, is best used for states and conditions (it *was* cold), not actions—the water *froze*.

Active Voice

For verbs to convey the action in a sentence, the subject should logically be the party doing the acting. Here the subject is Oklahoma Corporation Commissioner Jim Townsend; the action is grabbing a lead:

Oklahoma Corporation Commissioner Jim Townsend grabbed an early but substantial lead over challenger Charles Cleveland yesterday in the Democratic runoff for a two-year term on the utility rate-making panel.

Tulsa (Okla.) *World*

Too often, sentences are reversed so that the subject is what is being acted upon.

Weak:

An early lead was grabbed by Oklahoma Corporation Commissioner Jim Townsend yesterday….

A sentence is in the *active voice* when the subject does the acting—the man shot the deer. It's in the *passive voice* when the subject is the recipient of the action—the deer was shot by the man. As a rule, sentences work best when cast in the active voice:

Weak:

Support was expressed yesterday for a federal prosecutor by a group of black Richmond lawyers….

Better:

A group of black Richmond lawyers expressed support yesterday for a federal prosecutor….

Richmond (Va.) *Times-Dispatch*

Tense

Newspapers usually use the past tense, since most of the news they report happened at least hours before the paper reaches newsstands or doorsteps:

Four people *were killed* and three others critically *injured* yesterday in Gwinnett County when a southbound car on Interstate 85 *veered* across the median and *crashed* into an oncoming car.

The Atlanta Constitution

The past tense protects a newspaper from looking foolish. An action could end in the hours after the paper was written but before it hits the street. If, for example, a teachers' strike were settled at 4 a.m., a story in that morning's newspaper about the previous night's negotiations would be merely dated in the past tense. In the present tense it would be wrong.

Unacceptable:

Representatives of Lakewood's 247 striking teachers and the board of education *are continuing* talks in an effort to end the 65-day walkout.

Acceptable:

Representatives of Lakewood's 247 striking teachers and the board of education *continued* round-the-clock negotiations last night in an effort to end the 65-day walkout.

On occasion, however, newspaper reporters slip into other tenses. If, for example, it seemed certain that an action that took place yesterday would still be taking place today, a reporter might use the present tense to give the story more immediacy:

Loyola College *is negotiating* to buy the 200-unit Wynnewood Towers apartment complex.

The (Baltimore) *Sun*

Negotiations like these are not likely to end at 4 a.m.

A government report linking secondhand tobacco smoke to cancer *gives* an immediate boost to anti-smoking lawsuits nationwide.

USA Today

The effect of the report is not likely to change by 4 a.m.

Sometimes, especially when news is several days old, reporters will substitute the present-perfect tense for the past tense in the lead paragraphs of their stories so that the story sounds fresher.

Weak:

The First Reformed Church last week *converted* its basement into a dormitory for the homeless....

Better:

The First Reformed Church *has converted* its basement into a dormitory for the homeless....

One tense journalists should try to avoid is the future. We are not omniscient. We know what people say they will do, but we can't predict whether these actions will actually take place.

Unacceptable:

A plan that could save Northwest electric ratepayers $3 million to $4 million *will be presented* Monday....

Acceptable:

A plan that could save Northwest electric ratepayers $3 million to $4 million *is scheduled to be presented* Monday....

Better to be cautious than wrong.

Clauses and Interjections

If all the sentences in a section of a story used the same structure, the writing would be too choppy.

Weak:

The San Francisco Giants are the hottest team in baseball. *They were* suddenly discovered yesterday by the division's front-runners. *The Giants have* played the best baseball in the major leagues since June 27. *They have* come from near the bottom of their division to battle for first place with the Los Angeles Dodgers and the Atlanta Braves.

Clauses and interjections can help vary sentence structure and link related ideas.

Better:

The San Francisco Giants, *the hottest team in baseball*, were suddenly discovered yesterday by the division's front-runners. The Giants have played the best baseball in the major leagues since June 27, *coming from near the bottom of their division to battle for first place with the Los Angeles Dodgers and the Atlanta Braves.*

San Francisco Chronicle

But interruptions in the basic subject-verb-object flow of sentences can also get writers in trouble. The trouble usually starts when clauses and interjections grow too long, particularly when they are placed in the middle of a sentence, creating too much distance between subject and verb.

Roy Peter Clark, a former writing coach for the *St. Petersburg Times*, finds two elements to be "the keys to clear, effective sentences." One is the use of active verbs. The other is the placement of the subject and verb. "If there are problems of jumbled syntax or focus, I'll usually look at where the subject and verb are," Clark explains. "If the subject and verb are separated, all sorts of confusion and complications start to set in."

Unacceptable:

The Elmwood Park Homeowners' Association, *which has strongly opposed the present rent ordinance and recently was denied by the council a chance to place a referendum abolishing rent control on the November ballot,* is unsatisfied by the proposed law.

The (Paterson, N.J.) *News*

The subject of this sentence is the *Elmwood Park Homeowners' Association*; the verb phrase is *is unsatisfied*. The distance between them is 28 words. By the time the verb arrives in a sentence with such a long clause, readers may have forgotten the subject.

An 18-word prepositional phrase separated subject—*an ordinance*—and verb—*cleared*—in this poorly worded sentence, which began a front-page story in the (Chicago) *Sun-Times*:

An ordinance *to move 8,000 city workers under the blanket of civil service in the midst of [the mayor's] firings* cleared a City Council committee yesterday.

Sometimes problems can be solved by reworking a sentence (and in this case improving the wording):

In an apparent response to the mayor's attempts to cut the number of city employees, a City Council committee yesterday approved a plan to make an additional 8,000 city workers eligible for civil service protection.

More often, though, the solution is to split the sentence into two simpler sentences:

Acceptable:

The Elmwood Park Homeowners' Association, *which has strongly opposed the present rent ordinance*, is not satisfied with the proposed law. The council recently denied the association a chance to place a referendum abolishing rent control on the November ballot.

The first sentence in this rewrite uses a clause, but it is short enough not to interfere with readers' understanding of the sentence. Reporters do not have to shy away from using clauses and interjections. But they do have to be sure these interruptions are not unwieldy.

Points

Another way to sink sentences is to overload them with information.

Unacceptable:

The arrest of two men on murder charges and the discovery of a badly decomposed body yesterday afternoon ended a 10-day manhunt for an emotionally disturbed Massapequa Park man whose abandoned car was discovered on fire in a Suffolk park.
(Long Island, N.Y.) *Newsday*

It would be difficult for readers to follow this sentence the first time through. Indeed, the many points it tries to make are still a little confusing on second reading.

A sentence should not be asked to communicate more than a point or two. The fact that two men were arrested and charged with the murder is one point. The fact that the victim had been missing for 10 days is a second. When there are more points to make, more sentences should be used.

Acceptable:

Two men were arrested yesterday and charged with the murder of an emotionally disturbed Massapequa Park man for whom police had been searching for 10 days. Police said they believe a badly decomposed body discovered yesterday is that of the man, whose abandoned car was found on fire in a Suffolk park Aug. 13.

Sentence Length

How long should sentences be? Since there are so many different ways to write them, it is impossible to set any firm limits on their length. Nevertheless, there usually is an inverse relationship between sentence length and reader comprehension. The longer the sentence, the tougher it generally is to understand. It can't hurt, therefore, for beginning reporters to count words in their sentences. If they haven't typed a period by the time they reach 25, they should be looking for a place to put one. If the sentence has 35 words or more, there's a good chance that it will be difficult for readers to understand.

Unacceptable:

Gaunt, glassy-eyed and possessionless, they crouch in the heat amid thousands of others, hungry and diseased, when they're not stooping over small, dry plots of rock-hard soil or waiting in tight lines for hours to get today's ration of food from international relief agencies: a bowl of rice gruel, two bananas, a bucket of brown drinking water.

Writing is clearest when the sentences are kept relatively short. But string together too many very short sentences, and writing will become choppy.

Unacceptable:

They look gaunt. Their eyes appear glassy. Their possessions were long ago left behind. They crouch in the heat. Around them are thousands of others like them. They are hungry and diseased. They stoop over small, dry plots. The soil is rock-hard. And they wait.

They wait in tight lines for hours. They want a ration of food from international relief agencies. It will include a bowl of rice, two bananas, a bucket of brown drinking water.

They wait for doctors to heal them.

Good writers mix simple short- and medium-length sentences to create a sort of "prose rhythm."

Acceptable:

Gaunt, glassy-eyed and possessionless, they crouch in the heat amid thousands of others, hungry and diseased. They stoop over small, dry plots of rock-hard soil. And they wait.

They wait in tight lines for hours to get today's ration of food from international relief agencies: a bowl of rice gruel, two bananas, a bucket of brown drinking water.

They wait for doctors to heal them.

The (Louisville, Ky.) *Courier-Journal*
(See Chapter 22, Features)

CHAPTER 3 SUMMARY: THE LANGUAGE OF NEWS

Readers want information that is clear, crisp and precise. Good news writers never dally in delivering the point. To write effective stories:

- Use simple, exact language. If you're in doubt about a word's definition, look it up.
- Be concise. Don't use five words when one will do.
- Translate jargon and specialized language into everyday words.
- Don't clutter setences with too much detail or too many clauses. A sentence should make no more than one or two points.
- Write in the active voice: subject/verb/object.
- Active verbs power most strong sentences. Let verbs drive your sentences.

ADDITIONAL READING

The Associated Press Stylebook and Briefing on Media Law, Associated Press, Norm Goldstein, editor, Perseus Books, 2004.

The Elements of Style, William Strunk, Jr. and E. B. White, foreword by Roger Angell, Longman; 4th edition, 2000.

A Journalistic Approach to Good Writing: The Craft of Clarity, Robert M. Knight, Iowa State Press, 2003.

Language Maven Strikes Again, William Safire, Henry Holt & Co., 1991.

Newspaper Language, Nicholas Bagnall, Focal Press, 1993.

On Writing Well: 30 Anniversary Edition, William Zinsser, HarperCollins, 2006.

Writing as Craft and Magic, Carl Sessions Stepp, Oxford University Press, 2006.

You Could Look It Up, William Safire, Henry Holt & Co., 1989.

EXERCISE A

Circle the word in parentheses that best completes each of the following sentences.

1. Two rooms had to be closed to the public after fire (destroyed/damaged) the art museum.
2. The governor said the results of the public opinion poll would have no (effect/affect) on his decision.
3. The mounted policewoman had a difficult time (reigning/reining) in her horse.
4. Our team has (less/fewer) tall players.
5. The mayor spoke first, (as/like) he always does.
6. (It is hoped/Hopefully) the mall will attract shoppers to the area.
7. She handed out (more than/over) 1,000 fliers announcing the meeting.
8. Her body will (lay/lie) in state in the Rotunda.
9. The councilman could not choose (among/between) the three proposals.
10. It was the first (annual/of what was to be an annual) dinner commemorating the victory.
11. The council will hold (its/it's) weekly meeting tonight.
12. The (principal/principle) of the school was to be the (principal/principle) speaker in favor of the (principal/principle) of equal educational opportunity.
13. The two men reached (a verbal/an oral) agreement. They believed it was unnecessary to write out a contract.
14. Bill Clinton's picture was (hung/hanged) next to one of his predecessor, George H. W. Bush.
15. Water flowed (continually/continuously) from the stream into the lake.
16. The (robber/thief) sneaked in when we were all away.
17. Graduates of the two schools are different (from/than) each other.
18. She was (averse/adverse) to the idea.
19. He put his shoe (on/upon) his foot.
20. In his speech he (alluded/eluded) to the book.

EXERCISE B

Edit the following sentences to replace any incorrect wordings.

1. "I have no intention of voting for the bill," she charged.
2. He was drowned when he accidentally slipped into the pool.
3. The bride-to-be and her husband were inviting over 500 guests to the wedding.
4. The Saturday school program has been in affect for five years, she revealed. She claimed that her statistics were that more than 1,500 students had participated in it.
5. The vases were unique; there were very few others in the world like them.
6. The senator refuted the opponents of prayer in the schools.
7. Hargrove is an imminent attorney who includes many political leaders and movie stars among his cases.
8. Fellow workers surmised that he had a tendency to flout his aristocratic background and wealth on the job.
9. The suspect forced three customers to sprawl face down on the floor and then escaped with about $350 from the cash register, police noted.
10. The mayor reported that Donaldson was a disgrace to the city, adding that the parks had deteriorated severely under him. "I knew he was a bum when my predecessor appointed him," she stated.

EXERCISE C

Edit the following sentences where necessary so that they use clearer language.

1. He utilized the opportunity to endorse the president's prescription for economic recovery.
2. His home boys thought he was totally awesome—one rad guitar player.
3. The governor's presence before the august legislature was meant to win over recalcitrant party members.
4. After the rumble he split for the hospital.
5. The long debate only served to obfuscate the issue.
6. He is a specialist in ichthyology, especially the classification of gobies.
7. He hit a rope over the ivy and into the centerfield bleachers to win the contest.
8. He had dated a veritable plethora of women.
9. They are still studying the problem of recidivism among former inmates of the large correctional facility.
10. Males and females are both admitted to the club, but they are required to dine in different rooms.
11. Brilliant beams of sunlight struggled to penetrate the surface of the water while the divers searched for the body.
12. More juveniles between the ages of 13 and 19 were arrested this year than last.
13. He clearly tended to anthropomorphize any sentient being.
14. Shortly thereafter they found a justice of the peace and tied the knot.
15. There were two octogenarians and seven septuagenarians participating in the teaching program.

EXERCISE D

Edit the following sentences where necessary to make them more concise.

1. He said that up to this point he had been unable to locate the small, two-week-old puppy anywhere.

2. The general consensus of all those who were assembled at the meeting was that the superintendent of schools had overexaggerated the effect budget cuts would have on extracurricular activities.

3. When she heard the loud scream, she burst into the room in a split second but the intruder who had been there already was gone.

4. The Coast Guard captain said he had been experiencing difficulty in removing oil from the hold of the leaking ship because the operation involved pulling a Coast Guard cutter up along next to the listing vessel in high seas.

5. Nearly 400 demonstrators ventured forth to a gathering at the Jackson County Jail yesterday to protest against conditions there.

6. One speaker, the Rev. James Kim, said he had definite proof that a fire that completely destroyed a section of the jail's eighth floor could have been prevented if the jail had had a sprinkler system and sufficient guards.

7. The accident, which occurred at the corner of Waverly and Mercer streets, was not a direct or indirect result of the fact that it had been raining, the prosecutor said. He added that he would call witnesses in the near future to conclusively prove his contention.

8. She will move out of her soon-to-be vacant apartment after they are married in their wedding ceremony, which will be held at exactly 2 p.m. this afternoon.

9. The city's residents had experienced many dangerous tornados over the period of the last 15 years.

10. He is currently serving a life sentence.

11. The incumbent congresswoman pays a visit to her district once every week in an effort to remain close to the citizens who elected her.

12. He performed an autopsy to determine the cause of death.

13. The crash involved two cars that met head on.

14. It was a new first for the track team, a jump that set an all-time state record.

15. The company agreed to hold an annual meeting every year in a large major city.

16. He refused to engage in conversation with reference to the very last meeting.

17. The brand-new car that he had just bought represented an investment of $20,000.

18. She owns her own home.

19. If it were not for the unexpected surprise of the thunderstorm, the hot, burning fire might have caused a severe catastrophe.

20. The sideshow included little midgets, big giants, and funny clowns.

EXERCISE E

Rewrite the following sentences to improve their use of verbs.

1. The fire is still burning out of control.
2. The wildly moving car went from side to side down the street.
3. The ruling on the bill was made by a state appeals court judge.
4. The legislation was supported by the senator.
5. More than 200 Potsdam residents left their homes yesterday when police told them a tanker truck had had an accident, turning over and letting toxic fumes escape into the neighborhood after a sudden large fire started in the chemicals.
6. Chambers said that the worst attack was the one which occurred on Oct. 26 in which 33 Indians lost their lives in the barrage of bullets fired by government troops.
7. The pilot said the tensest moment of the trip was when he suddenly had to go around a passenger plane that he saw on his radar.
8. There was graffiti that was the work of two teenagers all over the walls and windows of the subway train.
9. The man lost his life when the building came down on top of him.
10. Firefighters from all over the county will arrive at the firehouse at 2 p.m. for a picnic, which will be followed, at 4 p.m., by a parade.

EXERCISE F

Rewrite the following sentences or passages to make them more direct.

1. The car, which had been repaired by a team of mechanics flown in specially by its manufacturer at a cost of more than $30,000, finally started after four days of work.

2. Sloane returned from the store at 7 p.m. He found the front door open. The room was in a shambles. The television set was gone.

3. Instead of vetoing the $10 million tax cut, which he had attacked in a number of speeches, the governor in a speech today said he would refuse to sign the bill, a move that would have the same effect.

4. The teachers and the board of education representatives, who had been meeting for six weeks on and off but had been unable to forge an agreement, met twice—at 8 p.m. and 3 p.m.

5. Waving last month's crime statistics, which he had promised to find, over his head, Martin, who had said that crime would be the number one issue in his campaign for Missoula city councilman on the Republican ticket, said robberies had increased 12 percent in nine months.

6. Mahler called the accusation that he is a free spender a lie. He said he actually would cut city spending if elected. Mahler criticized his opponent, Ellen Haggerty, for "dirtying up the campaign." He said he wanted a campaign of "ideas, not name-calling."

7. In an uncharacteristic move, the governor, who had said debate on the death penalty had already gotten too heated and created too much acrimony in the weeks since Hamilton had proposed the bill, said nothing on the subject.

8. In an effort to find support for the school budget, which faces a difficult test next week, the superintendent scheduled an open house.

9. Police arrested the suspect, who worked as a teller at the bank but had been on vacation the week of the robbery, after a two-week investigation, which they called the most detailed ever conducted for a bank robbery in the city.

10. The fire, which started in the basement and worked its way through the five-story building, was brought under control after a two-hour struggle by the Farmdale Fire Department, which received assistance from Woodlawn and Fairfield.

EXERCISE G

Using research materials or interviews with experts, write explanations that could be used in a newspaper article for the following terms (the field in which the term is used is given in parentheses).

1. Consumer Price Index (economics)
2. restraining order (law)
3. middle C (music)
4. crop rotation (agriculture)
5. full-court press (sports)
6. red shift (science)
7. vehicular manslaughter (law)
8. special education (education)
9. multiple-family dwelling (government)
10. behavior modification (psychology)
11. kilowatt-hour (energy)
12. three-four defense (sports)
13. second-degree burn (medicine)
14. tornado warning (meteorology)
15. iambic pentameter (literature)

EXERCISE H

Edit the following story to correct any errors in word choice.

It appears certain that the state legislature will adapt a proposal this session to curb drunken driving, but legislators are reticent to speculate on the provisions that will comprise the final bill.

Both Senate and Assembly committees have carried bills intended to make it easier to annul the licenses of drivers convicted of driving while intoxicated.

The principle feature of the Senate bill, which had been proposed continuously over the past five years by Sen. John Mackey, calls for the automatic revocation of a licensee within seven days following a conviction of drunken driving. Under the law presently in affect, a driver can drive for months while appealing the return of his license.

The Assembly's bill presents judges with the option of removing the license after a conviction. Beside this provision, the Assembly committee's law involves a plan intended to make it more facile for police officers to apprehend suspicious drivers and give them on-the-spot exams for drunkenness.

"Its too early to say what the final bill will look like," argued Sen. Mackey.

Mackey also declined questions on whether the bill might be combined with a plan requiring beer bottles to be returned to the store to protect the ecology from litter. "Your guess is as good as mine," he indicated.

Edit the following story so that it uses clearer language.

A vehicle, whose driver, police said, was intoxicated, smashed through the window of a downtown eating establishment, Paco's Tacos, yesterday, injuring two customers.

About 10 patrons were consuming their food and beverages at the establishment, at 63 Nicoli Ave., when the vehicle, a 1996 Toyota, crashed through the front window.

"At first I thought it was an earthquake, until I saw the front of the car next to my salad bar," said Ivan "Paco" Schwartz, the proprietor of the establishment.

Isabel Hannok, 32, of East Bedford, was seated at the table in closest proximity to the window when the car entered the establishment. Hannok suffered lacerations caused by the flying shards of glass, according to police.

Leland Beagle, 34, of Flushing, received abrasions and contusions when he dived under the salad bar, police said. Hannok and Beagle were both transported to Booth Hospital.

The alleged perpetrator was apprehended as he essayed an attempt to flee the edifice, according to Police Sgt. James Spoke. Sgt. Spoke identified him as Francis Jenkins, 24, of 13 Nicoli Ave.

"It was obvious that Jenkins had been drinking," Spoke said.

Edit the following story to make it more concise.

Incumbent Democratic Mayor Sheila Straus was re-elected yesterday by an overwhelming landslide vote of New Brook City citizens.

Mayor Straus triumphantly defeated her one and only challenger and rival in the Election Day balloting, Republican Councilman Jose Ramirez, by a margin of 9,034 of the 53,496 votes that were cast. Straus was the recipient of 31,265 of the citizens' ballots, while Ramirez was able to get only 22,231 losing votes.

"This is a victory for everyone who worked in my campaign," the mayor told her partisans and supporters in a brief two-sentence statement after her successful victory. "I want to thank you all very much."

Straus's vote total represented the very largest number of election votes ever obtained by a New Brook City mayoral candidate for election in history. She received 27,443 votes when she was elected to her first four-year term in the mayor's office four years ago.

Edit the following story to improve its use of verbs.

A proposal through which there would be a large monument in the Lawnville town park in honor of fireman George Kemp, who lost his life last week, was approved last night by the Lawnville Borough Council.

Kemp's death came in a fire that left a house on Mulberry Avenue destroyed. He was hit by a falling beam, Fire Chief Al Ramone said.

The plan to build the monument was passed by a unanimous vote by the council after a speech in which Mayor Almonds said positive things about Kemp's contributions to the town.

Fire officials say they have not determined the cause of the Mulberry Avenue fire. They say they have not been able to contact the owners of the house in which Kemp was when he died.

The monument will be completed by early next year. The cost will be $13,000, Almonds said.

Edit the following story to improve its sentence structure.

A state judge ruled yesterday that Ardsley Utilities, which has embarked on a major effort to protect its high-voltage power lines from interference and damage during severe storms, has the right to cut trees around those lines for that purpose.

State Supreme Court Justice Albert Farrow, after lifting a 15-month injunction barring the utility from removing trees without permission from the property owners, threw out a suit brought with the support of the county board of supervisors on behalf of 430 Ardsley County residents whose property abuts the power lines.

The property owners had decided to file the suit after the company chopped down two oak trees in Garnersville. They hired Montalia attorney Vern Jounce. They claimed the contracts that had been signed with the company in the 1950s allowed the utility only to trim branches, not to remove entire trees.

In his ruling, which company lawyers said could affect up to 300 trees mostly in the southern half of the county, Judge Farrow said that the wording of the contracts is "clear and to the point" in granting the utility the right "to fell whole trees as and when it sees fit within the boundaries covered by the contracts."

PART 2 LEADS

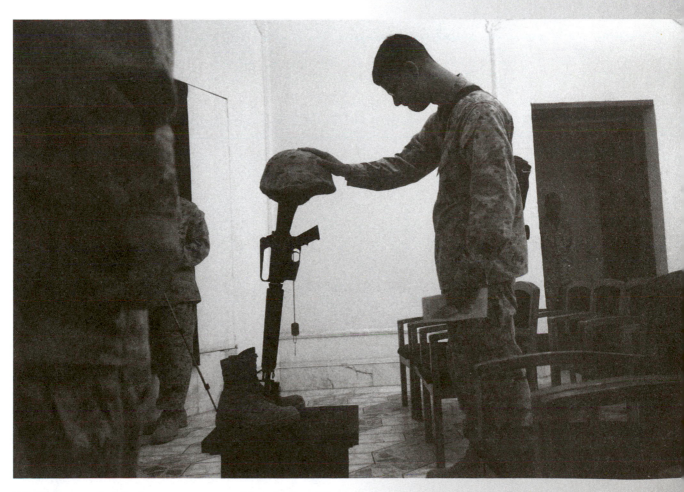

U.S. Marines pay their final respects at a memorial service for a fallen comrade on the outskirts of Ramadi, Iraq. The portfolio in which this photo appears won a Pulitzer Prize for breaking news photography; it contains work from 2004 by eleven Associated Press photographers.
(*AP photo by Jim MacMillan.*)

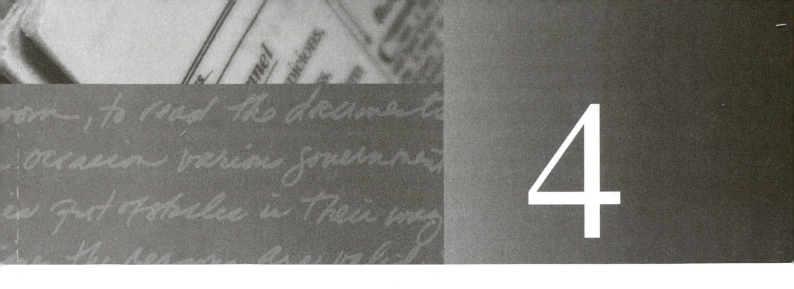

Traditional Leads

It is the rare news event that commands our attention regardless of the way it's presented. Masses of information tease our senses daily; much of it we let pass by. We pay attention to what we recognize—quickly—to be of interest.

Good reporters know this. They know few readers scan, let alone read, everything in the paper or on a news website. So reporters use a simple trick: They try to hook readers by placing their most newsworthy information at the top of the story—where the readers will be sure to spot it.

The top of the story, generally its first paragraph, is called the *lead*. In a story about three men, including a judge, who have been arrested for disorderly conduct, the judge's arrest will dominate the lead paragraph. The other two suspects are less newsworthy.

In a story about a press conference in which the mayor announces that she's promoting a police sergeant to lieutenant, ordering the pruning of oak trees on Main Street and firing the housing commissioner, the housing commissioner's dismissal will lead the story. The other two announcements probably won't even get in print.

In a feature story, reporters might best catch a reader's eye with an unusual description, an alluring little tale or a clever twist of a phrase. But stories about significant breaking events should not try to get fancy to attract readers' attention. The news itself demands attention. It shouldn't be obscured or hidden.

So reporters start most news stories with traditional, or *hard,* news leads—concise summaries of the most newsworthy information in the story, the most compelling hard facts.

Here is the lead to a story with some historic significance:

> Hijackers rammed jetliners into each of New York's World Trade Center towers yesterday, toppling both in a hellish storm of ash, glass, smoke and leaping victims, while a third jetliner crashed into the Pentagon in Virginia. There was no official count, but President Bush said thousands had perished, and in the immediate aftermath the calamity was already being ranked the worst and most audacious terror attack in American history.
>
> *The New York Times*

The choice of what to lead with and the wording of the lead are two crucial decisions in the writing of any story. "The lead helps the reader and writer find focus," says Roy Peter Clark, the former *St. Petersburg Times* writing coach, now vice president and senior scholar at the Poynter Institute for Media Studies in St. Petersburg, Fla.

LENGTH

Traditional leads must be tight. A flabby, overstuffed first paragraph is no way to seduce readers.

Unacceptable:

Five years ago, nurses at North Shore University Hospital in Manhasset voted that they wanted to be represented by the state nurses union. The hospital refused to recognize the union as bargaining agent for the nurses. Now the nurses have won the right to be represented by the union.

Hard leads are rarely more than one sentence long and almost never longer than two sentences. The first paragraph is the last place a reporter would want a wasted word or a redundancy.

Acceptable:

Nurses at North Shore University Hospital in Manhasset have won the right to be represented by the state nurses union after five years of resistance by hospital officials.

(Long Island, N.Y.) *Newsday*

Leads usually should be less than 35 words long (though there are exceptions). Often the shortest leads are the most powerful. Consider this lead from *The New York Times* on July 2, 1969:

Men have landed and walked on the moon.

Eight words can capture history.

CHOOSING THE LEAD

A reporter for *The Record* in Bergen County, N.J., received the following information from the Englewood Police Department:

"An alarm notified us at 12:36 this afternoon that there had been a robbery at the First State Bank at 1 State St. A car was sent and was unable to locate the suspect. Teller Andrea Dormis told us that she was working at a drive-in window at 12:31 when she was asked to turn over money. She gave the robber a paper bag filled with $5,500 in unmarked bills. She said the robber was a white male, wearing a black leather jacket, a scarf and riding a black motorcycle. She said he pulled up to the window, pulled out a gun and handed her a paper bag and a note reading, 'Fill this bag with money.' She did not know the make of the motorcycle and said she saw no license plate. She said the motorcycle left, heading east on Palisade Avenue. We are investigating."*

Choosing what information to include in the lead is an exercise in news judgment. (See Chapter 1, News Judgment.)

---

* The names of the people and the name and address of the bank in this story have been changed.

Unacceptable:

An alarm notified police yesterday that there had been a robbery at the First State Bank in Englewood.

The use of the alarm itself is not particularly weighty or unique. It should not be mentioned in the lead.

Unacceptable:

Police are investigating a robbery at the First State Bank in Englewood yesterday.

Police would be expected to investigate any crime. The fact that they are investigating this one is not very newsworthy.

Unacceptable:

The First State Bank was robbed of $5,500 yesterday, according to police.

The amount of money taken is important, but a $5,500 robbery hardly has much weight. What makes this story interesting is the unique method employed by the robber. That must be included in the lead.

Acceptable:

A man on a motorcycle rode up to the drive-in window of the First State Bank in Englewood yesterday, pulled a gun on the teller and rode off with $5,500, according to police.

The lead must include the most newsworthy elements in the story. When you are covering a big story, the problem often is which of a number of weighty facts to leave out of the lead. On lesser stories, the problem may be deciding which fact is appealing enough to get the reader's attention. There are plenty of close calls; two reporters covering the same story may come up with two different leads. But there still are right leads and wrong leads on any story.

Here is the wrong lead:

Two people were killed when a truck collided with a car yesterday in Mill County.

The right lead is:

A 10-month-old girl and her mother were killed yesterday when the car in which they were riding was hit by a truck in Mill County.

And another wrong lead:

Mayor Alfred Ellison announced today that Jim Barber has been appointed city attorney.

The right lead for this story is:

Mayor Alfred Ellison today fired City Attorney Roland Maston, who has been accused of conflict of interest in the Red River Dam case.

THE FIVE Ws

Journalists used to have a simple formula for writing a lead: Just answer the "five Ws"—*who? what? when? where?* and *why?* Here is a lead that does:

District health workers and 150 volunteers will sweep through many of the city's homeless shelters tonight to test residents for tuberculosis in a novel, high-stakes strategy to control the resurgent disease in one of its main breeding grounds.

The Washington Post

Who—health workers and volunteers; what—the sweep and tuberculosis tests; when—tonight; where—city homeless shelters; why—to control tuberculosis in one of its main breeding grounds.

Modern reporters, however, frequently will omit one or two of the five Ws to keep their leads from getting too cluttered. This lead from another issue of *The Washington Post*, for example, does not say when or why:

Pentagon officials have thought up a new way to persuade the military services to shut down excess bases: Let commanders keep control of the money saved.

Still, even if they are not all answered, it is helpful to consider the five Ws when writing a lead. These are questions readers will have on their minds. The "when"—usually yesterday or, on some newspapers, a stated day of the week—is particularly hard to ignore. It must be included in any lead worded in the past tense.

Chicago Tribune reporter Brendan McCarthy.
(*Photo by Peter Howard.*)

Unacceptable:

Three young sisters and their father, who had rushed back into their burning house when he heard screams for help, died in a fire in Northwest Baltimore.

Acceptable:

Three young sisters and their father, who had rushed back into their burning house when he heard screams for help, died *yesterday morning* in a fire in Northwest Baltimore.

The (Baltimore) Sun

And while it is inadvisable to strain to squeeze the answers to all the other five Ws into the lead, they will all have to be included somewhere in the body of the story. (See Chapter 8, Information Selection.)

DETAILS

The news is full of names, times, addresses and ages. Most of those details will be included in the story. Which should be included in the lead? Certainly, the fewer the better. The lead's job is to catch the reader's attention, and unfamiliar names or insignificant facts are not exactly grabbers.

As a rule, leave a proper name out of the lead unless it belongs to someone well known.

Weak:

*June B. Austin,** a Berkeley County woman accused of killing her newborn child, may be released on a $75,000 bond in two weeks, but only after she undergoes a psychiatric evaluation, *9th Circuit Judge A. Victor Rawl* ruled Thursday.

Better:

A Berkeley County woman accused of killing her newborn child may be released on a $75,000 bond in two weeks, but only after she undergoes a psychiatric evaluation, a judge ruled Thursday.

The (Charleston, S.C.) Post and Courier

Had the reporter used names in *The Post and Courier* lead, he'd only have slowed delivery of the news. Readers in a city Charleston's size would not have recognized them.

A newspaper in a small town, where everybody is relatively well known, will include more names in its leads than a newspaper in a large city.

Times, addresses and ages deserve mention in the lead only if there is something interesting about them. The peace treaty ending World War I was signed on November (the eleventh month) 11 at 11 a.m. The exact time might have made it into the lead on that story because of its historic nature—and because of the coincidence of the numbers.

Exact addresses are difficult to justify in any lead. Usually mention of the neighborhood or city is sufficient. Occasionally it is necessary to mention the street or the intersection in the lead—if, for example, there might be some confusion about which branch of the bank in a neighborhood was robbed.

This lead from a short item in *The Washington Post* violates three of these rules:

Anthony Brady, 18, of no fixed address, was arrested yesterday and charged with armed robbery of the Safeway store at 3830 Georgia Ave., NW, D.C., police reported.*

---

*The name in this story has been changed.

Only friends of Anthony Brady, people fascinated by the behavior of 18-year-olds, and patrons of that Safeway store would be likely to read on. In a city as large as Washington, that is not a large percentage of the paper's audience.

CONTEXT

News does not occur in a vacuum. Yesterday's news may be related to last week's or last year's. (See Chapter 10, Background and Context.) In some cases that tie-in is noteworthy enough to include in the lead. It provides the *context* without which the story cannot be properly understood.

> After an almost six-year manhunt, federal marshals in Orlando arrested a Chicago man Saturday who is thought to be the fourth suspect in the 1998 murder of an armored car guard, authorities said.
>
> *Chicago Tribune*

Sometimes the context is the most newsworthy element of a story:

> At a time when some employees soon may be required to take time off without pay to help ease Los Angeles County's budget problems, the Board of Supervisors is considering giving salary bonuses to selected department heads.
>
> *Los Angeles Times*

For many stories, the context or background is not newsworthy enough to earn a place in the lead.

Unacceptable:

A man on a motorcycle rode up to the drive-in window of the First State Bank in Englewood yesterday, pulled a gun on the teller and rode off with $5,500, according to police. *The First State Bank was last robbed two years ago.*

But on stories that *do* have a significant history, context and background may be needed in the lead to help readers who have not kept a scrapbook on the story.

Unacceptable:

A Baltimore widow has died of cancer.

Acceptable:

A Baltimore widow *who won an out-of-court settlement of an estimated $500,000 from an asbestos manufacturer* has died of cancer *she contended was caused by her exposure to the substance.*

The Associated Press in The Washington Post

In an age of rapid-fire, round-the-clock news, context helps put the news in perspective and allows newspapers that do so to compete against the immediacy of broadcast and the Web by offering greater insight.

---

* The name in this story has been changed.

THE LEAD'S LEAD

The way in which a reporter starts a lead often indicates what element of the lead that reporter considers most newsworthy. It is frequently useful for reporters to ask themselves which of the five Ws is most newsworthy in the story and then to begin the lead with that fact.

In many leads, the "what" is most important...and comes first:

> *The safer-sex announcements, posters and media ads used in the campaign to combat AIDS* appear to be losing their impact among gay and bisexual New Mexico men.
>
> *Albuquerque* (N.M.) *Journal*

Many stories are news primarily because of the importance of the people in them. This story from *The Providence* (R.I.) *Journal* begins with the "who" because the auditor general's views carry a lot more weight than might the complaint of a local accountant.

> CRANSTON—Auditor General Ernest A. Almonte has identified an error in the city's audit that he contends could jeopardize Cranston's bond rating.
>
> *The Providence Journal*

An increasing number of stories consider the reason for an action—its "why"—significant enough to emphasize in the lead. *The New York Times* is known for its use of "why" leads:

> SARAJEVO—*Citing reports of hundreds of deaths from cold and hunger,* the United Nations official who oversees relief operations in this embattled republic said today that he had urged NATO to consider dropping food and medicines by air.

The remaining two Ws, "when" and "where," rarely dominate the lead. Of course, there are exceptions, as in that favorite "when" lead on April 15:

> *Midnight tonight* is the deadline for filing federal income tax returns.

In most newspaper stories, "when" is yesterday. That fact is not newsworthy enough to begin a lead.

Unacceptable:

Yesterday, the Pearl River School Board ratified a new two-year contract with the union representing about 40 teaching assistants.

Acceptable:

The Pearl River School Board *yesterday* ratified a new two-year contract with the union representing about 40 teaching assistants.

The (Rockland and Putnam Counties, N.Y.) *Rockland Journal-News*

POINTS

Some leads make one point:

> Three men were wounded early Saturday in a shooting outside a north Wichita nightclub, police said.
>
> *The Wichita* (Kan.) *Eagle*

Some leads include two independent but related points, as does this lead on a flap in Texas:

> HUNTSVILLE—State prison officials denied Friday that their agency has been spying on state Comptroller John Sharp and said reports to that effect were "an inhouse joke that got blown out of proportion."
>
> *Houston Chronicle*

And some leads summarize a series of related points—here, the effects of a rainstorm:

> A wildfire started by a lawnmower burned at least 67 homes on the south shore of Shasta Lake and raged out of control Thursday, charring more than 7,500 acres and forcing the evacuation of more than 400 residents.
>
> *Los Angeles Times*

How many points should a lead include? The rule, as usual, is the simpler the better...the fewer points the better. A lead that makes one point will read better than a lead that makes two. But if more than one element of the story is newsworthy enough, it will be necessary to write a lead that introduces two or more primary themes in a story. (See Chapter 9, Organization.) In the California disaster story, the burned homes, charred acreage and evacuations all were quite newsworthy and, therefore, all belonged in the lead.

But multiple theme leads should be used only if the extra points are equally newsworthy.

Weak:

Three men were wounded early Saturday in a shooting outside a north Wichita nightclub and a half-dozen people were engaged in a fistfight in the bar when police arrived, officers said.

The fistfight may well belong in the story, but it hardly carries the same weight as the shooting of those three men.

LABEL LEADS

Too often beginning reporters, fearful of selecting the wrong information for their leads, fall back on a lead that includes no important information at all. Instead of reporting whatever significant actions were taken at a meeting, they begin by merely informing readers that the meeting took place. The leads they produce are called *label leads*. They label an event instead of reporting on it.

Unacceptable:

The Los Angeles County Board of Supervisors met yesterday in regular session in the County Building.

The fact that the board met yesterday is not news. The news is what happened at the meeting.

Acceptable:

The Los Angeles Board of Supervisors yesterday authorized reopening the Hall of Justice jail to house weekend prisoners.

Los Angeles Times

Unacceptable:

John Frankenheimer,* the out-of-work Iowa father whose suicide threat created an outpouring of sympathy across the nation, appeared yesterday in U.S. District Court in Minneapolis.

The news is not that this man appeared in court. The news is what happened to him there.

Acceptable:

John Frankenheimer, the out-of-work Iowa father whose suicide threat created an outpouring of sympathy across the nation, was indicted yesterday in U.S. District Court in Minneapolis on 18 counts of food stamp fraud.

The Des Moines (Iowa) Register

THE ANGLE

The decision all reporters must make on what points to include in their leads has an importance that extends beyond the initial paragraph—the story that follows will have to emphasize the same points that are emphasized in the lead. In other words, the lead must be written with the rest of the story in mind; it establishes the story's *angle.*

If the lead talks about an arrest for drunken driving, the story cannot switch and concentrate on the sentencing the defendant received. If the story is going to focus on the sentencing, then the lead must focus on the sentencing.

Reporters sitting down to write a lead must ask themselves: What is the most weighty, emotional or unique aspect of this story? What will readers want to know about it? The lead will establish this angle; the rest of the story will have to follow in the same direction—it will support the points made in the lead. (See Chapter 9, Organization.)

CHAPTER 4 SUMMARY: LEADS

Readers scan the news, looking for what's compelling and interesting. The lead, or start, of a story, must inform readers and grab their attention. Reporters know that:

- Leads should be lean and focused. In traditional news stories, they typically are a single sentence.
- Leads should typically make a single point and rarely make more than two.
- Leads focus on what's new and unique. Sometimes reporters determine this by considering which of the "five Ws"—who, what, why, where and when—are most important to the story.
- Leads contain only the most relevant details. Other details wait until the body of the story.
- Leads avoid clutter. Unfamiliar names, addresses, ages and times tend to clutter leads.
- When necessary, leads link what's new to information preceding it that's essential to understanding the story. This is called context.

---

* The name in this story has been changed.

ADDITIONAL READING

News Reporting and Writing, Brian S. Brooks, George Kennedy, Daryl R. Moen and Don Ranly, Bedford/ St. Martin's Press, 2004.

News Reporting and Writing, Melvin Mencher, McGraw-Hill Humanities, 2005.

Reporting for the Print Media, Fred Fedler, Harcourt College Publisher, 1998.

EXERCISE A

Rewrite the following leads to make them more effective.

1. Yesterday the City Planning Commission met to consider the fate of Redwood Corp.'s plan to build a new Pathmark supermarket on a site at 345 Jones Road in Albertson. The plan was approved by a vote of 5–2.

2. The wind storms yesterday knocked over power lines causing blackouts in Rosemont, broke branches off trees throughout the area, toppled an oak tree in Fairmont and knocked over some garbage cans. Power was off in Rosemont for six hours before the Rosemont Electric Company was able to restore service to the about 800 affected homes.

3. Maria Ramero, 23, of 154 East Lansing Blvd. in Riverdale, and her daughter, Jessica Ramero, 4, of the same address, were killed when their car collided with a milk truck at 4:13 p.m. at the corner of Wayne and First streets in Riverdale yesterday.

4. Hancock High School met Caldwell High School for the state women's basketball championship yesterday at Caldwell, and Caldwell won in double overtime by a score of 52–50.

5. Mayor Eliot Runsfeld announced yesterday that Highway Commissioner Judith Sand will remain one of his good friends and an important and trusted adviser to his administration, but that she will resign her position in the city government. City Attorney Melvin Battel had announced last week that he is investigating charges that Sand accepted bribes from contractors.

6. Jury foreman Henry Norton announced yesterday that Lawrence Addison, 28, was guilty of first-degree murder in the shooting deaths last fall of Frieda Krump, 16, Jon Hayworth, 17, and Linda Robbins, 16, all of Berkeley.

7. Gov. William Davis announced yesterday that he will not seek re-election to a second term as governor next year. Davis said he made his decision after discussions with his wife and "long and hard soul searching." "This is a 24-hour-a-day job and it leaves no time for family," the governor said. "I am simply not willing to give up my family life for another four years."

8. About 100 policemen from the state police barracks in nearby Canton under the direction of State Police Capt. Roger Thomas used machine guns and tear gas to regain control of the Danbury State Penitentiary at 3 p.m. yesterday from a group of rioting prisoners who had been demanding improvements in prison conditions.

9. The Nantucket Board of Aldermen voted last night to spend $100 on this year's July 4th children's party, to cancel its next weekly meeting because of the three-day weekend and to fire Police Chief Paul Eddings because of his refusal to enforce the city's ban on topless bathing.

10. Three people were killed in an auto accident yesterday. Their car hit a utility pole at the corner of Dwayne and Broderick roads. The three people were all seniors at Southside High School. They were driving home from a high school football game at Southside.

EXERCISE B

Write traditional news leads based on each of the following collections of information. In each case you are writing for a newspaper dated tomorrow and read in the town in which the events occurred.

ONE

1. Litchfield County Board of Supervisors met tonight at the County Building, 8 p.m.
2. A memorial minute was read for the late William Hussel, former county attorney, who passed away this week.
3. After discussion, the supervisors voted 5–0 to lengthen the hours of operation of all county parks by 15 minutes.
4. Parks will now be open from 7 a.m. to 9:15 p.m.
5. Beach parks at the lakes, however, will remain on their old hours.
6. County Agricultural Commissioner Graydon Hall made a special report.
7. Hall reported that gypsy moth caterpillars had recently been detected in sections of the county.
8. Hall says research he has done suggests the caterpillars could damage, by eating the leaves and ruining their health, thousands of trees in the county.
9. Hall warned that spread of the caterpillars could threaten the county's million-dollar apple industry.
10. Hall said only a few dozen of the pests had been seen in the county, but that he was afraid they would multiply.
11. This, Hall reported, was the first time gypsy moth caterpillars had been seen in this area in 10 years.
12. Hall said he would investigate aerial spraying alternatives but that nothing had been decided on what to do.
13. This was the first announcement of the sighting of gypsy moth caterpillars in the county.

TWO

Talked to Newton Fire Chief Amy Aratani. She told me: Fire today at Beekman Plaza Hotel, corner of Best and Spring Sts.; detected at 5:05 p.m., under control by 10:15 p.m.; hotel burned to ground; nearly 120 residents forced to evacuate hotel; none of residents dead, 22 residents injured, 12 injuries serious; one fireman killed when hit by falling beam, 3 other firemen injured, two of them seriously; fire started in kitchen; damage estimated at $5 million; Beekman Plaza is town's oldest hotel—built in 1887; dead fireman—George Honan, 43, of 23 Elm St., Newton, father of three, married.

THREE

1. Upton Mayor Jane Rosenquist held news conference today at 3 p.m.
2. Announced she will run for governor.
3. "I am convinced that I can best help the people of this city by working to solve problems on the state level," she said.

4. Quote from Rosenquist exactly three weeks ago: "It would be foolish for me to leave the people of this city behind and run for higher office. I will finish out my term. You have my pledge."

5. Rosenquist asked about her pledge: "I don't want to discuss that. I believe I have explained why I have decided to run."

6. Rosenquist, a Republican, said she will enter Republican primary for governor...primary held in June.

FOUR

Sgt. Howard Black of Worchester police provided all info: Robbery and assault; victim Sean O'Casey; location—in front of Fairview Housing Project in Southside section of Worchester; time—app. 9:45 p.m. this evening; all info. on assault Black says is from his own interview with O'Casey; says O'Casey not available to talk to reporters (check at hospital confirms this); O'Casey attacked by four youths as he was exiting house of parishioner; hit in face with chunk of ice thrown by one kid; forced to ground; hit, kicked and scratched by four youths; left bleeding on ground; youths fled with O'Casey's wallet, including credit cards and $38 in cash; O'Casey, a Catholic priest, St. Paul's Church in Southside; was wearing clerical garb; no suspects; Black says he is investigating; third attack this month on member of clergy in Southside (check of newspaper records confirms this); Black refused to discuss why clergy were targets.

FIVE

From a statement released today by the ownership of the Pavillion Restaurant, considered one of the better and more expensive restaurants in Jackson: "The Pavillion Restaurant, the city's finest eating establishment, has always been known for its fierce commitment to the best quality and freshest ingredients in its food. We want to state today that this commitment remains. We will use nothing but the best in our cooking. We also want to announce, in accordance with our policy of the utmost in concern for our customers, that after receiving a few reports of stomachaches following meals eaten at the Pavillion last Saturday, we investigated and found a batch of garden peas that was rotten. They apparently caused some mild cases of food poisoning. These peas pose no serious health hazard. But in accordance with a request of the city's Department of Public Health, we are making public the problem for the first time today and inviting any customers who experienced discomfort following a meal on Saturday to return for another meal *gratis*."

SIX

1. Construction work has been ongoing at the new Railway Hotel, at the corner of French Street and Conduit Avenue in Ralston for six months.

2. A 200-ft.-tall, 5-ton crane has been used in the construction.

3. The crane toppled over and fell to the pavement on Conduit Avenue at 7 a.m. today.

4. Damage: Serious damage to sidewalk and pavement on Conduit Avenue; two parked cars smashed and seriously damaged; two windows of shops on Conduit Avenue smashed by asphalt loosened by the crane.

5. No people injured, though crane landed within three feet of a group of four construction workers.

6. No explanation yet for what went wrong.

7. Driver of crane uninjured.

8. Crane owned and operated by Axel Construction Company.

SEVEN

According to Dave Humal, owner of the Flicks Theater in Chandler:

1. The movie *Please Don't* is a romantic comedy.

2. As of today it has now been playing at the Flicks movie theater downtown for 49 consecutive weeks.

3. In the 24 years the Flicks movie theater has been in existence, the longest playing movie had been *Home Alone II,* which played at the theater for 48 consecutive weeks in 1992 and early 1993.

4. That makes *Please Don't* the new record holder at the Flicks.

EIGHT

From a speech today by George Jeffers, a local businessman, running in the Republican primary for Galveston City Council president against incumbent June Ratner: "Councilwoman Ratner is clearly a nice woman. We all like her. But it is just as clear that she has been a poor city council president. I have done some research in the council meeting minutes and I have found that Ratner has missed 25% of the meetings, that she plays no leadership role and that she rarely succeeds in convincing other council members to follow her views." (A check of council minutes confirms that she has missed one in four meetings.)

NINE

From an announcement by Bismark Police Chief Andrew Haney today: "As you all know, the city's financial troubles have forced a 15-percent cutback in our uniformed force in the past year. Today I want to announce three measures designed to make better use of our police officers: First, we are going to end the practice of sending one officer each year to the FBI's special training school. Second, we are going to try to shift the burden of filling out the paper-work on arrests increasingly to our nonuniformed clerical personnel. And finally, we are going to reduce the number of officers in the department's patrol cars at any one time from two to one. We will now use one-person patrols exclusively, instead of our former two-person patrols. I want to emphasize that none of the changes will affect the number of police patrol cars patroling the city at any one time and, therefore, that they will not affect the safety of our citizens."

TEN

In excavation work for the foundation of the new Twenty-first Century Tower office building at 4th and Sugarmill streets in Park Slope, four unusual items were found, Tara Jenkins, spokeswoman for the Continental Construction Corp., said in an announcement today. The items were:

1. An Indian head penny, dated 1896.

2. Three Indian arrowheads, of indeterminate date.

3. A Brooklyn Dodgers baseball memento from 1951.

4. Five fossils of dinosaur bones.

Jenkins: "The penny, the arrowheads and the baseball memento have been donated by Continental to the Sugarmill Elementary School for use in their historical discussions. The bones have been taken to the American Museum of Natural History in New York City. Steven

Studwell, an assistant curator at the museum, has been here. All the items were found by construction workers within the past two weeks."

Steven Studwell, in a telephone interview: "Yes, I was there yesterday, and we're sure they are dinosaur bones—the first ever found in Ty County. They would be about one million years old. But more exact dating and identification will have to await our tests."

Carol Locazio, of the Coin and Stamp store on 4th Street, in an interview: "Yes, that coin, an 1896 Indian head, is probably worth about 25 cents today, depending on what shape it is in."

ELEVEN

Information from Eugene Police Sgt. Sam Wong:

1. Automobile accident on eastbound lane of Fremont Expressway, 200 yards from the Montville Road exit, at 10:32 p.m. this evening.
2. Green Chevrolet pickup truck, driven by Susan Harvey, 53, of 6 South Greenwood Avenue here, apparently spun around and smashed into red Ford Escort driven by Jim Hardwood, 29, of 3 Mill Valley Road here; both vehicles had been heading east on the expressway.
3. Also in Escort was: Hardwood's wife, Alison Hardwood, 26, of same address. Mrs. Hardwood was in her sixth month of pregnancy.
4. Both occupants of Escort were killed in accident. Occupant of pickup injured and taken to Beth Israel Hospital.
5. It had been raining for three hours previous to the accident and we believe pickup hydroplaned on wet road surface. Both cars going, we estimate, about 60 mph.

Information from Susan George at Beth Israel Hospital:

1. Susan Harvey is in fair condition with a broken shoulder and serious facial cuts.

TWELVE

1. Roberta and Alan Fine of 66 Hotchkins Drive in Harworth reported their son Jerome, 12, missing to police two days ago after he failed to return home from school in the afternoon.
2. Betty and Arthur Angelo of 89 Hotchkins Drive in Harworth had reported their son Sandy, 12—a good friend of Jerome Fine—missing at the same time.
3. Harworth Police Officer Ellen Saunders: "We had the whole force looking for those boys. I guess you could call it a full-scale search."
4. Jerome Fine and Sandy Angelo returned to their homes on their own today—they had been officially missing for two days.
5. Jerome Fine: "We decided we would go camping in the woods. I guess we didn't think about our folks. The camping? It was great, but boy I feel awful."
6. Sandy Angelo: "It was just a little camping trip, that was all. But I guess I see now we should have told somebody."

THIRTEEN

From a statement by East Brook School Board President Walter Schapp: "The science lab and computer facilities at the East Brook High School are simply inadequate for training young men and women who will have to deal with the scientific problems of the 21st century. We simply do not have enough money in our already-overburdened operating budget to upgrade these facilities and, therefore, I am announcing tonight that the School Board at its meeting tonight has voted 5–0 to ask the voters to okay next month a $2.5 million bond issue to fund a total revamping of the high school's science facilities. The money will enable us to build three new science labs, four thoroughly equipped new science classrooms and a state-of-the-art instructional computer center."

FOURTEEN

1. The Shelterbrook Town Library held its annual book fair today.

2. More than 200 people from all over the state attended, including Gov. Doris Elliott.

3. People had a chance to buy the library's excess books and to see a number of special exhibits mounted by the library's staff and educators throughout Shelterbrook.

4. This was the 150th annual Shelterbrook Book Fair.

5. Shelterbrook's is the oldest continuing book fair in the United States.

6. Special exhibits and a birthday cake were there in honor of the big birthday.

FIFTEEN

At a meeting of the Redding Friends of the Parks tonight, the following actions were taken (wording from official transcript):

1. To appoint Stanley Howard acting secretary tonight to take the minutes.

2. To change next month's meeting to an informal coffee-cake session on Sunday morning.

3. To write a letter expressing the RFOTP's extreme concern and dismay on the subject of Redding Mayor E. W. Getty's plan to close Riverside Park.

4. To write a letter praising the Redding Police Department for its "Keep Our Parks Safe" campaign.

5. To raise $150 to restore the softball backstop at East Franklin Field.

SIXTEEN

Firecrackers are a continuing problem in Ardsley ... According to Harold Marman, police chief, three teens—Alex Hurt, 18, Freddy Dorset, 18, and Samuel Block Jr., 19—were arrested this evening and charged with illegal possession of firecrackers. Marman said: "One of our cars responded to a report that two boys had been injured by firecrackers in front of Flashy's Video Arcade, on South Road. When they arrived they found Hurt suffering a hand injury and Block with injuries to the hand and face. Hurt had burns on the palm and three fingers of his right hand—second-degree burns, the hospital said. Block had second-degree burns on his right hand and on his right cheek. According to the two boys, a large firecracker, called an 'Ashcan,' they were playing with went off prematurely. Our officers found additional firecrackers on Block, Hurt and on another boy, Dorset. They all are being charged with possessing those firecrackers. Block and Hurt were taken to the hospital. Dorset was booked, then released." According to Susan Alphonse, of St. James Hospital, Hurt and Block are in good condition. Alphonse confirms Marman's description of their burns.

SEVENTEEN

From statement today by Sharon Mayor David Bernard: "We've all been reading these stories in the paper that Fire Commissioner Carl Dean, one of the finest public servants it has been my pleasure to know, slipped up somewhere on his handling of his personal finances, that Carl somehow ended up receiving a consultant's fee from a company that sold equipment to the Fire Department. Now I think those charges are false. I thing Carl Dean is innocent. But I know the county prosecutor is looking into the charges. We all read that in the paper yesterday. And just to avoid even the hint of any impropriety while she investigates, I'm going, and Carl agrees with me on this, to suspend Commissioner Dean, without pay, until the investigation into this by the county prosecutor is complete. Assistant Commissioner Jill Davis will run the Fire Department until Carl returns."

EIGHTEEN

1. Fontana Windows president Sylvia Sidney held a press conference today in Shreveport at 11 a.m.
2. "Business has not been good in the past three years," she said.
3. "Fontana has lost a total of $1.8 million in three years," she said.
4. "Clearly we have to cut back somewhere, and I am afraid our cutback is going to have to be here in Shreveport," she said.
5. "As of Monday we will be permanently closing our Shreveport factory," she said.
6. "This will enable us to keep open our two other factories—in Belldown and Green River," she said.
7. "Obviously Shreveport workers will receive full severance benefits in line with their contract," she said.
8. Fontana's factory here in Shreveport employs 108 men and women.

NINETEEN

District Attorney Jake Milborne announced today: "As part of my office's continuing investigation of governmental ethics I have to report that we have found two minor technical violations of the state ethics code here. Mayoral assistant Gail House failed to disclose a $3,500 loan she received from Reliance State Bank on her financial disclosure form. And city Recreation and Arts Director Doyle Victor failed to disclose earnings of $4,670 in interest and dividends on two investments on his financial disclosure form. We have found no evidence of conflict of interest in either case. We do not intend to prosecute, and both officials have refiled correct forms. But we have made these problems known to Mayor Hildy Brooks, and we are, as is our policy, making them public now."

TWENTY

Wow, was it ever a cold one today in Martin! Temps fell to minus four at 4:00 a.m. this a.m. The National Weather Service says that's the third coldest temp ever recorded for this date here…temp only hit 8 degrees for a high this afternoon … and the city certainly suffered, that's for sure: Parents and children alike suffered from red faces and running noses; kids had to be sent home before lunch from the Hill Street Elementary School and Westside Junior High when heating systems at the school proved unable to get the places warm enough; and didn't we all have trouble getting those cars and vehicles started? The local AAA reported that today it received more calls for assistance from motorists here than ever before in its history. Yes, cold may be good for polar bears and igloos, but it certainly takes its price on our town!

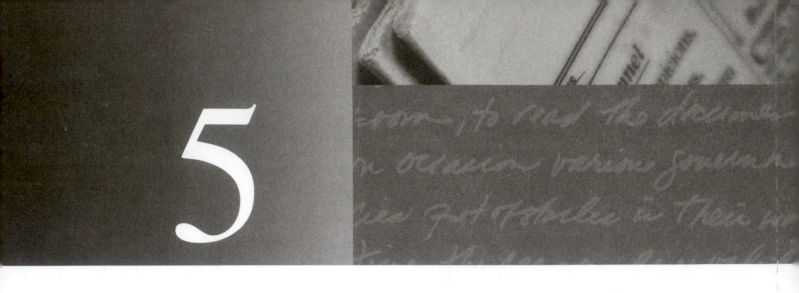

Other Leads

Justice is, after all, supposed to be blind. On Long Island, however, it has been charged that justice just couldn't keep its eyes open.

> It all happened in a Mineola courtroom at a divorce trial. Eyewitnesses say Supreme Court Justice George Krauss* fell asleep and snored loudly.
>
> (New York) *Daily News*

Not all stories begin by hammering home the hard facts. This lead has little in common with the traditional news leads discussed in the preceding chapter; it teases readers and withholds the most newsworthy facts until the second paragraph. But this lead is undeniably effective. The way it introduces the story of a judge who apparently took a snooze on the bench will certainly catch readers' attention. Written in the more traditional style, the lead would still be interesting but less compelling:

> A Supreme Court justice fell asleep and snored loudly during a divorce trial in Mineola yesterday, eyewitnesses reported.

Some reporters rely on a well-turned phrase or ironic twist—a *zinger*, as in that example from the *Daily News*—to hook their readers. Others lure readers into the story with a little tale—an *anecdote* intended to introduce the story's main theme through an example illustrating that theme. Still others begin by *setting the scene* of the story. And, on those rare occasions when an interview subject says something so striking and to the point that no paraphrase could communicate what the story is about so clearly, reporters may lead with a *quotation*.

All four of these types of leads—the *zinger*, the *anecdote*, the *scene setter* and the *quotation*—choose not to weigh in immediately with the hard news. They delay, for as little as a sentence or as much as several paragraphs, the delivery of the story's basic facts.

This lighter, more subtle delivery of the news is used at the top of many, if not most, timeless

---

* The name in this story has been changed.

stories, or features. (See Chapter 22, Features.) But some of these leads, particularly zingers, are frequently used atop news stories—particularly about offbeat events—in an effort to make them livelier.

Traditional or hard leads are just one paragraph long. Other leads, sometimes called *delayed* or *soft* leads, may go on for as many as four or five paragraphs. These leads generally end with a paragraph that clarifies what the story is about—that specifies how the turn of the phrase, anecdote or description at the top of the piece relates to the general theme of the article. This paragraph is called the *nut graf* (sometimes the *cosmic* or *billboard graf*). In the two-paragraph soft lead that opened this chapter, the nut graf is the second paragraph—it outlines the basic facts.

ZINGERS

Some leads grab readers with a snappy or clever phrase, often a play on words. This line led a news feature on the scarcity of blacks in the Mafia:

> The Mafia is not an equal opportunity employer.
>
> *The Wall Street Journal*

Zingers usually give readers a little surprise:

> Virginia City residents Mike and Rose Arp recently gave the state Board of Education a lesson in where to find lurid accounts of prostitution in Thailand.
> Their advice: Try a school library.
>
> *Las Vegas Review-Journal*

These leads are particularly effective in highlighting the unlikely or seemingly absurd:

> The U.S. Postal Service has added something to the snow, rain, sleet and gloom of night that it says will not stay its couriers from their appointed rounds.
> It is called nuclear war.
> …postal planners went before a House Post Office subcommittee yesterday to outline a 400-page plan for delivering the mail after a holocaust.
>
> *The Washington Post News Service*

To be effective, these punchy introductions must be kept short.

Unacceptable:

> The U.S. Postal Service has added something to that familiar list of trials and obstacles—snow, rain, sleet and gloom of night—that it says will not stay its hardy and tireless couriers from what are commonly known as their appointed rounds.
> In an effort to make the deterrent threat credible, it has introduced a plan for delivering the mail in the event of the unthinkable—nuclear war.

And a zinger must in fact zing, not plop.

Unacceptable:

> The old saying that the grass is always greener on the other side of the fence isn't necessarily true when it comes to utility rates.
>
> *The (Portland) Oregonian*

This is no place for tired or unclear writing.

ANECDOTES

Sometimes reporters try to interest readers in an issue by telling the story of one or more people whose experience makes the subject vivid. This dramatic lead to a story on avalanche science conveys just how dangerous avalanches can be:

> On a sunny morning in April 1967, Ron Perla found himself on ski patrol perched atop a block of snow, many hundreds of yards wide, that was itself perched above a long, slick ski run.
>
> Suddenly, the snow gave way under his weight touching off an avalanche. Beneath thick blankets of powder, Perla was carried half a mile down the Utah mountain at about 100 miles an hour. He fell unconscious. Rescuers later told Perla they had dug him out of an icy tomb—the fingers of his left hand were all that had shown above the snow piled at the bottom of the slope.
>
> In the years since the spill, Perla has retained a respect for avalanches that borders on awe.... "The power that soft, white snow can have during an avalanche is just astounding," he said, recalling why he chose to join the small band of men and women who have devoted their careers to avalanche science.
>
> *The New York Times*

The dictionary defines an anecdote as a short, entertaining account of an event. When these leads get long or dull they are in trouble.

Vanishing coastline at Gateway National Recreation Area on Sandy Hook, N.J.
(Courtesy of The *[Bergen County, N.J.]* Record)

SCENE SETTERS

Good writing communicates the feel of an event. Some leads, called scene setters or descriptive leads, draw readers into a story by painting a picture of where it takes place.
This visual image, like the tale in the anecdotal lead, introduces the flavor, if not the substance, of the story that follows:

> A red and white sign stands between the parking lot and the main bathing beach at Gateway National Recreation Area on Sandy Hook. Its message, "unprotected beach," is meant as a warning that the sands are unpatrolled. It could just as well be lamenting the beach's plight.
>
> Only a few giant steps are needed to span the distance between the sign and the high-tide mark. Along the narrow beach, tangles of utility cables and uprooted poison ivy, beach plum and bayberry are all that remain of last summer's dunes.
>
> A decade ago the water line was 300 yards away.
>
> The beach at Sandy Hook—along with many others along New Jersey's 137-mile coastline—is vanishing.
>
> *The* (Bergen County, N.J.) *Record*

These leads may provide an opportunity for creative, colorful writing: "Along the narrow beach, tangles of utility cables and uprooted poison ivy, beach plum and bayberry are all that remain of last summer's dunes." But they shouldn't be used as opportunities for verbosity and affectation. Sometimes leads that set the scene read like parodies:

> Emma and Alfred Mitchell are surrounded by broken beer bottles, crumbling cigarette packages and other rubbish. But even when trespassers start grass fires, the couple never complains.
>
> They can't. The Mitchells are buried in Mount Prospect Cemetery, Neptune Township.
>
> *Asbury Park* (N.J.) *Press*

The best scene setters leads are unforced; the power of the scene speaks for itself. This unconventional lead, from post-Katrina New Orleans, carries great power both for its tight focus and the searing image it's built around.

> NEW ORLEANS—In the downtown business district here, on a dry stretch of Union Street, past the Omni Bank automated teller machine, across from a parking garage offering "early bird" rates: a corpse. Its feet jut from a damp blue tarp. Its knees rise in rigor mortis.
>
> Six National Guardsmen walked up to it on Tuesday afternoon and two blessed themselves with the sign of the cross. One soldier took a parting snapshot like some visiting conventioneer, and they walked away. New Orleans, September 2005.
>
> Hours passed, the dusk of curfew crept, the body remained.
>
> A Louisiana State trooper around the corner knew all about it: murder victim, bludgeoned, one of several in that area. The police marked it with traffic cones maybe four days ago, he said, and then he joked that if you wanted to kill someone here, this was a good time.
>
> Night came, then this morning, then noon, and another sun beat down on a dead son of the Crescent City.

A nurse tends to a man awaiting transport to a medical evacuation area after Hurricane Katrina.
(Photo by John Rowland of The *[Lafayette, La.]* Daily Advertiser)

That a corpse lies on Union Street may not shock; in the wake of last week's hurricane, there are surely hundreds, probably thousands. What is remarkable is that on a downtown street in a major American city, a corpse can decompose for days, like carrion, and that is acceptable.

Welcome to New Orleans in the post-apocalypse, half baked and half deluged: pestilent, eerie, unnaturally quiet.

The New York Times

QUOTATIONS

Quotes should be used as leads only when they are short and to the point, and they should be used only in those *rare* instances when the newsmaker has said something that introduces the story better than the reporter can:

"Real jobs," said Gerald Detoia, with a touch of awe and hope. "They say that they have real jobs in there."

The 20-year-old Detoia has had quite enough in recent months of combing the classifieds, pounding the pavement and trying to track down people said to know people who think a job might open up somewhere. Finally he stood at a door with "real jobs" behind it.

Unfortunately he stood along with hundreds, then thousands of others as word spread fast that Marriott Hotels Inc. was hiring a complete staff for a new hotel next to the Nassau Coliseum.

The New York Times News Service in *The Milwaukee Journal*

Too often reporters resort to quote leads when they just can't seem to come up with a lead on their own.

Unacceptable:

"Their major concern was whether he had had extensive X-rays or radiation of that type," said an Arizona woman whose husband died of leukemia and who testified yesterday that her community was never warned that fallout from atomic tests in Nevada might create a health hazard.

This is a fine quote. It will be used high in the story (see Chapter 7, Quotations), but it does not get to the essence of the news; it does not belong in the lead.

Acceptable:

An Arizona woman whose husband died of leukemia testified yesterday that her community was never warned that fallout from atomic tests in Nevada might create a health hazard.

Associated Press

Occasionally a quote is so powerful that it calls out to be at the top of the story.

Weak:

When the Fremont couple put their 4-year-old to bed Aug. 17, she was happy and alert. The next morning she was dead.

At first, there seemed to be no explanation. Perhaps the child died during an asthma attack? But on Saturday, the parents stumbled upon a chilling entry in the diary they had just given their 14-year-old daughter for Christmas:

"Dear Diary: Well, it's the New Year so I'm going to start telling you everything dearest to me. I have to get something off my back. I killed my little sister...."

San Jose Mercury News

Better:

"Dear Diary:...I killed my little sister."

Wire service reports in *The Orlando* (Fla.) *Sentinel*

THE ANGLE

These leads are not just writing exercises. They have a job to do—the same task performed by a traditional news lead. A nontraditional lead, too, must engage readers by highlighting the most newsworthy element, or elements, of a story, and a nontraditional lead must also establish the angle that the story will follow.

If the story is about a daring rescue performed by a man in a wheelchair, it won't do to start with some largely irrelevant reference to why the man happened to be there in the first place.

Unacceptable:

Joseph Santos can't say why he decided to go in his wheelchair to the public dock at Bellmore Creek yesterday.

Newsday service in *The Milwaukee Journal*

Acceptable:

Joseph Santos was sitting in his wheelchair on the public dock at Bellmore Creek yesterday when he saw 5-year-old Kim Burke topple into the water.

The following anecdotal lead appears to be introducing a story about an interesting arrest.

Unacceptable:

A Hull police officer spotted the car at 5:12 p.m., on December 29.

The automobile was heading north on Shore Drive in Hull, travelling at an approximate speed of 10 miles per hour and weaving back and forth across the lanes of the road.

A breathalyzer test showed that the driver's blood-alcohol level was .26. Under Massachusetts law, a driver with a .10 blood-alcohol level is legally drunk. That's about three drinks in an hour's time.

The Boston Globe

The story, however, turned out to be about a local judge who, after announcing a crackdown on drunken driving, sentenced the car's driver to a year in jail. The lead here obscures rather than highlights the news.

A reporter's job is to communicate the news. No matter how clever or well written a nontraditional lead is, it is of no value unless it leads the reader directly to that news.

APPROPRIATENESS

Nontraditional leads can be used to discuss serious subjects:

IBM has more than just computers on its mind...

The struggling computer giant also wants to help deliver movies to your home, build cameras and put TV screens in airplanes.

USA Today

These leads can also be effective when the news is timely but of interest more because of its uniqueness or emotion than its impact or weight. The lead that opened this chapter began such a story.

But most editors agree that on fast-breaking and important news stories a delayed lead only gets in the way. Florida readers, for example, might have wondered why they were asked to wade through this zinger before getting to the pressing news that a frost was threatening their state's citrus crop and tourist industry:

The paunchy old men of the L. Street Brownies bath club won't need to test their stamina any more by dipping their toes in the wintry waters of Boston Harbor.

After today, they might as well mug for the camera in Miami.

The Miami Herald

There is another consideration in deciding where to use a nontraditional lead: These leads—especially zingers—often employ humor, and there are some stories in which humor simply doesn't fit.

Unacceptable:

Students aren't the only ones taking a holiday break this year.

Omaha (Neb.) *World-Herald*

That hardly seems an appropriate way to begin a story about 5,600 temporarily laid-off workers.

DILLY-DALLYING

An opening anecdote or description is intended to draw the reader into the story, not to be the story. Too many soft leads meander, testing the patience of readers.

One morning the *Los Angeles Times* kicked off its daily "column one" news feature with six paragraphs crammed with descriptions and details about a suit involving 27 Japanese appliance firms. A reader had to plow through to paragraph seven to confirm that this was a story about the difficulties of providing a jury trial in certain civil cases.

"I don't want to lay down a flat rule, but if you have to drift seven or eight grafs down the page, you begin saying, 'Why am I reading about this?'" concedes William F. Thomas, former executive editor of the *Los Angeles Times*.

Most editors agree that the nut graf—which pins down exactly what the story is about—should appear by the fourth or fifth paragraph, if not sooner. Anecdotes and descriptions at the top of a story shouldn't be allowed to wander indefinitely.

CONTROL

Some of the constraints of hard news writing are pushed aside when reporters choose a less direct approach to their stories. Nontraditional leads not only allow but demand greater freedom of style. It is this very freedom, however, that makes the writing of these leads so difficult for many reporters.

Too many writers strain, in the words of William Zinsser, author of *On Writing Well*, "to commit an act of literature." They fuss and fool around and use words and phrases they do not know how to control. The results can be woeful, as in the sentence from *The* (Paterson, N.J.) *News* that was first discussed in Chapter 3. It was used to lead a story about a baby abandoned a week before the New Year:

While most people were preparing to ring out the old, someone rang out the new this week. . . .

The solution, as usual, is simplicity. Many of the examples of acceptable nontraditional leads quoted in this chapter are colorful and creative, but none employs great poetry or spectacular prose. These leads are clear and simple. They use words the writer can control and they are dedicated to the news, not to literature.

CHAPTER 5 SUMMARY: OTHER LEADS

Nontraditional leads, or *soft leads,* grab readers' attention with a turn of phrase, a scene or a vignette that *shows* what the story ultimately will *tell.* But though these leads don't immediately summarize the news, they must be on point and resolve quickly so that readers know where the story is going. Four approaches often used in nontraditional leads are:

- *Zingers.* These are short and punchy, and are written to surprise.
- *Anecdotes.* These vignette leads are designed to illustrate the story's main point. They need to be clear and concise, getting to the story's main point within four or five paragraphs.
- *Scene setters.* These leads ground a story in a place and help readers see where the story is going.
- *Quotes.* These leads should be used sparingly. Quote leads only work if the quote is short, sharp and central to the story. Quote leads should not be used because the reporter can't figure out any other way to begin.

ADDITIONAL READING

America's Best Newspaper Writing, Roy Peter Clark and Christopher Scanlan, Bedford/ St. Martin's; 2nd edition, 2005.

"Jell-O Journalism: Reporters Are Going Soft in Their Leads?" Gerald Lanson and Mitchell Stephens, *Washington Journalism Review,* April 1982.

"Plotting the First Graph: Why Hard-Boiled Leads Aren't Necessarily Good Leads," Roy Peter Clark, *Washington Journalism Review,* October 1982.

Writing as Craft and Magic, Carl Sessions Stepp, Oxford University Press, 2006.

EXERCISE A

Rewrite the following leads, using traditional or other forms, to make them more effective.

ONE

"Boy, I just really can't believe this day is reality," said Charles Riggins. "I feel really lucky about having this chance."

A brisk breeze nipped at the sails of the S. S. Pinafore as Riggins and his son, Arthur, hauled up the anchor. She was a fine boat, 37 feet in length with a full-scale cabin sleeping eight below. There even was the most modern of kitchens, complete with food grinder, and a gas toilet to eliminate unpleasant odors that could cut appetite. Built in 1957 and reoutfitted last year, she showed none of the wear of her years at sea—a lucky thing, since the Riggins had 3,000 miles of ocean before them before reaching land again.

As a child, the older Riggins, 61, had begun to form his dream of following the route the Pilgrims took to this country more than 370 years ago. Now, after four months of preparation and 36 years as a pharmacist, he and his son were ready to set out from Plymouth, England, to Plymouth, Massachusetts.

TWO

No sunlight leaked into the room. The curtains were drawn and a dark green material covered the walls. Alex Victor was dressed in a maroon pullover sweater, as he sat alone at the square wooden table. The soft light left half his face in shadow. Victor opened the match by sliding a finely detailed white Queen pawn two spaces forward on the black and white checkered board. The clock was pushed, giving his opponent, Hans Astor, one hour to move.

Astor, a tall man with thinning hair, never moved. He wasn't at the Prescott High School gymnasium. Astor had refused to play the game, for the state championship, unless he was paid an additional $2,000 for expenses. He wasn't.

When the big hand on the timing clock returned to the twelve, the game was declared over, and Victor had won his first state championship. No state championship match had ever been so short—one move.

THREE

Hospital food. How he hated hospital food. But the nurse brought another tray and Jim Peller, a 9-year-old cancer patient at Elmwood Hospital in Duluth, ate some of it all the same.

Yes, the food at the hospital is hardly great, but today Peller had something to look forward to. A group of performers from the Midwest Circus was scheduled to give a performance in his room.

And, sure enough, at 2 p.m., right on time, the show started. A clown with orange hair, a huge purple nose and baggy red pants was the first to arrive in Peller's room. He was juggling four pink balls as he strolled in and stood at the foot of Peller's bed.

Two more clowns came into the room soon, along with a magician who made three tongue depressors and a thermometer disappear. Finally an animal trainer with three trained poodles came in, and the poodles walked on their hind legs all around Peller's yellow hospital room—number 253 in Elmwood.

The benefit performance—which lasted an hour and a half—was arranged by Davorah McNelly, manager of the circus, after she heard from hospital administrators that Peller was a circus fan and felt badly that he couldn't attend the show.

FOUR

First, sometime in December, the shiny, lightweight aluminum pots began to come out of the dishwasher with a faint, bluish-like film on them. That, recalls Irene Berg, thinking back to where it all started, was the first sign of the troubles that went on to plague her day in and day out ever since.

For the Bergs, a family of four who had lived 12 years at 43 Selmon Way in Lenox, things would only get worse. Next, a sweet odor, not unlike the ether that used to be used as an anesthetic in hospitals, emanated from their water pipes, wrinkling their noses.

The health inspector would not sample the water until he had been badgered by the Bergs for weeks. Then he sampled only for bacteria. The tests came back negative. Still, things didn't seem right. By March, Irene was finding herself the victim of searing, pounding headaches several days a week. Her younger daughter, Alissa, 12, a seventh-grader at Armonk High School, complained of dizziness and missed 12 days of school. Her husband, Robert, lost his appetite, she says, looking back.

Now, Irene Berg knows why. She feels vindicated but is scared. The city released the results of more far-reaching tests yesterday and the news wasn't good. The Bergs found their well contains the highest level of industrial solvent ever found in the state in drinking water.

FIVE

When Oscar Martin turned 5, his parents bought the beat-up, rickety and unpainted piano that still sits on the porch of their house on Sickles Lane. Oscar took to it immediately, crying when his mother told him it was time for bed. Within 24 hours, the tow-headed little boy, still in kindergarten, had picked out the melody of "Yankee Doodle," his favorite song.

As the years went by, Oscar began to study formally with Olivia Bartow, the music teacher at the grammar school. But if Beethoven, Bach and Brahms filled his lessons, beebop and boogie-woogie filled his spare time.

Even so, Oscar went off to college to study medicine. He lasted six months before the lure of his band, the "Martinettes," a six-member jazz ensemble, pulled him back. Within five years he'd progressed from the bars of Lincoln, Nebraska, to the Queen's Court in Buckingham Palace.

"I guess Oscar had a bug for music from the age he was in diapers," recalls his father, Handley Martin. "Even his crying was musical."

Oscar Martin returned to the two-story white house with blue trim on Sickles Lane in Decatur yesterday for his first visit in five years. Later, as 400 neighbors gathered around the bandstand in Van Dyke Park, he gave a benefit concert for the hospital auxiliary. And no one could miss the symbolism of the opening number of the now 32-year-old internationally renowned jazz musician. It was an old favorite with a new twist—Impressionistic Arrangement of Yankee Doodle in E Flat.

EXERCISE B

Write nontraditional leads for stories based on the following collections of information. In each case you are writing for a newspaper dated tomorrow and read in the town where the events occurred.

ONE

1. Emilia Staunton Grant celebrated her 95th birthday today at the Elmira Gardens, a nursing home at 397 Orient Ave., in Mansfield.

2. She was joined by six children, two of whom had come from out of state, 13 of her 15 grandchildren and six great-grandchildren.

3. Among her gifts was a cake, three feet in diameter with 95 candles. She blew them out with the help of an 86-year-old friend.

4. "If someone had told me I'd live to be 95 about 50 years ago, I'd have thought it was the devil talking," she said. "Then I'd learned to take it one day at a time. Maybe that's why I'm still around."

5. Fifty-one years ago, Mrs. Grant was told she had a rare form of liver cancer. Doctors operated but still told her she would be lucky to live two years. Six months later, without explanation, the disease went into remission.

6. Mrs. Grant's first husband, Alexander Grant, died in 1961 of a heart attack. She remarried at the age of 73 but separated from her second husband, Peter Randle, a year later on the grounds of incompatibility.

7. "Emilia Grant takes life in her own hands," said Gerald Poldin, a nurse at the home. "She is one spunky lady."

8. Mrs. Grant served as president of the school board from 1948 to 1960. She taught high school English for 28 years after her youngest child entered school.

TWO

1. Dominic Zaretti drives a taxi for the Golden Medallion Co. in Hamilton.

2. Every Friday afternoon before he gets off work, he stops for coffee at Sam & Louis's luncheonette and buys a $1 state lottery ticket on the way out, Zaretti said.

3. The state lottery helps raise money for education. Eighty percent of the weekly take goes to whoever picks the correct six numbers between 1 and 40. The other 20 percent goes to the state. If more than one person chooses the right combination of six numbers, the prize is split.

4. Last Friday when Zaretti bought his lottery ticket, no one had bought the right number in three weeks. The state lottery pool had risen to $12 million.

5. Zaretti said he was sitting at the counter filling out his lottery card when the waitress came up. Her name is Patricia Augusta, and Zaretti said he has known her for six years but only by her first name, "Pat." Sometimes he said he's shared his dreams with her of starting a restaurant if he wins the lottery.

6. Last Friday was Pat's birthday, Zaretti said. She told him to put down the month and day of her birthday as two of the numbers on his cards and the four numbers on his cab license as the other four.

7. Today Zaretti became the largest lottery winner in state history. He will receive $600,000 a year for the next 20 years or $12 million.

8. "Without Pat, I'd still be hawking fares," he said. "The first thing I plan to do is quit. The second is to open a restaurant and the third will be to make Pat manager. Oh yes, I'm giving her a $10,000 tip next time I stop by for coffee. That's the least I could do."

9. Zaretti is 46, divorced, and lives in a one-bedroom apartment in a two-family house in town.

THREE

1. Many Americans associate the fashion of nude and topless bathing with the stylish beaches of southern France.

2. Nude bathing isn't prohibited on French beaches.

3. Mark Nhu Research conducted a poll among 1,235 French adults over age 18 to get their views on nude bathing. The poll was conducted last month between the 13th and 19th of the month.

4. The poll was a random sample with a 5 percent margin of error, fairly typical for a poll.

5. In answer to the question, "Have you or would you ever bathe nude on a public beach?" 83 percent said "no," 12 percent "yes" and 5 percent, "don't know."

6. In answer to the question, "Would you be offended if others bathed nude on a public beach?" the answers were "no," 27 percent, "yes," 64 percent, and "don't know," 9 percent.

FOUR

1. This afternoon, Parker Bros., the manufacturer of the popular board game Monopoly, sponsored the first Monopoly tournament ever in Vineland.

2. Contest took place at the Holiday Inn on West End Avenue.

3. Match began at 10 a.m. and lasted until 5 p.m. There were four 90-minute games in which players were eliminated.

4. Winner is Nancy Rafferty, a graphic designer. Prize was $200. Her brother, Paul, also played. Nancy is 27; Paul 29. Paul is a pilot with United Airlines.

5. At the end of the final game, Nancy had $24,000 in Monopoly money stacked in front of her and owned most hotel chains on the board.

6. "I wish I could use some of this to pay my real rent," she says. "Or I'd use it to buy a ticket to Paris and eat on the banks of the Seine. Or maybe I'd just buy the Playboy Club in Atlantic City and turn it into the Playgirl Club. Complete with guys walking around in hotpants and muscle T-shirts."

7. "I suspect there's some kind of graft going on here," said Paul, joking. "Nancy has never won a family Monopoly game in her life. We've been playing since we were 10 and she always loses. Who loaded the dice?"

8. Twenty-five contestants began the tournament. Nancy is now eligible to enter the state Monopoly contest next month at the capitol. The grand prize? A week's paid vacation to Atlantic City.

9. The object of Monopoly, of course, is to become the wealthiest player by accumulating property. Nancy said she latched onto Park Place and Boardwalk early in the game and had the good luck of building hotels on both just before three people landed on them. Boardwalk and Park Place are the most expensive properties on the board.

10. "I've always had expensive tastes," said Miss Rafferty, who wore blue jeans and a Monopoly T-shirt to the tournament.

FIVE

1. Temperatures have been in the 90s in Louisville all week. Today they are supposed to break 100. It will be seven straight days of temperatures over 90, a record.

2. Sun rose at 6:03 a.m. today. At that time, temperature was 82 degrees.

3. Air thick and moist on 8:15 a.m. bus downtown. The air conditioner is broken and the bus, a No. 9 bus going from Elton Plaza to Main Street, is standing room only.

4. Ella Lewis is a passenger. She's a heavyset woman in her 50s. Sweat drips from her forehead. She pulls out a large red handkerchief and mops her brow. Her cotton blouse sticks to her stomach and is soaked under the arms. "I've always liked saunas," she says. "But they're always followed by a cold shower and a cool drink. I'm about ready to take my clothes off and run through town screaming." She declines to give her address or age.

5. Gene Patrick, 28, of 147 Ferguson Boulevard, also on that bus: "They always say there's two sure things, death and taxes. There's really a third. That's that the bus won't have air-conditioning on the hottest day of the year." Patrick is wearing yellow shorts, a blue polo shirt and sandals. He's carrying a leather briefcase and says he is a lawyer. He's also licking a raspberry popsicle. "It's like guerrilla war; you've got to adjust. I began eating these instead of cereal on Tuesday. At least your mouth stays cool. I'm not sure my partners are thrilled with my dress but my clients haven't exactly been wearing wool suits either." He works for Kassen, Bartley and Miller.

SIX

Two months ago. Call came in to the Shippenberg police station. Baby abandoned on steps of St. Mary's Church, Franklin Street. Police sent Officer Michael Shipmann, 36, to investigate.

"I couldn't believe anyone would just abandon a child like that," he says today. "But there she was, just perched on the step."

Baby girl, two weeks old, taken to Holy Name Hospital. Treated for exposure. Released to an adoption agency.

Shipmann and wife, Helen, 34, had no children. Filed to take in child as foster child along with 15 couples who read of incident in the paper. Agency, the Gladwin Home for Parents and Children, chose the Shipmanns.

No one ever claimed the child. Today, the agency called the Shipmanns and tells them they can adopt the child, whom they've named Martha. "This is the greatest day in my life," Shipmann says. "We had talked about adoption before but couldn't face the agencies, the waiting, the uncertainty. With Martha, the last two months have been wonderful and scary. Wonderful because we love her. Scary because there was always that fear someone would come back. Now that can't happen."

Talking in the living room of their home at 6 Parker Circle. Martha, 13 pounds, sits on Shipmann's knee in yellow footie pajamas. Coos from time to time. "I've never been a very religious person," Helen says. "But some things seem like providence. It's hard to remember all the free time we had and hard to imagine how we could have filled it."

Shipmanns given permission to adopt today. Tomorrow will go to Surrogate Court to file preliminary papers.

SEVEN

Bruce Ridley, 26, and his wife Kim, 27, moved into their new home at 66 Barkley Way, Hillcrest. Moved today. Interview with Mr. Ridley: "It was incredible. I went to the attic to check the roof and there on the beam I could just make out that someone had carved the name Hiram J. Ridley. I called the local Historical Society and sure enough my father's grandfather had built this house in 1889."

EIGHT

Tornado ripped up three trailers at Hunt's Corner this morning. Empty except for one. Alice Korn was baking bread in her kitchen. Miss Korn is 24 and works nights as a nurse at Hopkins Medical Center. That's where she woke up at 3 p.m., but she was in a hospital bed, in stable condition. You interview her at the hospital.

"It's a miracle really. Right out of *Wizard of Oz*. That's all I could think of, that and that I wondered how I would die. It was about 9:30 in the morning. The sky got black, absolutely black. The clouds were enormous and low and black. And then this funnel starts coming down, couldn't have been five miles away. It was monstrous, maybe a half mile wide. I ran out of the trailer and I was headed toward the gulley when I just was swept off my feet. Then I was in the cloud with everything swirling by and the ground passing below like in an airplane. A mattress went by and I just wanted to lay on it and go to sleep. Next thing I knew I woke up here. They told me a farmer found me lying in a cow pasture. Amazingly I didn't break anything. I sure feel like I went 15 rounds in a heavyweight fight though. I can't describe it really. I lost my home. I lost everything I own. I'm bruised and black and blue, but I feel real calm. I feel like I've gotten a second chance when I really shouldn't be here at all."

At Hunt's Corner everything is devastated. Miss Korn's trailer, which she'd been in minutes before the tornado hit, is bent around a tree in a V-shape 50 yards from its foundation. The field Miss Korn landed in is 225 yards to the northeast. She apparently was thrown out of the funnel as it bounced off a hill. Police estimate the damage at $180,000.

NINE

From interview with Green River Mayor Kenneth Denton today: "How many years have I been on this job now? Two. Well, I'll tell you something. I don't like it. I've had a lot of jobs in my life…been working for 36 years now…but I've never had a job as bad as this. There's tension and pressure from the moment I wake up in the morning to, you know, the moment I finally—and believe me it takes a while these days—fall asleep. I got to worry about whether taxes will go up, who should be fired, who hired, whether the police are doing their job, why that old lady was mugged downtown, whether the schools need more money, whether, you know, the Memorial Day parade should be on Sunday or Monday this year, whether the homeless need another shelter. On and on the worries go, and what do I get for doing, well, my level best to untangle all these problems? I get grief, that's what I get. I get grief from my fellow Republicans and grief from the Democrats, and grief from officials and grief from ordinary citizens. You know, I hear more complaints and nastiness in one day nowadays than I heard in a year in my other jobs. I walk down the street, and people must say to themselves, 'Hey, there's the mayor; let's toss him some grief.' Great job, huh? I hate it!"

TEN

1. Police officers Darrel Hanson and Jill Rivera arrived on scene at 3:46 p.m.
2. *Hanson:* "A crowd of, oh, I'd say 12 people had gathered around the tree. They were all looking up, so when we arrived we looked up, too. It was the damnedest sight. A white dog with black spots. I'm something of a dog lover myself. Looked to me like part fox terrier, part cocker spaniel. Got no idea how it got there."

3. *Rivera:* "We were called by a Susan Hersh; the tree was in front of her house. That's 1613 Willowbridge Road in Rosewood. She said she's never seen the dog before. It wasn't wearing a tag. So we had no way of identifying it. It was perched about a third of the way out on a thick branch about ten feet off the ground. Darrel was able to start climbing up the tree. He began calling to the dog. Called it 'Checker.' He tried to calm it and get a reading on whether it would bite. He let Checker sniff his hand, then gently grabbed the dog. Lowered it down to me."

4. *Hanson:* "None of the people there had any idea what the dog was doing up in the tree. I can't believe it could have climbed up by itself. Maybe some kids put it up there as a prank. The dog is going to the pound. Nice dog. Could use a good home."

PART 3 STORIES

Charlie Roduta, education reporter for *The Columbus* (Ohio) *Dispatch*, interviews students in a local classroom. *(Photo by Doral Chenoweth III for* The Columbus Dispatch*)*

6

Attribution

A 27-year-old man was arrested on Christmas Eve in South Carolina *on charges of* fatally shooting a Port Authority police officer Monday.

The suspect, George Redoux, of Elizabeth, N.J., was arrested at his brother-in-law's apartment in a housing project in Simpsonville, 10 miles from Greenville, *according to Detective Steven Harris of the Greenville Police Department.*

Detective Harris said Redoux, who *was described* as "armed and dangerous" in a multistate alarm, surrendered without resistance as police cars converged on the housing project at 7 p.m. Authorities had been alerted to Redoux's presence by an anonymous caller, *the detectives said . . .*

The Hudson County Prosecutor, Fred Zimmer, said that several witnesses had viewed a photograph of Redoux in New Jersey and had "positively identified" him as the gunman.*

The New York Times

A few days after this story appeared, George Redoux was released and all charges against him were dropped. The police admitted that they had arrested the wrong man. Yet *The New York Times* reporter who wrote the story could look back on it without embarrassment.

The story never says that Redoux had fatally shot the police officer, only that he was arrested on charges of having fatally shot him . . . which was true. The story does not say that Redoux was armed and dangerous, only that he was described in an alarm as being "armed and dangerous" . . . which was true. The story never says that witnesses had positively identified Redoux, only that a prosecutor said Redoux had been "positively identified" . . . and the prosecutor did say that.

This story was carefully written. All potentially questionable or controversial information was properly *attributed*—the source of the information was identified. The circumstances of the arrest were *attributed* to a detective who participated in the arrest. The evidence allegedly implicating Redoux was *attributed* to the county prosecutor. (The *Times*, of course, did publicize the fact that all charges against Redoux were dropped.)

---

* The names in this story have been changed.

Here are some additional examples of attribution:

Jimmy Daniels, a 7th grader at Sadler Junior High School, was dead at the scene with a bullet wound to the head, *said Detective Robert Medley.**

Tulsa (Okla.) World

Press Secretary Beverly Hubble said Grassley is to be treated for a tightening of muscles in his lower esophagus that interferes with the passage of food.

The Des Moines (Iowa) Register

Salt River floodwaters, which have swept away tons of garbage from landfills alongside the riverbed, will leave behind filthy pools of stagnant water laced with rotting material and hazardous bacteria, *according to a Valley environmentalist.*

The (Phoenix) Arizona Republic

WHEN TO ATTRIBUTE

In any story all the facts have a source. Some come from officials or witnesses, some come from records or documents, some come from reference sources. It would be possible to place attribution in every sentence in a story. But attributing every fact in a story would make the story almost unreadable.

Unacceptable:

The 1912 sinking of the Titanic took 1,517 lives, *according to an encyclopedia.*

The number of deaths on the *Titanic*, mentioned in a story on the death of more than 800 people on an Indonesian ship, is independently verifiable. There is no question or controversy about that number. The attribution adds nothing to the story.

Acceptable:

The 1912 sinking of the Titanic took 1,517 lives.

Associated Press

More often than not, however, information does have to be attributed. Here's why and when.

Opinion

Two people watching a basketball game would undoubtedly agree on which team had won. The final score, since it is independently verifiable, would not have to be attributed to the official scorer or the press information officer for one of the teams. But two people watching a presidential debate might very well reach different conclusions about who had won. Those conclusions would be subjective—opinions; they would require attribution. A reporter, guarding a reputation as an unbiased observer (see Chapter 2, Fairness), must attribute any opinions, any subjective comments, that appear in a news story.

Unacceptable:

The city should not ask for a federal license to build the dam and all studies should be stopped at once.

* The names in this story have been changed.

Acceptable:

The city should not ask for a federal license to build the dam and all studies should be stopped at once, *the utility said.*

The Seattle Times

Unacceptable:

D.C. Public Schools Superintendent Clifford B. Janey yesterday began fulfilling his pledge to fix disappointing management practices by hiring a corporate executive to work on contract procurements—free of charge.

Acceptable:

D.C. Public Schools Superintendent Clifford B. Janey yesterday *said he* began fulfilling his pledge to fix *what he described as* disappointing management practices by hiring a corporate executive to work on contract procurements—free of charge.

The Washington Times

Informing Readers

It seemed a simple fact: How many people were killed during one day's brutal sectarian violence in war-torn Iraq. But, as often happens in reporting on war, natural disasters and other catastrophes, the key statistic proved elusive.

SULAIMANIYAH, Iraq, June 4—Gunmen killed *21 people*—many of them high school students—after dragging them off buses northeast of Baghdad, *officials said.*

...*Serwan Shakir, the mayor of Qara Tappah...said* of those killed, 19 were Shiite Turkomen and two were Kurds.

Associated Press on *The Washington Post* website

BAGHDAD, Iraq, June 4—It was a brutal killing, even by the standards of this violent country. Gunmen set up a fake checkpoint north of here Sunday, stopped two minibuses and executed *20 passengers*, including students on their way to final exams.

The New York Times

Clearly the figure for those killed was wrong in at least one of these reports. But something else is different about them. The AP story tells readers where the information came from. The *Times* story, which focused more on analyzing the meaning and impact of these killings, does not. It deprives readers of a chance to assess the source of the news.

All of us trust some people more than others. Thorough identification of the sources of potentially controversial information in a story allows the reader to judge whether the information is believable.

Without careful attribution, readers don't find out about the potential biases behind the information sources provide. For example, in the bad old days when the *New York Post* was known for the subjectivity of its political reporting, it printed a statement claiming that a Democratic presidential candidate was "lying throughout the Great Debate." The charge was attributed to "an expert on detecting lies." Later in the story readers learned that the expert was "vice president of the International School of Polygraph Science." They did not learn that the expert also was a Republican candidate for the New York State Assembly and presumably no friend of the other party's presidential candidate.

In addition, attribution informs readers of the scope of the reporting that has been done to produce the story. If a reporter covering a rent strike by tenants has talked only with the landlord and the building's employees, that will show in the attribution, and the story will be revealed as potentially biased and underreported.

Michael Santino, 31, reflects amid a field of flags planted in Houston Heights in memory of American troops who lost their lives in Iraq.
(Photo by Johnny Hanson)

Protecting Newsmakers

People in the news are subject to countless charges and attacks. Politicians are denounced. Judges are accused of bias. Coaches have their intelligence questioned. Suspects are formally charged with crimes. Reporters should never just spread nasty rumors or pick up charges repeated on the street. (See The Basics, Section F, Law.) But some charges should be reported—particularly formal criminal charges. When any such controversial statement appears in the newspaper, it must be carefully attributed.

Unacceptable:

Flagrant violations occurred at polling stations across Ukraine.

Acceptable:

Officials for the top three candidates in the field of 24...denounced *what they said* were flagrant violations at polling stations across Ukraine. They cited numerous reports of harassment—and in at least one case a violent assault—against voters and election observers from both camps.

The New York Times

The need to use attribution to protect newsmakers becomes crucial when they are charged with crimes. Until the judicial system has had its say, there are no criminals, just suspects. No one can be identified as having committed a crime; only allegations of someone's potentially criminal behavior can be reported.

Unacceptable:

Andrew Fell was arrested after he slashed a shopkeeper with his pocket knife in a dispute over egg prices.

Acceptable:

Andrew Fell was arrested, *police said*, after he slashed a shopkeeper with his pocket knife in a dispute over egg prices.

Should the caveat "innocent until proven guilty" slip your mind, remember George Redoux... accused of a crime he did not commit.

Unacceptable:

A 27-year-old man was arrested on Christmas Eve in South Carolina for fatally shooting a Port Authority police officer Monday.

To protect the suspect's rights here, it is necessary to make clear that he is merely *being charged* with this crime. Technically this is not attribution—no source is indicated—but it does the same job.

Acceptable:

A 27-year-old man was arrested on Christmas Eve in South Carolina *on charges of* fatally shooting a Port Authority police officer Monday.

The New York Times

Protecting the Writer

Reporters are responsible for their decisions on whom to quote in a story. (See Chapter 7, Quotations.) But if a reporter has selected credible sources, that reporter certainly is not expected to stand behind every point those sources make. One purpose of attribution is to make clear that this is the newsmaker's point of view, not the reporter's. If the reporter has attributed the condemnation of a Presbyterian Church delegation to its source—in the following case the American Jewish Committeee—any angry responses can be sent to the committee, not the reporter.

Unacceptable:

The Presbyterian Church delegation that met with leaders of the terrorist group Hezbollah lent legitimacy to the A-Team of global terrorists and delivered a blow to peace efforts. The Presbyterian Church should repudiate the delegation's actions.

Acceptable:

The *American Jewish Committee* said the Presbyterians had "lent legitimacy to what *American government officials* call the 'A-Team' of global terrorists" and delivered "a blow to peace efforts in the region." *It called on* the Presbyterian Church "to repudiate immediately" the delegation's actions.

Associated Press in the *Charleston* (West Virginia) *Gazette*

The writer of this story in the *San Francisco Chronicle* has chosen to stand behind a rather strong claim made by a dentist:

A Beverly Hills dentist described in San Francisco yesterday his *vastly improved* version of invisible dental braces—attached not to the front but to the back of the teeth.

It is prudent to leave such claims to the newsmakers:

...what he called his vastly improved version...

Adding Credibility

Reporters borrow expertise on the subjects they are covering from their sources. Good reporters give credibility to their stories by seeking out the most authoritative sources and then attributing information to those sources so readers know that the information is, if not definitive, at least the best available. Attribution assures readers that these experts stand behind the information presented in the news.

Unacceptable:

If you want to talk about frightening numbers, try looking at the projected cuts the city would need to make if the proposed Palesky tax cap passes.

Acceptable:

If you want to talk about frightening numbers, try looking at the projected cuts the city would need to make if the proposed Palesky tax cap passes, City Manager Steve Bost said Wednesday.

Bangor (Maine) *Daily News*

When a story announces someone's state of mind, the reporter's credibility is always suspect. So statements about a newsmaker's thoughts, hopes or emotions should be attributed.

Unacceptable:

Thompson hoped to deliver his message later today.

Acceptable:

Thompson said he hoped to deliver his message later today.

St. Louis Post-Dispatch

GUIDELINES

The use of attribution often seems to confuse beginning reporters. Perhaps this is because the rules of attribution are applied more strictly in journalism than in most other forms of communication.

Here are some additional guidelines intended to eliminate the confusion.

Overattribution

While too little attribution can leave a story vague and subjective, too much attribution can make it seem sluggish and amateurish. As noted earlier, facts that are not subject to interpretation and can be verified independently should not be attributed. For example, it is not necessary to attribute the statement that Chicago is on Lake Michigan to an atlas.

While information connecting a suspect to a crime must be verified, some facts about that potential crime can be established and do not require attribution.

Unacceptable:

The victim allegedly died.

A person's death is independently verifiable. Facts that can be verified independently can be reported without attribution, if the reporter has done the verification.

Similarly, if the reporter was there to witness the event, attribution would rarely be necessary.

Unacceptable:

According to witnesses, including this reporter, the former hostages and members of their families in the audience applauded his remarks.

Acceptable:

The former hostages and members of their families in the audience applauded his remarks.

The Seattle Times

The amount of verification reporters demand for a fact before they will use it without attribution should depend on the degree of controversy involved. Applause is not generally a matter of controversy. But in discussing a crime committed in that audience, reporters would not want to rely on their casual observations of what happened.

Acceptable:

Police said two persons were wounded by shots fired in the audience.

For matters of record—such as criminal charges—reporters will rely on officials they trust. Information on specific criminal charges will appear, without attribution, based on the report of a trusted police official:

He was charged with armed robbery.

A cautionary note, however: Some facts that seem noncontroversial and independently verifiable may be less solid than they appear. For example, the official who tells a reporter how many people were killed in a train wreck two hours ago may not have the final figures. Death counts have a way of changing. The figure given in the story should be carefully attributed to that official. A week later in a follow-up article, after all the wreckage has been searched and the seriously ill treated, it will be safe to print the number dead in that crash without attributing it to an official. By then that statistic will be part of the verifiable public record.

All questionable or controversial facts in a story need attribution. But one attribution per fact is sufficient.

Unacceptable:

Sgt. Murphy said Walker *allegedly* ran away from the scene.

Acceptable:

Sgt. Murphy said Walker ran away from the scene.

Indirect Attribution

Rather than continually repeating phrases such *as according to* ... or ... *police said*, reporters occasionally use another means of indicating attribution.

The victim *was identified* as Burton Feroe.

Was identified here is shorthand for *was identified by police* or other officials. This *indirect attribution* saves words, yet still makes clear that the identification was not simply made by the reporter. The identification of a body is not independently verifiable, but it is generally not controversial. It is safe to use indirect attribution here.

Many forms of indirect attribution use the passive voice (see Chapter 3, The Language of News): *was reported*, *was scheduled*, *was listed in satisfactory condition*. Because they do not clearly identify the source of the information, these wordings should be reserved for noncontroversial information for which the source can be inferred.

Perhaps the most common examples of indirect attribution are adverbs such as *allegedly*, *reportedly* or *apparently*. These words do not do the job that standard forms of attribution do because they do not identify the source of the allegation or report. "He *allegedly* shot him," does not protect the suspect as effectively as "*Police said* he shot him."

Weak:

Gompertz *allegedly* walked off with the money.

Better:

According to police, Gompertz walked off with the money.

Allegedly should be used in a sentence in place of attribution only if previous sentences make clear exactly who is responsible for the allegation:

According to police, Gompertz robbed the store. He then *allegedly* walked off with the money.

Reportedly and *apparently* are even weaker words and are the least effective forms of attribution. They should not be used in discussion of something as controversial as potentially criminal behavior.

Unacceptable:

According to police, Gompertz robbed the store. He then *reportedly* walked off with the money.

One final note on *allegedly*: The word derives from the same Latin root as *legal*. It should be reserved for potentially criminal matters and not used for more frivolous charges.

Unacceptable:

He *allegedly* does not like chocolate.

Placement of Attribution

Attribution can be placed at the beginning of a sentence:

According to police, he was in the building at the time of the murder.

In the middle:

He was in the building, *according to police*, at the time of the murder.

Or at the end:

He was in the building at the time of the murder, *according to police*.

Attribution carries the most weight at the beginning of a sentence because the reader then knows who is responsible for the information before reading the information. So when the source is as important as the information itself, the attribution should come first.

Weak:

Not all crimes require police to shoot a fleeing suspect, *according to Police Chief Joseph G. McAtee.*

Better:

Police Chief Joseph G. McAtee said yesterday that not all crimes require police to shoot a fleeing suspect.

The Indianapolis Star

Attribution is also placed at the beginning of a sentence to alert readers when the reporter is switching sources. (See Chapter 7, Quotations.) Attribution is held until the end of the sentence in the *lead*, unless, again, the source is as important as the information. Otherwise placement of attribution is just a matter of style. It's wise to vary it to keep a story from sounding stilted.

CHAPTER 6 SUMMARY: ATTRIBUTION

All facts come from some source. Attribution makes clear to what newsmaker or published source a story's key information can be traced. It also helps readers decipher what point of view may be behind that information. Ultimately, attribution gives the news authority and protects reporters' credibility. In deciding when to attribute, consider:

- Whether the information is widely known fact or reliant on specific sources.
- Whether the information implies a point of view or opinion. (All opinion should be attributed.)
- Whether the information is subject to change. For example, numbers of dead and injured reported immediately following an accident often change.

EXERCISE A

Edit the following sentences where necessary to improve their use of attribution.

1. He was arrested for shooting her.
2. Police said they were told he was allegedly seen leaving the building.
3. Cole attacked his opponent, Mary Simmons, in a speech before the Chamber of Commerce. Simmons is a free-spender. She has no concept of the value of the taxpayers' money.
4. The police arrived and determined that Grimes had been drinking.
5. Officials of the state Agriculture Department discussed the threat posed by the fruit fly with reporters. That tiny bug could cripple the entire state's produce industry.
6. Anthea Jones died, according to Mercy Hospital spokesman Pete Kaplan.
7. The candidate then outlined plans for the most effective campaign this city has ever seen.
8. Police said Montoya left the store 20 minutes later. He apparently was carrying some stolen purses and wallets.
9. The state's economy will improve sharply next year, according to the governor.
10. The victim, Randall Peters, allegedly had stab wounds all over his body.
11. Police had no suspects.
12. Increasing labor costs are a serious problem in this area. The Coalition for a Stronger Economy presented a plan yesterday that, if approved by local governments, would help alleviate that problem.
13. According to the council secretary Robert Paxton, the council approved the park plan by a vote of 9–1.
14. Police said Menkin hit the other car after running a red light. Menkin then ran south on Orchard Street with police in pursuit.
15. The victim was identified as Michael Brewer of 13 Old Mill Lane.
16. The worst accident in the United States involving a commercial airliner occurred in 1972 when 357 people were killed in a midair crash, according to FAA records.
17. The mayor said his opponent had a history of waffling on the issues. He alleged that Olson had changed his position on a tax increase three times.
18. The three burn victims were listed in critical condition, according to a hospital spokesman.
19. The president said he supported covert aid to the rebels because the government intends to destroy their culture.
20. Zevin met with the press at midnight and discussed the tremendous impact of the campaign his opponent's arrest for drunken driving will have.

EXERCISE B

No attribution is included in the following stories, but the source for the information in each paragraph is listed to the left of the paragraph. Edit the stories, rewriting where necessary, so that they include proper attribution.

ONE

1. Police Officer Jane Shaw and arrest record

A 72-year-old man has been arrested and charged with robbing a shoe store in East Milford.

2. Officer Shaw

Eliot Anderson, a retired construction worker, entered the store, Jake's Shoes at 42 Milford Ave., at 2 p.m. yesterday, pulled out a knife and demanded that the store's owner, Jake O'Brien, hand over all the money in the cash register.

3. Jake O'Brien

"He looked like a nice old man, but then I saw the knife." O'Brien gave the man approximately $550, and then the robber hurried out of the store.

4. Officer Shaw

O'Brien quickly called police and gave them a description of the robber. Officer Jane Shaw spotted Anderson, who fit O'Brien's description, walking south on Milford. Avenue. He was carrying a four-inch knife and had $550 in his pocket.

5. Officer Shaw and arrest record

Anderson, who lives at 28 Forest St. in East Milford, was charged with robbery and released after posting $2,000 bail.

TWO

1. Report of local Environmental Commission released yesterday

The city is allowing too much development of low-lying areas, a practice that could lead to serious flooding.

2. The report

In the past year, nearly 70 acres of swampy land along Conshohocken Brook has been developed, raising the water table.

3. Articles in your paper two weeks ago

Two weeks ago, residents of Holly Court, which is about a half mile downstream from the newly completed Shady Grove condominiums, complained that the construction had flooded their basements and yards.

4. The report

Further construction in low-lying areas, such as the land near Conshohocken Brook, could raise water tables even more. If water tables go up, there will be more serious flooding.

5. Commission Chair Gladys Sternhell

"The Planning Board has approved a half dozen applications for new construction without even setting stringent drainage requirements. We urge the council to review these applications more carefully."

6. Planning Board Chair Johannes Pizetsner, in response

"Every town has its do-gooders and I guess they have their place. But this town needs more taxable property. It has one of the highest tax bases in the county."

7. Report on city finances provided two months ago by the City Council when it passed the budget

A homeowner currently pays $2,750 in city and school taxes on a home valued at $95,000, the average for the community.

8. City planning maps

Nearly 300 acres of city land remains undeveloped because of drainage problems. Most of it is along Conshohocken Brook.

THREE

1. Report of the state Assembly Oversight Committee released today

The housing inspection program run by the state cannot ensure the safety of tenants.

2. The report

The current system of spot inspections of rental properties leaves most apartments "uninspected and unprotected."

3. Five committee members from both parties and a copy of Assembly-woman Engoron's speech

The report was written by the Assembly Oversight Committee after a speech by Assemblywoman Annie Engoron expressed concern over state housing inspection policy.

4. Statement by Engoron, who is on the committee, yesterday

"The state Housing Department is pro-landlord and is not really concerned with protecting tenants."

5. Statement by Dick Fried, spokesman for the department, yesterday

The Housing Department is still studying the committee's report and will have no comment on it at this time. "But the charge that the department is pro-landlord is absurd."

6. Old newspaper stories in the paper's library

When the Housing Department's budget was cut by $150,000 last year, the department was forced to lay off 35 of its 124 inspectors and to switch from regular periodic inspections of apartments to irregular spot inspections.

7. The report

There are not enough inspectors in the field to maintain contact with all the state's rental properties. Landlords know they are no longer being watched as closely as before.

8. Transcripts printed in the report

The committee heard testimony from a number of tenants who complained their landlords seemed much less concerned with upholding standards in their buildings. Some complained of days without heat and hot water.

9. Transcript printed in the report

State Housing Commissioner Jake Wolf denied the tenants' charges in testimony before the committee. He told the committee that through more efficient procedures his reduced staff of inspectors is able to monitor housing at least as well as in the past.

10. Statement by Engoron confirmed by committee secretary

Assemblywoman Engoron has introduced a bill to increase funding for the Housing Department by $200,000 next year and to require yearly inspections of all rental property in the state.

EXERCISE C

Edit the following story to improve its use of attribution.

Brian McAuliffe, a chief inspector for the state's Industrial Control Board, said yesterday that the board has fined Serpico Chemical Co. $5,000 for failing to maintain air-pollution-control equipment and for installing other equipment without permit.

McAuliffe said yesterday that his inspectors allegedly found during a visit to the chemical plant last September that some pollution-control devices "had just literally rusted away." The inspectors, McAuliffe said, also found that the firm, located on State Highway 7 and Tuckerton Road, according to town maps, had installed or moved more than 40 pieces of equipment without obtaining state permits required for a change in operation.

Serpico President Allen Turner would not comment on the fine, which, lawyers for the state and company said, was negotiated by the attorney-general's office and company lawyers.

Deputy Attorney General John Gregson said that under an order signed by the company, the state would return 80 percent of the fine if Serpico installs new pollution equipment by March 1.

Anthony Armani, a senior environmental specialist with the Industrial Control Board, said that the company already has applied for permits for some new equipment.

McAuliffe and Armani said they did not know which of Serpico Chemical Co.'s processes had been operating without pollution-control equipment.

According to President Turner, the Industrial Control Board and records filed with the federal Environmental Protection Agency, Serpico manufactures about two dozen chemicals used in plastics. Nearby residents have complained for years about a sickeningly sweet odor that emanates from the plant on some days, old newspaper articles show. McAuliffe said the firm would be installing additional odor-control equipment.

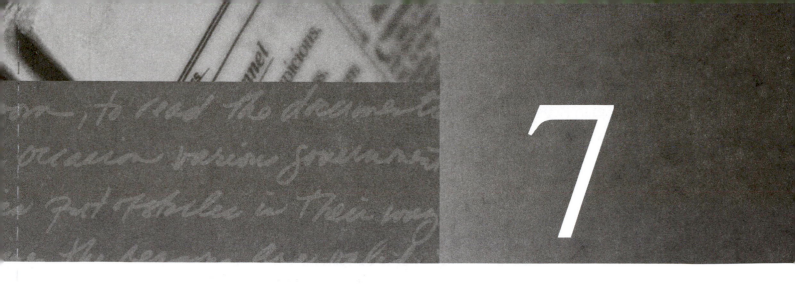

Quotations

> "It's kind of sad to think of Pluto as a Teamster."

That was the reaction of a visitor to Walt Disney World when she was asked about a vote by the park's employees, some of whom portray cartoon characters, to join a union. The Associated Press reporter who had sought the visitor's opinion must have known he had gotten a good quote. It expressed a personal viewpoint, and it did so colorfully. It helped bring the story to life.

Thousands of miles away, another AP reporter got this quote from a businessman worried about "undesirables" in town. "If we could get rid of the dirtbags and dopers, we'd be OK," the businessman said. Again, this comment, nakedly subjective, helped bring the emotions behind the news to life.

Much of the news is about the actions, ideas, achievements, travails and emotions of people. Often the best way of conveying people's thoughts and experiences is through their exact words. Quotes usually provide the spice and sometimes some of the substance of the news. Reporters listen as keenly for the original, vivid or funny remark—the "good quote"—as students listen for hints about what's going to be on a final exam.

DIRECT QUOTES

Direct quotes—quotes at least a sentence long—should be used when many of a speaker's exact words bear repeating. Sentences tend to be quotable when they fit into one of the following categories:

Colorful Statements

During the Revolutionary War, a colonial officer, William Prescott, ordered his troops at Bunker Hill to withhold their gunfire until the British troops were in very close range. Paraphrased, that is not a particularly interesting command. But the power of Prescott's language, in this direct quote, has kept his words alive for centuries:

> "Don't fire until you see the whites of their eyes."

A more recent United Press International story included the remarks a British explorer made upon returning from a 14-month trip around the poles and seeing his wife. Here the wry humor of his simple language made a direct quotation worthwhile:

> "How do you do? Are you my wife?"

Nothing the reporter could have composed could have captured the scene better.

Subjective Comments

Restrained by the rules of objectivity (see Chapter 2, Fairness), reporters must leave the expression of opinions to the people they are interviewing. Those opinions, and the passions behind them, are communicated best in the people's own words.

This direct quote was from a mother who was ejected from a restaurant for breast-feeding her baby in public:

> "You wouldn't want to eat your dinner in the restroom. Why should my baby have to?"
> Associated Press in the (New York) *Daily News*

And this statement was made by a 71-year-old artist who journeyed from Florida to Washington, D.C., to protest the president's budget cuts:

> "Our Social Security is down to $420 a month. Our food stamps were cut to $13 a month. I decided I was going to Washington on my broomstick to tell that man off."
> *The Washington Post*

There is no more powerful way of presenting this woman's case or of explaining her motivation.

The quote at the beginning of this chapter that it was "kind of sad to think of Pluto as a Teamster" obviously represented an opinion. Teamster members and supporters might find unionization "kind of nice."

Eyewitness Reports

Eyewitnesses were there the moment it happened. You weren't. Readers will want the drama of eyewitness recollections to enliven your more composed reconstructions.

Here, a policeman injured in a gun battle is talking:

> "I was in the doorway. We were firing directly at each other. There wasn't time to think about being nervous. He was trying to kill us."
> (Chicago) *Sun-Times*

Expert Knowledge

If someone knows more about a subject than the reporter does, it's often most convincing to let that person talk directly to the reader for a sentence or two. The prosecutor has more credibility than the reporter would have in explaining why criminal charges were dropped against two men accused of abducting a Salvation Army bell ringer:

> "We cannot prove this case beyond a reasonable doubt," said Richard Buchman, the assistant Ramsey County district attorney who dismissed the charges.
> (St. Paul, Minn.) *Pioneer Press*

Important Statements

The views of some people—the president, the mayor, the House majority leader, the head of a striking union—are so important that readers deserve to know exactly what such persons have to say about certain issues. Kentucky Gov. Ernie Fletcher ran into some turbulence in his race for re-election after he was indicted on misdemeanor charges. His lieutenant governor declined to run on the ticket with him again. But Fletcher was undeterred, as the Associated Press noted by quoting his own words:

> "I'm very excited about running and I've got the fire in the belly to do it and we're going to get it done," Mr. Fletcher told reporters.
>
> Associated Press in *The New York Times*

PARTIAL QUOTES

When reporters choose to quote just a word, a phrase or a fragment of a newsmaker's sentence, they are using a *partial quote*:

> Saying he wants to avoid *"even the appearance of inappropriate actions,"* State Auditor-elect Ralph Campbell has reimbursed the city for a trip to New Orleans in November.
>
> *The* (Raleigh, N.C.) *News & Observer*

There are three situations in which these partial quotes make sense.

Emerson College student Sandra Chen interviewing then Massachusetts Gov. Mitt Romney (left). The other man in the picture is Stephen Coltrin, a New York City public relations consultant.
(Photo by David Rosen)

Weak Sentences

Newsmakers cannot always be counted on to come up with a usable sentence. Sometimes only part of a sentence is worth quoting.

Unacceptable:

"It's a little something else, I guess I'd say, to have so much cheap politicking in so many expensive commercials."

In a case like this, the best option is to select only the compelling words, if there are any, to use as a partial quote.

Acceptable:

The candidate complained of what he called "so much cheap politicking in so many expensive commercials."

Key Words

Readers don't need to read the exact wording of an investigator's detailed description of the circumstances of a robbery. The reporter can paraphrase those circumstances, with attribution, more effectively. But the potentially controversial charge that the crime was committed by someone working at the place that was robbed is worth expressing in the investigator's own words:

In what investigators termed "*an inside job*," two men, one posing as a maintenance man, entered the cashier's office in the building…taped the mouth, arms and feet of part-time cashier Barbara Summers and took the money from an open safe, police said.

The Philadelphia Inquirer

Leads

In a traditional lead, there rarely is room for a complete direct quote. But a newsmaker's own words can be newsworthy enough for the top of the story. In such cases, it is generally necessary to pull out just the most important phrase or two.

Here is a lead that would have benefited from use of a partial quote.

Weak:

The chairman of the Alabama Ethics Commission on Tuesday accused state government of general dishonesty and immortality.

The Birmingham News

Better:

The chairman of the Alabama Ethics Commission on Tuesday said the state has "in many respects a dishonest and immoral government."

Partial quotes should never be used to cover sloppy note taking. It won't do to substitute a sentence spotted with partial quotes for the direct quote the reporter didn't quite get. Except in the lead, a good direct quote is usually more effective than a paraphrase sprinkled with partial quotes.

Weak:

Jim Clark's ability to "recognize defeat" is in question, Sen. Thomas V. "Mike" Miller Jr. said. He charged that Miller "can't count votes."

Better:

"Jim Clark doesn't have the ability to recognize defeat," said Sen. Thomas V. "Mike" Miller Jr. "He can't count votes."

The (Baltimore) Sun

PARAPHRASING

Quotes, despite their effectiveness, can't be allowed to take over a story. Most of the story can be better conveyed by paraphrasing, by communicating the newsmaker's ideas through the reporter's own more succinct, more direct sentences. Journalists are paid in large part because of their ability to write. Is it surprising that they can often write better than the people who interest them can talk?

Unacceptable:

"We followed the perpetrator to the building which he lived in and began a stakeout of the premises," explained Sgt. Rudolph Gomez. "After a four-hour wait he came out again and we apprehended him and brought him back to the station house."

There's nothing compelling in Gomez's words here. The reporter should paraphrase.

Acceptable:

The suspect was arrested after a four-hour stakeout of his home, Sgt. Rudolph Gomez said.

Paraphrasing should be used whenever the reporter can say it better than the newsmaker. Flat, dull quotes are worse than no quotes at all.

Unacceptable:

"I think it's a good idea," said Councilman Steve Robertson. "I'm voting for it."

Acceptable:

Councilman Steve Robertson said he would vote for the proposal.

Complex explanations are, generally, also best paraphrased:

For the first time in 12 years, the enrollment in the Milwaukee Public Schools went up this month, Lee R. McMurrin, superintendent of schools, said yesterday.

McMurrin said the enrollment on Sept. 17, the day the official enrollment is taken statewide, was 87,402, about 1,400 more than had been expected and about 100 more than last year.

The Milwaukee Journal

But if the quote is vivid or poignant, forget the paraphrase. Let the speaker talk:

Unacceptable:

White said there were many noisy and bold drug dealers, and she could watch them hide their drugs in nearby bushes and trees.

Acceptable:

"It was a jungle, a three-ring circus," White declared. "They were so bold and so noisy. We'd watch them hide their dope in our bushes and trees, and they'd look at you to let you know they saw you."

Los Angeles Times

FORM

In the body of a story, quotes generally are more effective when they lead off a paragraph, with the attribution *after* the first sentence of the quote. The quote is livelier than the attribution; it deserves to go first. This quote is from an Iowa crop duster who walked away from the crash of his light aircraft:

Weak:

He said: "This is a heckuva way to start a day. I must be getting better, must be doing something right because the last time I tangled with a power line I broke my hip and my arm."

Better:

"This is a heckuva way to start a day," he said. "I must be getting better, must be doing something right because the last time I tangled with a power line I broke my hip and my arm."

The Des Moines (Iowa) Register

The attribution should come *before* the quote when the person speaking is more important than what the person is saying and when some fact about the speaker must be explained at the start:

The mayor refused to answer the charge directly, but he did have this comment: "Somehow this issue always seems to rise to the surface during an election year."

Attribution also should come first when it is necessary to show that another person is not speaking.

Unacceptable:

"We certainly don't want all the parents sending their kids to school in fear," said William Hayes, who was running the meeting in the absence of the board president.
  "And we don't want to send our kids to school out of the district either," said Lemmo.

(New York) Saratogian-Tri-County News

This wording could confuse readers. It reads, at first, as if the second quote is also from Hayes.

Acceptable:

"We certainly don't want all the parents sending their kids to school in fear," said William Hayes, who was running the meeting in the absence of the board president.
  Added Lemmo: "And we don't want to send our kids to school out of the district either."

In a quotation more than a sentence long, attribution is needed only once in each paragraph and is usually found at the end of the first sentence.

Unacceptable:

"I'll be frank with you," he told the lawyers. "I don't think that's going to happen," he continued.

Acceptable:

"I'll be frank with you," he told the lawyers. "I don't think that's going to happen."

In many but not all cases, additional paragraphs in a long running quote are reattributed to the speaker. Each distinct time a person is quoted in a story, the quote requires its own attribution.

A note on capitalization: The first word of any *direct quote* should be capitalized, whether it comes *before* the attribution:

"A live power line is an emergency," he said. "A dead power line is not. A live power line dances and sparks. It's easy to detect the difference."

St. Petersburg (Fla.) *Times*

or *after* the attribution:

He said, "A live power line is an emergency...."

The first word of a *partial quote* in the middle of a sentence (unless it's a proper noun), however, is lowercase:

Former Gov. Edwin W. Edwards charged that he had made "sweetheart deals" with two campaign supporters for state contracts.

The (New Orleans) *Times-Picayune*

LENGTH

Weak:

"We could have gone anywhere in the United States but we chose to come to Bluefield," Gary Harrison, vice president of Flowers Industries,... said yesterday. "We could have gone to Bristol [Va.], Ashland [Ky.] or to Charleston, but we decided to come to Bluefield. There were two or three different reasons we did so. The trade area is good. We have an opportunity to sell baked goods here. And the manpower is here."

Bluefield (W. Va.) *Daily Telegraph*

This reporter seemed not to know where to start or end the quote. Quotes should rarely run more than a few sentences. The writer's job is to select the sentences that make the point most effectively. In this case, four sentences from Harrison could have done the job.

Better:

"We could have gone anywhere in the United States but we chose to come to Bluefield," Gary Harrison, vice president of Flowers Industries, said yesterday. "The trade area is good. We have an opportunity to sell baked goods here. And the manpower is here."

CHORUSES

A quote should never be attributed to more than one person—unless the people interviewed managed to answer in unison like a Greek chorus.

Unacceptable:

"The time has come for the government to stop ignoring the elderly," the protesters argued.

Acceptable:

"The time has come for the government to stop ignoring the problems of the elderly," one protester argued. Many of her fellow demonstrators said they agreed.

DISHONEST QUOTES

When readers see words in quotation marks they have a right to expect that they are reading the exact words of the person to whom the quote is attributed—not a paraphrase, an approximation or a fabrication.

Quotes should never be invented, or *piped*. Always avoid the temptation to create a fictitious and anonymous taxi driver to say what you think someone should have said about an event. Such dissembling poses a profound threat to the credibility of journalism.

If a reporter fails to catch the exact words of a quote, it is also dishonest to try to recreate what the newsmaker had said. Readers deserve quotes, not guesses.

Movie ads occasionally quote the lone positive comment from a review while ignoring the mass of slams and digs that surround it. Such practices certainly have no place in news reporting. Reporters must always be sure that quotes not only were taken verbatim, but that they are true to the overall meaning and context of the speaker's remarks.

If a member of the planning commission said this: "The new highway would simply create too many environmental problems for the city, though we see the highway's economic value," it would be unfair to quote only "We see the highway's economic value."

Reporters should apply the highest standards of honesty and fairness in reporting others' words.

EDITING QUOTES

Most editors would agree, however, that reporters can make some minor changes in the quotes they use, *as long as the meaning and tone of the quote truly represent those of the speaker*.

It is acceptable to correct a minor grammatical error in a quote. "The commission has to do *their* job" can become "The commission has to do *its* job." But more significant changes in wording must be placed in brackets within the quotation to indicate that those were *not* the speaker's words:

"I think the nursing care [at LaRabida] was more than reasonable," said Jacobsen.
Chicago Tribune

It is also acceptable, even advisable, to remove, without notice, the meaningless throwaway phrases with which some of us punctuate our conversations: "*Well*, it was, *you know*, one of the most frightening and sickening experiences I ever had." More significant deletions from a sentence used as a direct quote should be indicated by using an ellipsis: "It was one of the most frightening...experiences I ever had."

Minor editing of quotes must be practiced evenhandedly, or not at all. The reporter who corrects the minor grammatical errors in the quotes of one candidate but leaves the embarrassing little fluffs in those of his opponent is practicing a type of bias.

RESPONSIBILITY FOR QUOTES

It is your article. You must remain in control of it no matter who else is being quoted.

Reporters are not responsible for the opinions expressed in the quotes they choose, but they are responsible for deciding which opinions to present. Their selection must be informative and fair. (See Chapter 2, Fairness.)

Similarly, reporters—though they won't be totally satisfied with the wording of all the quotes they use—must be responsible for their clarity and relevance.

"But that's exactly what she said!" is not an acceptable explanation for why a confusing or misleading quote was used. She may have said it, but it was the reporter who decided to use it. Quotes must either be used in such a way that they make sense or not used at all.

The use of quotation marks is no excuse for sloppy journalism.

CHAPTER 7 SUMMARY: QUOTATIONS

Quotations provide color, insight and point of view to news stories. They shouldn't be used to convey basic information. That's why one of the authors of this book calls quotations "the salsa and not the chips" of good reporting. In selecting quotes, remember that:

- They are the speaker's exact words. If you're not sure what someone said, paraphrase.
- They are most effective when they are succinct and lively. Most quotes should be just a sentence or two long.
- They should be in plain English. Choose quotes readers will understand.

Full quotes (complete sentences) should generally be set off in their own paragraph.

They are usually preferable to partial quotes—key words within quotation marks—which are used to emphasize a specific phrase.

The quoted words typically precede attribution unless you are introducing a new speaker. In such cases, put attribution before a quote.

EXERCISE A

Rewrite each of the following passages to make it more effective. Use either a paraphrase, a partial quote or a direct quote. The sentences would each be part of longer stories.

1. *The governor's press secretary, Shana Haloran:* "The governor will not be commenting on the prison strike until 2 p.m. tomorrow, when he will have something to say on it."

2. *Mayor John Ahern:* "Well, c'mon now. You know, it's been 14 years since we've had a tax revaluation. I've thought it over enough; that's for damn sure. I decided we had waited long enough, OK?"

3. *Police Officer Sheila Aurora:* "We have picked up one suspect in the case—a white, 23-year-old male by the name of Conrad O'Leary, who was seen leaving the building. He has been booked and charged with homicide in the case."

4. *Principal Gregory James:* "Ah, students, students. Yeah, a flagpole sitter. No, no. No decision has been made on disciplining him yet, but very, very scary watching. I can tell you that."

5. *Joanne Page, president of striking Sewers Union Local 45:* "I just hope those bosses in there have got the message by now because I can't tell you how tired I am of repeating it. I mean, we've stuck by our guns from the beginning of this thing, right? I'd say our reluctance to go back is a mile deep and a mile wide."

6. *Coach Red Bernard:* "Well, I'll sketch it out a little for you if you'd like. You see we had the other end, Gene Bronowski, running a fly pattern, and we thought the quarterback he could get the ball to him deep. But he saw Miller open in the flat. Do you see how surprised I was?"

7. *Truck driver Amos Enders:* "Yeah, I was right behind them when they crashed. I've never seen anything like it. Frightening? When I saw them hit my heart skipped two beats; I'll tell you. No, I don't know what caused it. I'm not gonna guess for you. I can't believe anyone got out of those cars alive."

8. *Fire Chief Elma Sanborn:* "Our trucks arrived on the scene at 11 p.m. We had the fire under control by 1 a.m. But those were a tough two hours."

9. *Dancer Al Hawkins:* "Look, they can arrest me every day. They can come and stop my show every day, and twice on Sunday. They can walk right in here anytime they want. But I'm going to get on that stage. I'm going to take my clothes off. I'll do my act in jail if necessary."

10. *Meat Packers Association President Janet Glazer:* "Yes, looking for a convention site, our organization is. Yes, we've been around a lot in the search; all over, really. Yes, your town's Show of Shows Center, too! Yes, that's the snazziest one I've seen, all right."

EXERCISE B

Rewrite the information in each of the inserts in the following stories so that it can be used effectively at that place in the story. Use direct quotes, partial quotes or paraphrases.

ONE

The Rev. James Wilcox was appointed to fill an interim seat on the Lampley Town Council yesterday, making him the first black to serve on the council in the town's 147-year history.

The appointment, made by Mayor Hodding V. Martin, filled a seat left vacant by Councilman Rafer Anderson, who resigned two weeks ago for family reasons. Wilcox's term will run until November, when he will be eligible to seek re-election.

Insert:

Gerald Havermale, 45, Town Council member for 12 years, owns Havermale's Hardware Store at 656 Market Square. "I was real pleased about Wilcox's appointment. Reverend Wilcox is a close personal friend. I've known the guy for many years, ever since he became minister of our church. We've served on several committees together. He's, well, a very intelligent man, and there aren't many who have his knowledge of Lampley matters. I think he'll have no problem at all getting re-elected in November. He'll add an active, knowledgeable voice to the Lampley Town Council. Frankly, I have problems working with some of those guys, but I'm sure Wilcox and I will get along just fine."

Wilcox, 47, is the senior pastor of the First Congregational Church at 91 DePew Terrace. He has chaired the town's Task Force for Education and has served on many civic committees. He is married and has two sons, 13 and 11.

TWO

A two-ton crane lifting girders on top of a downtown bank building crashed onto the roof of the building yesterday afternoon, knocking loose pieces of brick and granite that then plummeted five stories onto South Avenue, battering cars, smashing store windows and snarling traffic.

The shower of stones caused an estimated $70,000 in damage. Nine cars were hit by the falling bricks and stones, and three store windows were shattered. A half-dozen pedestrians suffered minor injuries, police said.

The 140-foot crane hit the roof of the Midland Bank on 45 Cooper St. at about 3 p.m. Pieces of the wall around the roof, where the crane hit and came to a rest, fell to the street, sending pedestrians scurrying for cover and backing up traffic on downtown streets for several hours.

Insert:

Glenna Fox, 26, clerk in the city government building across the street: "I was on my way back from my lunch hour. Suddenly I heard a loud crash and everybody began running every which way. It was incredible. I said to myself, 'Oh, boy. I'm Chicken Little come alive.' The sky may not have actually been falling but an awful lot was coming out of it."

Emergency workers treated five people at the scene for cuts caused by flying glass. One man sprained his ankle while rushing for cover, police said.

Insert:

Anna Zirps, 56, owns and runs Joey's delicatessen two doors down from Midland Bank. She was cut by glass from the shattered front window of the deli: "I was just standing here, you know, serving customers and what not and then all of a sudden there's people screaming outside and stones bouncin' off cars. Then I heard a crash and my right shoulder felt like it had run into a cactus tree. I'm OK really, but the salami and fruit salad are a mess. Can you imagine? What a strange afternoon."

The cause of the accident is being investigated, according to a spokesman for Martel Industries, the firm supervising construction of a workroom on the roof of the five-story building. The crane had passed a safety inspection only two weeks ago, the spokesman said.

Insert:

Hugh Evans, 46, of 16 Baylor St., a burly redhead who stands 6 feet 2 inches tall and weighs 210 pounds, was part of the four-man construction crew working on the roof: "I don't know what caused it. Beats me. We were just loading a bunch of girders, something we do every day, and, all of a sudden, the crane tilted and started to wobble. Then it fell. The operator jumped out just in time."

THREE

More than 300 Newport State College students crowded into the waiting area at McNee County Airport last night to cheer the return of sprinter Evonne Simpson after her record-breaking performance at the National College Games.

Earlier in the day Ms. Simpson had run the 100-meter dash in 10.24 seconds, the fastest time ever by a woman collegiate athlete, at the meet in Philadelphia.

Insert:

Crowd of students, dressed mostly in blue jeans and button-down shirts, waved banners and yelled as Ms. Simpson and her coach, Hilda Baum, walked through the door into the waiting room from the runway. Crowd yelled in unison: "We want Evonne! We want Evonne!"

Insert:

Ms. Simpson, 20 years old, is a sophomore at Newport State. She is 5-foot-8, weighs 118 pounds, has brown eyes, and is wearing a red and white Newport State sweatsuit. She enters the waiting room and raises her right hand, curled into a fist, into the air, and shouts, "All right! All right!" She hugs several apparent friends in the crowd. While in the waiting room she says: "I am just so thankful for all the support and encourage-ment that all the students at Newport State have given me. This isn't just my record, it's their record, too, in a sense. It's funny to think back, but I almost didn't come to school here. I originally was interested in going to a bigger school, but the scholarship here just was too good. I certainly don't have any regrets now. I'll tell you something else: I thought I'd never be as happy again as I was after I ran that race, but the way I feel after this welcome here comes pretty close."

The race began at 1:30 p.m. at Franklin Field in calm, clear weather. Ms. Simpson broke first from the starting blocks and led throughout, beating her nearest challenger, Bernice

Duvall of UCLA, by nearly two meters. Ms. Simpson's time broke the former record, held by Betsy Meghan of the University of Kentucky, by 5-hundredths of a second.

Insert:

Coach Hilda Baum, 31 years old, a graduate of Newport in 1978 and a former state champion in the 100- and 200-meter dashes, says after arriving in the waiting room: "Wonderful! Wonderful! Just wonderful to see such a crowd of fans and supporters gathered here at the airport. You know, it's been a real boost to Evonne throughout her career here to have so much interest in track and field on campus. You know, I've thought this over carefully; Evonne is the most gifted athlete we've ever had at this school, and what is more amazing, you know, is that she works far harder than athletes with far less talent. This is no fluke; it was just a matter of time before she got the record."

A ragged motorcade of students' cars escorted Ms. Simpson from the airport to the campus, honking their horns along the way.

She was greeted at the main gate of the campus by still more students and Newport State President Lauren Sethkins.

Insert:

Dr. Sethkins, 43 years old, in her fifth year as president, says: "I watched the race on television and it was great, incredible. I must admit I'm quite a sports fan, and particularly a fan of Simpson's. I don't know if you're aware that she's not only a great runner, but a great young woman. And what a turnout we've had to welcome her. Well, in my five years here I've never seen this campus more spirited. I mean, this will be remembered as one of Newport State's finest days."

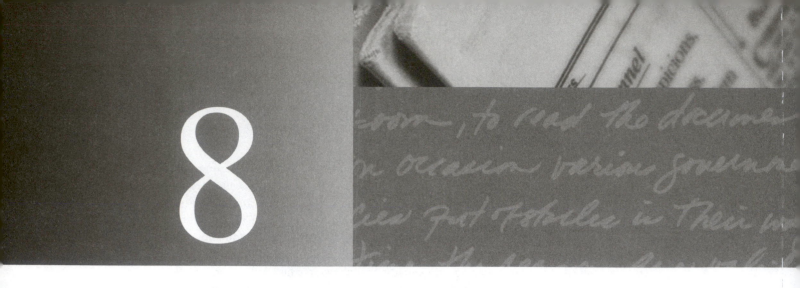

Information Selection

Any news event is surrounded by a mass of facts. There are the broader points that can be made—the story's primary focus (established in the lead), supporting information and secondary themes. And then there are the fine points—details such as times, ages, addresses, names and descriptions.

Decisions on what to emphasize in a story require news judgment. (See Chapter 1, News Judgment.) But reporters also must balance the need to answer readers' questions thoroughly against the need to communicate clearly in a limited space. Readers should neither be beaten down by a barrage of unimportant details nor left wondering about a point in the story that was raised but not explained.

SELECTIVITY

Here's the lead to a story that appeared in *The Dallas Times Herald*, a newspaper that had waged a spirited competition with *The Dallas Morning News* before it was shut down in the 1990s:

> Two Dallas men were killed yesterday when their single-engine airplane crashed in southwest Collin County shortly after takeoff from Addison Airport.

There are any number of points that might be made in a story about the crash of a small plane. The reporter might have considered the circumstances that brought each of the victims to the plane that day. The story might have touched on the safety history of the plane, the personal backgrounds of the victims and the actions of emergency crews.

But the story written for the *Times Herald*—just eight paragraphs long—mentioned none of these points. It confined itself to what the reporter considered the essential details about the crash and its victims. The story also noted that both victims were experienced pilots, that the area in which the crash occurred was well known as a place where pilots attempt aerobatic stunts, and that the Federal Aviation Administration would investigate.

The other points—optional information, which might have been included in a longer story—had to be scrapped. (Obviously, had the victims survived, the actions of emergency rescue crews would no longer have been optional.)

Journalism, it has been said, is the process of elimination. Any event significant or interesting enough to be labeled news trails behind it an almost endless train of circumstances and ramifications. What murder does not profoundly rattle a few dozen people? What governmental policy does not alter relationships in our society in some way? Reporters put hours into pursuing causes and effects. But though it can be painful to realize, many of these hard-won points simply won't fit in the story.

Although space limitations take most of the blame, journalists have another reason for restricting the number of points they allow in their stories—clarity. A story that tries to explain too much usually winds up explaining almost nothing.

Here is how the beginning of the story on that airplane crash might have read if the reporter had tried to squeeze everything in.

Unacceptable:

Two Dallas men, who left that city about 8 a.m. yesterday to drive 47 miles to Addison Airport for a day's flying, were killed when their 8-year-old, gray, two-seater, single-engine plane crashed in southwest Collin County shortly after taking off in clear but slightly breezy weather.

Collin County Justice of the Peace Andy Howard, 45, who knew some of the pilots at the airport and occasionally flew his own plane there as well, identified the victims as Gene Thomas, 37, about 6-foot-2 and 190 pounds, of 45121 King Lane, and Robert Clayburn, 46, about 5-foot-8 and 175 pounds, of 778 Seminole St. Collin County Sheriff's Deputy Joe Gergen, 31, who has participated in a state training program in emergency rescue, said Thomas was the pilot.

Gergen said both victims, one of whom had two grown children, the other of whom was single, were experienced pilots. He said Thomas, a math professor at Southern State University, who, colleagues said, had taught two courses that morning, had an airline transport pilot's license. Clayburn, who had had the day off before accepting an invitation to join Thomas on the flight, according to a friend, had a commercial pilot's license.

The plane, a two-seat Vitrol Skybird—a small plane with a strong safety record, according to its manufacturer—crashed about 7 p.m. It was the second crash of a small plane in the Dallas area this year.*

Good reporters have learned to avoid the temptation to say too much. They use their news judgment to rank the points that might be made about a story, and then, often ruthlessly, they slash off most of the lesser points. Although news stories will be full of facts, these facts will rarely be used to support more than a few points.

Acceptable:

Two Dallas men were killed yesterday when their single-engine airplane crashed in southwest Collin County shortly after takeoff from Addison Airport.

Collin County Justice of the Peace Andy Howard identified the victims as Gene Thomas, 37, of 45121 King Lane, and Robert Clayburn, 46, of 778 Seminole St. Collin County Sheriff's Deputy Joe Gergen said Thomas was the pilot.

---

* Names and other facts have been changed in this story, and some entirely fictitious details have been added in "unacceptable" examples.

Gergen said both men were experienced pilots. He said Thomas, a math professor at Southern State University, had an airline transport pilot's license, and Clayburn had a commercial pilot's license.

The plane, a two-seat Vitrol Skybird, crashed about 7 p.m....*

Dallas Times Herald

THOROUGHNESS

Reporters must be selective, but they also must be thorough. The information that a reporter *does* decide to include in a story must be fully explained. Those points that are made must be made clear. The basic questions readers might have about them must be anticipated and, where possible, answered. A story's *lead* might not answer all the five Ws—who? what? when? where? and why?—but the complete *story* must try to answer them all.

Not all readers will be interested in the details—names, addresses, ages, times. That's why they are usually held out of the lead. However, if these details contribute to an understanding of the story, they should be included in the story for readers who are interested.

Who

The identity of the protagonists in a news story can be pinned down in a number of ways, the first being the most obvious.

Names

Names usually will not be mentioned in a story's lead—the names of the two victims were not included in the lead of that *Times Herald* story on the airplane crash—but the full names of all the significant characters in a story must be given the first time each is mentioned in the body of the story. Full names are essential information.

The *Times Herald* story names the victims, the justice of the peace who identified the victims, and the sheriff who told the reporter who had piloted the ill-fated plane. There were, according to that sheriff, no witnesses, but if there had been witnesses to quote, they would have been named, too.

There are only three situations in which names might be withheld:

- If the person's role in the story is so insignificant that exact identification is unnecessary: Police reporting routine crimes they didn't personally investigate needn't be named.
- If the reporter has agreed in advance with a source to withhold a name. (See Chapter 15, Sources.)
- If identifying the person would, in the paper's view, be an unwarranted invasion of privacy. Most papers, for example, do not print the names of rape victims or of juveniles charged with minor crimes. (Some have taken issue with the common practice of withholding rape victims' names, arguing that it implies the woman has done something wrong.) Police may ask that the names of people who have died be withheld for a short time until police can get in touch with their relatives:

  The victims' identities were being withheld until relatives could be notified, Lt. Christiansen said.

  Associated Press

---

* This story has been reprinted with permission of the *Dallas Times Herald*.

Titles and Professions

Titles should be included whenever they are relevant, whenever a person is appearing in the story in a professional role. *Collin County Justice of the Peace* Andy Howard was on the job when he released the names of the two victims of the crash. His title is relevant. However, had *Assistant Store Manager* Fred Strauss seen the plane go down, his title would not have been included. His being a witness would have had nothing to do with his exact professional position. The story might, however, have included some less specific information on this hypothetical witness's profession—Fred Strauss, *who works at a nearby grocery store*—to give the reader an idea of where he fit in. The professions, though not necessarily the full titles, of the two victims of the plane crash are essential information in a story about their deaths so that readers have some indication of who these two men—central to the story—were.

Sometimes the mention of a profession is redundant, as in this story from the *Hartford* (Conn.) *Courant:*

> Dr. Carolyn Runowicz, *an author* and expert on cancer in women, and her husband, Dr. Sheldon Cherry, director of the University of Connecticut's Cancer Center, will discuss their book, "An Answer to Cancer," on Nov. 7.

Presumably, Runowicz could not discuss "her book" if she were not an author.

Race, National or Ethnic Background

These details are rarely mentioned in news stories—especially if they might serve to reinforce ethnic stereotypes. (See Chapter 2, Fairness.) However, if race, ethnicity or nationality is central to a story—if, for example, a professor complains about discrimination in a promotion or hiring decision on the basis of his background—then it should be mentioned.

Race and ethnicity also are sometimes mentioned when they are "firsts"—the first Japanese-American baseball player to win the batting title, the first Haitian-American elected to the state legislature, the first Dominican police chief. Identification of "firsts" can be overdone and condescending, and reporters are advised to discuss specific cases with their editors or, in the case of students, professors.

Here is an example of where such identification was considered germane:

> WORCESTER—Deval Patrick, a political novice whose campaign for governor has stirred the grass roots of the Massachusetts Democratic Party, won a strong endorsement at the state convention yesterday, outpacing two well-established and well-funded political figures.
>
> ...The victory makes Patrick the *first African-American* to be endorsed by a major political party for governor in Massachusetts history.
>
> *The Boston Globe*

Ages

Ages are newsworthy when they are surprising—an 83-year-old marathoner, for example—and when they help establish a profile of a major figure in a story. Readers should be told the ages of the victims of the plane crash—not only to satisfy curiosity about the tragedy but because their ages further establish the victims' exact identities. However, the age of the justice of the peace is irrelevant.

Readers want to know—and should be told—the age of a woman suspected of robbing a bank; they won't require the age of the councilwoman who introduced a bill.

When former Secretary of State Henry A. Kissinger was hospitalized for coronary bypass surgery, *The New York Times* erred in not giving his age. Clearly age is essential in a story about the health problem of a prominent person.

Addresses

Addresses estabish a person's exact identification. It is necessary that important characters in a story—victims and suspects, for example—be identified by age and address so they won't be confused with others who have similar names.

Gene Thomas of *45121 King Lane* died in that plane crash. Any readers who know another Gene Thomas can rest assured. Justice of the Peace Andy Howard's address is not necessary, however. His title helps keep him from being mistaken for someone else. But more importantly, the consequences of any mistaken identity in his case would be insignificant.

What

Readers will always want to know exactly what happened:

> The plane, a two-seat Vitrol Skybird, crashed about 7 p.m. . . . in a maize field.
>
> *Dallas Times Herald*

The "what" is often the most obvious question to answer in a story. But like most questions, it can have more than one answer. Beginning reporters occasionally make do with the most superficial answer and miss the story. (See Chapter 4, Traditional Leads.)

Unacceptable:

The City Council met for three hours yesterday at City Hall to discuss the municipal budget.

Acceptable:

Trash collection is scheduled to be cut from three to two days a week in an effort to reduce a deficit in the city's budget, the City Council decided yesterday.

When

Every news story needs a "when" of some sort. Sometimes "yesterday," "last night" or the day of the week will do. But in stories describing sudden and dramatic events, exact times should be given. In the plane crash story, it is of some interest to note, as the reporter did, that the plane crashed at about 7 p.m. and that the victims were pronounced dead at about 7:45 p.m.

Where

It's not necessary to repeat the address of city hall in every story. But readers normally should be told *exactly* where a fire broke out, where traffic is being detoured or where a plane crashed. In the *Times-Herald* story, the plane crashed "in a maize field 120 feet from Baccus Road and about one and a half miles west of Preston Road."

On less dramatic stories, such as a speech, the "where" should be included, but a *detailed* address is not necessary:

> "The cost of medical care is increasing at an astounding rate," Stein told a convention of the American Medical Association at the Sheraton Plaza Hotel on Route 17.

Why

This is often the hardest question to answer for readers, but reporters must try. The reporter who wrote the *Times Herald* story was unable to get much information on why the plane crashed, but readers were told what the reporter did find out: that the area where the plane crashed was considered a good spot in which to attempt aerobatic tricks, that both men were experienced pilots and that the plane in which they were flying was capable of performing such tricks.

"Why" must always be asked, and the answer should appear prominently even when it is "we don't know":

> The spokeswoman refused to discuss why the product was withdrawn.

CHAPTER 8 SUMMARY: INFORMATION SELECTION

In reporting any story, journalists have to pick and choose what's most important to emphasize and where to place it in the story. Good stories develop a single dominant theme and try to answer any questions about it that readers might instinctively raise. To select information appropriately, reporters should:

- Think about the answers to the basic five Ws and an H: who, what, where, when, why and how.
- Determine which of these are most important to the story. Rarely if ever are all crammed into the first paragraph. If a story is breaking news, the key element is typically what happened.
- Be thorough. While the lead summarizes key information, the body of a story needs to provide relevant details. For example, in conveying the "who" of an accident, the reporter should provide the name, age and address of each accident victim so that a victim can't be confused with others of the same name.
- Provide all titles relevant to the story. Key sources of news gain authority when it is clear what they do. Attributing an opinion to Mary Jones doesn't tell the reader much. Attributing it to investigating detective Mary Jones tells a lot.
- Give exact locations of events if they help readers understand the story or where it took place. The more local the news outlet, the more likely the reporter is to provide exact addresses.
- Let the reader know when answers aren't available. Reporters also tip their readers when authorities aren't releasing certain information.

EXERCISE A

If a story were to be written based on each of the following sets of facts, which facts definitely should be included? Which might be included, depending on how much space was available for the story? And which should not be included? Write "yes" next to the facts that would be essential; "maybe" next to those that would be optional—depending on length; and "no" next to those that should be ignored.

ONE

1 _____ A silver-and-gold chalice was stolen from a church on the west side.

2 _____ The gold-lined cup has a cross at the base. Several large diamonds adorn the outside.

3 _____ The church is 87 years old.

4 _____ The chalice was stolen only minutes after it was used during Mass.

5 _____ The church's name is St. Catherine's.

6 _____ Police say they have no suspects in the case.

7 _____ The church has three similar chalices.

8 _____ The chalice was valued at $2,500.

9 _____ The church last reported a theft four years ago.

10 _____ The church is located in a neighborhood that has been hard hit by unemployment.

11 _____ About 150 people attended the mass.

12 _____ Chalice believed stolen at about 11:30 a.m.

13 _____ Address of church is 295 Hunter Street.

14 _____ Church is a beautiful granite building.

15 _____ Chalice noticed missing by an altar boy, John Gibbons.

16 _____ Information came from police.

TWO

1 _____ Rome Councilwoman Sheila Albers announces that she will run in the Democratic primary to seek the nomination for lieutenant governor.

2 _____ Albers is best known for her support of the gay rights bill in the Rome Council. She says she will work for a similar bill if elected to state office.

3 _____ Rome Mayor John Raymond also has declared his candidacy for the Democratic nomination for lieutenant governor.

4 _____ Albers attended Antioch College. Raymond attended George Washington University.

5 _____ Albers is 38, Raymond is 49.

6 ____ Albers ran unsuccessfully against Raymond for mayor last year.

7 ____ Albers says she supports the president's economic program.

8 ____ Albers has served for six years on the council. Before that she managed a record store in Rome.

9 ____ Albers says that the state needs to increase its aid to local school districts.

10 ____ Albers says she is concerned about the plight of "guest workers" in Germany.

11 ____ Thus far no other candidates have declared for the primary.

12 ____ Raymond declared two weeks ago.

13 ____ Raymond is a lawyer.

14 ____ Raymond served on the council 12 years before winning mayor's election.

15 ____ Raymond has been a bitter opponent of Albers in city meetings.

THREE

1 ____ Information provided by police.

2 ____ Officer spoken to was Joseph Altobelli.

3 ____ He is 29 years old.

4 ____ A gas station was broken into over the weekend.

5 ____ It was closed at the time.

6 ____ Station on Greenwood Turnpike in Kanesville.

7 ____ Police have no suspects.

8 ____ Police said they will investigate.

9 ____ Burglar entered by forcing the lock.

10 ____ Station had a soda and candy machine. Nothing taken from them.

11 ____ Burglar did break into a safe with a hammer and chisel.

12 ____ $679 in cash stolen.

13 ____ Most of the money was in $5 and $10 bills.

FOUR

1 ____ Allen Rodgers sued the Town of Valley Stream yesterday.

2 ____ Rodgers is 13 years old.

3 ____ Rodgers lives on 19 Myrtle Ave.

4 ____ Rodgers's hobby is stamp collecting.

5 ____ Rodgers is black.

6 ____ On April 9, Rodgers and his friends were playing baseball in Memorial Park.

7 ____ Rodgers plays on that field frequently.

8 _____ Running between first and second base he tripped and shattered his kneecap on a rock protruding from the dirt.

9 _____ It was a Tuesday afternoon.

10 _____ Part of his kneecap was removed.

11 _____ He was on crutches for six months.

12 _____ It was raining the day he was hurt. The field was muddy.

13 _____ Rodgers was wearing baseball spikes.

14 _____ The field is owned and maintained by the Town of Valley Stream.

15 _____ Suit contends town was negligent in not removing the rock from the basepaths.

16 _____ Rodgers's father, Noel Rodgers, is a lawyer.

17 _____ Noel Rodgers is 43 years old.

18 _____ The town says no one has ever been injured on the field before.

19 _____ His doctor says Rodgers will walk with a limp for the rest of his life.

20 _____ Suit asks for $2 million in damages.

FIVE

1 _____ State legislature approved plan to impose a 1 percent state sales tax yesterday.

2 _____ Bill had been proposed by Assemblyman James Jones of Murdoch [the city in which your paper is published].

3 _____ Jones's age—41.

4 _____ Jones's address—15 Amber Road.

5 _____ Governor must still sign the bill.

6 _____ Governor's name—Bill Freeman.

7 _____ Governor's age—53.

8 _____ If approved, tax would go into effect May 1.

9 _____ Tax would cover all products except food.

10 _____ Vote on tax—48–44.

11 _____ Bill had been opposed by Assemblywoman Ellen Glassman of Murdoch.

12 _____ Glassman's age—45.

13 _____ Glassman's address—1267 Robin Court.

14 _____ Glassman said tax would be paid by the poor.

15 _____ Jones said tax needed to maintain city services.

16 _____ Jones a Republican.

17 _____ Glassman a Democrat.

18 _____ Freeman a Democrat.

19 _____ Governor has not announced his position on the bill.

20 _____ Bill approved by legislature at 3:45 p.m.

21 _____ Legislature meets in state capitol, at One State Street.

22 _____ After approving the tax, the legislature approved a motion to adjourn for the day.

SIX

1 _____ An apparently crazed cat wreaked havoc on an apartment building in Freeport yesterday.

2 _____ Information from officer at 3rd Precinct.

3 _____ Officer's name—Sgt. Nick Pollard.

4 _____ Cat entered first apartment at 4:30 p.m.

5 _____ Apartment belonged to Sally Real.

6 _____ Cat tore down curtains.

7 _____ Cat scratched Real's two children.

8 _____ Children's names—Aaron and Emilia.

9 _____ Children's ages—4 (Aaron) and 6 (Emilia).

10 _____ Sally Real's age—32.

11 _____ Real is divorced.

12 _____ Cat entered second apartment at 4:55 p.m.

13 _____ Apartment belonged to Joe and Mary Sipser.

14 _____ Joe Sipser—52, Mary Sipser—54.

15 _____ Sipsers have no children.

16 _____ Cat bit and scratched Mary Sipser.

17 _____ Cat jumped onto Joe Sipser but did not hurt him.

18 _____ Cat escaped into hallway and into street.

19 _____ Cat was black Siamese.

20 _____ Owner's name George Grover.

21 _____ Grover's age—83.

22 _____ Grover says cat had never misbehaved before.

23 _____ Cat's name—Tabby.

24 _____ Cat's age—3.

25 _____ ASPCA searching for cat.

26 _____ Building's address—68 Front Street.

27 _____ Building six stories tall.

28 _____ Real lives on second floor.

29 _____ Sipser lives on first floor.

30 _____ Grover lives on first floor.

31 _____ Real children not seriously injured, not hospitalized.

32 _____ Mary Sipser treated at Booth Hospital for severe cut, then released.

33 _____ Booth Hospital's address—1 Booth Street.

SEVEN

1 _____ Car crashed into telephone pole yesterday.

2 _____ Man killed in car.

3 _____ Victim's name—Arthur Fredericks.

4 _____ Victim's address—60 Redfern Road, East Albens.

5 _____ Victim's age—24.

6 _____ Victim's race—white.

7 _____ Victim's profession—plumbing supplies salesman.

8 _____ No other passengers in car.

9 _____ Police officer on scene—Dean Rich.

10 _____ Officer's address—4 Palace Court, East Albens.

11 _____ Officer's age—35.

12 _____ Officer's race—black.

13 _____ Rich says car skidded for 30 yards on wet pavement before hitting pole.

14 _____ Rich says victim was dead when he arrived at Lincoln Hospital.

15 _____ Rich says no sign of foul play and no sign victim had been drinking.

16 _____ Rich says victim had stopped for gas at service station four miles from scene of accident.

17 _____ Scene of accident in front of house at 33 Blackburn St., East Albens.

18 _____ Allen and Sarah Fredericks live next door, 31 Blackburn St. They were victim's parents.

19 _____ Time of accident—6:30 p.m.

20 _____ Had been raining steadily for six hours before the accident.

21 _____ Victim had no criminal record.

Organization

A look through any newsroom in the hours before deadline will inevitably turn up a few reporters with eyes upturned, as if searching for inspiration in the ceiling. No one who attempts to turn events into words can completely escape these moments of perplexity.

News writing, however, has a structure and order designed both to reduce the number of questions reporters need to ask the ceiling and to make it easier for readers to follow the stories reporters eventually produce. This chapter will explain the mechanics of composing and organizing the short paragraphs that are characteristic of newspaper journalism. It will outline strategies for structuring information so that readers get the news quickly—and neither reader nor writer gets lost along the way.

PARAGRAPHS

The paragraphs used in newspaper journalism are shorter than those used in most other types of writing. Often newspaper paragraphs are just a sentence long; rarely do they go on for more than a few sentences.

Each paragraph, or *graf*, usually should contain only one idea; a new thought, a new person talking, and it is time to start a new graf.

Notice how the paragraphs are divided at the beginning of this historic story:

> WASHINGTON—Richard Milhous Nixon, the 37th president of the United States, announced last night that he had given up his long and arduous fight to remain in office and would resign, effective at noon today.
>
> Gerald Rudolph Ford, whom Nixon nominated for vice president last Oct. 12, will be sworn in tomorrow at the same hour as the 38th president, to serve out the 895 days remaining in Nixon's second term.
>
> Less than two years after his landslide re-election victory, Nixon, in a conciliatory address on national television, said that he was leaving not with a sense of bitterness but with a hope that his departure would start a "process of healing that is so desperately needed in America."
>
> *The New York Times*

Newspaper paragraphs are kept so short for three reasons: Short grafs make it easier for busy readers to follow what's happening; they make it easier for editors to add, delete and rearrange information; and they help break up the mass of "gray" print crammed in the narrow columns used by many papers.

But paragraphs can certainly be too short. Every sentence does not deserve a graf of its own.

WEAK:

Shortly after noon, Ronald L. Ziegler, the president's confidant and press secretary, his face saddened and weary, appeared in the crowded White House press room and announced that the president would go on national television tonight to address the American people.

As with most previous such announcements, he did not say what the president would talk about.

Two sentences on the same thought, such as these two, should be combined into one graf. But any change in idea, occasion, outlook or person commands a change of paragraph.

Unacceptable:

At 11 a.m. today, as crowds for the third day gathered along Pennsylvania Avenue outside the White House, President Nixon summoned Ford to his Oval Office and officially informed him that he would submit his resignation tomorrow to the secretary of state, as provided by federal law, and that Ford would become president. Shortly after noon, Ronald L. Ziegler, the president's confidant and press secretary, his face saddened and weary, appeared in the crowded White House press room and announced that the president would go on national radio and television tonight to address the American people. As with most previous announcements, he did not say what the president would talk about.

Acceptable:

At 11 a.m. today, as crowds for the third day gathered along Pennsylvania Avenue outside the White House, President Nixon summoned Ford to his Oval Office and officially informed him that he would submit his resignation tomorrow to the secretary of state, as provided by federal law, and that Ford would become president.

Shortly after noon, Ronald L. Ziegler, the president's confidant and press secretary, his face saddened and weary, appeared in the crowded White House press room and announced that the president would go on national radio and television tonight to address the American people. As with most previous announcements, he did not say what the president would talk about.

The New York Times

Paragraphing should not be difficult once beginning reporters learn to accept the idea that a graf can end after a sentence or two.

THE INVERTED PYRAMID

In most news stories, reporters do busy readers a favor: They present the most newsworthy information first and relegate less crucial facts to the bottom of the story. An essay works toward a conclusion; a work of fiction builds to a climax; but a news story often winds down to facts of less and less importance.

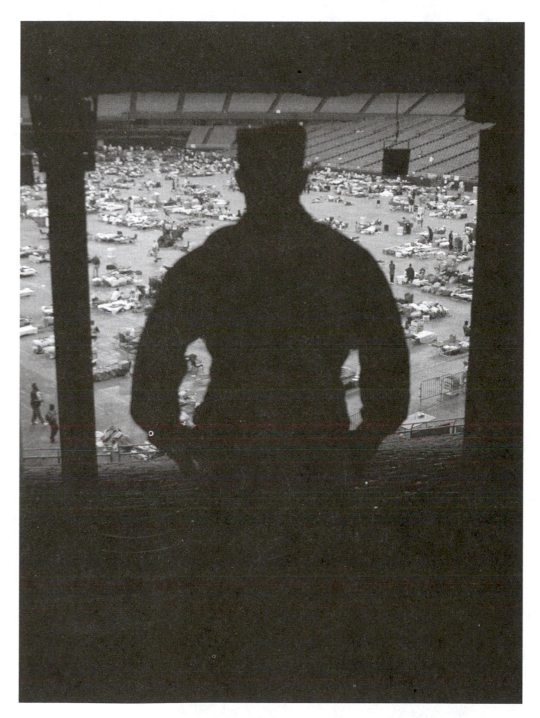

Army National Guard Sgt. Raymond Chopane looks on as evacuees from Hurricane Katrina begin arriving at the Houston Astrodome.
(Photo by Johnny Hanson)

This special technique for organizing stories—in which information is presented in descending order of newsworthiness—is called the *inverted pyramid*. An inverted pyramid is big at the top and gets smaller and smaller toward the bottom. Most news stories have the big news at the top (see Chapter 4, Traditional Leads) and present facts of decreasing importance as the stories continue toward their end.

This concept, taught to journalists for so long that it has become something of a cliché, can be oversimplified. But the inverted pyramid should be kept in mind when it comes time to organize facts into a news story. Reporters usually will informally rank the information they have by its news value and then proceed in approximately that order.

This *USA Today* story, which appeared several weeks after Hurricane Katrina pummeled New Orleans, provides a useful example of how the inverted pyramid and related organizing principles work:

1. Louisiana's governor asked the federal government Tuesday to move tens of thousands of Hurricane Katrina evacuees out of shelters and into hotels.

2. Gov. Kathleen Blanco's request comes after state officials said it could take months to prepare trailers and other temporary housing for evacuees. Blanco wants the Federal Emergency Management Agency to pay for hotel rooms for 90 days for each individual or family.

3. "It's just not moving fast enough," said Jerry Jones, the governor's director of facility planning. "We don't want to warehouse these people. We want them to be in a place where they can thrive and get back to normalcy."

4. Ron Sherman, FEMA's housing coordinator in Louisiana, said the idea could work and vowed to review it. FEMA already is paying for thousands of evacuees to stay in hotels for up to 60 days. The American Red Cross is paying hotel bills for thousands of others.

5. If accepted, Blanco's recommendation would allow displaced Louisianians living in shelters in their state or elsewhere to move to hotels identified by FEMA. It is unclear how many people would be eligible for hotel stays. Nearly 100,000 people are staying in 1,042 shelters in 26 states and the District of Columbia, according to FEMA....

6. Arkansas has 7,992 evacuees in shelters. Texas had 13,182 shelter residents Monday but was planning to move 7,000 to Arkansas and Tennessee to keep them safe from Hurricane Rita.

7. Blanco's hotel request reflects the state's growing concern that Louisianians staying in out-of-state shelters will find permanent housing in the communities where they are sheltered.

8. People would be more likely to move back to Louisiana if they could stay in hotels for 90 days and then be able to occupy a trailer in their home state, said Jones, the governor's aide.

9. "This buys us time....We want to entice them to come back home," he said.

10. Sherren Bartheleny, 49, sitting on a plastic chair outside a shelter in downtown Baton Rouge, said she was skeptical of the governor's plan because she fears it will take much longer than 90 days for the government to find appropriate housing for evacuees.

11. "If [Blanco] can put me in a trailer back in Plaquemines Parish after 90 days, I'll go to a hotel," said Bartheleny, whose home was destroyed. "I want a written statement from the governor."*

The most newsworthy point in this story is succinctly summarized at the top—Louisiana's governor wants the federal government to move tens of thousands of evacuees from shelters into hotels. That is all the lead tells us.

The paragraphs that immediately follow explain why and fill in who the governor is, what agency in the federal government she approached, and how long she wants the federal

---

* *USA Today.* September 21, 2005. Reprinted with permission.

government to pay for the evacuees. Less important issues—how many evacuees can be found in shelters in surrounding states, the governor's interest in drawing Louisianians back into the state and the reaction of one evacuee to the plan—are explored lower in the story.

The arrangement of information in descending order of news value or importance helps editors as well as readers who have no time to read from beginning to end. Editors forced to cut a story's length could, if rushed, simply start chopping from the bottom up without fear that vital information would be sacrificed.

Had *USA Today's* editors needed to, they could easily have shortened the story of the governor's request without stopping to rearrange the information in it. In fact, this piece could have been ended after any paragraph from the second on. It still would have been a sound, self-contained story, though fewer details would have been available to readers.

SUPPORTING THE LEAD

The lead represents a decision on what is most newsworthy in a story. (See Chapter 4, Traditional Leads.) It can be seen as a promise to readers of what is to come. The paragraphs that immediately follow the lead must deliver on that promise—they must *support* the lead.

If the lead is about a drug arrest, the next few paragraphs can't wander off into a discussion of the problem of drugs in schools. If the lead is about the school board's decision to eliminate courses in Spanish, much of the rest of the story will have to be about that decision, not about wage negotiations with the teachers' union.

Support paragraphs fill out the information provided in the first graf. They bolster the lead's credibility and fill in some of the details.

Look back, for example, at the first two paragraphs of the story about the governor's request. The lead summarizes it—governor asks federal government to move evacuees. Further details would clutter the lead, obscuring the main point of the news.

By the second paragraph, though, it's time to begin providing these details. Here we learn the governor's name (Kathleen Blanco), the reason she's making the request (it could take months to prepare trailers and other temporary housing for evacuees), what agency her request is directed toward (FEMA) and how long she's asking the government to pay (90 days).

That paragraph is followed by a quote from the governor's director of facility planning. This adds further authority and color—"it's just not moving fast enough"—dual roles strong quotes often play high in a story (see Chapter 7, Quotations). It also supplies further "lead support," by giving more detail in answer to the question "why." Finally, the paragraph adds credibility, a kind of proof, to the information by attributing it to a specific member of Blanco's staff.

Stories that fail to support their leads promptly can frustrate and confuse readers. This story from the *Houston Chronicle* takes much too long—until grafs 6 and 7—to support its lead by explaining *what* happened:

> BALTIMORE (UPI)—Three maximum-security inmates and five guards were shot in an attempted breakout at the Maryland Penitentiary, officials said. Four of the guards were shot by other guards.
>
> No escapes or serious injuries were reported in yesterday's incident, police said.
>
> "It was horrifying, terrible," said Ken Neal, who was visiting his brother. "We saw guards running about with shotguns. My brother figured it was an escape."
>
> Earlier, officials [had] recommended the dismissal of 14 guards at an adjacent prisoner reception unit. The guards had staged a sickout last week to protest staffing [cuts] at the main penitentiary.

A despondent evacuee from New Orleans sits outside the Cajundome in Lafayette, La., a few days after Hurricane Katrina.
(Photo by Claudia B. Laws, The (Lafayette, La.) Daily Advertiser)

Corrections Commissioner Jon P. Galley said, "Any report, whether done by union or management, will prove that staffing is one of the major causes for escapes and inmate uprisings."

The shooting began at about 1:30 p.m. when the inmates—two convicted killers and an armed robber—took a female guard hostage in the prison yard and commandeered a shotgun and a revolver, said prison spokeswoman Beverly Marable.

The inmates shot guard George Bellows, who returned fire, hitting the inmates in the legs and the female guard in the foot, [Marable said.]...

For a more dramatic example, *The Washington Post*, during the second year of Ronald Reagan's presidency, led a story about his national security adviser with this information:

...William P. Clark has dampened the internal power struggles and policy disagreements that marred much of Reagan administration policy during its first year.

* The names of the prisoner's brother and the guard in this story have been changed.

The *Post* story that followed included *no* facts supporting this claim—not in the next few grafs or anywhere else.

Supporting the lead should be the first priority when composing the beginning of the body of a news story. Here is a simple story that does the job thoroughly:

> Weekend service on the trolleys that use the subway-surface tunnel routes will be interrupted for the next two weeks, SEPTA officials said yesterday.
>
> Service on Route 10, 11, 13 and 36 trolleys will be interrupted between Juniper and 40th streets from 10 p.m. Friday to 5 a.m. Monday because of Center City Commuter Tunnel construction, officials said.
>
> Passengers can take the Market-Frankford line to 40th Street and transfer there to the trolleys.
>
> *The Philadelphia Inquirer*

ELABORATING

Once the lead has been supported—its main points solidly grounded—the reporter can begin broadening the basis of the story. Additional information can be supplied; less pressing questions can be answered.

In the *USA Today* story about the governor's request, grafs 4 to 6 elaborate on the current status of the evacuees. We learn that some already are in hotels and that nearly 100,000 are in shelters in 26 states and Washington D.C., many of them in the nearby states of Texas and Arkansas. Grafs 7 and 9 provide more information about the governor's interest in bringing the displaced residents back to Louisiana.

The information in these paragraphs gives interesting background and insight into the governor's request, but is not essential for the reader to grasp the baseline news.

Indeed, not all stories or all main points made within a story require elaboration. It may not be worth the space. Lead support is required. Elaboration—the addition of extra details and explanation—is an option.

SECONDARY THEMES

If the story is long enough, after supporting the lead and elaborating on the main themes, reporters can begin introducing secondary themes.

Paragraphs 10 and 11 of the Katrina evacuees story develop a new theme, what one evacuee thinks about the plan. In a longer story, the reporter might have talked to several New Orleans evacuees, some of whom longed to return to the state and others who were skeptical about the plan. But if the story were shorter, this one evacuee's response probably wouldn't have been noticed or missed.

As discussed in Chapter 8, Information Selection, the number of points that can be made in a newspaper story is limited. Readers are busy, their attention span limited. If there is room for secondary points, they should be covered one at a time, and only after the main themes of the story have been dealt with.

So a simple story should be organized along these lines:

1. Lead
2. Support

3. Elaboration (if any)

4. Secondary themes (if any)

LIKE IDEAS TOGETHER

Good stories start with a design. Experienced reporters may not take the trouble to write out an outline in advance, but they certainly keep one in their heads. They decide what ideas they plan to cover, and they organize these ideas so that they are developed one at a time.

Nothing breaks the flow of a story more effectively than the jumbling of ideas.

> **Unacceptable**:
>
> Gov. Kathleen Blanco's hotel request reflects the state's growing concern that Louisianians staying in out-of-state shelters will find permanent housing in the communities where they are sheltered.
>
> Sherren Bartheleny, 49, sitting on a plastic chair outside a shelter in downtown Baton Rouge, said she was skeptical of the governor's plan because she fears it will take much longer than 90 days for the government to find appropriate housing for evacuees.
>
> Arkansas has 7,992 evacuees in shelters. Texas had 13,182 shelter residents Monday but was planning to move 7,000 to Arkansas and Tennessee to keep them safe from Hurricane Rita.
>
> Ron Sherman, FEMA's housing coordinator in Louisiana, said the idea could work and vowed to review it. FEMA already is paying for thousands of evacuees to stay in hotels for up to 60 days. The American Red Cross is paying hotel bills for thousands of others.
>
> "It's just not moving fast enough," said Jerry Jones, the governor's director of facility planning. "We don't want to just warehouse these people."

Related ideas were kept together in this story as it appeared in *USA Today*. For example, the three paragraphs discussing where evacuees had fled to came one after the other. So do the three paragraphs elaborating on Blanco's concern that Louisianians staying in out-of-state shelters might ultimately settle in those states.

It makes no sense to ignore the natural connections between ideas when organizing a story. It is difficult enough to make a story read smoothly when it does proceed logically from idea to related idea.

TWO OR MORE PRIMARY THEMES

The stories discussed so far in this chapter make one basic point in their leads. A story must be organized somewhat differently when it raises two or more points of such equal, or nearly equal, importance that they all are introduced at the top of the story.

These additional main elements may be incorporated in the lead (see Chapter 4, Traditional Leads):

> Teachers struck at all three schools in Waldwick, N.J., yesterday, while striking teachers in the Deer Park Union Free School District on Long Island suspended their walkout, which began last Friday.
>
> *The New York Times*

Or they may be introduced in the second graf:

Theme A

> NEW YORK (UPI)—A stickup man dressed as a police officer stole antique jewelry valued at $1 million from a Manhattan antique store yesterday, police said.

Theme B

> In another heist reported by police yesterday, a Park Avenue firm was broken into over the weekend and art objects valued at nearly $2 million were stolen.
>
> (Long Island, N.Y.) *Newsday*

Each of these elements must then be supported, and possibly elaborated on, in the story. All the primary themes introduced in the lead should be developed before secondary themes are introduced. And—following the *like ideas together* rule—each should be developed completely before the next is considered.

Here is how the reporter proceeded after the first two grafs in that *Newsday* story:

Support theme A

> In the jewelry theft, Lt. Frederick Stein of the East 67th Street station house said, the "police officer" arrived at Ares Antiques, 961 Madison Ave., at the store's 10 a.m. opening time.
>
> Stein said the store was still locked, but the clerk on duty opened the door and admitted the stickup man without question when he saw the uniform. The robber pulled a handgun, handcuffed the clerk and ordered him to lie on the floor, according to Lt. Stein.
>
> The robber and an accomplice then scooped up antique jewelry valued at $1 million, mostly crowns and necklaces, from two opened safes and fled, Lt. Stein said.

Support theme B

> In the art theft, officials of the William B. O'Boyle Co. at 99 Park Ave. reported $1.8 million worth of art objects, along with 10 Krugerrands and $2,000 in cash had been taken. The art objects included 37 pieces of pre-Colombian art.

A basic dual-element story, then, will be ordered like this:

1. Introduction of theme A and theme B in first graf or two
2. Support for theme A
3. Elaboration on theme A (if necessary)
4. Support for theme B
5. Elaboration on theme B (if necessary)
6. Secondary themes (if any)

A story with three main elements will follow a similar pattern:

1. Introduction of themes A, B and C in first graf or two
2. Support for theme A
3. Elaboration on theme A (if necessary)
4. Support for theme B
5. Elaboration on theme B (if necessary)
6. Support for theme C

7. Elaboration on theme C (if necessary)

8. Secondary themes (if any)

CHRONOLOGY

Purely chronological stories begin at the beginning of an event and end at the end—a rarity in journalism. This technique is used most often in features. (See Chapter 22, Features.) But occasionally, news stories also flow chronologically:

> GRAND MARAIS, Minn. (AP)—Drawn by messages from "some higher power," Mitchell Irving and Esther Sklaire drove last month from St. Paul to the frozen wilderness of northeastern Minnesota to wait for a flying saucer, authorities say.
>
> For more than four weeks they waited in their car, apparently eating vitamins and drinking water from nearby Loon Lake.
>
> On Monday, a motorist found Irving, 38, an electrician from West St. Paul, semiconscious on Gunflint Trail, 41 miles northwest of here. Rescue squad members found Sklaire, 48, dead in the front seat of the car a few hundred yards off the main road.
>
> An autopsy determined she died from a combination of hypothermia, dehydration and starvation.*
>
> (New York) Daily News

More frequently, chronological accounts are mixed with nonchronological sections of news stories. After the basics of the story are laid out in the lead and in one or more support paragraphs, a writer may switch to a narrative, chronological recounting of the event. This technique is particularly effective in police, fire and disaster stories and in any other account in which the narrative itself is compelling enough to hold the reader's interest. It has been dubbed the "hourglass" story form by the Poynter Institute in St. Petersburg, Fla. The top of the hourglass summarizes the news in the same way as the inverted pyramid. But then the writer starts again in chronological order, going into the story in greater depth.

Here's an example, written with a hint of irony:

> TARPON SPRINGS – When they heard the screams, no one suspected the rooster.
>
> Chona James, 2, was toddling down the sidewalk Monday lugging her Easy Bake Oven when she became the victim in one of the weirder animal attack cases police can recall.
>
> In the cluster of beige houses at Lime Street and Safford Avenue where Chona lives, man and chicken have coexisted peacefully for years in quiet defiance of city ordinance.
>
> That ended Monday afternoon, when authorities apprehended the offending rooster, named Rockadoodle Two, and its sister, named Hen. Hen was not involved in the attack, police said.
>
> *Chronology begins:*
>
> The rooster struck around noon as Chona ventured from her house in the middle of the cluster to visit her Uncle Tony, waiting in the driveway. It's a short walk, even if you're 3 feet tall and carrying a toy oven.*

---

* The names in these stories have been changed.

Tony Allen, 44, heard the little girl shrieking, spun around, and saw the rooster.

Rockadoodle Two had knocked the 27-pound girl flat on her belly and was pummeling her with beak, claws and blue-black wings.

"He was beating the crap out of her," said her mother, Alicia Swift, 27. "A freaking rooster, you know"....

St. Petersburg (Fla.) *Times*

Chronological accounts can be effective in organizing complex events into a coherent story. Readers may find a confusing series of occurrences easier to follow if they are presented in the order in which they happened. A reporter may choose to tell most of the story chronologically or to devote simply two or three grafs to a chronological account. It is perfectly acceptable to mix these accounts into a story that otherwise follows the inverted pyramid.

The rooster story stayed with chronology straight through until the end:

Chona was shaken after the attack but is recovering fine. Her scratches are almost gone; her right eye is barely puffy.

She hid in the house after the attack but said chickens don't worry her now.

"He's gone," she said of the rooster. "The police got him."

TRANSITIONS

Here are two consecutive paragraphs from a *Los Angeles Times* story:

Continuing his attacks on gang graffiti, City Attorney Ira Reiner yesterday announced a plan for Los Angeles business leaders to pay for paint and other materials to clean up messages left by street gang members.

The Los Angeles County Board of Supervisors voted to continue funding for a separate anti-gang program, the $1.3-million Community Youth Gang Services Project.

These two paragraphs, making two separate points, seem to fit together poorly. There is no flow. The solution? The *Times* reporters who wrote the story solved the problem by adding one word: *meanwhile*. That word, placed at the start of the second paragraph eased the switch from thought to thought.

Meanwhile is an example of a transitional word. Without such words, which serve to ease sometimes abrupt shifts from idea to idea, many stories would be choppy and confusing. The *Los Angeles Times* reporters used three other transitional words at the beginning of paragraphs in that story—*while, although* and *but*. These words, and others like them, help stories flow.

Logical Connections

All transitional words work by emphasizing a relationship between thoughts. Some underline a logical connection between ideas, as does this introduction to a paragraph in *The Philadelphia Inquirer* that followed a discussion of a complex strike:

As a result of the labor differences....

These transitions also call attention to such direct connections:

therefore   so
consequently   because

Time Connections

Some transitions point to a relationship in time. Here are three examples from a different *Los Angeles Times* article:

> *At the time*, the government announced that Israeli forces had been ordered in....

> *Meanwhile*, Zev Schiff, the military correspondent of the [Israeli] newspaper *Haaretz*, reported....

> *Before* the government's earlier decision....

and some other time transitions:

while	over the years
at the same time	since
concurrently	following
then	later
the previous day	afterward

Place Connections

Other transitions point to relationships in location. It may be a direct relationship:

in the same building	nearby
also in Washington	across the street

Or the transitional word may simply indicate to the reader that the location has switched by mentioning the new location:

on Capitol Hill

in Beirut

Contrasts

Among the most commonly used transitions are those that indicate contrasts:

> For 47 years, the Hells Angels have roared down the road as the biggest, baddest outlaw motorcycle gang.
> *But* the Oakland-based club has a quieter, law-abiding alter ego....
> *San Jose Mercury News*

Other such words include:

however	in contrast
nevertheless	on the other hand
nonetheless	still
notwithstanding	despite

Additions

A final group of transitional words indicates that the reader is about to get more:

> The grand jury...was scheduled to adjourn this week....
> *Another* grand jury will be sworn in next week....
> *The Washington Post*

Other examples are:

also	in another development
in addition	besides
and	moreover

Natural Connections

Some transitions work smoothly without transitional words because the wording refers to something mentioned in the previous paragraph:

> Rockefeller...discussed the organization's programs at a luncheon *meeting* of the Women's Forum....
>
> *The meeting* was the fourth of a series of "Newsleader" luncheons held by the Women's Forum....
>
> The New York Times

No transitional words are needed when paragraphs can be made to fit this snugly.

Unacceptable:

> Rockefeller...discussed the organization's programs at a luncheon meeting of the Women's Forum....
>
> The meeting, *in addition*, was the fourth of a series of "Newsleader" luncheons held by the Women's Forum.

Pitfalls

Transitional words have their own special meanings and must be used with the same care as any other tools in the language.

Unacceptable:

While he was tired, he still finished the task in three hours.

Acceptable:

Although he was tired, he finished the task in three hours.

Unacceptable:

She received the award for the fourth time. *However*, three other winners were named.

Acceptable:

She received the award for the fourth time. Three other winners were named *as well*.

It is easy to overuse transitions. A story that has a transitional word in front of every paragraph sputters like a car with a flooded gas line. But beginning reporters generally use too few rather than too many transitional words. They often fail to take advantage of this simple trick for keeping paragraphs from grinding against one another.

BULLETS

Just as lists help us organize our lives, they can help reporters organize stories. To make lists clear in newspaper stories—and to set them off from the rest of the story—each point is indented and preceded by a small, dark circle (indicated by an asterisk on the typewriter or keyboard).

These little circles are called *bullets*. They give reporters a means of organizing and setting apart a series of similar points. Here is an example from a story on the expansion of recycling in the city of Toledo, Ohio:

The new neighborhoods and pickup days are:

- East Toledo, near White High School, on Monday.
- The Westmoreland area south of Ottawa Park, on Wednesday.
- The Douglass and Tremainsville roads and Sylvania Avenue area, on Thursday.
- The Library Village area north of Sylvania Avenue, on Friday.

The Toledo Blade

Bullets should be used selectively. Points should be arranged as bullets only if they can be made in a sentence or two. Bulleted items also should exhibit parallel structure. Finally, bullets should be used only when three or more points need to be made.

Unacceptable:

In other action last night, the council:

- Voted 5–3 to close Memorial Park each night at 10 p.m. The council's action followed reports that teen-agers have been terrorizing residents living next to the park by breaking their windows and shooting holes in their garbage cans. Councilman John Rose called the actions "disgraceful," but said some means should be made to keep the park open for "decent kids."
- In an action that angered some and delighted others, lifted an ordinance forbidding video-game parlors in the borough.

The solution here is to forget the bullets and return to normal paragraphs and prose.

AFTER SOFT LEADS

Stories that begin with zingers, anecdotes, descriptions or quotes (see Chapter 5, Other Leads) must still obey most of the rules outlined in this chapter: The story must follow and support the angle established—no matter how cleverly—by the lead; themes must be elaborated on…one at a time; like ideas should be kept together. (Actually, the rooster story above qualifies as having a zinger lead.)

Nevertheless, most features found in newspapers (see Chapter 22, Features) differ from a news story in one crucial way: Such stories rarely follow the inverted pyramid. Instead of petering out, they may build to a climax or conclusion. In this way, they may be more similar in form to an essay or a work of fiction. This means that a feature story may introduce some important themes far down in the story. (The lead, though, must still indicate the overriding theme of the story—see Chapter 5, Other Leads.)

There are a number of strategies for organizing feature stories. Some features, as previously mentioned, begin at the beginning and end at the end. They are chronological. Others use spatial relationships to lend order. A piece about the changes in a neighborhood over time, for example, might move the reader from north to south or from east to west. Still others move from the statement of a problem to consideration of its solutions.

A well-crafted feature also may return at the end to the incident introduced in its lead. In this way, the final paragraphs help tie together the story. These final grafs—sometimes called the *snapper* or *kicker*—are often viewed as second in importance only to the lead.

Here are the first four paragraphs of a substantial *New York Times* feature about home sharing by the elderly:

> MONTICELLO, N.Y.—When 74-year-old Joan Howitt broke a hip last winter, the fear of not knowing where she would live when she left the hospital almost broke her spirit.
>
> Mary Beaman, 72, said the stillness of her rambling house, near Sackett Lake, where she has lived for 50 years, began to grate on her last January.
>
> Now the two women are living together, sharing Mrs. Beaman's house, thanks to a match made by a Sullivan County project for the elderly.
>
> Having a companion, Mrs. Beaman said, "gave new life to the old house."
>
> Like Mrs. Howitt and Mrs. Beaman, a growing number of elderly people in the New York metropolitan area and nationwide are sharing homes—to save money, stave off loneliness and avoid going to a nursing home, according to social workers and other authorities on problems of the aging....

And here are the last three grafs of that story. Notice how the writer manages to wind back to where she began:

> ... "Sometimes it just doesn't work," said Enrico DeGironimo, assistant coordinator of the Community Outreach Program for Senior Adults ... in Piscataway, N.J.
>
> "Older people have set habits. Sometimes finances force them to consider shared housing, but then they feel like someone has moved into their territory. Or from the home-seeker's view, they may feel displaced."
>
> Mrs. Howitt said, however, that even though she could hardly see, the corners and turns of Mrs. Beaman's house had become familiar to her. "It's become my home," she said. "And Mary has become my family."

CHAPTER 9 SUMMARY: ORGANIZATION

The news is compact and direct. It's organized in a way to get key information quickly and efficiently. In organizing stories:

- Summarize key information in the first paragraph.
- Support, or elaborate on that key information in subsequent few paragraphs, fully developing the primary theme before tackling others.
- Keep one idea to a paragraph. Newspaper "grafs" are short and direct, often just a single sentence long.
- After establishing the key news, organize information for the rest of the story in one of two ways. In the inverted pyramid, information is organized in descending order of importance, with the primary theme followed by secondary themes. In the hourglass structure, the reporter reverts to a storytelling format—chronology—after establishing the news.
- Try blocking or outlining your information to keep like ideas together.
- Use transitional words or phrases in moving from one idea to another. There are various types of transitions. For example, geographic transitions, *across the street, up the block* and *below him* establish movement in space. Contrast transitions, *meanwhile, on the other hand, however,* make clear a contrast is coming.

- Use bullet points to organize loosely related ideas. This chapter summary is using bullets—succinctly presenting loosely related points.

ADDITIONAL READING

News Reporting and Writing, Brian S. Brooks, George Kennedy, Daryl R. Moen and Don Ranly, Bedford/St. Martin's Press, 2004.

News Reporting and Writing, Melvin Mencher, McGraw-Hill Humanities, 2005.

Reporting for the Print Media, Fred Fedler, Harcourt College Publisher, 1998.

Writing and Reporting News: A Coaching Method, Carole Rich, Wadsworth, 2003.

EXERCISE A

Indicate where new paragraphs should begin in each of the following stories.

ONE

As soon as Mayor Kennely left the city yesterday for three weeks at his vacation home in Raleigh, workmen moved into his office in City Hall to begin installing a new wooden floor. The floor, being installed by Freemont Floor and Ceiling at a cost of $1,250, will replace the vinyl flooring placed in the office at the beginning of Mayor Kennely's first term, six years ago. The mayor's office had had a wooden floor since City Hall was first built in 1905, but Kennely's predecessor, Angie Lairmont, an avid golfer, had left many cleat marks on the floor of the office, where she often practiced her putting, according to Mayor Kennely. Kennely said he had decided to install the vinyl, at a cost of $460, to cover the cleat marks. "Now we finally have the money in the budget to restore this beautiful room, owned by the people, to its original condition," the mayor said, before leaving for his summer home. The construction work is expected to take all of the three weeks Kennely will be away.

TWO

Royal Plumbing Supplies Co. is expected to report a record $100,000 profit this year, Blake Securities Co. said in a forecast released yesterday. Blake's report said Royal's total sales should reach a company record of $900,000 by the end of the year. It predicted that Royal will sell more than $200,000 in supplies out of state this year. Royal made a profit of $55,000 last year. Earlier this year the company's president, Elena Hargrove, had predicted that Royal would do substantially better this year.

THREE

An East Waldwick woman, Helene Beegle, yesterday became the first $2 million winner in the state's Get Rich Instant Lottery. Beegle scraped the lottery ticket she bought at 1 p.m. yesterday at Sam's Stationery Shop, on Rickles Road, and saw the numbers "2,000,000." "I almost fainted," Beegle recalled at state lottery headquarters. "I hugged Martin Silver, who owns the store, and then I ran to the phone to call my husband." Beegle, 37, of 23 Hayloft Lane, is manager of the 7-Eleven store on Rickles Road. Her husband, Woodrow, is assistant manager of the store. The money, the largest prize in the history of the state lottery, is to be paid out in $100,000 installments every year for 20 years. "We haven't yet decided what we'll do with the money," Beegle said. "But we sure won't be selling any more coffee at 7-Eleven."

FOUR

Elizabeth Burma, who was convicted of murdering a policeman, was sentenced today to life in prison. In sentencing Burma, Judge Robert Hendricks called her crime "heinous," but said the fact that she is a mother convinced him not to give her the death penalty. Burma, 31, who has a 9-year-old son, was found guilty Friday of shooting to death Patrolman James Ganey last March after Ganey tried to arrest her for child abuse. Burma's son, Joseph, has been living in a foster home since the incident. Ganey's widow, Maryann, attended every day of the two-month trial, "I think it's a farce," she said after the sentencing. "Burma should be killed." In an interview with reporters after he handed down the sentence, Hendricks defended his decision. "I simply cannot condemn any child, no matter what his mother has done, to be an orphan," the judge said. "I hope he never lives with his mother again, but at least he'll know she is alive." Burma will be eligible for parole in 25 years.

FIVE

The City Council yesterday approved a plan to sell the Hightop Elementary School building to the county to be used as an arts center. Under the plan, the county's Artistic Development Agency, which will pay $214,000 for the building, will rent studios in the building at below-market rates to artists, musicians, craftspeople and writers. "We think this is a great thing the county is doing," said Council President Sarah Levine after the vote. "And we hope it will help make Andersonville a center for arts in the state." The council approved the plan unanimously. Mayor Robert Scortino, a supporter of the arts center, is expected to sign the bill within the week. Athena Harris, director of the county agency, told the council that the county is ready to buy the school immediately. The arts center could begin operations early next year, Harris said. The Board of Education closed the Hightop School two years ago because of declining elementary school enrollment in the area. Levine told the council that the board envisioned no future need for the building. Levine said the council still must decide how to allocate the $214,000. An amendment to the bill, proposed by Councilwoman Sheila McGee, under which the money would have been used to purchase new uniforms and training equipment for all the city's high school sports teams, was defeated by a vote of 4–1.

EXERCISE B

Number the grafs (not written in final form) in the order in which they should appear in each of the following news stories.

ONE

_____ Jordan was charged with second-degree murder, auto theft and motor vehicle violations.

_____ The bus, which was empty, was stolen from its depot on Broadway at 8:30 a.m. Suspect is Leon Jordan, 32, of Ellington Avenue, police said.

_____ After a 20 minute chase, police said, Jordan finally forced to curb on Belair Street and Broadway.

_____ A man who apparently was drunk stole a city bus yesterday morning and drove it wildly down Broadway, killing a pedestrian and injuring three other people, police said.

_____ Dead identified as Juliana Franck, 76, of 8205 Broadway. She was struck while crossing Broadway a block from her house.

_____ Franck declared dead on arrival at Lady of Mercy Hospital.

_____ Three persons slightly injured when the bus hit a taxi cab 10 minutes later at Broadway and Hudson Street.

TWO

_____ Police said Ramirez was helping his sister, Angelita, 26, the owner, close up the store at 10 p.m. when the three armed men approached.

_____ Ramirez lived with his relatives uptown.

_____ Police said that "for no apparent reason" the gunman assigned to guard Ramirez and his sister shot Ramirez through the head.

_____ One of the robbers, all of whom wore ski masks, forced the brother and sister to lie face down in the store's aisle, police said.

_____ A grocery clerk who arrived here from Mexico six weeks ago and went to work in his sister's store was shot to death yesterday. He was shot by one of three robbers who escaped with $500, police said yesterday.

_____ The robbers escaped on foot.

_____ Miguel Ramirez, 24, was pronounced dead on arrival at the Jonas Salk Medical Center after he was shot in the head at Angelita's Grocery on 252 Sycamore Boulevard.

_____ The robbers drew guns and demanded money, police said.

_____ Miss Ramirez told them there was a bag with $500 behind the register. Two gunmen went to look while the third watched the brother and sister.

THREE

_____ Lewis Browning, 35, of 29 W. 9th St., and Thomas Browning, of 261 Pontiac Court, were charged with conspiring to force Anatoli Povorsky, 72, from her two-bedroom apartment in the building they own at 16 Dyer St.

_____ The indictment alleges that the damage was done March 16 when Povorsky was on vacation. It says the brothers entered the apartment with plumbing tools in order to jimmy the kitchen sink, causing it to run constantly. They also destroyed the vegetable drawer and rack in the refrigerator and clogged up the toilet, the indictment charges.

_____ The indictment, handed up in Superior Court, charged the brothers with drawing up a false lease and with breaking the sink, refrigerator and toilet in the apartment in an effort to show Povorsky did not take care of the premises.

_____ Povorsky, who is protected under city rent control statutes, pays $175 a month for the apartment. She has lived there 45 years. Equivalent apartments in the building not protected by rent control statutes are being let for $845 a month.

_____ Two brothers indicted yesterday; charged with illegally attempting to force out elderly tenant in building they own.

_____ The Brownings also own four other buildings on Dyer Street, including Dyer Tower, one of the most expensive and fashionable apartment buildings in city.

FOUR

_____ In Denver, residents were digging out from a record-breaking 38 inches of snow that fell in just 22 hours.

_____ The National Weather Service is predicting continued wet weather and below-normal temperatures over all parts of the country other than the Northeast in the next 30 days.

_____ In Sapulpa, Okla., hailstones the size of baseballs cracked car and shop windows and sent a dozen people to the hospital, where they were treated for cuts and bruises.

_____ Strange spring weather continued to plague the Mountain and Plain states yesterday with snow in Denver, hail in Oklahoma and near hurricane-force winds in New Mexico.

_____ The storm in Denver, officially a blizzard, left motorists stranded in cars for up to 13 hours, closed Interstate 40 and obliterated the first signs of spring. Three people were believed to be missing.

_____ A wind storm, with gusts up to 72 miles an hour, buffeted Alamogordo, N.M., tearing down trees and power lines and leaving sections of the town without electricity for more than eight hours.

FIVE

_____ Downtown, only the tops of parking meters were visible and shop owners could be seen rowing down Main Street, trying to salvage what they could.

_____ It was believed to be the worst flood in Sheridan's history.

_____ A family of three whose one-story bungalow at 4 Elm St. was less than a block from the river was reported missing and believed drowned. They were identified as Allie Ng, 36; his wife, Sue, 34, and their son, Ted, 4. By morning water covered all but the roof of their home.

_____ The water swirled into the homes of hundreds of residents as they slept at about 3 a.m. when the river suddenly poured over embankments at First Street and at Main Street.

_____ "The damage just on Main Street could well run into the hundreds of thousands of dollars," said Mayor Robert Ridley. "I have asked the governor to declare Sheridan a disaster area."

_____ The Beaverhead River, swollen from a week of constant rain, overflowed its banks early this morning and flooded downtown Sheridan, leaving at least two dead and three missing.

_____ The Beaverhead has not overflowed its banks since 1918, when only 400 people lived in Sheridan.

_____ Nellis Chandler, 24, of 815 Aubrey Road, and his cousin, Dana Chandler, 28, of 34 Carson St., had been attempting to reinforce the First Street embankment when they were caught in the turbulent water and drowned.

EXERCISE C

Add transitions where necessary in the following sets of paragraphs.

ONE
"The new transit plan will cut traffic and save gasoline throughout the state," Gov. Pressman said.

Mayor Hugh McCarthy argued, in a press conference following the governor's announcement, that the proposal would hurt rather than help transit in the city. "Our taxes will go up, and our buses will remain just as slow," McCarthy said.

The mayor said he will fight the plan.

TWO
Police said Runnion entered the store at 1 a.m. He pulled a gun and demanded all the money in the cash register, they said.

Runnion left on foot and was arrested two hours later, according to police.

THREE
Nole's Hardware owner, Jim Nole, reported that Christmas business has declined 40 percent compared to last year. He said he was not sure he could afford to stay open.

Art Blaine, of Blaine's Shoes, said that he has seen some positive signs that the shopping center could recover from its Christmas-season slump this year. Blaine said that he was sure he will keep his store in the center.

FOUR
"I am going to end this slump and put the people of the county back to work," Fredericks told the cheering crowd.

He promised to cut crime throughout the county.

FIVE
The top floor of the building was destroyed, fire officials said. There was serious smoke and water damage in every room on the ground floor, they said.

Classes are unlikely to resume in the building this year, according to Superintendent Smith.

SIX
The damage in Redding included five willow trees uprooted, three windows smashed and two cars dented by falling branches, according to the Redding Fire Department.

Redding police reported that traffic was blocked on the Freemont Expressway for 45 minutes by some large branches that had fallen onto the roadway.

An undetermined number of trees fell and one house, at 6 Pine Road, suffered structural damage in Hastings, according to the Hastings police.

SEVEN
For Jennifer Sandusky, 8, of 127–63 E. Motor Ave., the snow meant a day off from school and a chance to perfect her snowball-throwing technique. "I wish it snowed like this every day," she told a reporter.

Her father, William Sandusky, 45, looked like he was not having much fun as he attempted to remove the mounds of snow from his driveway.

EIGHT

Howard's Hardware Store, at 34 Ridge Road, was the first store the robbers visited, police said. According to police, the three men pulled a gun on the owner, Axel Howard, and made off with $340 from his cash register.

They moved on to the Safeway supermarket, at 60 Ridge Road, where five customers were robbed of a total of $705, and $3,300 was taken from the store's safe and cash registers.

The owner of the Downtown Lunch Place, Pat Singleton, was robbed of $450 before the three men escaped from the area.

NINE

The labor leader called on the city to pay more attention to the problem of unemployment and less attention to the problems of golfers and tennis players.

His speech was the first sign that local union heads are willing to criticize the Democratic mayor.

TEN

The comet may be visible from parts of the state on the nights of May 3 and 4 this year, according to the astronomer.

Halley's Comet, which is due to make one of its periodic visits to our section of the solar system, may be visible this year.

EXERCISE D

Add transitions where necessary in the following story.

Newport Schools Superintendent John Alvers has reported that he has received two death threats following Newport High's first losing football season since World War II.

Alvers said yesterday that both threats were made in calls to his office. Both callers, he said, threatened his life if he did not fire football coach Red Molman, whom Alvers hired last year.

Alvers maintained that he is perfectly satisfied with the job Molman has done with the team. Newport High had a 3 and 5 record in football this year. The team won 7 games and lost 1 last year, under coach Blandon Phillips. It was 7 and 1 the previous year.

Sgt. Harry Elms said Alvers's report is being investigated. There is little likelihood of tracing the source of the calls, Elms said.

Security has been increased in his offices, Alvers reports. He said he does not believe he is in any real danger.

The Newport High Alumni Association has called for Alvers to fire Molman. The Boosters Association voted in a meeting last week to advise Alvers to give Molman a chance.

EXERCISE E

The leads are already written for the following stories. Use the facts listed after the lead to complete each story.

ONE

A truck loaded with live chickens overturned on the Ventura Freeway here yesterday, filling the freeway with chickens and causing rush-hour traffic delays of up to one hour.

1. Truck and chickens owned by Acme Farms of Ventura; driver was Anthony Devaldi, 36, of Ventura.

2. From interview with Police Sgt. Fred Gompers on scene: "The truck was driving north when Devaldi seems to have lost control. It skidded for about 50 yards before overturning a quarter mile south of the Freemont Street exit. This was at 4:05 p.m. Devaldi was unhurt. No other vehicles involved."

3. More from Gompers: "Many of the chickens were killed in the crash, but about 60 chickens escaped onto the road. We have no word on exactly how many chickens were on the truck. My partner and I immediately called for help. Three other squad cars arrived, and two officers directed traffic and supervised the removal of the truck while four of us chased chickens. You had to sort of fall on top of them and give them a good hug. Then we stuffed them back into cages from the truck. Most seemed sort of dazed, so they weren't that hard to catch."

4. More from Gompers: "For a while the freeway there looked like a chicken farm. But we had it cleared of chickens and the truck towed away by 5:15 p.m. The truck and chickens had completely blocked northbound traffic for at least 45 minutes, and southbound traffic was partially obstructed by the chickens for about that long. Some drivers were delayed up to one hour. Nothing longer than that."

5. Gompers says no criminal charges will be filed.

6. Devaldi and representatives of Acme say they don't want to talk about the accident at this point with the media.

7. From interview with Sally Burrows, of East Harrington, a driver in northbound lane of freeway who says she was delayed 45 minutes by accident: "You had to see it. I have never seen anything like that: four police officers chasing these dozens of chickens around the Ventura Freeway. Yeah, I'll be late getting home, but, you know, it was worth it for the entertainment."

TWO

The Bullock Pipe factory and the Hardwood Lumber Products factory here say they'll be expanding their workforce this month to meet increased demand.

1. Bullock is located on Greene Street. It now employs 104 people here in Bloomsbury. Hardwood Lumber employs 88 here. It is on George Avenue.

2. From a statement by Bullock Vice President James Robertson: "Our sales increased 28 percent last month over the same period last year. People are buying more and more of our pipe. We are going to need 25 new workers here by the end of the month to keep up with demand. The positions will all be on the assembly line. They will be full time and they will pay a starting wage of $15 an hour."

3. From an interview with Joan Nedelka, president of Hardwood Lumber Company: "Yes, what you heard is true. Hardwood is having a solid year, a very solid year. Our new chestnut coffee tables are leading the way, but our line of traditional furniture is selling better than ever also. Sales for the last quarter were up 17 percent over the same time last year. Yes, that's the quarter that ended on the first of last month. So we plan to add 15 workers. Eight openings will be for experienced carpenters and seven will be on our production lines. Salaries commensurate with experience."

4. From the interview with Robertson: "Things are looking good for our company, and we think that that means things are also going to be looking up for this town's economy. We hope to hire additional workers in the coming months if sales continue to rise."

THREE

The crowd of about forty people cheered wildly as he crossed the finish line on Howard Road and collapsed into the arms of his mother.

The runner then waved feebly to acknowledge the cheers, sat down on the pavement and took off one of his legs.

Julian Nance, 19, who lost his right leg in an automobile accident three years ago, ran the 14 miles between Hartford and Westbrook alone yesterday in an effort to raise money to improve Westbrook's facilities for the disabled.

1. Nance ran using an artificial leg; run took 2 hours 10 minutes.

2. Nance visited local business people before run. He got pledges for total of $6,500, if he finished run.

3. Alice Woodward, owner of Woodward Hardware, who pledged $300 in an interview after run: "How could you not respect a boy like this? He fought so hard to come back from what happened to him. I wanted to help out his cause."

4. Nance in interview after run: "Well, I guess I did it. I never had run more than 8 miles in training. But those people cheering sure made it easier. I'll tell you though, that fake leg got to feeling a little sore. But right now I feel great."

5. More from Nance interview: "You know, I haven't decided exactly what I'm going to do with the money. But there surely are enough things in this town that need to be done. We need a social center for the disabled. We need a transportation vehicle to enable people in wheelchairs to get around. We need more ramps on our sidewalks and in our buildings for these people. I'm lucky. I can still walk and run. Some people are stuck in wheelchairs."

6. Friends of Nance, some in wheelchairs, along route. They cheered him on before finish line and gave him cups of water.

7. From interview with Maureen Nance, 43, his mother: "Proud? I think this is the happiest day of my life. To see that boy come back from what he's been through and do something like this for what he believes in, I am just thrilled by it. Until that accident, I didn't know he had it in him. Now, I see that he won't let anything stop him from doing what he believes in."

8. Crowd starts to move to cars and leave; Nance's mother helps by picking up artificial leg; she hands Nance crutches; he takes two wooden crutches and starts walking, using them, to car; mother gets behind wheel; they leave.

9. Facts on Nance: Sophomore at Westbrook Junior College; political science major; lost father when he was 12; lost leg at age 16 when bike he was riding hit by a car; in hospital then for eight months; founder of Westbrook Disabled Person's Rights Association—has 28 members; never ran or jogged before his accident.

EXERCISE F

Write stories based on each of the following collections of information. In each case you are writing for a newspaper dated tomorrow and read in the town or county where the event occurred.

ONE

From interview with Chief Andrew Phegley of East Meadowbrook Fire Department: "Men were called at 10 this morning to answer an alarm at 4 West 10th Street, downtown here.... When we arrived we saw flames coming from window on second floor of two-story frame house.... Were able to control fire in 20 minutes.... When we went inside we found severe damage to most of the top floor of the house...then we found the body.... He was 18 months old, name: Sam Robbins. My guess is smoke inhalation killed him. An autopsy will be done. No adults were home when we arrived...neighbor turned in alarm.... Mother, Rebecca Robbins, 28. She arrived minutes after we did. She was crying wildly and we had to restrain her from running into the flames. Managed to tell us she'd put Sam down for a nap at 9:30 and gone shopping for some groceries.... Father she said is Eric Robbins, 29. He works at King's Shoes.... Mother says the family had a wood-burning stove on. We're investigating whether it could have caused the fire.... Let me tell you, seeing that baby's body was one of my worst experiences in 35 years of firefighting."

TWO

All information supplied by Sgt. Whit Russell of the Paoli Police Department: "There was a bad accident at the Paoli train station today—22-year-old kid, a senior at Havermore College here, was killed trying to be a Good Samaritan. Seems as if he was waiting for the east-bound commuter train to come in, the 8:23, when he noticed this guy lying on the tracks. He jumped down on the tracks to help him and found out the guy was just soused. At 8:15 in the morning. Guy had an empty bottle of Jim Beam in his hand. Just then people on the platform heard the train whistle—it's a local-only stop, and the train was an express—and started yelling to the kid to get off the track. He picked up the drunk and threw him to the side. I guess he figured he had time to jump after him, but the train just ran over him. The local would have been slowing down and he would have had time. But the express must have been going through at 30 or 40 miles an hour. Victim's name was Danny McGruder. Like I said, he was 22, a senior at Havermore College majoring in economics. Lived on campus. Nice kid, played soccer, served on the student council. His family lives in 427 Chestnut St. in Philadelphia. No, the drunk wasn't hurt at all. We're still not sure of his identity, but no question McGruder saved his life. I guess you could say he was a hero, but life isn't always that kind to heroes, you know."

THREE

This is for a Rockland County newspaper. The source is county Police Officer Judith Bergman.

1. Quite a wind storm hit the southeast corner of the county this morning. Real freaky. Was quite calm when winds began howling about 8:45 a.m. Clocked at between 45 and 63 mph. Gusty.
2. Kids had a hard time walking to school. Some had to chase hats that blew off.

3. Winds broke off some power lines; 5,000 customers of Orange Electrical Co. had their power interrupted from about 9 until 4:02 p.m. All the customers were homes and businesses in towns of Nyack, Piermont and Sparkill in the southeastern corner of the county.

4. Rush hour also was messed up. Big tree branches broke off along Route 9W and Route 59.

5. "It certainly wasn't a day to go for a drive. I got in my car, you know, to check for speeders on 59 before it hit and before I knew it I was out there directing traffic. When the power went out so did the traffic lights, and with the tree limbs down all over everything pretty much came to a standstill for an hour. It was the kind of rush hour when you wished you owned a horse."

6. Tree house came down in James Smith's back yard. He lives at 343 Wellington Place, Nyack.

7. "Some people were lucky and didn't lose power, but most of the electricity in those three towns was out all day."

FOUR

Transcript of a speech by Democratic Mayor Harrison Fredericks of Jonesville at 11 a.m. at City Hall: "I have an important announcement to make to you today. As you all know, the drug problem downtown in River Park, or as it's sometimes called, Needle Park, has gotten totally out of control in recent years. Our police staff, under the fine leadership of Commissioner Jane Lovejoy, has done its best, but has still been unable to prevent the open exchange of drugs in what should be a place for city residents to enjoy themselves and escape some of the pressures of city life. I think I speak for most of the decent people of this city when I say that I have had enough. Starting tomorrow I am going to order Commissioner Lovejoy to triple police patrols in the area. I am going to ask Governor Richard Ramos to increase the penalties for drug use and drug sales in this state. And right now, I am warning those people who persist in using illegal drugs that this city will no longer tolerate their immoral and irreligious behavior. We have had enough. Thank you. Any questions?"

The mayor is asked where the additional police patrols will come from. He replies: "Sure, we are not in a position, without raising taxes, to increase the size of the police force, but I am confident Commissioner Lovejoy will be able to find the additional officers for the park without weakening protection in other parts of the city. As to the exact number of police who will be assigned, I'm not at liberty to say that."

Commissioner Lovejoy is contacted. Lovejoy says she welcomes the mayor's plan and, of course, will follow his orders. She says there is now one officer in the park at most hours of the day. She says she is not sure where she will find the additional officers on her 68-person force.

Republican City Council President Frank Shapiro is contacted about the mayor's plan: "Is that what he said? It sounds like another publicity stunt to me…. Robbing Peter to pay Paul. To fight crime in this city we need more police officers, not just a reshuffling of the ones we have."

FIVE

The following on the telephone from Grover Brandon, director of press relations for Howell County Airport near here: "Did you hear? Here's what happened: A Midwest Airlines 727 jet (the plane was carrying 73 people plus 5 crew members from Chicago) had some trouble here today. No, nobody seriously hurt. I'll tell you what happened. The plane is coming in for a landing—perfect weather, sunny, no clouds or fog—but it comes in much too late on the runway—was using our main runway—number two. It landed maybe 150 yards further down the runway than it's supposed to land. The problem is that it just ran out of runway at the end. The plane, of course, wasn't able to slow down in time. So, it kept going past our runway…right onto the soy field—owned by John McPherson—that abuts the airport. We estimated that it ran 75 yards through the soy fields before stopping. Hey, this is why you want—they encourage it in fact—to have flat land near airports, in case something like this should occur. So, we had no damage to the plane. After the boys from the FAA take a look, we'll just get a little tractor and move her to the terminal, no problem. Five people on the plane say they were hurt a little—soy fields are a little bumpier than airport runways, you know—but only one was taken to the hospital. Wait, I think I have her name here—it's Helen Bennett; she lives at 51 First Drive here in Howell. So, as I said, the Federal Aviation Administration will want to look this over—they said they'll have some people down here tomorrow. We don't know what went wrong."

A visit to the scene, and the Boeing 727, painted orange and black, can be seen, after long tire marks, sitting in the soy field. One passenger, Jack Frankel, 58, from Chicago, still at airport. Frankel in interview: "We didn't know what happened. We were landing okay and then suddenly everything started to get incredibly bumpy. A few people screamed, but soon we came to a stop."

Midwest Airlines official says pilot's name was George Hancock, refuses to comment further, says Hancock is not available for an interview, says no crew members are available, says it was flight 505 from O'Hare Airport, says incident occurred at 1:35 p.m.

A call to Howell Hospital: Spokeswoman Hilda Ringel says passenger, Helen Bennett, 38, had a broken wrist bone set, has since been sent home.

No answer at Bennett's house.

SIX

Meeting of Millsburg Recreation Committee this evening at which following action is taken.

1. By a 5–0 vote, additional $35 given to swing fund for Oak Street Playground at the corner of Kings Row and Presidents Street.
2. Committee member Steve Fairmont: "That is one of the most used playgrounds in the city. Let's make sure the kids who use it have decent, safe swings."
3. By a vote of 4–1, city's annual Memorial Day parade is canceled this year.
4. Committee member Jill Peters (supported proposal): "It was just a disaster last year. We had one band, a few firefighters and no more than 50 spectators watching the parade. I love parades, but if the people of this town would prefer to stay home and watch baseball on TV, why should we spend $500 preparing for a parade?"
5. Committee member Willa Creel (supported proposal): "I agree with Jill. It's not our job to force things down people's throats. If they don't want to come watch the parade, why go to all the trouble? Many of us put in long hours on the parade last year, for what?"
6. Committee member Alona Irving (opposed proposal): "I don't like this one bit. What are we doing here? That parade has been held in this city for 58 years. OK, we had one bad year. I wish we would try to publicize it better and maybe make it more attractive—maybe include some rock bands for the younger people—rather than just give up on it."

Some research in the newspaper clips confirms the committee members' statements about the age of the parade, the cost of last year's parade ($500) and the number of spectators.

A call to Mayor David Jones gets the following: "It's the committee's job to decide things like this. I don't want to comment on it."

A call to Alan Greenwood, president of local chapter of Veterans of Foreign Wars, gets the following: "Yeah, I heard they were going to cancel the parade. What can I say? The sad thing is that they couldn't get enough people to show up at the parade last year. I guess people don't much care about Memorial Day around here anymore."

7. Meeting was at City Hall at Municipal Plaza. It began at 8 p.m. and lasted until 10:25 p.m.

SEVEN

1. Sherri Hall is an active citizen of Sterling.

2. She is 37, grew up in town, lives at 7 Garber Hill Road, husband is Vernon Hall, sales manager at Scott's Chrysler-Plymouth in Sterling.

3. Sherri and Vernon have three kids: Tom—8; Suzanne—10; and Shelly—11. Sherri is a housewife.

4. Six months ago Sherri Hall was ejected by a guard from a Sterling Town Council meeting for refusing to sit down and stop talking during a council discussion of the budget for the town's parks.

5. The council voted to cut expenditures on the parks by 12 percent. Town has four parks totaling 65 acres for its 13,000 citizens.

6. Sherri was an opponent of the cut.

7. "Parks are the heart of any town," she had told a reporter after the meeting. "Our parks need more, not less money. I can't just sit by and watch them fall apart further."

8. After that meeting Sherri formed Citizens for a Green Sterling. This organization has picketed Town Hall twice for more support for parks.

9. Text of speech this afternoon by Sherri Hall in front of crowd of 16, including supporters, passersby and reporters on steps of Town Hall: "Hello. How are you all? I think you all know something about the history of my involvement in Sterling's politics. For 36 years I was just another ordinary citizen. I don't think I had attended more than two Town Council meetings in my life. Then suddenly I was on the front page of the local paper and the radio station wanted an interview. I have always cared about this town. I had assumed our politicians cared as much as I did. But when I heard about that plan to actually cut the parks budget six months ago, I decided I better see for myself what they were up to. Well, I saw. And as you all know I was so outraged by what I saw that I couldn't hold still. Later with the help of some of you I formed the CGS.

"Well, we've accomplished a lot. But it soon became clear to me that there's plenty more to be done. They approved that 12 percent cut as you know. The parks are in awful shape. The schools and libraries and buses and benches of this town aren't in such good shape either. Something has to be done. We need government leaders in this town who care about this town. We need officials who aren't just interested in dollars and cents and all that politician talk. We need officials who care about schools and libraries and buses and benches...and about the heart of Sterling—its parks.

"So that's why I'm announcing today that I've decided to run for mayor of Sterling. I'm going to run against Mayor Jerome Barrett—who supported that cut in parks—in the Democratic primary on the 11th of next month. If I win I'm going to make sure this town spends more money on parks and things used by its people. They threw me out of Town Hall once. But I'm going to be coming back."

10. Reporter asks Sherri where she plans to find the money to spend on the improvements she detailed. Sherri's reply: "We are studying that and we will release a detailed plan soon."

11. Barrett in telephone interview after Sherri's announcement: "I welcome her into the race. I think it's good for the town to have as many as possible of its citizens involved in

politics. I don't think she understands municipal finance at all, but the voters will have plenty of time to educate her about that."

12. In Sterling, mayor chairs Town Council meetings.

EIGHT

1. Burglary at 103 Gedney St. in Howorth. Happened sometime between 10 a.m. Saturday and 6 p.m. today.

2. Owner away on vacation at Grand Lake, Colo.

3. House a two-story colonial on a half-acre at the end of Gedney. Borders River View Country Club.

4. Owner, Richard Phelps, 62, returned with wife, Patricia, 59, at 6 p.m. Saw nothing amiss.

5. At 7 p.m. Phelps went to office in house and noticed door to small safe ajar. Personal papers and stock certificates untouched. TV, radio, cash in bedroom drawer also untouched.

6. Taken from safe: gold jewelry valued at $4,300 and a collection of early English and American coins valued at $15,500. Figures come from appraisal done for Phelps by Deemer, Stein & Goltz, Inc.

7. All information above from Detective Hugo Kolk, who investigated. Kolk said that one or more burglars entered house by kicking in a basement window in northeast corner facing golf course of country club.

8. Kolk: "This looks like a professional job to me from all the evidence I have so far anyway. Used a window away from neighbors, selective pickup, no fingerprints, you name it. Right now we are at square one. You gotta believe the person knew about that coin collection though. There was no dilly-dallying here."

9. Phelps: "What can I say? A hell of a way to end a vacation. I've been collecting those coins for 35 years. They mean more than money to me."

10. Phelps is attorney for the city of Howorth, a part-time position. He also has his own law firm.

NINE

1. Meeting of Albertson Village Council. Held at Village Hall, 1 Van Dyke Drive.

2. Began at 7:35 p.m. Ended 10:19.

3. Minutes of last meeting approved.

4. Council votes 5–0 to send letter of thanks to Jennifer Rowe for donating new American flag for pole in Conners Park.

5. Douglas Marsico, 36, of 19 Oak Brook Road, read the council a petition signed by 14 residents on Oak Brook Road. Five of his neighbors were among the audience of 12 people.

6. Petition: "Dear Mayor and Council: Last September the village agreed to construct a curb along Oak Brook Road between Hill Street and the cul-de-sac. We who live on the block had requested the curb to prevent erosion of our lawns and to keep parishioners of St. Ann's Church from accidentally parking on our lawns. Some of us now wish we had not sought the curbing. With all due respect, it was not installed properly. It is now extremely difficult to enter any driveway on the street with any car without scraping a muffler or tailpipe. We've discussed this with the Department of Public Works and they've hemmed and hawed. It's time to do more. We ask that the curb be lowered by whatever amount necessary so that we can once again use our driveways without ruining our cars."

7. Mayor DeLong suggests that Department of Public Works Director Andrew Cobb be asked to investigate and report in 14 days. Other members of council agree.

8. After meeting. Interview with Mayor Ralph DeLong: "This, frankly, is the first I've heard of the problem on Oak Brook. As you heard, we've instructed Andy Cobb of the Department of Public Works to look into the matter and report back to us in two weeks. Who did the work? I really don't remember. You should check with Mr. Cobb."

9. Andy Cobb: "Yeah, it was O & D Construction Company. They won the contract on bid. They were the low bidder for paving and curbs for the area. I've got it here. They bid $35,500 on the job. This was just a small part of it. Some people just aren't satisfied no matter what you do for them."

10. Marsico: "Did he say that? People should only have enemies like he is our friend. Here's the facts. I've started parking on the street because the curb knocks the stuffing out of my muffler every time I pull into the driveway."

TEN

Study by the National Teachers Association released today:

1. Average income of public school teachers in U.S. five years ago: $28,227.

2. Average salary this year, $32,530.

3. Damon Josephson, president of the NTA, an organization representing some 275,000 teachers nationwide: "These figures don't say much for public confidence in education. During these five years inflation was a total of 22 percent. Teachers' salaries rose 15 percent. How can the public ask for quality education when it isn't willing to pay for quality teachers? I'll tell you how I think public education can begin to change for the better in this country. When teachers get a decent wage."

4. You check with state NTA. Average salary in your state is $32,860 this year, slightly above national average, says Gertrude Beer, president of the state NTA.

5. Figures for local teachers here in Green River, provided by Supt. Jane Bidlack. Average salary for 152 teachers in district is $31,275 this year. Bidlack: "Yes, we are below the national and state average but the figure is misleading. This is one of the few areas in state where enrollment is growing. Lots of our teachers are young and vital. They have little experience so they are less expensive. We hired them because they are good though, not because they are cheap."

6. Bidlack: "Average starting salary in district is $24,350 this year."

7. NTA study: Average starting salary nationwide is $23,425.

8. Survey based on responses from local NTA chapters in 17,032 districts. Represents 93 percent of all districts in the country.

Background and Context

Most news stories center on a set of facts that emerges the day the story is written. Yet few stories are complete when they stand on those facts alone. News must be placed in perspective. It must be weighed against what has happened already, what will happen next and what of a comparable nature is also happening currently.

When such explanatory information gives depth to a story but is not essential to its meaning, it is known as *background*. Background facts usually are placed near the bottom of a story; they can be cut if space is tight. (See Chapter 9, Organization.) For example, the following paragraphs from a story about an 11-month-old girl who received a new liver and a new lease on life are valuable but not *required* to understand the story. They are the 25th and 26th paragraphs of a 26-paragraph story. They provide background:

> Two children are waiting for livers at the Minnesota hospital. Forty-nine adults and children are waiting at the University of Pittsburgh.
>
> "Since our liver program began in 1981," a Pittsburgh spokesman said, "32 adults and 16 children have died waiting."
>
> *The Washington Post*

Sometimes background information is essential; it is needed to place the breaking events in *context*. This contextual material provides a framework necessary for understanding the news. Context usually appears at the top of the story—sometimes in the lead. (See Chapter 4, Traditional Leads.)

When, for example, officials weakened a plan to limit ship emissions, the *Los Angeles Times* pointed out that the action apparently contradicted the mayor's vows to reduce pollution. That provided context.

> *Despite Mayor James K. Hahn's vow to reduce air pollution at the harbor,* Los Angeles officials last week weakened a plan to limit emissions from ships at a much touted new "green terminal" intended as a national model.
>
> *Los Angeles Times*

A reporter who had merely noted the weakening of the plan without the context of Hahn's vow would have missed a major portion of the news.

THE PAST

Many stories stretch on for days, months and even years. So each time the subject is revisited, reporters must restate the basic facts of the story. Readers cannot be expected to have read and remembered each previous installment.

While this *background* information will likely appear low in the story, the reference to the original event may be needed as *context* much higher. Such was the case in this story about an unresolved lawsuit filed over the deaths of three ironworkers in a construction accident:

> MADISON—*More than five years after three ironworkers fell to their deaths when the Big Blue crane collapsed at Miller Park*, the lawsuit spawned by the tragedy remains unsettled.
>
> *Milwaukee Journal Sentinel*

The background of this highly publicized accident was then summarized in the fifteenth paragraph.

> Most Milwaukeeans are familiar with the events that led to the tragedy. The Big Blue crane lifting a 450-ton roof piece collapsed after the pieces started swaying in the wind. The three workers had been suspended 200 feet in the air in a man-basket hoisted by another crane. Falling debris collided with their basket, sending the men plummeting to their deaths.
>
> *Milwaukee Journal Sentinel*

The secret is always to provide this little history lesson thoroughly enough so that a reader who has read nothing else on the subject will be able to understand the story, but briefly enough so that those who have been keeping up will not be bored. It wouldn't do to devote a significant portion of each new story on the lawsuit to a review of the accident that spurred it. Generally the relevant past history of a much-reported event can be summed up in one to three paragraphs. Less familiar stories may require more background.

Context also helps measure change over time, an essential ingredient of news. Consider this lead from *The Denver Post*:

> Denver residents enjoyed some of the cleanest air in a quarter-century this summer—just one year after the metro area violated a tough new federal ozone standard.

An eye for historical context can prove particularly useful in covering politics. Politicians are pragmatic people. Their views have been known to change from year to year, if not month to month. Their visions of the future are not always realized, their promises not always kept. Part of a reporter's job is to keep politicians and other newsmakers honest. One way of doing that is to compare statements and predictions made by newsmakers with their past pronouncements...as recorded in the electronic files of old newspaper stories and in the literature provided by the politicians themselves. (See Chapter 14, Research.)

When a Florida sheriff announced plans for widespread layoffs, a reporter for the *Sun-Sentinel* in Broward County, Florida, was prepared to set his announcement in context:

> Broward County Sheriff-elect Ron Cochran, *who promised there would be no "bloodbath" if he was elected,* said that about 80 employees will lose their jobs after he takes office on Tuesday.

A reporter works on a story in the newsroom at *The* (Bergen County, N.J.) *Record.*
(Courtesy of The *[Bergen County, N.J.]* Record)

COMPARISON

The weight of an event (see Chapter 1, News Judgment) is often best indicated through comparison. It is incumbent on the reporter to tell readers if a race was run in the *fastest* time ever, the tax increase was *twice as large* as last year's or the plane crash was the *worst* ever in the state.

Here the comparison *is* the news so it was placed in the lead:

> Domestic new-car sales continue to sputter, with the five major automakers yesterday reporting *their lowest daily selling rate for mid-October in 24 years.*
>
> The (Bergen County, N.J.) Record

When sales of Marlboro cigarettes took a dive because of price undercutting by competitors, *The Wall Street Journal* waited only a little longer—until the second paragraph—to note that "it was the steepest drop in the brand's history."

Comparisons, however, must be valid and specific to be of any value. No useful insights can be gained, for example, from comparing the murder rate in different years on a *single* day in a *single* city. The statistical sample is too small: Whether one, two or five people are killed on that day is a matter of chance and says nothing significant about trends in violence.

But that didn't stop the *New York Post* from making such a comparison on New Year's Day 2004:

Weak:

New Year's Eve turned into New Year's Evil...in 2004 with a horrifying series of shootings, stabbings, slashings and two murders....In the breathless night of mayhem, the NYPD reported 11 shootings, including two murders, as well as five stabbings—all within the first six hours of 2004....

This year's orgy of crime far outstripped the violence at the start of 2003, when four people were shot and no one was stabbed.

Some comparisons are not worth making.

Even worthwhile comparisons demand specific information. In this story from (Long Island, N.Y.) *Newsday*, the absence of specifics makes the comparison almost useless:

> *An unusual number* of primary contests have emerged in Nassau County this year, election officials said yesterday.

For readers to gain a clear understanding of the political situation in Nassau County, the reporter would have had to come up with some numbers: how many primaries this year, how many in previous years. "Unusual" tells us little.

PATTERNS

The news tends to be repetitious. Sometimes, however, that repetition seems to be more than a matter of chance. If five buildings burn down on the same block within two months, a pattern has emerged regardless of whether police have established a connection among the fires. Reporters should let readers know something unusual is going on, and they should let them know prominently in the story:

> An abandoned warehouse on Gatlin Road burned to the ground early yesterday morning in a fire police described as being of suspicious origin.
>
> *It was the fifth fire in a four-square-block area in the past two months.* A mother and her two children were killed Sept. 24 when a fire raced through their second-floor apartment two blocks from yesterday's blaze at the Cherney Co. warehouse on 235 Gatlin Road.
>
> Fire officials said yesterday that they do not know whether any of the five fires are connected. They said, however, that all appeared to be the work of arsonists.

THE FUTURE

Our legislative and judicial systems are as much process as product. A verdict may be overturned on appeal; an amendment passed by an assembly committee may lose in the assembly only to be approved in the state senate, approved when resubmitted to the assembly, and then vetoed along with the rest of the bill by the governor. For stories to be meaningful, this process—or at least the next steps in it—must be explained within the first several paragraphs of a story:

> SAN MARCOS—The county Registrar of Voters Offices has determined that there are enough valid signatures to qualify a referendum for the ballot aimed at blocking construction of a Wal-Mart store in the Southwest of San Marcos.
>
> *The measure will now go to the City Council, which has the choice of rescinding its 3-2 vote approving the store or placing the issue on the March 2 ballot. The council will probably consider those issues Nov. 18.*
>
> The San Diego Tribune

The future, in other words, can also place events in context.

CHAPTER 10 SUMMARY: BACKGROUND AND CONTEXT

News doesn't exist in a vacuum.

Today's story is often closely connected to the past and will have implications for the future. Sometimes that connection is central to understanding the news. In such cases, this context needs prominent play, a place in the story's lead or support paragraph (see Chapter 9, Organization). Context plays an important role in stories that:

- Measure change through comparison, such as a report on a sharp drop over a decade in a city's murder rate.
- Establish achievement, such as the fastest time ever in the 100-meter dash.
- Note patterns, such as a series of arson fires in the same neighborhood.

At other times, information from the past provides *background* that's important to the story but not essential to understanding its purpose. For example, a story on the efforts of a neighborhood devastated by a hurricane to rebuild a year later would focus on rebuilding efforts, not what happened during the storm. But lower in the story, a few paragraphs on the storm itself would provide valuable *background* information.

EXERCISE A

Which of the following background facts definitely should be included in stories on the following subjects? Which might be included, depending on how much space was available for the story? And which should not be included? Write "yes" next to the facts that would be essential; "maybe" next to those that would be optional—depending on length; and "no" next to those that should be ignored.

ONE

Police Commissioner Steven Leary orders officers not to fire their guns unless first fired upon.

1 _____ Leary appointed to job when predecessor resigned to run unsuccessfully for mayor.

2 _____ Leary's nomination as commissioner had been opposed by some community groups because they considered him too much of a "hard-liner," too much of a "law-and-order man."

3 _____ Leary had served as assistant commissioner in Columbus, Ohio, before accepting this job.

4 _____ One week ago a teen-ager was killed by a policeman who said he thought the youth was about to pull a gun on him. No gun was found on the teen-ager.

5 _____ The mayor has said he will review Leary's handling of this situation.

TWO

Local high school senior Mark Egan runs the mile in 4:04 to win the mile race at the state high school championships.

1 _____ Egan transferred here from an out-of-state school two years ago.

2 _____ Egan's time would have set a record for high school students in his old state.

3 _____ This was the fastest he has ever run the mile.

4 _____ His time tied the record for the fastest mile ever run by a high school student in this state.

5 _____ Jack Renaldo, of Oakdale High, ran a 4:04 in a meet in this state three years ago.

6 _____ Egan plans to run in the national high school championships in June.

7 _____ The third fastest mile ever run in the state was run by Steven Wild, also of Oakdale, two years ago.

THREE

Two people are killed when the car in which they are riding slams into a wall next to a curve on the Shoreline Highway.

1 _____ There had been two other fatal accidents at that curve in the past three years.

2 _____ The state had been scheduled to widen the curve, beginning next week.

3 ____ Anti-nuclear demonstrators had marched on that section of Shoreline Parkway last week.

4 ____ Money for widening the curve had been approved by the state Highway Department six months ago.

FOUR

The scores of city high school juniors on a standardized national test drop 1 percent from previous year's scores.

1 ____ Scores on test nationwide were the same as in previous year.

2 ____ Scores in the city had dropped an average of 1 percent in each of previous four years.

3 ____ New reading and math programs were introduced here this year to stop declining scores.

4 ____ School Supt. Sue Jamison, just before scores were announced, called this test "not perfect, but certainly not something we can ignore."

5 ____ Scores in a neighboring city increased 1 percent this year.

FIVE

President of local bank dies of heart attack while getting out of his limousine in business district.

1 ____ Two other local bank presidents have died of heart attacks within past decade.

2 ____ Bank had recently announced profit for year of $130,000.

3 ____ Bank president had a history of heart trouble.

4 ____ Bank president had recently instituted an employee physical fitness program, citing lessons he had learned from his own condition.

EXERCISE B

Additional contextual or background information is listed after each of the following stories. Add the information, if needed, at the appropriate spots in the stories.

ONE

A 43-year-old priest waiting for a bus on upper Green Street was robbed at knifepoint last night by two teen-agers, police said.

The priest, Rev. Peter Santangello of St. Mary's Church on East 87th Street and Parker Boulevard, was dressed in clerical garb when he was held up at 11:45 p.m. at the deserted bus stop near the corner of Centre Avenue, according to Sgt. Raoul Valenzuela.

Santangello was not injured, Sgt. Valenzuela said.

Valenzuela said two youths, both about 16 years old, approached Santangello and demanded a bag he was carrying. When the priest refused, one of them pulled a knife, while the other grabbed the bag, Valenzuela said.

Police said they have no suspects.

Additional information:

1. This was the fourth robbery of a priest in the city this month.
2. Rev. Ambrose McIntyre and Rev. Joseph Santos were held up while working late at St. Francis's Church in the suburb of Cherry Woods, five miles from the site of last night's robbery. Rev. Stephen Riley was robbed while walking home from St. Paul's a mile further south on Centre Avenue three weeks ago. None of the priests was injured.
3. Police say they have no evidence of a connection among the robberies.

TWO

Police investigators will be interviewing hundreds of residents of the Point Pleasant area today in an effort to find someone who saw 8-year-old Cindy Wolf before she disappeared Thursday afternoon.

According to Lt. James Flaske, investigators will concentrate on an eight-block area around the child's home at 324 West Meadow Road. They will be looking for someone who may have seen the thin, blonde-haired girl after she got off her school bus at 3:20 p.m. Thursday on West Meadow Road, Flaske said. Cindy was wearing an orange slicker and had her hair in braids.

Lt. Flaske said that police have no leads in the case.

Additional information:

1. Cindy Wolf's parents, Henry and Alma Wolf, reported her missing Thursday evening when she failed to return from school.
2. She was last seen by school bus driver Richmond Avery, getting off the bus.
3. Henry Wolf was the prosecutor responsible for sending five reputed members of an organized-crime family to jail last summer, but police have no information linking his daughter's disappearance to that case.

THREE

Mayor Ellen Goodman has endorsed Sam Streeter in the runoff election for the Democratic nomination for city controller.

Streeter, a local businessman, is running against former Councilman George Harris for the right to face incumbent Arthur Greener in the November election.

"Streeter's business experience makes him the best person for the job," Goodman said in a press conference at City Hall today.

Streeter welcomed the mayor's endorsement. "I think it gives my campaign a big boost in these crucial final days," he said. The runoff election will be held next Tuesday.

However, Harris discounted the significance of the mayor's move. "Voters in this city are going to make up their own minds," he said.

Additional information:

1. Streeter received 34 percent of the vote in the Democratic primary two weeks ago; Harris received 22 percent; the rest of the vote was split among three other candidates.
2. The mayor had declined to endorse any of the candidates in the primary.

FOUR

The City Council voted last night to impose a 3-percent sales tax on all retail sales in the city.

The council approved the new tax by a vote of 4–3.

Councilwoman Greta Almalfi, who gave no indication of how she would vote during the debate, cast the deciding vote in favor of the new tax.

Councilman William Ruckham, the most vocal proponent of the sales tax, which would take effect on January 1, estimated that it would raise $350,000 in its first year. "This tax will finally give the city the money it needs to keep its schools and roads in decent repair," Ruckham said during last night's debate.

Opponents of the tax argued that it would hurt business in the city and place an unfair burden on the poor. "If we need a tax, and I'm not sure we do, let it be a graduated income tax," said Michele Flurenski, head of the council's Finance Committee. "A graduated income tax would spare those who cannot afford to pay and would protect the retail businesses that are so important to this town."

However, Al Freedberg, another supporter of the sales tax on the council, defended it as "the simplest, least painful way for the city to pay its bills."

Almalfi refused to discuss her vote after the meeting.

Additional information:

1. The city has never before had a sales tax.
2. The council defeated similar proposals twice in the last six months, by votes of 4–3, with Almalfi voting against them both times.
3. The tax bill must still be signed by Mayor Hedrick Armstrong, a long-time supporter of a sales tax.
4. The tax bill must also be approved by the state legislature, which rarely has interfered with local tax plans in the past.

FIVE

The rock group The Rage announced yesterday that it will play a concert here on May 26 to benefit Municipal Hospital.

According to lead singer Owl Saul, the concert at the Music Factory could raise as much as $50,000 for the hospital. All receipts from the show will go to the hospital.

"We care about the people of this town," Saul said. "We recognize that we have a debt to them. This is our way of expressing that care and repaying some of that debt."

Municipal Hospital Director Alison Burt said she was pleased to hear of the benefit concert. "We are working to upgrade our facilities, and this money will be a big help in that effort," Burt said.

Additional information:

1. The Rage had the best-selling record album in the United States last month.
2. Last Aug. 16 two people were injured in a stampede to the stage at a Rage concert at the Music Factory; one—19-year-old Seymour Hamilton, who lived on West Street—later died.
3. Both the people injured at the concert were treated at Municipal Hospital.

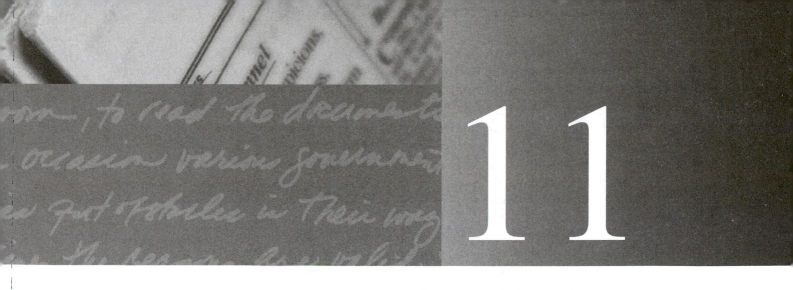

11

Reporting in a Multimedia Age

In the spring of 2006, a news report painting a bleak picture of the state of American journalism created a buzz in the corridors of academic journalism.

Titled "Journalism's Crisis of Confidence: A Challenge for the Next Generation," the Carnegie Corporation report began: "If 1775 was...both the best of times and the worst of times for the English and French citizenry, then 2005 may be called simply the worst of times for American journalists."

Others soon echoed the report's sense of urgency and gloom, with the loudest warnings aimed at the venerable newspaper industry.

The *American Journalism Review*, one of the country's few journals devoted to critiquing the news profession, devoted a cover story to warning editors and publishers to "Adapt or Die."

And a few weeks later, Jim Romenesko's widely read blog, a compilation of articles, reports and other tidbits on the media at www.poynter.org, circulated a memo sent to the news staff of Dow Jones, publisher of *The Wall Street Journal* and other leading business publications. It called for far-reaching change.

"We live in a digital age that is fundamentally changing how people get their news and information," the Dow Jones executives began. "Consumers now expect to get news however, wherever and whenever they want it....This is the right time to take a step back and re-evaluate our news strategy in a comprehensive way."

As authors of this text, we share the sense of urgency about change in 21st-century newsrooms. We don't share the gloom. More than a decade into the new newsroom culture of what's still called new media, online journalism has allowed newspaper companies back into the competitive arena of up-to-the-minute news. It's given their reporters a chance to talk directly to readers about their work and share original documents on which it's based. And it's allowed those readers to interact with the news and the people who report it in ways unimaginable just a decade or two ago.

Listen to Michelle Johnson, who served as the first editorial manager of boston.com, the online news site of *The Boston Globe*.

"Compare 1996 versus 2006 and you see this gigantic leap," she says. "[Online news] has become a lot more multimedia, a lot more eye-catching and interactive compared to where we started. And that's all a result of the changes in technology.

"The news cycle now is 24-7 and that didn't used to be true on the print side. Print is operating more on the broadcast model....I keep wondering what all this is morphing into because you've

171

got print people doing video and audio and broadcast people writing for the Web.... It's really interesting to see all these different elements come together."

If there is one certainty about the future of journalism at the start of the 21st century it is this: Things will keep changing.

That's why neither we nor anyone else can tell you precisely how news will be written and packaged in 10 years. As Johnson says, "New technologies keep coming down the pike to transform it."

Nor can we tell you what form your news will come in, though it's a fairly safe bet you'll get more and more news in some kind of digital form and with the opportunity to call it up in more than one medium.

We can't even tell you *where* you'll get your news a decade or two from now. (Will the supersized and digitized cell phone make the laptop passé? Will the BlackBerry or some yet-to-be-invented successor corner the market? Will home computers print out personalized versions of what used to be the mass-market newspaper?)

But one thing we can tell you: This a century in which the audience will be increasingly calling the shots. And that changes the way reporters think about, report, package and write the news.

Today's journalists, especially those working online, are in some ways analogous to modern-day travel agents. In the pre-Internet age, travel agents held the expertise: Consumers heading to an unfamiliar destination or embarking on a complicated journey turned to the travel agent to map out all the details. For most travelers, the agent designed the trip from arrival to departure, booking trains, hotels, entertainment and tours. In essence, though not phsyically there, the travel agent drove the tour bus as the traveler sat passively behind, taking in the sights.

Fast forward to contemporary travel. Few surviving agents still try to drive the bus—few, that is, tell the traveler, without give and take, what to see and where to go. Instead, they're sitting alongside the new tour drivers—the tourists themselves—making suggestions about how to travel cheaper, where to find the most scenic route, and where to find (and not find) the most charming places to stay. Today's tourists, well-armed with their own Web information on cheap fares, travel hideaways and exotic sites, might not buy into all a travel agent's suggestions. But if the travel agent has ideas that prove distinctive or fun or special, the tourists will keep coming back.

Reporters, producers and editors of online news sites find themselves in a similar position today: They offer a broad-based menu to choose from rather than a prescribed journey of what the audience should read. Newspapers have just so much space; the *news hole* is fixed. No matter what the news, the stories are attached to specific pages. That's not true of news on the Web. Readers map their own journey. And in doing so, readers are changing their relationship with the journalists who provide the options.

Says Johnson: "[Editors are] putting the information in front of the reader and saying, 'OK. You can come over here and read this blog. You can go here and watch this slide show, over here is a forum you can join.... They're giving people different places they can go, more choices."

Even on traditional newspaper pages, editors are seeking to offer more *entry points*, more ways to scan the page, picking out graphic elements that break out information and highlight key statistics for the busy reader.

Whereas news in the 20th century allowed the journalist to be the *gatekeeper*—the expert in charge of what audiences read, listened to and viewed and in what form—news in the 21st century is designed to leave much of that decision up to audience members themselves. When they click online, these news consumers are much like modern-day tourists, traveling at their own pace through a myriad of sites carrying a variety of news, opinion, graphics, links, archives and other opportunities to interact.

The impact of this changed relationship already has been profound. Fifty years ago, most American consumers defined their news by a name or a brand: Cronkite (as in Walter Cronkite at CBS news), *The New York Times, The Herald Tribune.* Whatever news outlet those consumers had given their allegiance to took on the role, within the individual's specific format and standards, of providing the day's news. Today we live in a world of *surfing,* whether our physical home is oceanfront Los Angeles or landlocked Laramie, Wyo. This surfing is guided by a mouse as each surfer darts from entry point to entry point on the page, looking at what's of interest, then jumping someplace else. Readers expect and demand to be able to move around freely and at their own pace, but they also seek out sites with a good reputation and a clear roadmap (or *site index*). Online news audiences want to set their own course, but they don't want to get lost any more than other travelers. They often want to travel fast, to just skim the news highlights. But they also want to be rewarded with breadth and depth if they decide instead to dawdle and wander off the beaten path.

In other words, today's news consumers want choices. On an unprecedented scale, they are defining where they go for news, how long they linger and what they look for. And by doing so, they have much to say about how news is written, produced and presented.

WRITING FOR THE INTERNET

For newspapers and their reporters to survive the Wild West competition for audience online, they'll will need to embrace not only new technologies but, we are convinced, some old skills. Succinct writing will count. Clear writing will count. Lean sentences driven by strong, active verbs will count. Accuracy will count.

"I tell my students, 'Don't give up the basics. Don't throw away the ethics. Don't ignore what you've learned in journalism classes,'" says Johnson, who today, in addition to writing a column for *Computer World*, teaches new media at Emerson College. "You still have to have a decent lead. You still have to have your facts straight. The basics are still part of this."

Why can't newspaper Web sites afford to be wrong sometimes in that competition to be first? Because reader trust and confidence are what give traditional news organizations an edge online. And there are signs that edge is slipping. That Carnegie report mentioned at the start of the chapter noted that the number of Americans who told one polling company that they believe

Michelle Johnson, teacher and Web journalist.
(Photo by Jonathan Satriale, Emerson College)

most of what they read in a daily newspaper dropped from 84 percent to 54 percent in the two decades between 1985 and 2004.

So our first advice in writing for the Web is this: Don't sacrifice accuracy for speed. Here are some other tips:

1. Draw readers with sharp, simple headlines, subheads and bullet points. Web surfers scan. Don't practice subtlety on them. As their eyes dart across pages on the Web, the information, says Columbia University Professor Sree Sreenivasan, must be "absolutely explicit and clear."

That is why *USA Today's* "Bush Vetoes Stem Cell Bill," worked better on July 19, 2006, than another headline the same day in the *San Diego Union-Tribune* that read: "Bush Casts First Veto of Career." The first head was slightly shorter *and* more specific.

THE CHRISTIAN SCIENCE MONITOR — csmonitor.com

WORLD | USA | COMMENTARY | WORK & MONEY | LEARNING | LIVING | SCI / TECH | A & E | TRAVEL | BOOKS | THE HOME FORUM

Aug. 3, 2006   About Us/Help | Archive | Subscribe | Feedback | Text Edition | **Search:**   Go

Special Offer: Subscribe to the Monitor for just 43 cents an issue.

TERRORISM & SECURITY
A DAILY UPDATE

Leaked memo: Civil war in Iraq most likely
British ambassador also predicts country will break up along sectarian lines.

Why effort to rebuild Iraq came up short
Reconstruction funds from the US have been diverted to security operations.

Where the next Castro may take Fidel's Cuba
Some analysts say Raúl could open up the country's economy and start to ease hostilities with the US.

New Treasury head eyes rising inequality
In his first major speech, Henry Paulson pushed America's wide income gap onto the agenda.

Antarctica under siege
Stunning beauty and the promise of minerals and oil are bringing people to the once-pristine continent.

Pakistan turns to its people in quake relief
The government is paying victims directly to help them rebuild, but some say more money is needed.

More photos   Mary Knox Merrill - Staff

People tried to stay cool despite temperatures in the 90s at the Melnea A. Cass swimming pool in the Roxbury neighborhood of Boston.

When the heat hits, city hall to the rescue
Some cities' responses to extreme heat resemble those used for terrorist attacks or natural disasters.

As A/C whirs, budgets tighten
Utilities and advocacy groups are trying to help consumers cope with double-digit increases in electric bills.

ISRAEL, HIZBULLAH CLASH

Israel carving out buffer zone
It aims to push Hizbullah beyond the Litani, because the river creates a natural geographical boundary.
* Hizbullah guerrillas wait amid ruin

The next man to lead Japan?
Shinzo Abe, a conservative politician who is hawkish on foreign policy, will most likely be tapped in late September.

News updates: AP's The Wire

China faces suspicions of organ harvesting
A Canadian legal duo has released a report alleging that practitioners of Falun Gong are being murdered for their organs.

CLOSING THE GAPS
Structured work and play helps boys thrive
A study program works with boys in middle school to prepare them for high schools and college.

Students in Ohio get a taste of college
The Barbara Byrd-Bennett Scholars Program helps young men avoid detours that lure away their peers.

The dog days of a Scottish summer
Shepherds and their border collies compete in Scottish sheepdog trials.
Photo gallery

BACKSTORY
An electrifying job atop an American icon
We make the rounds with Bill Tortorelli, the Empire State Building's chief electrician.

→ All of today's headlines
→ Past five editions
→ Corrections

Headlines and read-out lines on the Aug. 3, 2006, home page of *The Christian Science Monitor* concisely summarize the stories, making clear to readers what they'll get if they go to each link.

In an essay at www.poynter.org, Jonathan Dube, the founder of CyberJournalist.net and a visiting faculty member at Poynter, writes, "Make sure you tell people what they are going to get." Otherwise, they'll never stop by.

2. **Write concisely and directly.** Web journalists can't waste words. For one thing, says Johnson, "it's hard to read much text on the [computer] screen." That's why her first advice to students is always "write it shorter." Think in screenfuls, in short chapters, in packages that break material out.

Sreenivasan says writing for the Web mixes techniques of broadcast and print. (See Chapter 27, Broadcast Journalism.) "It's getting people the information fast," he says.

In his Poynter essay, Jonathan Dube writes: "You can't afford to bury the lead online because if you do, few readers will get it. When writing online, it's essential to tell the readers quickly what the story is about and why they should keep reading—or else they won't."

3. **Think in more than one layer.** If Web stories should be short, they can—and should—link to material that provides depth and added context for the serious reader. We call this the *bifocal effect*—one set of lenses for the person scanning what's on the surface, another for the person looking deep into the story.

Even as they structure brief summary stories, Web journalists should think about ways of breaking up the material in their news packages. Stories can be linked to sidebars or be linked directly to related information—charts, original records, related stories—embedded in the story's text. This lends depth and context that individual stories online may not have room for.

"Sometimes you can't go into the depth you have in a print piece, but you can replace that with pointers to related information," says Johnson. "I try to get [my students] to think about how to get the reader sort of beyond their story, to link them to [related] types of information....You can incorporate that into the writing as you think about how you're going to structure your story."

In 2006, when the collapse of concrete ceiling tiles crushed a motorist in one of Boston's notorious Big Dig tunnels, the state of Massachusetts began a massive inspection of bolts holding up ceiling tiles throughout the multi-billion-dollar project. Inspectors kept finding more deficiencies, and *The Boston Globe*, through its website, boston.com, updated readers throughout the day.

This AP story was posted at boston.com in midafternoon on day 12 of the saga:

> BOSTON—Gov. Mitt Romney on Thursday ordered an immediate shutdown of eastbound lanes the Ted Williams Tunnel, days after 12 tons of ceiling tiles fell from a connecting tunnel, crushing a motorist.

But even as it kept readers up to date on breaking developments, *The Globe's* website offered context and depth by creating a "special report," titled "Big Dig Tunnel Collapse," complete with "A History of Big Dig Problems," video, graphics, maps and a message board.

Among its features, noted here in the kind of *bullets* that work well on the Web, were:

- A discussion board allowing readers to speculate about whether companies were staggering shifts to offset traffic snarls caused by the tunnel's closure.
- Photo galleries, showing how and where the concrete ceiling tiles collapsed and recording the emotional wake and funeral for the woman killed by that collapse.
- An article looking at the cost to the city of Boston in rerouting traffic.
- Video newscasts of the collapse and subsequent investigations provided by New England Cable News, *The Globe's* broadcast partner station.
- An information graphic explaining how the bolts work and how they're inserted into the concrete. (Infographics are illustrated in the next section.)
- A graphic showing closed portions of the local highway grid.
- Another graphic showing where hundreds of other suspect bolts had been found holding up ceiling tiles.
- A survey asking readers whether they'd continue driving through the tunnel (presumably when it reopened) in light of the ceiling collapse.

In other words, even as boston.com's periodic daily updates kept the news fresh, the special section on the site, which archived related stories, pictures, graphics, video and discussion, offered as much depth as the patient reader wanted and a chance to voice an opinion, that important interactive component of the Web.

4. Be yourself. It's possible to be succinct without being stiff. The Web lends itself to less formality; a conversational style fits the give-and-take of an interactive medium. And since the Web remains reasonably new and continues to evolve, it's also a place that encourages a bit of boldness.

"Online audiences are more accepting of unconventional writing styles," Dube writes in his Poynter essay. He adds later, "Challenge yourself and your colleagues to question the way things are being done and to stretch the boundaries of what can be done. There are no rules, only ideas. Take risks. Try something different."

Tom Regan, a columnist and blogger for *The Christian Science Monitor*'s website, has done just that: writing in praise of cell phones, for example, or even letting his 8-year-old daughter post, on a trip to Africa, on his blog. "I think the key thing about writing for the Web is actually WHAT you can write about, not how," he noted in an e-mail. The Web, he suggested, gives writers greater range of choice than does the sometimes more tightly constrained realm of traditional news.

5. Think in more than one medium. In a book primarily about print journalism, it may seem a sacrilege to say so, but written words don't always tell the story best. The Web has the power to break out data that readers can manipulate in interactive games, quizzes or maps. It can show information in time or space on maps and timelines. It can accompany words with streaming video or audio, or sound clips from participants in the story. When these work with the story, they enable the writer both to keep the writing's focus tight and to give readers/viewers more opportunities to pick their own path. Note the bulleted list in item 3, above. How many of the things listed rely strictly on words?

Technological advances continue to make it easier for the nontechie to produce varied content on the Web. For example, Johnson says blogging technology has enabled reporters in the newsroom of *The Globe* to post updates on boston.com without going through Web producers. No Web coding skills are needed with these automated methods of posting online.

In mid-2006, Web applications known as mashups were gaining momentum. These applications join together content from more than one source to present public data in new and interesting ways, sometimes interactively.

As one example, Johnson suggested that a mashup might overlay a database of crime statistics on a city map so that users can display crimes by street or neighborhood. One mashup, discussed by *The Washington Post*, used Google maps in a way that readers could click on a country and call up recent news from that area.

While print can't offer the same range of options, editors and designers have spent more time in recent years figuring out how to tell parts of the news visually in an effort to make newspapers more accessible to their audiences, too.

USING GRAPHICS TO TELL THE STORY

When the *San Jose Mercury News* set about making sense of the sweeping changes measured by the latest census in California, the newspaper reached beyond standard text to interpret the numbers for readers. It turned to charts, maps and *highlight boxes* to home in on some of the most critical information and to help tell the story.

Readers who wanted to know whether their town's household income had risen and by how much compared with neighboring communities had only to consult a chart. Or they could view color-coded maps showing the relative distribution of wealth in the newspaper's primary readership area. Those with just a few minutes to spend on the story could turn to a "census snapshot" highlight box that told them a few highly pertinent facts: the overall increase in state and county income, for example.

Today, the vast majority of American newspapers have borrowed at least a page or two from the game plan of *USA Today*, the once-controversial national newspaper that led a revolution in newspaper design in the 1980s. More and more papers have hired graphics editors whose job is to help reporters and editors better understand how to present the material in their stories visually. In part, this job category reflects well-documented concern that busy readers don't have time to wade through inches of text to find a key nugget of information. In part, it reflects research showing that well-*packaged* stories—stories that draw together photographs, maps, graphics and words into one readable design—convey information most effectively. And in part, it reflects changes in the newspaper industry, as the multimedia culture increases in importance and graphics prepared for print appear in some form online and vice versa.

The smartest reporters don't bother to wait for graphics editors to suggest ways their stories can be better understood. They understand that graphics can enhance rather than detract from their prose.

"I used to tell reporters they wanted graphics because it would help readers, but I've found it works better to tell them that with graphics their stories will get better play [placement in the paper]," jokes David Yarnold, the former executive editor of the *San Jose Mercury News*. "Stories with graphics also can relieve a narrative from the obligation of presenting dense statistical material and let the reporter concentrate on writing."

Sometimes the graphic alone can be the story. Throughout much of the Iraq war, the opinion pages of *The New York Times*, for example, periodically ran a graphic that compared and contrasted information in a given month to the same period a year and two years before.

The graphic, compiled by scholars at the Brookings Institution, measured indicators of progress or lack thereof in areas as diverse as the number of U.S. troops killed in combat to the hours of electricity service in Baghdad.

More often, graphics enhance stories, enabling the writer to keep the text shorter and sharper and to break out key information for the busy reader. This is particularly important in an Internet-driven age when the online reader may look at nothing but the graphic.

The *San Jose Mercury News* used numerous graphics in a special section on earthquake safety, "We Are Not Prepared," which helped the paper win the 1990 Pulitzer Prize for local news coverage.

HIGHLIGHT BOXES

Highlight boxes are short, printed checklists that are surrounded or *boxed* with a dark line, or rule. These graphic devices do what the name implies, providing busy readers with both design and informational value. They make a gray page less imposing *and* provide a quick summary of the story's main points. Some effective highlight boxes go beyond these summaries and provide additional, related information on the story.

A highlight box from "We Are Not Prepared" looked at how one model Santa Clara County city had prepared for a big earthquake.

Sunnyvale Sets a Good Example

Five ways Sunnyvale has prepared itself for the Big One:

- **Self-help program:** 110 volunteer groups trained in first aid, search and rescue, and damage assessment for their neighborhoods.

Sunnyvale Sets a Good Example (continued)

- **Shelters:** containers stationed at eight schools with cots and blankets for 3,600 people.
- **Amateur radio:** antennas in place at all fire stations and most schools.
- **Full-time staff:** seven city employees working only on emergency planning.
- **Seismic retrofitting of city buildings:** more than $10 million in strengthening projects already completed on overpasses and city buildings.

CHARTS AND INFOGRAPHICS

Even the most assiduous reader would quickly lose interest when confronted with a story listing the number of potentially dangerous, unreinforced masonry buildings in five or six dozen California communities. But readers might have great interest in the dangerous buildings located in their own communities. The solution? The *San Jose Mercury News*, in its earthquake safety section, presented the list in the form of a simple chart. Readers could pick out what interested them and skip over the rest. Other charts looked at buildings by type, assessing how much it would cost to earthquake-proof different building designs.

The special section also contained a diagram combining words and drawings. This *infographic*, or informational graphic, showed and told how a building can be quake-proofed.

Mourners at the scene of The Station nightclub fire in West Warwick, RI.
(*Providence Journal photo by John Freidah*)

When a horrific fire swept through The Station, a club in West Warwick, R.I., trapping and killing many of those crammed inside, designers at *The Providence Journal* built an informational graphic that showed and described what had happened.

Reporters aren't expected to know what kind of chart or graphic works best with their stories. Leave that to the artists, whose repertoire extends well beyond the classic pie charts we all were introduced to in school. It does help, however, for reporters to know what kinds of information are best suited to graphic presentation.

"There are probably graphics hiding in any story heavily based on numbers, pegged to a specific location or dependent on one or two key people," says David Yarnold of the *Mercury News*. Here are some examples:

1. Key dates in a project or a career can be shown in a timeline.
2. Numbers that change over time can be arranged in a chart or graph that makes it easy to compare them. This is true whether you are comparing changes in different communities' standardized test scores, housing prices, budget outlays or population.
3. Explanations of how things work can be combined with drawings in infographics. These can show anything from how the brain functions to how architects plan to redesign city hall.

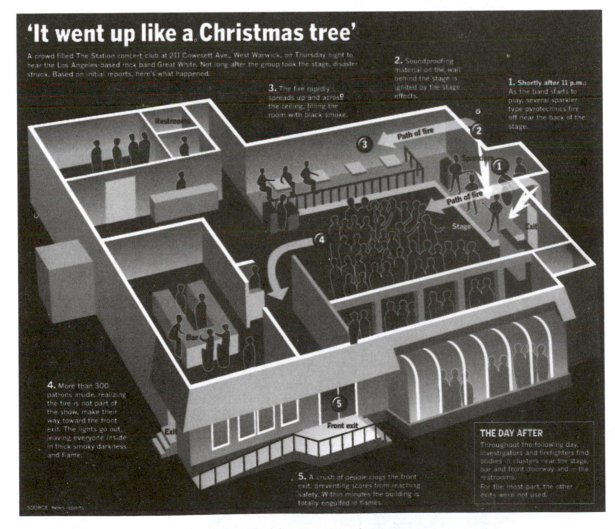

An infographic detailing the fire at The Station nightclub in West Warwick, RI.
(Providence Journal *photo by John Freidah*)

4. Differences of opinion can also be illustrated in chart form. For example, one way of quickly comparing the views of the four candidates for the school board is to ask each one the same few questions and put their answers side by side in a chart.

When *The New York Times* in its Week in Review section looked at the growing debate over illegal immigration in the United States, it used multiple graphics packaged together to convey the nature, scope and geography of the issue. Different elements showed the size and origins of the illegal immigrant populations, what jobs the people were taking in the American work force, what they were being paid, and what the American public thought about it. The entire graphic is reprinted below.

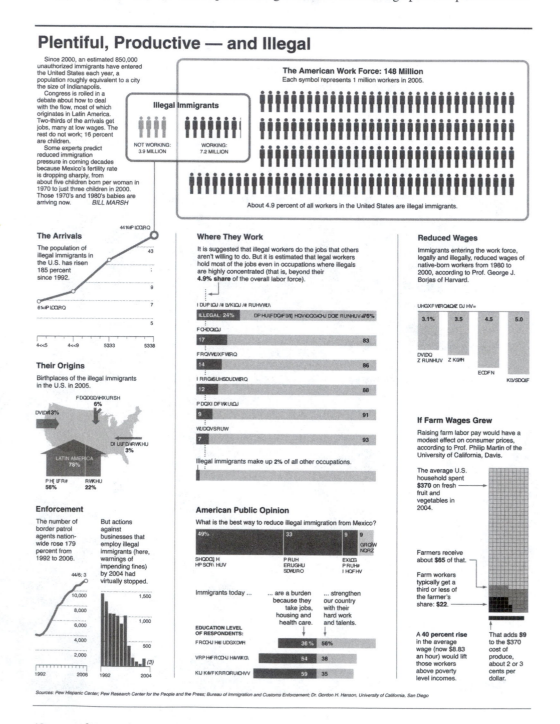

Plentiful, Productive — and Illegal

(Courtesy of New York Times *News Service*)

MAPS

It is hard to describe an intersection in words. Whether the story is about an accident, a fire, a shootout or a traffic tie-up, one of the first things a reporter should do is request a map showing readers where the incident took place.

Locater maps show no more than that. Other more complicated maps might show, for example, an army's strategy for overwhelming an enemy or the landmarks and demographic factors that clarify patterns of crime associated with drug use in a community. Most newspapers today can use color graphics, which makes it possible to convey a variety of information attractively on the same map.

In its special earthquake section, the *San Jose Mercury News* used color coding to show both the scope and the intensity of damage that might be expected from earthquakes of different intensities in the Bay area.

In the map in plate 11.6, which ran with *The New York Times* package on illegal immigrants, *The Times* used shading to what states are believed to have the highest number of illegal immigrants.

Online, many maps take on an interactive component, usually allowing the reader to dig a few layers deeper. When war broke out between Israel and Lebanon, for example, *The New York Times* offered an interactive map on its web site that allowed readers to see where bombing attacks had taken place each day of the war, what kinds of missiles were being used, what their range was, and what the population density was at the site of their targets. The reader clicked on icons at various points on the map to gather this information.

Restricting licenses for illegal immigrants

Immigrant rights groups Wednesday attacked the Senate's passage of new driver's license rules that would require states to verify that people who apply for a license are in the country legally. More than 10 million undocumented immigrants are already in the country with more arriving monthly.

Estimated illegal immigrant population (2000)
☐ Less than 25,000   ▨ 100,000-250,000
▨ 25,000-99,999   ■ Over 250,000

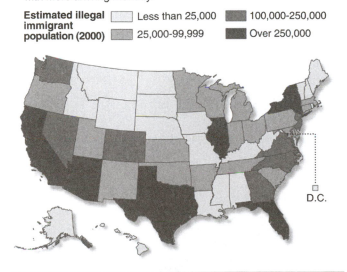

D.C.

SOURCES: U.S. Citizenship and Immigration Services   AP

(Courtesy of New York Times *News Service)*

CHAPTER 11 SUMMARY: REPORTING IN A MULTIMEDIA AGE

The relationship between news organizations and readers is changing rapidly and radically in the 21st century. Today, audiences expect more say about what they read. They want an opportunity to interact with news organizations and the news itself. That is why newspaper web sites emphasize multimedia content and interactive elements. And it is why today's newspapers talk about news packages—including maps, graphics and photos as well as stories—not just articles.

In reporting and writing for the multimedia age, reporters should:

- Get to the news quickly and clearly. Internet readers particularly expect clear headlines and direct leads.
- Look for ways of separating the news into smaller, bite-sized chunks. Bullets, such as you are reading now, work well online to summarize key points. So do *links* to charts, related stories, audio clips of newsmakers, original source material, *photo galleries* that tell a story through pictures and words, and *interactive elements*, such as mediated or unmediated reader chats, games and quizzes.
- Think of the news as layered. Provide short, summary stories for the busy reader; *link* or, in newspapers, *refer* inside to more thorough, contextual material for the reader with time to engage.
- Write conversationally. News is never formal. But online reporters tend to take more chances, write more colloquially, cover topics sometimes ignored by papers of record for their communities.
- Think visually and graphically at the start of the reporting process, not the end. It will allow you to write better stories and get better play on the page.

ADDITIONAL READING

Convergence Journalism: Writing and Reporting Across the News Media, Janet Kolodzy, Rowman and Littlefield, 2006.

Conversations on Convergence: Insiders' Views on News Production in the 21st Century, Stephen Quinn, Peter Lang Publishing, 2006.

News in a New Century: Reporting in an Age of Converging Media, Jerry Lanson and Barbara Croll Fought, Pine Forge Press, 1999.

Visual Editing: A Graphic Guide for Journalists, Howard Finberg and Bruce Itule, Wadsworth, 1990.

Writing News Online, Jonathan Dube, www.poynter.org, July 14, 2003.

EXERCISE A

Define the following terms and discuss their implications for news.

1. Mashup
2. Media convergence
3. Highlight boxes
4. Media consolidation
5. 24-7 news
6. Entry points
7. Infographic
8. Photo gallery
9. Surfing

EXERCISE B

Look for stories in a local newspaper that are not accompanied by any type of graphic or other visual element. List any information that might be shown graphically, improving understanding of the stories. Then think about how the story might effectively be told in a multimedia environment online. What additional reporting would you consider? How might the information be presented differently?

Ask yourself these questions:

1. Might the reader have gained additional background information or context through links to original reports, related stories or organizations mentioned in the story?
2. How might the reporter have interacted with the audience online?

   - Could readers have been encouraged to test their knowledge through an interactive quiz?
   - Would an informal, interactive poll of reader viewpoints have made sense?
   - Does the story lend itself well to a mediated online chat?
   - Might supporting documentation be organized in a way that the reader could ask additional questions to get further information from the data?

3. Do statistics, historical or geographical information in the story lend themselves to presentation as:

   - A timeline—measuring how things have changed over time or noting key dates?
   - A map that shows relationships in space (and perhaps allows the reader to interact for further background information)?
   - A graphic or chart showing a relationship?

4. What kinds of multimedia might enhance presentation of the story? Would it benefit from?

   - Audio clips—perhaps sound bites from participants in the story or "man-in-the-street" responses to a new movie or show?
   - Photo galleries—related photographs, with cutlines, on which the reader can click forward or backward?
   - A video stream to show something related to the story?

EXERCISE C

List what highlight boxes, charts or maps might be used to accompany the following story in a newspaper read in the area where the events occurred. Note what information would be included in each graphic. Also indicate what additional information might be shown graphically, were it available.

Then think about how the story might best be told online. What audio, video or galleries of still photography might accompany the print version? Would the story be written differently? Would other voices be sought? In what ways might the news organizations interact with readers or allow those readers to interact with the information?

SAN FRANCISCO—The storm of the decade continued to pound Northern California yesterday, as rain turned parts of this city into a lake, and snow, whipped by 70-mile-an-hour winds, paralyzed highways from Mount Shasta in the north to the Sierra Nevada in the east.

Three inches of rain fell in 6 hours starting at 2 p.m. yesterday, flooding city streets, closing the Army Avenue on-ramp to Highway 101 and forcing dozens of motorists in the Marina District to abandon vehicles in 3 feet of water.

"I think it's safe to say it is the worst storm in a decade and one of the four or five worst this century," said Brad O'Leary of the National Weather Service in Redwood City. "At least we're getting rain instead of snow, and we need the water."

In the Santa Cruz mountains, 50 miles south of the city, 6 inches of rain fell, spawning mudslides that closed Highway 17 near Summit Road and forced the evacuation of a dozen homes.

"I know we need water," said Clover D. Hobson, 56, who has lived in the mountain region for 27 years. "But this is ridiculous."

In the Sierra, the California Highway Patrol closed Interstate 80 eastbound at Auburn and westbound at Truckee. Highway 50 also was closed.

And to the north, motorists poured into the city of Redding, as ice and snow blocked travel on Interstate 5.

Ski operators rejoiced in the snow but regretted that there was so much of a good thing that almost no one could struggle to the slopes. "Talk about powder skiing," said Shirley Blossom, one of the handful of enthusiasts waiting by the lift at Franconia ski area. "I've never skied up to my armpits in light powder here before. I can't see a thing but who cares."

Among the areas reporting, Franconia said it had received 11 feet of snow in the last 72 hours, Alpine Meadows 10 feet, Squaw Valley 11 feet, Sugar Bowl 8 feet, Heavenly Valley 8 feet, Homewood 7 feet, Donner Summit 7 feet and Boreal 7 feet. The huge storm has brought the snowpack to 220 percent of normal for this time of year, sweet music to the ears of water officials worried about a reservoir system that stood at 24 percent of normal statewide before the storm.

In the Santa Clara Valley, where six years of drought have forced three years of strict rationing, water district spokesman Scott Hurm said the storm hadn't ended the drought though it had put a dent in it.

"We haven't had this much water in Lexington Reservoir since 1987," he said.

Water levels in that reservoir were at 47 percent compared to just 8 percent at this time last year, he said. He said levels also were up at the water district's nine other reservoirs.

The five-day forecast calls for more rain and snow toward the end of the week.

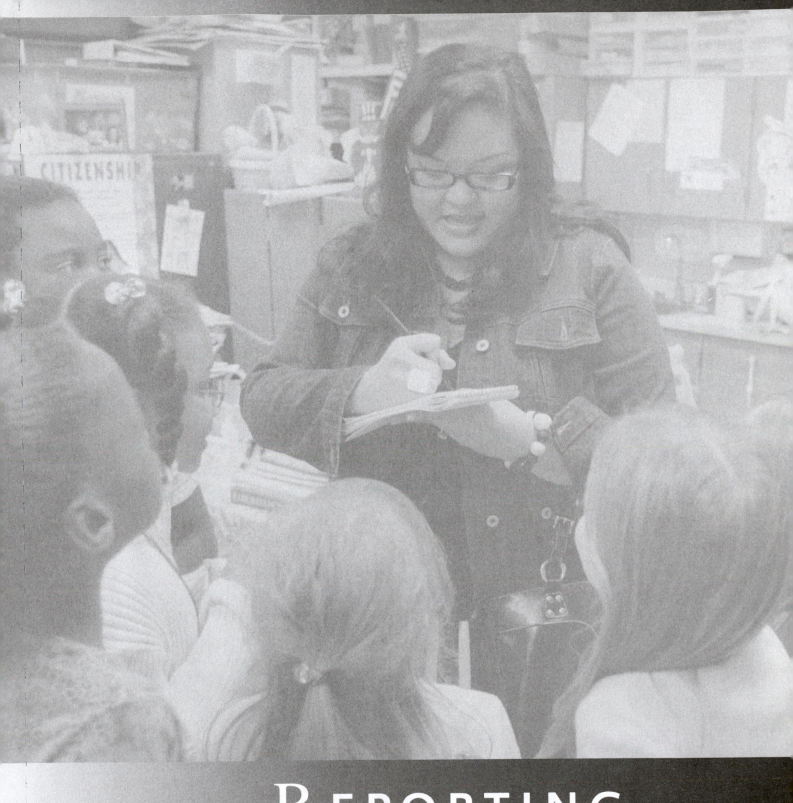

REPORTING

PART 4 TECHNIQUES

Tremeshya Eurings, 8, of New Orleans, walks past a line of Texas Army National Guardsman assigned to help evacuees from Hurricane Katrina.
(Photo by Johnny Hanson)

Facts

Jimmy is 8 years old and a third-generation heroin addict, a precocious little boy with sandy hair, velvety brown eyes and needle marks freckling the baby-smooth skin of his thin brown arms.

The Washington Post

So began *The Washington Post* story that in 1981 was awarded one of journalism's most respected prizes, a Pulitzer. It was a powerful story. It also was untrue: Jimmy did not exist. The prize was withdrawn; the paper's pride shaken.

Journalism is about things that are true. Not the elemental truths of artists and philosophers—the police stations, city halls and business offices where reporters pick up their information do not generally deal in eternal *verités*. A journalist's truths are tentative, clapboard structures banged together out of stripped-down, unvarnished facts. It is a fact that the suspects were arrested and charged with murder. Six months from now they may be found innocent of the charge, and that will be a fact. Similarly, it is a fact that the governor said she would veto the proposal. It is a fact that the fire was at the corner of Miller Avenue and 43rd Street. It is *not* a fact that a *Washington Post* reporter found an 8-year-old heroin addict.

Reporters should be suspicious of any story that can't be tied to solid fact. They should be uncomfortable with predictions, speculations and attempts at mind reading. The best reporters continually struggle to cut through the evasions and the distortions of newsmakers, but they do so by piecing together patterns of facts, not by voicing an opinion. Their struggle becomes that much more urgent in an era when anyone can grab a megaphone by starting a blog and discourse about news has become that much louder (but not that much clearer) on all-talk TV. Ultimately, facts *do* matter. They are the basis of news.

CHECKING

Joseph Pulitzer, the renowned editor and publisher, used to say there were three things he demanded of his reporters: "Accuracy, accuracy and accuracy." As Pulitzer undoubtedly realized back in the last years of the nineteenth century, those are not simple demands. Facts are notoriously slippery. They can get lost while being transmitted from someone's memory to someone's mouth and from that mouth to another person's ear. They can wander off somewhere before hitting a note pad. And if reporters get them wrong, they can ricochet through newspaper databases for years, multiplying the initial mistake. All are reasons why reporters handle facts with so much care.

Many a reporter has jumped out of bed at 3 a.m. and grabbed a telephone book or scrolled through an online database to check for the third time to make sure that a name was spelled right. Facts make reporters paranoid—and they should. The reporter who made up that story about the young addict was fired. Reporters who can't get addresses right don't last long, either.

For a start, reporters must check the spelling of the name of every unfamiliar person they meet on a story. Many interviews begin with the request, "Before we get started, could you just go over the spelling of your name?" And many interviews end with, "May I just make sure I spelled your name right?" Reporters will ask a police officer for the spelling of the name of a victim or suspect, then double-check with the arrest record (facts seem a little more reliable when they are written down). If the victim was hurt or killed, the hospital or coroner also may be consulted.

And names are just a start. The address, the age, the name of the place where someone works, the time, the cause of death, the name of the hospital, the attribution, the explanation—stories are masses of facts, and each one must be worried over:

> A Chicago fireman was killed yesterday by a flash of fire when he rushed into an empty burning home on the Far South Side after neighbors reportedly told firemen that three children were trapped inside.
>
> Sidney Brown, 32, of 7915 S. Peoria St., assigned to Engine Co. 75, was pronounced dead at 4:20 p.m. of burns and smoke inhalation in Roseland Community Hospital.
>
> *Chicago Tribune*

Getting the facts right does not depend exclusively on asking and reasking, checking and rechecking. It may take some thought: "Hey, the police are saying it happened at Shady Knoll Road and Strawberry Lane in Southbrook, but those two roads intersect in West Orange!" Then it's back to asking and reasking, checking and rechecking.

Reporters soon realize that no matter how solid their understanding, how engaging their writing, how great the quotes they've obtained, if one digit in a number, one letter in a street name, is wrong, somebody is going to spot it. There may be a letter; a correction may have to be run. A reporter's credibility rests on every fact.

PROOF

Not all facts are as straightforward as a name, an address or an age. Where people's reputations are at stake, information requires corroboration as well as attribution, no matter how carefully it's reported.

Charges against people, unless they are made during trials or other official proceedings (see Chapter 21, Courts), are not just double-checked to make sure they have been transcribed properly. They must be, in some sense, proven.

During their celebrated Watergate investigation, Bob Woodward and Carl Bernstein of *The Washington Post* refused to report any charge until it had been confirmed by two sources—two reliable sources. That should be taken as a minimum standard for any reporter who has been handed some ready-to-fling mud. When records are available, such documented proof is even better. One source saying that the state attorney general is a hidden partner in a race track invites

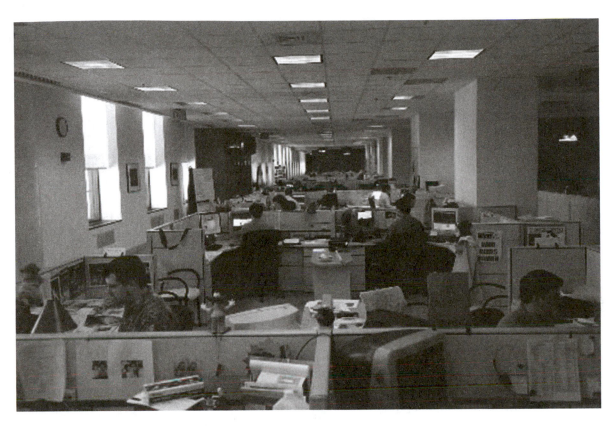

Newsroom of *The Christian Science Monitor*.

further investigation, not a story. A trustworthy form of confirmation, and an interview with the accused person, will be needed before the charge can appear in print—carefully attributed, of course. Much more than the reporter's credibility rests on the confirmation of such a "fact."

INTERPRETATION

Newspaper readers will not always be satisfied with simple accounts of who said what to whom when. They often have seen the newsmakers themselves talking on television the previous evening. When their newspaper comes out the next morning, they may want a little more: Why did they say that? What did it mean? Newspaper reporters increasingly are asked to *interpret* the news.

There are dangers here. Interpretation too often leads to guesswork and subjectivity. For an example we turn to an event some years ago: a presidential visit to Britain by Ronald Reagan. In writing of that visit, one *New York Times* reporter said that "In style, Mr. Reagan pleased and almost charmed Britain" with his "genial and relaxed manner." Three days later, another *New York Times* reporter wrote that British newspapers, in assessing the same visit, "commented on the lack of spontaneity or common touch to his [Reagan's] appearances."

Where are the facts there? Where are the facts when the *Los Angeles Times* concludes that a speech by Reagan before the British Parliament was "generally well-received," while *The New York Times* reports a day later that the same speech "stunned many Britons, including a number of leading conservatives."

Too frequently, reporters take their orders to explain causes and effects as license to take leave of the facts. They certainly do their readers no service with unsupported and possibly unfounded speculation that a speech was "generally well received."

As usual in journalism, the solution is to include more facts. Facts do not just fill all the little holes in a story; they anchor it and keep it from wandering too far from observable reality. Instead of indulging in guesswork, R. W. Apple of *The New York Times* managed to say something about reaction to that speech Reagan gave by noting the generally overlooked fact that "only about 30 of the 225 members of the Labour Party" chose to show up to hear the U.S. president address Parliament.

It is more difficult to find a fact illustrating reaction to a speech than simply to take a stab at summing up that reaction yourself. But good reporters always are ready to make the extra effort. The order to interpret, to analyze, to explain the news should be seen as an order to find more, not fewer, facts—to conduct that extra interview in search of a quote that might explain why, to read that extra document in search of a crucial explanation, to observe the scene more closely in search of a telling detail.

Reporters are people who watch, read, ask and listen, with notebook out and pen in hand. They should also be interested in nuances, concepts and ideas, but they should be looking to translate these subtler thoughts into what is essentially the language of journalism—the language of facts.

CHAPTER 12 SUMMARY: FACTS

Reporters don't traffic in predictions, speculation or mind reading. They build their stories around facts. In reporting:

- Double-check all key facts. Reporters who misspell names and misrepresent titles don't last long. Accuracy is sacrosanct in journalism, and a reporter's credibility hinges on every fact he or she presents.
- Use facts and not opinions to demonstrate the evasions or contradictions of newsmakers. The reporter will present evidence that the politician reversed her position on enforcing stricter immigration laws by showing how she voted on the issue now and two years ago. The reader can then determine whether that politician is "absolutely consistent" as she claims. The reporter does not need to give an opinion.
- Avoid interpretation not supported by fact. With the Web and broadcast news issuing up-to-the-minute reports, newspapers are increasingly asked to interpret the news. This can be dangerous territory because it can lead to guesswork and subjectivity. The solution is to find more facts and build conclusions around their evidence.

ADDITIONAL READING

The Elements of Journalism: What Newspeople Should Know and the Public Should Expect, Bill Kovach and Tom Rosenstiel, Atlantic Books, 2003.

"Trust Me Journalism: The Hidden Dangers of Increasing Analysis and Interpretation in the Daily Press," Gerald Lanson and Mitchell Stephens, *Washington Journalism Review*, November 1982.

EXERCISE A

Interview a classmate or colleague and obtain answers to the following questions. Then allow that person to check your facts.

1. Full name
2. Age
3. Father's name
4. Mother's maiden name
5. Place of birth
6. Date of birth
7. Names, ages and occupations of any brothers and sisters
8. Schools attended
9. Employment history
10. Address
11. Religion
12. Hobbies
13. Major in college
14. Minor in college
15. Career goals

EXERCISE B

Use a dictionary, almanac, encyclopedia, atlas or other reference materials to correct any factual errors in the following statements.

1. Iceland is located just north of Greenland.
2. Raphael, an Italian painter, lived from 1493 to 1520.
3. The New York Mets were in the World Series in 1969, 1971 and 1986.
4. The highest judicial position in the United States is chief justice of the Supreme Court.
5. The sitar is a Moroccan stringed instrument.
6. Texas has the largest land area of any state in the United States.
7. Ronald Reagan had no children by his second marriage.
8. The singer Madonna's last name is Ciccone.
9. The United States purchased Alaska from Russia.
10. Bill Clinton was the youngest governor in the history of the United States.

EXERCISE C

ONE

Note what is wrong with the facts in this description of a robbery provided by a witness:

"Yeah, sure. I remember the exact moment it occurred. I was the only customer in the store. It had just opened. I was standing in front of the supermarket—by the milk—and it was exactly 8:22. . . . I know because I was looking at my watch . . . when these two Hispanic guys dressed in purple pushed through the doors and ran up to one of the checkout girls. One pulled out a pistol from beneath what looked like an army overcoat, aimed it at the nylons of the checkout lady and shouted something like "Vite! Vite! Or you'll never walk again." The manager jumped down from his booth and the second guy pulled a rifle, I believe it was a Colt, so he couldn't get near her, while the first guy was covering all the rest of us who had stopped shopping and had run over to see what all the banging was about. Anyway, the checkout woman looked at the gun on her and started clearing out everything in her drawer . . . lots of loose bills and checks and food stamps . . . and all these coupons and even the money from her pants pockets. . . . The manager was there reaching into the drawer too and stuffing things into these white A & P bags yelling, "Don't shoot!" as the robber just sits there smoking a cigarette. . . . And then they were gone . . . these two tough guys . . . you could see their muscles . . . and they drive away in a 1989 Toyota Accord with green California plates . . . sorry, I just couldn't see the number."

TWO

The desk sergeant for the state police gives you this story. Note what's wrong with his facts.

"Yeah, we arrested a woman for driving while intoxicated on state Route 45 in Ainsley. Weird story. Do you know the highway? It's straight as an arrow for miles, two lanes and a shoulder on each side and a grassy area dividing the north- and southbound lanes. It's 3:22 a.m. and the highway is deserted. Well, Officer Keith Bart was driving southbound, all by himself, when he looks out the driver's window and sees this green car driving right toward all the traffic on the northbound lane. Officer Keith didn't waste any time. He crossed the grassy median and put his car sideways so this green car couldn't get around him. . . . Luckily no one else was on the road although they probably would have spotted him because it was getting light. Keith jumps out and just in time. The blue car smashed right into the side by the door. It pushed the police car about 20 feet, slamming it into Keith's partner, Leslie Locke. She sprained her knee. The woman driving the car seemed dazed. We found some marijuana in the glove compartment and it was clear she was stoned out of her mind. Her name was Elizabeth Aramor. She's 42 and lives in Stanton in the High Tor apartments. She's already been convicted at police headquarters."

EXERCISE D

Write a story based on the following information. You are writing for an issue dated tomorrow of a newspaper read in the town where the event occurred.

1. Basketball game tonight between Hawthorne State College (located here in Hawthorne) and Raintree College (located in Raintree County in this state).

2. Before the game Hawthorne one game behind Raintree in Central Conference. Raintree in first; Hawthorne in second. Before game, four games to play before end of season for each team. Conference winner automatically in national college championship tournament this year.

3. Last night final score: Raintree 72, Hawthorne 75.

4. Half-time score: Raintree 52, Hawthorne 37.

5. Raintree ahead until 2:38 left in second half.

6. Raintree high scorers: Al Kosman—14, James Gutworth—10.

7. Hawthorne high scorers: John Coleman—28, Ralph Stokes—10.

8. From interview after game with Kosman: "Okay, I'll talk with you, but only for a minute. I hated it, OK? It was awful. It felt like someone put a lid over our basket in the second half. Nothing we put up would go in."

9. From interview after the game with Coleman: "Hey, I'm still in shock, or something. I just wanted the ball, if you understand what I'm saying. You know, I've had big nights before, but to do it against Raintree was really something special. Hey, we're number one."

10. After game Hawthorne's record: in conference 10–2, overall 17–6; Raintree's record: in conference 10–2, overall 19–5.

13

Story Origination

Good reporters don't wait for the news to come to them; they search for it.

Editors do assign many stories, of course. But reporters have to learn to develop their own stories, too, both out of those assignments and in areas that their editors may know nothing about. An editor may assign a reporter to cover a press conference, but it's up to the reporter to determine what news is there and whether the news might be part of a larger trend or pattern worth pursuing the next day.

And reporters who are assigned a *beat*—a specific area of coverage such as police, the courts, city government or a whole town—will be responsible not only for knowing when press conferences and meetings are going to be held but also, when possible, for breaking a story beforehand.

Plenty of news is never announced. Stories about the trends, the squabbles, the dirt and the subtler movements and fluctuations that lie behind events are uncovered by reporters who know whom to listen to and how and where to look.

"[Former *Philadelphia Inquirer* editor] Gene Roberts used to say that really important things seep and creep," recalled the late Molly Ivins, a nationally syndicated columnist who once worked with Roberts at *The New York Times*. "No one ever held a press conference to announce that there was an enormous migration of blacks from South to North."

This chapter will talk about ways of finding the news. Some are conventional: These are strategies for winnowing the news from the thickets of often self-serving information that sprout or are planted under the light cast by any news organization. Some are unconventional: The biggest stories sometimes go to reporters who can spot the news that grows, untended and overlooked, in the shade.

PRESS RELEASES

In our society of sellers, promoters and campaigners, almost everyone seems to have a message to transmit, and almost everyone seems conscious of the media's ability to amplify that message. Hundreds of messages find their way into newsrooms each day in the form of press releases, emails and faxes. They announce a rock star's new manager, the findings of a government study or the date of the elementary school's next PTA meeting. Many are written by public relations professionals—people whose job it is to spread news of their clients.

Many press releases are designed to appear as complete news stories from the dateline at the top to the *30* at the bottom. (See The Basics, Section A, Format.) They are intended to slip unedited into a hole in a lazy journalist's newspaper. The vast majority are more likely to end up in the newsroom's garbage bin.

Press releases are usually worth scanning, however; they just might plant the seed of a good story. But they should be read with the understanding that long or short, frivolous or serious, from the government or from a company, all press releases have two limitations: First, they are unlikely to tell the complete story; you are not going to learn from the press release that that rock star has already fired four different managers. Second, press releases don't merely pass on information; they pass it on in a way that reflects favorably on the person or organization that sent them. Or, in the case of potentially negative or alarming news, they downplay its impact. The press release's description of that star as "the best dancer since Jennifer Lopez" should not necessarily be swallowed whole; nor should a reporter automatically give credence to a company's insistence that it decided to file for reorganization under bankruptcy laws so that it could "emerge even stronger."

Jerry Lanson, one of the authors of this book, was covering the environment for *The Record*, in Bergen County, N.J., when a press release, excerpted here, arrived from the state Department of Environmental Protection.

> TRENTON—The Department of Environmental Protection (DEP) today released the initial results of a major statewide ground-water testing project which is examining 500 wells for selected toxic and cancer-causing chemicals.
>
> Environmental Protection Commissioner Rocco D. Ricci said results from the first 250 wells tested in 12 counties show that water quality, in most cases, was found to be far better than federal drinking water standards. No wells were found to pose an immediate danger to human health, Ricci emphasized.
>
> Ricci said 20 violations of the federal standards were found and DEP is now conducting follow-up testing at these sites to identify the sources of pollution. None of the contaminated wells are sources of potable water supplies. Ricci said....

Press releases like this should be viewed as potential starting points for stories, not as anything approaching finished products. First, reporters glance through them to see if there is any news. Sometimes, the news may not be what the release's author chooses to highlight.

In this case, the reporter knew enough about the subject to see beyond the cheery statements in the release's second paragraph. He knew that meeting federal standards was not that impressive because for most of the chemicals no federal standards existed. And he knew that the presence of any amount of these chemicals in drinking water was cause for some concern.

The intriguing news in the release was that "almost all of the wells tested contained traces of some of the chemicals under investigation," a fact the release did not get around to mentioning until its fifth paragraph.

If a release leads to a trail worth following, the next step for reporters is to find someone who can guide them in the right direction. Every release designates someone as a press contact and gives that person's phone number. Reporters should call either the press contact or someone they know to be more knowledgeable. A call, if nothing else, verifies that the release is authentic. It also starts the real reporting.

When Lanson received the release from the New Jersey environmental agency, he chose to call Dr. Peter Preuss, who had supervised the testing program, instead of either Commissioner Ricci or the agency's spokesman. In an interview with Preuss, Lanson tried to determine what wells had been tested, particularly in his area of the state, as well as what levels of contaminants had been found and how great a danger they posed.

Here is how his story began:

> TRENTON—A sampling of the state's underground water supplies has revealed that they are widely contaminated with low levels of potentially cancer-causing chemicals.
>
> State-sponsored tests of 250 public and private wells for 50 toxic and potentially cancer-causing chemicals have shown that almost all contained at least traces of some of the chemicals, according to a report released yesterday by the Department of Environmental Protection (DEP).
>
> Eight of the wells sampled are in Bergen County, and 11 are in Passaic County. The report said none of the 250 wells presented an immediate threat to public health.
>
> But Dr. Peter Preuss, head of the DEP's cancer program, said the presence of even trace quantities of potentially cancer-causing substances raised the possibility of long-term effects on health.
>
> "I think [the test results] are a cause for concern and that it will require a fair amount of effort to determine the boundaries for that concern," he said. "If you have a large population exposed to low levels [of potentially cancer-causing chemicals] over a long period of time, then there will be some added risk of cancer. We don't know what that risk will be."
>
> *The* (Bergen County, N.J.) *Record*

Most press releases are more straightforward: Someone has been hired, fired or honored; something has been scheduled or accomplished; something has changed. But all press releases should be examined and, when newsworthy, reported with a critical eye.

TIPS

All good reporters have troops of sources they rely on to alert them regularly to potential news. (See Chapter 15, Sources.) Veteran police reporter Mike Cox of the *Austin American-Statesman* was at home when a former prisoner who had filed a widely reported suit that led to prison reform in Texas was arrested again and charged with armed robbery. One of Cox's sources in the police department quickly gave him a call, and the next morning Cox had a front-page story. Cox expects such tips from his sources ("I'll get angry if I don't get a call," he says), and he knows to what extent he can trust the information he gets from the sources on whom he relies.

Sometimes tips come from a relative stranger. One morning in Lufkin, Texas, a local builder walked into the newsroom of the *Lufkin News* and started telling a story about his nephew who he claimed had died while training with the Marines in San Diego. Ken Herman was the only reporter on duty, and he was called in to listen.

"It's not unusual for someone to walk into the newsroom unmolested on a small newspaper," Herman explains. "Some you can't help. Some you don't believe. This was one where we were able to pursue it and we got some answers." The *Lufkin News* pursued this tip on questionable Marine training tactics well enough and found enough answers to win a Pulitzer Prize.

People who think they have a story try to corral reporters in person, they try to reach them on the phone and they try to contact them by mail. Doreen Carvajal, who covered the police for the *St. Petersburg Times*, once received a letter maintaining that a veteran police sergeant had resigned after being arrested a second time for indecent exposure. Few reporters will ignore such tips—this is one route to scoops—but all good reporters will check them out thoroughly and obtain solid corroborating evidence before allowing a tip from any source to get into print (see Chapter 12, Facts). "Sometimes tips check out, sometimes they don't," says Carvajal. "This time it checked out."

Lessons from the Pros

Ric Kahn, *The Boston Globe*

As a reporter for *The Boston Globe's* City Weekly edition, Ric Kahn always has his eyes open for a story. Kahn uses the techniques for finding news outlined in this chapter. He calls his sources regularly, trolling for tips. He reads press releases with an eye for what's buried deep within them. He looks for ways to follow stories in his own paper. And, as often as possible, he gets out of the newsroom and goes to the scene.

Ric Kahn
(*Courtesy of* The Boston Globe)

"Sometimes you aren't sure if something is a story until you go to the scene and are open to all of the possibilities," he says. "You see the people, the action. One time a kid fell off the roof of a house. My story started as a profile of Freddy, 14, who was drunk and fell off this roof. But after going to the scene my story changed to be about the 'corner culture' in that neighborhood. Generations of residents have hung out on this one corner."

Kahn offers other suggestions for finding news:

- **Unearth stories embedded in other stories.** "There was a story in the paper about a man charged with sticking a cop with an AIDS needle. The story quoted the man's brother, who was a reverend. So I wrote a feature about the tale of two brothers—one with a drug addiction, the other a reverend—and how their lives could have been reversed."
- **Read the news briefs.** Kahn found a brief about a homeless man charged with assaulting two people. After doing his own reporting, Kahn said he discovered that the man had a long rap sheet and preyed on other homeless people. "There was a nugget in the story just waiting to be mined."
- **Visit a municipal court.** Kahn said this is where he finds and develops unconventional sources (see Chapter 15, Sources), from drug addicts to prostitutes.
- **Go to local meetings.** These aren't always worthy of a story in themselves. But, points out Kahn, "You can meet neighborhood people who are outraged about an issue."
- **Read junk mail.** "Anything can become a good story. Don't discard something because it sounds boring on the surface."
- **List your phone number and listen.** Though Kahn acknowledges that crank calls can be an occupational hazard, he adds, "Even a call from someone who sounds crazy can amount to a good story. If you hang with them you could get a kernel of a good story to go off of."

RECORDS

When Bruce Maxwell was hired as an investigative reporter for the *Rochester* (Minn.) *Post-Bulletin*, he had a hunch that he could find his first story before ever setting foot in the state.

Maxwell, who was completing a graduate reporting program in Washington, D.C., visited the Nuclear Regulatory Commission's public documents room and asked for the *reportable occurrences* file for the Prairie Island nuclear power plant located near his new newspaper. In the file, which contains documents related to any problems at a plant, a single sentence caught his attention: It said a used radioactive fuel assembly had come apart nearly two years earlier while being moved underwater in a storage tank.

That single sentence in a NRC report led three months later to a four-part series that began like this:

> Nearly two years ago, a nuclear fuel assembly containing highly radioactive fuel elements broke in two while it was being moved at the Prairie Island nuclear power plant.
>
> No one knows what caused the failure, even though several investigations have been conducted during the last 20 months...
>
> The weight of scientific opinion says that mishaps like that at Prairie Island do not threaten public safety.
>
> Instead, the significance of the Prairie Island incident lies in the fact that it serves as a microcosm of problems plaguing the U.S. nuclear industry.

Reporters can find somewhat less difficult stories by, for example, spotting a well-known name or an unusual crime in police or court records, an unusually large number hidden in a business's otherwise ordinary quarterly report or an exceptionally high expense account filed by the city manager.

Although the federal government has made it more difficult to obtain some federal records in the post-Sept. 11 era, records covering everything from building projects under review in the city of Boston to the names of sexual predators in the city of Orlando, Fla., are available online. (See Chapter 14, Research.) Still, many records, census data, for example, can best be understood and applied with the help of experts in the offices that compile them. (See Chapter 15, Sources.)

LOCALIZING

When federal, state or county governments pass laws, enact regulations and appropriate funds, their actions eventually affect the lives of people. Too often, though, newspapers dutifully print blow-by-blow accounts from the wire services of legislative battles only to lose interest when the impact of the change begins to be felt at home.

There are exceptions: When the National Commission on Excellence in Education issued a report decrying the state of public education, many newspapers reacted by looking at problems and solutions in their own schools. "When a national commission puts out a report talking about a rising tide of mediocrity in the schools, it suggests local stories you almost have to do," says Saundra Keyes, who was education writer for *The Courier-Journal* in Louisville, Ky. "One suggestion was that students waste their electives. So you go to your own schools and see what's happening. Another issue was merit pay for teachers, which raises the issue of how local teachers are paid and evaluated."

The effects of recession, inflation and unemployment are just a few other national stories that reporters can localize, and humanize, by looking at how people are coping in their readership area.

Such localizing can be overdone. Reporters can grow so consumed with uncovering local manifestations of national trends that they lose sight of the idiosyncrasies that make their area distinctive. But as long as reporters use national trends as tools to understand better what is happening locally—instead of trying to force a national perspective on local events—these national and regional stories can be useful sources of local story ideas.

REGIONALIZING

In the era of suburban sprawl, the regional newspaper, serving several dozen or more independent communities, is fast taking the place of the urban newspaper that serves a single, cohesive metropolitan area. Papers like *The Record* in New Jersey and *Newsday* on Long Island serve no single dominant community. And major metropolitan papers such as *The Washington Post*, the *Los Angeles Times* and *The Philadelphia Inquirer* have sections tailored to meet the tastes of their expanding suburban audiences.

It becomes virtually impossible to provide thorough municipal coverage for dozens of small towns whose residents read the same paper; newspapers aren't thick enough for that. It also isn't good business. Residents in Carle Place, Long Island, don't much care about a run-of-the-mill school budget fight in Hicksville, Long Island.

Faced with the challenge of building a cohesive readership out of an audience with disparate municipal loyalties, most regional newspapers encourage their reporters to look for *trend stories*—reports on issues that cut across the borders separating suburban towns. In other words, reporters on these papers are asked to *regionalize* their stories. If they come upon a dispute in the town they cover about the difficulty elderly people are having finding affordable housing, reporters might examine the problem of housing for the elderly in other towns in the region as well. And if they hear a complaint at a city council meeting about shopping centers hurting local downtown shops, reporters might look into whether other Main Street shop owners in the region are facing hard times.

Story ideas, then, travel in both directions in journalism: Local stories grow out of events and decisions at a national, state and regional level, and regional stories evolve from what starts as a local issue.

FOLLOW-UP

Reporters needn't look past the same day's newspaper for many of their best story ideas. That is because most stories demand *follow-up*.

When Hurricane Katrina overwhelmed the levees around New Orleans and flooded the city, the natural question was, "Why?"

Like other major national newspapers, *The New York Times* turned to this question early and returned to it often. After all, it was the levee's breach, more than the storm's force, that devastated one of America's most unique and colorful cities. This article appeared on Page 1 a few days after Katrina made landfall.

WASHINGTON—When Michael D. Brown, director of the Federal Emergency Management Agency, returned in January from a tour of the tsunami devastation in Asia, he urgently gathered his aides to prepare for a similar catastrophe at home.

"New Orleans was the No. 1 disaster we were talking about," recalled Eric L. Tolbert, then a top FEMA official. "We were obsessed with New Orleans because of the risk."

Disaster officials, who had drawn up dozens of plans and conducted preparedness drills for years, had long known that the low-lying city was especially vulnerable. But despite all the warnings, Hurricane Katrina overwhelmed the very government agencies that had rehearsed for such a calamity. On Thursday, as the flooded city descended into near-anarchy, frantic local officials blasted the federal and state emergency response as woefully sluggish and confused.

Survivors of Hurricane Katrina, evacuated by boat, are offered a perplexing choice of directions as they approach a sign on a roadway buried by water.
(Photo by Brad Kemp of The *[Lafayette, La.]* Daily Advertiser)

"We're in our fifth day and adequate help to quell the situation has not arrived yet," said Edwin P. Compass III, the New Orleans police superintendent.

The response will be dissected for years. But on Thursday, disaster experts and frustrated officials said a crucial shortcoming may have been the failure to predict that the levees keeping Lake Pontchartrain out of the city would be breached, not just overflow.

The New York Times

Piecing together answers to this vital question, of course, was just one part of covering perhaps the worst natural disaster in U.S. history. Any major news story suggests dozens of follow-up stories, from hard-hitting investigations to moving feature stories.

In the case of Katrina, newsroom reporters and editors across the country immediately began asking questions: Who died, how and where, and what was the extent of the damage? Who were the heroes in the hurricane's aftermath? What weaknesses in emergency preparedness by the Federal Emergency Management Authority, the state of Louisiana and the city of New Orleans contributed to the devastation and the suffering of survivors? What drama was captured on 911 tapes? Where did communication break down? Why did the city fail to anticipate the force of the hurricane in its evacuation plan? How did the city's police and fire departments perform in the crucial hours and days after the city was flooded? What is the impact on oil supplies? Why are more severe hurricanes hitting the Gulf Coast? What can be learned from the tragedy of New Orleans in preparing for severe hurricanes in the future?

Gradually, these questions have given way to others: What is the future of New Orleans? Who has returned and who has stayed away? Who is helping to rebuild the city and how? What challenges are residents facing in cutting red tape, getting bank loans and finding jobs in the storm's aftermath? Did the race and class of New Orleans evacuees play a role in their treatment and care in the hurricane's aftermath? What's been done to reopen schools and city services?

Once again, the list is almost endless.

Not only stories of broad-ranging impact demand follow up: When the city council passes an ordinance requiring dog owners to scoop up after their pets, the natural follow-up is whether people are complying with the law. When a student is shot at a local high school, the time may be right to investigate whether weapons are a problem on campuses.

One trick in finding these follow-up stories is for reporters to ask themselves these questions: Why did the event happen? What larger forces were behind it? And what are its implications?

Journalists for the *Reno* (Nevada) *Gazette-Journal* asked themselves about the implications of a massive snowstorm that struck the Sierra Nevada. Then they gave readers a full page of articles on the snow's effect on drought conditions, ski areas, wildlife and strained state and county budgets. Here is an excerpt from one of these articles:

> The Nevada Department of Transportation has spent $200,000 on snow removal since the series of heavy storms began three weeks ago.

That's follow-up.

UNANNOUNCED STORIES

Some reporters just seem lucky.

When Ric Kahn of *The Boston Globe* took his son shopping at a Boston-area mall one day, he noticed several customers laying down a few dollars for items costing a penny or two less and then watched them walk away from the checkout line without bothering to collect their change.

"I wondered how much money stores make on that extra penny," he said.

And so he tried to find out. He couldn't find anyone who had ever studied the issue. But Kahn didn't give up on the story.

"I wrote a feature about the poor penny being hijacked," he recalls. "I interviewed a guy who doesn't want pennies so he throws them out. I also found an Internet group called Citizens for Retiring the Penny [that] wants to round off prices to the nearest nickel."

He also discovered the average U.S. household has nearly $100 in "idle change" sitting around. The total amount nationwide added up to more $10 billion.

There is a certain amount of luck in reporting. But because good reporters do things to increase their chances of getting lucky, good luck often seems to follow them around. And while some of the stories they stumble onto are merely cute—the plight of the lowly penny, for example—they also are refreshingly original precisely because they are unexpected and are not derived from conventional news sources.

Here are some ways to improve your "luck."

Staying Alert

"If you keep your eyes and ears open, if you ask about things, you'll come up with good stories," says Doug Rainey, who was city hall reporter for the *La Crosse* (Wis.) *Tribune*.

A reporter's alertness paid off one snowy night years ago when Rainey was an editor on *The Hutchinson News* in central Kansas. Rainey recalls that the reporter, while driving home, had noticed a city plow clearing the public golf course, although plenty of people were still trapped in their homes by the snow and people were not exactly lining up at the first tee.

"It was a totally useless activity, and at the same time people were calling and complaining that streets weren't being cleared," says Rainey. The paper ran the story. Well before the following winter, Hutchinson had a new director of public works.

Routine meetings needn't be covered routinely either. A reporter for *The Record* in New Jersey took note when a lawyer in the audience at a town government meeting strayed from the agenda to complain that new maps designating certain areas of the town a "floodplain" might keep his client, a shopping center, from expanding. The comment took all of five minutes, but it piqued the reporter's curiosity. He did some research and the result, months later, was an award-winning series on how state and federal flood-control programs were placing restrictions on land use that could devalue millions of acres of developed and undeveloped land around the country.

This story was perhaps too subtle to have been heralded by press conferences and demonstrations. It was one of those stories that, in Gene Roberts' words, "seep and creep."

Brainstorming

Sometimes a reporter's brain, a reporter's creativity, requires a little nudging. In a memo to reporters at *The Boston Globe*, Donald Murray, who served as the paper's writing coach, suggested, among other things, that reporters find story ideas by sitting down and working up a quick list of topics that might interest local readers—crime, commuting, property taxes, public schools, shopping.* They then could pick one topic and do some free associating, getting as specific as possible.

It might work like this:

Public education.
For gifted children?
Special programs?
More or fewer than a decade ago?
Are they more or less conventional?
Do these students get bored in school?
Do they leave a year early to attend college?
How do they do in college academically if they enroll early?
What about emotionally?
Has anyone ever traced what happens to students who enter college before age 16?
Can I find students who left area high schools early and enrolled in college?

While few reporters may actually play this particular game, most find some time to think about readers' interests and to let their minds wander over those interests, looking for fresh angles.

Wandering

Sometimes, Murray advises, story ideas can be found by letting your body as well as your mind wander. Take some free time and visit a video game parlor, a retirement home, a bowling alley. If you usually drive to work, walk or take a bus. Drive through an area you haven't been to before. A few more ideas, suggested in Murray's memo: "Shop in a supermarket where people

---

* Murray's ideas are spelled out in his book *Writing for Your Readers* (see Additional Reading).

on welfare shop. Stand in line at an unemployment office and listen to what people are saying. Sit in a waiting room at a clinic. Watch a ballgame from the bleachers."

A story idea is just a fresh perspective on some aspect of life. Sometimes all it takes is a break in the routine to obtain that new perspective.

The Globe's Ric Kahn practices what Murray preaches. As often as possible, he varies his route and his mode of transport to work to see what is going on.

One day, riding the No. 66 bus from the neighboring city of Brookline, Kahn noticed an ad with two smiling women. A front tooth of one of them had been painted black.

Most reporters would have shrugged. But Kahn decided to take the bus line again the next week, and on a different bus saw the same ad with the same distinctive graffiti. At the local bus depot, he found about a dozen altogether.

"I knew I had a story there," Kahn said. "Was the artist a boyfriend gone bad? Copycat graffiti? Demented dentist? If the woman whose tooth has been blackened doesn't know about her ad, then you get her reaction in the story. If she does know and is pissed, you can see if she knows why this is happening and still get her reaction."

Kahn said the woman was aware of the ad and thought someone who worked for the bus station had done it. The story had no definitive ending, but its hint of mystery made it a good read.

"I wasn't looking for a story while riding the bus," Kahn said. "I was just aware that anything can turn into a good story. So I just relax and let things hit me by looking and hearing what is around me all the time."

Reading

There are thousands of magazines, trade publications and specialized websites in the United States, and they cater to a wide variety of interests. Occasionally reporters can find a fresh slant on a story just by looking through a magazine they wouldn't normally read—perhaps one read by bird-watchers, hang-glide enthusiasts or health-food lovers. Murray suggests buying a different magazine every week.

To find story ideas, reporters increasingly track blogs (web logs), discussion groups and hyperlocal news sites, "published" online by so-called citizen journalists. For example, more than 700 "place blogs," sites devoted to coverage of and community chat about a geographic area, existed in U.S. towns by mid-2006, according to Lisa Williams, one of the pioneers in this kind of blogging.

Many other virtual communities are joined by common interest instead of common geography.

Sometimes these sites themselves become the news, particularly when they raise questions about privacy and safety.

> Teens love showing off their MySpace profiles to their friends—friends of friends are welcome, too. But is it OK for parents to look at what their children are posting to this very public Web site that now has more than 43 million members?
>
> *Sacramento* (Calif.) *Bee*

In trolling for ideas, don't forget the ads. One freelancer developed a story on computerized voice boxes after she saw an ad for one in a science magazine.

Questioning

Just walking down the street with a good reporter can be enlightening. Like 3-year-old children, many reporters seem to question everything: What are they building over there? Who owns the new office building next to it? Is this new development putting a strain on the roads? Where do all the people who work there park? Where do they eat lunch?

Most questions will lead to simple, unsurprising answers, but some might lead to a story. For example, after talking to people in that new office complex, a reporter may find they *are* having trouble parking, getting on and off the highway, and getting a bite to eat. The new construction may have left services seriously overburdened. An important story, but no one was going to send out a press release about it; no one was going to stage a demonstration.

Alert reporters tend to get "lucky."

CHAPTER 13 SUMMARY: STORY ORIGINATION

Good reporters find news before it finds them. Here are some ways of staying ahead of the pack instead of running with it:

- Scan press releases, but remember they give only one perspective and should serve only as a starting point for a story. Look for buried story angles, or approaches, that might make for a story more interesting than the one the organization sending the release is trying to sell.
- Keep an ear open for tips. Often they're provided by people you've cultivated as sources by calling them regularly and showing an interest in what they do.
- Look for regional and local angles to stories.
- Follow the news. Often the best source of original stories is your own newspaper. Think about what questions initial stories don't answer. Think about whom the news affects.
- Make your own luck. You'll do this by approaching your community or your beat like a visitor on foreign soil. Look, listen, read. Think about what catches your attention and what has changed.

ADDITIONAL READING

Convergence Journalism: Writing and Reporting Across the News Media, Janet Kolodzy, Rowman and Littlefield, 2006.

News in a New Century: Reporting in an Age of Converging Media, Jerry Lanson and Barbara Croll Fought, Pine Forge Press, 1999.

Writing for Your Readers: Notes on the Writer's Craft from The Boston Globe, Donald Murray, Globe Pequot, 1992.

EXERCISE A

In a sentence or two, identify the most newsworthy information from a local perspective in the following local press release, record and national story. List the people you would contact and the questions you would ask to develop these stories.

ONE

ALLIED BUS CORPORATION

Press contact: Judy Ringold
Phone: 403-3423

The Board of Directors of the Allied Bus Corporation, the leader in public school transport in this area, proudly announced today that it has selected a new president, James T. McLintock.

Mr. McLintock served as vice president of Allied for the past five years. Before that he was the company's treasurer.

Mr. McLintock joined Allied in 1976 after ten years with the Reynolds Trucking Company here. He is 44 years old and a graduate of Pennsylvania State University.

"I am proud to be offered this wonderful opportunity to serve the company and to work closely with the Board of Directors," Mr. McLintock said. "I am also honored to be following in the footsteps of Bill Howard. He is a fine man and but for all this foolishness would still be in this job. Now it's time to look ahead."

The Board of Directors also announced today that it had accepted "with extreme regret" the resignation of President William Howard. Mr. Howard submitted his resignation today so that he can devote all his energies to discrediting what he called the district attorney's "systematic campaign of leaks and innuendo" intended to raise questions about the propriety of Howard's dealings with the Remington Board of Education. In submitting his resignation, Mr. Howard reiterated that he had offered no bribes and made no promises in negotiating a contract with Remington school officials.

The news?

People to contact?

Questions to ask?

TWO

Agenda for Potter City Council meeting this evening:

1. Adoption of minutes from last week's meeting.
2. Moment of silence for Patricia Real of Hillbrook Elementary School, who passed away on Sunday.
3. Approval of Zoning Commission's waiver of regulations to allow completion of Westview water tower.
4. Police and Fire Committee reports on Marine fitness tests conducted among all uniformed men and women.
5. Housing Committee report on full occupancy of the Seally Project.

6. Salary Committee report on proposal to raise council salaries 15 percent.
7. Environment Committee report on plans for Earth Day planting of a tree.
8. New business.
9. Adjournment.

The news?

People to contact?

Questions to ask?

THREE

WASHINGTON, D.C.—The nation's taverns and bars are experiencing their worst year in a half century, according to a report issued today by the Retail Alcoholic Beverage Council.

The RABC said up to 12 percent of the taverns and bars will face bankruptcy this year unless the public starts drinking more in public again. The number of these establishments has declined 9 percent in the last five years.

The report attributed the decline to the increasing tendency of Americans to stay home in the evening and watch television. It said, "the era of the neighborhood bar may have passed...."

The news?

People to contact?

Questions to ask?

EXERCISE B
Story Ideas

1. Walk through an unfamiliar neighborhood and talk to people who live and work there. Compile a list of four story ideas about life there or about how things have changed in the last decade.

2. List two stories you might write on each of these topics in your area.
   a. College dating patterns
   b. Commuting
   c. College enrollment and recruitment
   d. Health awareness in diet
   e. The use of food stamps
   f. Changing tastes in popular music
   g. The probation system
   h. Job discrimination
   i. Malls
   j. Unemployment

EXERCISE C

Write a story based on the following collection of facts. Assume you are writing for a newspaper dated tomorrow and read in the city of Culver.

The following press release was received yesterday in the newsroom:

> The Office of Mayor Robert Gold
> Contact: Roberta Feinstein, Press Secretary
> Phone: 456-9898

Mayor Robert Gold announced today that he has succeeded in arranging for the United Filmmakers Company to use Culver for 12 days of on-location shooting for their new film, "Terror Downtown."

Mayor Gold said he estimates that United Filmmakers will bring $900,000 worth of business into the city while they are filming.

"This is another major step in our economic recovery," Mayor Gold exclaimed. "I want this to be the city film companies turn to when they are looking for a scenic downtown area."

The agreement comes after four days of intense negotiations between the mayor and his special cultural adviser, Susan James, and "Terror Downtown's" executive producer, Hilda Mae Brown. "Terror Downtown" will be directed by Jonas Sawyer. The cast has not been announced.

Filming will begin July 23. Three full blocks of Main Street between First and Fourth Avenues will be shut to all pedestrian and automobile traffic seven days a week from 9 a.m. to 4 p.m. during the filming, so that the filmmakers can shoot "a realistic version of what would happen if a very small nuclear device exploded in an American city." The filming will end Aug. 3.

"We realize that there will be some inconvenience associated with the filming, but we will try to make sure that all workers in the small affected area use back exits and arrive at work before the filming begins," the mayor said. "We have received every assurance from the filmmakers that there will be absolutely no danger to the public in making this important movie.

"United Filmmakers has agreed to compensate all merchants along Main Street in accordance with what we believe to be a very fair formula," the mayor added.

From interview with Gold: "Now, you tell me, isn't this just the sort of thing our town needs? Do you realize how much business these folks are going to bring us? Do you think there's a chance in the world any mayor would say 'no' to such an offer? Yes, the name of the movie is a little disconcerting, but from our point of view it's all about business, money downtown, not terror downtown. Maybe some of those workers will be a little upset, but I have to think of all our citizens, right? I'm thinking about $900,000, not about a few people having to use back exits. No, I can't disclose the compensation formula; Susan's still working on that."

From interview with Brown: "I want to emphasize that this is a very serious film, about a serious subject—nuclear war. We were looking for a plain, average, routine if you will, American city. We found it. Viewers will see what would happen to such a city if the unthinkable happened. No, no, there's no danger. This is a movie. We could end the world on a soundstage; we certainly can fake nuclear war in a small city. Still, you have to realize that any film is quite a production, and this one will certainly make its presence felt in the city. We're bringing in a lot of people, and we're trying to show something that isn't pretty. What will it look like? Not at all pleasant. Just this side of obliteration. No, we haven't finalized the compensation agreement yet, but our lawyers know what's fair. Now I can't go into exactly how we will transform your downtown, or exactly what our logistics will be like. Jonas will be working on that, now."

From interview with Fred H. Lane, head of the Main Street Merchant's Association: "Yes, Bob and Susan have told us about this. I can't say we're excited. Apprehensive is more like it. I told Susan to be very careful on what she said 'yes' to. We all hope she was. We've scheduled a meeting for a week from Friday to sit down and talk with Susan and Bob, the mayor, about all this. There are certainly some questions we're going to want answered. How much is the film company going to pay each of us? What is it going to do to our business, for those of us in retail? (Lane owns Lane's Shoes at 78 Main.) Will there be any damage? Will we be able to get to work?"

14

Research

The *Online Journalism Review* has called him Columbia University School of Journalism's "tech guru." He writes a column on Web research for the highly respected Poynter Institute for Media Studies in St. Petersburg. He's the official "tech guru" of WABC-TV in New York City. His own website, www.sree.net, is a repository of "surfing tips" that can help guide reporters through countless streams of online information.

But Sree Sreenivasan, a professor and dean of students at Columbia, has no illusions that the Internet is the be-all and end-all of journalistic research.

"Young people think all research is all about search engines and it isn't," cautions Sreenivasan. "You combine it with good old-fashioned reporting, with phone calls, with face-to-face interviews and, God forbid, a visit to the old-fashioned library."

In a world of endless stores of information and Internet "hits" quickly tallied in the hundreds of thousands, a journalist's challenge in research isn't merely to get information. Information is cheap; it's everywhere. The reporter's challenge is to get the *best* information. And the source of the best information varies. Sometimes it can come from something as old-fashioned as a phone book. Sometimes it's best provided by a local expert. Sometimes it can be found in your paper's proprietary archives, it's *clips*, so named because before the computer age, newspaper librarians would clip each article and file it in an envelope in the paper's *morgue* or library of old stories. (Today, of course, these databases are electronic.)

Still, in this online age, where personal computers more and more seem an extension of our fingertips, often the best starting point to finding answers *is* online. The question is, Where do you look? The answer isn't always immediately obvious.

"My dad is wrestling with a bout of gout," Sreenivasan says. "He was going to go online and type in 'gout' or something like that. I said, 'Why don't you go to someplace like the Mayo Clinic?'" The trip he was suggesting was virtual—to www.mayoclinic.com, where the clinic's experts provide current information and news on health topics. But it was a lot more direct than a Google search that likely would have identified millions of options.

Sreenivasan has devoted much time in recent years to being a virtual tour guide for journalists seeking information. He knows that more often than not, the World Wide Web, used effectively, can be an excellent starting point for reporters to get their bearings on a story, to background it, to get leads to fresh angles on the story, to find key facts, and to locate key sources. But he also knows there are risks—mistakes in a name or a fact can quickly be magnified hundreds of times over by sloppy journalists picking up someone else's mistake. And those

Professor Sree Sreenivasan, Columbia University School of Journalism.
(Photo by Roopa Unnikrishnan)

facts on "Readmywebsite.com," may be generated by a 13-year-old trivia buff, who has more fun building a website than verifying the information it passes off as fact.

"The Web," Sreenivasan counsels, "is not a place to find answers. It's a place to find clues to answers."

Reporters should never check their skepticism, along with hat and coat, at the door. When they find startling facts or leads online, they know they *might* have a story. But one of the first steps is to establish the source of those "facts" and verify them with further reporting. The Web, in short, is starting point, not an end point.

Reporters, student and professional, conduct journalistic research for everything from finding out statistics that underpin a story to finding people who can give insight into what those statistics mean. This chapter will move from introducing the most basic research tools—a desktop dictionary is still an awfully good place to determine the spelling and definition of words—to introducing sophisticated digital research tools, such as the computer-assisted reporting used by investigative reporters to sort through enormous quantities of computerized data in order to establish patterns on everything from housing discrimination to gasoline price gouging.

As central as computers and the Web are to every contemporary reporter's life, the chapter won't start and end with your keyboard. Because as Sreenivasan points out, the first step in conducting research on any project is to think.

FIGURE OUT A SEARCH STRATEGY

"The first thing I tell people," Sreenivasan says. "is think for 10 seconds before you touch the keyboard and you'll save yourself 10 minutes. Most people's instinct is to type the word of the topic [they are interested in researching] into Google or Yahoo. . . . What I tell people is that if you can think of great starting points, you'll save time."

Let's say, for example, your goal is to research and write about the Albanian immigrant community in your area. Sreenivasan recommends looking for an ethnic newspaper representing that community as a starting point ("Most people will type Albania into Google and get about a million hits"). The editor of that ethnic newspaper will know a lot about the issues facing the community locally. And if you are interested in knowing about the background of those immigrants, he suggests, go to Nation Master (www.nationmaster.com), for a quick primer on the history and statistics of that country. ("Check in out," Sreenivasan says. "It's not about Dick Cheney.")

Figuring out a search strategy, especially for a beginner, isn't always obvious or easy. That's why every library—public and university—has *reference librarians*. These are people trained in reference materials, both online and in print. They are people worth talking to regularly and, for a beginning municipal reporter, worth cultivating as sources in their communities (see Chapter 15, Sources). Reference librarians can save a lot of time and a lot of false starts.

In addition, many journalism organizations have compiled helpful online guides to sources to help reporters doing research on timely topics such as "covering terrorism" or "covering immigration." The American Journalism Review, at www.ajr.org, links to a reasonably comprehensive list of such organizations on its home page. At one such site, the Poynter Institute (www.poynter.org), you can find tip sheets on such diverse topics as the following:

"Handling Race in Political Coverage"

"Tips for Covering Cops"

"Covering the Environmental Fallout of Hurricanes"

Poynter also provides extensive bibliographies for backgrounding a wide range of issues journalists face.

And individual reporters and journalism professors, such as Sreenivasan at www.sree.net, offer a wide variety of targeted links and tips on how to use them. Sreenivasan, in fact, links to several of the better-known individual sites. Two are Power Reporting, Pulitzer Prize winner Bill Dedman's site (http://www.powerreporting.com), and the logically organized site of Christopher Callahan (http://reporter.umd.edu), author of *A Journalist's Guide to Internet* (see Additional Reading).

Again, research doesn't start with Google, not even Google's advanced search (which allows you to search for specific phrases or titles). Nor should it end there.

FIND THE BEST TOOLS
Basic References
A Dictionary

Call us old-fashioned. But Internet or no Internet, we believe every reporter needs a well-worn dictionary by his or her side. Any one of a number will do. *The Oxford English Dictionary* is the most comprehensive, but it's also 13 volumes. *The American Heritage Dictionary of English Language* is useful because it includes proper names and the votes of a distinguished review board of writers impaneled to consider which modern usages are "acceptable" in good writing. Most newsrooms will have an unabridged dictionary on hand, often *Webster's New International*, which the Associated Press recommends. Why keep a pocket dictionary on your desk? Well, you may need to know what a jacaranda is five minutes before deadline. (It's a tropical tree.) And if you take the lazy way out and type "apple" + "definition" into Google, the answer could surprise you: "A computer company, maker of the Macintosh line of computers," comes back the answer at www.cals.ncsu.edu/agexed/aee226/terms.html. And here we thought it was a piece of fruit. If you truly have an aversion to paper, try Merriam-Webster online at www.m-w.com.

An Encyclopedia

The name is Wikipedia (www.wikipedia.com). It's widely used—and hotly debated—as that online encyclopedia that just about anyone can edit. Sreenivasan says that when he visits newsroom to coach reporters on Internet research, he'll call up Wikipedia "and edit things and scare the heck out of people."

"But I use it every day," he adds. "It is a starting point."

If you want confidence in a more authoritative encyclopedia reference, he suggests, try *Encyclopedia Britannica.* "It's relatively inexpensive, and a lot of universities have accounts."

Encylopedias can help you with background on what to expect from that lunar eclipse everyone is excited about and provide brief history of Iraq under Saddam Hussein's rule.

So, you wonder, what does Wikipedia have to say?

> As president, Saddam ran an authoritarian government and maintained power through the Iran-Iraq War (1980–1988) and the Gulf War (1991). Saddam's government repressed movements that it deemed threatening, particularly those of ethnic or religious groups that sought independence or autonomy. While he remained a popular hero among many Arabs for standing up to Israel and the United States, some in the international community continued to view Saddam with deep suspicion following the 1991 Gulf War. Saddam was deposed by the United States and its allies during the 2003 invasion of Iraq.

Not exactly, um, encyclopedic, you say? Well, it's a start.

A Phone Book

This is another forgotten asset in the world of instant online access.

Most people, including some prominent public officials, list their phone numbers. So if a key source won't give out a home number, try the white pages of the phone book: They may be more forthcoming. And that number will be nice to know should an emergency—a jail break, a toxic spill, an earthquake—make it necessary to suspend normal rules of etiquette and seek information at an odd hour.

A quick Google search might be as effective if you know what town your source lives in. In the regular search field, type rphonebook: (the r is for residential), followed by a colon. Then type the last name, city and state (abbreviation), and up pops a number and street address. At least it should if the number is listed. Google's listing system worked for both authors of this book. It didn't work, however, for Boston Mayor Tom Menino. Darn.

The system, in any case, hasn't overcome all its kinks. Type in *bphonebook, starbucks, Boston, MA:* and the phone numbers and addresses of Boston Starbucks (the b before Starbucks is for business) should pop up. Presumably, they do—among 1.2 million hits.

That's one reason it still makes sense to keep the phone book nearby.

Phone books, in any case, provide more than numbers. They are a good place to double-check the address or the spelling of a source's name. Phone books have rescued more than one reporter returning to the newsroom late at night after a heated municipal meeting at which a half-dozen unfamiliar people spoke. (Names of public officials can be checked in the *city directories* distributed by municipalities.)

Newspapers also will buy special *reverse directories*, in which listings are arranged by address in geographical order, rather than by name in alphabetical order. If there's been a fire, a reverse directory can quickly provide the names and phone numbers of the people—possible eyewitnesses—who live next door. And if the state has decided to turn Anderson Avenue into

Anderson Freeway, this is one way of tracking down—in a hurry—the names and numbers of the people who will be most directly affected. If you're on your own, try the reverse directory at White Pages (www.whitepages.com/10001/reverse_phone).

Maps

The Web can take you a lot further in finding your way around town.

Type in the address of your starting point and your destination at Mapquest (www. mapquest.com) and a set of directions, complete with distances and driving time, will be in front of you in seconds. If you want to see what that address *looks like*, try going to www. googlemaps.com. There, you can magnify specific satellite images to an extraordinary degree. Want to see your own house? Check it out. But leave yourself a little time to sort through the navigation system.

Backgrounding

Leon Wynter, who covered business for *The Wall Street Journal*, has this advice for new reporters: "The *first* thing you do is start reading your own publication."

Reporters don't read their own publication solely to keep up with the news. They delve into its electronic archives, which, for a fee, can also be accessed today by student reporters and other members of the general public. These archives contain important *background information*, for example, for the reporter working on a Sunday piece about a nursing home cited for negligence in the death of one of its patients. Has the nursing home ever run afoul of state regulators before? And what about that labor strife six months ago when many of its nurses quit? The "clips," in this case called up electronically under the nursing home's name, likely will help. Good reporters verify facts even if they've appeared in their own paper. But the clips offer historic context and background for the stories reporters write. They also offer leads to what to ask next.

And, of course, reporters don't want to be caught *pitching*, or suggesting, a story the paper wrote three of six months ago. That's why a reporter, before suggesting a story on a summer midnight basketball league wants to make sure she didn't miss a story on it while on vacation. The clips will provide the answer.

Reporters also monitor the competition, both daily by reading several papers online or on the printed page. Most newsrooms and college libraries are equipped with *Lexis-Nexis*, a subscription full-text-retrieval database that has catalogued decades of articles from hundreds of newspapers (that's Nexis; the Lexis part focuses on legal research). Users type in key words and apply search tips that allow them to search for words within a certain distance of each other in a story, search for exact phrases, and eliminate words (for example, Rivers, but NOT water if looking for stories about a person named Rivers).

A reporter who sets out to write about the explosion of ethnic newspapers in his city might first want to see who else has written about the phenomenon in his city or region or elsewhere. Such backgrounding helps shape the direction of reporting, helps inform a reporter's questions, and may offer leads to fresh story *angles* or approaches (the real story may be that ethnic newspapers are abandoning their print efforts and flocking online) and sources, who may have appeared particularly knowledgable or interesting in stories written elsewhere.

Reporters who are monitoring the competition during a breaking story might turn to news. google.com, where, for example, a quick search of "sectarian violence" and "Iraq" might pull up several hundred articles from around the world filed the previous day. The site allows reporters to monitor constantly updated news at 4,500 news websites.

In an article called "Better Googling Tips" on his website, Sreenivasan counsels reporters monitoring a particular topic over time to sign up for Google Alerts at www.google.com/alerts. By doing so, the reporter receives e-mail alerts from Google when the specific phrase crops up in articles on Google news or on websites or on discussion groups (the reporter can determine which). So, for example, that reporter working on the story of alleged negligence at the nursing home might type in "nursing home negligence" and variations of that phrase to keep tabs of other cases cropping up around the country.

The reporter can determine the frequency of these alerts by clicking once a day, once a week, or "as it happens."

Finding Sources

Sometimes reporters rely too heavily on what's been reported before. This can be particularly true when it comes to sources.

"One of the problems with journalists is that everybody wants to be first on a story, but nobody wants to take a chance on a new source," Sreenivasan says. "I like to think of it as the Nexis virus. They go into Nexis and they only interview the people [who've been interviewed] on Nexis. I find that very irritating.... That's why we end up with the same five guys on the Sunday morning talk shows."

The same happens in print. Too often reporters, in mining old clips, also mine the same old sources. This limits the range of viewpoints put before readers and, sometimes, also gives too much credence to the "old boy" networks, whose members (older white men) have been less than eager to give up their grasp of the top rungs of influence in politics, business, the law and other professions.

It's not that difficult, however, both to be a careful researcher and to find new sources with credibility and expertise. One excellent starting point, Sreenivasan says, is the Rainbow Diversity Sourcebook. Compiled by the Society of Professional Journalists (SPJ), the source-book, which can be found at www.spj.org/divsourcebook.asp, provides contact information for "qualified experts on key news topics from populations historically underrepresented" in the news media. These are not primarily sources for so-called minority issues, but experts on issues ranging from technology to telecommunications and from law to labor who also happen to be of color. Reporters using the sourcebook can choose from among five dozen areas of expertise and also look for sources in a specific geographic area.

So if you are writing about consumer issues in Arizona, the sourcebook will provide you with an Arizona expert on consumer issues. Sreenivasan notes that for far too long in an increasingly multicultural America, the news media have sought minority voices only on minority issues.

"We'll interview black folks only for black issues and Hispanics for so-called Hispanic issues. We'll see Hispanics in immigration issues but not Social Security stories.... That kind of thing."

The sourcebook allows reporters—including student reporters—to change that.

Another excellent source of expert sources, but one limited to professional reporters, is Profnet (www.profnet.com). As the name suggests, Profnet is primary a clearinghouse that links reporters and experts on university campuses throughout the country (21,000 in all). It also links to the latest news on the PR newswire. The rub, however, is that you'll need a sign-in to use the service. And you'll need an affiliation with a news organization to get one.

An easier route for students and journalists alike often is to contact the public information offices of universities in your area. Colleges love to see their faculty members quoted as experts. It enhances the reputation of the institutions as well as the individuals. Sources developed as student journalists also may prove the best ones to return to on your first job.

One marvelous superlink to sources and source directory has been compiled for reporters of the *St. Petersburg Times*. Here you'll find direct links to the prestigious Brookings Institution (http://brookings.edu/index/scholars_byresearch.htm), where you can search for scholars by issues ranging from Afghanistan to anti-trust regulation, and link directly to their backgrounds, their bios, their publications and their e-mail in a matter of seconds. Or, you can balance those views with a visit to a guide compiled by the more conservative Heritage Foundation (http://www.policyexperts.org), where with a few more clicks you can come up with a phone number for that Afghanistan expert as well.

You'll find the National Press Club's Directory of Reporter's Resources at http://npc.press .org/library06/resources.cfm, where, if you have a question about anti-Semitism, you'll quickly learn that Myrna Shinbaum, director of Media Relations and Public Information for the Anti-Defamation League of New York, is a good source to whom to direct your query.

And a lot more, too.

That old-fashioned library, with its books, also can be helpful in tracking down sources. If you're trying to figure out what associations represent ornithologists (scientists who study birds) or hang-gliding enthusiasts, a great place to start is the Encyclopedia of Associations. Among its more than 135,000 nonprofit membership organizations worldwide are the American Association of Aardvark Aficionados and the Musical Box Society. Addresses, phone numbers and the names of key personnel—potential sources—are included. And yes, with patience, and perhaps the help a representative whose e-mail address is given at the website, you can search online, too.

In covering any beat, one of the first requests is for a current directory—of a city government, of a school district, of a government agency. These may be online. Ask. Current directories tell you who is in charge of what office and how to reach that individual. Local libraries sometimes have older directories in which you can find the names of those who've left an agency or organization. These people often know lots and are less constrained from sharing what they know.

Finding Statistics

If sources provide insight, credibility and colorful or provocative quotes in news stories, statistics give the news a sense of authoritativeness. No one wants to read only that the test scores in their children's school districts have gone "up" or gone "down." They want those scores quantified. Numbers shouldn't weigh down stories so they're unreadable. Often these figures can be broken out in charts or graphs that accompany a story (see Chapter 11, Reporting in a Multimedia Age). But they can't be left out, either. One mark of an inexperienced reporter is stories that are laden with generality but light on specific data.

Perhaps no newspaper relies as heavily on statistics as the national daily *USA Today*. Each day on its front page, *USA Today* publishes a graph that it calls "USA Snapshots: A look at statistics that shape the nation." Many of the four- and five-paragraph news items that dominate the paper also rely on statistical reports:

> Nearly half the people who crowd into emergency rooms don't need emergency treatment, says a national survey.
>
> A General Accounting Office survey of 1,025 hospitals found that...43 percent of emergency room patients were categorized as "non-urgent."
>
> Nearly 85 percent of these hospitals had an increase in such patients, most uninsured or underinsured.
>
> *USA Today*

As does virtually any statistical story, this piece concentrated on those few numbers considered of greatest interest to readers. Just as reporters covering a meeting pick two or three morsels of news from a page-long menu of topics (see Chapter 18, Meetings, Speeches and Press Conferences), reporters culling through a report look only for numbers most likely to satisfy readers' hunger. Typically, these compare something this month or year or decade with something last month or last year or last decade. (Reporters must be careful that such comparisons are valid. It wouldn't do to compare last year's crime rate in the city with this year's if in the interim the city annexed three suburban counties.)

So where do all the numbers in newspapers come from? Many, perhaps most, can be found in the voluminous reports filed by all levels of government each year. And, in this electronic age, more and more of these reports can be found online. A few cautions are in order before you start looking.

First, bureaucracy tends to be slow. Sometimes the statistics released to the state's public health website are two or three years old. If these are the latest statistics available, let your readers know that.

> Why talk about 2004, rather than more recent experience? Unfortunately data on the distribution of income arrive with a substantial lag; the full story of what happened in 2004 has only just become available.
>
> *The New York Times*

Before "talking about 2004," however, always follow your background research online with a phone call or e-mail to find out whether more recent statistics are available.

Second—and we know we're repeating ourselves here—don't become so enamored of numbers that you overwhelm your readers.

Unacceptable:

> There were 538,051 reported felonies in New York City last year. Of these, 1,422 were murders, 3,833 were rapes and 78,816 were robberies. During the same year, 9 people were murdered in the subways, 21 were raped there and 5,999 were robbed.

Percentages might work in a lead, but often it's best to lead simply with words—words that tell readers what the numbers mean:

Acceptable:

> There is an image of New York City's subway system, derived in part from the appearance of the trains and stations, as a lurid underground kingdom ruled by murderers, rapists and muggers where a subway rider's life sometimes has less value than a token. But the crime statistics belie at least part of that image. The subways are not the cleanest transportation system in town, but they are often the fastest and, by any measure, the safest.
>
> *The New York Times*

Only after hooking the readers did the *Times* reporter include the key numbers to back up the lead. One good rule of thumb: Don't force more than three statistics into any one paragraph—and spread your statistical material through a story. But do include statistics.

Here are a few good places to find them. There are hundreds more:

Robert Niles' Guide to Data on the Internet (http://nilesonline.com/data/)

This site can help you pinpoint all kinds of statistics and other data.

"How far is City A from City B? Your answer awaits here," reads the site. The link is to http://www.indo.com/distance/. Going from San Francisco to San Juan, Puerto Rico? The distance, you'll find in seconds, is 3,638 miles. Oh, and yes, in case you're curious, San Juan is 8 feet above sea level, San Francisco, 63.

Looking for weightier data? How about "incident-based crime statistics from the FBI, another of Niles' subcategories. Click the word "FBI," and you're immediately linked to a list of Uniform Crime Reports, organized by year. Click "2005" and you'll learn that U.S. law enforcement agencies reported an increase of 2.5 percent in violent crimes over the previous year.

Niles' site is loaded with links succinctly explained to visitors in such ways as "query national health statistics at the Centers for Disease Control's National Center for Health Statistics" http://www.cdc.gov/nchs/datawh.htm or "the basic skinny on every nation on Earth is in the CIA

World Factbook," https://www.cia.gov/cia/publications/factbook/index.html (And you thought the CIA searched only for weapons of mass destruction). There you will find that Christmas Island, population 1,493, is a territory of Australia named in 1643 after the day of its discovery. Almost two-thirds of the island has been set aside as a national park.

FedStats (http://www.fedstats.gov/)

You'll find this on the Niles site, too, but we thought it worth giving its own recognition. Niles says of FedStats, "If you go to just one site for U.S. government data," let it be this one. He is right. The home page describes itself as "the gateway to statistics for over 100 U.S. federal agencies."

Among your options is to click "Topics A to Z—a direct link to statistical data on topics of your choice." Interested in teen births? There were 414,580 in 2003, the last year for which data was available. (Remember, this is the U.S. government. Data often is a few years old and not all links work.)

Writing about what it's like to look for work with a criminal record? The U.S. Department of Justice can provide these handy statistics: At the end of 2004, 7 million Americans were either in jail or prison or on probation or parole. That is 3.2 percent of the entire adult population (one out of every 31 people). And were the number of people going to jail increasing or decreasing as of 2005? You got it: increasing (at an annual rate over the previous decade of 3.4 percent).

Too many numbers, you say. You are right. We just violated our own rule. That is why as a reporter, your job is to pick numbers carefully and use them sparingly.

Refdesk (http://www.refdesk.com)

This is one of Sreenivasan's favorites. It bills itself as "the single best source of facts." It's certainly one of the most enjoyable. Each day it will provide a site of the day, an article of the day, a prominent birthday of the day, the day in history and a thought of the day (on the day we stopped by it was "Excess on occasion is exhilarating. It prevents moderation from acquiring the deadening effect of habit"—by E. Somerset Maugham.) The search area in the upper right-hand corner allows you to query by "reference desk" (from genealogy to quotations, maps to medicine) or by tool (another website, www.answers.com, comes up first).

Fun facts and gadgets aside, Refdesk best value may be as a megasite with well-organized links to other sites. Click "government" and FedStats is on the list, along with GovEngine (http://www.govengine.com/), a compilation of federal, state and local government sites on the Internet. This well-organized site can provide you with the names and phone numbers of every state representative, the laws passed in recent legislalative sessions, links to municipal home pages (which in some cases include visiting hours of council members), and a whole lot more. There's also Thomas' legislative information on the Internet (http://thomas.loc.gov/), provided by the U.S. Library of Congress. Here you can search for any bill before Congress, look up statements made by your local representative or senator on the floor and browse key committee reports.

Not all the links on refdesk are so earnest. For fun, try out CreativeQuotations.com (www.creativequotations.com), where among the categories parsing 50,000 quotations from 3,000 men and women, is one called "creative wit." There you'll find such quotes as "Success is a great deodorant. It takes away all your past smells"—Elizabeth Taylor; and "Adolescence is just one big walking pimple"—Carol Burnett.

Blogs and Discussion Groups

Where there is a topic of interest—hurling, curling, hot cars, cold storage—there likely is a discussion group on the Internet to which aficianados flock to talk about that topic. In this world where anyone and everyone can be a publisher, you also can get a front-row seat at anything from World Cup soccer to the savage violence on the streets of Baghdad. The self-publishers writing about what they see, hear and feel are not trained journalists.

They are *bloggers,* participants in a form of citizen journalism—web logs—that has swept the Internet in the last decade. (Others participate in less formal online chats and discussion groups.) Some bloggers write trivia, untruth and nastiness. Many offer interesting insights into scenes and situations mainstream journalists know little to nothing about.

The trick, whether monitoring blogs, discussion groups or chats, is to look at them for ideas, emotions and potential "real-people" sources to interview, not facts. None of the facts have been verified. Often these "facts" are simply drawn from somewhere else or from what someone said. On the other hand, a good education writer *not* monitoring FaceBook (www.facebook.com) or MySpace (www.myspace.com) to find out what the kids have to say about life, their school (OK, and about each other), isn't doing his job well.

For a good portal for sorting out discussion groups, try http://groups.google.com.

There are ethical implications to such journalistic voyeurism. Reporters should not take material they've gathered by lurking online or searching social networking sites (where participants draw their own profiles) and use it indiscriminately. Many students view these sites almost as diaries and are unaware that the things they say just might end up in newspaper columns. (Indeed, the vulnerability of such sites, and the concerns of parents about them, has been topic of more than one newspaper article.) Reporters shouldn't contribute to their vulnerability by irresponsibly exposing what individual students are saying. But these sites can be good places to find intelligent sources and interesting story ideas outside the realm of officialdom.

COMPUTER-ASSISTED REPORTING

Like most good reporters, Chris Schmitt started with a hypothesis. In California, legal sources had told him, justice still was being meted out unequally to minorities despite laws intended to ensure similar sentences for similar crimes.

A good tip to be sure, but one that even veteran reporters would have been hard-pressed to *prove* or *disprove* a few decades ago. Careful interviews with dozens of sources might have bolstered a perception of bias. Tips would have led to court records providing scattered examples of unequal justice. But proof? California is a big state with tens of thousands of cases heard each year.

So Schmitt, an investigative reporter at the *San Jose Mercury News,* turned to one of the newer tools of reporters in their struggle to ferret out authoritative information: computer-assisted reporting.

Schmitt started with the raw data, recorded in state of California computer files, about the disposition of criminal cases. State law (see The Basics, Section F, The Law) requires that such information be made available to the public.

Schmitt obtained the records of nearly 700,000 criminal cases in California, from the state Bureau of Criminal Statistics and the Board of Prison Terms. Then he set about making sense of it. By hand, it might have taken Schmitt the rest of his career to plow through all the material he had amassed. That's where his personal computer came in.

"The computer isn't very smart," says Schmitt, who taught himself the skills necessary to manipulate computer data. "That's still the reporter's domain. But the computer is very fast. Any time you have large amounts of data that need to be cross-tabbed and sorted, it's a tremendous help."

It is the tabbing, sorting and review of such data has been dubbed *computer-assisted reporting.* The state's information was already online. By organizing the data into various subsets and comparing them by means of database management software, Schmitt was able to analyze the disposition of these cases.

"We looked at the severity of punishment," he recalls. "Who was sent to jail? Who was sent to prison? Who received probation? Who was sent to drug diversion programs? We also looked at when charges were dropped. Virtually everywhere we looked, whites did better than anyone else, in some cases by a substantial margin."

Schmitt had his proof; he was ready to write. But before his articles ran, they needed a reality check: Computer-literate reporters like Schmitt don't only crunch numbers; like other reporters, they rely on knowledgeable people (see Chapter 15, Sources) to help them place what they've learned in context.

Knowing his findings would be controversial, Schmitt and his editor invited experts—judges, public defenders, district attorneys, law professors, civil rights leaders—to critique the *Mercury News'* data. "In some cases they gave us something to think about, and we went back and reviewed and in some cases changed our analysis," says Schmitt. "What you find out sometimes is that when you look at the real-world situation, there was an entirely appropriate reason for the outcome. Maybe one [suspect] was particularly violent but that didn't show up in the records."

Still, the story was sound; the computer had spit out enough evidence to make it unassailable. Schmitt's three-part series, which took six months to complete, began like this:

> In California, justice isn't colorblind.
>
> As more and more cases are decided by plea bargain, whites as a group get significantly better deals than Hispanics or blacks who are accused of similar crimes and who have similar criminal backgrounds, a *Mercury News* analysis of nearly 700,000 cases shows.
>
> Such deals between prosecutors and defense lawyers now occur in more than 95 percent of serious criminal cases, and in the great bulk of less-serious cases, according to statistics and attorneys.
>
> So, instead of judges or juries handing down verdicts, the fates of hundreds of thousands of defendants a year often are negotiated over the telephone, in hurried hallway or parking lot conversations or in closed-door meetings.
>
> What happens?
>
> At virtually every stage of pretrial negotiations, whites are more successful than non-whites.
>
> *San Jose Mercury News*

Schmitt, who regularly uses computers in reporting, also has reviewed hundreds of thousands of records to investigate California's state pension funds and the state's enforcement of toxic-waste regulations. But though he respects computers as a powerful tool, he warns young reporters that they are useless without common sense and that they cannot completely take the place of street reporting.

"The two caveats are always check it out and don't get so wrapped up you lose track of reality, because you are not an expert," Schmitt says. "As much as you can, run your conclusions by people who are."

RECORDS

The front lines in reporters' endless battles to keep those who hold power honest are not found at the televised press conferences, but in computer memories—and sometimes, even today, in dusty back-room filing cabinets. Most of the actions of government, and many of the actions of business, must be recorded. The "dead bodies" buried by officials can often be exhumed only by a search of these records.

"Some beginning reporters think they can hang out a shingle reading 'investigative reporter' and then sit back and wait for Deep Throat to walk in the door," notes Bruce Maxwell, who was an investigative reporter for the *Rochester* (Minn.) *Post-Bulletin*. "It simply doesn't work that way."

No matter how carefully you phrase the question, you are unlikely to get the mayor to admit that he owns some of the land at a site he's pushing for a new shopping center. But proof might exist in the county records of deeds and mortgages. No one will put out a press release announcing inequities in the town's reassessment of all the homes in its boundaries; but a search through the records of the local tax assessor might show the homes of certain city officials assessed at below the value of comparable properties. The hospital may deny any knowledge of drugs being diverted by its staff; but the forms the hospital must file with the Drug Enforcement Administration may reveal theft of drugs as a major problem. Did the congressman rely heavily on the contributions of oil companies in his re-election campaign? Federal Election Commission reports will tell. Is it true that the mayor opposed the convention center while a councilman? Check the minutes of the council meetings.

"Often reporters don't realize what a gold mine of information there is in public records," says Louis Rose, of the *St. Louis Post-Dispatch*.

Good reporters like Rose know where records are and know how to use them. Some of the written information available to reporters is discussed in Parts 5 and 6, Coverage and Specialized Coverage, respectively. For additional information on records and their uses in investigations, we suggest membership in the Investigative Reporters and Editors (IRE) association, located in Columbia, Mo. Membership includes a subscription to *The IRE Journal*, which regularly features articles on where and how to look for potentially newsworthy information.

REPORTERS' FILES

Reporters who cover a *beat*, a prescribed area of coverage, whether it is city hall or science, also develop their own files, in their computer memories, on backup CDs, and—still—in paper printouts and files. These can be enormously helpful in finding the right source on deadline (see Chapter 15, Sources), in seeing connections or patterns in the news, in organizing the inherently fragmented process of making sense of constantly shifting patterns of news.

It must have been a disconcerting experience to watch the late I. F. Stone read a newspaper. Stone, who covered Washington with great skill for many years for his own newsletter, didn't so much read a paper as rip it. The stories he tore out—and he seemed to pull as many as he left—were destined for a place somewhere in his personal files. Today, reporters following Google Alerts on a topic of interest can do the same thing more quickly and more efficiently.

Any reporters who want to develop areas of expertise—and that should mean *all* reporters— should create laptop folders and printed-out files. Reporters simply can't allow all the potentially useful information that passes through the hands of well-read people to get away from them. It makes no sense to be assigned a story on the safety of a local bridge and then to have to sit around searching your brain to remember where you read that article about a bridge somewhere that collapsed, killing 18 people. File systems, to borrow Marshall McLuhan's concept, are a necessary "extension" of a reporter's memory.

CHAPTER 14 SUMMARY, RESEARCH

Research is a process of thought before action. Though the Internet has brought access to endless information to our fingertips, it doesn't always make it easier to find the best information. That's where the thought comes in. It's why "googling" something is *not* the first step in journalism research.

Here is what you should do:

- **Think about the information you want and the best place to get it.** Writing about how many consecutive sellouts the Boston Red Sox have had? You *could* go to The Red Sox website or type Red Sox + sellouts into a search engine. You *should* call the Red Sox public information office or ticket office. Who would better know and be able to give you a quote as well? Not all research is done best online.

- **When you do go online, focus your search.** Going directly to the right place saves considerably time and avoids having to wade through thousands of inapplicable hits. Looking to find out whether Wolf Blitzer, anchor for CNN, spells his first name with one *f* or two? You could type what you thought was the right spelling into a Google search. You *should* go to CNN.com and look it up because Blitzer's employer presumably will spell his name right.

- **Use supersites when you aren't sure where to start.** Some sites are designed to help you narrow your search for information. If you're looking for data on median income in Detroit but you aren't sure what agency can provide it, try FedStats, mentioned in the chapter. It's a megasite for statistical research on the federal government.

- **Look back in order to look forward.** Research can help you find story ideas, sources and key statistics for a story. Often, however, its greatest value is in showing you what was written about something before and what's being written about the topic elsewhere. A newspaper's clips are the best resource for past stories in your readership areas. Databases such as Lexis-Nexis can tell you what has been written elsewhere, and Google Alerts can tell you what is being written now.

- **Double-check.** Data online is often dated. You may have gotten it from a site last updated two years ago. Or the data itself may be old. Once you've found what you think you want, follow up with a phone call to the source to make sure the information is still correct. And if you use data a year or two old, explain why (e.g., "It's the most recent statistic available").

ADDITIONAL READING

Find It OnLine: The Complete Guide to Online Research, Alan M. Schlein, Facts on Demand Press, 4th edition, 2004.

A Journalist's Guide to the Internet, Christopher Callahan, Allyn & Bacon, 2nd edition, 2002.

The Investigative Reporter's Handbook, Len Bruzzese, Brant Houston, and Steve Weinberg, Bedford/St. Martin's, 4th edition, 2002.

The New Precision Journalism, Philip Meyer, Indiana University Press, 1991.

Qualitative Research in Journalism: Taking It to the Streets, Sharon Hartin Ioro, Lawrence Erlbaum Associates, 2003.

Web Search Savvy: Strategies and Shortcuts for Online Research, Barbara G. Friedman, Lawrence Erlbaum Associates, 2003.

EXERCISE A

Locate the following websites or reference books (in a local public or college library), and then answer these questions for each:

What general information do they contain?

How is the material organized and searchable (by key word, author, subject, title, etc.)?

In what ways did you find it useful?

In what ways is it interactive (if applicable)?

What are two specific examples of information (not mentioned in this chapter) available from the source?

1. Hoover's (www.hoovers.com)
2. *Research Centers Directory* (http://library.dialog.com/bluesheets/html/bl0115.htm)
3. *Dictionary of Music and Musicians*
4. The Poynter Institute for Media Studies (www.poynter.org)
5. FedStats (www.fedstats.gov)
6. *Black's Law Dictionary*
7. The American Journalism Review (www.ajr.org)
8. *Jane's All The World's Aircraft* (http://jawa.janes.com/public/jawa/index.shtm)
9. *Stedman's Medical Dictionary*
10. Google maps (www.google.com)
11. Wikipedia (the free encyclopedia—www.wikipedia.com)
12. Merriam-Webster online (www.m-w.com/)
13. The World Fact Book (www.cia.gov/cia/publications/factbook/)
14. The Washington Information Directory (www.cqpress.com/product/Washington-Information-Directory-Online.htm)
15. Congressional Quarterly Weekly (www.cq.com)

EXERCISE B

Use references available at the library or online to answer the following questions. Indicate the source you used and the page the answer appeared on.

1. How many murders were reported in Houston, Texas, last year?
2. What is the longest river in the world, and how long is it?
3. When and where was Angelina Jolie born?
4. How many pounds of potatoes were grown in Idaho last year?
5. Who is the president of Peru?
6. Who is the governor of Hawaii? What party does he or she belong to?
7. What is the population of Aix-en-Provence, France? What "departement" (or province) in France is it a part of?
8. Who said, "There is no substitute for hard work"?
9. What is the state tree of Florida?
10. How many cars did Japan export two years ago? What company exported the most cars?
11. What is the population of Cleveland, Ohio?
12. Who won the Academy Award for best actor in 2005?
13. What baseball team was in first place in the Eastern Division of the American League on July 4, 2003?
14. What are the ages of the president of the United States and the prime minister of Japan?
15. Who won the gold and silver medals in the slalom at the 2006 Winter Olympics? What was the time of each winner?

EXERCISE C

Write a story based on the following report, released today, and interviews. Assume you are writing for a newspaper in the town of Worley.

The United Teachers Association has compiled a report comparing the starting teachers' salaries at 198 school districts in your state. Starting salaries in all the districts in Boone County and their ranking compared with other districts in the state are listed. The statewide average and the high and low for the state are included.

School District	This Year		2005	
	Starting Salary	State Rank	Starting Salary	State Rank
Boonton	$37,145	99	$33,280	78
Compton	$37,890	63	$34,100	61
Crosby	$39,430	9	$35,690	12
Evergreen	$40,050	1	$35,600	13
Fulton	$38,045	54	$34,995	34
Monroe	$39,170	18	$36,200	5
Narberth	$37,675	78	$33,775	66
Norwood	$38,900	27	$35,100	24
Ringtree	$39,660	7 (tie)	$35,500	15
Salem	$38,675	38	$34,395	56
Westminster	$39,800	3	$36,500	1
Worley	$37,250	96	$32,300	112
State average	$37,100		$32,750	
State high	$40,050		$36,500	
State low	$35,400		$30,970	

Worley Supt. of Schools Michael Morrisey: "I think the report shows we are ready to compete for quality teachers. In 2005 we ranked 112 of 198 schools in the state and were below the state average. Now we rank 96th in the state. In both percentages and in pure dollars we've increased salaries more than any other district in the county during that period. You do the math and you'll see that I'm right."

Vera Brookes, president of the Worley Teachers Association: "I didn't know being mediocre was something to be proud of. The only reason we've come as far as we have is that we threatened to strike in 2005 after five years of 2 percent wage increases. Let's face it. This is one of the wealthier school districts in the wealthiest county in the state and we still rank—if I'm right—almost dead last in the county. Sure the board has made improvements, but I think this demonstrates it has no right to rest on its laurels."

EXERCISE D

Using records available at a local city hall or municipal building or online at the city's website, answer the following questions about the mayor or the elected head of the town government.

1. Did the mayor support or oppose the municipal budget last year?
2. What is the mayor's salary?
3. How much is the mayor's house assessed for? How much are neighboring houses assessed for?
4. Does the mayor or the mayor's family own any other property in town?
5. Does the mayor receive an expense account? How much was spent in expenses last year?

EXERCISE E

1. Select a report available online from the General Accounting Office, an investigative arm of Congress (www.gao.gov) and, acting as though the report were released today, write a news story for tomorrow's paper on its findings. At the end of the story, list five follow-up questions you would want to ask and the people you would contact for answers.

2. Identify a candidate seeking federal office in your community and write a story about his or her fund-raising efforts, using the reports of the federal election commission at www.fec.gov as a starting point.

15

Sources

Bob Greene's break came under the letter *V:* Vizzini. Salvatore Vizzini.

When Greene spotted the name in his well-worn source book, it brought back memories of "a pretty fair evening" of eating, drinking and talking more than a decade earlier. Greene was an investigative reporter; Vizzini had been a federal narcotics agent who kept tabs on the international drug trade. At the time, Greene had had no interest in writing about Vizzini's work. But Vizzini's name had found its way into Greene's thick collection of names, telephone numbers and addresses. They had exchanged Christmas cards, Vizzini's arriving from around the world.

Now Bob Greene was trying to trace the international heroin trail for a series of articles in *Newsday*. He contacted Salvatore Vizzini, who would turn out to supply the road map for a *Newsday* story. Vizzini opened doors to people familiar with the Turkish underworld; he opened doors to undercover police in France. He helped Greene win a Pulitzer Prize.

It was no accident. Bob Greene knows what sources mean. He was one of the founders of IRE, Investigative Reporters and Editors, an organization devoted to helping reporters worldwide take on important and difficult depth reporting assignments. When he retired as an assistant managing editor of *Newsday*, Greene still was sending out Christmas cards to a "trimmed down" list of about 1,800 people a year. Many on the list got personal notes.

All reporters need tips; they need quotes; they need people to be their eyes and ears in the places they aren't. They need sources.

"If you tell students one thing, tell them how incredibly important sources are," says Tim Belnap, who covers courts for the *Detroit Free Press*. "You have to develop them—take them to lunch, call them—even when you aren't working on a story."

This chapter is about how to find sources, how to train them and how to deal with them. The coverage chapters in Part 5 will discuss in more detail the types of sources available on different beats.

WHO

Journalism is detective work. Simply figuring out whom to contact about that plan to turn the downtown shopping district into a mall can take the industry and astuteness of a sleuth.

Reporters might start with the officials for and against the plan at city hall and, perhaps, at the Chamber of Commerce. Then they might stroll around the area interviewing store owners, residents and shoppers. That's easy enough, but good reporters will want to find out more. A good way of deciding whom to ask is to figure out what questions need to be answered:

Will the mall affect traffic? People in the planning office or the police traffic division may have opinions. They also may know where to uncover studies on the impact a mall might have on the local environment.

Will the mall push up rents? Landlords and tenant groups might have something to say about that; housing officials, too.

Will the mall help revitalize the business district? An expert on urban redevelopment could offer an educated guess based on the experiences of similar cities.

Who stands to make money? Local realtors might know; so, obviously, will the owners of the property the mall would be built on (city tax records can be used as a first step in finding out who they are).

With such questions in mind, reporters will make a list of the types of people they will want to talk to on a story. One way of building this list is to break it into three subheadings. The *players* list would include those directly involved, those who stand to benefit. This list might include the mall's owner and the realty company that's just snatched up a lot of adjacent land. It also might include the politician pushing the mall who just got a big contribution from the developer. The *experts* list includes those with specialized knowledge about development and its impact but no vested interest in the project. The *real people* list includes those who might be affected, positively and negatively, from neighboring residents to shoppers. These are not the financial movers and shakers behind the project but they are people who may have strong, personal reactions to the plan.

The next task is finding actual names. A reporter looking for an expert on urban redevelopment, for example, might start with a call to the sociology or urban planning department at the nearest university or to the federal department of Housing and Urban Development in Washington. Or she might put in a query to Profnet, one of a myriad of expert sources databases that provide fast and efficient means of finding experts (see Chapter 14, Research).

It can take ten calls just to track down a source whose comments may be boiled down to a single quote in the article. This could be a hundred-call story. Many are. Good sources are hard to find.

Reporters should spread a wide net. A story on the mall that quotes only boosters of the project will, assuming the project has some critics, be flawed. Sources should be chosen to represent various hues on the political spectrum, various interest groups, officials and nonofficials, and people from a wide range of racial, ethnic, religious and economic backgrounds. (See Chapter 2, Fairness.)

It's hard work to start every story from scratch. That's why reporters—especially those assigned to cover a regular *beat* such as police, the courts or local politics—fill their phonebooks with the names of people who can provide regular guidance and tips. These people—faithful, reliable sources—are accumulated over time. Reporters start by pumping their predecessors on the beat for names. At the *Chicago Tribune*, for example, a list of sources and their phone numbers is kept for each beat and passed on from reporter to reporter. But reporters might not share their best sources, and it's better in some ways to find your own: Personal chemistry has something to do with who helps whom.

Good sources can be found almost anywhere, not just in the largest offices or the fanciest houses in town. The mayor's secretary can be an excellent source; he may know as much about the inner workings of city hall as the city council president. The woman who pumps gas outside the police station may know a lot about who passes in and out the station doors.

Nurses in the hospital emergency room know who is getting sick and who is getting shot. "The wonderful thing about journalism," said the late columnist Molly Ivins, "is that it gives you a chance to talk to all kinds of people."

To do that, it's imperative that reporters get out of the office. Some of the best sources can be found on leisurely strolls through the territory, by stopping and chatting and learning who knows whom and who knows what. One source inevitably leads to another. And at each stop, reporters should pencil the names and phone numbers (home number, too, if possible) into their phone books, first alphabetically by name, then alphabetically under the subject—housing, unions, arson—that is a source's special area of interest or expertise.

It's equally imperative that reporters push beyond their *comfort zones*. The Jewish reporter should make a point of visiting a mosque, of spending time there and familiarizing herself with the imam and members of the congregation. The Islamic reporter should visit a temple and get to know its rabbi. Ivy League–educated reporters should spend time at the bars and restaurants frequented by workers in a nearby auto plant. Caucasian reporters should spend more time in largely African-American neighborhoods, and vice versa. And everyone should listen more closely to both teenagers and the elderly.

Diversity of coverage means much more than covering stories about how "other people live." It starts with reaching out and seeking sources across cultural, ethnic and racial lines in all fields. That Vietnamese-American doctor at the local hospital may be just as good an authority on a new kind of neurosurgery as her white, male counterpart. But the odds are she hasn't gotten the same exposure if the reporter on the beat is white, male and the product of upper-crust schools. It shouldn't be that way. One complaint about today's well-educated reporters is that they've lost touch with the communities and people they're trying to reach.

Don't let that happen to you. Reporters sometimes chafe at the notion that they need encouragement to seek sources with backgrounds different from their own. But as Robert Maynard, the founder of the Maynard Institute in Oakland, Calif., noted toward the end of his life, all people tend to view the world through the lens—what he called the *fault lines*—of their own ethnic or racial, generational, geographic and economic background as well as their gender or sexual orientation. By seeking sources from a wide variety of backgrounds, reporters can begin to stretch their own sense of what's news and what perspectives they should seek out about that news.

Lessons from the Pros

Brendan McCarthy, *Chicago Tribune*

Brendan McCarthy hates the word "source." He prefers "contact," someone he can "talk to any time," not just someone who is going to drop an exclusive story on him in a dimly lit garage. McCarthy never stops introducing himself to people who might be able to help him do his job better.

"When I'm not on duty or work, I still talk to people," he says.

That's one reason why McCarthy was the second youngest reporter in the *Chicago Tribune* newsroom when he was hired at age 23, the fall after graduating from Emerson College in Boston. McCarthy never tires of asking questions to find out who has an interesting story to tell.

He offers simple advice about sources: "Sources are people." They are people, he might have added, who should be treated with respect and interest, not manipulated to get information.

Brendan McCarthy,
Chicago Tribune.
(*Courtesy of the* Chicago Tribune)

Lessons from the Pros (continued)

One year into his career at a major metropolitan daily, McCarthy has done a number of things to build the breadth and depth of his sources:

- He collects and hands out business cards wherever he goes.
- He makes personal notations to remember a new source and make connections the next time he and the source talk. "I write down if a cop goes by the name Rocky or likes jazz music," he says. "You'll encounter people who are not always apt to talk to reporters. They can be a little crusty.... So you look for those things that you may have in common."
- He calls regularly, not just when he's looking for information.
- He treats everyone with equal respect, whether the person is a sanitation worker or the mayor. When he calls people at home, McCarthy always apologies for the inconvenience. He tries to walk a fine line between being persistent but not badgering ("You don't want to burn bridges"). When a source is too busy to talk, he leaves his cell phone number and asks for a callback.
- He follows up when people initially say no.

"The more you can empathize and put yourself in someone else's shoes, the better your writing [will be]," he says. "In mayhem stories of the day, accident-type stuff, I always remember that it could be someone knocking on my door, that it could be my mother or brother. You can't lose your emotions. Think with your emotions and write with them. Treat people with the same emotion that you would want them to treat you with."

CULTIVATING

There is no law that requires anyone to talk to a reporter. But most people will talk, and for a variety of reasons: Some like the publicity and the sense of self-importance; some want revenge against a political or personal rival; a few believe the public really ought to know what's happening. Reporters have to be prepared to understand and mine all these motivations. In addition, however, they hope to find informed people who will talk because they respect the reporter's work and perhaps even because they like that reporter as a person.

"I think you have to see people out of the courtroom," says Walter Fee, who covers the courts for *The Milwaukee Journal*. "Jog with them, play racquetball with them, hike with them, anything you like. If you are really interested and not a phony, then do it. It takes time away from family, but I've found no alternative."

This is called *cultivating* sources. A jogging partner is much more likely to help you with a story than someone who doesn't remember your first name. Some reporters make it a practice to jot down the names of the spouse and the children of the people they deal with on their beat. "Then," says Bob Greene, "when you call the mayor and his wife answers, you say 'Hi, Charlotte, how are you? I feel like I know you. Can you tell me where I can reach Charlie?'"

Reporters also cultivate sources by staying prepared and keeping up on the programs and policy initiatives of those they cover. One reporter for the Syracuse (N.Y.) *Post-Standard* kept a running chronology on his computer of individual sources and when he'd last talked to them. This allowed him to get a running start on each subsequent interview. It would go something like this: "Councilwoman Sproul. The last time we talked you were studying whether to seek funding for a bilingual program in Spanish and English in the middle school. Are you still pursuing that?"

Virtually all prospective sources have at least one thing in common—an appetite for good food. "There's a great American institution called lunch," says Leon Wynter, who covered banking and financial services for *The Wall Street Journal*. "I keep setting up those lunches whenever I can."

When things get too busy for lunch (the newspaper, incidentally, should pay), there's always the phone or even a quick e-mail to follow up, for example, on what happened on the playing field after your source broke off an interview to coach her daughter's soccer game. Such courtesies count.

The consistency of contact also can be important. "The key thing with all sources is to call even when you don't have a story in mind," Greene says. "It shows sources you have a personal interest in them. If you have free time, why not just spin through the As and then the Bs and so forth."

Obviously some sources are more essential than others. Greene suggests compiling a primary list of the top 20 or so sources. "Those," he says, "you tickle every week."

AVOIDING BEING CULTIVATED

Walter Fee of *The Milwaukee Journal* was writing a story about a man accused of having organized crime connections when he came across information that the alleged mobster had worked as a court commissioner for a district attorney. The district attorney was one of Fee's sources. Fee knew he risked losing this valuable source if he included high in the story the damaging fact that the DA had hired a reputed mobster. Still, the damaging fact appeared high in the story.

One of the dangers of cultivating sources is that they also begin cultivating you. Just as sources grow to like reporters, reporters grow fond of many of the people with whom they spend their days on the beat, especially if they've shared lunches or jogs. It is easy to soak up the perspective of these new friends, to begin taking their side—*cronyism* it's sometimes called. And it's hard to take the risk of alienating these friends or cronies with a tough story. More than friendship is at stake; an offended official can make a reporter's job difficult by withholding information.

But difficult though offending a source may be, neither affection nor fear can be allowed to influence reporters' work. Journalists are ultimately obliged to their readers, not their sources. Fee's decision was the only decision a good reporter could have made.

"On any beat you will be working with people over and over," notes Saundra Keyes of Louisville's *Courier-Journal*. "You may like them and you may come up with a story they won't like. But that's never kept me from writing a story. You have to say, 'I'm sorry, but I have to write this.'"

GROUND RULES

As a matter of course, reporters should expect the people they interview to attach their names to what they say. (See Chapter 6, Attribution.) When people say things *for attribution*, or *on the record*, their statements take on greater credibility. People also are likely to be more honest when they can be held responsible for what they said. After identifying themselves, reporters therefore should always assume that the material they gather for a story is *for attribution* and *on the record* unless a news source pushes for a different relationship. Even then, reporters should agree sparingly and only after their sources give cogent explanations of why they do not want to speak publicly.

Lessons from the Pros: Reporting Across Cultures

Jessie Mangaliman covers immigration issues for the *San Jose Mercury News*. Maureen Fan works out of Beijing, China, as a foreign correspondent for *The Washington Post*. Though one focuses on local and regional issues and the other is covering the world's largest country, they face similar challenges in developing sources: Both must cultivate relationships with people whose backgrounds, experiences and native languages are different from their own.

Maureen Fan,
The Washington Post.
(*Courtesy of* The
Washington Post)

Jessie Mangaliman,
San Jose Mercury News.
(*Courtesy of the* San Jose
Mercury News)

"It takes a long time to work sources in these communities," says Mangaliman, who came to the United States from the Philippines as a teen-ager. "People won't talk to you unless they know you. People won't talk to you unless they know your face. It's very, very grass roots."

Yet despite the special nature of both his beat and Fan's, those challenges likely will be shared by any good reporter covering the news in the 21st century. Today, a neighborhood reporter in rural Maine just might encounter a community of Somalian refugees. And a local reporter in Omaha, Neb., almost certainly will cross paths with Latin American immigrants working in its meatpacking plants. It's not just cities like New York, Chicago and Los Angeles whose texture is a rich cross-web of cultures.

Developing sources across cultures presents special challenges. And judging from the rapid growth of ethnic media news outlets, mainstream news outlets don't always step up to those challenges.

Often the first is language. Even after nine months of intensively studying Mandarin, Fan says, she is a relative beginner. Sometimes, she says, the Chinese are particularly hard on her—as an American of Chinese parentage—for not speaking the language better. She says her Caucasian colleagues, who don't *look* like they should speak the language better, are sometimes given an easier time.

Mangaliman makes a point of at least learning to say hello when he visits a source of another culture. He loves to travel and always tries to come home with a few new words.

But the barriers of reporting across cultures only start with words. Ignorance of history, of culture, of tradition can quickly foil reporters' efforts to develop new sources. And reporters must guard against oversimplification and stereotyping as well. In covering any ethnic or racial group, reporters must start by realizing that the diversity of viewpoints within the group is likely to be just about as varied as the number of people they add to their source list.

Fan and Mangaliman offered these tips to reporting effectively across cultural lines:

- **Read widely.** If you cover people of a particular ethnic group regularly, read widely about their history and culture. "I have a huge list of things I still have to read through," Fan says. Ask your new sources what books they believe best characterize their culture.
- **Be sensitive to cultural expectations.** In some Asian cultures, Mangaliman said, no one wears shoes in the house. That's usually obvious from the line of shoes at the door. But other cultural cues are harder to discern. Is it a sign of respect or disrespect to look someone in the eye? To shake hands? Mangaliman says he remains alert to cues around him and is careful not to impose his own cultural expectations on others. When he started an 18-month project on a community of Hmong refugees, for example, none of

the women shook his hand. But after he gained their trust, and they became familiar with U.S. customs, that changed. Early in her assignment, Fan learned that it was a sign of respect in China to offer her business card with both hands.

- **Break bread.** In many cultures, sharing a meal is the start of sharing a relationship. "The Chinese are obsessed with food," Fan wrote in an e-mail. "People who aren't curious or aren't interested or perhaps are fincky eaters won't necessarily miss the story but they'll probably get less color, less detail." Mangaliman says he will always eat some of the food he's offered in the homes of strangers, whether it appeals to him or not. "These kind of gestures when writing across cultural lines go a long way," he says. "People will remember that you ate their food in their home."

- **Spend time in new communities off deadline.** Shortly after starting her assignment in Beijing, Fan noted in an e-mail that "people like it when you go see them without asking for anything. It's good to make an effort to get to know them first before [you] 'use' them as a source." Mangaliman says building trust is essential on his beat as well. He does it at work, meeting new sources over a cup of coffee, and off duty, helping new communities learn how to write press releases or place an item in a community calendar as part of volunteer work for the Asian American Journalism Association. The payback of such source building comes later.

- **Use one source to meet to meet others.** When Mangaliman grew interested in a new Serbian refugee community in San Francisco Bay area, he enlisted the help of a woman named Sonia who ran a social service agency that helped the Serbs. She invited him to "have coffee at this Serbian place." Soon Mangaliman was asked to a folk dance, began learning about Serbian customs and developed an expanding circle of sources in the community.

- **Write about the cultures of others through their eyes, not your preconceptions.** "We all bring to the table certain notions because we think that we know something about a culture," Mangaliman cautions. "I think being aware that that could happen when you meet a source across cultures is important and the best defense against putting your foot in your mouth."

    Another mistake, he suggests, is to write about other cultures as if they are outside the mainstream—to cover their festivals instead of their cultures. Mangaliman calls it "freak-factor reporting."

    "These are our new readers," he says of immigrant groups. "We can't cover them as if they arrived from Mars last night and write, 'Oh my God, they're putting fish sauce in their food.' That's the kind of reporting that goes nowhere. You're freaked out if someone is wearing an hijab (a head scarf worn by Muslim women), freaked out by people who eat blood sausage or gefilte fish or whatever."

    Instead, he says, reporters have to check their stereotypes at the door and be open to learning from and about people of other backgrounds and experiences. "Go out there and meet people," he says. "it's the only way. Learn a thing or two about a new culture."

Sources can be particularly valuable when they are willing to tell secrets—such as the boss is double-billing his travel expenses or a superior has not been enforcing state conflict-of-interest statutes—that can get them into trouble. Sometimes a source's name can't be attached to these secrets unless the source is willing to become unemployed. It is then that reporters negotiate different levels of source protection.

It is, for example, not difficult to imagine why this "official," criticizing the Canadian government's submarine purchases from Britain, did not want his or her name used:

> A senior federal official says [Prime Minister] Jean Chretien's government was largely bamboozled into buying four faulty and rusting submarines in 1998, one of which caught fire this week, killing a Canadian seaman.
>
> The official, who was close to the original deal, compared the British endorsement of the subs to someone relying on a used-car salesman to do the tire-kicking.
>
> Then-defense minister Art Eggleton was "pretty much hoodwinked," said the official, who did not wish to be named.
>
> *The Toronto Sun*

Reporters in recent years have been criticized, and rightly so, for relying too heavily on anonymous sources and for allowing these sources to use their anonymity as a shield from behind which to criticize others. An inquiry into just who "outed" CIA agent Valerie Plame after her husband, Joseph Wilson, questioned the Bush administration's claims of a link between weapons of mass destruction and Saddam Hussein led into the offices of some of Washington's most powerful presidential and vice-presidential aides, the indictment of one, and the jailing of *New York Times* reporter Judith Miller, who refused to divulge her sources.

Many newspapers today are taking greater care to at least find out why a source was granted anonymity, something *The Toronto Sun* may have considered in the foregoing example.

A first step is understanding what ground rules exist for dealing with confidential sources.

Background

Information accepted on *background*, or *not for attribution*, can be used in a story but cannot be linked to the source of that information by name. The reporter may, however, use a nonspecific description that gives readers a sense of the source's position without revealing who the source is. A deputy mayor might be referred to as a *high city hall official*, as a *source close to the mayor* or merely as *an official*, according to the ground rules worked out in advance. The head coach of the local high school football team might be referred to as *someone familiar with the school's athletic policies* or as *a member of the athletic department* or simply as *one coach*.

Reporters press for permission to use the clearest attribution possible. Calling people simply *sources* may have a conspiratorial ring, but readers learn next to nothing about the importance, credibility or knowledge of that source. Be as specific as the source allows. A *high-ranking official* presumably carries more weight than *an official*:

> "It's a done deal," said a *high-ranking University of California administrator who has seen the proposed contract....*
>
> *Los Angeles Times*

Deep Background

Sources who provide information on *deep background* will allow reporters to use the information they provide but without any attribution whatsoever. If the deputy mayor reveals on deep background that the mayor is planning to retire, the reporter could write no more than: "It has been learned that Mayor Cassidy is not planning to run for re-election when her term ends next year."

Reporters dislike stepping out on a limb like this...and for good reason. Deep background allows government officials to test new policies without taking any responsibility for them. If Mayor Cassidy changes her mind, she doesn't look bad; the reporter who wrote the story does. Reporters can't afford to have their credibility undermined like this very often.

Information obtained on deep background can be useful when reporters are trying to confirm statements they obtained with attribution elsewhere, or when they are looking for leads to further investigation. Bob Woodward and Carl Bernstein of *The Washington Post* used a deep background source—referred to in the newsroom as "Deep Throat"—for these purposes in their Watergate investigation.

Off the Record

If sources say, "This is *off the record*," ask what they mean. The term is frequently confused with *background*. "Sometimes people really mean background when they say off the record," notes Fred Barbash of *The Washington Post*.

Material that is really *off the record* cannot be used in the story, period. On routine stories, many reporters will simply walk away if a source insists on staying off the record. Others will stick around in the hope that their new knowledge will help them with future stories. Only if off-the-record material is developed independently, from *another* source, can it be used. Then the information should be attributed—but to the second source only. (Reporters who receive off-the-record confidences should honor them in personal conversations as well as in print. Too often, beginning reporters tell colleagues of interesting off-the-record tales that they can't write. This is risky. Sources may be upset if they learn that their secrets have become newsroom gossip.)

Ground rules should be agreed upon *before* information is exchanged. In theory, reporters assume all comments are for attribution, *on the record*, unless a source sets some other condition beforehand. Sources who deal regularly with the press usually are held to this rule. But in interviewing people who are inexpert in dealing with the press, most reporters will be a bit more generous.

CHAPTER 15 SUMMARY: SOURCES

Reporters need tips, information and insight from others. The people who provide these on a regular basis are known as *sources*. The word *source* is more than a fancy synonym for *person*. True sources are people whom reporters contact regularly, people with whom they have an ongoing relationship.

In identifying potential sources and building source lists, reporters should:

- Recognize that anyone can be a source. Secretaries and clerks of those in power often are more interested in sharing information than the power brokers themselves. Don't overlook them.
- Think of sources in three broad groups. *Players* are those central to any story. They stand to benefit or be harmed financially or politically. They have a vested interest. *Experts* hold specialized knowledge about a topic but do not have a vested interest. *Real people* are the citizens affected, whether the story is about a vote on a new school tax or transportation program for senior citizens.
- Seek sources across a broad spectrum of ethnic, racial, religious, economic and generational backgrounds. Reporters should work assiduously to push beyond the boundaries of their personal contacts and experiences in seeking sources.
- Collect cards and hand out their own. This is an essential way to build a source list.
- Set up a system of notation that facilitates remembering sources and details of interest to them in their personal or professional lives.

- Touch base with key sources regularly, not just when working on a story.
- Assume that sources are on the record, but be prepared to negotiate a different relationship if the source is in a vulnerable situation.

ADDITIONAL READING

News in a New Century: Reporting in an Age of Converging Media, Jerry Lanson and Barbara Croll Fought, Pine Forge, 1999.

EXERCISE A

Find the name and telephone number of a person in your area who could provide each of the following types of information.

1. Information on what has to be done to get a name on the ballot in the state Democratic gubernatorial primary.
2. Information on the safety of nuclear reactors.
3. Information on licensing procedures for doctors in the state.
4. Information on local civil defense plans.
5. Information on the knowledge required to pass the state bar exam.
6. Information on the safety of local drinking water.
7. Information on the average income levels of welfare recipients in the area.
8. Information on the chances of severe drought in the area.
9. Information on the way the decision on which police cars to purchase is made in a local town.
10. Information on how international basketball rules differ from collegiate rules.
11. Information on the movie that was most successful at local theaters last year.
12. Information on the health consequences of a diet rich in cholesterol.
13. Information on fatality rates on local highways.
14. Information on what the French mean by *nouvelle cuisine*.
15. Information on state hunting regulations.

EXERCISE B

Write a list of the names and telephone numbers of officials, community group leaders or experts who should be contacted to report each of the following stories locally, and a list of places you might go to find any additional sources who would be useful.

1. How are the elderly responding to rising prices? Are their Social Security and pension benefits adequate? Are they having difficulty paying for food or housing?

2. Have local police departments invested in bulletproof vests? Why or why not? How much protection do the vests provide? What are their disadvantages?

3. How have local school boards responded to health warnings against high-fat, low-fiber diets? Have the lunches they offer students changed?

4. How common is the use of marijuana among local teen-agers?

5. How serious is the injury problem in high school football? Are students suffering injuries that may have long-lasting health consequences?

6. What is the quality of the air in the area? What steps are being taken to monitor air quality? What are the main sources of local air pollution?

7. Who are the likely candidates in the next election for mayor in a local town or city?

8. Have television, cable television and videotape recorders hurt business at local entertainment places?

9. How does local unemployment compare with that in the state and in the nation? Is unemployment here increasing or decreasing? What factors affect the local unemployment rate?

10. Is the dog and cat population in the area decreasing or increasing? How serious is the problem of strays? When was the last reported case of rabies?

EXERCISE C

Write a story based on the following collection of facts. You are writing for a newspaper dated tomorrow and read in the city where the events occurred.

Alice Batsel, press secretary to Mayor Georgina Desjardin, a Republican, agrees to discuss the mayor's upcoming decision on whether to run for re-election to a second term, but only off the record. You agree. Here's what she says: "Of course, she's going to run. Desjardin just ain't the type to cut and run, not when there's work left to do in this city. But we've got some *t*'s to cross and some *i*'s to dot before we make the announcement, got to get a campaign organization in place. We'll announce sometime next month. But she's told me it's definite."

From interview with Desjardin: "Well, I'm sorry but I just don't have anything to say on that. Yes, I enjoy this job. Yes, there's still work to be done. But there are a number of personal and family considerations that will go into the decision as well as political consideration. I haven't made a final decision. I'll be sure to let you know when I do."

From interview yesterday with Robert Barkley, the mayor's executive secretary: "OK, I'm willing to talk about this with you, but only on background. You can call me someone who works in the mayor's office. Just don't say a secretary. OK, you can say that I am familiar with her thinking. That's for damn sure. Yes, she is going to run. Yes, it is going to be announced next month. No, I don't think a date has been set yet. Yes, I'm sure she has no doubt about it. She told me separately and all of us together that it's definite."

From interview with Deputy Mayor Jacob Ambler: "I will discuss this subject only on deep background. You heard right—Georgina's running again. She told me a few days ago. I don't know any details about the campaign, just that she'll be heading our ticket in the city."

The Republican mayoral primary will be held Sept. 9. No other candidates have announced that they will run yet.

16

Interviewing

The best answers regularly get saved for reporters who ask the best questions. Those questions take preparation.

Not that reporters don't have to think on their feet. But more often than not, good interviewers have done plenty of thinking before they ever get on their feet to go to an interview, and they'll do some more after it ends.

Indeed, interviewing really is a three-step process. First a reporter spends considerable time finding the right people (see Chapter 15, Sources), reading about them and their views, and plotting a rough line of questioning. Next comes the actual face-to-face, or voice-to-voice, interview. And finally, in the minutes and hours that follow, reporters sort through their notes to see what's missing and whether a follow-up call is needed to fill in holes.

Lessons from the Pros: Getting Started

Jack Encarnacao

Jack Encarnacao's first big test came on his first day on the job at the *Quincy Patriot Ledger*. Fresh from college, Encarnacao discovered the town he'd been assigned had called an emergency meeting. Repairmen fixing a water tank had botched the job and, as a result, lead-contaminated water was sprinkling out into the surrounding neighborhoods.

"It was an Erin Brockovich-type of big thing because it was poisoning the neighborhood," Encarnacao said.

Encarnacao didn't wait. He started asking questions, conducting interviews.

"I had the whole story before I went to the meeting, which was important because while other reporters were scribbling furiously what was going on, I was just waiting for stuff to add to my story," he said. "I jumped on the story when I first heard about it, and it unfolded from there."

Jack Encarnacao, now reporting for the *Quincy Patriot Ledger*, speaking as his class valedictorian at Emerson College.
(Photo by David Rosen)

Encarnacao says part of starting out is to know when to ask for help. That's why his first tip in carrying out interviews is, "Work with your editor."

"It is very valuable to ask an editor what questions they would ask," he says. "They know what story they want and how to do it. . . . The worst thing is to pretend you can handle it and then miss things that go right over your head."

He offers these other tips for preparing and carrying out interviews:

- **Figure out what you need to know before the interview.** Beginning reporters sometimes confuse what they'd like to get with what they need to get, he says. Get the basic information, he adds, before shooting for the sky.
- **Get to know the key players quickly.** "Once you spend enough time covering a certain area and get a sense of responsibilities, you develop a sense of who the town would send to fix a problem."
- **Don't start at the top.** Top officials are often tougher to reach and less accommodating than those lower down in the chain of command, Encarnacao says. In police stories, he looks for the department's lieutenants: "I quote them ten times more [than the police chief] because their job is to know everything happening in the town."
- **Keep reasking questions in different ways.** "You make a story different by asking questions in an interesting way."
- **Push for good quotes.** "It has been one of the real key things that sets me apart. I read other stories and the quotes are not interesting. They can have solid reporting, nice writing and solid facts, but no quotes. You have to make sure that the impression the source leaves on you is also left on the reader."
- **Learn from your mistakes.** "You interview someone endlessly and then realize it was the wrong thing to do. But, then you learn who the right person to interview is for next time."

THE PREINTERVIEW

Inevitably, there is a direct relationship between how much the reporter knows *before* an interview and how much that reporter will find out *during* the interview. Reporters who don't know the politics of the politician they are interviewing, who haven't read the books of the author they are questioning, who haven't looked up the background of the business executive they are profiling, are hardly in a position to persuade these people to be forthcoming.

Homework

Sometimes it is wise to build up to a key interview. When Stuart Diamond, a reporter for *Newsday*, wrote a series on the Long Island Lighting Company's difficulties in building the ill-fated Shoreham nuclear plant, he didn't interview officials from the utility until he had most of the facts. "I literally brought 150 pounds of material to LILCo for the interview," he recalls. "You have to know enough already so that you can penetrate the answers you are getting and get to the truth. In my series I was able to get their admissions because I was able to say in response to some of their answers, 'You are wrong.'"

This isn't to say that reporters should never hazard an interview without first gathering several carton-loads of documents. However, those who are out to prove that they know more law than lawyers or more business than businessmen frequently will lose track of the simple things readers need answered to understand a story. Reporters should enter any interview ready to learn. They should never make believe they understand something when they don't. But learning, nevertheless, takes homework. It is one thing to ask the mayor to explain some of the ramifications of that new zoning ordinance; it is quite another to waste time asking the mayor how he voted on the ordinance two nights ago—information that appeared in yesterday's paper.

Writing Out Questions

Preparation for an interview should also include thinking about what questions you are going to ask. Jot down a list of potential questions. These rarely will be used exactly as they are written out or exactly in the same order—good interviewers always are open to new avenues of questioning, should these develop. But a list of questions serves as a guide to keep an interview on track, as a fallback should the reporter become momentarily flustered, and as a check at the end of an interview to determine whether everything has been covered.

"I not only write down questions in the order I might ask them, but I think about what the answers might be," says Diamond. "I try to envision the course an interview might take."

Getting Through

Most people who participate in public life, or who find themselves in the news, are glad to talk with a reporter. They want a chance to state their case or to gain a little publicity. But some people, generally people whose portrayal in the paper is likely to be less than flattering, just don't want to talk. Anyone has a right to remain silent, but aggressive reporters often won't accept an initial "no" as a final answer. (Such aggressiveness becomes obnoxiousness when interview subjects are victims of tragedies, of course. These people should be approached gently and never hassled. See Chapter 20, Police.)

Sometimes the problem is simply getting to talk to the source. Many secretaries are programmed to intercept the timid and hesitant caller. It may help to sound confident and personable. Reporters also have learned to take an end run around secretaries by calling an office before 9 a.m., during lunch or after 5 p.m.—times at which these gatekeepers are less likely to be around.

With certain people, e-mail can be an effective way of making initial contact and setting up an interview. Most people still read their own e-mail. And those who deal in complicated information, people such as scientists, doctors and academics, sometimes are reassured when reporters first write to them and outline the scope and nature of their interview. Don't send specific questions, however. (See the section that follows, Choosing Tools.)

The closer a reporter can get to a potential source, the harder it is for that person to turn down an interview. That's one reason aggressive reporters can sometimes be seen interviewing associates of their targets—they hope that news of their inherent wisdom and fairness will filter back. Nor does it hurt to "just happen" to be walking by a prospective source's house about the time he or she usually heads for work: "Aren't you Ms. Honeycutt? What a coincidence. I've been trying to arrange an interview."

When all else fails, a bit of forcefulness can't hurt: "Ms. Honeycutt, the story will run whether or not you respond to the charge. I just thought it would be better and fairer if it gave your side as well."

Choosing Tools

The first decision every reporter about to conduct an interview faces is whether to do it in person, by telephone or by e-mail.

E-mail is the easiest, and worst, choice. Avoid it, unless you are looking for no more than the confirmation of a fact or two. E-mail interviews tend to be devoid of spontaneity and serendipity, and both are important. What's more, e-mailed questions allow subjects to turn to their PR practitioners to craft answers that make them look smart; such responses are anything but spontaneous.

The telephone has one advantage: It's fast. That's an important consideration when working on deadline or on a story that may require dozens of interviews. And if a source won't talk or has little to add, on the telephone you haven't wasted much more than the time it takes to say "Hello" and "Goodbye."

But for an important interview, there is no substitute for being there in person. It is easier to size up people when you can see their faces, and people are more likely to open up when they can see your face. Proximity builds trust. In addition, an in-person interview gives reporters a chance to observe and collect the descriptive detail that can enliven a story.

If the zoning board decides to postpone a monthly meeting, the telephone probably will do. But a feature on a trapeze artist shouldn't be reported on the telephone. Neither should a story about the closing of a welfare hotel.

Tape recorders also present reporters with a decision. Nothing can compare with a properly functioning tape recorder for an accurate and complete record of key interviews. On timeless stories—a feature or a long-term investigation, for example—tape recorders can be invaluable. For an article profiling a person, tapes may capture the eloquence or the idiosyncrasies of the subject's speech and free the reporter to listen and look more closely. In investigations, tapes may provide evidence needed to protect the newspaper's and the reporter's credibility.

Still, few newspaper reporters use tape recorders regularly. Some argue that the physical act of writing down what someone says makes them more attentive. Others live in fear that the tape recorder in front of them will self-destruct. And some sources grow nervous at the thought of having their words recorded for all to hear. The main advantage of settling for pen and pad, though, is that of saving time—a tape must be replayed. For shorter interviews, therefore, veteran reporters almost invariably trust in their handwriting.

Lessons from the Pros

Tracy Breton, *The Providence Journal*

Tracy Breton has spent more than three decades as a reporter for *The Providence Journal*.

She's interviewed a man who was serving time for "chopping up" his wife and a lawyer who stole money from a quadriplegic client. No matter what the subject, Breton follows the same rules: Be prepared, be polite and never leave without asking your toughest questions.

These are among the reporting techniques that have served Breton well. She's been invited to speak on interviewing at National Writers' Workshops, teaches at Brown University and has been awarded journalism's highest honor, the Pulitzer Prize.

But if homework counts, says Breton, so does the ability to listen and adjust. Even the most informed reporter, she says, sometimes is better off discarding the script.

"Too many reporters make the mistake of thinking they know what someone is going to tell them ahead of time," Breton says "Be prepared to punt, and throw away your questions and come up with new questions."

Tracy Breton,
The Providence Journal.
(Photo by Mary Murphy)

Lesson from the Pros (continued)

Understanding a subject's motivation can help. Breton says most people agree to interviews for three reasons: "vanity, fear and loneliness."

To improve their odds of success, Breton encourages her students to:

- **Interview their subject face to face whenever possible.** "It's hard to build that rapport over the phone, and interviews are also built on observation."
- **Start by finding common ground.** "If it's the kind of interview where you want them to open up, start with a lot of chitchat before pulling out the notebook," Breton says. "Talk about the things on their walls, or their pets, whatever you can come up with to build trust."

    Since "no two interviews are alike," Breton says, this advice doesn't always hold. Politicians, for example, are busy people and don't often take time to schmooze. Interviewing people who are targets of an investigation is likely to be even briefer: "If they agree to talk to you at all, it may be for only five minutes."
- **Avoid asking questions that can be answered with "yes" or "no."** Open-ended questions that explore the why or how of someone's thoughts or actions, she says, elicit more interesting and useful answers. "By asking open ended questions that are simple and direct, you will get a much better interview."
- **Allow the interview's silences to linger.** "You may be tempted to fill in silences, but when a question you ask elicits silence, don't try to fill it in."
- **Save the tough questions until the end.** "If you ask a stranger hard questions right off the bat, you might lose the interview," Breton says.

But, she adds, be sure to ask those questions.

INTERVIEW STRATEGIES

The questions experienced reporters ask are anything but haphazard. Whether the reporters have had a chance to prepare or are responding to a breaking story, their interviews usually follow a strategy.

Ease In

There are many ways to conduct an interview. But one that almost never works is to open with an accusatory question. If your first question to the president of the board of education were to be: "How can you talk about improving education when the board has recommended a 10 percent cut in school funding?" the president is hardly likely to be forthcoming in the remainder of the interview.

Reporters instead should start with an easy, comfortable question that gets the source talking. The hope is that the source will keep talking later in the interview when it comes time for those tough questions. Get that board president to open up by asking, "What improvements do you think are needed in the school system?" By starting with a less confrontational question, reporters ensure that they'll leave the interview with some answers, even if the source clams up or walks out later when the hard questions begin.

In an in-person interview, there's often time to open with a little small talk. The offices or homes of people who sit for interviews are filled with potential conversation pieces—a picture of family members, a framed degree from the University of Hawaii, a piece of art from Mexico. A few minutes' conversation about what interests the interviewee can make that person comfortable (See Lessons from the Pros: Tracy Breton.)

Telephone interviews often call for a different technique; it may make sense to be more direct. "The only way I can keep a high-powered person on the phone is to ask questions that might interest him," says *Newsday*'s Diamond.

An Overview

"The biggest mistake beginning reporters make," says Ron Harris of the *Los Angeles Times*, "is that they arrive on the scene, interview someone and begin to ask a series of minor, picky questions. They end up with a series of disjointed facts. Instead, what they should do first is say, 'Hey, guy, what happened?' Let him tell you the story, then you can go back and ask questions to fill in the missing details."

In other words, if a dam has collapsed, don't begin by asking the person in charge, "How many gallons of water escaped?" then, "What time did the first crack appear?" then, "What is the dam made of?" Instead, open with "Tell me what happened," or "How did it start?" Let that official say, "We got our first warning that water had begun to leak at 8:45, then we looked out and saw the crack...." Get the basic scenario—preferably in chronological order. Make sure you understand essentially what went on. "You want to start by getting an overview," says Harris. Then you can worry about exactly how many gallons of water escaped.

Obviously, reporters will need an overview in a hurry when they first arrive at a breaking event like a dam collapse. However, getting an overview can also be a priority on more leisurely but more complex stories. Leon Wynter, of *The Wall Street Journal*, says he often opens with general questions when conducting interviews on his beat—bank regulation: "I have people explain the structure, background and philosophy to me before getting into the specifics."

The Goal

When they do get down to specifics, reporters are looking for information that suits the needs of the stories they will write. From an interview with the union leader, they may need facts on the position of workers in a dispute and a tough restatement of that threat to strike. From an interview with one of the workers, they may want emotional quotes and specific complaints. And from an interview with the company's president, they may seek a reply to the specific charges.

Reporters have a much better chance of getting what they want from an interview if they know what their goal is. If they're looking for subjective comments, the interview should be filled with questions like: "What was it like?" "What were you feeling at the time?" "How did you react?" "What would you compare the experience to?" If the goal is expert analysis, however, most of the questions will use words like *explain, interpret, predict* and *analyze*.

It's important that reporters attempt to clarify their goals as they plan an interview, but it's just as important that they remain flexible enough to respond to unexpected, but newsworthy, information that may come up as the interview progresses. If that worker whose union is threatening a strike happens to mention that the company routinely dumps chemical wastes in a local pond, reporters will put aside their plans and goals and head off in a new direction.

A Trap

Despite what the movies and television shows would have you think, not every journalistic interview is an attempt to make a person sweat, twitch, tremble, and break down and admit guilt. In fact, the majority of interviews are just friendly attempts to get some helpful information and some usable quotes. But sometimes you do want to get newsmakers to say something that they might not have wanted to say. Sometimes you're laying a trap.

In *Interviews That Work: A Practical Guide for Journalists* (see Additional Reading), Shirley Biagi discusses a few possible strategies for trapping newsmakers. When interviewing a police officer said to have beaten a suspect, for example, a reporter might open with some general questions about suspects and the proper way to treat them...and then get more and more specific about what is alleged to have happened. The strategy is to force the subject into a corner, to place on the record general statements that will make it more difficult to evade the specific questions that follow—"Then how can you justify the rough handling that someone obviously gave that accused murderer?" Biagi calls this a *funnel* interview.

In the *covertly sequenced* interview, the trickier questions are spread throughout the interview to surprise the newsmaker or lead the newsmaker into contradictions. For example, the reporter might ask early on whether the officer has known of any police officers who have used physical force with a suspect already in custody, then, after some more innocuous questions, ask whether the officer himself has ever felt a desire or a need to use physical force with a suspect in custody, then, after another interval, ask about how he treated that accused murderer.

A third technique—we'll call it the *machine-gun* interview—is to weigh in at some point with a series of tough questions, leaving little room for evasion: "When did that suspect arrive back at the station house?"..."Were you ever alone in the room with him?"..."Did he get you angry?"..."Did you ever hit him?" But hold your fire! The *machine-gun* technique should not be used at the start of the interview.

Which technique a reporter chooses depends on the person and the situation. For example, if newsmakers are threatening to walk out, the detective-like approach of boring in might not work. But if newsmakers are confident and evasive, it might make sense to hit them with a series of rapid-fire questions.

The point is not that reporters should announce to themselves, "I'm going to do a covertly sequenced interview." These techniques can be mixed and matched, their names ignored. The point is that beginning reporters, at least, should devote considerable prior thought to what they are trying to accomplish in an interview and how best to accomplish it.

QUESTIONS

A reporter's "body language" in an interview can make a difference, as Biagi notes in her book. Alert and attentive, leaning forward, head nodding—these are gestures reporters may use to encourage interviewees to open up. On the other hand, appearing stiff, uncomfortable, bored or distracted can easily turn off a source. "You want to establish a rapport," says Ron Harris. Small talk can help; so can flattery—in small, controlled doses.

Nevertheless, the success of an interview is more likely to rest on the quality of the questions reporters ask than on their posture or their ability to chat about the weather. Some questions do the job. Some don't.

Direct

The more convoluted the question, the more convoluted the answer is likely to be...if the subject is able to understand the question at all. If you want a clear, direct quote, don't ask: "So, if the toxic wastes from your company were diverted by the B & R Hauling Company, which we have discussed as a possibility, though not a probability, and if your company suspected that something was amiss in the terms of the contract, then, if I may backtrack a bit, about your original decision to sign on with them, how does it look?" Instead ask: "With the benefit of hindsight, what more might have been done to assure that all your wastes were disposed of properly?"

Open or Closed

If a reporter is looking for quotes, it's wise to ask questions that require some explication. These are called *open-ended questions*. Don't ask high school students whether they are for or against a local busing plan. Ask them what their views on busing are and why. "Yes" and "no" make lousy quotes.

But in the search for facts, or confirmation of facts, *closed questions* can be efficient tools. Ask the superintendent of schools about her feelings on the starting date for the busing plan and you could be in for 15 minutes of soul searching. If all you need is confirmation of the date, ask: "Is the busing going to start on the first day of school, Sept. 7?"

Getting Specifics

Good interviewers get more than just facts and quotes; they get *the* facts and quotes that will best communicate to readers the meaning of a story. Abstract, vague responses won't do that job. Reporters are after *specifics*. They are constantly working to keep their subjects' feet on the ground, to force them to illustrate their ideas, theories and characterizations with concrete examples.

The bank president who has just reported that more than $10,000 was embezzled from his bank might be asked what *specifically* he remembers about the suspect teller. "He was always the first teller here in the morning, and he always brought his own lunch," tells readers a lot more than just "He was a fine employee."

A reporter interviewing a rescue worker at the scene of a flood might ask for a description of some of the *specific* things the rescue worker saw. "All that was left of one house was the garage and the chimney," is a lot more powerful than, "A number of houses suffered severe damage."

When interviewing a local high school student who is making $50,000 a year as a model, ask her to try to recall a *specific* example of when her work and her studies conflicted. An anecdote usually makes the point better than a statement: "One day we worked shooting some jeans ads till 10 at night. Everybody else went home to relax, I went home to read a chemistry book. We had a test the next day."

"Could you be more specific?" "Could you give me an example of that?" "Can you describe exactly what it was like?" "Can you remember exactly what happened?" "Can you recall a specific incident?" These are questions good reporters will ask again and again.

Questions are not the only way to obtain concrete examples. Sometimes all a reporter at an interview has to do is look around. In features in particular (see Chapter 22, Features), physical details—clothes, furniture, mannerisms—can add to the picture painted by the subject's own words. Here are some of the details spotted by a *USA Today* reporter interviewing author Jackie Collins: "She is drinking pink champagne and eating smoked salmon. She touches a pink napkin to her peach colored lips. All her furniture is cream colored. There are prints, paintings and figurines of leopards everywhere in her house."

Follow-Ups

Make sure you understand the answer. Sometimes newsmakers will hide behind an unclear answer. More often their answers are unclear simply because they have difficulty explaining themselves. In either case, reporters have to be prepared to ask *follow-up questions*.

Follow-ups can be used to translate jargon: "But what exactly is blood doping?" To clear up confusion: "Wait a second, so you're saying these blood transfusions did not violate Olympic rules?" Or to respond to evasions: "OK, but let me repeat my original question: Did you or did you not see these athletes take blood transfusions before their races?" In addition, follow-ups are sometimes used specifically to get a better quote: "Could you tell me again, why you didn't tell anyone about the blood doping?"

Ask. Ask. And, if necessary, reask.

NOTE TAKING

People being interviewed talk faster than most reporters can write. One way of keeping up is to learn shorthand. Many reporters even concoct their own brand of shorthand. And even the large majority of reporters who have no such formal system for recording what people are saying will use abbreviations and leave out some words to save time. They learn to jot down information in clear but compact form.

Here's part of a statement by Police Chief Brad Jovens:

> We have information that Bernard Levin, a teller at the First State Bank here left for Brazil Friday evening. Bank officials suspect that he was the perpetrator of an embezzlement plot at the bank. The suspect, Bernard Levin, is 35 years old, with no criminal record.

And here's how that part of the statement might be recorded in a reporter's notes (handwritten, of course):

> Chief Brad Jovens:
> Bernard Levin, teller, 1st State Bnk, left for Brazil Fri. eve.
> "Bank offic. suspect that he was the perp. of an embezzlement plot at the bank."
> 35, no record

Ron Harris suggests another technique that can help the interviewer who is desperately trying to play catch-up with a fast-talking newsmaker: "Throw in a throw-away question." The subject has just said something marvelous. You're struggling to get it all down in your notes, but you have to say something so that there isn't too long a lull in the conversation. Ask an unimportant, even irrelevant question, Harris advises ("I imagine you've had a lot of time away from your family on this one, huh?"), and, meanwhile, keep writing down that quote.

Nevertheless, the real secret for getting down on paper the important information disclosed in an interview is to learn to recognize what information is worth recording, and what can be forgotten. The first words reporters will write in their notebooks are the name—with correct spelling—and exact title of the person they are interviewing. After that, what they take down will depend on what they might need in their stories. Beginners usually try to scribble down everything. While they are struggling to record the trivialities, the important points fly by. Good reporters think before they scribble.

Facts

Reporter: "How much exactly did you lose?"

Bank president: "Let's see...I have that information right here. I know it's over $10,000. Oh yes. Ten-thousand four-hundred and twenty-three dollars. Is that exact enough for you?"

Reporter: "Yes, thanks. Do you know over how long a period the money was being taken?"

Bank president: "Six months, approximately. From the beginning of January to the beginning of July. I can't give you exact dates. We've had police here every day this week, and those are the dates I told them. . . . I mean that's the approximate period."

That bank president, discussing the embezzlement of some money from his bank, didn't say anything quotable in this section of the interview, so what he said can be boiled down to a few facts. Forget those that have no chance of making the story—of course, police have been spending a lot of time at the bank. Jot down the rest, being careful to indicate what the numbers and dates refer to and to include the qualifications—those dates are only "approximate." Here's what might have appeared in a reporter's notebook:

> Amount lost—$10,423
> Taken over approx. 6 months, begin Jan. to begin July. No exact dates.

Quotes

Reporter: "What did you think of Levin, before you heard he had left for Brazil?"

Bank president: "He was a fine employee. We never suspected anything. We have a lot of fine employees; yes, I can certainly say that. And let me add, we hire people we think will be good employees."

Reporter: "What specifically do you remember about him?"

Bank president: "He was, let me see, always the first teller here in the morning, and he always brought his own lunch. I remember that . . . yes."

Reporter: "What was your reaction when you heard he was in Brazil?"

Bank president: "I was shocked. You can quote me on that. I mean . . . it was just . . . I'm a bank president not a . . . Well, what else can I say? It was shocking."

Besides facts, interviews are designed to produce quotes. Reporters will take the time to write out the exact wording of any potential quotes (minus such excess verbiage as, "yes, I can certainly say that"), but there's no need to waste time jotting down the irrelevant ("We have a lot of fine employees"), the obvious ("we hire people we think will be good employees") or the poorly worded. (See Chapter 7, Quotations.) Here's what a reporter might have noted about this section of that interview:

> "He was a fine employee. We never suspected anything. He was always the 1st teller here in the morn., and he always brought his own lunch." When heard in Brazil: "I was shocked."

STAYING IN CONTROL

You're in the newsmaker's office or living room, taking up the newsmaker's valuable time. It's easy, in gratitude, to let the newsmaker control the interview, to smile and say "thank you" a lot and then leave, still smiling, with a useless collection of digressions, reminiscences and lectures.

Forget how important that newsmaker is. Forget how thankful you are to have been granted this interview. You're the one who is asking the questions. You will have to write the story. You are in charge.

It's your job to make sure the interview stays on track. You certainly don't want to offend the person you're talking with, but you also don't want to listen to a 15-minute discourse on the value of hard work when you're there to learn about a holdup, either. You may have to politely but firmly break in—especially if pressed for time. Wait for the end of a sentence and then jump. If that doesn't work, it may be necessary to actually interrupt. And if newsmakers continually filibuster, you might suggest, in so many words, that they keep answers short and stick to the subject.

Reporters don't want to be perceived as boors, but they can't be so polite or shy that time runs out on their interview before they get the answers they need.

LISTENING

Reporters have a lot on their minds during interviews. They might be thinking about their plan for their interview, about whether they are getting the facts and quotes they need. They may be trying to decide on their next question, or still mulling over the previous one. And all the while they're straining to take notes.

There's a limit to the number of things humans can do at once. Something's got to give. And often what happens, strangely, is that reporters forget to listen to what the person they're interviewing is saying. The mayor's last comment, that she has decided not to seek re-election, might even have made it into their notes, but their minds are too busy trying to think of what else to ask her about this waterfront development plan to have really *heard* what she said. So the next question is something about ports and parks when it should have been: "Wait a second! When did you decide that you weren't going to be a candidate next year?"

Ron Harris, who has run an internship program for the *Los Angeles Times*, says he often has to give inexperienced interviewers this seemingly obvious advice: "Listen to the answers." Reporters often have to forget the next question and the answer to an earlier one for a moment for the sake of paying attention to the answer to the question they just asked.

If reporters have the time, they might ease up enough so that they actually lose themselves in the conversation. "I like to let the conversation run," says Karen W. Arenson of *The New York Times*. "In a lot of interviews I like to just follow people's logic, to find out why they are thinking what they are thinking."

Part of the art of listening is certainly learning when to hold your own tongue. It is foolish to start debating with an interviewee who happens to say something you disagree with. Reporters are there to elicit someone else's two cents, not to add their own.

THE END

Here are two things to remember as the interview is drawing to a close.

End Tough

Now's the time to follow Tracy Breton's advice (see Lessons from the Pros: Tracy Breton). You saved the tough questions for the end; don't neglect to ask them. By the end of the interview you have less to lose by alienating subjects, and after a long interview they might be more inclined to let down their guard.

The Last Question

Before "goodbye," always ask: "Do you have anything to add?" or "Is there anything else I should have asked?" Sometimes there is. Then warn your subjects that you may have to call back with a follow-up question or two, ask for their home phone numbers, and leave your phone number in case they think of something else. And keep listening once you've closed your notebook. Sometimes, subjects suddenly relax and leave you with a nugget of information or a gem of quote that has eluded you during the interview.

THE POSTINTERVIEW

Many reporters start to collect their thoughts by typing up their notes soon after an interview ends. That way they also can decipher their scribbles before the words that inspired them have been forgotten, and they can check whether there are holes in the information that might necessitate a follow-up call or additional interviews. Others highlight key facts and quotes before they even drive away in their cars. They check for holes, too.

Most sources will be impressed rather than annoyed by a diligent reporter who calls back to clarify points. It also is appropriate to read sources passages of a story to check the accuracy of what you have written, particularly about a complicated issue. However, reporters should never surrender final control of an article to sources by promising them a chance to retract statements, censor paragraphs or read a final manuscript before the article appears on the newsstand.

CHAPTER 16 SUMMARY: INTERVIEWING

There is a direct relation between how much a reporter knows before an interview and how much that reporter will find out during the interview. To be successful, reporters need to find interesting and knowledgeable subjects. They need to get those subjects to talk. And once the interviews begin, they need to ask compelling and original questions, designed to dig out specific details, lively quotes and surprising insights. All of that takes thought and preparation *before* an interview begins.

Usually, the most successful interviews are:

- **Face to face.** Interview by phone if you need basic information and a quick quote. But for real insight and depth of information, meet your subject somewhere that shows something about his or her work or interests. Limit your use of e-mail to setting up an interview or verifying a fact of two. E-mail interviews reveal little.

- **Well focused.** Enter an interview with a clear sense of what your goals are. Are you looking for insight and explanation? Are you looking for facts? And do you have a clear sense of your subject? An interview is not a fishing expedition.

- **Polite but controlled.** Be friendly, but don't be a friend. Don't mistake an interview for a conversation. Your job is to gather information, to learn something. So you should listen much more than you talk. If the answers veer off course, politely lead your subject back to what you came to talk about.

- **Thorough.** Never leave an interview without asking the questions you came to ask. And before you close your notebook, ask if there's anything else your subject wants to share, ask for a phone number so you can check back if you have further questions, and be sure to leave your subject a number where you can be reached.

ADDITIONAL READING

The Art of the Interview: *Lessons from a Master of the Craft*, Lawrence Grobel, Three Rivers Press, 2004.

Creative Interviewing: *The Writer's Guide to Gathering Information by Asking Questions*, Ken Metzler, Allyn & Bacon, 1996.

The Interviewer's Handbook: A Guerrilla Guide: Techniques and Tactics for Reporters and Writers, John Brady, Kalmbach Publishing Company, 2004.

Interviews That Work: A Practical Guide for Journalists, Shirley Biagi, Wadsworth, 1991.

Talk Straight, Listen Carefully: The Art of Interviewing, M. L. Stein and Susan F. Paterno, Iowa State Press, 2001.

EXERCISE A

For each of the following interviews, write a list of the questions you would ask in roughly the order you would ask them. Then note any other people you would talk to before writing the story.

ONE

There is a crowd outside the police station chanting, "Conrad must go!" They hold up signs saying, "Kid Killer" and "Murderers belong in jail, not in blue." Three days ago, Police Officer Frederick Conrad reportedly shot and killed a 12-year-old boy. Police Chief Alan Rouchet has said Conrad reported that he thought the boy—who was walking through an alley when he was shot—was pulling a gun on him. Conrad had responded to a call for help after a delicatessen was robbed three blocks away. The shooting took place at 7:30 p.m. at twilight. Police accounts have not made clear what Conrad was doing in the alley. The boy, Peter Cairns, was shot in the head. The bullet entered above his left ear. No gun was found near the boy's body.

Conrad has been suspended from the force with pay, pending the outcome of a departmental investigation. You've dealt with him before, three years ago when he climbed a tree to rescue a cat that had been up there for 24 hours. He liked the feature you wrote. Conrad has been on the force five years. His record is free of prior disciplinary actions.

You haven't been covering the story (your beat is now city hall), but Conrad's lawyer called to say Conrad will give one interview—to you.

TWO

The sculpture has been smashed into—the police say they counted—132 pieces. Someone knocked it off its pedestal, in front of Amville City Hall, late at night two weeks ago. Police say it was smashed with a hammer after it fell. They report no suspects, but the words "Amville art for Amville" were sprayed in red paint on the sidewalk where the pieces of the sculpture lay. A number of local artists had protested the awarding of the commission for the sculpture three years ago to Ellen Dinkins, who lives in Holland. The sculpture—a representation of a pioneer woman—had been in place for only 18 days when it was smashed.

Dinkins is arriving in Amville today to investigate the chances of restoring or reconstructing her work, and she has agreed to an interview.

THREE

School board president Julia Hines has just made the following statement: "As you know, my opponent in next week's school board elections, Stanley Wise, has been running around saying, in essence, that he's going to turn Central High into a high school Harvard. Wise wants to change everything: If there's a computer in room 103, he'll move it to room 102. The football team will wear red shirts and white pants instead of white shirts and red pants. He says he's going to upgrade the level of education. Anyone familiar with education knows he's just going to create chaos.

"We've had a chance to look over Mr. Wise's record closely in the past weeks. He's certainly had a great career: president of his own trucking firm, director of the Ridge Road Country Club, father of two fine kids. The mystery is what he knows about education. He has a B.A.

in business; I've got a masters in education. He's worked in trucking; I've been a college professor. He's spent his spare time worrying about Ridge Road's sand traps; I served as president of the PTA. And I've had four years' experience at this job.

"Does Stanley Wise know anything about science education, advanced placement programs, accountability in education, physics labs, fitness programs, et cetera, et cetera? If he does, he must have read it in the newspaper."

A story on Hines' charges and Wise's response will appear in tomorrow's paper. You're interviewing Wise.

FOUR

Yesterday an overpass of the Spruce Highway—the most used road in the city—gave way, and a large truck fell 25 yards to Richard Road. The driver of the truck was killed, a section of the highway was closed in both directions, and traffic was backed up for more than five miles during the evening rush hour. The story in today's paper included speculation from Highway Department inspectors that rusting beams had caused the overpass to give way. City budget cuts have reduced the funds available for highway maintenance. Highway Commissioner Frank Elliott—who is responsible for local highways and traffic patterns—was not available for comment yesterday. He has agreed to an interview today.

FIVE

A student you know at the local high school calls with a tip: "Coach McKinley has done it again," he exclaims. "He just cut three of his best basketball players—of course, they happen to be the only Hispanics on the team."

You get a list of this year's players from your source and use the phone book to call the homes of as many as possible. You reach two, including Willie Alvarado, a starting forward and one of the players cut. "The man had two standards," Alvarado says. "Yes, I was late to practice a few times and I missed a curfew, but so have other players. But he didn't see it that way. Twice he said, 'Willie, you're different. It's going to be tougher on you out there so you've got to be that much better.' He also told me I'm talented but that talent needs to lead. Then he pretty much stopped talking to me, and after I came late one day he just said, 'That's it.' There's no room for discussion with that man."

You ask about the other two players cut, Albert Reyes and Juan Ramon. "I don't know what he had against them," Alvarado says. "He claims they just aren't good enough, but I think that's bull. They may not be stars but they're solid players. I really think he sacked them because they stood up for me. McKinley can't tolerate anyone who stands up to him on anything."

The other player you reach is John Richman, a sophomore who sees limited playing time. "McKinley has always been fair to me," he says. "He's really hard driving, but that's why this school has had winning teams for the ten years he's been here. We're one of the smallest schools in the division, too."

He balks when you ask about the three players kicked off the team, but cautiously answers when you assure him his name won't be used in the paper. "McKinley's an egomaniac," he says. "He's a talented egomaniac but he's an egomaniac. He wants things done his way or not at all. All three of those guys wanted some basic respect. They wanted to be treated like individuals with individual needs. To McKinley, every player is a member of a team. They have roles, not personalities. . . . But is the guy a bigot? I just don't think so."

You call McKinley and he says it's true that he dropped three members of the team: "It's a long story," he says. "Their behavior was simply not up to the standards that we require of people who are going to represent this school. Why don't you stop by and we'll talk about it."

You agree and on the way you check the clips. An article dated five years ago reports that students staged a sit-in in his office one afternoon to protest what they said was his policy of not playing the Hispanics on the team.

EXERCISE B

Write stories based on the following interview assignments.

1. Interview the person responsible for security at a local library or bookstore about the problem of book theft and possible ways to prevent it.
2. Interview a successful student athlete about the pressures involved in combining training with academic work.
3. Interview a local bar owner about how drunks and minors looking to buy alcohol are handled.
4. Interview a police official responsible for investigations about the problems of dealing with informants.
5. Interview a representative of a high school or college English or journalism department about reports of declining writing skills among students.
6. Interview the manager of a local supermarket or grocery store about changes in customers' buying habits.
7. Interview an official of a community or university counseling service about changing attitudes toward psychological counseling.
8. Interview the owner of a new business about the problems and challenges of getting started.
9. Interview the manager of a local movie theater about local tastes in films.
10. Interview a fire department official about the problem of false alarms.

EXERCISE C

Write a story based on the following collection of information. You are writing for a newspaper dated tomorrow and read in the city where the events occurred.

Text of an interview today with Pottstown Police Chief Daniel Workman:

Reporter: "We just got a call saying you're quitting. Anything to that?"

Workman: "Well, yes. I just told my staff today. I gave my resignation today to Mayor Joseph Ashburn."

Reporter: "Why?"

Workman: "Well, it's quite simple really. When I came here eight years ago I said my goal was to improve the morale of this staff and try to lower crime in this city. Well, it's been a tough eight years, even tougher than I expected, but they've been rewarding years, too. And the point is that I think I've done what I set out to do. Now it's time to move on."

Reporter: "Can you detail how you think things have changed?"

Workman: "Let's see. We have a staff of 28 full-time officers here. They were quitting at the rate of four a year in the five-year period before I arrived. Only two officers have quit in the past five years. I think that says something about morale."

Reporter: "And the crime rate?"

Workman: "Well, you know we instituted this "crime watch" program here six years ago—where citizens are encouraged to stay alert for crime, particularly burglars. Since then the rate of burglaries in the city has declined 31 percent."

Reporter: "If you believe things are going so well, why leave?"

Workman: "As I said, it's time to move on. I'm 45 years old. I think there might be a couple of more challenges ahead for this old boy before he hangs them up for good."

Reporter: "What kind of challenges are you looking for?"

Workman: "Well, you know, I don't think I want to get too specific on that just yet. I want to stay in law enforcement, though."

Reporter: "There's been talk that you're in line for the post of police chief in Omaha. Any truth to that?"

Workman: "Well, I've talked to them. But I assure you I have no definite job offers at this time."

Reporter: "When will you be leaving?"

Workman: "I've told Ashburn I'll stay until my replacement arrives."

Reporter: "Any idea who that will be?"

Workman: "No."

Reporter: "Is there anything else you have to say about this?"

Workman: "No."

Reporter: "Can I give you a call if any other questions come up?"

Workman: "Sure, glad to help."

Text of an interview today with Mayor Joseph Asburn:

Reporter: "How's it going? Heard you had a bit of a shocker today...."

Ashburn: "I'm with you there. It was bad news for this city. We're going to miss Dan Workman. He has been an outstanding police chief for us. But I understand his decision, and wish him the best of luck. You can say I accepted his resignation with a good deal of regret."

Reporter: "Where's he going?"

Ashburn: "Hey, you know I couldn't tell you that, even if I knew. That's Dan's business."

Reporter: "Who's going to get his job?"

Ashburn: "We'll begin working on that tomorrow. Right now I don't have any idea. It could be someone now on the force; it could be an outsider. Those are going to be hard shoes to fill."

PART 5 **COVERAGE**

The collapse of the Cypress viaduct in Oakland, Calif. This shot was taken Oct. 17, 1989, immediately after the elevated roadway collapsed in the Loma Prieta earthquake.
(Courtesy of the San Jose Mercury News*)*

Obituaries

Death is probably the oldest regularly covered news story. In some preliterate societies the relatives of the deceased immediately take to wailing. This serves both to satisfy the heavens and to notify everyone within hearing distance that a tribe member is no longer with them. We spread this news through obituaries.

Obituaries also serve as a final remembrance of a person's life. They provide, in the words of the late Alden Whitman, who turned obituary writing into something of an art form at *The New York Times*, "all the characteristics of a well-focused snapshot," capturing the character and personality of subjects, as well as their achievements.

FORM

Obituaries are the most formalized stories in newspapers. Most follow a standard pattern, which is why they often are the first stories assigned many news clerks and beginning reporters. But the form can be as entrapping as it is reassuring. Just as young composers can follow the design of a fugue to perfection and still create bad music, obit writers can master the form of an obituary and still fail to capture the essence of a subject's life. "Many obituaries suffer from dullness," warns Whitman in his book *Come to Judgment* (see Additional Reading). "They are little more than...a *curriculum vitae* wrestled into print."

Still, learning the form of a fugue or of an obituary is a starting point to composing such a work successfully.

Claim to Fame

For the purpose of our obituaries, each of us is assumed to have had a *claim to fame*. Some of us have accomplished a great deal:

> Thurgood Marshall, *pillar of the civil rights revolution, architect of the legal strategy that ended the era of official segregation and the first black justice of the Supreme Court,* died yesterday.
>
> The New York Times

Most of our accomplishments prove more modest. But even if our "fame" does not extend beyond immediate family and business associates, we all have some attribute or, as would be the case with a noted criminal, some flaw worth noting.

Jane Fonda's claim to fame will probably be that she was an Academy Award–winning actress known for her outspoken support of liberal political causes and her energetic and commercial advocacy of physical fitness. Eminem's claim to fame may be that he helped bring hip-hop into the mainstream. Bud Miller, a long-time grocer in Shamberg, will be recorded as "a grocer who worked for 38 years in Shamberg."

This is no time to get nasty. Miller's claim to fame is not that he had a reputation for drinking too much. But obituary writers do have to be honest. For all his years in office, Richard Nixon's claim to fame at his death was anything but laudatory.

> Richard Milhous Nixon, the 37th President of the United States, who was the only President in more than two centuries of American history to resign from office, died last night at New York Hospital-Cornell Medical Center.
>
> *The New York Times*

"Saints we are not in life," wrote Whitman. "Nor should we be in death."

However unusual it is, the claim to fame goes in the lead. Traditionally, it is compressed into a phrase in the first paragraph:

> Sybil Leek, *who proclaimed herself a witch and wrote and lectured widely on the occult, the mystical and the supernatural*, died of cancer yesterday at the Holmes Regional Medical Center in Melbourne, Fla. She was 65 years old.
>
> *The New York Times*

However, obituaries increasingly are being topped with nontraditional leads, which often take a slightly more leisurely approach to telling the story of a person's life:

> STILLWATER, Okla.—Henry Iba began playing basketball on the dirt courts of rural Missouri, wearing uniforms sewed by his mother. He became one of the great coaches in history, a man whose influence is still felt amid the glitz of today's multimillion-dollar game.
> Iba died of heart failure early yesterday. He was 88.
>
> Associated Press in *The Philadelphia Daily News*

People's claim to fame may have nothing to do with their recent past. When Constance Carpenter died at the age of 87, she was remembered for a Broadway role she had made famous 41 years earlier:

> Constance Carpenter, an actress *whose roles included a starring performance opposite Yul Brynner in the original Broadway production of "The King and I,"* died on Saturday at Lenox Hill Hospital in Manhattan. She was 87....
>
> *The New York Times*

Age and Cause of Death

These are two topics about which people get secretive. Age is still a touchy subject for some of us. And some causes of death—particularly cancer, for reasons that are difficult to comprehend, and AIDS, because of homophobia—are viewed as something of an embarrassment.

Reporters have to press, firmly, if politely, to get this information from a funeral home or from family. Obituaries are news. Readers deserve to know at what age and why someone died. When, for example, AIDS is repeatedly underreported as a cause of death, the disease's true toll is hidden from the public. A few newspapers have now gone so far as to refuse to print obituaries unless relatives are willing to divulge the age and cause of death.

The Knight-Ridder news service took extra care in an obituary that appeared in *The (Charleston, S.C.) State* to print both the officially released cause and the apparent underlying reason this well-known person died:

> Rudolph Nureyev, the titan of dance, died Wednesday in a Paris hospital.
>
> The Russian-born dancer, 54, was widely reported to have been suffering from AIDS. He died of "cardiac complications, following a cruel illness," said Michel Canesi, his physician. Canesi added, "In accordance with Mr. Nureyev's wishes, I can't say any more."

When age and cause of death are included in an obit, they belong in, or right after, the lead.

Developing the Claim to Fame

If an obituary is long enough—some run only a few grafs—the reporter's next job is to provide some more details about that claim to fame. In essence, the reporter supports the lead just as is done in any news story (see Chapter 9, Organization):

> Leek, a native of Stoke-on-Trent, Staffordshire, England, once described herself in an interview as "just an ordinary witch from the New Forest of England," saying her family had been involved in witchcraft since 1134....
>
> Leek wrote more than 60 books, including "The Diary of a Witch," published in 1968, and works on numerology, phrenology and astrology. One of her most recent books, written with Bert R. Sugar, was "The Assassination Chain," which discussed theories behind the assassinations of President Kennedy, Robert Kennedy and Martin Luther King.
>
> *The New York Times*

Chronology

At some point, the obituary, again provided there is sufficient space, will jump back to the beginning of someone's life and detail major events such as birth, marriage, degrees and jobs—in chronological order:

> Born March 17, 1938, supposedly on a train traveling near the Mongolian border, he grew up in the industrial city of Ufa, in the Urals. His parents were poor, and his father, a soldier, disapproved of the boy's inclinations toward dancing.
>
> Young Rudolf persisted, however, studying wherever he got the chance. He did not receive first-rate training until 1955 when, at the advanced age of 17, he was admitted at the academy attached to Kirov Ballet in Leningrad....
>
> *Knight-Ridder News Service in The State*

Survivors

Any obit, at the end, will include a paragraph naming the person's closest relatives and often telling where they live. Newspapers generally have their own rules on who is mentioned and who is left out. Wives and husbands, children and parents always are named. Siblings usually are. Grandparents and grandchildren generally are not, although the number of them surviving sometimes is mentioned.

Pet dogs, no matter how beloved, don't make the list, nor do cousins. Either a spouse who has died previously or the closest living relative—usually a spouse, parents or children—comes first in the list of survivors. Previous marriages normally are noted, but the names of divorced husbands and wives aren't included among the surviving family members.

Sybil Leek's husband died before she did:

> Her husband, Brian Leek, died in England in 1974. She is survived by two sons, Stephen, of West Palm Beach, Fla., and Julian, of Melbourne Beach, Fla., and two grandchildren.
>
> *The New York Times*

Funeral Arrangements

Particularly in smaller cities, a significant proportion of readers may want to know what they can do to pay their respects. The final paragraph or two of a local obituary almost always will be devoted to information on who is handling the funeral, when it will be and whether the family would appreciate donations to a favorite charity.

Here is how the front-page obituary of Ernest W. Hahn, a California developer, ended:

> A rosary is to be recited at 7 p.m. today at the Immaculata Catholic Church at the University of San Diego. A Mass is planned for 11 a.m. Wednesday, followed by a private burial service.
>
> *San Jose Mercury News*

Lessons from the Pros

Julie Polovina, intern

Julie Polovina had just started a six-month internship at *The Boston Globe* when she was assigned her first story. She wasn't sent to a fire or told to race to a crime scene. She was handed a press release from a funeral home that said a prominent Boston lawyer had died.

Polovina's first instinct was to interview the man's family and learn more about his life outside the courtroom. She discovered that he hadn't gone to law school until his late 20s, didn't marry until he was 39, and, at age 70, joined a rowing program.

With these details in hand (they would become the second paragraph of her story), she began the obituary like this:

> Willard "Bill" Stievater was a late bloomer.
>
> *The Boston Globe*

Julie Polovina, intern,
The Boston Globe.
(Courtesy of *The Boston Globe*)

Many a new reporter in the newsroom has been judged by how well they've marked the passage of someone's life. Polovina, for one, found the obituary desk a terrific first experience.

"It's really good training for writing a news story," Polovina says. "You have to interview family members, and they can be a tough interview that takes sensitivity. You have to gather facts, and you have to put together a story that tells somebody's life."

Polovina honed her ear for colorful quotes and learned to triple-check all facts. And finding the right "claim to fame"—what made her subject interesting—helped her sharpen her overall news judgment.

In writing obituaries for *The Globe,* Polovina always tried to heed the advice assistant Metro editor Janet Walsh gives all the paper's interns when they sit down to report and write an obituary. Among Walsh's tips were:

- **Check—and recheck—your facts.** Mistakes of any kind tarnish a newspaper's reputation. Mistakes in obituaries can devastate already grieving families.

- **Convey the essence of the person's life.** It is the specific details of someone's life and achievement that bring their past to life.
- **Don't shy from public controversy.** If a person's failings are what they're known for, they belong in an obituary as in any other story.
- **Always confirm the person has really died.** More than one newspaper has been burned by a planted hoax announcing someone's premature death.
- **Be sensitive.** The reporter who can skillfully interview members of a bereaved family will likely have similar success at accident and disaster scenes.

GETTING THE INFORMATION

During his 12 years as an obituary writer at *The Times*, Alden Whitman traveled across continents interviewing movie stars, prime ministers, authors and presidents, and returned to write obituaries thousands of words long that were stored in *The Times'* files until the subjects died. (*The Times* has about a thousand advance obituaries on file.)

However, few obituary writers have the luxury of getting to know the people they will eventually be asked to write about. Instead they usually rely on facts phoned in to the paper by the local funeral director handling the arrangements. These facts may be the only information available or necessary for a three- or four-paragraph obituary. But reporters should still remember to check the clip files just to make sure some newsworthy fact about a person is not being missed. (See Chapter 14, Research.)

If there will be room for a story more than a few paragraphs long, a reporter should push for more information. In some cases, magazine articles or books have been written by or about the person who has just died. That person also may be listed in the series of biographical books called *Who's Who* or in some other biographical index. It's all right to google a person for leads as well. But don't rely on it. There's nothing authoritative about a funny story about the deceased on his brother Bob's blog (if, in fact, that really is his brother).

Speaking of family members, there is no substitute for calls to them, along with friends, doctors and business associates to gather facts, anecdotes and quotes that help develop that "well-focused snapshot" Alden Whitman always tried for:

> Keven McKenzie, artistic director of the American Ballet Theater, said Nureyev's contribution was inestimable: "He was responsible not only for bringing ballet to the awareness of the general public but for single-handedly creating legions of dance fans over four decades."

The Knight-Ridder News Service also drew on past printed interviews in compiling its obituary of Nureyev:

> Nureyev attributed the force of his personality on stage to his Tartar blood, which he said "somehow runs faster." Some of his colleagues said he simply jumped higher than anyone else. But his most famous partner, the late Margot Fonteyn, believed that the Nureyev magic had to do with transformation.
>
> "When I am dancing with him," she once said, "I don't see, as I do with others, a man I know and talk to every day. I see the ballet. He is how I would like to dance."

ENTERPRISE

The term *enterprise* is used in this book to refer to stories on which reporters spend extra time and effort, stories in which they attempt to give readers a deeper look into events than may be possible in routine news gathering under deadline pressure. There is room for such enterprise even within the confines of a format as tight as that of the obituary. The best obit writers distinguish themselves through the thoroughness of their research, through the quality of their description and quotes, and through their ability to communicate the texture, as well as the highlights, of someone's life.

This is from an obituary on the newspaper publisher Samuel I. Newhouse:

> Despite the vast scope of his holdings, Newhouse was an unobtrusive man, with no central office except his battered brown briefcase. He preferred to live and do business relatively quietly. "That's the advantage of being a shrimp," the 5-foot, 3-inch, self-described "newspaper businessman" once said. "Nobody notices you."
>
> Moreover, unlike some press lords, Newhouse did not use his newspapers as a megaphone to expound his thinking on public matters.
>
> "I am not interested in molding the nation's opinion," he said. "I want these newspapers to take positive stands of their own; I want them to be self-reliant...."
>
> *The New York Times*

CHAPTER 17 SUMMARY: OBITUARIES

The best obituaries capture a person's life. They are in some ways the most important articles any newspaper writes, recording and recounting the lives of those who have passed on. Obituaries demand thorough research; sensitive reporting; and careful, accurate and at times colorful writing.

In writing an obituary:

- Report thoroughly and sensitively. Like all newspaper articles, obituaries are built on facts.
- Mine clips and other accounts of the person's life. Then seek information and quotes from those who best knew the person who died.
- In writing your lead, identify a person's "claim to fame," the contribution, positive or negative, for which that individual will be best remembered. Crafting the claim to fame in the lead is perhaps the obituary writer's greatest challenge.
- Include selective details and stories that elaborate on that claim to fame and, in a sense, bring the subject to life. The key word here is *selective*. An obituary is not a résumé of someone's entire life.
- Remember that an obituary is news. Such information as a person's age, the place of death and the cause of death should be obtained and included high in the obituary.
- Use chronology as a means of organization after you've established the person's claim to fame.

ADDITIONAL READING

Come to Judgment, Alden Whitman, Viking Press, 1980.

The Dead Beat: Lost Souls, Lucky Stiffs, and the Perverse Pleasures of Obituaries, Marilyn Johnson, HarperCollins, 2006.

EXERCISE A
Writing Assignments

Write obituaries based on the following collections of facts. In each case, the obituary is being written for tomorrow's paper in the town in which the person lived. All of them died on the day you are writing.

ONE

The editor tells you Charles L. Maxwell, a photographer who used to own The Photo Shop on Dexter Street here in Easton, has died. He tells you to take down the information from funeral director Frank Mansfield at Oberhurst Funeral Home:

"Charles L. Maxwell, 87. He died in his home after a long illness. What illness? Well, I guess the family won't mind. He had lung cancer. Lived at 207 High St. He was born in Springfield, Wisconsin, and went to high school there. Attended U. of Wisconsin in Madison and served in the army after he graduated. He married June Bailey in 1946 and moved here that year. He'd learned photography in the army apparently. Anyway, he worked as a freelance photographer for eight years and in 1954 he opened The Photo Shop. Ran it by himself for five years and gradually expanded to where it had seven employees when he sold it in 1981. His wife, June, would help in the summer. She taught English at the high school.

"Maxwell was an active guy. He was a member of the Masons and a former vice president of the Rotary Club. He also helped design stage sets for the local theater group, The Prime-Time Players. Nice fellow. A couple of hundred people came to his house a few years back when he and June celebrated their 50th.

"June's still alive. He also had two sons; Brock lives in Houston and Larry lives at 12 Pepper Drive right here in town. Brock has three kids, Daniel, Susan and Leila. His wife's name is Anna. Larry has no kids. Isn't married for that matter. Maxwell is at the funeral home now. Friends can stop by here Friday from 9 to 11 a.m. and 3 to 6 p.m. The funeral will be Saturday at St. Luke's Catholic Church on Sellars Street. It's at 10 a.m. Oh, our address is 95 Hanneman Road. Burial will be for the family only."

You check the clips and find the only piece on Maxwell was a brief item that appeared on the People Page in 1967. Seems his hobby was photographing kids. He is quoted there as saying: "Their faces are alive. The joys, the anguish, the love are there for everyone to see."

TWO

From Sheila Benson, the funeral director at Van Saun Funeral Home, 69 Webster St.:

"Esther Randolph. She died in a head-on automobile accident on Route 7 near Bennington, Vt. She was spending the week with her son. Her home here in Croton Lake was at 17 Roundabout Drive. Here's what we have: Born, July 9, 1916, in Pottstown, Pa. She was married in 1944. Her husband, Lionel, died in 1990. She has two sons, Jack Randolph of Bennington, Vt., and Lionel Randolph Jr. of Philadelphia, Pa. Neither has kids. Her maiden name was Bell, and her parents' first names were James and Elaine. They're both dead. Background? She went to high school in Pottstown, Pa. Earned a degree in nursing from

Thomas Jefferson University's School of Nursing and did graduate work at Johns Hopkins University. Worked at the Veterans Hospital in Philadelphia during World War II. In 1952 she joined the Red Cross in Philadelphia and served as its director of nursing services.

"Later she became a specialist in, what do you call it, nursing recruitment. Let's see, she moved to this neck of the woods in 1959. In 1960 she became director of the Red Cross in the southeast portion of the state and then six years later, that was in 1966, she took a job with the state health department, where she was hired to set up the Community Nursing Services in the state. I've got here that this was the first time anyone had found a way to help the elderly poor people who were sick with home nursing. Here is how it was set up: Elderly people who couldn't afford a private nurse could contact the state and arrange for a nurse to visit them at their home. The service was for up to eight hours a day, and the nurses would do all sorts of things—prepare meals, change bedding, you name it. It kept a lot of people out of the hospital. Mrs. Randolph ran the program—she was its director—from 1966 to 1970, coming over from the Red Cross. Then she supervised all community health programs for the state from 1970 to 1980, but still spent most of her time on that Community Nursing Services. Other programs were flu clinics, an educational program for the high schools, the Doctors on Wheels clinic. She retired in 1980.

"Awards? She got lots of awards. The latest was a leadership award from the American Association of Nurses when she retired. Let's see. She was a charter member of the National Association for the Advancement of Colored People and a member of the American Civil Liberties Union and the American Association of Nurses."

You check the newspaper's clips and find an article on the Community Nursing Services from 1972. It quotes Mrs. Randolph: "No one wants to fill a hospital bed. If we can bring nursing care to people in their homes, we'll cut medical costs, free hospital beds and help make the elderly healthy. There's no better medicine than to live in your own home." Article confirms funeral director's information.

You call M. Fremont Louis, commissioner of the state Department of Health, and a colleague of Mrs. Randolph's for many years. He's glad to talk.

"It's hard to think of Esther as dead," he says. "She was a dynamo. Always helping people and never looking for credit for it. I saw her last month, and she was still running rings around people half her age. She did everything to start that Community Nursing Services program. She wrote the federal grant proposal, she recruited the nurses to work in it and she publicized it through the senior citizens' community centers. The elderly and public health care in this state owe her a lot."

A callback to the funeral director is necessary to confirm that Randolph will be buried Friday at All Saints Cemetery on 12th St. That's after they hold the service at 10 a.m. at All Saints Episcopal Church on 12th Street. The family says it doesn't want any flowers sent. Instead, it suggests donations be made to the National Health Council.

THREE

From Fred Logan, funeral director at Logan Funeral Home on 499 Broadway:

"Sun Tang Koo died in his home here in Redwood City...lived at 3144 Shore Blvd. He was 99. Quite a fellow. He graduated from the U.S. Army Corps of Engineers college equivalent training program in 1929...traveled to China by ship the next year.... Taught at Tsing-Hua University in Beijing from 1929 to 1931. Then he taught at the University of Shanghai from 1931 to 1953. He taught civil engineering at both places. He was an elder at the First Presbyterian Church in Shanghai. He was actually born in the U.S., incidentally. In San Francisco. Anyway, he returned to the U.S. in 1953 and taught Chinese studies as a lecturer at

San Francisco State University from 1953 to 1975. He was something of a self-taught expert on China. His book, "The Rise and Fall of Nationalist China," was published by Putnam in 1963....He contributed articles on civil engineering, China and Christianity to a number of international journals. He was also a member of the Chinese Christian Fellowship and president of the Fellowship of Chinese-American Understanding from 1967 to 1974 in San Francisco. He was a member of the West Side Presbyterian Church here. Services will be at the church on Wednesday at 10 a.m. That's at Geiger Square. Burial's going to be after the service at Willows Cemetery on Route 46. The family doesn't want flowers. Suggests that contributions be made to the Fellowship of Chinese-American Understanding in San Francisco instead. His wife, Kim, is still alive. He also leaves three children, two sons, William and Peter, and a daughter, Ellen Alpert. All of them live in San Francisco. He had seven grandchildren and three great-grandchildren. He died of cancer."

You call Lois Richmond, a long-time professor of Chinese studies at San Francisco State: "Yes, I knew him. We still corresponded, occasionally. He was something of a legend when he taught here. A true renaissance man. He didn't have any of the degrees of the rest of us, but I've never known anyone who knew more about China and its people. He also did a great deal to improve Chinese–American relations in the Bay area. He personally worked out a compromise busing plan when the Chinese community downtown objected to being bused five miles to school in the suburbs. Instead, an exchange program was worked out with another city school."

Kim moved here in 1980.

FOUR

You are in the office of Mayor Tom Jackson when you learn that Michael Lazar, chairman of the planning board, has died of a heart attack. He was just 67. Died in his home at 9 Dickerson Terrace here in Ducayne.

Jackson: "He should have listened to his doctor. He's been telling Mike to lose 45 pounds for a number of years now. But Mike did everything in excess. He ate well, he drank well and he fought hard for this town. Mike Lazar loved this community like few people do. He understood the history here and, I mean, practically convinced the merchants single-handedly to restore the downtown. Look at business today. Up 50 percent from five years ago. I'd like to take the credit but I can't. He'll be sorely missed and impossible to replace."

You stop down at the Planning Office and tell Martha McCarthy, the office secretary, the news. She says: "His temper did him in. Boy, could he blow. But he was as tough on himself as anyone. If we didn't have something for a meeting he could go through the roof. But he was just as quick with praise as he was with criticism."

You call John DeLuca, a Republican council member, because you know Lazar, like Jackson, was a Democrat. He says: "It's a real loss. Mike fought hard but clean. And he was full of new ideas. Frankly, we asked him to run for council as a Republican but he didn't want to hold elected office for anyone."

DeLuca agrees that Lazar was instrumental in restoring the downtown business district in 1989. So does Rita Tandy, who owns Tandy's Antiques. "He'd come by and say, 'Look, you want business, then help yourself. Strip off this ugly paint, put some trees out front, get some nice storefronts.' After a while the Merchants Association began to listen, and he helped us get some state Historical Preservation funds. He was the spark-plug who got us started."

You call Hannemann Funeral Home, 88 Sickles Ave., for more information. Find out Lazar has lived here since he was 5. Moved with his family from Durango, Colo., where he was born. Went to the local elementary and high schools and then to University of Chicago and University of Chicago Law School. Served in the Air Force. Was stationed in Germany. Returned in 1970 and opened his own law firm. Mainly did real estate and personal law. Appointed to the planning board in 1987. Chairman since 1990.

His wife Mae and daughter Anne live at home. His son Thomas lives in Nyack, N.Y., and another son, Peter, lives in Boulder, Colo., where he's in graduate school. A second daughter, Heather Wilson, lives in St. Louis and owns a boutique. Lazar also has three sisters. We don't know their names. And three grandchildren.

He is going to be buried at Friends of Israel Cemetery Friday, but the public is not invited. There will be a memorial service at City Hall Saturday at 10 in the morning.

EXERCISE B
Story Assignments

1. Write an obituary of yourself. Assume that you died yesterday of a heart attack and that services will be held at a local funeral home. Otherwise, stay true to the facts of your life. You can interview friends, relatives, employers and teachers for quotes.

2. Choose a person from your area in one of the following categories and write an obituary of that person based on interviews with people who know him or her. (You might tell people you are working on a profile rather than an obituary.) Choose a sudden heart attack as the cause of death and a local funeral home for the funeral.

a. mayor
b. a school superintendent
c. a barber
d. a chef
e. a judge

f. a corporation president
g. a member of the clergy
h. an artist
i. a scientist
j. a professor

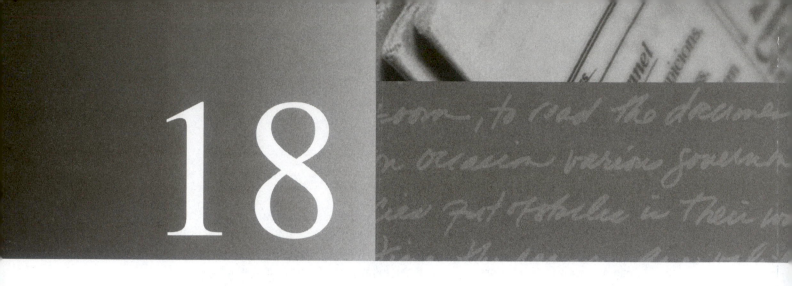

Meetings, Speeches and Press Conferences

Things got out of hand at the Sherrodsville, Ohio, Village Council meeting:

> The mayor was attacked, the village solicitor was pummeled, the fire station's pool table collapsed, a village councilman was charged with assault and the councilman's father was hospitalized with a heart attack.
>
> "I'm not used to having that kind of breakdown in authority," said the solicitor, Brad Hillyer, after last night's council meeting [at the fire station] in this northeastern Ohio village.
>
> Associated Press

The meetings that government bodies, school boards and other organizations hold; the speeches their officials make; and the press conferences that these officials call generally are quieter—and safer—affairs than this tumultuous meeting over a proposal to disband the two-man Sherrodsville Police Department. Mayors are not usually attacked. Village solicitors are rarely pummeled. Still, these functions are major sources of news. This chapter explains how to cover them.

MEETINGS

Most of the business of organizations, from the U.S. Senate to the Ridgewood Shade Tree Commission, is taken care of at meetings. That means reporters, inevitably, will spend much of their time sitting in the audience.

Reporters covering their first meeting are often so impressed by the attention the participants are paying to matters ranging from the selection of a new deputy assistant parks commissioner to the proper hour to begin next week's meeting that they return to write a thousand-word stenographic account of what went on. Usually it will end up being reduced to a few paragraphs by a grim-faced editor. Obviously, it's better to exercise news judgment beforehand.

What should be included in a story about a meeting? What's important to look for? Here are a few tips.

Keep a Tight Focus

The council may have passed three ordinances last night, but unless they were awfully important, the lead and most of the story are going to be devoted to the fact that council members voted to fire the police chief. Reporters have to remember that their job is not to keep the minutes of the meeting but to pick out one or two newsworthy developments to share with readers.

Unacceptable:

The Wilmar City Council last night voted unanimously to rename Carter Street, hired a new secretary and defeated a plan to monitor downtown with closed-circuit cameras.

Acceptable:

The Wilmar City Council last night rejected a plan that would have made Wilmar the first small city in the United States to use closed-circuit TV cameras to monitor its downtown area.

The Minneapolis Star and Tribune

It's always a mistake to return to the newsroom from a meeting with a couple of paragraphs worth of information on each of the five or ten items that were discussed. A coherent story can't be constructed out of such a hodgepodge. At some point as the meeting progresses, reporters have to decide what their story is likely to focus on. Then they must gather enough information on that subject to make sure they can treat it thoroughly, even if that means slighting one or more less newsworthy agenda items.

Don't Just Sit There

The news at a meeting will usually be found in the more heated debates between participants and in the votes that follow those debates:

The Los Angeles City Council voted 9 to 4 to approve an agreement over noise control with the Burbank-Glendale-Pasadena Airport Authority despite strong objections from some members of the council that the agreement has no teeth.

Under the terms of the agreement, the airport authority will attempt to reroute departing flights away from city neighborhoods....

Los Angeles Times

Nevertheless, covering a meeting well will require more than just jotting down who says what and tallying the votes. Reporters will want to have prepared themselves before the meeting begins with information from sources and documents, and they will use breaks in the meeting to solicit additional quotes and explanations from the participants. Participants can also be corralled when the meeting ends. And after the meeting, good reporters will attempt to contact anyone not in attendance who was directly affected by a decision taken—the police chief who was fired, for example. (With deadlines approaching, these follow-up interviews are usually conducted by telephone.)

Shortly after the council vote on that airport-noise-control agreement, the *Los Angeles Times* reporter was able to speak with a particularly important source:

Charles Aalff, the Federal Aviation Administration's air traffic manager for the airport, said in an interview that the change in direction requires aircraft maneuvering, to get quickly above nearby mountains, that many planes may not be equipped to do so safely....

Don't Ignore the Audience

Sometimes the audience's behavior is the most interesting aspect of a meeting. If the audience is unusually large or small, count it. The number becomes part of the story. And note applause, jeers, catcalls or unruliness. The reporter who covered that Village Council meeting in Sherrodsville also had to note that a councilman's father, sitting in the audience, had a heart attack; that the councilman's wife, also in the audience, then began yelling, "Are you people satisfied?" at the mayor; and that the councilman allegedly jumped at the mayor, causing both men to fall on a pool table, which collapsed.

At more orderly meetings, there is often a special slot in the agenda for audience complaints or suggestions. These comments frequently lead to stories, whether they represent the views of one frustrated citizen or of an organized and indignant group:

> Rosemary Donohue called it an incentive to clean out her garage.
> Barney Walsh called it a constitutional right.
> And to another Glen Rock resident, a garage sale seemed "as American an institution as apple pie."
> A coalition of private property protectionists, weekend browsers and peddlers joined forces in Glen Rock last night to win at least a temporary victory over a Borough Council attempt to restrict that bastion of free enterprise—the garage sale.
>
> The (Bergen County, N.J.) *Record*

Find Out What's Next

There is often a long distance between a council or board's discussion of a proposal and a final decision. Sometimes discussions drag on without any formal action. Sometimes organizations vote to *table* issues—postpone them to another date. And even if a proposal is passed the first time it is considered, it may have to go through a public hearing and a final vote.

Reporters must always find out what happens next: When will the issue be reconsidered? When is the hearing scheduled? Is the mayor's signature required before the proposal becomes law? This information should be placed prominently in stories (see Chapter 10, Background and Context):

> A proposed $17 million bond issue to pay for a five-year capital improvement program apparently will be submitted to Roanoke voters in a November referendum.
> The City Council voted yesterday to schedule a public hearing to get citizens' views on the proposed bond issue.... The hearing will be June 25 at 2 p.m.
>
> Roanoke (Va.) *Times & World-News*

The work of covering a meeting often begins well before the meeting actually takes place. Reporters will want to call some of the participants to see what is scheduled. Sometimes there's something controversial on the agenda:

> Paramus Mayor Joseph Cipolla wants to rid his community of smut. He thinks it offends the "average person" with average community standards. But a tough pornography ordinance that he and the Borough Council are expected to introduce tonight has sharply divided many presumably "average" people.
>
> The (Bergen County, N.J.) *Record*

The best way to cover a meeting, of course, is to attend it. But reporters staring at a list of the meetings held in a large town—meetings of the waterfront board, the environmental commission, the Memorial Day committee—quickly realize that they will want to call around to see what is scheduled. The presence of a controversial item on the agenda may itself be news:

Jim Flagg, who covers city hall for *The Express* in Easton, Pa., gets agendas of all city meetings sent to his offices as soon as they are printed. He follows up by checking with people who will attend or have attended. The best practice is to place two phone calls—one before the meeting and one after. The first call—"What am I going to miss?"—might go to someone on the board that's meeting or to the public official that board oversees. (The full-time health officer might know more about what the Board of Health will discuss tonight than the citizens who volunteer for the board.) The follow-up call after the meeting—"What did I miss?"—obviously must go to someone who attended.

If something newsworthy did in fact take place, many additional phone calls will follow.

Not All Meetings Provide News

Many regional newspapers are pushing reporters to cut down on the number of meetings they actually cover. These papers are looking for stories—about the environment or education, quality of life or public safety—that cut across several communities rather than being centered on one. They want more *enterprise news,* news that bubbles up from the community, and less official news. Even so, reporters new to a beat can't afford to ignore the public officials and engaged citizens who hold and attend meetings.

Meetings are high on the list of places where reporters meet new sources (see Chapter 15, Sources) and pick up on issues that demand development (see Chapter 13, Story Origination).

Lessons from the Pros: Getting Started

Andrea Gabbidon-Levene and Katie Oliveri

As a town reporter who began with *The New Jersey Herald* in Newton, N.J., right out of college, Andrea Gabbidon-Levene figured out quickly that meetings were a crucial part of the job. While covering her first meeting, she learned that one local town didn't have a generator to use if the community lost power. That in itself wasn't news for this regional newspaper. But after checking around in surrounding communities, Gabbidon-Levene discovered she was on to a trend of sorts: Other towns didn't have generators either.

Andrea Gabbidon-Levene, *The New Jersey Herald.* (Courtesy of The New Jersey Herald)

Katie Oliveri, *Battle Creek Inquirer.* (Courtesy of the Battle Creek Enquirer)

"It was an issue worth tackling because people living in this town watch TV and saw Hurricane Katrina and want to make sure they are not in a similar situation," she said.

Katie Oliveri covered 20 school districts in 15 towns, as well as higher education, in her first job out of college for the *Battle Creek Enquirer* in western Michigan. She also finds meetings helpful and sometimes important: "I think that education reporters should attend as many school board meetings as they can," she says. "I will attend them even if I am not

Lessons from the Pros: Getting Started (continued)

writing a story because that is when you find out what is going on with the school—changes with the curriculum, for example. And if you miss it, you may not get the information."

Gabbidon-Levene and Oliveri, who at Emerson College served as editor and managing editor, respectively, in putting out the college newspaper, offered these tips to young reporters:

- **Do your homework.** "You should never walk into a meeting not knowing what is going on," Gabbidon-Levene says. "It is always good to also call the mayor of the town before you go because it is hard to write an actual story without the background first."

- **Write before the meeting.** Many meetings end minutes before deadline, leaving new reporters clutching the phone and frantically leafing through their notes. One way to avoid this is to write early, to lay down background. "I do a lot of prewriting during day," Oliveri says. "If I know the board is considering curriculum changes, then I get the facts beforehand....I [write] some context so I can come back after the meeting and plug in just the details about what happened at the meeting."

- **Come prepared for a long night.** Oliveri says she never goes to a meeting hungry and always carries a water bottle. She also brings a tape recorder if she knows the meeting could be contentious. "Be prepared to be there, and don't be cranky," she says.

- **Pay attention.** "A lot of times the meetings are boring because [the participants] spend three hours on an issue they can't decide," Oliveri says. But, she warns, important information can turn up at any point of the meeting. The reporter who lets her mind wander may miss the moment the board lets slip that it is considering closing a school.

- **Get it right, even on tight deadlines.** "Take time after the meeting to make sure you have everything correct," Oliveri says. Names in particular are easy to misspell. Double-check names and titles.

SPEECHES AND PRESS CONFERENCES

People give speeches when they want to sell themselves, their organizations or their ideas.

COLUMBIA—Midway through her speech Monday, B. J. Reed, a member of S.C. Mothers Against Drunk Driving, broke from her prepared statement to relay a personal message to the crowd gathered at the Statehouse.

Reed was speaking at a rally in support of the Nov. 2 referendum question to strike the minibottle regulation from the state constitution. She told the crowd that on Nov. 2, 1996, her younger sister died in a car wreck caused by drunken driving.

"That day is always a sad occasion for our family," she said. "But this year, on that day, we have a chance to do something about this state's problem with drunk driving. If we vote 'yes' to the referendum, then maybe my sister's death will have some meaning."

The (Charleston, S.C.) *Post and Courier*

This story reported on a governor's annual State of the State speech:

Saying Ohioans are "battling for our economic survival," Gov. Bob Taft used his State of the State speech yesterday to advocate training 200,000 workers, limiting lawsuits to shield businesses...and creating a nonprofit corporation to market the Buckeye State.

The Columbus (Ohio) *Dispatch*

People hold a press conference when they have an announcement to pass on or when they have decided it's time to face reporters' questions:

> Keith Gilbertson's tenure as University of Washington football coach will end at the conclusion of the season, a decision that was announced Monday in a news conference attended by Gilbertson and UW athletic director Todd Turner.
>
> *The* (Portland) *Oregonian*

Reporters have two jobs: They have to pass along the speaker's message; but they also have to help readers examine that message.

Preparation

Speeches and press conferences are sometimes scheduled so close to deadline that reporters won't have time to pursue thoroughly whatever news the speaker makes. As with meetings, it helps to find out beforehand what's likely to be said. "If you can get the person holding it to preview for you—off the record—what *will* be said, it's a big help on deadline," says Jim Flagg, whose deadline for *The* (Easton, Pa.) *Express* is 11 a.m. "It allows you to prepare, check clips and line up a few people for interviews ahead of time."

Reporters may be able to obtain a draft of a major speech in advance—with the understanding that no story will appear on that speech until after it is given. This can be a help, but reporters must make sure they still follow what the speaker actually says. Big news can be made in variations from prepared texts.

Finding the News

Politicians and officials always have a purpose when they give a speech or hold a press conference. But reporters are there for their own purpose—to find the news. On some occasions, the news that reporters find in a speech or press conference is not what the newsmaker intended them to find:

> *Without offering specifics,* he pledged also to strengthen the program....
>
> *The New York Times*

This presidential candidate did not plan to have his lack of specifics highlighted.

Nor presumably was Ohio Gov. Bob Taft anxious to have *The Columbus Dispatch* highlight what he did not bring up in his State of the State address:

> To spark a turnaround, the two-term Republican offered no sweeping proposals or major new spending in a 31-minute speech that focused heavily on jobs and the economy. Instead, Taft called for tweaking existing programs, shifting state money, and revisiting two proposals that have languished in the legislature—lawsuit and tax reform.

The lead in a story about a speech might come from a remark two-thirds of the way through the address that contradicts something that person said a month ago; or reporters might choose to emphasize the reaction of the crowd or comments from the audience; or their stories might be based on answers to questions, not the speech or announcement itself.

Often the newsmaker's purpose and the reporter's purpose do coincide: The mayor has called a press conference to announce that the city will be constructing a new municipal swimming pool. Fine, that's news. But if the police chief emphasizes in a speech that the local burglary rate is down 3 percent and lets slip afterward that armed robberies have doubled in the last year, the reporter's story is going to focus on robberies, not burglaries.

Getting information and quotes from a speech or press conference, especially when no prepared text is available, will provide a stern test of reporters' note-taking abilities. (See Chapter 16, Interviewing.) The secret is to apply news judgment while taking notes and to jot down only potentially newsworthy material. The reporter's notes should not turn into a transcript or even a summary of all the points the speaker has made. Forget the governor's rhapsody on the beauty of this part of the state in springtime. Forget her tribute to the state's "hardworking law enforcement officials." But make sure you return from that speech prepared to write *in detail* about her attack on the mayor for wasting state funds.

Questions

When the questioning begins at a press conference or after a speech, a well-prepared reporter sometimes takes over. This is no time for timidity. Good questions are concise and to the point (see Chapter 16, Interviewing); they may be used to force the newsmaker to clarify or defend points that have been raised or to pursue issues the newsmaker seemed to ignore.

When the applause starts or the questioning stops, good reporters will usually be dashing for the podium to conduct a brief private interview with the politician or official. If possible, they will have arranged for such an opportunity beforehand. Alone with the newsmaker, reporters can pursue new angles, check quotes or ask questions they might not have wanted to share with the competition.

Follow-Up

The reporting of a speech or press conference often is not complete when the reporter leaves the room: The mayor has to be contacted for a reaction to the governor's charges; the clips have to be checked for background on the dispute.

When Easton's mayor and police chief held a press conference to announce that they had broken a *police* burglary ring, they dutifully disclosed the charges that had been filed against police officers but said little else. Only by checking the affidavits filed with a lower village official was Jim Flagg able, in a follow-up story, to include details of what had been stolen and how:

> Two Easton policemen described by their peers as quiet and uncontroversial used their positions on the night shift to carry out a series of bold burglaries, according to Easton police investigators.
>
> On several occasions, the two patrolmen, Fred Curry and Harvey Gogek, allegedly filed police reports on crimes in which they had played a role. Sometimes, police officials say, the target of the crimes was the department itself.
>
> That portrait of an extensive crime ring is *sketched in affidavits filed this week* by Easton police with an Easton district judge.*
>
> *The Express*

In writing up a speech or press conference, reporters should be particularly careful not to clutter the lead with too many details. (See Chapter 4, Traditional Leads.) What's most important usually is who spoke and what newsworthy point that person made.

---

* The names in this story have been changed.

If regionalism is to work in Northeast Ohio, Cleveland's suburbs must help the city deal with unemployment, homelessness and a cash-strapped school system, City Council President Frank Jackson said Friday.

The (Cleveland) *Plain Dealer*

Usually, such details as where the speech was given and how many people attended are worked into the second or third paragraphs, along with information that supports the lead. (See Chapter 9, Organization.) Here are the second and third grafs of the *Plain Dealer* story:

"We're wasting our time if we don't deal with the substantive things," Jackson said in a speech at the City Club.

Jackson's 30-minute speech was delivered to more than 300 people, including Mayor Jane Campbell and U.S. Rep. Stephanie Tubbs Jones.

Speech or press conference stories should take advantage of the abundant quotes available. The *Plain Dealer* story began quoting Jackson in the second graf. Context for the speech is provided in the fourth graf:

It marked the first time Jackson has spoken at length about the ongoing discussions on regional cooperation. He has tremendous sway in the debate; as council president, he can block any legislation necessary for Cleveland to participate in regional projects.

Finally, when writing up a story about a speech or press conference—or a meeting, for that matter—the secret is to remember that the news is usually what was said, not the event itself (see Chapter 4, Traditional Leads):

Unacceptable:

Gov. Robert L. Ehrlich Jr. gave his second State of the State address yesterday.

Acceptable:

Gov. Robert L. Ehrlich Jr. yesterday called on the Democrats who control the Maryland State House to abandon the partisan feuding that marked his first year in office and join him in pursuing a centrist agenda focused on reining in state spending, cleaning up the Chesapeake Bay and protecting services for children, the poor and the disabled.

In his second State of the State address, Ehrlich, R-Md., traded his usual joking banter for a more thoughtful speaking style. He detailed the accomplishments of his young administration and laid out what he described as a broadly inclusive vision for the future that he said should appeal to everyone in the heavily Democratic state.

The Washington Post

CHAPTER 18 SUMMARY: MEETINGS, SPEECHES AND PRESS CONFERENCES

Meetings, speeches and press conferences are the staple of much municipal and government-related reporting. In covering meetings, reporters often have to pick nuggets of newsworthy information out of hours of sometimes monotonous dialogue and debate. Speeches and press conferences require a related but not identical skill: the news the speakers want to get out may not be what's important to readers.

In covering these events, it's important to:

- **Know the issues going in.** In covering meetings, get an agenda in advance and read it. In covering a speech, try to get an advance copy. In covering a press conference, see if someone will tell you in advance why it's being called.

- **Prepare.** Read clips, check documents, talk to key sources. Meetings, in particular cover a lot of ground. The reporter who is completely unprepared going in will likely produce a muddled story.

- **Write early when possible.** Meetings, and press conferences in particular, often end minutes before deadlines. Sometimes this is by design; it leaves reporters, as some newsmakers know, little time to check details or get reactions. One way reporters guard against this time crunch is to write background material in advance.

- **Pay attention to the audience.** Sometimes they provide the news. Those residents lined up at the microphone to protest city council plans to cut a branch library may be the lead. So, too, might a sharp exchange between reporter and news subject at a press conference.

- **Come early, stay late.** There is no substitute for hard work. Reporters who buttonhole sources to get a response or clarification of a board's actions or a speaker's comment will file a more interesting story.

- **Look for key actions.** In meetings, it's often the votes that are not taken or the matters that are tabled. Look especially for contested votes. Knowing the divisions on any city council or other public board can help lead you to the news.

EXERCISE A
Writing Assignments

Write stories based on each of the following collections of information. In each case you are writing for a newspaper dated tomorrow and read in the town where the events occurred.

ONE

The following is a transcript of tonight's meeting of the Plainfield City Council:

Council president Shelly Shumar, Democrat, called the meeting to order and asked that the minutes of last week's meeting be approved. They were.

Councilman Greg Hawthorne, Democrat, chair of Council Police Committee: "I don't have too much to say here. We had a robbery and a handful of burglaries this week. It looks like we're going to need at least one new police car soon though. One of those old Dodges seems to have blown its transmission. I would suggest that we consider replacing them all at once, rather than just handle the problem piecemeal. We could get rid of all four of those five-year-old Dodges, and probably get a good deal on some new cars. Save ourselves a lot of problems. If it's OK with you folks I'll have the chief start looking at prices." (Other council members nod their heads.)

Councilman Robert Reese, Democrat, chair of Council Department of Public Works Committee: "OK, we have the second architect's report on the new DPW garage, and it's pretty much the same as the first one two months ago. Ardmore and Penn Inc. is the firm's name. Headquarters in Boynton. I'll read you the last paragraph: 'We conclude that renovation of the existing structure would be inadequate to handle the department's current and future needs. We believe a new structure should be constructed on the site. And we believe the new structure could be completed for approximately $400,000.' OK? The original firm said $380,000, they say four hundred. Both say we have to do it. There's danger to men and equipment in that old garage. I say let's go."

Shumar: "Are you introducing a motion, Bob?"

Reese: "I move that we authorize the Department of Public Works Committee to begin accepting bids on the construction of a new DPW garage on the present site, completely replacing the current garage."

Hawthorne: "Second, Shelly."

Councilman David Fayles, Republican: "Wait a second, Bob. We're just not with you on this one. Three hundred and eighty to four hundred thousand dollars. That's going to raise our property taxes, Bob. You know that. These consultants just love to take things down and build. I've looked that building over, and it looks to these eyes like it can be easily renovated. How old is it anyway?"

Reese: "28 years."

Fayles: "I say let's get another one of these firms to tell us exactly how much a renovation would cost."

Reese: "Come on, David. Let me read to you from the report of the first architectural consultant—Main Line Designs of La Port: 'A renovation of such a deteriorating structure would simply not be cost effective. The department now has six trucks in its garage. They barely fit, and it is reasonable to assume more trucks will be needed in the future. Even if the structure could efficiently be renovated, it is inadequate for the department's needs.' Roof tiles are falling down, David. We had a garbage truck scratched by one, last month. The roof leaks. It's an incredible eyesore. Let's vote."

The motion is carried by a 3–2 vote, with Shumar, Hawthorne and Reese voting in favor and Fayles and June Bryson, Republican, opposed. Mayor Jonathan Rose, Democrat, must still sign the proposal. Rose was at the meeting and said he would sign it as soon as it reached his desk. The meeting adjourned shortly afterward.

TWO

The following is the text of the public participation portion of tonight's meeting of the Dawson Town Council:

John Goldsmith, 42, of 271 Lanier Road: "Mr. Mayor, council members, I've come before you here tonight to question the town's recent increase in parking fees from 5 cents to 25 cents per hour. Ladies and gentlemen, that is a 500 percent increase. And I didn't get a 500 percent raise last year. Yesterday I parked for what must have been all of 2 minutes on Gedney Street to buy the Sunday paper. I didn't bother to feed the meter because who wants to spend 25 cents for 2 minutes? That comes to $7.50 an hour. Well, I came out to find a $5 ticket on my windshield. The cop must have been hiding behind a tree because he was gone. My question is this. Why don't you put in meters with slots that will take nickels for 10 minutes, dimes for 20 minutes and quarters for an hour? I'd really appreciate it."

Councilwoman Barbara Moffett: "I guess as chairperson of the Police Committee I'll speak to that. I would say, Mr. Goldsmith, that you had bad luck. I'd guess your chances of getting a parking ticket in 2 minutes are about as likely as your odds of winning a million-dollar lottery. This town has a police force of 14, and I don't think any of them have been assigned to harass you. As for the change in the meters, yes, it is 500 percent. But look where we started. Can you make a 5-cent phone call today, buy a 5-cent candy bar? We'd like to keep taxes down in this town, and one way to do it is get some revenue from all the shoppers who enjoy the personal attention they get on Main Street. I'm sorry you had bad luck, but I'm afraid there isn't much we can do about it."

Averill Worshom, 78, 12 Decatur Ave.: "Mr. Mayor. As you know, sir, I've lived in this town 43 years now. When I first came here, Decatur Avenue was a rural road with so little traffic that you hardly had to look both ways before crossing the street. No more. Dawson has grown, which I don't mind, but I do mind not being able to cross the street to visit with my neighbors. I'm not as spry as I once was, and those kids from Upper Regional High School don't seem to care a hoot about the speed limit or about being polite. Would you please look into the matter? It would help, I think, if you would consider putting in a stop light or at least a stop sign at Decatur and Meadowview Road. And unlike the gentleman who just spoke, I'd like to see a few more traffic tickets around here."

Mayor Russel Todd: "Mrs. Worshom, it's good to see you. I don't know about the part of your being less spry. You still keep one of the best vegetable gardens in town. Joking aside, though, we are well aware that traffic is getting to be a serious problem out your way. The council appointed a Traffic and Advisory Committee last month to look into just the kind of problem you are talking about, and we expect a report in another two or three weeks. I know the intersection you are speaking of can get very busy, and I expect it will be one of several that will get close consideration for a stop sign or stop light."

Angela Barbaro, Chair of the Town Parks Committee: "Last year I came before you at this time to urge you to consider lifting all curfews at Landers Park. It seemed particularly appalling to us that kids could not use the park in the summer after 8 p.m., and you agreed. I'd like to say the trial we agreed to has been a resounding success, but I'm afraid at best I'd have to call it a mixed bag. Use of the park in general is up this year, and the new playground for pre-schoolers is simply packed during the day. Vandalism also has increased again, though. Last week we took an inventory at the playground for older kids next to Ridge Road and I was truly shocked. Five of eight swings had been ripped from their support. The large slide was covered with some of the foulest graffiti I've ever seen, and there must have been a dozen shattered beer bottles under the jungle gym apparatus. I've discussed this with [Police] Chief [Eugene] Banks, and he says he simply does not have the manpower to assign a patrol car full time to the park in the evening. Reluctantly, therefore, I'd like to ask you, on behalf of the Parks Committee, to reinstitute a dusk-to-dawn curfew at the park. I hate to do it because most of the kids in this town would benefit from fewer constraints on their lives and more breathing room, but the minority in this case has ruined it for all of them."

Councilman Robert Lansberg: "Mrs. Barbaro, thanks for your forthright report. I agree with you that the situation at the park has gone sour again and, as you know, we can't buy a new set of swings every month. I'd therefore like to propose a motion that the council reinstitute a curfew at Landers Park on Wilson Boulevard from dusk to dawn. We can't take away the park from parents and younger children in this town so a pack of unruly teen-agers can have a place to break beer bottles."

Councilwoman Moffett: "I second."

The council votes 5–0 in favor of the motion.

THREE

The following is the text of a speech delivered yesterday to unemployed people, in meeting hall at headquarters of Local 14 of the Fast Food Workers Union at 748 West Humphrey Street in Columbus, by Dolores Mandel, executive director of the new National Union of the Unemployed, founded just three months ago:

"Hello, brothers and sisters. We've gotten some press coverage lately, so you probably know something of what this is all about. The media can't handle things if they get too complex, so we've been keeping it simple. The simple version—are you listening, reporters?—is that we're starting a union of unemployed people. That we're uniting a group of people who tend to disappear for the 29 days of the month between the monthly releases of unemployment figures. That we're going to make a lot of noise and maybe even cause some trouble—the media just eat up that kind of talk—until people, one, start to recognize that the statistics have families and feelings and real human needs, and, two, until people start to listen to our demands, instead of just calling us names."

"Here's the complicated version: We aren't going to wait around for the do-gooders to have their periodic pangs of conscience anymore. We aren't going to wait around for our broth-ers and sisters in the other unions to think of us anymore. Though we thank the Fast Food Workers for the use of the hall, these other unions represent people who are lucky enough to keep a job in these crazy days. Those of us who have gotten the pink slip are an afterthought to them. We aren't going to wait. We're going to do what people have always done when they were oppressed and ignored. We're going to organize. We're going to unite. We're going to tell the world that we aren't going to be the doormat on which this insane, high-tech, global economic madness wipes its feet. We're going to shout a simple message—here we go, reporters—We want jobs! We want jobs! [Crowd joins in chant.] We want jobs! We want jobs! And we're going to get the millions of others of our unemployed brothers and sisters to shout it with us until...until...until they listen."

Crowd of 125 cheers wildly. They line up at tables in the back of the hall to sign up for new union. Later Mandel announces that 97 unemployed people joined her union at the meeting and that it now represents 22,000 unemployed nationwide.

From interview after speech with Walter Hall, former worker with Atlas Ball-Bearing here, laid off three months ago, unemployed: "Are you kidding? Of course I'm signing up. This woman talks sense. I haven't heard so much sense come out of anybody's mouth in a long time. We want jobs! I need a job."

From interview after speech with Mandel: "What power do we have? Would a couple of hundred thousand unemployed people sitting down on Wall Street have power? Would a couple of hundred thousand unemployed people paying a visit to those computer whizzes in the Silicon Valley have power? We can't go on strike, but we have lots and lots of power. We just have to decide how best to use it. Our demands? We want jobs to become a priority in this country again. We want a tax system geared to creating jobs, not getting people to buy more computers. We want an economy geared to creating jobs, not raising the rate rich people can earn on their investments. We want a government putting its money into job programs not missile programs."

Membership dues are $15 annually, she says.

EXERCISE B

Story Assignments

1. Watch a televised presidential press conference or a Sunday morning interview show. Write a news story based on the newsmakers' comments.

2. Attend a meeting of a local government body such as a city council or school board. Write a story.

3. Find someone giving a speech in your area by calling the local Chamber of Commerce, political clubs, a local college or the public school system. Attend the speech and write a story based on what is said and, if possible, on a follow-up interview.

19

Government and Politics

For decades James Reston wrote a column on Washington and the world for *The New York Times*. Don Melvin covered City Hall for *The Burlington* (Vt.) *Free Press*. Both subscribed to the same philosophy of covering government and politics.

"You study the record," advised Reston, a much revered political writer and editor in his generation. "You start by finding out what the officials have done. You look at the clips. [See Chapter 14, Research.] You find out where politicians came from, what their districts are like, what people know them. You call up their offices and say you'd like a copy of their speeches."

Most beginning political reporters will find themselves covering officials who "came from" no place more exotic than the other side of town and who have not necessarily preserved copies of their speeches. For the beginning reporter, covering government and politics almost always means covering *local* government and *local* politics. Still, when Don Melvin was sent to City Hall in Burlington, he followed a routine quite similar to that Reston prescribed. Melvin checked clips on local politics and politicians in his newspaper library. He sought out some political science professors at the University of Vermont who had studied local politics in Burlington for more than a decade. He took the leaders of each of the city's three political factions out to lunch. He set up weekly meetings with the mayor. And he spent as much time as he could wandering around City Hall, meeting and talking with officials and people who knew those officials. All this "homework," to use Reston's term, was hardly done at his leisure. Melvin was assigned to the beat just three months before a hotly contested local election.

Covering government and politics generally requires keeping up with an endless parade of meetings, speeches and press conferences. (See Chapter 18, Meetings, Speeches and Press Conferences.) It also requires deciphering budgets and audits, and following campaigns and polls—skills discussed in this chapter. Whatever the task, however, our strongest suggestion is that beginning reporters do the homework—talk to the sources, read the records and documents—that will help them make sense out of the rush of politically charged events.

SOURCES

Professors moan about "politics" at universities. Business people complain of "politics" in corporations. What they are lamenting is a style of behavior that emphasizes manipulation of

292

others, self-promotion, the creation of false appearances and the selective application of power. Politicians are often people devoted to the public good, as they perceive it. But they are also people who have chosen to spend much of their lives engaging in "politics." This is true as well of elected officials, who are, after all, just the politicians who managed to win the last election.

It is difficult to report on these people, whose behavior is often highly controlled and rehearsed, simply by showing up at their public performances. Fortunately, in the privacy of their offices or their favorite hangouts, most politicians love to discuss the "game" of politics with reporters whom they've come to know personally. That's why, when Jim Flagg was assigned the City Hall beat for *The* (Easton, Pa.) *Express*, he set out to meet potential sources away from the public gatherings where their posturing is likely to be most pronounced.

"I went around to almost every office at City Hall and tried to make contact with the people there face to face, from secretaries to the mayor," he recalls. And, as Flagg became more experienced, he began to look beyond those in office to the people who try to influence their decisions and to the people affected by those decisions. "As I've progressed as a reporter, I've begun to shy away from stories that start with 'City Hall said last night. ...'" Flagg explains.

The Chief Executive

Within the limitations imposed by the "checks and balances" of Congress and the judiciary, the president runs the federal government. The governor, with similar restraints, is in charge of

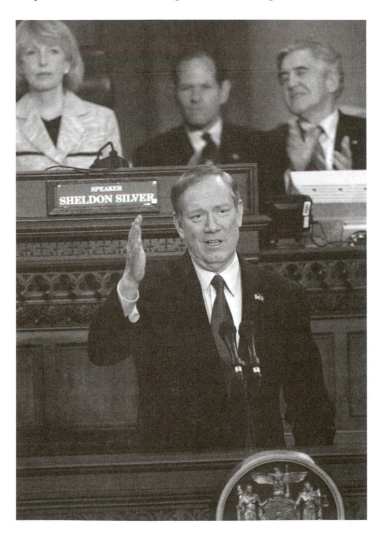

Former New York Gov. George Pataki delivers a State of the State address.
(Photo by Tom Killips, The Troy [N.Y.] Register)

a state government. Finding the boss on the local level may not be that easy, however. Often *county managers* have a major say; often the elected mayor is just a part-timer and the city or town is run by a full-time appointed *city manager*.

The first thing any reporter on the beat must do is find out who holds the *real* power: Who makes the day-to-day decisions? Who hires the people who occupy the government offices? Who draws up the budget? A starting point in finding answers is to read up on the local form of government and how it's organized.

The Council or Legislature

Councils and legislatures can be great sources of information because they are filled with politicians, each of whom is struggling to gain recognition and a say in policy. The two or more sides of an issue that reporters usually look for (see Chapter 2, Fairness) are frequently represented on the council or in the legislature. For example, when Mitt Romney, Massachusetts' Republican governor, presented his 2006 State of the State address, the overwhelmingly Democratic legislature was quick to react. Articles in *The Boston Globe* that recorded these reactions gave readers a glimpse of what they could expect in the legislative battles ahead:

> ...Democrats, pointing out that Romney declined to attach price tags to many of his proposals, said it may be difficult to pay for all of them, given a projected $600 million hole in state's fiscal 2006 budget.
>
> "While all elected officials undoubtedly would like to create jobs, whether we have the fiscal resources to provide the backbone to the governor's proposals remains the unanswered question," said Rep. Eugene L. O'Flaherty, Democrat of Chelsea. "We have to make sure the state has the money to create those types of programs, given the structural deficit."

Reporters should review past votes and election statements to determine where the divisions lie in a council or legislature. This also allows them to seek out a fair range of views on future stories.

Other Government Officials

The people who pass laws aren't necessarily the people who know the most about how the laws are enforced. Reporters will want to get to know the heads of city departments, from the police to the health department, to monitor how well policies are working in practice and to keep in touch with problems that may grow into issues. (See Chapter 23, Municipal Services.)

The *city attorney* is another important source. In this age of litigation, few governments refrain from suing or escape being sued. The city attorney is privy to information on all legal disputes affecting a government and is responsible for advising officials of the limitations and requirements imposed by various laws. And the *city clerk* is a valuable source for background on issues and for access to city records.

It's also crucial to know who keeps track of the money and who is spending it. Most cities have a full-time *financial officer* or budget officer. It's wise to know who heads the finance committee of the city council, too. And the *tax assessor* can be useful because he or she keeps track of property values in town and the records showing how much each property owner is paying in taxes.

Boards

Boards or commissions are usually appointed by the mayor, council or some combination of the two. Boards often function as advisory bodies and don't have the final say:

> The Richmond Planning Commission *recommended* yesterday that the city transfer ownership of Parkers Field to the Richmond Metropolitan Authority as part of the plan to replace the ballpark's decrepit stadium.
>
> Richmond (Va.) *Times-Dispatch*

Two of the most important boards in any municipality are the *board of adjustment* (in some areas called the zoning board) and the *planning board* (or commission), which between them monitor development. A variety of additional boards, often staffed by volunteers, oversee everything from the operation of the library to the preservation of historic sites. Controversy can crop up on the library board just as it can on the council, and such controversies generate news.

Former Elected and Appointed Officials

Politicians lose as well as win elections. And top appointed officials are likely to be swept out of office with them when a new party or new administration takes power. These former officials understand how government works from the inside and are often anxious to share their views. Some former officials, of course, sound off just to get even. Their charges, nonetheless, help balance the self-congratulations of those in power:

> The former head of New York City's Off-Track Betting Corp. charged yesterday that the mayor was attempting to "rewrite history" by claiming that OTB is free of political patronage.
>
> (New York) *Daily News*

Power Brokers

Possibly the single toughest task in covering government and politics is discovering who holds power—and manipulates the visible politicians—behind the scenes. Candidates and officials are buffeted by a variety of interest groups on a wide range of issues. The people whose interests regularly prevail, or who broker the deals between the politicians and the interest groups, often prefer to keep themselves out of the limelight.

The first place to look for these *power brokers* is in the local political parties. Find out which members of a party have served on the county committee and are most active at party functions. The presidents or political liaisons of the Chamber of Commerce, the local board of realtors, the merchants' association and any local banking organization also are likely to be influential behind the scenes. These people have a considerable stake in their communities and often provide financing for candidates.

Candidates are required to report campaign contributions over a certain threshold, as well as the names of the donors. At a federal level, these can be found at the website of the Federal Election Commission (www.fec.gov). Find out what state, county and city offices monitor election contributions and check regularly to see who the big contributors are. They usually wield influence.

Community Groups

The influence of various community organizations ebbs and flows with the news. Some, like the League of Women Voters, are worth contacting periodically. Though the League commonly avoids partisan positions on issues, its members often attend and monitor meetings reporters might miss. Active League chapters also prepare reports on a variety of problems in government and sponsor candidate debates.

The importance of most other groups varies. A local merchants' association might suddenly emerge as a major force during a council dispute over whether to build a downtown parking garage. Taxpayer groups are most vocal and visible at budget time. And block associations, some of which grow overnight, are heard from when there's a perceived need for better police protection or snow removal, or a concern over intersections without traffic signals or parks that have become hangouts for teen-age beer drinkers. In New York, members of the Good Old

Lower East Side preservation group turned out in force to oppose a proposal for a city shelter for the homeless in their neighborhood:

> "We on the Lower East Side have never turned our back on the homeless but it is unfair to expect our community to absorb most of the city's homeless population," said Susan Leelike of the Good Old Lower East Side preservation group.
>
> *The New York Times*

Reporters should try to maintain contact with these community groups even as they hibernate, waiting for an issue. The people in these organizations can help reporters make connections to people living in homes where governmental decisions are actually felt.

In seeking out community groups, it helps to identify the places in which they gather. Church, synagogue and mosque basements, senior centers, community centers and coffee shops are just a few. Spend time in the places your community's engaged citizens go to talk.

RECORDS AND DOCUMENTS

"Whenever anything comes up, I ask, 'Is there anything on paper?'" says Jim Flagg of *The Express* in Easton, Pa. "A ruling from the attorney, memos between departments … if it's on paper it saves time." If it's online, of course, it saves even more time. And documents do more than save time. They provide the seed of a story idea, the context to build the story's frame, the authority that the spoken word sometimes lacks. Records and documents, whatever their form, can be the basis of stories. Here are some categories of record and documents to seek out.

Ordinances

Ordinances are the laws on the books in a locality. Typically they become news when they are proposed and debated before a council or legislature. But old laws, too, can become a source of fresh controversy. (Is it *still* illegal to sell beer in town on Sunday?) And study of a town's ordinances—its ban on massage parlors, for example—can help reporters become acquainted with the issues that have been important in the area they are covering.

Development Plans

Development plans can spark fierce controversy in communities. Some invariably favor attracting more businesses and industries to town because new enterprises bring jobs and pay taxes, lowering the residential tax rate. Others oppose development, fearing that it will change the character of a community or will bring traffic and pollution. These battles inevitably generate reams of paper and computer files.

Every municipality has a *master plan* designed to set out, in broad terms, how the community should grow. In theory, but not always in practice, that plan is reflected and enforced by *zoning regulations*, which establish areas, or zones, restricted to such buildings as one-family homes, apartments, businesses or factories.

Anyone interested in building anything from a one-story house to a thousand-unit apartment complex must submit a *site plan* to the planning board or commission even if the development conforms to existing zoning. Planners will review whether the proposed project conforms to requirements on lot size, height and distance from roadways. Those whose projects conflict with existing zoning regulations must file for a *variance*, or exemption. Such requests usually are reviewed by a *board of adjustment*. Decisions of both the planning board and board of adjustment often must be ratified by the town's governing body.

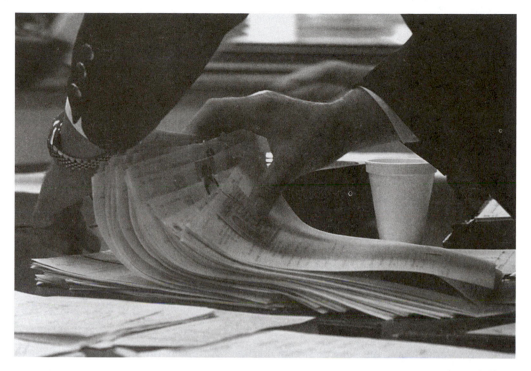

A member of the Kalamazoo, Mich., Gun Board looks through a stack of applications for a concealed weapons permit.
(Courtesy of the Battlecreek Enquirer*)*

If projects are controversial, they can be fodder for stories. Site plans and variance requests on file with the municipality's planning office inform reporters about who has asked to build and where. Reporters also should talk with the people who keep the files to find out whether the city has received any written opposition to the proposed construction:

> A Moslem congregation has proposed that a $1.5 million marble mosque be built near Seven Corners....
>
> The proposed Dar Al-Hijrah mosque, with a 60-foot minaret and a one-story administration building, is planned for the corner of Leesburg Pike (Rte. 7) and Row Street, near two churches, a shopping center and high-rise apartment buildings.
>
> Two letters of opposition and one of conditional support already have been received by the Fairfax County Board of Zoning Appeals, which will hold a public hearing April 17. ...
>
> *The Washington Post*

Tax Records

Reporters can't go poking around in people's income taxes—these are private. But the value at which various properties in town are assessed for real estate taxes is public information, and that information can lead to important stories.

Jim Flagg says he regularly checks the tax rolls in Easton to see who pays *no* taxes. The issue is controversial in Easton because huge chunks of property are tax exempt. Flagg used the city's tax records to report this story:

> Here's a moot question: If the City of Easton could collect taxes on tax-exempt property [this year], how much richer would the city be?

> Answer: $925,000—enough to balance the city budget without hiking the property tax and water-sewer fees.
>
> Here's another question, and it's not moot: How much longer will Lafayette College, the YMCA, cemeteries and every church and synagogue and non-profit institution in Easton enjoy freedom from property taxes?
>
> Answer: Maybe forever. But sides are forming in a debate on this question led by two administrations—that of Dr. David Ellis at Lafayette College, and that of Mayor Philip Mitman at Easton City Hall.
>
> *The Express*

Tax assessors often have two sets of tax records: One is arranged by location; it shows the taxes on each property and lists the owner of the property (or the person paying taxes on it). The other shows *all* the holdings and taxes paid by a particular property owner. Reporters who want to see how much the chair of the local Republican Party pays on the properties she owns (and that should include all government reporters) can easily find the answer in this latter set of tax records. The other set of records can be used to find out what the party official's neighbors pay on similar property.

Audits

It's always worth finding out what *audits* are done on government programs and when. Audits are report cards. They tell whether a program—welfare, aid to farmers—is being well managed or has problems, and they indicate whether that program is operating within its budget. State and local governments along with various independent agencies have to be audited if they receive substantial funding from the federal government.

"The real news is when you get a critical audit," Flagg notes. "But you always get tips on what's going on, even from a positive audit." Flagg says he routinely reviews several audits a year, including an audit of city financing, an audit of the federally funded Community Development grant program and audits of three employee pension funds.

BUDGETS

The budget is a blueprint of a city's costs and revenues in the coming year. A superficial reading of the budget tells how much taxes will increase, whether state and federal revenues are increasing or decreasing, whether more or less money will be allocated to different city departments, and whether the city's debts are mounting. A detailed analysis can offer a wealth of information about the quality and quantity of services, such as how much it costs to collect a ton of garbage and how many police officers the city has for every thousand residents.

Reporters should not think of budgets as documents that miraculously appear one day at a city council meeting. Instead, they should look at a budget as a process that goes on for months and should be written about all along the way.

This process begins when city department heads draw up what they consider to be their budgetary needs. Beware: The tendency at this stage is to inflate requests because all the players in the game know that budgets end in compromise. Next these requests are reviewed by the finance committee of the city council or the city manager, and a tentative budget is drawn up. Only then is it introduced to the public at a council meeting and discussed at a series of public hearings. There are stories all along the way.

"I try to track what kinds of increases each department is asking for and what kind of effects each increase will have on taxpayers," says Doug Rainey of the *La Crosse* (Wis.) *Tribune*. "I try to put it on a level the taxpayer can understand."

The single most important budget issue to most local readers is whether and by how much their taxes will rise, or, in rare cases, decline. Readers should be told of the change in general terms:

> The proposed tax increase in the municipal portion of the budget is $348,000, or 5.5 percent.

More importantly though, readers also should have the changes in the tax rate translated for them into terms they can use in thinking about their own budgets. Such changes are reported in terms of *assessed value*, which is a determination of a property's relative value for tax purposes, and is typically lower than a property's real, or *market*, value.

> If the proposed budget is adopted, taxes will increase from $4 to $4.22 per $100 assessed property value, or an increase of about $440 on a home assessed at $200,000.

Such translations require the command of one powerful tool—arithmetic. The "average" reader might not be very excited to learn that municipal taxes are going up $348,000. But tell readers that taxes on a typical house in town will increase roughly $440, or 5.5 percent, and the public hearing might be packed.

In addition to keeping track of changes in taxes, reporters should ask other, basic questions about each year's budget:

1. How much have expenses increased or decreased, both in dollars and as a percentage of the total budget? Expenses will fall into three broad categories. Every city has operating expenses—the day-to-day costs of providing services and maintaining equipment. Salaries invariably make up the largest single operating expense. Cities also have capital costs—money spent on major new equipment and on construction. And finally, like most of us, cities have debts. The debt service shows how much money the district must pay as principal and interest on old loans, typically bonds issued for construction projects.

2. Where will revenues come from, and how have the sources of money changed? Though cities rely primarily on local taxes, they also get help from the state and the federal government. Cuts in state and federal programs can be a direct cause of tax increases on the local level.

3. What changes in services or staffing will result from budgeting changes? To answer this question, reporters first must compare this year's figures with those from previous years. Is the city library getting more or less money? The next step is to find out what effect this change in funding may have:

> City Library Director James White says he plans to recommend reductions in services and hours of operation in response to budget cuts.
>
> *La Crosse* (Wis.) *Tribune*

Remember, budgets affect people—people who use libraries, for example.

4. Did department heads request additional funds that were left out of the final budget proposal? What will the consequences be? Is any department head complaining?

5. How much money does the budget set aside for salaries? Does the salary line reflect anticipated raises or money for more personnel?

BIDS

The city council, tired of wearing overcoats during its meetings, wants to install Thermopane windows in City Hall. Who should get the job? Most of the council members would be happy to give the job to the mayor's brother-in-law, who owns No-Draft Windows. But the law requires that any major public purchases be put out for competitive bidding. Municipalities must advertise for *bids* and must supply *specifications* that make clear the type of material or work they need. In their sealed bids, competitors for the contract set out what they can deliver and at what price. All things being equal, the low bidder should get the job.

But, as in any process in which someone stands to gain substantially, the opportunities for abuse are considerable. Occasionally, overt corruption dictates who is awarded a bid. More often, a governing body will draft "exclusive specifications" designed to favor a particular company. That city council might insist that the window company be located in town and have a staff of at least six people—a specification that only No-Draft Windows meets. Such exclusive specifications are illegal.

In covering the bidding procedure, reporters should seek the help of an expert not competing for the job. Among the questions worth asking: Are the specifications exclusive? Did the low bidder meet the specifications? Does the contract drawn up after the awarding of a bid require the contractor to purchase *a performance bond* (a sum of money put aside as an assurance to the city that the work will be completed as promised)?

In many cases, the awarding of a contract is routine. But when the low bidder is denied the contract or when only one bidder applies for a job time after time, a story—and further investigation—may be warranted.

While large contracts require advertised bidding, many day-to-day purchases, from toilet paper to thumbtacks, are simply written up on *purchase orders*. The monetary limit on such unadvertised—and unpublicized—purchases varies from city to city, but it can be in the thousands of dollars.

It's also not unknown for city officials to treat themselves to fringe benefits in the form of expensive lunches, junkets to check on services in other cities and exorbitant dry-cleaning bills for clothes ostensibly soiled in the line of duty. Such lavish spending would show up in expense and travel *vouchers*—statements of money spent.

Sometimes surprising corruption can show up in surprising ways and in surprising places:

> When he was hired last summer as a $63,150-a-year deputy administrator in New York City's Human Resources Administration, he called himself Courtney Isaac Saunders. His colleagues knew him as "Ike" and say he spoke well, dressed well and worked well.
>
> Yesterday, city officials announced that the former official had been arrested Thursday night in Washington under his real name.... The New York City warrant accused him of falsifying his past history and relying on his city title to run up thousands of dollars in personal debts he charged to the city.
>
> *The New York Times*

If they had looked into the official's expense accounts when he was asked to resign four months before the story ran, reporters wouldn't have had to wait for the city's announcement.

CAMPAIGNS

Politicking is a year-round occupation for most elected officials. Whether they are in Washington, D.C., or Burlington, Vt., they try to stay in the news by issuing press releases, leaking information or scheduling events such as speeches, press conferences and ribbon cuttings that the media are likely to attend.

But politicking takes on a special fervor in the months preceding an election. Even the most close-mouthed officials suddenly have something nice to say to potential supporters or something nasty to say about the other side. And, as Don Melvin found after "parachuting" into the middle of a hotly contested local race in Burlington, politicians are just as comfortable working reporters as they are working a crowd. "Certain folks tried to lean on me a little at first to see what I'd do," says Melvin. "They were testing me. What they were doing was a little like yelling at the umpire and hoping for a better call next time."

Fairness

It is difficult enough to cover a campaign fairly, even when politicians are not leaning on the reporters. Charges and countercharges must be balanced, if not in a single story, certainly in the course of the campaign's coverage. (See Chapter 2, Fairness.)

Charges in campaigns always fly between members of opposing parties. Rifts also appear within a single camp, particularly during primaries, and they too must be covered fairly. Here is an example from *The Boston Globe's* coverage of a 2006 Democratic primary fight for the gubernatorial nomination.

> FALMOUTH—Democrats Thomas F. Reilly and Deval L. Patrick traded heated accusations over ethics yesterday in a gubernatorial candidates forum sponsored by the Massachusetts AFL-CIO.
>
> Reilly, who filed legislation yesterday to toughen state ethics disclosure rules, hammered Patrick for his ties to Ameriquest, a controversial mortgage lender that recently agreed to a $325 million settlement with 49 states, including Massachusetts, over predatory lending practices.
>
> Patrick, for his part, accused Reilly of not doing enough to control huge cost overruns on the Big Dig and raised the prospect that Reilly was influenced by campaign contributions from Big Dig contractors.

Attention in the newspaper must be divided among the various candidates and camps in a campaign on the basis of some consideration of the newsworthiness of their respective pronouncements, the excitement they seem to be generating *and* the public's right to hear what each has to say. (See Chapter 2, Fairness.) Finding this balance is not an exact science. For example, in the 1992 presidential election, there appeared to be some truth to the Libertarians' bitter charge that Ross Perot's billions had in effect bought him a podium at the presidential debates while longer-standing minor parties, like theirs, were left out.

Political reporters must be particularly careful not to allow their own political and personal opinions of the candidates to color the stories they turn out. "It's inevitable that if you travel with a candidate, you'll develop some feeling one way or another for that candidate," notes David Espo, who has followed presidential candidates for the Associated Press. "You have to check yourself." And, of course, reporters can't allow themselves to be influenced by politicians who attempt to lean on them.

What They're Saying

Political reporters get themselves in trouble when they begin to place too much emphasis on their feeling that they've seen it all and that they know it all. After covering a candidate for a few weeks, a reporter may have heard the same speech a dozen times. It is easy to forget that readers probably have not heard the speech once and that they may never have been presented with that candidate's major proposals. Similarly, it's easy for reporters to become so entranced by their own speculations about *why* candidates are saying what they're saying that they forget to report *what* the candidates are saying. (See Chapter 12, Facts.)

An important part of the reporter's job is to pass on the candidate's message to readers so that readers can evaluate it *themselves*. Here a candidate for the U.S. Senate in Colorado:

> Although [Ben Nighthorse] Campbell generally backs civil rights measures, he voted to curb public spending on "pornographic" art. "To me, if a person is paying for it himself, out of his own pocket, I stick pretty much with free speech," Campbell said. "But with taxpayers' money, there should be limits on the degree of pornography."
>
> *The Denver Post*

What They're Not Saying

In addition to this basic "he-proposed, she-proposed, he-charged, she-charged" coverage, good political reporters will provide their readers with enough facts to place candidates' statements in perspective. They might try to pin down politicians by measuring their campaign statements against their records—legislative and spoken. The candidate may be promising to upgrade the schools, but if he voted against the past three aid-to-education bills and attacked school spending in a speech last year, that claim sounds rather hollow.

While reporting on the proposed second-term domestic policy of President George W. Bush on the campaign trail in 2004, the *Los Angeles Times* also noted some of what he was *not* saying:

> With only a week to go before the Republican National Convention, the *lack of details* in President Bush's second-term domestic policy agenda has left some conservative activists worrying aloud about the Vision Thing.

Political coverage might also include a look behind the curtain at what's going on backstage in a campaign: Who is running the campaign? Who is paying for it? How is it being organized? What is the candidate's strategy? This isn't easy to do. It requires extremely thorough reporting to determine the strategies of rival candidates as they jockey for position. An interview or two won't do.

And there are dangers in these analytical stories. Too often, when the facts aren't there, the analysis disintegrates into conjecture. (See Chapter 12, Facts.) Also, in concentrating on what's happening backstage, reporters tend to lose sight of the politician's actual performances. They forget their responsibility to report what the candidate *is* saying.

"Political writers can focus so much on the strategies and aims of the candidates' staffs that they lose track of what the candidates are trying to do," says Steven R. Weisman, former White House correspondent for *The New York Times*.

One of the most basic, and one of the best-read, election stories is the announcement of the results. The lead of that story obviously should tell who won, for what office and by what margin. The vote totals, the turnout and quotes from winners and losers usually follow close behind. Space permitting, some of the major issues of the campaign also are recapitulated. As in any story, the unusual alters the basic formula. If it is an election outcome that defied the pollsters, the lead should note that it was an upset.

Even in such seemingly straightforward stories as these, reporters can get in trouble with characterizations or judgments. Note these two accounts of the results of the same New York City primary election:

> Chalking up large margins in many of Brooklyn's black neighborhoods, former Rep. Elizabeth Holtzman headed for a narrow victory early today over Norman Rosen in the hotly contested Democratic primary for Brooklyn district attorney.

With 99 percent of the 1,519 election districts reporting, Holtzman had slightly more than 52 percent of the vote to Rosen's 48 percent.

(New York) *Daily News*

Former Representative Elizabeth Holtzman won the Democratic nomination for Brooklyn District Attorney last night with a comfortable margin over Norman J. Rosen. With 1,504 of 1,519 districts reporting, the vote was:

Holtzman...93,788
Rosen 85,084

Holtzman pieced her victory together by showing strength in the Flatbush and Park Slope sections of the borough, which made up her old Congressional district.

The New York Times

Both these reporters would have been on firmer ground had they stuck to the facts—the percentages of the vote—and left to the reader the decision on whether that was a "comfortable" or a "narrow" victory.

POLLS

Many reporters have written, and many readers have read, stories about the reaction of a few members of the public to an event in the news. Should the mayor run for governor? Should the United States develop weapons in space? Who should win an Academy Award? This the proverbial person-in-the-street interview. Here is what the wait staff at Stan's Restaurant in Columbus, Ohio, had to say about the 2004 presidential election:

[Judy] Cole, a 10-year Stan's waitress, said she probably will drive to her polling place today still not knowing for whom she will vote.

"I have no idea," Cole said. "Well, I have an idea and then I change my mind and go back the other way. I'm in my 60s, and I guess I'll decide on who's best on the things that are going to affect me down the road—Social Security, Medicare, things like that."

Co-owner Kevin Trombley, 43, who started as a busboy at Stan's 27 years ago, said he, too, is undecided.

"I'll probably go into the voting booth, close my eyes and point."

The Columbus Dispatch

Such reaction stories are people stories. They can be colorful, poignant, funny. They are filled with quotes and descriptions. And they are next to useless as a measure of the greater public's views.

Reporting of polls, informal and formal, has progressed in the last few decades. Few reporters these days will make the mistake of presenting street-corner, come-as-you-will interviews as anything more than cute color stories. Those who try to treat them as a serious reflection of opinion are quickly dressed down by their editors.

Recognizing the need to look for a scientifically representative sample of the population, many large news organizations such as *The New York Times* and CBS, *The Washington Post* and ABC, *USA Today* and CNN have hired experts to design regular polls gauging public reaction to a wide range of issues. And newspapers regularly write up the results of polls by such large organizations as those founded by Louis Harris, George Gallup and Burns Roper. In fact, polls have come to dominate national, state and local political campaigns. Every candidate with a wisp of a chance has hired a pollster. Candidates listen ... and so do reporters. Barely a week passes without a new assessment of who's in first. (A number of websites such as www. realclearpolitics.com amass polls for those tracking the progress of what is known in politics as the *horse race*.) This poll appeared 10 days before a Milwaukee mayoral primary:

> The poll shows [Tom] Barrett, a former member of the U.S. House, and [Marvin] Pratt, the acting mayor, both with support from 23 percent of likely voters. [David A.] Clarke [Jr.], the Milwaukee County sheriff, follows at 17 percent—but undecided voters, at 28 percent, top them all.
>
> *Milwaukee Journal Sentinel*

Although the journalistic use of polling has expanded, the results of polls are still not always well understood. Reporters too often suspend their natural skepticism in reporting polls. They tend to treat the numbers as if they are more authoritative and meaningful than even the pollster would claim.

Take the poll reported above in the *Journal Sentinel*. It said that both Barrett and Pratt were backed by 23 percent and Clarke was backed by 17 percent. But, as the newspaper noted, 28 percent of those polled were "undecided," meaning that this election was still completely up for grabs with just over a week to go.

The poll also was based on *likely voters*, a category that was not defined by the newspaper, and it had a *margin of error* of plus or minus 5 percentage points, meaning each candidate's actual support could have been 5 percentage points *higher* or 5 percentage points *lower* than reported. Pratt or Barrett, in other words, could have been leading by as much as 16 percentage points over Clarke, or trailing Clarke by as much as 4 percentage points. (The paper did note the race was statistically a dead heat.)

All of which raises a host of questions about the value and use of polls. In interpreting the poll, the *Journal Sentinel* wisely refrained from anointing anyone as the front-runner. Instead, it made a valid comparison with an earlier poll, noting that it had shown Pratt to be trailing by 12 percentage points.

Polls, as a rule, tend to be snapshots of a given moment of a campaign. When their numbers are sagging, candidates typically say they pay no attention to them. But, of course, they do. And as political campaigns progress, polls sometimes are used as weapons. An optimistic poll might cause a candidate's supporters to become overconfident and stay away from the ballot box. A pessimistic poll might scare away voters who don't want to waste their vote on a loser. That's why candidates *selectively* feed poll results to reporters. It is also why the misreporting of polls is of such concern.

The best advice for reporters writing about polls is simply: Be cautious. Even though a poll has been conducted "scientifically," its results should hardly be treated as absolute truths. During the final days of the 1992 presidential campaign, for example, rival news organization polls portrayed the race between incumbent George H. W. Bush and challenger Bill Clinton as anything from a dead heat to a potential landslide, with Clinton leading by a dozen points.

A dozen years later, polls of those exiting the voting precincts projected victory for Sen. John Kerry, who lost his bid to defeat George W. Bush.

One reason for such discrepancies in polls is that people are not test tubes. It is impossible to find a tiny sample of a population that will perfectly mirror the views of the entire population. The inaccuracies inherent in such efforts can be estimated by a statistical formula that is expressed as the *margin of error*. But polls can err in many ways that cannot be expressed statistically.

Sometimes people do not have firm views on a subject. Embarrassed to appear ignorant, they may offer an answer to a question they have limited interest in and little knowledge about. And people without firm views can quickly change their minds. "The results of polls are unstable when the property they measure—opinions—is unstable," one pollster has noted.

In addition, people can be influenced by who asks a question and how it is asked. "Do you support the mayor's plan to provide equal education for all children?" will undoubtedly get a different response than "Do you support the mayor's plan to bus white students to black schools?" In discussing the limitations of polls, Burns Roper of the Roper polling organization has reminded journalists of the old saying, "Ask a stupid question, get a stupid answer."

It is not enough that reporters themselves be aware of the limitations of a poll. They must make sure their readers have the same opportunity to evaluate and question the results. That's why stories about polls should include the following information:

1. What is the poll's margin of error? A 56 to 44 percent lead with a 4 percent margin of error might be significant; 56 to 44 percent with an 8 percent margin of error means little.

2. How many were undecided? A large group of undecided voters means the electorate is, to use one of the pollsters' favorite words "volatile"—in other words, don't place your bets.

3. What group was being sampled? The proportions of the opinions of a sample of "likely voters" might be different from those of a sample of "eligible voters," for example. Some of the discrepancies in polls before the 1992 elections were attributed to different ways of predicting who was "likely" to vote.

4. What was the size of the sample? Readers deserve to know that this prediction, however scientific the survey, was based on interviews with only 537 people. Such numbers help keep poll stories humble.

5. If findings are presented for any subgroups—people with incomes of under $20,000 a year, for example—what was the size of the subgroup sample, and what is the margin of error for conclusions about it? Undoubtedly, that sample will be smaller and the margin of error higher.

6. When was the poll taken? For example, was it before or after that debate between the candidates? Might the results be dated?

7. What key questions were asked and how were they worded?

8. Who paid for the poll? If it was candidate Smith himself, that should give readers pause.

The New York Times regularly answers most of these questions for readers in a short article titled "How the Poll Was Taken" that runs alongside every poll story. Here is the beginning of one such article:

> *The New York Times* survey of Democratic delegates is based on telephone interviews conducted June 14 through July 9 with 1,561 delegates. This includes 523 of the 568 unpledged delegates and 1,038 of the 2,276 pledged delegates. The pledged delegates interviewed were those reached among a randomly selected sample of 1,125 such delegates. . . .

Polls are probably the best device available for finding out what that amorphous Public, with a capital *P*, is thinking; but reporters and their readers must keep the limitations of those polls in mind.

CHAPTER 19 SUMMARY: GOVERNMENT AND POLITICS

Whether covering government or covering politics, reporters must always measure what officials or candidates are *saying* against what they've actually *done*. Supplying this context requires a command of public records that capture past action, the curiosity to look backward more and to speculate less on what's to come, and the willingness to politely challenge the assertions of candidates and elected officials who have a tendency to "spin" or distort things to make themselves look as good as possible.

Reporters covering government and campaigns also should:

- **Seek sources across the political spectrum.** A new reporter in town always wants to identify and then *mine the seams*, working on all sides of the political fissure lines between those of different parties or political outlooks, different administrations or different interest groups.

- **Learn the system, whatever that system is.** Reporters need to know, for example, that a local ordinance becomes law after a *second* reading and vote and not after a first. They need to know when the leading vote getter in a primary has really won and when she must face her top opponent in a runoff. They need to know how the municipal budget is prepared.

- **Follow the money trail.** Politics and government increasingly are fueled by private money. Track down who the big contributors are.

- **Seek out those affected.** This often requires peeling back multiple layers of a community's citizenry. Every community has its movers and shakers—local business owners and neighborhood association presidents, ward leaders and Parent Teacher Association presidents. In a country and world in flux, it's important to look further, to seek out new immigrant groups, those on the poorer side of the tracks, and others who, lacking political clout, may get less than their fair share of government attention.

ADDITIONAL READING

Beyond the Front Lines: How the New Media Cover a World Shaped by War, Philip Seib, Palgrave Macmillan, 2004.

Feeding Frenzy: Attack Journalism and American Politics, Larry Sabato and Larry J. Sabato, Lanahan Publishers, 2000.

A History of News, Mitchell Stephens, Oxford University Press, 2006.

Municipal Yearbook, International City Managers Association, published annually.

The Press, Geneva Overholser and Kathleen Hall Jamieson, editors, Oxford University Press, 2005.

The Press Effect: Politicians, Journalists, and the Stories That Shape the Political World, Kathleen Hall Jamieson and Paul Waldman, Oxford University Press, 2002.

"'Trust Me,' Journalism," Gerald Lanson and Mitchell Stephens, *Washington Journalism Review*, November 1982.

"We're All Postmodern Now," Mitchell Stephens, *Columbia Journalism Review*, July/August 2005.

EXERCISE A
Research Assignments

ONE

Using research materials or interviews with people familiar with government, write explanations that could be used in a newspaper article for the following terms.

1. Run-off election
2. Fiscal year
3. Block grant
4. Line-item veto
5. Zero-based budgeting
6. Grandfather clause
7. Millage rate
8. Matching grants
9. Spot zoning
10. Nonconforming use

TWO

Use research materials or interviews with people familiar with local government to obtain answers to the following questions for a city or town in your area. Illustrate some of the answers with quotes.

1. What form of government does the municipality have? Is the mayor elected by the public or by the council? Is the mayor a part-time or full-time employee of the municipality? Is there a city manager who runs day-to-day affairs?
2. How many council members are there? How often are they elected?
3. Is the government partisan or nonpartisan? (In other words, are there competing political parties or no political parties?)
4. What council members are responsible for overseeing which departments of government? What formal and informal systems exist for this oversight?
5. How often does the council meet? When and where?
6. What were the last five ordinances passed by the council? Who voted for them and who voted against them?
7. Who are the presidents of the local Democratic and Republican clubs? Have they ever held elective office?

THREE

Use research materials or people familiar with the financing of local government to obtain answers to the following questions for a city or town in your area. Illustrate some of the answers with quotes.

1. When must department heads submit their budget requests to the municipality's principal financial officer?
2. Who draws up the budget?
3. When is it first submitted to the mayor and council?
4. By when must it be adopted?
5. What percentage of the current budget is spent on salaries? What are the salaries of the mayor, the council, the chief of police and the chief administrator of the municipality? How do these compare with the salaries of five years ago?
6. How much money will the municipality receive this year from the federal government? From the state government? As specifically as possible, find out what it is being spent for.
7. What major construction projects are planned in the current budget year? How much is being spent on them?

EXERCISE B
Writing Assignments

Write stories based on each of the following collections of information. In each case you are writing for a newspaper dated tomorrow and read in the town where the events occurred.

ONE

The following budget information was just released by the town of Kalispell. An interview with Town Manager Robert Wajsblat follows.

Town of Kalispell Budget Revenues

Source	Actual Budget Current Fiscal Year	Proposed Budget Next Fiscal Year
Water Commission	58,790	61,230
Building permit fees	21,500	22,575
Municipal parking	3,250	3,250
Fines and forfeitures	12,768	13,200
Delinquent tax collection	27,890	33,000
Other revenue	83,645	85,300
Tax levy	590,000	700,000
Total revenue	797,843	918,555
Federal revenue sharing	146,500	89,000
Prior year surplus	27,000	0
Grand total	971,343	1,007,555
Property tax (per thousand dollars assessed valuation)	28.10	33.33

Expenditures

Salaries

Town Manager	30,000	31,500
Police Chief	30,000	31,500
Supt. Public Works	27,500	28,457
Water Commissioner	25,000	25,825
Mayor and Council	9,000	9,000
Police	112,200	123,420
Public Works	122,000	126,270
Town Clerk	18,000	18,630

(continued)

Town of Kalispell Budget Revenues *(continued)*

Source	Actual Budget Current Fiscal Year	Proposed Budget Next Fiscal Year
Waterworks	76,000	78,660
	449,700 (total)	472,362 (total)
Utilities	22,800	28,500
Streets and Roads	28,615	21,500
Insurance	62,900	65,035
Legal	2,700	3,500
Buildings and Grounds	7,950	7,950
Municipal court	14,500	14,500
Recreation	5,700	5,700
Fire	17,635	17,635
Planning Office	7,500	7,500
Waterworks	27,890	27,890
Plowing	3,750	3,750
Overtime pay	42,000	42,000
Other expenses	25,000	25,000
Debt service	253,625	253,625
Grand total	971,343	1,007,555

Wajsblat: What do I think of the budget? Frankly, I don't much like it, but this town is paying for cuts in the federal budget. Look at our federal funds next year. They are being cut almost in half because of cutbacks passed by Congress. Where are we supposed to go? That's more than $50,000. More than 5 percent of our budget in one fell swoop. Yes, I think it would be fair to call this an austerity budget. Take a look at expenditures. They'll be rising all right—3.6 percent. But it's beyond our control again. You know as well as I that the police department held us all up for a 10 percent pay raise. Ten percent. Heck, everyone else in town is getting 3.5 percent and the mayor and council haven't asked for a penny more, even though $1,500 is a joke for the time they put in. And when utility bills and insurance go up we either pay the piper or shut down. We already have to cut back on street repair—sharply. And most other items are stuck where they were, which with inflation will have to mean some cutbacks.

Yes, it is unusual to have no surplus. Don't blame me, though. I just got here this year. Maybe, just maybe, the town shouldn't have borrowed what it did for the new fire engine last year and the expansion of the municipal building the year before and the new fire station the year before that. Maybe our debts are coming back to haunt us. No, I don't think the residents of this town are going to like the looks of the tax increase they face. Hey, the average house here is assessed at $70,000. That means everyone will have to pay a bit more. You figure it out. When they complain though I'll just show them the numbers ... tight as a drum. The only other choice to raising taxes is to cut the uncuttable. Sure we could save a few thousand getting rid of the summer recreation program. Or we could let the snow pile up when it snows. Or we could fire one of our six police officers. But I wouldn't suggest any of them.

"The waterworks. Yes, that could become an issue. Our expenses for it were nearly double revenues last year, but it could be inevitable. If we raise water rates to lower taxes, then the public is just paying another way. It's possible though that we should sell all 12 wells and the treatment station to County Waterworks. I've suggested that the council consider it. You hate to see that though, if for no other reason than the commissioner and four men in the plant could lose their jobs."

TWO

1. Thomas Staney, Republican, is running against Ruth Paps, Democrat, for sheriff of Camden County.

2. Incumbent George Director, Republican, is retiring.

3. Three weeks until the election.

4. Staney in speech yesterday before county Republican Club in Briarsville: "It's time we brought the great unstated issue in this campaign onto the table. It's time we discussed whether this woman—Ruth Paps—is really qualified to be a sheriff. A sheriff has to run a large county department. Ruth has been a community activist for a few years. I've been a deputy sheriff for five years. A sheriff has to wear a gun and be ready to arrest dangerous persons. Ruth has raised three children. I've personally arrested two bank robbers—with gun drawn. We're not electing someone to the school board here. We're choosing the county's top law enforcement officer, who will help protect all of us against lawless elements. Voters have to consider the qualifications of the candidates for that job."

5. Al Lansan is campaign manager for Staney.

6. Lansan in interview after Staney's speech: "Yeah, I think it's fair to say this is a change of tactics on Tom's part. We've been trying to be chivalrous up to now. But this is starting to look like a close election, and we felt it was time to play some hardball. To start making clear to voters exactly what choice they're facing here. We laid off of Paps till now. But now she's going to have to take the heat."

7. Paps in interview a few hours after Staney's speech: "Yes, I heard about his speech today. I don't want to get into a name-calling contest here. Tom has every right to be proud of his work as a deputy sheriff, but the point is who will do the best job of running this department, not who has arrested the most people. Let me just say that my experience as head of the Neighborhood Protection Association—which has worked closely with the Sheriff's Department and other law enforcement agencies—is a pretty strong qualification. If a woman can be a Supreme Court justice, she can be a sheriff."

8. A check of the clips confirms all the factual statements made by Staney and Paps.

THREE

Evelyn Anderson is running for City Council in Rahway as an independent. Her opponents, Democratic incumbent Keith Parkins and Republican Alice Jones, have come out in support of a 137-unit, eight-story luxury apartment complex with accompanying arts, crafts and clothing boutiques proposed by KBC Developers for four acres of city-owned land a quarter-mile east of downtown. Anderson opposes the project. She has been invited by the local Preservation Council, a nonprofit group interested in preserving the town's heritage, to give a speech explaining her views. About 85 people attended the speech this evening at Volk House at 343 Jefferson St.

Anderson: "Good evening. It is nice to speak this evening at a place that stands for the history and traditions of our fine town. I'd guess that if he were alive today Erasmus Volk would have trouble identifying with the town he helped incorporate 123 years ago. Yet the changes—expensive townhouses, boutiques catering to the wealthy and the tourist, too much pavement and too little greenery—have only begun. There's still time for us to stop our town from becoming a haven for the wealthy urbanite instead of for the families of many religions, races and cultures who have called it home for the past several generations."

"When I was a schoolgirl here—dare I say 35 and 40 years ago—North Tucker was still a wooded grove. A 65-acre farm occupied what is now the Crescent Drive development. And the biggest building in town stood four stories. Times have changed, and when KBC Developers moved to speed that change by proposing to put up an eight-story apartment building in the only remaining wild parkland, I decided someone had to speak for those who have long lived in and long loved this town. Unlike my opponents, I have no vested interest in this town. Unlike Mr. Parkins, I do not own a real estate firm that stands to benefit if property values in this town are pushed beyond the reach of its average citizens. Unlike Mrs. Jones, I do not own an antique shop that relies on wealthy tourists for business. I am a native of this town. I've put three sons through its public schools. And I've taught in those schools for 12 years now, teaching some of your children in elementary school art, in fact."

"Let me make my position clear. I am not against development per se. Far from it. I am for the preservation of this town's independent and heterogeneous character. Over the years, as you know, I've been a member of your organization and, from 1998 to 2002, its vice president. I was part of the committee that lobbied the council to seek grants to restore and upgrade the turn-of-the-century brick buildings along Main Street. I have long fought to get the council to put a town recreation building on the very four acres KBC now wants to turn into a luxury apartment complex."

"Why should we oppose the KBC plans? My opponents say it would bring down taxes in this town by attracting wealthy residents. I say hogwash. Our schools already are filled to capacity. What will the cost be to build a new elementary school for the complex's children? Who will pay those costs? What will the cost be to provide additional sanitation and snow removal and police protection for this complex? Who will pay those costs? The answer frankly is that no one knows. At the council's urging, the Planning Board already has pushed through the KBC proposal without the benefit of an economic or environmental impact statement. Is this sound development?"

"I say let's look at impact, let's look at alternatives. This town has proven unique in its ability to mix people of different socioeconomic backgrounds. Bring in an exclusive apartment complex designed to lure the wealthy from the cities, and it is only a matter of time before those of us of moderate means will be forced to move elsewhere, only a matter of time before a horde of like-minded developers turns our once-rural town into a high-class asphalt playground."

"What about the specific four acres in dispute? It is an informal playground to dozens of children on the east side of town. As you know, it is the only open play area east of Main Street. Isn't that something worth preserving? Isn't that something worth developing—as a playground, a nature walk, a teen recreation center? At the very least, I can promise you that if elected to council I will be an independent voice—independent of the developers, independent of the party hierarchies and independent of the commercial interests who would stand to gain customers. I ask for your vote. Thank you."

A check of the clips confirms Mrs. Anderson's statements about the KBC development plans and the current use of the property. It also shows that KBC's plan has been approved by the Planning Board but still must be approved by the City Council. No date has been set for the council's vote.

The clips further confirm that Parkins owns High Road Realtors and that Mrs. Jones owns The Highboy antique store.

FOUR

Three candidates have been running for a single seat on the Granby Village Council. On the basis of the following interviews with the candidates, clips and election returns, write a story for the local paper. Your deadline is before all the votes will have been counted.

The candidates are Douglas Jermack, 46, incumbent Democrat of 5 Cedar Lane, first elected to council in 1998; Republican Glen Armaleo, 52, born in Granby, lives at 19 Garth Boulevard; Sandra Liscomb, 34, independent, of 23 Moonshine Terrace. ...96 percent of the vote has been counted. Here are the returns so far—Liscomb 124 votes, Jermack 4,729 votes, Armaleo 6,412. Voter turnout, 46 percent. Previous low turnout, 51 percent.

Armaleo, at Republican headquarters: "What do you say, quite a herd of elephants, huh? We've come a long way, baby, ya know. I'll tell you, I'm ecstatic. This vote shows that the public wants fiscal responsibility and fiscal restraint. There are just so many extracurricular school and recreation activities this town can afford to support."

Jermack, reached at his home: "I'd like to congratulate Glen for campaigning hard. I have already conceded defeat. Frankly this hurts pretty bad, but I'll be back. If the Democrats had cared enough to vote, I'd be serving four more years. Still, the people have spoken and I accept their verdict. Perhaps I took my opponent too lightly."

Liscomb can't be reached for comment. Clips show the following.

Jermack operates an antique store at 256 N. Broadway and is a member of the Elks, the Rotary Club and the Granby Softball League. He is married and has two sons. In the race he spoke in favor of the high school budget and of building six new tennis courts in Riverview Park. He argued from time to time that the courts would pay for themselves within 15 years as a result of the fees that the village would collect for their usage. He also supported a 9 percent raise for the town's 25 police officers.

Liscomb works part-time for John Henneman, a CPA in neighboring Spring Valley. She is a tax clerk. She has three sons and two daughters and is divorced. She ran primarily to oppose a new shopping center planned in her neighborhood. (No mention is made in the clips of Jermack's or Armaleo's views on the shopping center.)

Armaleo is a partner in the law firm of Jones & Armaleo, Esq. on North Main Street. He is a scout leader of Boy Scout Troop 83, an American Express Gold Card holder, and a member of the Rotary Club. He is married and has a daughter and a son. Armaleo supported the police raises. He campaigned for increased police protection in the Cross Arms apartment complex, in which there have been two dozen burglaries in six months among the 256 units. He opposed plans to build the six tennis courts to be operated by the village, and he led a successful effort in September to defeat the school budget.

FIVE

The following poll was conducted by Wilson Lynch Inc., a major national polling organization, for your paper, the *Burnsville News*. According to Harrison Stewart, a senior poll analyst for the company, the poll was conducted among 945 adults (over age 18) in the state selected at random from the telephone book. The poll was conducted by telephone between last Tuesday and Friday. The margin of error—5 percent. Last Monday, the federal government announced plans to build a nuclear waste repository 200 feet underground in a salt bed 45 miles west of Burnsville. The repository would store radioactive wastes from nuclear power plants in this and neighboring states. The paper commissioned the poll to measure public response to that announcement. Here are the questions and responses.

In your view, can nuclear power help eliminate U.S. dependence on foreign oil?

Yes	*No*	*Don't Know*
54 percent	33 percent	13 percent

Do you support continued use of nuclear power plants in the United States?

Yes	No	Don't Know
48 percent	46 percent	6 percent

Would you support a plan to build a nuclear power plant in Burnsville?

Yes	No	Don't Know
42 percent	56 percent	2 percent

Did you know the federal government has proposed building a repository for nuclear wastes 45 miles west of Burnsville?

Yes	No
73 percent	27 percent

Would you support construction of such a waste site?

Yes	No	Don't Know
28 percent	69 percent	3 percent

Comment by Stewart: "We've seen similar patterns in a half-dozen cities in other states. The message seems to be 'it's not so bad in principal but….' Certainly nuclear waste continues to be the Achilles heel of the industry from the public's point of view."

EXERCISE C
Story Assignments

1. Find out what, if any, federal grants a local city or town has received. Track down the last audit of the largest grant program and write a news story based on that audit. If the municipality has not applied for or has not received any major federal grants, write a story about why none of this has happened.

2. Find out how much a local city or town has borrowed in the last five years, why it has borrowed the money and what the repayment terms are. Check the last five municipal budgets to determine whether the service, or repayment, of the municipality's debts (this is found in the debt service line of the budget) has increased or decreased. Interview the chief financial officer to determine why. Also find out what percentage of the municipality's expenses go toward serving the debt. Write a story based on your findings.

3. Write an article on a meeting of a local planning board or planning commission. Stop by the planning office the day before the meeting to get a copy of the agenda. Ask to see any letters or communications about the projects on the agenda and also ask to see site plans. Interview people familiar with or affected by items on the agenda before or after the meeting.

20

Police

A jewelry store had been robbed, and a detective with the Austin Police Department was making a statement for the microphones of the local broadcast media. Mike Cox, a reporter for the *Austin American-Statesman*, listened as the officer announced that a white male had come in, taken an undetermined amount of jewelry and escaped. The reporters with the microphones said "Thanks" and left.

Cox stayed. "How did it go down in there?" he asked the detective, now that they were alone. Cox learned that the robber had come in with an attaché case and had pistol-whipped the store manager. He also learned that three other store employees had been locked in the restroom.

"Did he tie them?" Cox asked. The detective acknowledged that the employees had been handcuffed by the robbers. After getting a few more details, Cox had his story—a better story than the competition's.

Mike Cox's father also was a police reporter. So was his grandfather. Cox knew that was what he wanted to be before he could even type. "I grew up hearing stories about how exciting it is to cover police," he recalls.

It is the rare reporter who hasn't spent some time coaxing details out of the police or counting the survivors and the victims of a fire. On modern newspapers this may not be a glamour beat, but there are few sterner tests of basic reporting skills—the ability to obtain and care for facts, to turn often-difficult people into useful sources, to function efficiently with blood, smoke or tears flowing around you.

"You do get kind of callous," Cox says. "The other day I was bantering with a homicide detective just three feet from the body of a dead wino."

BEAT CHECKS

Police reporters probably spend more time than any other reporters worrying about the stories they might have missed ... and with good reason. It's a small city, indeed, in which a day goes by without a crime, a fire or an accident serious enough to make news. And crime and disaster are unpredictable. They can occur at any time. To protect themselves, almost all reporters on the police beat devise a system of regular checks, a monitoring system they use to ensure that no murder or major fire somewhere on the fringes of their beat escapes them.

An hour-long police chase down Interstate 45, south of Dallas, ends in a car crash.
(Photo by Johnny Hanson)

Calls

One morning each week Doreen Carvajal, a police reporter for the *St. Petersburg Times*, takes her turn calling every one of the 20 or so law enforcement agencies in the area—various local police departments, the highway patrol, the Coast Guard. The next day another reporter will make the calls.

Beat calls are so much of a ritual in the lives of police reporters and of police and fire departments that both sides could probably play the game in their sleep: "Got anything for me? Anything up?" asks the reporter. "Nope, quiet, just the way we like it," comes the typical response. Reporters will be lucky to get one solid lead in a few dozen such calls. But that lead can wake them up in a hurry: "I'd come right down to the station if I were you. We had a little visit from the mayor early this morning, and it wasn't exactly in his official capacity. The charge was drunken driving."

Telephone calls have definite limitations: Controversial stories are often reserved for reporters whose faces as well as voices are familiar. Beat calls are no substitute for efforts to cultivate sources. And officers are often telephone shy to begin with. They know that in many cases their calls are being taped by their departments. Nevertheless, these regular phone calls provide one important way for reporters with a lot of departments to cover to help protect themselves against missing stories.

The Radio

Next to Carvajal's desk is the speaker of a police radio. There's also one next to a copy clerk's desk and others near the desks of the other police reporters. The exchanges on the various police frequencies in the area crackle away in the background as these journalists go about their business. Carvajal listens with some fraction of an ear for a tightening of someone's voice or for a code number indicating something serious has happened, such as a robbery in progress or a murder.

Records

Police keep a running log, traditionally called a *blotter*, of the events of the day. Though the amount of detail in them varies greatly from city to city, blotters should always include at least a line or two noting a suspect's name, the charge and the time of an arrest; the time, place and parties involved in any accident; and the source, time and nature of any complaint. The blotter is open to the public and typically is maintained by the sergeant at the main reception desk. Reporters scan blotters for unusual complaints, prominent suspects or repeat offenders.

Other police reports that may or may not routinely be made available to reporters are *investigation reports*, *arrest reports* and *accident reports*. These give details about what happened, and the names of the witnesses, suspects and officers involved. In some states and municipalities, reporters can get some of these reports online. But personal contact, working the beat (see next section, The Rounds), is an essential part of developing trust with police sources.

Since the records of Austin police are computerized, Mike Cox checks the blotter each morning by sitting at his computer. He punches in the code 01 to learn if any murders have been committed; 02 for rapes; 03 for robberies. "I usually won't go beyond robberies," Cox says. "Austin's so big I wouldn't generally even write about a robbery unless someone was killed, a bank was hit or the robber was wearing a Mickey Mouse suit."

Even with the basic police information a keystroke away, Cox knows that any good police reporter has to show his face, too.

The Rounds

At 5:30 every morning, Mike Cox walks into the press room at police headquarters. An officer will be waiting to brief him on what's happened overnight. Later, he might stroll by the criminal investigations bureau, stop by homicide to see what they're working on and poke his head in to check with robbery detectives. This is the in-person equivalent of making beat calls.

Reporters keep regular rounds to get access to the police reports only the trusted reporters see and to pick up on bits and pieces of the news the printed record doesn't hold. They listen to police investigators gripe about their problems in gathering information and their frustrations when they end up with not quite enough evidence to make a charge stick. And in the process, reporters begin to understand better the workings of a police department; and they begin to replace the formal relationships of routine news gathering with something warmer and, most likely, more productive.

In smaller cities, police reporters regularly stop by all the divisions. They might learn from "traffic" about plans to install signals at two hopelessly congested intersections. The officers at "juvenile" may peddle a "nice" story about a special program designed to encourage vandals to work off the damage they've done. "Operations" may want to show off a new computer linking the town with national crime data from the FBI or Law Enforcement Administration.

These visits lead to legitimate news. They also can lead to valued sources.

SOURCES

Doreen Carvajal recalls that she was once asked by police to hold a story on a hospital employee being held on narcotics charges. The police said they were hoping to turn the employee into an informant. Carvajal checked with her editors, and they decided, properly, to go with the story. Unless they are convinced people's lives are at stake, newspapers can't get into the habit of censoring themselves when it suits the police.

"Everyone seemed to understand that that's the rules except this one sergeant," Carvajal says. "He ended up blaming me. When I had to deal with him a few weeks later on a story about a man arrested for trying to get minors into porno films, he wouldn't return my calls. I had to go to an assistant chief, who ordered him to talk."

Police officers operate in an extremely tense, occasionally dangerous, highly insular and highly politicized world. Many police officers aren't sure just what place reporters have in that world. It's not hard to find officers who believe they've been burned by reporters and who are antagonistic toward them. Reporters have to try to win these officers over. They also have to know their rights, and they have to keep an eye out for sources outside the police ranks.

Local Police

Long-time police reporters often reach the point of being able to count on officers to supply them with the information they need. "When there's a two-alarm fire at 2 a.m., if somebody doesn't call me at home, I'm going to be angry," says Mike Cox.

Newer reporters have to work to build up that trust. "You can't go in with a chip on your shoulder," says Carvajal, who at times has faced special problems as a working woman dealing with what she calls "macho" men. "You have to try to develop a style that uses a sense of humor, because that's the way they deal with their job. If they can identify elements in you that they find in themselves, then they'll talk to you. I think you can still ask the tough questions, but you can ask them in ways that make clear you aren't screwing them."

Carvajal also goes out of her way to do legitimate news stories about the police that aren't confrontational. "When I first came, I did a story on the canine school and spent some time with the guys training new dogs," she recalls. "People like dog stories, and I also made some contacts that way."

Some officers, by the nature of their job, are more likely to have newsworthy information and are more likely to share it than others. Detectives generally are the most helpful people on the force. They are experienced officers, often less concerned about what their boss will think than street patrolmen, and more knowledgeable about ongoing investigations. Their job in some respects resembles that of the reporters who cover police stories. They, too, call strangers and try to piece together information.

Other important police sources are the head of the local Patrolmen's Benevolent Association—essentially the police union—and the attorney for the association. They're often willing to air their members' gripes about departmental policies.

Other Law Enforcement Officials

Just as the branches of the armed services like to outdo one another, law enforcement agencies with overlapping jurisdiction tend to compete. A reporter who has been "stonewalled" by the local police department should consider whether any other law enforcement personnel might be involved. Once, when the public information officer of the St. Petersburg police refused to release information about a strange child-abuse case, Carvajal developed the story with the help of other sources—including the county sheriff's department. "You can rely on rivalry between the agencies," she says. "It's important to talk to all of them."

Witnesses, Victims and Suspects

"Too many police stories rely on just one source," says Carvajal. "Always try to avoid using *just* what the police say about an incident. Go back and talk to a neighbor or someone who was involved. You can usually flesh things out."

There are risks here. Reporters must be careful not to accuse anyone of a crime on the basis of an account by someone who happened to have been standing across the street. But what that witness saw, in his own words, can help dramatize the more formal account provided by police. Quotes from nonofficial sources—friends, relatives and neighbors of victims, for example—help communicate the tragedy of an event. This is from the neighbor of a 13-year-old boy who was found dead after having been missing for almost a week:

> "I prayed for him every night, for the dear Almighty God to let him come home safe, let him come home safe.... You can't trust nobody today, it's the God's truth."
>
> *The New York Times*

The danger of cronyism (see Chapter 15, Sources) is at least as great a risk on the police beat as on any other. It is all too easy to parrot the perspective of the police on their work and on the people they arrest, especially since police can be so sensitive to criticism. One way to preserve a balance is to maintain a wide range of outside sources.

CRIME

It is not for reporters to try to create a new race of humans who do not want to read about pistol whippings or murders; that would be like trying to create people who do not stop to rubberneck at the scene of gory accidents. The ability to cover a jewelry store robbery or a murder is a skill all reporters—even the most serious minded—must have.

Basic Facts

Crime stories are about emotion and drama, but they are also very much about detail: names, addresses, ages, times. (See Chapter 8, Information Selection.) Reporters covering a crime will want to make sure that by the time they are ready to write, they have made an effort to obtain *all* the relevant basic facts. In covering the murder of a South Philadelphia man, three *Philadelphia Inquirer* reporters clearly made that effort. Here was their lead:

> The body of a man who had been shot to death was found early yesterday on a back road in Camden County, about a mile from the site where reputed organized-crime figure Salvatore Testa was found slain Friday, police said.

The following is a list of the information that reporters should *try* to gather. (The examples are from the *Inquirer* story.)

1. Name, age, address, closest relatives and profession or claim to fame (see Chapter 17, Obituaries) of any victims.

   > The victim was identified as Marvin T. Wicks, 21, of the 400 block of Bar Street, South Philadelphia, by Luis A. Rodriguez of the homicide division of the Camden County prosecutor's office....*

2. The exact time and place of the crime and of the discovery of the crime, including a description of the scene.

   > Wicks' body, found near Hickstown and Erial roads in Gloucester Township ... at 6:48 a.m., was lying on a 3-by-4-foot pallet just off the shoulder of Hickstown Road, in front of a roofless, gray, concrete structure at the edge of the now-closed Gem's Landfill ...
   >   Wicks was found lying on his back with his right arm by his head, according to [Gloucester Township Police Chief Seth] Stichler, who said $170 was scattered on the ground inside the crook of his arm.

3. Detailed description of the circumstances of the crime, including any weapon used, method of entry, method of escape, and, in the case of death or injury, the official cause and time.

---

* The name and address of the victim in this story has been changed.

An autopsy by the Camden County medical examiner's office showed that Wicks died of the two bullet wounds from a small-caliber handgun. There was no estimate of the time of death.

4. Description of any damage to property or loss of property—with dollar amounts if possible.
5. Name and identification of any witnesses, particularly the persons who discovered the crime. (Wicks' body was found by "an unidentified bicycle rider.")
6. Description of the police investigation of the crime, including any possible motivation for the crime, any possible clues and the names of officers involved in the investigation.

Assistant Camden County Prosecutor Dennis Wixted said officials were investigating whether the two slayings were linked. Philadelphia police, cooperating with Wixted's investigation, said the second slaying was not connected with Testa's gangland-style execution ...
Stichler said investigators had made impressions of what appeared to have been automobile tire tracks near the site where Wicks' body was found.

7. Name, age, address and profession of suspects, if any, plus exact charges against them.
8. Descriptions of the circumstances of the arrest, if any, and of the *booking*—when suspects are brought to the police station and information about them and their alleged crime is recorded. Reporters should also know the schedule for the *arraignment*—when charges are presented before a judge and bail is set.
9. The response of suspects to charges against them, if available (perhaps through their attorneys).
10. Any additional consequences of the crime resulting from death or injury, loss of or damage to property.
11. Any unusual circumstances involved in the crime (to use Mike Cox's example, robbers wearing Mickey Mouse suits).

Not all the preceding information, of course, will be available on every crime in time for reporters to make their deadlines. The point is that they should try to get as much of it as *is* available or pertinent. All the important questions readers might have about a story must be answered even if the only answer police can provide is "We don't know" or "No." The reporters from *The Philadelphia Inquirer* covering the Wicks murder told readers that "no weapon was found at the site." They also made clear where police were stymied ("There was no estimate of the time of death.") or holding back ("An item had been found there, but [the chief] declined to describe it.").

Can police be expected to cooperate with reporters as they search for these facts? Generally, yes. Groups of journalists and law enforcement officials in most states have agreed on certain basic guidelines for helping the police determine what they should and should not say to reporters about arrests. Reporters should be able to get a copy of these guidelines from a local press or bar association, and they should be able to hold police to them. Here are some standard rules on what information officers should be expected to release:

1. The defendant's name, age, residence, employment, marital status and similar background information—unless the defendant is under age.
2. The substance of the charge as contained in the complaint or the indictment (see Chapter 21, Courts).
3. The circumstances immediately surrounding the arrest, including the time and place, resistance, pursuit, possession and use of weapons, and a description of items seized.
4. The identity of the person filing the complaint—unless that person is under age or the victim of a sex crime.

Such guidelines also generally discourage officers from releasing information that may prove prejudicial to a defendant, such as statements about the character or reputation of the accused person, admissions or confessions the accused may have made, and speculation or opinions concerning the evidence that might be used in a trial.

Terminology

The facts about crimes will often be communicated in legal jargon. These terms can be tricky. Here are some pairs of terms that police reporters must be particularly careful not to confuse (see Chapter 21, Courts, particularly the chart on pages 344–345, for discussions of additional legal terminology).

Charges/Indictment

Charges are accusations made before a judge at arraignment. A *grand jury*—a deliberative body of citizens—usually must decide whether there is enough evidence to warrant pursuing the charges before an *indictment* is issued, formally charging the person who has been arraigned.

Felony/Misdemeanor

Felonies are more serious. Violent crimes—murder and rape, for example—are *felonies*. So are major crimes against property, such as robbery, burglary or car theft. Reporters rarely will be concerned with *misdemeanors*, such as shoplifting. People convicted of *misdemeanors* generally face only fines. People convicted of *felonies* often are sent to prisons or penitentiaries.

Robbery/Burglary

Robbers threaten or use force. *Burglars* sneak in and out. (See Chapter 3, The Language of News, for more discussion of terms for stealing.)

Murder/Manslaughter

Murder means killing with malice: *first degree* if it was premeditated, *second degree* if it was not. *Involuntary manslaughter* indicates an accident; *voluntary manslaughter* is an intentional killing done without malice—in the heat of passion, perhaps. All these killings are *homicides*.

Parole/Probation

Only people who have been serving jail or prison terms can be *paroled*; but people who have been convicted of a crime can be placed on *probation* instead of being locked up. If a person fails to meet the terms of the parole or probation, both forms of conditional freedom can be retracted.

Suspect/Criminal

This is the most crucial distinction reporters covering crime will confront. No one is a *criminal* until he or she has been proven guilty of a crime. People who have been arrested and charged with crimes are *suspects*, to be considered innocent until proven guilty. And *suspects* are not arrested for *committing* crimes. They are arrested *on charges* of having committed crimes, or, if no charges have been filed, *in connection* with crimes. Similarly, all allegations of potentially criminal behavior are just that—*allegations*—whether they come from police, from witnesses or, in that rare case, from the reporter's own observations. And allegations must always be carefully attributed. (See Chapter 6, Attribution.)

Troy, N.Y., firefighters hose down the remains of a house in which an 8-month-old baby died in a three-alarm blaze. *(Photo by Tom Killips, The Troy [N.Y.] Record)*

FIRES, ACCIDENTS AND DISASTERS

When something is burning down, crashing or collapsing, reporters don't want to have to rely on the telephone or police reports. They want to be there. But "there" more often than not will turn out to be a chaotic scene of smoke, shattered glass and sirens. Drawing a coherent story out of that frantic confusion is quite a different task from conducting interviews across desks and coffee tables.

Upon arriving at the scene of a fire or disaster, the reporter's first job is to determine what is most *perishable*—what is least likely to stick around. If the fire is still burning, a reporter will want to begin by jotting down some observations before it goes out. If overturned cars are still on the highway, blocking traffic, a reporter will note the scene and try to determine how long the backup is. Then it's time to start talking to people.

Officials

A reporter's most important official source will be the person in charge. The chief or captain, if there's one there, will have access to the most information and will have authority to release the most information. If you don't know the chief, ask any officer or firefighter. Or just head toward the person in the white hat.

From this interview, and supporting interviews with other officers or firefighters who may be able to supply more firsthand information, reporters primarily will want a rundown on the basic facts. (See Chapter 8, Information Selection.) But the professionals who handle tragedies can occasionally provide a dramatic quote as well:

> Trooper John Pfanz of the Pennsylvania State Police, who spent yesterday morning sifting through the charred rubble, said: "It's devastating to stand there in someone's home and know that a few hours earlier, there was a family and now there's nothing, and to know that a battery could have saved them."
>
> Firefighters found one smoke detector, without batteries, on a wall in the second-floor hallway.
>
> *The Philadelphia Inquirer*

The facts reporters are looking for start with the dead, the injured and the property damage. These usually will appear in or near the lead, with death always taking precedence:

> Two children, aged 7 and 9, who apparently had been left unattended, were killed last night in a fire in their Brooklyn home that they may have set themselves by playing with matches, officials said.
>
> (New York) *Daily News*

Notice the cause of the fire in the *News* lead. That's the next question, though fire officials won't always be willing to speculate.

> East Whiteland Fire Chief Donald Fonda ... said the fire may have been started by an overloaded electrical outlet, a malfunctioning television or video game, or by a cigarette.
>
> *The Philadelphia Inquirer*

Questions aimed at filling in other details follow: What's the address? When did the fire start? How many people lived in the building? How many escaped? How many fire companies responded? How quickly did they respond? When was the fire brought under control? What are the names and addresses of the dead? Officials can help piece together these facts by recounting events chronologically (and reporters may decide to employ that chronological organization at points in their stories—see Chapter 9, Organization):

> A few moments later, the first fire truck arrived, and Brunstetter and other firefighters entered the front door, where they found Mary Catherine's body. Her brother was lying at the top of the stairs.
>
> *The Philadelphia Inquirer*

The fact-gathering pattern is the same at car accidents and plane crashes as at fires, though the exact questions asked of officials obviously will vary somewhat. In an automobile accident, reporters would want to know the types of cars, their speeds and destinations, and the conditions of the road. (Reporters should be cautious about using speculation from police at the scene of an accident that implies criminal intent—"it appears she was drinking.") The necessity to get down all the details, though, remains, no matter what the incident:

> Police say Hatridge apparently lost control of the car on a curve in the 17200 block of New Halls Ferry Road about 9:15 p.m.
>
> *St. Louis Post-Dispatch*

Three fire scenes.
(Courtesy of The [Bergen County, N.J.] Record)

Survivors and Witnesses

Interviewing survivors and witnesses is no fun, but it has to be done—delicately. Survivors of a fire, an accident or a disaster usually can be spotted by their glazed appearance. "Was anyone in there?" "Did anyone see what happened?" These are two questions reporters may ask everyone they see until they find someone who answers, "Yes, me."

Sensitivity obviously is all-important in interviews with people who have just lived through a horror. "So how does it feel to have lost everything you own?" won't do. Reporters have to be sympathetic and gentle; there's no substitute for real human compassion. A touch of someone's hand, an offer of coffee or a blanket, can help. Survivors and witnesses also need room to gather their thoughts and express their feelings. An initial question followed by silence can be much more effective than a barrage of staccato questions. Vivid memories should require little prompting:

> "There was just a huge ball of flames coming from the rear of the house. I came out thinking I would take the family into my house. But nobody came out."
>
> *The Philadelphia Inquirer*

Reporters want emotions and descriptions from the people at the scene. Facts will have to be checked later with officials.

Hospitals

After checking with survivors, witnesses and officials at the scene, reporters covering an accident, fire or disaster will likely head for the hospital where the injured were taken. There may be more interview possibilities at the hospital, usually in the emergency room, where survivors who were not seriously injured and the relatives of victims may be gathered. Afterward, hospital officials should be consulted for the facts on the injured.

Most hospitals have established procedures for releasing information. Often the supervising nurse or the head nurse in the emergency room will be responsible for handling the press.

The Health Insurance Portability and Accountability Act (HIPAA), which established certain privacy rights of patients, includes regulations that have made it more difficult for the press to find out medical information. These rules, which began taking effect in early 2003, apply to any health care organization that transmits records electronically, including hospitals and doctors' offices. But they don't apply to police departments or fire departments unless such agencies are acting in a medical care capacity.

Hospitals and other agencies generally cannot release the name, specific address or specific medical condition of a patient without the person's consent. They can confirm that a person whose name a journalist provides is in the hospital. They can release the patient's general condition (in order of increasing severity: good, satisfactory, fair, poor, serious or critical), the patient's general address (state or region) and an age range.

The terms used by hospitals to label a patient's condition are one set of jargon reporters can*not* attempt to translate. *Stable*, one word that's often used, can be applied to a person with a cracked ankle or a person with a cracked skull. Reporters don't have the expertise to make sense out of this confusion. If they can get through to a doctor, they might be able to wheedle out details of the injuries, but otherwise all they can do is pass on what the hospital is saying:

> Two passengers were admitted to Christian Hospital-Northwest, where they are listed in serious condition.
>
> *St. Louis Post-Dispatch*

Hospital officials should *not* be expected to speak to legal questions: Was he drunk? Was he shot from close range? Was it a suicide? While hospital officials may offer a tip, the official word on these questions should come from police.

The websites of the First Amendment Center (www.firstamendmentcenter.org) and the Radio-Television News Directors Association (www.rtnda.org) have further information about journalists' rights under HIPAA.

ENTERPRISE

The police beat has plenty of room for more challenging reporting, too. Though they will make few friends in doing it, the best reporters on the beat eventually will turn their attention to the police department itself. Are its crime statistics accurate? Are its salaries competitive? Does it offer equal protection to all parts of town? Are there any crimes that seem to be overlooked? Are suspects treated properly and victims treated with kindness?

Sometimes police officers are too callous; sometimes they get nasty; sometimes they are accused of being corrupt:

> Indian County Sheriff Keith Stephans and his department's investigations chief, Sgt. Alvin Crews, were indicted yesterday on charges of stealing weapons from the department's evidence locker....*
>
> (Denver) *Rocky Mountain News*

These can be tough stories that may cost reporters friendships and blow useful sources. At a few papers, like the *Los Angeles Times*, "police politics" has been made a separate beat in recognition of this problem.

In an article in *feed/back*, a San Francisco journalism review, David Johnston, the *Los Angeles Times* reporter assigned to cover police politics, lamented a "failure [by newspapers] to look upon the police with the same questioning viewpoint that is routinely applied to elected politicians, school administrators and others who work for government." Yet, Johnston noted, "police costs often consume one-third of a city's operating budget."

And serious reporting on the police beat needn't be limited to stories of overspending, malfeasance and brutality. In-depth features have traced the lives of criminals in an effort to explain "why," have reconstructed the trail of clues police have followed to solve complicated crimes and have taken a closer look at the victims of crimes:

> Two days before she was killed, Alison Jay wrote an essay for her English class in which the young woman described her frustrations about violence in Des Moines.
>
> At one point in the essay, the 18-year-old senior at Technical High School said she was becoming scared to walk the city's streets.
>
> Her fears came true last weekend. Jay's nude body was found Saturday morning about four blocks from her home. Authorities said she had been strangled.
>
> Her classmates and teachers at the school said Monday the essay was typical of Jay, who did not share her thoughts or concerns easily....**
>
> *The Des Moines* (Iowa) *Register*

---

* The names and county in this story have been changed.
** The name in this story has been changed.

CHAPTER 20 SUMMARY: POLICE

The police beat never sleeps. Police reporters need to monitor the news around the clock. They keep an ear open to police scanners, call the station several times a day and check the police *blotter*—the register where daily police activity is logged—with regularity, either online, in jurisdictions where it's available, or in person. No matter how good a reporter's access by phone or Internet, there is no substitution for face-to-face beat calls.
In covering the police beat:

- Work to establish good source relations. It doesn't hurt to have a sense of humor or to write a few legitimate positive stories when new to the beat. "Ride along" stories both help develop sources on the beat and give the reporter a close-up view of how an officer works her beat. Stories about a department's canine or mounted unit, or its technological advances, inform the public and help build trust.

- Seek out accident reports, arrest reports and investigative reports to provide the details of a crime or accident. Look for names, ages, exact locations. Look also for the name of the officer who took the report and the names of witnesses you might contact.

- Try to be specific and polite in all requests. Many police officers are somewhat suspicious of reporters. They have an aversion to reporters who approach them with what they perceive to be a hunting expedition for records. As a rule, speaking softly will get you much further than waving a big stick about your rights under the law. In fact, many police records, those pertaining to an ongoing investigation, for example, don't have to be released.

- At the scene of a fire, an accident or a disaster, determine who is in charge. Start by asking what happened, and try to get the information chronologically. Once you have an overview, push for more specific information. Finally, look for witnesses and surivors at the scene for drama and color. But approach them respectfully. Sometimes the best you can do is leave a card and ask them to call you later.

- Hold your ground, but again, do it politely. Don't censor information because police ask you to unless they can provide a strong rationale. Even then, discuss the request with your editor.

- The more specific your request for information, the more likely police will comply. But remember: Police do not have to release information, for example, of an ongoing investigation.

- Master police scanner codes and criminal legal terms. Use them correctly. And remember that a suspect is just that, a person who is innocent until proven guilty.

ADDITIONAL READING

The Biker Who Shot Me: Recollections of a Crime Reporter, Michel Auger, Translated by Jean-Paul Stewart, McClelland & Stewart, 2002.

Best American Crime Writing; 2004 edition, The Year's Best True Crime Writing, Otto Penzler and Thomas H. Cook, editors, Vintage Books, 2004.

The Corpse Had a Familiar Face: Covering Miami, America's Hottest Beat, Edna Buchanan, Random House, 1987.

Covering Violence: A Guide to Ethical Reporting About Victims and Trauma, Columbia University Press, 2000.

Crime Scene: On the Streets with a Rookie Reporter, Mitch Gelman, Times Books, 1992.

"On the Police Beat," David Johnston, *feed/back*, Winter 1983.

Understanding Crime Statistics: A Reporter's Guide, Kurt Silver, IRE, 2001.

EXERCISE A
Research Assignments

ONE

Use research materials or interviews with people familiar with police and fire department work to write explanations that could be used in a newspaper article for the following terms.

1. Reckless endangerment
2. Saturday night special
3. Controlled substance
4. DOA
5. Released on own recognizance
6. Airplane's black box
7. Miranda rights
8. Third-degree burns
9. Three-alarm fire
10. Triage

TWO

Use research materials or interviews to obtain answers to the following questions for a police department in your area. Illustrate some of the answers with quotes.

1. How many police officers are on each shift?
2. How many of those officers are actually on patrol at any one time?
3. Are all parts of town regularly patrolled?
4. How many people work for the police department, and how do they break down by rank?
5. What are the salary scales for the different ranks?
6. How many women and members of minority groups work as police officers?
7. What training is required to become a police officer?
8. Do police have special procedures for dealing with rape victims?
9. What percentage of reported crimes leads to arrest?
10. What percentage leads to convictions?

THREE

Use research materials or interviews to obtain answers to the following questions for a fire department in your area. Illustrate some of the answers with quotes.

1. Is the fire department volunteer or paid?
2. If it is paid, what are the salary scales for the different ranks? If it is volunteer, what clothing or other expense allowances are the firefighters entitled to?
3. How many firefighters are on duty or available to respond to alarms at various times of day and night?

4. What is the average response time to a fire? Has that response time changed in the past five years?

5. What kind of equipment does the department have? What is the oldest and what is the newest piece of equipment?

6. What training is required to become a firefighter?

7. What is the name of the fire chief, and what can you learn about his or her background?

8. What percentage of its time does the department spend answering false alarms?

9. What was the most serious fire the department was called to in the past year?

EXERCISE B
Writing Assignments

Write stories based on each of the following collections of information or police reports. In each case, you are writing for a newspaper dated tomorrow and read in the town where the events occurred.

ONE: Robbery Report

POLICE DEPARTMENT

1. Complaint No. 57693	2. Mun. Code 0207	3. Phone No. 768-5000	4. UCR	21. Prosecutor's Case Number		22. Department Case Number		
5. Crime/Incident Armed robbery		6. NJS		23. Victim/s/ Frank Berry DOB		24. Age 43	25. Sex M	26. Race Blck
DATE AND TIME	7. Between / At	8. Hour 10:30pm	9. Day Today	27. Victim/s/ Home Address 47 Michaels Way S. S. No. 109-75-1927		Phone 968-4482		
13. Crime/Incident Location Keough's Pharmacy, 13 Castle Heights Rd.				28. Employer Albert Keough		Phone 968-1843		
14. Municipality Lawrence	15. County Dubuque		16. Code	29. Person Reporting Crime/Incident Frank Berry		30. Date and Time 10:38 p.m.		
17. Type of Premises Pharmacy	18. Code	19. Weapons–Tools Handgun	20. Code	31. Address		Phone		

32. Modus Operandi

Went to Keough's Pharmacy in response to phone call from Frank Berry, the night pharmacist. Berry said he had been robbed, at gunpoint, by a white female as he was counting receipts for the day at closing time. Arrived at store at 10:55. Berry gave following account:

He was alone in the store at 10:20 when a caucasian woman of medium height and build entered store. Suspect was wearing black leather pants and motorcycle jacket, a helmet and goggles. Took off goggles and stood for five or ten minutes looking at rack of birthday cards. Suspect then glanced out front door and walked to register with two cards after slipping goggles back on. Upon reaching register pulled out silver pistol with right hand and told Berry to empty the register into a paper bag. Suspect apparently knew of store's alarm system. Warned pharmacist not to push silent alarm to right of register. After Berry handed suspect bag, she told him to lie face down, close his eyes and count to 500 if he wanted to see his kids again. She apparently escaped on foot. Berry gave this description: "She was a cool customer, polite but real scary. Her voice was honey but she said, 'this shoots bullets.'"

33. Vehicle	34. Year	35. Make	36. Body Type	37. Color	38. Registration Number & State		39. Serial Number or Identification	
VALUE STOLEN PROPERTY	40. Currency $425	41. Jewelry	42. Furs		43. Clothing	44. Auto		45. Misc.
46. Total Value Stolen $425		47. Total Value Recovered	48. Teletype Alarm		49. Technical Services	50. Technician–Agency		
51. N.C.I.C. Check	52. Rain Check	53.	54.	55.		56.		
57.	58.	59.	60.	61.		62.		

63. No. of Accused	64. Adult	65. Juvenile	66. Status Crime	67. Status Case	68. UCR Status Month ___ Year ___	69. Date Cleared
70. Name		Address			71. Age 72. Sex 73. Race 74. DOB	

75. Name Sgt. Charles Birns Signature	76. Badge Number 36	77. Page ___ of ___ Pages	78. Date Report 12/15	79. Reviewed By
		80. Weather	81. Car No. 54	82.

TWO: Accident Report

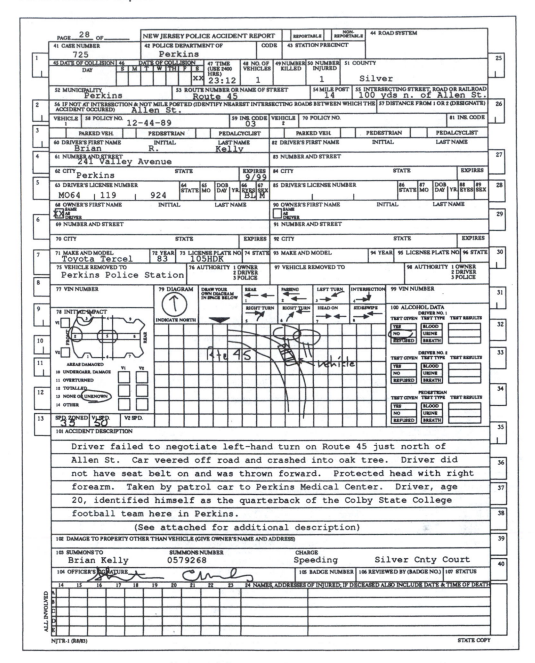

Officer Stanton Charles: "Clocked driver going 50 in 35 mph zone as he passed Allen St. Pulling out to ticket him when he hit the tree. Impact sheared off right side of car. It probably would have killed a passenger, but driver was alone. Driver appeared stunned, but only serious injury was right forearm, which apparently hit and cracked windshield.

"Said he was returning home from Ricco's Pizzeria on Water Street, where he and friends had gone to celebrate victory over Butler College today. Said he had argued with a teammate over his game plan and was distracted. Driver apparently had not been drinking. I drove him to the hospital for X-rays. Police tow truck took car to police station."

From call to hospital: Nurse Clara Milkey: "Kelly has broken two bones in his right forearm. He is in stable condition but is being kept overnight for observation. Yes, he will have to wear a cast. No, I don't know how long, but he surely won't be throwing footballs again this winter."

From clips: Colby State had a record of 3 wins and 3 losses this year in football. (You know the team won 16–13 this afternoon.) Kelly, a junior and the first-string quarterback, had passed for 8 touchdowns and 1,037 yards and run for 268 yards this year. He is the team's dominant offensive player. The team was 2–1 in the Small College Conference and had six games remaining, all in the conference. Kelly is right handed.

THREE

The Movies is a movie theater complex that shows seven films at once at 77 Transom Road in Burlington, Vt.

From an interview with Officer Janet Flannery: "We had a report of an incident at The Movies at 10:45 p.m. this evening ... we arrived and found that the theater's cashier, Amos Rob, had experienced a robbery at 10:30 p.m. in which he lost all the funds in his cash box—an amount totaling $346. The perpetrators, Rob has told us, were two white males ... one of whom was wearing glasses, the other of whom we are told was wearing what appeared to Mr. Rob to be a black Mickey Mouse hat. There were no patrons in line at the time ... the theater's last show begins at 10:15.... Mr. Rob said the robbers came up to his ticket window. The guy with glasses aimed a black revolver at him and demanded all the money he had. Mr. Rob said he turned over the money quickly. The robbers stuffed it in a white plastic bag and then ran off.... Rob said he did not get a good look at the two men, because he was nervous, but that the one without the hat seemed to have dark hair and they both seemed to be in their early 20s. He said he did not recognize them as patrons of the theater. There were no other witnesses. We have no record of this theater being robbed before. The theater's guard and ticket taker were both inside the lobby at the time of the robbery. We have no suspects at this time, but we are investigating. Yes, the Mickey Mouse hat is a possible clue ... though I would imagine the fellow has taken if off by now."

Amos Rob in interview: Gives his age as 22. Confirms Flannery's account, and adds: "The robbers' exact words? 'Let's have all the money!' That's all they said. Yes, I'm sure it was a Mickey Mouse hat. I've seen them at Disneyland, actually. It was black, with two, large, black, round ears and a picture of Mickey Mouse on the front. I think I'm going to have nightmares about Mickey Mouse hats. Let me tell you, this was the scariest thing that ever happened to me."

One of the seven theaters that makes up The Movies is showing a Disney film, *Snow White*, with a Mickey Mouse cartoon called *Mickey Goes Camping*.

FOUR

Smoke streaming out of the top story of factory.... Orange flames dance out of the bottom floor ... it's 6:23 a.m. Chief Robert Salant of the Turnbull Fire Department says the fire began at about 5:25 a.m.... four trucks are here aiming water at the factory ... it is the Regal Fire Alarm plant....

Salant: "Yeah, the alarms went off and all, but when we got here the fire was pretty well along." Can still hear occasional fire alarm going off inside [Salant confirms that that is the noise] above the din of workers and flames....

Salant: "Our information is that there were two watchmen inside the place when she went up. Both men got out without injury. No firefighters have been injured either."

It's 7:10 a.m.... still smoking like a chimney from the top floor, some of which is charred and eaten away. The flames are gone though ... firefighters climbing ladders, knocking out windows and pushing in smoldering walls. The building is brick and timber.

Firefighter Alan Caldwell: "No, we didn't find any sign that there was anyone else in there, but there are certainly a lot of melted fire alarms. The whole place is black and the machinery looks useless."

You are told a lady from Regal has arrived.

Hildy McGomery, vice president of Regal Fire Alarms: "It's awful, just awful. We're just glad our two men got out on time. This was a $3 million plant. We'll have to see what's left of it. Our fire alarm system might have saved the life of those two men, but it just goes to show that fire alarms can't prevent fires."

The two watchmen already have left scene, you discover. At 7:30 Salant says the fire is completely out. He says the fire trucks arrived at 5:40 but that the fire already was going strong.

Salant: "It's obviously much too early to determine for sure what caused this thing, but we're going to look very closely at the electrical wiring. This had all the signs of an electrical fire." He summarizes the damage: bottom floor gutted, structure seriously damaged; other floor, top floor, contents about half gone. Address of plant: 62 Commerce Street in an industrial park in Turnbull.

FIVE

1. Frank Richards is the 21-year-old son of Councilwoman Celeste Richards, a Republican and a close friend and political ally of Republican mayor Ralph Hamilton.

2. Frank is a student at the University of Chicago. He's in his junior year and returned to Dayton yesterday for a short vacation.

3. Late last night attendants aboard US Air flight 505 flying Frank to Astor Airport near here informed the pilot that the young man was in some trouble.

4. Lucille Audrey, a flight attendant aboard the plane, a 727, said the following in an interview: "All I can tell you is what I saw. This well-dressed young man ... we later learned that his name was Frank Richards ... suddenly slumped over in his seat and began moaning quietly. About 15 minutes later he vomited in his lap. The woman sitting next to him ... her name was Adora Campis ... called me over in something of a panic. It was clear we had a medical emergency. I checked his pulse and made sure his breathing passages were clear. Then I notified the captain—who radioed ahead for an ambulance on the ground—and I stayed with him until we landed half an hour later. By then he was awake, though groggy, and he refused medical help and made his way off the plane, where a friend helped him to a car. He didn't even get his luggage. Look, I'll tell you what I told police—it looked to me like a drug problem."

5. Sgt. Gerald Stern, a detective with the police here, said in an interview: "We had reports of a medical emergency that looked like a drug problem aboard US Air flight 505 from Chicago, which landed here at 11:55 last night. We went before Judge Elliot Robinson in Superior Court early this morning and obtained a warrant to search the luggage of Frank Richards, the man in question. The bags were clearly labeled, and he had left them at the airport. We searched and found some suspicious materials, which were analyzed for us this morning at the police labs on Center Street. Our report states that his luggage contained a significant quantity of heroin, I can't say exactly how much right now, but enough to keep even a moderately heavy user happy for a week or so.

   "We have notified Mr. Richards, whom we reached at his mother's house at 10:30 a.m. today, and he arrived at police headquarters with his parents at 11:45. He was fingerprinted and booked on one count of possession of heroin, a felony. He was released to the custody of his parents and told to appear in court at 2 p.m. tomorrow for formal arraignment.

   "No, I haven't discussed the case with either of his parents. Yes, normally we would set bail in such a case, but we know Mr. Richards' family and we are confident he will report as required."

6. A call to the Richards house at 63 Chestnut Drive. The man who answers the phone says no one there wants to talk to the press, but the family lawyer—Walter Fields—can be contacted.

7. Walter Fields, in an interview, says: "Look, this is a good kid, from a good family. He's never been in trouble in his life. I don't know what this business is all about, but we'll be there at 2 p.m. tomorrow and give our views to the judge. That's all I have to say."

SIX

You are making your morning telephone checks and the guy who answers at Fire Department headquarters has put you on hold. To your surprise, Chief John Crowley comes to the phone. Here's what he says.

1. A fire broke out at 5 a.m. this morning in a three-story frame apartment building in Lambertsville. Brought under control at 5:46.

2. Twelve residents escaped uninjured.

3. "We don't know how it happened," said Crowley. "But we know it seemed to start by the front porch. Anytime a fire starts outside a house at 5 in the morning, well, you can't help being suspicious."

4. Three people were killed in the fire. They were all children. Three sisters who lived in a third-floor apartment: Cynthia Evans, 12; Lynette Evans, 8; and Tania Evans, 1. The building was at 29 Mercer St.

5. *Crowley:* "Tania almost made it. Her mother had her in her arms, but then she stumbled in the heavy smoke and dropped the baby as she was groping down the stairs. The little girl was pulled out a few minutes later, but she died on the way to Good Samaritan Hospital. Apparently smoke inhalation. The two older kids were trapped in their third-floor bedroom. The mother, Alicia Evans, 33, is OK now. She's with relatives. The father, Mark, he's 32, was rescued from a third-floor ledge by firemen. All the other residents lived on the first two floors and managed to escape through the doors or out windows."

6. *Crowley:* "We had three trucks and 15 men there within four minutes of getting the alarm, but it was hopeless. This thing went up like tinder. One more thing. We've cited the landlord for negligence for failing to install smoke detectors. His name is Arthur Hopkins, and he lives on McDonald Avenue. I don't have his exact address. The city code here in Lambertsville requires all landlords to install fire detectors in any multiple-dwelling building. The fine will be $500. It doesn't seem like much for three lives. Damage looks to be about $200,000."

7. By now deadline is just an hour away and you know you have time for just another call or two. You run to the reverse directory and get through to two people living in the adjacent apartment at 27 Mercer St.

8. *Jennifer Markus, 53:* "I woke up coughing and ran to the window. I thought *our* house was on fire. The smoke was just pouring out the windows. You could hear the flames popping inside."

9. *Jon Kaunitz, 29:* "I heard people screaming that there were kids in there. I wanted to help, but the smoke was so dense I couldn't get close."

SEVEN

It's 11 p.m. Halloween night and you've just finished editing a feature on Rent-A-Costume, a new store specializing in monster outfits. The newsroom is nearly empty. The night rewrite man went home with a stomachache after eating too much candy. Only your boss, the night city editor, and a clerk remain. That means you get to do the police checks.

You reach Sgt. Stanley Richman at Marion police headquarters. He's just returned from the scene of an accident. You are only an hour from deadline so you know you'll have to cover it by phone. Here is what he says:

1. The accident occurred at 10 p.m.
2. It involved two cars, a green 2005 Toyota Corolla and a black 2003 Volvo 740.
3. The Corolla was being driven by Margie Simmons, 32, of 14 Bashaw Terrace in Marion. Her sons, Paul and Stephen, both 9, were in the backseat. Mrs. Simmons was driving northbound on Route 9W in Marion and had just crossed Arlington Road when the crash occurred.
4. The Volvo was being driven by Maurice Vialle, 43, of Garden Road in Marion. He had no passengers in the car.
5. Mrs. Simmons and her two sons were killed in the collision. They were pronounced dead at Parsons Valley Hospital but actually probably were killed on impact.
6. Vialle was taken to Parsons Valley Hospital as well. Richman isn't clear what his condition is.

You ask how the accident occurred.

Richman reminds you that Route 9W is lined with trees and barely two lanes wide for about a one-mile stretch just north of Arlington Road. Vialle, driving south, apparently never completed a sharp curve to the right, Richman says. His car, obscured by the curve, crossed the divider and entered the northbound lane directly in the path of the oncoming Toyota.

Richman said of Mrs. Simmons: "She never had a chance to swerve, if you know what I mean. It must have all happened in seconds." He said that when he arrived, the Toyota had rolled onto its side. Its crushed roof was leaning against a pine tree beside the northbound lane. The front end was caved in. The door and fender on the passenger's side of the Volvo were caved in and the car, blocking both lanes, was spun around so that it was facing northbound. Richman: "This is what we have: It appears as if Mrs. Simmons hit Vialle as he crossed in front of her."

You ask whether any charges will be filed. He replies that the accident is under investigation. You ask how fast the cars were traveling. "It's impossible to judge exactly," Richman says. "But from the violence of the impact, I would have to guess at least one of them was speeding. The speed limit there is only 35 miles per hour, and those cars were totaled."

Richman says he knows nothing about Mrs. Simmons or Vialle. As you're about to hang up, you remember reading an article about two months ago. "Haven't there been accidents on that stretch of road before?" you ask. "Yes, a couple," he replies. "Mayor Long has been applying for state money to widen the road there for a couple of years."

You call Parsons Valley Hospital and learn that Vialle is in critical condition. The night nurse won't disclose the nature of his injuries. You call the Simmons home. No answer.

You rush to the reverse directory and call a phone listed under the name of Charles Balint, of 16 Bashaw Terrace. A woman answers. Hesitantly and gently, you identify yourself and tell her that her neighbor and her neighbor's children have been killed in a car crash. You ask whether you might ask a few questions so that your story can be as accurate and complete as possible.

"I'm in shock," says the woman, who later identifies herself as Janice Balint. "The police called about 10 minutes ago. Margie was my best friend. She was always kind, always ready to listen and help out. It makes no sense."

She continues. You learn that Margie Simmons had been a fashion model for local department stores but gave up her career 11 years ago when she married her husband, Alfred. She had carrot-red hair, green eyes and was of medium height.

"She was an excellent seamstress. In fact, she made both the boys' Halloween costumes. That's why they were on Route 9W. They went to the south part of town to go trick-or-treating with friends, and they must have been on the way home. Margie was so proud of the witch costumes she made herself. She wanted to see the expressions of the people when they opened the door. She was in a cheerful, bubbly mood when she left off Alice."

You ask who Alice is and find out that Alice, 6, is Mrs. Simmons' daughter. She had a bad cold, so Mrs. Simmons left her with the Balints to take the boys trick-or-treating. You also learn that Alfred, an executive for Exxon, is in Houston on a business trip. The boys, freckle-faced, red-haired twins, were classmates at Douglass Elementary School. They were good students but "a bit mischievous." They would sometimes switch identities to confuse substitute teachers.

You hang up and try the Vialle house and one or two neighbors. No one answers. You rush to the library and pull out the clips for accidents. You find that this is the third fatal accident at the same location in six months. Two months ago, four people were killed when seven teen-agers in a car driven at 50 miles an hour (well above the speed limit) failed to complete the same curve and crashed into the trees. Four months ago, one person was killed and another critically injured when their cars collided during a rainstorm.

You have a few more minutes and then you absolutely must start writing. You decide to call Mayor John Long. It turns out to be a stroke of luck. He says he had met Vialle, who moved to Marion six months ago from Paris, France, leaving his family behind. He worked in foreign trade and had planned to return to France at Christmas to move his family to this country.

"The senselessness of it, what a disaster, what a mess," he says. "They should name that stretch of road 'death curve.' The state's supposed to maintain it, and I've been writing to them and calling them for several years. There's not even a sign warning of a sharp curve. If they don't do anything this time, I'll go out there with a pick and shovel and widen it myself."

EXERCISE C
Story Assignments

1. Check the blotter at a local police station. Ask to see the report on an incident that interests you and write a news story based on the report and interviews with police officers and others connected with the incident.

2. Compare this year's crime statistics in a town with last year's. How have things changed? Are the numbers of certain crimes up or down? Is the number and percentage of crimes solved up or down? Develop a story from some aspect of the reports.

3. Write a story on some aspect of police procedure. How are the officers assigned? How frequently do their shifts rotate? How much overtime do they work? Do they have any quotas to fill? Has new technology changed the way the station operates? What reports do officers have to fill out? Do they feel as if they are buried in paperwork?

21

Courts

Few institutions are as formal and tradition bound as the courts. Grand juries hand up indictments; judges—in their old-fashioned black robes—hand down decisions. Bank robbers and drug smugglers, few of whom presumably know any Latin, find themselves seeking writs of *habeas corpus* (statements from the judge that they are being illegally held). Companies, not anxious perhaps to fight a government charge that they polluted nearby water supplies, plead *nolo contendere*, meaning that, while they do not admit guilt, they do not contest the charge against them.

Reporters wandering around a courthouse will confront many such unfamiliar rites and obscure terms each day. Each offers reporters an opportunity to err, and the consequences of such errors can be particularly severe here, where people's money, reputation and freedom are so often on the line. That plea of nolo contendere, a reporter may learn too late, was not exactly a guilty plea after all.

To make matters worse, procedures can differ from court to court and from state to state. A reporter trained in California, where the Supreme Court is in fact the top state court, might be taken aback to learn that in New York the state Court of Appeals is above the various Supreme Courts.

Most reporters approach the courts without the benefit of any legal training. Tom French says he did not even know how many people sit on a jury (12 on most criminal juries) when he took over the court beat at the *St. Petersburg Times*. Beginning court reporters have to get hold of any documents they can find on the structure and procedures of the courts in their jurisdictions. (The chart on pages 344–345 provides a rough outline of the path suspects might travel through the criminal justice system.) Reporters also must consult a good legal dictionary (see Additional Reading) to help penetrate the jargon. And they must be prepared to sit down with a notebook and some friendly lawyers or court clerks to run through the structures and practices of the courts they are covering.

"Look up everything! Ask about everything!" advises Fred Barbash, who covers the Supreme Court for *The Washington Post*. "When I have trouble writing something clearly is when I don't really understand it." Tom French echoes Barbash's advice: "Don't feel stupid. Lawyers are good at explaining things. They're anxious that you get it right."

Reporters covering the courts must stay on top of all the jargon and ritual, but at the same time they can't allow it to set the tone of their reporting. For behind the Latin terms and the rigid customs are some of the rawest, most compelling events and decisions in our society. "Courts are a repository of human drama, a window on everything!" Barbash exclaims.

This is a difficult beat. It should not be a dry beat:

> Allen Paul Henry, weeping on the witness stand, admitted yesterday that he had stabbed a waiter to death with a kitchen knife last summer, but he pleaded that it was a "tragic misunderstanding" born of his lifetime of exposure to prison violence.*
>
> *The New York Times*

RECORDS

"First," says Ted Rohrlich, who has covered the courts for the *Los Angeles Times,* "you want to learn where the records are kept and which are open to public inspection and which are not." These records include search warrants [statements that there is enough cause for suspicion to search someone], arrest warrants [statements that there is enough evidence to arrest], affidavits [sworn statements], indictments [formal charges by a grand jury], depositions [sworn statements by witnesses], civil suits [complaints filed by one private person or company against another] and the transcripts of hearings or trials.

The court clerk usually has responsibility for keeping track of most of these documents and should be asked for help in determining where they are filed. In many if not most courts, the lawsuits themselves are available on computer databases. The court clerks can help explain this system, too. And court clerks also should have information on which records the public, and therefore a reporter, has a right to see. It's wise to double-check, however. Clerks can be a bit more protective of the privacy of their files than the law is.

Some courts have boxes in which they file material of interest to reporters—major decisions and indictments, for example. All court reporters routinely check the court's calendar of scheduled cases and the docket [a listing of cases to be tried]. "But," warns Walter Fee, who covered the courts for six years for *The Milwaukee Journal,* "depending on the calendar is like depending on a New York City subway schedule. It's written in Sanskrit."

Often armed with tips from sources, reporters go beyond boxes and calendars and dockets to the files of warrants, indictments, suits and other documents themselves. Ted Rohrlich calls it "the mundane process of regularly checking the records." As Rohrlich knows well, what is in those court records can be anything but mundane. It was during one of his regular visits to the files that Rohrlich discovered allegations of a scheme to sell phony tickets to Dodger games. There are exclusives hidden in those files.

"So many stories are there," says Tom French of the *St. Petersburg Times.* "You can get a lot of great human detail and emotion and quotes from the records."

And most court records are privileged—they can be quoted in a story without fear of libel (see The Basics, Section F, Law). As a result, even when other sources are available, court reporters stick as closely as possible to the printed word. "Documents are absolutely crucial," says Fred Barbash of *The Washington Post:* "Since you are reporting things that are terribly damaging to people, the only way to protect yourself is to rely on privileged information."

SOURCES

It was a case no one was supposed to find out about.

"It wasn't on the court calendar," Walter Fee of *The Milwaukee Journal* recalls. "No reporters or members of the public were in the courtroom." This mystery hearing, Fee says,

---

* The name in this story has been changed.

was a contempt of court proceeding against a juror, an unemployed veteran, who had arrived late in court after calling and explaining that his car had broken down.

"The judge took umbrage, cited the juror for contempt and fined him $3,000," Fee says. And the public never would have found out about this severe action had Fee not had a source, a bailiff, one of the court officials in charge of jurors and prisoners.

Courthouses are filled with people worth knowing: not only the judges who hear cases and the lawyers who argue them, but the court clerks who file them, the judges' law clerks who help review them, even the vendors who sell coffee and pastries to judges and lawyers and hear plenty of the gossip that passes between them in line. A major part of a court reporter's job is cultivating people. (See Chapter 15, Sources.)

Judges

Many judges will agree to talk periodically with reporters on background. (See Chapter 15, Sources.) Some, Fred Barbash has found, "like a little publicity." Every now and then they will want to call a reporter with a story," he says. "You want to be the one they think of calling." When Barbash was assigned to the U.S. Supreme Court, the first thing he did was introduce himself to each of the justices.

Lawyers

A lawsuit is an adversarial proceeding. In court, prosecutors and defense lawyers try to influence the judge, play the jury and play the press. But the reporters who ultimately gain the respect of both sides are the ones who listen carefully to the arguments and write their stories "down the center." "I think some reporters tend to side with defense lawyers and others side with prosecutors," says Walter Fee. "Try to avoid that."

Most of the news originates with prosecutors—the district attorneys and U.S. attorneys who conduct investigations, announce indictments and prosecute trials. Reporters want to get to know them and their staffs, particularly their investigators.

Defense lawyers tend to be, as Rohrlich puts it, "a little defensive" and therefore more reticent than prosecutors. Nonetheless, as the prosecutor begins to weave a web of evidence implicating someone, particularly if that evidence is leaking out on background, it is crucial at least to attempt to get the accused's version of events into print. Fairness and innocent until proven guilty are the operative commands here.

In civil cases, the attorneys for both sides, obviously, need to be approached. And even lawyers who are not directly involved in a particular case can be useful as sources of legal information, gossip or general guidance.

"Most court reporters make rounds," Barbash says. "They take a little walk around the building every day. You walk into the U.S. attorney's office, and he'll say he's got an important indictment coming down. Almost all stories come that way."

If suspects will talk, what better source is there for an account, however one sided, of the events in question? One warning though: Accepting such information off the record (see Chapter 15, Sources) can be very risky. If someone were to confess to a crime off the record, the reporter would be left with knowledge of a crime and no ethical way to report it. Usually lawyers will try to protect suspects from the press.

Witnesses

After a crime or disaster (see Chapter 20, Police), witnesses can be crucial sources of information and quotes. But reporters on courthouse beats see the witnesses who are about to testify in court somewhat differently. Attempts to beat the court to prospective testimony leave reporters with an additional responsibility: the burden of checking and balancing what witnesses say,

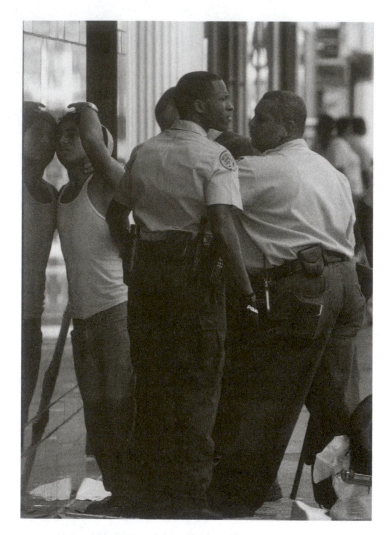

New Orleans police with a suspected looter in the days after Hurricane Katrina.
(Photo by John Rowland of The *[Lafayette, La.]* Daily Advertiser)

a job that during a trial would be handled by means of the adversarial process. Unless there is a compelling reason to move faster—a reporter's own investigation, intense competitive pressure, a suspicion that the prosecutor is holding back—reporters generally will wait to hear witnesses out during the trial.

Clerks

Court clerks and judges' clerks are repositories of information on new cases, on schedules of hearings and trial dates, on the whereabouts and availability of courtroom exhibits (which generally are kept separate from the rest of the files), and on the operation and, sometimes, the finances of the court. They are the best source of tips on new cases and a good source of tips on when decisions are about to be handed down. When a new law reducing the waiting period for marriage licenses went into effect unannounced in Florida, Tom French was the first reporter in the state to get the story. His secret: A clerk, whom he had befriended, called and told him about it.

Courtroom Regulars

Most courthouses attract a group of people, usually retired, who entertain themselves by spending the day watching trials. Fred Barbash often has taken advantage of their expertise. "They are remarkable for their knowledge of what's going on, who is going to testify, and where," he explains.

CRIMINAL COURT

People accused of threatening the well-being of society end up in criminal court. This is where prison and occasionally even death sentences are handed out. The road from criminal charges to sentences is long and has many possible turnoffs, detours and roadstops. The chart on pages 344–345 has a detailed outline of the criminal justice system. Each turnoff, each detour, each roadstop may contain a story.

The first story—the arrest and charging of a suspect—is discussed in Chapter 20, Police. Police reporters often stay with the story through the initial court hearing at which the suspect is arraigned, or formally charged, before a judge. From then on, reporters on the courthouse beat usually take over.

Indictments

In serious cases, or felonies, the prosecutor often must develop the case twice. First, a grand jury, a panel of citizens, decides behind closed doors whether there is enough evidence to formally charge or indict an individual. (In some states, a prosecutor can file charges directly by means of a formal accusation called an information.) Then, the case is presented in open court before judge, jury, spectators and the press. The release of a grand jury's indictment often makes news:

> A suspended Boston plumbing inspector was indicted yesterday by a federal grand jury on charges of racketeering and extortion.
>
> *The Boston Globe*

So, too, should a decision by a grand jury not to indict, a decision by a prosecutor not to pursue a case or a decision by a trial jury not to convict. Newspapers have an ethical responsibility to follow up the outcome of any case in which they report that someone was arrested and charged with a crime:

> A charge of arson was dropped yesterday in the case of Paul D. Searford of Dorchester, a 23-year-old roofer who had been accused of setting the fire that destroyed St. Bartholomew Church in Newburyport on Jan. 24.*
>
> *The Boston Globe*

Pleas

The vast majority of cases never get to a jury. In some major cities, it's been estimated that as many as 90 percent of all cases are dispensed with through plea bargaining—a process in which prosecutor and defense attorney agree to allow the defendant to plead guilty to a lesser charge. A suspected drug pusher might be allowed to plead guilty to possession of narcotics, which carries less severe penalties. A murder suspect might accept a five-year sentence for manslaughter.

The reasons for plea bargaining are complex. Sometimes it results when the evidence is not as airtight as the prosecutor might like. Often it's a means, however imperfect, of meting out some form of justice in a criminal courts system that is suffering from too many cases and too few judges.

---

* The name in this story has been changed.

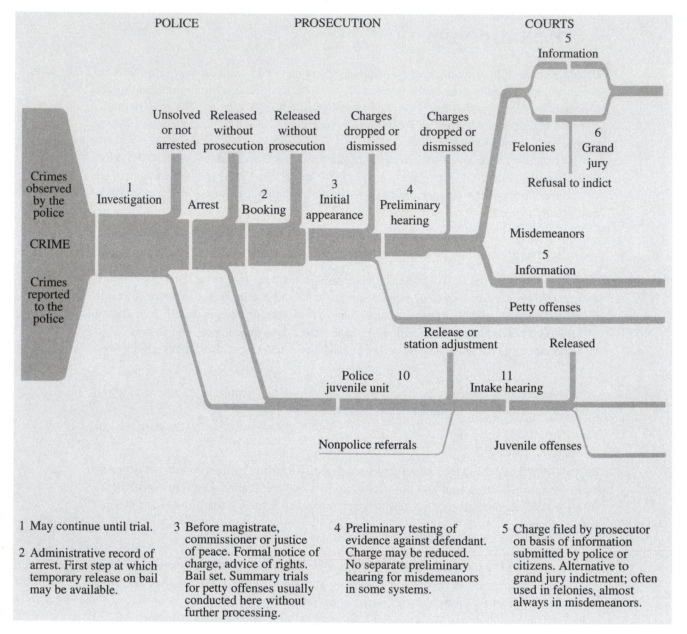

This chart, prepared by a presidential commission, shows how cases move through the criminal justice system—from detected and reported crimes to prosecution, the courts and the corrections system. Procedures in some states may vary from those outlined here. The varying weights of the lines reflect estimates of the relative numbers of cases that reach each stage in the system.
(The President's Commission on Law Enforcement and Administration of Justice, The Challenge of Crime in a Free Society)

Guilty pleas, whether or not to a lesser charge, make news:

> A Hancock Park mother of four who police believe is responsible for distributing 80 percent of the nation's child pornography pleaded guilty yesterday to a felony pornography distribution charge in Los Angeles Superior Court.
>
> *Los Angeles Times*

Trials

No criminal court story generates as much interest and electricity as a major trial, especially a trial involving a prominent defendant. The media pack that descends on such stories can be so

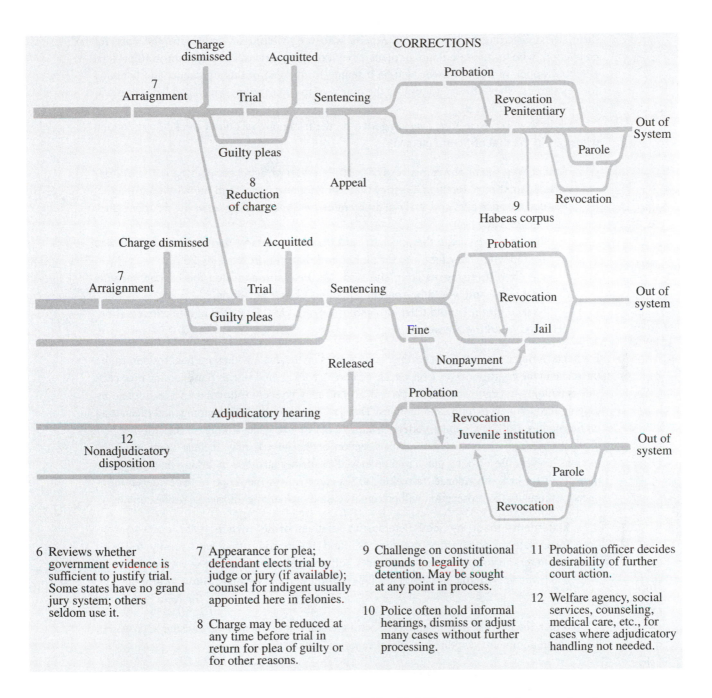

CORRECTIONS

6 Reviews whether government evidence is sufficient to justify trial. Some states have no grand jury system; others seldom use it.

7 Appearance for plea; defendant elects trial by judge or jury (if available); counsel for indigent usually appointed here in felonies.

8 Charge may be reduced at any time before trial in return for plea of guilty or for other reasons.

9 Challenge on constitutional grounds to legality of detention. May be sought at any point in process.

10 Police often hold informal hearings, dismiss or adjust many cases without further processing.

11 Probation officer decides desirability of further court action.

12 Welfare agency, social services, counseling, medical care, etc., for cases where adjudicatory handling not needed.

large that it even boosts the local economy, as *The New York Times* noted in this unusual angle (see Chapter 13, Story Origination) on the announcement that the trial of Scott Peterson, eventually convicted of killing his pregnant wife, Laci, would be held in San Mateo County, Calif.:

> Tourism officials in San Mateo County cheered wildly on Tuesday when a judge announced that the murder trial of Scott Peterson would be moved there.
>
> "You couldn't hear us screaming?" asked Anne LeClair, president and chief executive of the San Mateo County Convention and Visitors Bureau, which is in Burlingame, about 15 miles south of San Francisco. "This is wonderful."
>
> Ms. LeClair predicted the trial—or more precisely, the news coverage of it is expected to generate—would inject at least $8 million into the county's economy...."

Covering a major trial amid all that competition can be emotionally draining for any reporter. Days are spent in court: watching as the defense and prosecution lawyers develop their cases; listening to a parade of experts who try to build or undermine the case for conviction, who try to erase doubt or plant enough of it to sway even a single juror. Reporters, notebooks open in front of them, will be listening for the gist of the arguments and listening for key quotes. They also try to capture the drama of the courtroom, which can be as compelling as the evidence itself:

Here is how *The New York Times* reported on the testimony of one of the key prosecution witnesses in the trial of Scott Peterson:

> Amber Frey, the onetime mistress of Scott Peterson who has cooperated in the murder case against him, testified Tuesday that Mr. Peterson romanced her with champagne, flowers, surprise gifts and a tearful moment in the weeks leading up to the disappearance of his wife, Laci.
>
> Ms. Frey, a massage therapist…, said that Mr. Peterson had told her that he was unmarried when they first met for dinner and dancing on Nov. 20, 2002.
>
> Less than three weeks later, she said, Mr. Peterson confided the he had recently "lost his wife" and would be spending his first Christmas alone….
>
> "I asked him if I could trust him with my heart," Ms. Frey said of one conversation. "He said I had the answer to that."

Evenings during a trial are spent writing: news stories on the day's witnesses, features describing the scene in the courtroom (see Chapter 22, Features), background stories that examine how each side is building its argument. Weekends and days off may be spent following up a lead found by digging through new exhibits and motions. The case can become all-consuming, and it can drag on for months. Still, few good reporters covering a hot trial consider asking off the story.

Trial coverage sometimes starts with selection of the jury. It may include mention of the motions lawyers file—asking that a trial be moved to another jurisdiction, asking that charges be thrown out for lack of evidence, or seeking to widen or narrow the scope of the evidence introduced. Eventually the prosecution will present its case (with defense attorneys cross-examining):

> Statements made by Scott Peterson to relatives of his missing wife, Laci, were so inconsistent, one family member testified Wednesday, that he secretly followed Mr. Peterson to a shopping mall and a golf course to see if anything was amiss.
>
> "I was very suspicious from the first night," said the relative, Harvey Kemple….
>
> *The New York Times*

And then the defense gets its chance. Scott Peterson's attorney took an unusual approach in his opening arguments, captured by *Times* reporter Dean Murphy:

> There are certain unflattering facts about Scott Peterson that even his lawyer, Mark Geragos, considers beyond argument.
>
> Like the fact that Mr. Peterson had an affair and can come across as boorish and like a cad, to use two of Mr. Geragos's descriptions.
>
> "We are not going to dispute that," Mr. Geragos told a jury here on Wednesday in his opening statement in Mr. Peterson's trial.
>
> But Mr. Geragos went on: "He's not charged with having an affair. The fact of the matter is this is a murder case, and there has to be evidence."
>
> The long-awaited defense in the long-awaited trial of Mr. Peterson, who is charged with killing his wife, Laci, and her fetus in December 2002, was outlined in San Mateo County Superior Court in blunt and rapid-fire fashion.

After the defense presents witnesses and the prosecutor cross-examines them, each side is allowed to bring back witnesses to rebut the opposition's arguments. (Reporters try throughout to give approximately equal play to the arguments of both sides.) Finally, after closing speeches to the jury by both attorneys, the jury will consider a verdict. That verdict generally is the biggest story of all:

> Scott Peterson, the Modesto fertilizer salesman whose murder trial stoked the nation's appetite for real-life courtroom drama, was found guilty on Friday of killing his wife and unborn child in 2002.
>
> The jury found Mr. Peterson, 32, guilty of first-degree murder for the death of his wife, Laci, who was eight months pregnant, and of second-degree murder for the death of the fetus. He could be sentenced to life in prison or death by lethal injection after the jury reconvenes on Nov. 22 for the penalty phase.
>
> Mr. Peterson, wearing a dark suit and smiling when he entered the courtroom, showed no emotion as the verdict was read.
>
> But gasps and loud sighs echoed through the courtroom, and Sharon Rocha, Ms. Peterson's mother, sobbed quietly as her son Brent placed his arm around her shoulder. Like all parties in the case, they were ordered by Judge Alfred Delucchi not to speak with reporters.
>
> Outside a crowd of several hundred people let out a roar when news of the verdict hit the street. Reporters and crews from several hundred news organizations were in and around the courthouse. Local newspapers printed special editions.... Several television stations had offered to send notice of the verdict by instant message to mobile phones.
>
> *The New York Times*

Notice that verdict stories mention prominently not only what the defendant has been cleared or convicted of but also the maximum (and often the minimum) sentence. The date of sentencing, if set, also rates prominent attention. Quotes from the judge, jurors, defendant or attorneys, if these people are willing to be interviewed, can be invaluable in bringing out the emotions that fill a courtroom on verdict day. That's probably why the *Times* reporter made a point high in this story of noting that the judge had ordered all parties not to talk. Readers otherwise would have expected some reaction.

Even the story of a five-month trial such as Scott Peterson's never assumes the reader has all the background information (see Chapter 10, Background and Context). Here are three of the seven paragraphs of background *The Times* included in the Scott Peterson verdict story:

> Public interest was high from the moment Ms. Peterson, a 27-year-old substitute teacher, was reported missing. On Dec. 24, 2002, her husband told the police, he returned home from a solitary fishing trip on San Francisco Bay to find the family dog wandering near the couple's home and his wife nowhere to be found.
>
> The police were almost immediately suspicious of Mr. Peterson, who it turned out had been having an affair with a massage therapist named Amber Frey.
>
> The remains of Ms. Peterson and her unborn son, whom the couple had planned to name Conner, washed ashore in April 2003, a few miles from where Mr. Peterson told the police he had gone fishing. He was arrested later that month while driving near his parents' home in San Diego. His dark hair was dyed reddish-blond, and he had about $15,000 with him.

Many trials don't get the gavel-to-gavel coverage accorded the case against Scott Peterson. That's where reporters' sources come in. "Ideally you don't want to miss a minute of what goes on in court," says Ted Rohrlich. "But in practice, with 20 trials going on in the building at once, you may miss a lot. In that case you want to develop communication with the lawyers and court personnel so you can have a sense of when important or newsworthy witnesses will come up."

A man convicted of murdering his wife is led from the courthouse in Warren County, N.Y.
(Photo by John Carl D'Annibale of The Albany (N.Y.) Times-Union)

Appeals

Court coverage rarely ends when the verdict is announced. Readers will be interested in the sentence that is handed out if the defendant was found guilty. And readers should be informed if the verdict is overturned by a higher court on appeal. For example, Claus von Bülow, the Newport, R.I., socialite and millionaire, was initially convicted of attempting to murder his wife. But that conviction was overturned on appeal, and *The New York Times* reporter who covered the trial was there with that part of the story.

> PROVIDENCE, R.I.—More than two years after the long and dramatic trial in which Claus von Bülow was convicted of twice trying to murder his wealthy wife, the Rhode Island Supreme Court overturned the jury's verdict today and ordered a new trial.

Claus von Bülow was found innocent in that new trial.

Good court reporters also try to keep track of the lives of the people they have been covering after the legal process has come to a close. They may visit prisons for interviews, and they remain alert for parole board decisions determining when convicts will be released.

CIVIL COURT

Civil court is where people and companies use the legal system to settle disputes. Often these lawsuits—filed by individuals or companies against individuals or companies—involve efforts to collect damages for injuries or for failure to comply with contracts. There is no role for a prosecutor here, and, unless someone is held in contempt of court for interfering with the process, no one goes to jail. Still civil court can make big news.

AT&T was dismembered in civil court, and former Israeli Prime Minister Ariel Sharon lost a multimillion-dollar libel suit against *Time* in civil court. This is where Microsoft, the software giant, defended itself against charges of unfair trade practices. It is where Johns-Manville Corp. filed for reorganization under bankruptcy laws, in large part because of the hundreds of millions of dollars in civil suits filed against it by former employees who worked with the cancer-causing fibers of asbestos used in many of the company's products.

"Civil court is not as sexy as criminal court, but a lot more important to your readers," says Tom French, who has covered both. Yet, since it rarely is the setting for movie or television scenes, the workings of civil court may be more perplexing to reporters.

Fred Barbash says he has seen too many reporters write that someone was found guilty in a civil case. Here is an example of that error from the lead paragraph of a lead story in the *Los Angeles Times* on a judgment in a "civil case":

> The flamboyant Hunt brothers of Texas, whose combined riches once totaled an estimated $6 billion, were found guilty in federal court Saturday of attempting to illegally corner the silver market eight years ago....

No one is guilty or innocent in civil court. In this case the jury concluded that the Hunt brothers had violated fraud, commodities and anti-trust laws; therefore it "found in favor of the plaintiffs." If the plaintiffs win, as they did here, the defendants may be liable for huge sums of money in actual damages—compensation for losses actually suffered by the plaintiffs—and punitive damages—additional compensation designed, presumably, to teach the defendant not to do it again.

> A jury has ordered the manufacturer of a one-ton robot that killed a worker at a Ford Motor Co. plant to pay the man's family $10 million.
>
> *The Philadelphia Inquirer*

Among the thousands of civil suits that may be filed, reporters look for cases in which unusually large amounts of damages are sought, in which unusually prominent individuals or businesses are involved or in which the issues seem particularly significant or likely to set a precedent:

> Television anchorwoman Christine Craft won $500,000 yesterday in a suit against her former employer, who she claimed demoted her for being "too old, unattractive and not deferential enough to men."
>
> (Chicago) *Sun-Times*

The need for reporters to stay with stories after verdicts is no less important in civil court. Craft's victory was overturned upon appeal, although she eventually won $325,000 in damages after a new trial.

ENTERPRISE

"The main thing," advises Barbash, "is that there is always drama associated with the courts. It's important not to get so consumed with the legal issues that you neglect to dramatize and make relevant these cases."

Barbash has flown to South Carolina to interview victims of "brown lung" disease in order to dramatize discussion of a Supreme Court case on cotton dust and job safety. Tom French evaluated the effectiveness of Florida's new, supposedly tougher drunken driving law by following through the courts the first two dozen cases to be prosecuted under the law:

> The law was clear about Alfred L. Aspiro, a jack-of-all-trades and three-time convicted drunken driver. Arrested in a Dodge van in July 1982 with a bottle of vodka at his side, he was supposed to spend at least 10 days in jail.
>
> Instead, a Pinellas County judge sentenced him to probation.
>
> He was supposed to be fined a minimum of $1,000. The judge fined him $250.
>
> He was supposed to lose his driver's license for 10 years or more. The judge suspended it for six months.
>
> What happened to Aspiro was no isolated case. Thousands of other drunken drivers in Florida are escaping even the minimum sentence required by a new, year-old law. And the ones who stand the best chance of escaping the minimum sentences are the most dangerous drivers—the ones who are repeatedly caught drunk on the road....*
>
> *St. Petersburg Times*

Some of the drama in the courts lies in the legal system itself and in its weaknesses and blind spots. Here are some examples of questions reporters might ask about the courts they cover:

1. How do sentences for white-collar crimes compare with sentences for violent crimes?
2. Do judges differ in the sentences they impose? How significantly?
3. Which judges are frequently overruled by higher courts?
4. Who owns the hotels that sequestered jurors are sent to?
5. What is the average sentence actually served for different offenses?
6. How does plea bargaining affect sentencing?
7. How much do trials cost?
8. Are the fines defendants are asked to pay actually being noted in the records?
9. What is the conviction rate of the prosecutor? How does that compare with that of prosecutors in other jurisdictions?
10. How are judges selected?

Here is how the *Los Angeles Times* began a story about one problem courts face—nuisance suits:

> Two Houston football fans, upset over a referee's call in a championship game which their team lost, sue the referee and the National Football League for "consumer fraud."
>
> A happily married woman in Boston, after falling and breaking her pelvis, sues her husband for $35,000 for failing to keep the sidewalk clear of ice and snow.
>
> A 24-year-old Boulder, Colo., man sues his parents for $350,000 because he doesn't like the way they brought him up.
>
> These are some examples of what many critics of the American legal system might regard as frivolous lawsuits, lawsuits that are increasingly clogging court calendars and delaying justice in more important matters. ...

---

* The name in this story has been changed.

Odd cases can make stories in their own right. When being interviewed for this book, Tom French, who has a taste for the offbeat, was pursuing a story about a doctor who was sued not only for malpractice but for stealing a patient's ligament.

CHAPTER 21 SUMMARY: COURT REPORTING

Most reporters who are assigned to cover courts do not have legal training, and the process of grand jury indictments, criminal and civil suits, affidavits, pleas, depositions, sentences and appeals is complicated and filled with legal jargon. Court reporting requires precision but not drabness. The high-stakes world of courtroom trials is filled with drama and tension for accusers and accused. Only one side can win.

Reporters covering the courts can prepare themselves by:

- Developing sources, from court clerks to judicial clerks, from defense attorneys to prosecuting attorneys, who can tip them to stories, help explain arcane legal matters, and provide context and balance.
- Learning where the records are kept and how the system in a given state and jurisdiction works. Courts follow different procedures and, from state to state, have different names. Start by reading up on the courts where you live and work.
- Relying on legal documents to lay out the framework of the case. Reporters who report from records and trial testimony are much less likely to make mistakes that are, at least, embarrassing and, at most, can lead to lawsuits.

It is essential in covering the courts to avoid taking sides. Just as lawyers attempt to build an argument around the evidence, reporters should explain what that evidence is and how lawyers use it in making their cases.

ADDITIONAL READING

Black's Law Dictionary, Henry C. Black et al., editors, Thomson West Publishing Co.; 8th edition, 2006.

Covering the Courts: A Handbook for Journalists, S. L. Alexander, Rowman & Littlefield, 2003.

Gideon's Trumpet, Anthony Lewis, Random House, 1989.

Press and Media Access to the Criminal Courtroom, Warren Freedman, Quorum Books, 1988.

The Reporter and the Law: Techniques of Covering the Courts, Lyle W. Denniston, Columbia University Press, 1992.

EXERCISE A
Research Assignments

ONE
Use research materials or interviews with people familiar with the courts to write explanations that could be used in a newspaper article for the following terms.

1. Warrant
2. Surrogate court
3. The bar
4. Chambers
5. Summary judgment
6. Class-action suit
7. Restraining order
8. Note of issue
9. Taking the Fifth
10. Eminent domain

TWO
Use research materials or interviews with people familiar with the courts to obtain answers to the following questions about a state court system.

1. What is the name of the highest court?
2. How many justices sit on the highest court? What are their names?
3. How are justices selected for the highest court?
4. What are the names of the other state courts?
5. Does the state impose the death penalty? For what specific crimes?
6. What is the penalty in the state for possession of less than an ounce of marijuana?

THREE
Choose a local municipal or state criminal court and obtain answers to the following questions through research materials and interviews with people who work at the court. Illustrate some of the answers with quotes.

1. What is the name of the court?
2. How many such courts are there in the state?
3. What are the names of the judges who preside at this particular court?
4. How were these judges selected?
5. How long must defendants at the court wait to stand trial? Is there any backlog of cases?
6. What is the name of the prosecutor or prosecutors at the court?
7. How were the prosecutors selected?
8. Do prosecutors at the court frequently engage in plea bargaining? Give an example.

EXERCISE B
Writing Assignments

Write stories based on each of the following collections of information. In each case you are writing for a newspaper dated tomorrow and read in the town where the event occurred.

ONE
You discover the following information from a source in the municipal building and confirm it with police and with court records:

1. Robert Lowry, 19, of Logan, Utah, has been sentenced to serve 30 days in the county jail on Blanchard Street here in Wheeling. He was sentenced three days ago, but no one found out about the case.
2. Lowry was arrested two weeks ago at a Wrigley's Convenience Store, 1400 Woodley Road in Wheeling.
3. Judge Helene Broussard heard the case in Municipal court and handed down the sentence.
4. Lowry was a Bible salesman for the New Order of Christian Hope, headquartered in Austin, Texas.
5. He was sentenced for trying to steal three packages of Hostess Cupcakes and a package of cheddar cheese. The total value of the items was $3.45.

Both the judge and store officials refuse to comment on the case. You are, however, able to reach Lowry by telephone at the jail. Lowry: "I was starving, if you know what I mean. I had a place to sleep but it was going on two days that I hadn't eaten and my boss wouldn't advance me any money."

Lowry said he had lost his previous week's paycheck of $237 in a poker game. His boss wouldn't lend him money, and his mother wouldn't accept a collect call, he said. He had no credit cards and the motel he was staying at, the Crestview on Calvary Lane, didn't have a cafeteria or restaurant, he added.

Lowry said this is the first time he had asked his boss, Anne Jones, for an advance. When you reach her by telephone, she also declines comment.

TWO
1. Last day of trial here in East Brunswick of Andrew Doomas, 98 East Brunswick Ave., East Brunswick, for involuntary manslaughter. Trial in East Brunswick Superior Court had lasted three days, total. (Trial was covered daily in your newspaper.) Doomas is 38.
2. Victim: Jennifer Jacobs, 7, of 34 East Brunswick Ave., in East Brunswick.
3. From closing statement of prosecutor, Asst. Dist. Atty. Joan Shelton, 58: "The defense has not contested the fact that the defendant's white Honda Accord driving east on East Brunswick Ave. hit young Jennifer as she was crossing East Brunswick Ave., at corner of Mulberry Street, on August 28th. The time was 3:15 p.m. We have shown, through five witnesses—three of Jennifer's friends, Susan Shaw, Nicola Wainright and Georgina

353

Wainright; one driver of another car at the intersection, Ralph Handleman; and one pedestrian standing on the corner, James Hampton—that Jennifer was walking, not running across the street and that if the defendant's car stopped at the stop sign there, it stopped very briefly. We do not mean to suggest that Mr. Doomas had any malice toward young Jennifer, only that he was careless in his driving, horribly careless. The only witness the defense offered to challenge any of what you heard from five people who were on the scene was the defendant. Think about that."

4. From closing statement of defense attorney, John Anderson, 29: "Yes, you have heard the testimony of the few obviously horrified and upset people who had fuzzy glimpses of the events on August 28th. But you also have heard the testimony of Andrew Doomas, the vice president of the First State Bank branch in our city, the father of a three-year-old boy himself; a man whose life has been changed by this accident, by this unfortunate, horrible accident; a man who has had, as he told you, difficulty getting behind the wheel of a car again. Andy Doomas remembers events of those moments clearly. He remembers little Jennifer dashing out, running wildly, in front of his car, after he had stopped and looked both ways at that stop sign, before he could stop his car again. Andy Doomas certainly has suffered enough."

5. Jury talks it over for one hour and forty-five minutes. Returns to courtroom at 3:53, and jury foreman Janice Freedman says they have found the defendant guilty.

6. Tears can be seen on defendant's face after verdict.

7. Judge Judith Jones, 62, says she will announce a sentence next Monday.

8. According to the law books, maximum sentence for involuntary manslaughter in state is four years in prison and a $10,000 fine.

9. Defendant, his family and attorneys will not comment after trial, except Anderson says, "Don't worry, we are going to appeal this decision." Gives no details.

10. Shelton, interviewed after verdict: "Obviously, we're satisfied with the jury's decision. We have nothing against Mr. Doomas except that he and others like him must learn to drive properly and protect this city's children."

11. Freedman, interviewed after verdict (no other juror will talk): "It was pretty simple really. There was no real disagreement among us. We just went over the evidence and the evidence said he was guilty. We heard five people there say she wasn't running and that he didn't stop much at that stop sign. What could we do but believe them?"

THREE

The following printed statement was released today by the office of Robert McHenry, Commissioner of the Department of Public Works here in Selma:

"The Department of Public Works, under the leadership of Robert McHenry, as part of its unceasing efforts to serve the citizens of this area, is launching a suit, filed today in Superior Court, against the Reliable Tire Outlet, of 262 South Street here.

"The cause of the suit is the unconscionable problem we are facing here with a shipment of 64 truck tires ordered one year ago for use on large vehicles employed by your DPW. In the year since we made the order, 16 of the tires have leaked air—a satisfactory rate of only 75 percent—well below any acceptable standards. We have removed all 64 tires from our vehicles and are asking Reliable, in our suit, for damages of $19,450 to cover the cost of the tires and the labor involved in installing and removing them, plus $100,000 in punitive damages, so that this company never does likewise to another municipality.

"We say that implicit in the contract we signed with Reliable Tire Outlet is the understanding that the tires would be acceptable. When the satisfactory rate is only 75 percent in a year, that is not satisfactory. It is breach of contract, and that is the ground of our suit.

"We have tried for two full months to get Reliable Tire Outlet to relieve this problem in gentlemanly fashion. They have said 'No.' We have, consequently, no choice but the courts."

From interview with Jane Sheraton, president of the Reliable Tire Outlet: "McHenry wants to take this thing to court. Fine. We will say in court the same thing we have been saying in our talks with him and his people: Fourteen of those sixteen tires that leaked were on trucks that frequently visited the East Side Dump. The dirt path to that dump is covered with glass, sharp stones and plenty of old nails. No tires could stand up under such punishment. There is nothing wrong with our tires."

From interview with McHenry: "I'll tell you. When you buy truck tires from people, you got to think you are getting tires that are going to last more than a year. I'll tell you something else, I have never, in my fifteen years in this job, been so angry about a deal we made. She says the problem is the road to the dump. Sure, there's glass and some sharp stones and nails on that road. It's a dump. What do you expect, a red carpet? I'll tell you, we bought those tires for 'heavy-duty use.' Those words are used in the contract. We used them heavy duty. They didn't hold up. What did she think she was doing, selling tires for golf carts?"

A visit to the East Side Dump shows there to be many pieces of broken glass, many sharp stones and many nails scattered about on paths seemingly used by trucks.

A reading of the contract for the purchase of the trucks (a copy is provided by McHenry's office) shows the following paragraph:

> These tires shall be consistent with standards for heavy-duty work by large industrial vehicles.

From a second interview with Sheraton: "Is he talking about golf carts again? My Lord! As I've told McHenry time and time again, heavy-duty use for tires does not mean driving over glass and nails. We sell heavy-duty tires—the best you can buy. We do not sell tires made of concrete."

FOUR

Julia Mead-Smith. She is twenty-seven. First day of trial in Superior Court. Judge Benjamin Roberts presiding. Tried on charges of robbery. Charges say she held up local welfare office—Department of Human Services here in Westport, 4 West Franklin Street, a state office, on September 28 at 3:45 p.m. Charges say that she walked in waving a gun, aimed it at cashier downstairs, that she ran away, that she made off with $768 from cashier ... was arrested two days later ... money not found.... In opening statement, District Attorney Shelly Fortrand, 45, the prosecutor, said: "Our case against Miss Mead-Smith rests on the testimony of the two people in the best position to say who robbed the Department of Human Services office here on September 28: the cashier who was robbed and the guard at the door."

In his opening statement, court-appointed defense attorney James Bronklin, 58, said: "We will show that Ms. Mead-Smith was not anywhere near the welfare office on the afternoon it was robbed. We will show that the two witnesses who claim they saw her there were mistaken."

First witness called is Susan Bolin, 38, cashier at welfare office. The following from transcript of her testimony:

Fortrand: "Mrs. Bolin, what is your profession?"

Bolin: "I work as a cashier at the Department of Human Services."

Fortrand: "Do you remember what happened on the afternoon of September 28th?"

Bolin: "Sure do. I was sitting at the counter. When this woman comes rushing up to the counter. Didn't take me long to see she had a gun. She said, 'You better give me that money, honey, everything you got,' in this weird, phonied-up voice. I didn't think twice. I was shaking so bad. I just emptied out everything we had in the drawer, lots of fifties and twenties, and gave it to her in a plastic bag. Then she ran out. The whole thing couldn't have taken more than five minutes."

Fortrand: "Could you describe the woman?"

Bolin: "Well, she was white; she had straight brown hair; dark eyes; must have been about my—I couldn't see her clothes below the counter—height, five-foot-five."

Fortrand: "Had you ever seen this woman before?"

Bolin: "Yup. She was what we call a regular. One of those who never gets off welfare."

Bronklin: "Objection, Your Honor."

Judge Roberts: "Mrs. Bolin, please stick to the question."

Bolin: "I'd seen her before. She was one of the people I worked with, cashed checks, gave out spending money."

Fortrand: "Is this woman in the courtroom now?"

Bolin: "Yes."

Fortrand: "Could you point to her?"

Bolin: "There." (Points in direction of defendant.)

Fortrand: "Did you know this woman by name before you were robbed?"

Bolin: "I had to. I cashed her cheeks. Julia Mead-Smith."

Fortrand: "No further questions."

Bronklin: "Ms. Bolin. This woman you say robbed you. Was she wearing anything unusual?"

Bolin: "Yup. A mask."

Bronklin: "Could you describe that mask please?"

Bolin: "Well, I don't remember what color it was, but it went from just below her eyes to, well it covered the rest of her face. You know, like the cowboys wear."

Bronklin: "So all you saw of this woman was her eyes and her hair?"

Bolin: "Yup. She was wearing a mask, as I said."

Bronklin: "You say she had dark eyes and long brown hair?"

Bolin: "That's right."

Bronklin: "Do you know any other women with dark eyes and long brown hair?"

Bolin: "Sure, plenty. Hey, wait a second, …"

Bronklin: "You say she was about your height, five-foot-five?"

Bolin: "Yup."

Bronklin: "You sit on a stool behind the cashier's counter, is that right Ms. Bolin?"

Bolin: "Right."

Bronklin: "You say you couldn't even see this woman's clothes behind the counter, and you were sitting on a stool. How could you tell that she was about your height?"

Bolin: "Well, after a while you sort of can estimate."

Bronklin: "So you sort of estimated her height, is that right?"

Bolin: "OK. I guess so."

Bronklin: "This long brown hair. How do you know it wasn't a wig?"

Bolin: "I don't know. Looked real enough to me, but I guess you can't really tell. It all happened so fast and I was nervous, of course."

Bronklin: "Ms. Bolin, you say you knew the defendant. Did you like her?"

Bolin: "Oh, no. None of us do. She always gave us a hard time. Always was trying to get away with something."

Bronklin: "So it's fair to say that you had a strong dislike for Julia Mead-Smith before you identified her as the woman who robbed you? Is that correct?"

Bolin: "Yeah, OK."

Bronklin: "No further questions, your honor."

At that point court adjourned until tomorrow. No stories have been written on this case since Mead-Smith's arrest.

EXERCISE C
Story Assignments

1. Find a trial in progress at a local courthouse. Sit in on a day's activities at the trial, interview people involved in or familiar with the case, and write a story about events in the trial that day (remembering to include sufficient background on the case).

2. Find the records of civil suits that have been filed recently at a local court. Select an interesting case and write a story about it based on the records and on interviews with people involved in or familiar with the case.

3. How long does it take for cases to move from arrest to trial in a local court? Why does it take that long? What are the consequences of any delay? Write a story on this subject based on research in court records and interviews with people working in and served by the court system.

4. What sentences are people arrested for drunken driving likely to receive in your area? Do sentences vary from town to town? From judge to judge? Is there any connection between the sentence and the background of the defendant? Write a story on this subject based on research in court records and interviews with people at the courts.

22

Features

She took him to dinner on his 50th birthday. Later, after his story had run, he took her to lunch on her 21st.

With a Pulitzer Prize and three decades of reporting among his credits, Tom Farragher knows well that reporters often tread a fine line in their relationship with the subjects of their stories. But when your subject is a Harvard freshman who has survived a malignant brain tumor that left her legally blind and you have set out to tell the story of her freshman year as a math major at an elite American university, the rules bend just a bit.

"Now that the story's published, we have a different relationship," says Farragher, who works as a special projects reporter for *The Boston Globe*. "I like her as a person, and I've come to know her. … [But] I told her family at the beginning, 'If Emily is elected class president I'm going to write that and if she's bounced out for selling dope, I'm going to write that. Whatever happened was going to be on the pages of *The Globe*.'"

Emily Crockett's journey produced a subtler but no less powerful story than one of triumph or tragedy; real life tends to be like that. As he chronicled her first year, Farragher acknowledges, it was sometimes tough to distance himself as a reporter (it took Emily Crockett's father to remind him, for example, that it wasn't his role to help carry Emily's couch into the dorm).

But as a feature writer, Farragher also knows that reporters who want and demand extraordinary access to their subjects can't always check their humanity at the door. Feature writing, after all, is the craft of capturing and chronicling people's lives and experiences. It often demands an intimacy of interaction in reporting far greater than that typically required in the daily bustle of news. It also often demands greater intimacy and subtlety in writing—the very reason that Farragher, from the beginning, laid out his ground rule of no-holds-barred reporting with the subject and her family.

As the line between news and feature writing blurs in 21st-century American newspapers—storytelling leads, for example, are often found on the front page (see Chapter 5, Other Leads)—good feature writers must bring an expanded set of skills to the task of both news gathering and writing. Like news reporters, feature writers dig for facts. But they also are looking to capture detail and emotion that entices readers to turn the page—that *shows* the story rather than merely *telling* the story. Getting those details, capturing that emotion, demands access, sensitivity and an ability to tap the senses—to watch, to listen and to bring readers to the scenes that unfold before the reporter.

It requires patience. And it demands the eye and ear of a storyteller. Like all feature writers, Tom Farragher knew he would need to take his readers with him—onto the Harvard campus, into Emily Crockett's room, and through the ordeal the bright, determined and sometimes mischievous young woman had gone through to make it there. Showing a bit of his own humanity during that reporting process didn't hurt.

Here is how Part I of Farragher's three-part series began:

> Numbers fly through the late-morning air and Emily Crockett, in a cocoon of shadows, leans forward in her classroom seat and tries to catch them as they sail by.
>
> Vectors and matrices, cosines and coordinates, integers and real numbers.
>
> This is mathematics in multiple dimensions, and even here, among the bright lights of Harvard, the material can be mind-bending.
>
> The teacher is enthusiastic, almost theatrical, effortlessly filling three panels of blackboard with a dense tangle of algebra.
>
> As the figures multiply, Emily sits near the back of the auditorium in historic Harvard Hall, where John Hancock once dined with Lafayette, and struggles to keep them straight in her head.
>
> More than for most of her classmates, her mind is her dwelling place. It has been her blessing, a repository of rare brilliance. And it has been her betrayer.
>
> When she was just a small child, a golf-ball-sized malignancy formed near her brain stem. Doctors told her parents to plan for her next birthday as if it would be her last.
>
> The tumor would eventually leave her legally blind, paralyze the left side of her body, and forever shift the axis of her world.
>
> But it had no power to obscure the essence of Emily: her fierce sense of fairness. Her impish sense of humor.
>
> And her singular determination that her life would not be defined by the malignant star-shaped cells that linger in her brain or by the long, thin cane with which she now navigates the well-groomed quadrangles of Harvard, to her a blur of marble, brick, and green.
>
> "I've learned a lot about life," she wrote in the application essay she sent to the university. "I've learned that the future is completely unpredictable, and that we should never take anything for granted. But instead, we should embrace and make the most of whatever we are given because anything, including our lives, may be taken away at any time."
>
> That hopeful code has proven invaluable since the day last fall when Emily moved to Harvard from her house in Worcester—a simple home of soulful music, mischievous laughter and middle-class clutter—where her parents ran a relentless support operation, a war room to protect her health and promote her education.
>
> Making her way at Harvard would prove harder than Emily could have imagined when she applied, almost on a whim. There would be health scares, and more surgery. There would be practical hurdles: How do you follow a math lecture when you can't see the blackboard? And perhaps hardest to bear, there would be the threat of heartbreaking isolation on a sprawling campus where the academic pace can sometimes outrun compassion.
>
> Not that Harvard left Emily to make it on her own. For the university, this would be a year of patient experimentation and delicate introspection in which boundaries

Emily Crockett.
(*Photo by Suzanne Kreiter—The Boston Globe*)

would be tested and the meters of fairness recalibrated. How much should be done to help a young woman, for whom doctors once held no hope, keep up?

Now, as the math class concludes, students stream out of the lecture hall into a brilliant, late-autumn morning, buzzing about student politics, about a late-night party that broke up just hours earlier, and then scatter down a crowded stairwell. Emily pulls on a black waistcoat and her backpack and walks alone across the bright and blustery Harvard Yard, determined to digest the numbers dancing deep in her head.*

Good feature writing is impossible without thorough reporting and precise communication. The reporting entails more than gathering information; it entails gathering scenes and the selective details that build them.

"You can't get it all obviously, but some things you must get," Farragher says. "My editor often uses the word *cinematic*. If this were a movie, what would be the key scenes in that movie?"

"In Emily's story," he continues, "[one scene was] the moment that [her parents] found out Emily had cancer. I knew I would have to portray that. I talked to them a lot about who sat where, what was the doctor's name, what floor of the hospital was Emily on, what did the room look like. ... I went to Amherst where the doctor lived and talked to the doctor. That's the kind of detail you need."

In this case, Farragher had to *recreate* a scene that had taken place years before he met Emily or her parents. The opening scene in the story itself, of Emily in a Harvard math class, he observed. He watched. He listened. He used his senses. And as he did so, he jotted some of the details he observed in his notebook. ("Emily arrives w/by herself ... cane, black waist coat and backpack ... she sits by herself.")

---

* This story is reprinted with the permission of *The Boston Globe*.

Here are a few pages of his notes.

Wed, Dec. 15, 2004, 11am
  Math class
  Room 202
  Harvard Hall
  John Boller is instructor.

19° frigid, blustery, 2 bright day just before official start of winter wintry nonetheless

Large, panel window seat
  All but one shade drawn: Fluorescent light
  Seats similar to theater cinema seats
  3 black boards

Pre-class chatter
  Boller talks w/student @ Pedro Martinez's [?] for millions to the Mets
  New York Mets
  Students bundled in hooded sweatshirt?

Emily arrives w/(by herself)
  Coat, black waist coat
  Back pack

Sits in 4th row from the back and on the aisles
  She sits by herself
  Boller is an enthusiastic lecturer

Vector spaces
  "I want to start with a nice, easy, Euclidian geometry problem."

Pythagorean theorem
  The norm of the vector
  2 vectors in 2 dimensional space

    Though Farragher would rely on his personal observation in grounding the story on the Harvard campus, his reporting—like all thorough feature writing—was grounded in painstaking research, which he organized into a detailed chronology of Emily's life.
    "As a reporter you're lucky if you've got someone who is smart, articulate, introspective," he says. "Emily is the whole package."
    But even with wonderful subjects, great stories don't tell themselves.

PREPARATION

All reporters grab the clips (see Chapter 14, Research) on the way out the door. Those seeking to tell stories need more than the few facts or paragraphs of background the clips might provide.

As he talked with Emily and her parents, Farragher made clear that to tell her story effectively, he'd need complete access—to her medical records, to family journals, to Emily's journals, to e-mails.

Much of what he read simply helped him understand. Some of his research, however, helped tell his story. Here is an example, a description of Emily Crockett's first surgery as a child.

> Emily Crockett was wheeled into (Dr. Alan) Cohen's fifth-floor operating room on the morning of November 13. He made an incision on the right side of her head just in front of her ear. Using a small drill, he bored a silver-dollar-sized hole in the bone, removing a "trap door" piece of skull. It was placed in a bowl of antibiotic solution and replaced later with titanium plates and screws.
>
> Working with magnifying lenses and, at times, a surgical microscope, Cohen worked his way into his 6-year-old patient's head. He opened the linings to Emily's brain and calculated the trajectory to her tumor.
>
> In some places, Cohen recalled, the tumor looked very much like normal brain tissue. In others, its texture and color were distinct. Cohen had to calculate how far to go and when to stop. On the other side of the tumor lay critical neural pathways.
>
> "You can do a lot of damage in a few minutes in surgery ... that can take years to be undone," he said in an interview.
>
> Once inside the mass, Cohen used a variety of equipment to emulsify the tumor from the inside out, eventually suctioning it out.
>
> "We want to take out the bad stuff and leave the good stuff alone," said Cohen, now surgeon-in-chief at Rainbow Babies and Children's Hospital in Cleveland.
>
> And after a five-hour operation, he believed he had done just that.
>
> *The Boston Globe*

The research, in other words, helped Farragher tell the parts of the story he could not observe and helped him verify and expand on details the Crocketts discussed during interviews.

"Become encyclopedic about your subject," he counsels.

OBSERVATION

It may sound relatively easy: "Just write a feature on that." The pressure of collecting facts on a breaking event is off. You just have to get the "sense" of things. No problem.

Wrong. Getting the sense of something, as reporters quickly learn, takes at least as much work as getting the basic facts. All good reporters *overreport*; they collect much more information than they actually will use. But this is never more true than in reporting features. Then, writers will sometimes find themselves discarding five, 10 times as much as they use. That is because observations that speak to a story's essence can be difficult to find.

"I want to marinate in my subject," Farragher says. "I want to be with them as much as I can. ... It's this thing about having a sense of place. You want to put the reader in the place [with your subject]."

At times, with Emily Crockett, that would prove difficult. Part of the story of her first year at Harvard was her sense of isolation. So while Farragher made sure to accompany Emily on her first visit to Harvard, to visit her in her dorm, to observe her in the classroom, he also was conscious that his very presence might skew her experience by casting him in the role as surrogate friend rather than reporter. He guarded against this, too.

"There were times I would just go to Harvard and watch her without telling her I was there," he said.

Whether joining Emily or observing her from afar, Farragher's goal was the same: to capture the details that brought readers into the scene. Here is how he described her on her first visit to Harvard:

> "She walks with a pronounced limp, her left foot held steady in a white plastic brace. Her left hand is withered and tucked against her stomach. And she is smiling."

Whether writing about a blind freshman on her first visit to the Harvard campus, a clown amusing a gaggle of kids, a marathoner struggling through the race's closing miles, writers approaching feature assignments always look for the right details, those that transport the reader to the person and place the writer seeks to capture.

Look and Listen

When working on features, reporters jot down just about everything. Even seemingly unimportant details can later help build understanding and interest in their story: Sometimes these details get turned into a lead.

> SAN DIEGO—They talk with their hands. One hand follows the other, swooping, diving, climbing, turning—the fingertips of one constantly seeking a kill shot on the other wrist.
>
> Reliving the day's flights in the officers club at the Miramar Naval Air Station, fighter pilots are conspicuous—less for their olive drab flight suits or khaki uniforms than for their restless hands. . . .
>
> *Los Angeles Times*

If the observations are not there in a reporter's notebook, no amount of skill in writing can compensate.

On Sept. 10, 2004, the day Emily Crockett left her Worcester, Mass., home, Farragher was there. In his notebook he wrote: "Bedroom stuffed w/ stuffed animals ... w/Bambi over headboard + a picture of Minnie and Mickey Mouse as well."

Listen and Learn

Feature writers, like all reporters, will be looking for good quotes. More than other reporters, they will need snappy anecdotes.

Their job is not done, though, when they've gotten the lively quotes and telling anecdotes. They have to keep an ear out for deeper meanings that can enable them to step beyond surface appearances. They have to keep listening.

As a young reporter for *The Courier-Journal* in Louisville, Ky., Joel Brinkley was sent to Thailand to write about thousands of Cambodian refugees massed in squalid camps along the border there. Brinkley, who had never reported overseas, deftly took detailed notes that described what he saw. But he still had to make sense of it.

"If a reporter is writing about people readers don't normally know about," Brinkley explains, "he ought to get inside the heads of these people to understand what makes them tick, rather than just settling for recording what they say." Brinkley says it took him days of conversation with the Cambodian refugees before he grasped the essential point that they found their misery in the refugee camps far preferable to the horror of life in their own country.

BUILDING THE STORY

Feature stories must live up to the same standards of proof and factuality as news stories (though the rules for attributing states of mind are a bit more liberal—Farragher writes that Emily's "mind is her dwelling place," not that "she says her mind is her dwelling place"). And features use the same language and basic format of news stories—words are simple and precise, sentences direct and concise, and paragraphs short and logically ordered.

How then do features differ? For one thing, they use nontraditional leads (see Chapter 5, Other Leads), like Farragher's:

> Numbers fly through the late-morning air and Emily Crockett, in a cocoon of shadows, leans forward in her classroom seat and tries to catch them as they sail by.

> **Not:**
> A Harvard freshman yesterday was forced to master the equations in a Harvard math class without benefit of blackboard or notepad, one of the many challenges of entering the esteemed university legally blind.

Then, feature stories differ in that they forsake the *inverted pyramid* form used in writing news. Instead, features tend to build to conclusions and to end strong (see Chapter 9, Organization). This is how Farragher concluded the first of three articles on Emily Crockett, who endured severe headaches during her first semester, leaving her unable to complete her coursework and at the mercy of college administrators.

> "Right now, I am just trying to salvage as much of my education as possible," Emily would later write in an appeal to her freshman dean. "It has been my lifelong dream to be a math concentrator, and I am not willing to give up on that simply because a few obstacles stand in my way. I have conquered a lot to get here. And I am not going to stop fighting now."

This quote from the letter helped Farragher build tension to draw the reader into the next day's story. It also brought the story full circle, returning to the special challenges Emily faced because of her choice of concentration. This technique of returning readers to where the story began is sometimes called *bookending* a story.

Color

Reporters working on features are trying to achieve a particularly intense form of communication with their readers. They frequently want their readers not just to *know* but to *feel*. One direct route to the feelings is through the senses, and good feature writers evoke images that refer to the sensory experiences of readers, bringing these readers to the scene.

Consider these paragraphs from a story by Joel Brinkley about Cambodian refugee camps, one of the series of stories that earned him a Pulitzer Prize for international reporting.

> But what kind of sanctuary is this?
> For many, it's a rectangle of hard, bare ground the size of a desk-top.
> It's a plastic sheet for cover, so low overhead that it rubs the noses of some who sleep.
> It's the searing odor of sweat, defecation and death. It's the ceaseless buzzing of a million flies and the hack of 10,000 coughs.

It's row upon row of blank-faced sufferers whose futures hold no promise or respite.

The Courier-Journal

Notice how Brinkley is using all his senses here to bring his reader to the place he's been.

Sight (aided here by analogy):

... bare ground the size of a desk top.

Touch:

... a plastic sheet for cover, so low overhead that it rubs the noses of some who sleep.

Sound:

... the ceaseless buzzing of a million flies and the hack of 10,000 coughs.

And smell:

... the searing odor of sweat, defecation and death. ...

It seems strange to refer to these grim images from Brinkley's story as "color," but clearly they take readers a step beyond a mere black-and-white recounting of the politically significant facts of the camps. They bring the story to life.

Such descriptions, of course, would not have been possible had Brinkley not put so much energy into observation. And the descriptions would not have been effective had he not communicated them in such simple, direct language. (See Chapter 3, The Language of News.)

> **Unacceptable:**
> Their tawdry plastic sheets sagged precariously over their bodies at a height that frequently left them grazing the very tip of their noses as they lay in repose.

Anecdotes

We have already discussed the use of anecdotes as nontraditional leads to stories. (See Chapter 5, Other Leads.) They are equally effective in the body of a feature story. Little stories help make larger stories comprehensible.

Here is an anecdote from Farragher's story that illustrates how Emily Crockett acquired a love of math.

> When she was a little girl, spending long afternoons in doctors' waiting rooms, Emily Crockett would busy herself with equations and word problems her mother devised to divert her from the medical matter of the moment.
>
> At 4, Emily was learning fractions. At 6, she was solving equations with two or three variables.
>
> [Her mother] tried to make it fun: One dog has three times more bones than another. Another has two fewer than the next. And so on. How many bones does each dog have?
>
> Emily, who loved dogs, loved the math, too. It would become her passion.

Specificity

Feature writers should frequently remind themselves to avoid abstractions, to make events real, to be specific. Instead of writing about industrial production, they might focus on events in a single steel mill. Instead of writing abstractly about hunger, they might focus on the story of a hungry person. Feature stories usually are most effective when ideas are discussed in terms of the people who hold those ideas and when organizations and movements are discussed in terms of their members.

One of the strengths of Brinkley's series was his constant effort to describe an almost incomprehensible tragedy through a series of real, easily understood images—the plastic sheet rubbing against noses, for example—and through the experiences and words of specific people. Readers may have some difficulty relating to massacres and refugee camps, but they can picture what it is like to live under a plastic sheet.

Farragher doesn't merely write that Emily is often by herself. He gives substance to her receding dreams halfway through her freshman year.

> As winter tightened its grip on the quadrangle beneath the windows of her room, there was little left of the buoyant plans Emily had for freshman year.
>
> She auditioned for the Radcliffe Choral Society. But when rehearsals interfered with her class schedule, she bowed out.
>
> She considered joining the Environmental Action Committee. But the group meets on Thursday nights, when she often is scurrying to complete math homework due each Friday.
>
> And her plans for political activism on campus never gained traction. Increasingly, Emily finds herself alone in her room. . . .

TONE

News stories all have pretty much the same tone; they are straightforward recountings of the facts:

> The Department of Housing and Urban Development said yesterday there are 250,000 to 350,000 homeless people in the United States.
> *The New York Times* News Service in *The* (Baltimore) *Sun*

Feature stories, however, give their writers the option of selecting whatever tone seems most appropriate to their material. Many features are far less serious than Farragher's or Brinkley's. It depends in part on the subject matter. Some tongue-in-cheek humor, for example, seemed called for in this account of efforts to mate two lowland gorillas at the Houston Zoo:

> On Wednesday, in their first appearance before the local news media, Vanilla countered Abe's romantic moves with a couple of punches to her 350-pound suitor's head.
> *Houston Chronicle*

A *Boston Globe* writer approached this story on "the new face of work" produced by technological changes with a sense of informed wonder:

> This is the first industrial revolution to be covered and analyzed in the newspapers. It is also the first whose agenda has been published in advance.

Short, fast-paced sentences can set the tone, and help bring out the drama, in more emotional stories. This feature accompanied longer news stories on the attempted assassination of then President Gerald Ford:

> SACRAMENTO, Calif.—The day was sunny and beautiful, and the tiny woman in red waited with other spectators for President Ford to walk by.
> Most of the well-wishers wanted to shake Ford's hand.
> The woman in red had a gun.
>
> United Press International

Brinkley enhanced this dramatic effect in his series through the use of repetition:

> They wait in tight lines. . . .
> They wait for doctors. . . .
> Some wait for news of family. . . .
> They wait for another assault by Thai soldiers. . . .

Strong verbs that drive sentences also convey a terse sense of drama. Here is how Farragher captured the reaction of Emily Crockett's parents when they learned their first-grade daughter had brain cancer.

> Walter *collapsed* in tears. Valerie *struggled* for her breath.

In choosing a tone, feature writers are establishing their *point of view* in the story—*point of view* in this case meaning perspective, not opinion. In choosing to use humor, the author of the *Houston Chronicle* article expressed a decision to concentrate on the funny aspects of efforts to mate two gorillas in captivity rather than on the brutality or pathos that might conceivably have been found in the situation.

Once they select a tone or point of view for a feature story, reporters must be careful to stick to it. One word in this paragraph of the *Boston Globe* story on the new face of work seems to violate the story's tone:

> For, say, 6000 years, work was mostly a matter between men and the soil; then, for 200 years, it was symbolically a confrontation between men and machines, though, of curse, many *folks* still farmed.

The word "folks," which might have been appropriate in a less formally written story, seems too colloquial amidst the knowing historical pronouncements here. (The word *men* is objectionable for an entirely different reason—*women* have worked, too.) A feature should not suddenly switch from informed wonder to folksiness or from humor to drama.

Another way to go wrong is to lay it on too thick.

WEAK:

> . . . Vanilla, no loose woman she, countered Abe's apelike romantic moves, made with all the subtlety of a bulldozer, with a couple of well-placed punches to her 350-pound Romeo's love-addled head. It looked more like tag-team wrestling than romance.

Lessons from the Pros: Writing the Feature

Tom Farragher, *The Boston Globe*

In his three decades as a reporter, Tom Farragher has told the stories of people whose lives have been cut short by war and stories of people who have fallen from high places because of their misdeeds. He's written stories about oft-covered politicians and stories about ordinary people. He offers this advice on approaching the writing of a feature article:

Tom Farragher
(*Courtesy of* The Boston Globe)

1. Approach your story with a thesis. Though it may change, your thesis—your angle—will shape who you'll talk to and what you'll ask them. For example, when Farragher wrote a series of profiles of New England families who had lost a child in Iraq, he and his editor knew they did not want the stories "to be another recapitulation of who they were and how they died." Instead, Farragher recalls, the theme of the piece "was more like what does it feel like when the war comes back home in this manner? That completely governs the questions you're asking people."

2. Be open to the unexpected. "Some things you know you're going to use in a piece and some things are serendipitous. You can't predict them." The serendipitous may be a detail in your notes that stands out as a lead or ending.

3. Before writing, outline. "Even if I'm doing a Sunday piece [rather than a project], I do a skeletal outline at least. Even if it's five words. Something as a guidepost to point you along the way of where you're going. Otherwise it is very easy to get lost."

4. Avoid the temptation to overwrite. "You want to show rather than tell. You want the characters in your story to be rich enough so that you don't need to get in between the subject and the reader. Just let the power of the narrative propel the story without the showiness of your words interfering. That's the goal."

TYPES

Features are opportunities for reporters to step back from breaking events and concentrate on the people and issues behind those events, to step back from the insistent and timely and focus on the offbeat and timeless. The main account of the death of 35 illegal immigrants abandoned in the desert without water would be written as a news story. But a survivor's recollection of events would be written as a feature. So might follow-up stories on the routes taken by immigrants, on the problems faced by border patrol officers, on the hardships encountered by immigrants even if they succeed in their journey, on the legislative confusion over how to handle illegal immigration and on a legendary person who guides illegals across the border.

Profiles

A *profile* is a portrait of a person in words. Tom Farragher profiled Emily Crockett. Like the best painted portraits, the best profiles capture the character, spirit and style of their subjects. They delve beneath the surface to look at what motivates people, what excites them, what makes them interesting. The problem is that lives are hard to fit into newspaper articles, no matter how much space is allotted for them.

Reporters who simply try to cram into a profile all the facts they can come up with inevitably end up with something more like a résumé than a story.

Unacceptable:

Laurel Coburn has operated The Tea Shop on Smith Street for 28 years. She has lived in Weston her entire life and graduated from high school here before enrolling in Smith College in 1951. It was there, as a magna cum laude English major, that she first developed an interest in tea.

Like all other stories, profiles have to have an angle, a primary theme. (See Chapter 4, Traditional Leads.) That theme should be introduced in the lead; it should be explored, and often it will be returned to at the end of the story. Something of a person's character, spirit and style will then be revealed through that theme.

Even with 11 months to report and write and more than 10,000 words—an enormous amount of space in the world of newspapers, where 700 or 800 words is a more typical assigned feature length—Tom Farragher had a theme: He looked at Emily Crockett through the lens of her efforts to succeed as a rather remarkable math major at Harvard.

Sometimes finding a theme takes considerable thought. When *Providence Journal* reporter Tracy Breton profiled the wife of a somewhat flamboyant Rhode Island governor for her paper's Sunday magazine, it would have been easy to settle on the somewhat fluffy angle of her role as the state's first lady. But instead Breton captured her as a woman of contradictions—one who had grown up with little and in many ways remained down to earth, but who now enjoyed the trappings of wealth and power. When the governor's wife served Breton a lunch of Domino's Pizza on priceless Limoge china, Breton knew she had one of many details her piece needed to capture the inherent contradictions in her subject's lifestyle. (And she got that detail by turning over her elegant plate to check on its manufacturer.)

At other times, a profile's theme is easy to pin down. It has everything to do with the reason why the story was assigned. This woman is in the news for one reason: She sells machine guns.

SALEM, Va. (UPI)—The first thing you notice when you enter Joan Davis' office is her friendly smile. Then you see the machine guns.

The (Memphis, Tenn.) Commercial Appeal

Through an exploration of the subject's interest in machine guns (done mainly through quotes), the writer is able to give readers insights into this 38-year-old mother of four:

"I absolutely love it but I look crazy sometimes," Ms. Davis said, referring to the stares she draws when moving the guns from her office to a bank vault. "It's like fishing. If you ever get into it, it doesn't let go of you."

The craftsmanship and history of each weapon are what fascinate her, not the gun's destructive capability.

"A lot of people think you're dealing with instruments of death," she said. "I don't look at it that way at all. People who collect old cars don't think of them as things to travel in, they consider them as pieces of history, and that's the way I feel about machine guns. ..."

Whatever the theme, it takes a thorough understanding of a person's life to create a revealing sketch of that life. If given the opportunity, reporters will want to spend time with their subjects in their private as well as their public lives. In this profile of the legendary stripper Tempest Storm, William Burrows led his readers backstage:

> When she first appeared, the woman might have been dressed for an inaugural ball, looking and moving with the controlled grace that is often called "class."
>
> But she is perspiring under the spotlight now, and if those watching from the darkness have noticed, they do not care. The black, full-length coat, the velvet gown, gloves, rhinestone necklace and fur stole have been discarded, leaving the woman in a white negligee. Three musicians grind out "Stormy Weather," which is her song, as the negligee—almost all that is left to separate her from the people in the darkness—slips off her shoulders.
>
> The people have been waiting to see that negligee fall away, so its removal is celebrated with loud applause and some whistling. They look up at her body with varying degrees of appreciation as she sways and twists with the piano, saxophone and drums for a few seconds more.
>
> Lips that glisten a moist, mandarin orange part and smile warmly back at faces her dark blue eyes can barely see. She is absorbing the applause like a sun worshipper basking in the heat, knowing that she has brought her audience to its peak just moments before the curtain takes her away, leaving the people out there alone again.
>
> Then Tempest Storm, the reigning queen of a dying art, picks up her clothes, climbs to a small, electric blue and white room, and drops onto a folding bed whose soiled sheet is marked with a predecessor's lipstick. She uses a tissue to mop the perspiration from her face and from under her long, red hair, while a single fan tries to dislodge thick dust and push around hot, stale air.
>
> *The Wall Street Journal*

Good profiles are spiced with the words of family, friends, enemies and the subjects themselves. Tempest Storm told Burrows she had little use for the explicit sex of X-rated films:

> "I think taking off all your clothes—and I've never taken off all my clothes—is not only immoral but boring. There has to be something left to the imagination. ...."

In a profile of another master of a dying art, Burrows talked to the wife of Hungarian-born Vincent Nemeth to capture the passion Nemeth held for making barrels.

> "Working on barrels doesn't pay much," says Mrs. Nemeth, "but with Vincent, it's a labor of love. My Vincent is a barrel nut."
>
> *The Wall Street Journal*

Sidebars

It's snowing. It's been snowing for six hours already. Twelve inches on the ground, and the storm shows no signs of letting up. The weather bureau is now predicting that 18 to 22 inches will collect on city streets before the storm finally moves up the coast. The previous record snowfall here was 20 inches.

A storm of this magnitude clearly deserves a hard-news story—detailing how much has fallen and is likely to fall in various parts of town and summarizing the effects of the snow on the city. But along with this news story—the *mainbar*—editors will assign a series of *sidebars*—stories discussing in detail one aspect of the larger story. One sidebar might consider people stranded at local airports and hotels; another might use clips and reference materials to describe the other large snowstorms that have hit the city. A third sidebar might focus on people who make money

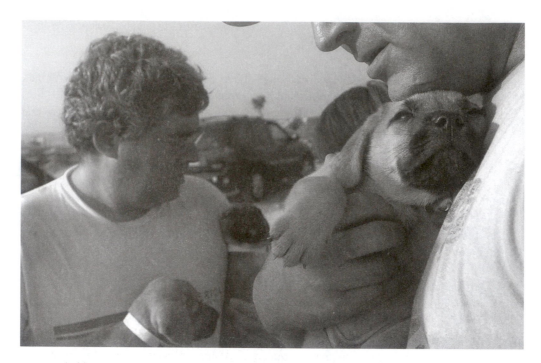

Rescuers hold puppies pulled from a building in Gulfport, Miss., more than a week after Hurricane Katrina. (*Photo by Steve Jacobs of the [Albany, N.Y.]* Times Union)

from a storm—snow shovelers and plowers; another might look into why weather patterns have been unusual this winter. Most sidebars are written as feature stories.

In the following case, the mainbar reported on the funeral of a family killed in their car by a drunken driver. The sidebar is about a stranger in the crowd:

> Abel Garcia shook his head knowingly as he stood on a knoll near the graves of Melanie Cravens and her daughters.
> He'd seen this before.
> And it still hurt.
> "It happens every year," he said, "and nothing seems to happen."
> Eight years and one day before Cravens and her daughters were buried, Garcia had lost his wife and 6-year-old daughter in an alcohol-related auto accident. The memories and the reality, he said, brought him to Sunset Memorial Park to pay his last respects.
>
> *Albuquerque* (N.M.) *Journal*

Sidebars after Hurricane Katrina included stories about families searching for loved ones, stories about families who returned to salvage their homes and efforts to rescue some of the hundreds of pets lost in the storm.

Backgrounders

The events had played out repeatedly on television screens and the front pages of American newspapers. Readers knew about the jury's acquittal of four cops despite their videotaped beating of Rodney King. And they had seen graphic photographs of the violence erupting on the streets of Los Angeles. But the rapidly developing hard news had left reporters little time or opportunity to cast light on the conditions in the city that underlay the riots. So for the Sunday paper, five days after the riots began, editors at the *San Jose Mercury News*, 300 miles to the north, assigned a *backgrounder* on Los Angeles to give their readers a better understanding of events. Here is an excerpt:

> When the streets finally exploded this week, the myth of the harmonious, multi-ethnic, 21st-century community that the city had manufactured for itself lay shattered among the gutted buildings and lives lost in the violence. As looters peeled the metal security gates away from business doors, they exposed a fragmented, leaderless, dysfunctional city with large chunks of its population struggling in poverty and competing for small pieces of its fabulous wealth.
>
> *San Jose Mercury News*

Reporters might be assigned to write a backgrounder on the impact of downtown sports arenas during a debate over whether to build one locally. They might be assigned a backgrounder explaining the history of the national debt during a congressional discussion over what to do about it. And they might want to write a backgrounder on alternate forms of student evaluation and their success during a break in a board of education battle on eliminating traditional grading. Backgrounders rely heavily on research. They may be the closest reporting comes to scholarship.

News Features

If researchers at a local university make a major discovery today about the causes of cancer, that would be a hard-news story in tomorrow's paper. But if a reporter decides to look into new approaches to cancer research at several institutions—even though there has been no major discovery—that story, a *news feature*, could run tomorrow or it could run a month from tomorrow. Such a story is newsworthy, but it needn't appear on any particular day. It is looking at a trend, rather than at a breaking event. This is probably the major factor that distinguishes news features from hard news.

News features are used to investigate subjects that simmer instead of exploding. They may take on one of the larger issues of the day—abortion or drug use, perhaps—or they may focus on changes in lifestyle—from the spread of hip-hop to the "gentrification" of Hoboken, N.J.

> HOBOKEN, N.J.—In this town of steel-toed work shoes, shot-and-a-beer taverns and an occasional beehive hairdo, the invasion of the quiche-eaters continues.
>
> Lured by rows of relatively inexpensive brownstones convenient to Manhattan, young professionals and artists have been moving in droves to the left bank of the Hudson River. And Hoboken, which some local residents look upon with pride as perhaps the least fashionable city in the country—if not all of New Jersey—is becoming positively trendy.
>
> *The New York Times*

Human Interest

Profiles paint pictures of individuals. Human-interest stories, or slice-of-life stories, tell about particularly interesting circumstances in people's lives. A Texas child's 100-mile walk to raise money for the Muscular Dystrophy Foundation is a human-interest story, so is a man's decision to donate one kidney to an ailing twin or a fireman's rescue of three children from a burning building. Human-interest stories often can be written either as hard news or as features. But stories about human beings' aspirations and achievements usually are more interesting when a feature approach is used.

Weak:

A 14-year-old Odessa girl walked 100 miles in the last three days in order to raise $4,500 for the Muscular Dystrophy Foundation.

Better:

Mindy Sackler says she's already forgotten the blisters, the muscle cramps, the endless roads.

Yesterday the 14-year-old 9th grader sat exhausted in the rain for nearly 45 minutes after finishing a 100-mile, three-day walk that took her from the high school hockey field in suburban Odessa to a ranger station in the wilds of Stockton State Park.

Today she was fresh and smiling as she presented a check for $4,500 to the Muscular Dystrophy Foundation, compliments of 112 friends and supporters, some of whom were betting she couldn't finish. ...

Brights

Newswriting can be awfully solemn. As the name implies, brights are designed to provide relief from the earthquakes, crimes, fires and recessions that often seem to fill the papers. Their goal is usually to elicit a smile if not a laugh.

The world, fortunately, is filled with potential brights: hot-chili-eating contests, attempts to set a record for nonstop pingpong playing, parakeets that escape and then fly back home, mock presidential elections in elementary schools, a Halloween parade.

In the first part of this century, many newspapers would mix in a few short brights to lighten up their front pages. *The New York Times* once ran a short front-page story about the president being hit by a pea.

Like all feature stories, brights are opportunities for reporters to loosen up, to show a little style, to experiment. If reporters are self-critical enough to throw their failed experiments in the garbage, their successful experiments can add charm and humor to a newspaper.

Here's the start of a bright about a raccoon who became a regular visitor to the apartment of a former police detective:

In the early-morning darkness, the masked burglar huddled on a ledge outside the open window. Slowly, stealthily, he parted the drawn drapes and slipped silently into the room.

Little did he know he was walking into the presence of a man who, in 24 years of service with the State Police, had captured many a midnight marauder.

Little did he care.

In fact, Roscoe the Raccoon didn't even notice the astonished occupant of the East Greenbush apartment ...

That was two months ago, ... Roscoe has been dropping in two or three nights a week ever since ...

(Albany, N.Y.) *Times Union*

CHAPTER 22 SUMMARY: FEATURE WRITING

News stories *tell*. They convey information. Good feature stories *show*. They convey information and emotion. They immerse the readers in a place, a scene, a person's life, a story. They often convey the effect of news on readers' lives, or they convey the story behind the news. And like any good story told to a friend, features don't attempt to front-load information in the same way a news story summarizes material for a busy reader.

In approaching a feature story:

- **Background thoroughly.** Know what's been written about your subject so that you can find a fresh perspective, a new "place to stand" in telling the story.
- **Find a single focus.** Good features are about one thing. They lose shape and purpose if the writer's focus is not clear. Try writing a focus statement—a single sentence that summarizes where your story is going.
- **Overreport.** Good feature writers discard much of what's in their notes. But if the details don't get into their notes they can't get into the stories.
- **In reporting, use your senses.** Feature writers fill their notes with observations, concrete details of what they see, smell, hear. To do this, it's essential that feature writers go to the scene whenever possible. Features are hard to report over the phone.
- **Push for specific examples and anecdotes.** Features are built around vignettes. They ultimately are stories, although they convey specific information.
- **Establish a tone and stick to it.** The best feature writers guard against overwriting or changing the nature of their writing in midstream. Features can be funny or serious, written in first person or as a fly-on-the-wall, folksy or more formal. But they can't be all of these in one.

ADDITIONAL READING

America's Best Newspaper Writing: A Collection of ASNE Prizewinners, Roy Peter Clark and Christopher Scanlan, Bedford/St. Martin's; 2nd edition, 2006.

The Art & Craft of Feature Writing: The Wall Street Journal Guide, William E. Blundell, NAL-Dutton, 1988.

Getting the Whole Story, Cheryl Gibbs and Tom Warhover, Guilford Press, 2002.

Intimate Journalism: The Art and Craft of Reporting Everyday Life, Walt Harrington, SAGE Publications, 1997.

The New New Journalism: Conversations with America's Best Non-Fiction Writers on Their Craft, Robert Boynton, Vintage Books, 2005.

Writing for Story: Craft Secrets of Dramatic Nonfiction, Jon Franklin, NAL-Dutton, 1987.

Writing to Inform and Engage: The Essential Guide to Beginning News and Magazine Writing, Conrad C. Fink, Westview Press, 2003.

EXERCISE A

Go to one of the following places and spend a few hours there as a *passive* observer. Ask no questions, but take notes on what you see, smell and hear.

1. A hospital emergency ward
2. A local welfare office
3. A roller rink
4. A police station
5. A park
6. A busy store
7. A factory
8. An athletic team's practice
9. The lingerie department of a store
10. A pawn shop
11. A church on Sunday
12. A third-grade classroom
13. A dance school
14. An aerobics class
15. A video arcade

EXERCISE B

Write down a list of features you might write if the following events took place in your town.

1. A tornado tears through a trailer park, killing two people.
2. Local unemployment rises 2 percent, to 10 percent overall.
3. A water main break leaves Main Street without electrical power for two days.
4. Next week is Halloween.
5. Town passes a strict anti-graffiti ordinance.
6. The Federal Aviation Administration issues a report saying training and safety standards at many airports around the country are subpar. Assume there is a small airport in your county.
7. Drought damages the corn crop in the area.
8. The mayor proposes a plan to develop the waterfront.
9. The mayor proposes an ordinance to ban garage sales in town.
10. Town to celebrate its 100th birthday.

EXERCISE C

Locate and write a profile of one of the following people.

1. A chimney sweep
2. A piano tuner
3. A rap singer
4. A long-distance runner
5. A disc jockey
6. A bartender
7. An airplane pilot
8. A magician
9. A person on welfare
10. A police officer
11. A househusband
12. An undertaker
13. A female firefighter
14. A computer hacker
15. A pool shark

EXERCISE D
Story Assignments

Write stories based on the following assignments.

1. Assume a local police officer shot and killed a suspect in a minor crime. Write a sidebar on local police regulations for using guns.
2. Write a human-interest story on the strange things local sanitation workers find in people's garbage.
3. Write a seasonal bright about a local resident who works with the homeless or disadvantaged during the holidays.
4. Assume a local zoning board has decided to allow industrial development in a previously all-residential area. Write a backgrounder on the history of local planning and zoning.
5. Write a news feature on the problem of teen-age pregnancy locally.

EXERCISE E
Writing Assignments

Write feature stories based on each of the following collections of information. In each case you are writing for a newspaper dated tomorrow and read in the town where the events occurred.

ONE

It's summer and it's hot—been in the low 90s for three days. Local boy, aged 11, Danton Roberts, 33 Randolph Street, in Delmore, set up a stand in front of his house yesterday. He's selling fresh orange and grapefruit and carrot juice. Uses parents' juice maker, charges 50 cents per glass, 8 ounces in glass. Says this is his first business venture. It's working.

Randolph Street is a through street to Delmore's downtown business district. Plenty of shop owners and shoppers drive and walk by. Yesterday Roberts made $21. Today he's made $16.50 by 2 p.m. He says he paid $9.65 for both days' supply of fruit and carrots, thinks he'll have enough to last until end of day ("My parents don't charge for the juice maker."). Sign on his table reads: "Fresh Juice—Cheap." He's rigged up an orange and yellow pool umbrella to keep off the direct sun.

Roberts in an interview: "I thought this over carefully, but I never thought I'd be this busy. I might keep going all summer. My first thought was how hot and thirsty everybody standing at the bus stop at the corner looked. So I figured I'd set up a lemonade stand. Ya know. There's always these cute stories about kids selling lemonade. But I thought, 'Who do I know who really likes lemonade? It's either too sour or it's half sugar.' So I decided on fresh juices. Everybody seems to like it well enough. What will I do with the money? That depends on how long I stay at it. I've already got enough for a new video game cartridge, but I might save up for a new bike."

Roberts says he and his family are health conscious. He says there are lots of joggers in the area and some of them have been customers in the evening. So have his friends, but about half his customers are drivers who stop when they see the sign. Roberts is "almost 5 feet tall," has dark brown hair that hangs in bangs over his forehead, wears blue jeans, running shoes and a tee shirt reading "I love nature."

At 2:05 two customers are lined up. One is Mildred Kaye, 31, of 14B Bothels Way on the west end of town. She works part-time at Andrews Antiques three blocks away on River Road and catches the 2:20 p.m. bus at Randolph and Perkins, a half block away. Kaye, smiling: "I guess you could call me a regular. Yesterday I bought the orange. Today I think I'll be really brave and try the carrot. No, I don't drink carrot juice at home. But you don't have to be a health food nut to want a cool drink after walking up from River Road. My boss may have to sell me as an antique if this heat keeps up. Maybe I can convince this kid to sell fans to the bus company as well."

Second person buys an orange juice, waves away questions and drives off in car by curb. "Need those vitamin Cs man. It's a busy world," he says.

TWO

Guess who is playing second base for Kennedy High School's varsity baseball team? Christine, that's right, Christine Malley. And Christine Malley, your editor has just informed you, is to be the subject of a feature you are to write this evening.

You stop at the athletic director's office on the way to the practice field at Kennedy, and, wouldn't you know it, they've put out a press release. It reads:

> Kennedy High School's Athletic Director Richard Mooney announced today that junior Christine Malley has made the school's varsity baseball team and will be the starting second baseman in the school's first contest, against Johnson Industrial High, next week.
>
> Miss Malley, who survived tough competition for the squad, under the leadership of Coach Rod Saunders, will be the first female to play on a varsity baseball team in the history of the state.

End of release. Before you left the newsroom, you checked through the clips and called the state education department. She *is* the first in baseball. In 1990, Virginia Rogers played varsity *basketball* for Wheatley High School for two weeks and then quit the team.

There's the team, all decked out in the school's colors—purple shirts and white pants. And there's Malley fielding grounders to the right of second base, her uniform fitting snugly. You watch for a few minutes. She handles seven balls … makes no errors. Talks a lot on the field, too. In those few minutes you hear her say, "This one's mine." "Hit it to me will ya." "Look alive everybody." "Come on, try to get one by me." "Can't you hit 'em any harder than that?"

You head for the man with the gray hair. Here's what Coach Rod Saunders, 5'6", 47, has to say: "Hi, you know you're the first reporter that's come by. Look, my position on this was simple: I simply chose the best men, oh, I mean the best peoples, ah persons, for the team. I had talked to her gym teachers. I knew she could pick it, but she had to prove it during the tryout and she did. Made my decision yesterday. Do you see her out there? She's really something. A real pepper pot. Keeps the whole team alive with her chatter."

You ask the coach who the second-string second baseman is, and you head for him, by the batting cage. Name, John Accosta, senior; says he started all last year, doesn't seem anxious to talk with you: "Coach thinks this lady's better than me, OK? What am I gonna say? We finished 12 and 8 with me out there last year. Let's see how we do with the lady, OK? That's all I got to say."

You wander out to the outfield and find starting shortstop and number three hitter Ted Mostrieli shagging flies. Mostrieli: "I have nothing bad to say about her. Can she handle the pivot on the double play? Yes. Can she go get balls in the hole? Yes. Me and Johnny felt like a real comfortable team out there. But I guess me and Christine will do fine, too. I tell ya, she is one tough little woman. And I'll tell you something else, too: If anybody on another team says anything nasty to Christine, there are gonna be quite a few of us who are going to quiet them down."

You can hear her chatter louder now: "Throw that ball." "Let's see some hustle." "Come on, hit it to me." You watch her for a while and again she fields without errors, gracefully. Then she starts walking toward the batting cage, and you get ready to watch her swing.

She looks less comfortable hitting: mostly ground balls, one fly to short center that Mostrieli catches easily. You walk back over to Mostrieli and ask about her hitting. "That's a problem," he says.

You walk over to the coach and ask the same question. Saunders: "Well, we're batting her at the end of the order, and we don't need much production from the number nine spot. But Christine is going to have to work on her hitting."

Practice is ending and you catch up with Malley as she heads toward the locker room. "These last few days must have been pretty exciting for you," you say.

"Sure have, and now I'm having the time of my life." Malley, who says she is 16, looks to be about 5'5". She has light brown skin, dark brown eyes and black, curly hair.

"Where did you learn how to play?"

"My dad taught me, though he died when I was 10. Been playing baseball with the boys in the lot down the block since I was 7. Played Little League with the boys, too."

"Why did you decide to do this?"

"Cause I love baseball. There wasn't much thrill playin' intramural softball with the girls last year. I think I batted about .990. These guys can play and I think I can play with them."

"Anybody give you any trouble?"

"I got plenty of dirty looks when I showed up for the tryout. Got some more when Saunders announced I made the team. But a lot of the guys congratulated me, and nobody's said anything."

You're getting near the locker rooms, so you ask the obvious question.

"Hey, Saunders says he'll arrange for me to use the girls locker to change everywhere we go."

And finally: "Have some trouble hitting this pitching?"

"Working on it. I'm working on it."

While you're waiting outside the locker for Malley to shower and change, you meet Al Reynolds, a senior here, who you soon learn is her boyfriend. You ask him how he feels about all this:

Reynolds: "Great, great, think it's great. I'm not much of an athlete myself, but Christine's good at it, and she deserves to play with the best. I've never seen her so happy as last night after she got the news." Malley comes out, wearing black pants and a metallic green blouse, and you ask if she sees this as an important step for women. Malley: "I'm glad if this will help some other girl somewhere, but I gotta say I did it for me. I wanted to play, and now I'm playing. What could be better?"

"You make a lot of noise out there."

"Love the game. I really get into it. Look, I'm having the time of my life."

Malley and Reynolds walk off together. You go to a pay phone and call her mother, Sally Malley, 43. Mrs. Malley: "Of course, I'm happy for her. I would never keep her from doing what she wants to do. She's always been a strong-willed girl. She gets what she wants. She's also always loved baseball. Can't say any of this surprises me."

Finally, you visit the athletic director, Tom Mooney, 46, in his office. "Did this cause any problem for you?" you ask.

"Life is full of problems. Life is full of change, too. Out with the old, in with the new. Go with the flow. These aren't the 1950s. The girl wanted to play. Coach Saunders says she was good. Her grades are OK. Who am I to stand in her way?"

"Did you consult with the district's attorney?"

"Hey, there's no law problem here. This is baseball. This is modernity; the new generation; women's lib; femininity. No chauvinist pigs in this school. I didn't ask anybody's permission. Just got to read the papers. The times are changing. McKerney saw the press release and he said, 'Good job, Mooney.' Told my wife last night and she said, 'Good job, Mooney.' So I guess all Mooney's done is a good job."

You head back to the newsroom hoping you won't start writing like Mooney talks. One last call to Supt. Gene McKerney at home to get the following: "We support the girl 100 percent. We support Coach Saunders 100 percent. And we support Mr. Mooney 100 percent. I personally think this is a wonderful development."

Now you write ... for tomorrow's paper.

THREE

Stats out today ... unemployment up 1 percent nationwide in last month ... call unemployment office in town ... get name of man laid off this month for feature on human side of statistics. Unemployment center director Jill Roberts: "Joseph Schwartz is the kind of man we love to help, and the kind of man it hurts not to be able to help. He is supposed to come in here once a week; sometimes he comes when he doesn't have to just to check to see if we have any jobs." She says Schwartz was fired from the Hastings Pipe factory in town three weeks ago.

Bob Hastings, president of the company, on the phone: "No, I don't know Joseph Schwartz by name. Why did we fire him? Same reason we fired 146 other workers this month. We ain't selling enough pipes. Our orders were down 43 percent last month from the same month a year ago. I ain't running a charity, and frankly I can't say chances are good these folks are going to get their jobs back."

Schwartz OKs an interview. Sitting in living room of small, Cape Cod style house. Has blond hair, blond beard, no hair on top of head, says he is 6'6", looks it, says he is 36. Schwartz: "I have never been fired from a job in my life. I worked at that factory for nine years, before then I did some traveling in Europe and the States. We knew business was bad but no one expected this. Why am I so gung-ho on finding a new job? Because I have three young kids: Jeremy, 4, Theodore, 2, and Katherine, 3 months. We haven't saved anything recently. I'm not saying we're going to starve, but I got to build a family." Schwartz's wife, Susan, 36, enters the room with Katherine. Schwartz continues: "One of us has got to find a job soon, and Susan is breast-feeding the baby. It's too early for her to go to work. I've been to every factory in the area. They all say they're firing not hiring. I'll take anything at this point." Susan Schwartz: "We're not trying to get sympathy. We're not starving. There's plenty of food in the house. My parents have helped us out some. I have diapers for the two little ones. But you've got to buy new clothes, school things. We believe in nursery school. We may want summer camp, someday. We just want to live normal lives, and this sort of throws those plans out the window, in a sense."

Next day ... with Schwartz as he visits local supermarket that advertised packing job ... ten people on line for interview. While on line, Schwartz says: "You know, when I was a kid, I thought work was a joke. I traveled and lived off my wits. But, this hurts me. I look at those kids and this hurts me. What kind of a father am I if I can't buy them what they want?" Man in front of Schwartz on line turns to him and jokes: "I hear they're paying packers $40 an hour here." Schwartz: "Yeah, and expense account lunches, business trips to Paris, retirement at full salary at the age of 55." Schwartz's turn to interview comes, and he learns they are paying $8.50 an hour. Made $12.50 an hour at Hastings.

Schwartz, while walking home: "Fun, looking for a job, huh? Looking for a job is the worst job I've ever had in my life. Begging, I always feel like I'm begging. Asking for favors. All these lines. I want to go to work in the morning, that's all, and come home every week with a little paycheck. Look, I believe that the economy will turn around. Has to, right? I'll find something, or I'll move. We don't own our house. I'll rent in Dallas or Phoenix or Kuwait." Walking slower as he gets close to home. Walks in door. Susan Schwartz: "So? What happened?" Joseph Schwartz: "What always happens. They said I could call tomorrow. I'll call tomorrow. Anything else in the paper this morning?" Next day on phone, Schwartz says that he called and that he did not get the supermarket packing job. Call to Kile Dobson of Fresh and Fast Supermarket, who is in charge of hiring and who says: "Yes, I remember the tall guy. He was nice. I liked him. But the guy we hired seemed really excited. Can't hire everyone can you?"

PART 6 **SPECIALIZED COVERAGE**

Central American migrants headed north on their way to the United States try to climb aboard a train on the outskirts of Mexico City.
(AP photo by Dario Lopez-Mills)

23

Municipal Services

Some newspapers do little more in reporting on municipal services than react to crises—a drought cuts water supplies, a building collapses, garbage collectors go on strike, a snowstorm ties up the city. Readers deserve more than this mad scramble, under deadline pressure, to figure out what went wrong.

If the press is to be a watchdog on government, the basic services provided by government should be high on the list of things worth watching. Day in and day out, little that governments do has as much effect on citizens as such municipal services as garbage collection, public transportation, street and highway maintenance, housing inspection and regulation, park operations and the supply of water.

On smaller papers, the important task of covering these services may be left to already overburdened city hall reporters. (See Chapter 19, Government and Politics.) Larger papers may assign a reporter specifically to the transportation beat or to housing. General assignment reporters pick up the rest.

SOURCES

All municipal services should be reported from the inside, that is, through interviews with officials and workers, and from the outside, through interviews with the people who regularly use those services and are affected by them.

Many of these "inside" sources can be found in the same building—city hall, the municipal building—as sources for political or governmental stories, but they tend to inhabit smaller offices. A reporter will probably want to visit the mayor for a comment on a story about the city's failure to fill last winter's potholes. The head of the Department of Public Works will know more about the story, however, as might the DPW's purchasing agent, its public information officer (if there is one) and the men and women who drive the trucks and lift the shovels.

Reporters responsible for evaluating government's performance in providing these basic services will want to know their way around all levels of the sanitation department or the traffic, transportation, parks, health or housing departments. Housing or health inspectors, for example, are in a particularly good position to be helpful, as are the scientists who test the quality of local water and the engineers who check the safety of bridges. Their jobs are to evaluate services, and although their work is not always publicized, they may have the most precise answers to reporters' questions.

It is also wise to cultivate sources in the county, state and federal governments as well as at city hall. County, state and federal officials are themselves responsible for maintaining some services (some roads and parks, for example) and for evaluating the city's performance on others (water quality, for example).

Remember, government officials won't always be the best or most honest judges of the quality of the services their departments provide. Citizens groups and professional organizations that monitor services offer a different and valuable perspective. Reporters covering traffic and transportation will want to know the leaders of the local AAA as well as representatives of commuter groups that might be affected by changes in bus lines, construction of roadways or new schedules for commuter trains. Here is what representatives of two community groups had to say about possible cuts in service by the Chicago Transit Authority:

> Cutting service "would have a massive impact on people, especially in black and Hispanic communities," said Rev. Leonard DeVille, pastor of Alpha Temple MB Church in Englewood and head of a coalition seeking to maintain CTA service levels on the South Side. "It would be a tremendous burden. What they seem to fail to understand is that Chicago was built on public transportation. ..."
>
> A spokesman for the Civic Federation, a taxpayer watchdog group, had a different assessment.
>
> "We don't want service cuts, but the system has to function in a fiscally responsible manner," said Myer Blank, a federation research associate. "The shrinkage may have to be looked at as an option."
>
> *Chicago Tribune*

Reporters writing on housing will find landlords, tenant groups and community activists to be essential sources. And individual citizens, too, can be of invaluable assistance. The sanitation commissioner can explain why Wednesday garbage pickups were ended. The head of the local community association can protest. But the best quotes on the effects of that decision are likely to come from a frustrated homeowner who is staring at a collection of overstuffed garbage cans at about 6 o'clock Wednesday evening.

RECORDS

The reports filed by city inspectors after they check the safety of buildings or elevators, the sanitary conditions in restaurants or the quality of air or water can be a fertile source of stories about municipal services. The findings of these inspections are announced only sporadically, but they are available to reporters. They can lead, for example, to stories about an outbreak of food poisoning at a local restaurant or a landlord who has shut off the heat at a nearby housing project.

Inspection reports also provide evidence of how well—or how poorly—health and safety standards are being enforced. Before examining the reports, find out what inspections are required under state and local statutes and when they must be carried out. It may turn out that the building or restaurant or elevator that has *not* been inspected in a decade is more newsworthy than the building, restaurant or elevator that's been cited for minor violations of code.

A city worker installs a left-turn signal at an intersection in Battle Creek, Mich.
(Photo by John Grap of the Battle Creek *Enquirer)*

Two questions may be more appropriate: "Why hasn't it been inspected?" and "Who owns it?" The potential for graft is evident here.

There are other records municipal reporters will have occasion to pore through: maintenance records of city buses, records of public hearings (a good place to look for potential sources), hiring records and, of course, ordinances, zoning variances and budgets. (See Chapter 19, Government and Politics.) The city or town clerk should know where most of these are filed in a smaller municipality. In larger cities, reporters may have to search out the records at each department.

BASIC STORIES

The municipal services beat is not without its breaking news. Sometimes these services cause controversy. Sometimes they break down. And the public also has to be told about efforts to keep them in shape.

Controversy

> The Romney administration today will be slapped with a slew of lawsuits charging that the state has reneged on several transportation improvements promised as mitigation for Big Dig air pollution.
>
> *Boston Herald*

Such controversies should automatically send reporters off in search of the other side. In the case of this *Boston Herald* story on a huge and trouble-plagued highway system, that meant a spokesman for the governor's office:

> "We've made significant progress so far and we are committed to building on that progress," Executive Office of Transportation spokesman Jon Carlisle said.

Breakdowns

As a rule, readers expect municipal services to work. They expect their town to fill those potholes on Main Street before people start popping tires. They expect water to go down storm drains, not bubble up sewage onto the street. And when they board the bus or subway, they expect to get to work, not get stuck in traffic or in a tunnel. When things don't work, the problems make news:

> A 12-inch water main beneath 28th Street and Eighth Avenue burst early yesterday, disrupting subway service and cutting off water to dozens of businesses in a one-block area.
>
> (New York) *Daily News*

Since the basic services governments provide—sanitation, transportation, water—are so crucial to readers' lives, the extent as well as the location and time of the interruption in service becomes a crucial part of these stories. The *Daily News* reporter considered these questions in his lead and then again in later paragraphs:

> Yesterday's water main break spilled hundreds of gallons of water onto uptown subway tracks on the IND Eighth Avenue line. A Transit Authority spokesman said local trains were rerouted onto express tracks between West Fourth Street and 34th Street, bypassing the 14th Street station, between 6:20 a.m. and 7 a.m. ...
>
> Arturo Lopez, of 213 W. 28th St., one of the few residents on the block, said he was forced to take buckets to a nearby hydrant to get water. "The situation could have been worse," he said. "At least most of the businesses on this block are closed for the weekend."

"Why" is always an important question when the government or its equipment fails:

> [Department of Environmental Protection spokesman Andrew] McCarthy said the cause of the break was not immediately known, but he noted that "traffic and subway vibrations, combined with the old age of some of the mains, is the usual diagnosis in that part of Manhattan."

Projects

Alongside these controversies and calamities, the municipal services beat has its share of news stories that inform readers about the plans for, or progress of, municipal projects—the digging of a new municipal well, the rebuilding of a playground or the improvement of a road:

> The facelift of U.S. 31 in Hoover is half complete and should be finished in April, according to the Alabama Highway Department.
>
> *The Birmingham News*

These stories must be covered—people need to know when they can expect some improvement in traffic conditions on U.S. 31. But reporters interested in government services must also find the time to dig deeper.

ENTERPRISE

It is not possible to measure the adequacy and efficiency of municipal services merely by writing about subway protests, water main breaks and highway improvements. Here are three basic questions reporters might pursue to get beyond such discrete events.

How Have Things Changed?

Is service better or worse than it was? Statistics, if available, are an important starting point for such investigations, though they must be elucidated and illuminated with interviews and observation. Are parks used more or less frequently in recent years? Is mass transit more or less reliable? Has traffic on local roads increased or decreased in recent years?

> A $1 parking fee, new permit rules and a new gate were successful in decreasing traffic and other problems at Willamette Park last summer, city and neighborhood association officials said.
>
> *The (Portland) Oregonian*

That's the kind of change city officials are all too happy to announce. But sometimes things deteriorate. And often even when they improve, it's because someone prodded government, not because city hall decided on its own to act.

How Are Services Perceived?

Compare the points of view of officials in charge of services and inspections with those of the people whose homes and businesses are being affected. Such an effort often will uncover wildly conflicting statements. Good reporters try to verify who is correct through further research, but even the feelings themselves can provide the basis of a lively story:

> The elderly who once spent much of their time in their neighborhood parks now sit on benches at their perimeters and say the dirt disgusts them and those who use the parks frighten them. Young people say they have known the parks only as disreputable gathering spots and see no reason to protect or preserve them.
>
> *The New York Times*

How Do Conditions Vary?

Are parking regulations the same in upper-class, middle-class and poorer areas of town? Are streets plowed as quickly and maintained as well? Are building codes enforced as strictly?

> Despite the fact that there are more people on the West Side, there are fewer sanitation men and trucks than on the East Side and only three pickups a week compared to five on the East Side.
>
> *The Westsider* (a weekly in New York City)

STORY APPROACHES

Here are some more specific questions that might be worth pursuing for each type of municipal service.

Sanitation

1. If the system is public, what is its operating budget and how much is it costing taxpayers? How do costs compare with those of neighboring communities? Ask a leading private firm what it would charge to pick up the area's garbage.
2. If the system is private, how is the franchise awarded? Is there usually more than one bidder?

3. What is the average daily pickup per truck (in tons)? How many workers are on each truck? How frequent are pickups?

4. What disposal system is used? If there is a town dump, are there any problems with odor or pollution of nearby water sources? Has the presence of the dump had an effect on property values? Is there enough room?

5. Has the town made any effort to recycle garbage? If so, has it been successful?

Traffic

1. Are there chronic traffic problems? What can be done? Ask experts. What is being done? Ask officials.

2. Is there sufficient parking? Do merchants believe that customers have easy access to the business district?

3. Where are the trouble spots in town? Are there bad curves or intersections that have been the scene of an unusual number of accidents?

4. Does traffic cause air pollution problems downtown? Have any planning studies been undertaken to improve the flow of traffic?

5. Who is empowered to enforce traffic rules? Who decides where to put up signs?

6. Are traffic signs effective? Locating misleading or inaccurate signs can make a good news feature. If signs are missing, how long does it take to replace them?

7. Who decides where to put traffic signals? What input does the public have into the system? (Parent groups are chronic complainers about the inadequate stop lights near schools and playgrounds.)

Transit

1. What proportion of funding is local, and what proportion is state or federal?

2. If a transit company is privately owned, what is its history? Who is on the board of directors? What firm provides its insurance (and who owns the insurance company)?

3. What is the local history of fares, and what are the procedures for increasing fares?

4. How many people work for the company, and how does their pay compare with that at other companies?

5. What is the system's safety history, and how does it compare with that of similar transit systems?

6. How old is the equipment, and what percentage of the time is it out of commission?

7. How often are the buses, trains or subways late, and by how much? How frequently do they run?

8. What percentage of riders uses the system during rush hour? What percentage of revenue is derived from rush-hour fares? (Off-peak fares may be lower, so these two percentages are not always the same.)

Water

1. Is the supply well water or surface water? Are the watershed or the wellfields (the places the water comes from) protected from pollutants?

2. What are the system's reserves? Are they adequate? In case of drought, how long could the system hold up?

3. What chemicals are tested for in the water? Does the water meet or surpass mandated federal or state standards?

4. How many inspectors are there to check the watershed and make sure it is pollution free?

5. What are the charges for water use, and how do they compare with those of neighboring communities? Is the water company publicly or privately owned?

6. How is the water treated? What levels of chlorine and fluoride are added?

7. How old are the treatment plants and the lines? How much water is being lost to leaks throughout the system?

Public Works

1. Does the town have regular programs to fill potholes, clean culverts (roadway drains), repair curbing and widen roads?

2. Are there flooding problems in the town? How has the town addressed them?

3. How old is the municipality's equipment, and what is the town's record for repairing and maintaining this equipment?

4. What is the town's reputation for clearing the streets after a snowstorm? Does it use salt and sand? How much of each? Any complaints about these quantities?

Parks

1. Is there an organized recreation program? Is there adequate equipment for recreation?

2. What other activities are offered in the parks (concerts, plays, races, bingo)?

3. What is the town's park acreage? Is parkland evenly distributed around the community? Are there any plans to expand the park system by buying land?

4. What type of parks are there (conventional playgrounds, open space)?

5. Are the parks well maintained?

6. Are they safe?

7. Are they used?

8. How can they be improved?

Housing

1. What are the housing codes, and how strictly are they enforced?

2. What are the town's zoning laws? Do they conflict with the town's master plan? What do officials plan to do about any discrepancy?

3. Is there any public housing in the community? What is the community's attitude toward public housing? (Usually public housing proposals result in heated arguments between proponents of home rule and those looking for financing from the state and federal government. Beneath the surface of such arguments are often strong sentiments about the social and economic integration of the community.)

CHAPTER 23 SUMMARY: MUNICIPAL SERVICES

For the press to fulfill its role as a watchdog of government, reporters must look beyond politics and the pronouncements of elected officials to the performance of city workers and their delivery of services, from clean water to safe roads and public transportation. Understanding how the system of services works and who is in charge of different services is a good start. Thinking of who is affected by city services and how they're affected can take reporting to the next level. You'll succeed in covering the municipal services of the towns or city you cover if you:

- Meet with and learn the responsibilities of department heads and their deputies in all areas, from sanitation and transportation to health and housing.

- Find out what citizens' groups have formed to demand better conditions or to respond to perceived weakness in services. Listen, in other words, not only to city officials but to the people they are pledged to serve.

- Know what records are available and what office controls them. Start by asking what records are available online. Try to get a master list of what records are kept even if they're in dusty file cabinets.

- Use the budget as a measure for gauging what services may be getting short shrift. The annual budget is a blueprint. It tells you what areas of services are growing and what areas may be neglected (for example, a 20 percent cut in parks maintenance can be measured in broken benches and untrimmed lawns).

- Don't wait for the news to come to you. Look for stories about how services are getting better or getting worse. Use your eyes and your ears. Listen to the people who use the parks, ride the buses, wait for their trash to get picked up.

- Follow the money trail. When new contracts are awarded, find out if they always go to the lowest bidder, and ask competitors whether they believe the bid awards were handled fairly.

ADDITIONAL READING

Making Local News, Phyllis Kaniss, University of Chicago Press, 1991.

EXERCISE A
Research Assignments

ONE
Use research materials or interviews with people familiar with municipal services to write explanations that could be used in a newspaper article for the following terms:

1. Gridlock
2. Building permit
3. SRO hotel
4. Paper streets
5. Right-of-way
6. Carbon-filtration system
7. Recharge basin
8. Certificate of occupancy
9. Roller-bearing failure
10. Sewage sludge

TWO
Use research materials or interviews to obtain answers to the following questions for a city or town in your area. Illustrate some of your answers with quotes.

1. Where does the water come from? Who supplies it?
2. Who inspects restaurants, and how often?
3. How many building permits were issued in the past month? What types of projects are most of them for?
4. Who is the municipal official responsible for the parks?
5. How large is the staff of people who clean the parks? Are there more or fewer people than five years ago?
6. Which of the roads in the area are under the control of the city or town government? The county? The state? The federal government?
7. Who provides the bus service?
8. How many bus routes are there?
9. Are all parts of the city served equally well?
10. Does the town have any municipal pools?
11. If so, how often is the water tested?
12. Where are the reports on water tests filed?
13. How many potholes were filled last year? Is that more or fewer than the previous year?

THREE
Select either an abandoned or particularly rundown building or a building that houses a pornography shop or a disreputable bar, and find out who owns it through the following steps:

1. Determine where the local property records are kept.
2. Locate the street address in a guide to lots and blocks in the city (property is catalogued in city records by lot and block, not address).
3. Take the block and lot number to a directory of deeds, mortgages and other papers. It is in reverse chronological order. You must go through it until you find the last time the property changed hands or was first registered. NOTE: Once you find the record of the last sale of the property, it may list the principal owner, or it may merely list a corporation. If it lists a corporation, proceed to step 4.
4. Find out where local records of businesses and corporations are kept. A list of corporations will provide you the names of the principal owners and officers.

FOUR

Call the local bus company and ask for the schedule of a bus that travels along a major thoroughfare and a bus that travels an out-of-the-way route.

Stake out each route for two hours, with a watch, and observe whether the buses are on time. You might also observe whether they are crowded and in what condition they appear to be (dirty, falling apart, noisy, spewing fumes or perfectly fine).

If the buses are *not* on time, call an official of the bus company and ask, "Are there any problems in running on time?" The answer should provide either an explanation for what you observed or a revealing contradiction.

If the buses *are* on time, try to find out how long the schedule has been in effect. Do riders have to wait a longer or shorter time than they did five years ago?

(To extend this exercise, you might try to locate through newspaper clippings critics of the bus system and interview them; conduct interviews with riders; or visit the company garage and talk to drivers, mechanics and supervisors about changes they've perceived.)

EXERCISE B
Writing Assignments

Write stories based on each of the following collections of information. In each case you are writing for a newspaper dated tomorrow and read in the town where the event occurred.

ONE

A press release issued by the Columbia Department of Highways today:

> Highway Commissioner Frank Rothman, as part of his continuing effort to improve the city's roads and bridges, announced today that a $535,000, six-month reconstruction program will begin next Monday at 11 a.m. on the four-mile-long stretch of the Westside Expressway between East 4th Street and River Road.
>
> The program will make major structural repairs to the roadway, much of which is elevated, to repair damage caused by the 42 years of wear and tear accrued since the section was constructed.
>
> "When this is done this section of the Westside Expressway—the most used road in the city—will be the par of any in the state," Mr. Rothman said.

From an interview with Rothman: "No, we're not adding anything new onto the expressway. Just fixing it up. Oh, traffic. Yes, traffic. Yes, we will have some problems there, of course. But Westside has six lanes. We may have to close two in each direction for much of the time, but we will always have at least one lane of the expressway open in each direction. Backups? Well, look, a lot of cars use this road, and we may have backups during rush hours. People might have to put up with quite a bit of inconvenience for a while, but if we hadn't done this we could have had some serious trouble with the Westside Expressway. Yes, I think it is fair to say that motorists who take the expressway home from the downtown area at River Street can expect some significant delays Monday evening. You got to break some eggs, you know."

From an interview with Ronald Coleman, president of the Columbia Automobile Association: "Good news, that's what we call it. Sure, there are going to be traffic troubles. We will be urging our members to find other ways home from work from Monday afternoon on—10th Avenue would be a good alternate route. But anyone who has driven on that stretch of Westside lately can see that it needs work."

TWO

You make a routine call to the Parks Department here in Lincoln and are surprised by what sounds like a nonroutine piece of information: the department has decided to pave over all the grass area in Oak Tree Park ... this according to public information officer Mike Chevra.

Chevra explains why: "This is the problem. ... The grass has just turned into a sleeping area for derelicts and drug users. We have decided that the park will be a cleaner place for all if we can get them out. ... And the first step is getting the grass out ... at least that's how I understand the thinking here. The paving will begin on Monday and should be completed by the end of the month. We expect it to cost about $12,000."

You call Pauline O'Shea, the parks commissioner. She says: "Look, I love grass. I wouldn't have taken this job if I didn't love grass, but I can't see a park turned into a dormitory for degenerates. If it takes getting rid of the grass to get rid of the degenerates ... that's what we're going to do. This was my decision, and mine alone."

Time to visit Oak Tree Park. It runs between Lincoln Avenue and Jefferson Avenue on Forsythe Road. It's a half-block-large piece of grass and trees with some asphalt paths winding through. It's two blocks west of the downtown shopping center, and it's bordered by a row of shops on Lincoln, a three-story apartment building and some pretty ramshackle frame buildings on Forsythe, and a warehouse on Jefferson. Not the nicest part of town, but you've seen worse.

It's sunny, about 11 a.m., and you spot one man sleeping on the grass. A woman seems to be sleeping on one of the few dozen benches scattered throughout the park. She's clutching a stuffed shopping bag.

Two women with strollers are sitting on a bench at the outskirts of the park. An elderly gentleman is on the bench next to theirs. Otherwise the park is empty. You try to talk to them all:

One woman with stroller: "Yeah, I come here most days. No, I hadn't heard they were going to take out the grass, but it's fine with me. Look, this is the only park for blocks around here ... otherwise you wouldn't catch me here. There are some awful people who hang out in this park and maybe paving it over will get rid of them."

She reluctantly gives her name, Sheila Rhodes, but will say only that she "lives in the neighborhood." Her friend refuses to be interviewed.

Elderly gentleman: "Sure I'll tell you my name. I'm Fred Strauss, I live a block from here at 328 South Broadway, I'm 72 and I've been coming here almost every day since I retired five years ago. No, I don't sit in the middle of the park, but I walk through it sometimes though. It's the only green place around here.

"They're going to what? Of all the bone-headed schemes. Let me tell you something. If they'd put a cop here during the day to shoo these people, they'd solve the problem easy enough. There's little enough grass. Let them use all that asphalt to fix some of these streets."

The woman with the shopping bag is sitting up now. The shopping bag seems to contain clothes and papers. Her dress is stained and wrinkled. She gives you a suspicious glance but answers your question: "Nah, I don't need nobody knowing who I am and I have no address, but I do got something to say about what you're telling me. And that's that it's no surprise. They'd close the whole city down just to keep us from finding a lousy place to sleep. I know I'm not the prettiest sight but I haven't hurt anybody. They kick us out of here, where are we gonna go? You got a room at your place? You see the city finding any place for us? Let 'em pave over the whole city." She falls silent.

Man sleeping on the grass curses and refuses to talk to you.

You check with Friends of City Parks and reach the organization's president, Michael Oh, who is also president of Fargo Bank, downtown: "Yes," he says. "O'Shea has discussed the plan for Oak Tree with me, and I'll tell you what I told her. It's ridiculous. Let them fight derelicts, if that's their problem, with police, not asphalt. Our organization believes this city needs more grass and greenery, not less."

You check with the mayor's office and confirm that the city does have an ad hoc program for providing shelter at night for homeless people. Anyone who shows up at the city's Greene Street unemployment office at 9 p.m. is taken to a local church or synagogue. The office is at 49 Greene St.

You call back Chevra to check the details of the plan: "All the grass areas will be paved but none of the trees, bushes or benches will be affected," he says. "And it's a special playground asphalt like they use on some tennis courts. It's got more give than the old-fashioned kind and isn't as punishing if you fall on it. Yes, the plan is definite. We've already ordered the materials. As for Oh, I can't comment on the record. Off the record, I think he wants to run for council, so this will make him look good."

THREE

Someone on the phone who refuses to give her name. She says she works in the New City Transportation Department. Says: "Listen, you should look into this. Something terrible is happening. The new commissioner and his people have a new policy. They send the old buses to the black areas of town and the new buses to the white areas. Nothing on paper of course. But I've heard them discuss it with people who do the routing. As a matter of fact, I'm a dispatcher myself and they told me. But you can't say that. Just call me someone in the department."

You decide to stand on the corner of Blaine and Harrison streets in the middle of a predominantly black section of town. You count 21 buses in four hours from 2 p.m. to 6 p.m. None of those buses looks new, 10 look very old. The next day, also a weekday, you pick a corner—Elm and Spruce roads—in an almost exclusively white neighborhood. This time 25 buses come by during the same period. Twelve look almost brand new, none seems to look as old as the ones you saw the previous day.

You call up the transportation department and learn that the city purchased 22 new Japanese buses last year. It also owns 45 GM buses that are nine years old and 20 buses bought from GM 20 years ago. You ask if there's any way to tell the nine-year-old buses from the 20-year-old buses and are told the really old ones all are painted dark blue in the back, while the nine-year-old ones are painted light blue.

Next day you are back counting again, during the same hours, at Blaine and Harrison—no Japanese buses, 10 light blue backs, 10 dark blue backs. Next weekday at Elm and Spruce, same hours: 13 Japanese, 12 light blue backs, no dark blue.

You call a source at the transportation department and ask for names of some dispatchers, the people who send the buses out. The first three you call won't talk. A fourth, Gil Hawkins, agrees to talk—on background. He's willing to be identified as a dispatcher. Says: "Look, no one's ever come over to me and told me in so many words what buses to send where. But the commissioner himself came by about five or six weeks ago and said, 'You know we have a lot of important people riding these buses on some lines, and we also have some people who don't work too hard on others, if you know what I mean. Let's make sure the right people get the right buses.' He was saying the same sort of thing to other guys, also about three weeks ago. I nodded. I don't like it, but I want to keep my job. I have been sending the new buses mostly on the lines that go through Riverdale and Plainfield. Four Corners gets the older ones. Everyone I know here is doing the same."

Riverdale is where Elm and Spruce roads are; Plainfield is another well-off, predominantly white neighborhood. Blaine and Harrison are in Four Corners. You ask the dispatcher if there might be some other explanation for the difference in buses assigned to the different routes. His answer: "I wish I could say there was, but all the routes in this town are designed to be of roughly equal length and equal difficulty. The only difference between the route that passes through Blaine and Harrison—the number 4 bus—and the route that passes through Riverdale—the number 10—is the people who ride the bus. They are both 12-mile routes and they both end up at the downtown depot at Elm Boulevard and Jesse Road."

You try to interview some of the bus drivers on the 4 and 10 routes. Most won't talk. One on the 4 route does complain: "Of course we get the older buses ... does that really surprise you?" He won't give you his name. Another driver, James Rosen of the 4 line, says: "Yeah, I'll talk. Let them fire me if they want. Shortly after that guy Cransfield … is that his name? … took over, all of us noticed something was up. I have a lot of friends who are dispatchers, so I know exactly what's going on: The old buses go for the blacks and through the working-class neighborhoods of town, white and black. The new buses go for the executives in Riverdale and Plainfield. The executives get to work on time, and the working people get stuck when one of those old GM jobbies breaks down … happened to me two days ago. A busload of people had to wait for another bus because of a busted starter on one of these ancient number 4s."

Transportation Commissioner Herbert Cranston calls just before you were going to call him: "What's this I hear about your interrogating all my men?" he asks. You present your facts.

Cranston says, "A—That's absurd. B—I would never say any of these things. C—If you print any of this garbage you will have one hell of a libel suit on your hands!" He hangs up.

Cranston calls back a half hour later: "Hey, I'm sorry I got so angry. Look, I checked with some of my people, and they tell me that it is possible that we do have more of our new buses on some of our lines, not because of any discrimination, of course, but because of the different needs of drivers on those lines. But believe me we will investigate this carefully, and if there is even the hint of any unfairness, I can assure you, I will insist on changes in our bus scheduling." Cranston said he can't be more specific on the different needs of drivers on the routes: "These are very technical issues."

You call three other people you know at the department, all of whom deny, on background, that there's any difference between the bus routes that might justify the imbalance of new buses and old buses. All are prepared to be identified as Transportation Department officials. Then you drive through Four Corners to Suffern and also take the route past Elm and Spruce to Riverdale. The first takes you past a few miles of apartments, stores and factories and then winds through a section of two- and three-bedroom brick and stucco houses on tenth-of-an-acre lots. Most of the people you see along the route are black. The other route heads east along Main Street and then north through a wooded area, past the municipal golf course and into an area of split levels and two-car garages. Neither route seems to have very many hills. You return to the office and begin to write.

Cranston was appointed commissioner two months ago when the new mayor, Republican Albert Fauk, took office. (You try to reach the mayor but he's out of town on business.)

EXERCISE C
Story Assignments

1. Obtain information on the schedule and record of a local city bus company or private bus line. How often are the buses on time? How many buses are there? How frequently are they supposed to come? Compare the current information with information about previous years. Write a story based on the comparison.

2. Interview municipal officials in charge of either transit, transportation, housing or parks and then interview the people who are affected by the services they provide. Write an article about different perceptions of the service.

3. Pick two areas of a city or town with roughly equivalent populations but sharply differing income levels. After interviewing local officials or officials of the companies that provide the services and after personal observation, write a story comparing one of the following services in each of the two areas:

   a. Sanitation
      - frequency of pickups
      - number of workers
      - cleanliness of streets

   b. Buses
      - number of lines
      - number of stops
      - frequency of service
      - crowds on the buses
      - quality of the buses in use

   c. Parks
      - number and size of parks
      - upkeep of parks
      - number of employees assigned
      - number of benches
      - athletic facilities

   d. Roads
      - state of repair of major streets
      - traffic
      - number of officers handling traffic
      - enforcement of parking rules

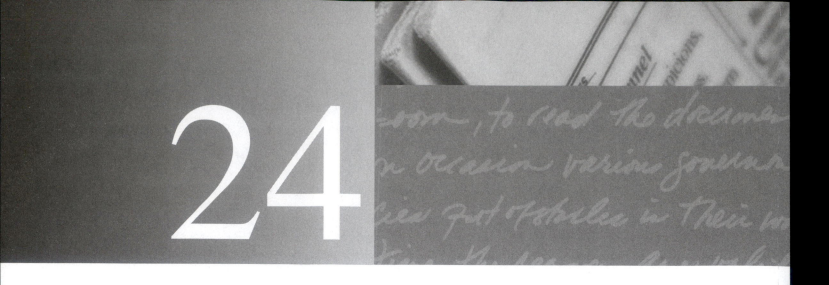

Education

Few public issues command the attention of parents more than disputes over the quality of their children's education. And school policies also can stir up nonparents; homeowners in most towns pay more local taxes for public education than for anything else.

Yet until the last few decades, many reporters dreaded an assignment to the education beat as much as a starting pitcher might dread being relegated to the bullpen. They saw no glory in it ... and often with reason. Education coverage on many papers more often than not meant attending school board meetings and writing occasional fluff features on slow news days. Few education stories other than those on desegregation battles and teachers' strikes made Page 1.

But when journalists begin looking for the factors that most influence our society, they increasingly find themselves staring at the schools, especially as state and national standards for measuring performance have taken center stage and debates over everything from whether to support bilingual education to whether to teach "intelligent design" alongside evolution have made their way to the front page. Gradually, editors and reporters have begun to realize that the only thing wrong with the education beat is the way it has been covered.

"There are too many *school district* reporters and too few *education* writers," laments Dale Rice, who covered education for the late *Dallas Times Herald*. "Too many reporters get so caught up in the politics and infighting ... that they forget the effect of policy when it filters down and hits the kids."

Rice, who spent more time in the schools than at the board of education, considers himself to be part of a generation of education writers intent on opening what he calls "a real window to the school system." Another member of this generation is Michelle Guido, who covered education for the *San Jose Mercury News*.

"The easiest trap is to get all your ideas from the district office," she says. "Their job is to make things really rosy, and things are not really rosy in California education right now.

"I try to cover education mostly from the classroom. It's more interesting for readers to know what's going on there than to know what pencil pushers are doing in the district office."

After covering the courts for the *St. Petersburg Times*, Tom French moved to special projects. He spent one year at one high school. Here is a small piece of what he found:

> Kids still go to pep rallies, write gushy notes and forget their locker combinations. But today, high school is also another kind of place, where kids decked out in gold

jewelry have beeper numbers, where baby-faced girls talk quietly about abortions, where students resist any assignment that makes them pay attention for longer than the latest MTV video. "Do you want to work at McDonald's for the rest of your life?" someone yells in the hall at Largo High. Several voices shout the answer: "Yes!"

It's rare for editors to give reporters a year to look into anything. But most education writers can at some point manage to find a week or two to investigate an aspect of education from within the schools. For example, Guido spent two weeks enrolled in a San Jose high school as a student. She also spent two weeks observing a special class in juvenile hall and over one school year periodically wrote about a class of immigrant students who had never before been to school.

Another approach for education writers is to periodically stop by a school to build a project over the course of a year. Charlie Roduta of *The Columbus* (Ohio) *Dispatch* decided to explore the remarkable success of Japanese students in the town of Dublin. The children of employees at a nearby Honda plant, most of these students spoke relatively little English when they arrived in Dublin. But as Roduta learned while interviewing the school's guidance counselor about something else, their performance was regularly outpacing that of their American peers.

After researching the story on and off for a few months, Roduta met two sisters, new arrivals from Japan, on the first day of school. "I met them maybe a month after they'd arrived in Dublin and charted their progress through the school year," she said. The project, she added, attempted to show "what are the study lessons they bring from their country, how do they apply them here successfully. I wanted to explore this through the eyes of several students."

Lessons from the Pros: Building an Education Beat

Charlie Roduta, *The Columbus Dispatch*

When Charlie Roduta arrived at *The Columbus Dispatch* in Ohio to cover education, she'd already learned a fair amount about the eight suburban school districts that she'd be covering. She'd researched each of them online, learning as much as she could about their demographics (size, population makeup, income), their test score performance and their educational missions.

Building sources and gaining trust in eight districts, all distinct, took time, Roduta says. But nearly two years into her beat, she now counts on board members and community members in some towns to call her

Education writer Charlie Roduta interviews a student. (Photo by Doral Chenoweth III, The Columbus [Ohio] Dispatch)

regularly with tips. She gathers "string," bits and pieces of ideas for dozens of stories that gradually find their way onto the weekly beat memo her editors request. And, in addition to the three or four daily and one weekend story she's expected to produce each week, she's completed a major project.

Roduta, who at 27 has been reporting for six years, gives these tips in building an education beat.

Lessons from the Pros: Building an Education Beat (continued)

- **Ask your editor's advice.** Roduta, who came to Columbus from a smaller newspaper in Indiana, says her editor taught her lots about the nuances of covering education in Ohio. "He told me how [Ohio] school funding works, the state's testing system, the state's accountability system. ... He was such a great resource because he gave me thumbnails of the districts and told me what he perceived to be the bigger issues that we hadn't reported on. It gave me a leg up."

- **Establish trust by showing up.** At first, Roduta recalls, she went to school board meetings, had coffees with principals and district public information officers, met with each of the superintendents. "I told them a bit about who I am, how I cover my beat, how I could work best with them." She also listened.

- **Listen for stories as you get acquainted.** "I always try to listen to things that make a school unique." One day, at the end of an introductory meeting, an elementary school principal mentioned that two third-grade girls in the school had dunked their heads in the toilet to gain acceptance. "That ended up turning into a story on girl troubles, mean girls ..."

- **Gather and review key documents.** "Even though budgets may not be the sexiest thing to cover, they are just full of stories," she says. "How much are administrators spending on trips or cell phones or credit cards?" Roduta says she's developing a story on field trip requests—"how much are districts spending, where are they taking students, how have field trips changed? ... I've found out that one district has students in a contemporary literature class go into the city where low-income people were living, at homeless shelters, and study them. I was kind of astonished at that."

- **Be thorough and be fair.** Roduta says she still regularly covers school board meetings in one particularly contentious district because often 30 or 40 residents attend. Her sources there include parents, PTA (Parents Teacher Association) members, parents of former students, former board members and the current board members. "This was an administration that was very wary of the press, but I was able to build a relationship with the board president and from there on gradually build a relationship with the community. ... I measured my success by the range of sources I was able to develop."

- **Get into the schools and talk to kids.** "I take the old-fashioned approach to covering education," Roduta says. "I like to hear what kids are saying. If I have time, I'll go into a high school lunchroom and just talk to kids." One day, after finishing reporting on a different story, Roduta went to a lunchroom and asked the students how high gas prices were affecting them. "That ended up turning into a story about kids doubling up on part-time jobs to pay for gas."

- **Read blogs.** Roduta says she regularly goes to www.technorati.com to scan the blogs written by students in the districts she's covering. All she has to do is type in the name of the district or a particular school, and technorati's search engine will pull up any blogs that mention the school's name.

SOURCES

Most teachers say they relish the independence of their job. Nonetheless, a complicated assortment of economic decisions and social pressures affects their ability to do the job well. Good education reporting requires an understanding of those decisions and pressures and of their impact on the classroom.

The Board of Education

"One of the first things you want to know is where educational policy is made," notes Saundra Keyes, a former English professor who covered education for *The Courier-Journal* in Louisville, Ky. No group will have more to say about that policy than the local board of education.

Members of the board either are elected or are appointed by elected officials to make basic decisions about the schools and to oversee how they are run. Divisions among board members usually reflect disagreement in the community over the direction and financing of education. "Most school boards tend to be divided along some kind of line," says Rice, the former *Times Herald* reporter. He suggests that new education writers check clip files to get a sense of these factions and then meet individually with board members, perhaps leaving pen and notebook behind. "Ask them what they think of the board and its problems," he suggests. "I think people are sometimes more relaxed when you don't approach them for a specific story."

Central Administration

Though they often are relied on too much, the administrators of a school system certainly can't be ignored. The superintendent and his staff interpret and put into effect the broad policies of the board of education. The system's purse strings also are opened and closed in the administrative domain. The superintendent and the deputy superintendent for curriculum usually top the hierarchy. But there are other important sources in the administrative offices.

An education reporter will want to know the district's public relations person, if it has one. It may be necessary to call daily to keep tabs on breaking news. And the district's finance officer can help interpret and bring to life the mass of numbers in the budget. Staff assistants and secretaries also can help lead a reporter to news. Rice recalls that early in his career, he befriended a school secretary in Syracuse, N.Y., who would often lend him books ... with xeroxed copies of school documents inserted between the pages.

Teachers

Teachers should know more about what's really going on in the classroom than their bosses. They may be tougher to meet than administrators—most don't spend much time in an office—but it's worth the effort to track them down after class or at home, Rice notes. He suggests that new reporters on the beat ask leaders of the local teachers' union to arrange an informal get-together with several active teachers from different schools in the district.

Students

When an irate mother arrived in a Dallas classroom with a loaded gun, Rice knew of the incident—and of what led to it—before police had arrived at the scene. A student reporter saw the principal escort the woman from the room and called the *Times Herald*. "You will not believe the loyalty you can develop among school kids, especially among would-be journalists," says Rice. "Find out what the best student newspaper is, talk to the students on the staff and say, 'Listen, anytime you need information or help, call me and I'll get you information.'" Such favors get returned many times over, Rice adds.

In his year at Largo High, Tom French was reporting on students, so naturally they were his primary sources. Here's a disconcerting conversation with a student French devoted considerable attention to, a student he describes as "well on his way to failing all his classes":

"If you could have whatever you wanted,... what would it be?"
"I don't know."

Lessons from the Pros: Interviewing Kids

Katie Oliveri, *Battle Creek Enquirer*

In an effort to deal with one of the highest rates of teen pregnancy in Michigan, the school system in Battle Creek started a sex education class to teach high school students about protection and reproduction. Katie Oliveri, a 22-year-old education reporter for the *Battle Creek Enquirer*, jumped at the chance to sit in on one of these classes and hear the discussions students were having.

Katie Oliveri (with notebook) conducting an interview. *(Courtesy of the* Battle Creek *[Mich.]* Enquirer)

"The STD rate was high, teen pregnancy was high, but it was the only district in area not offering health or sex curriculum," Oliveri says.

But Oliveri didn't want her presence to inhibit the students. So she decided to sit down, blend in and listen. After awhile, the students forgot she was in the room.

"It was interesting how much they didn't know, but they were [still] having sex," Oliveri recalls.

After class students came up to Oliveri and freely gave their reactions about the class, teen pregnancy and other issues the teacher raised.

"Kids are really willing to talk because a lot of people usually won't listen to them," Oliveri says. "And if they have a place where they can be heard, they enjoy that."

Oliveri believes her ability to make students comfortable in talking to her allows her to do a better job of covering her beat. She offers these tips.

- **Find out what the rules are for talking to students.** Oliveri said her town has a rule that reporters need parental permission before speaking with anyone under 16 years of age. Also, some schools require students to sign a media waiver before being interviewed.

- **Don't always name names.** Oliveri said she wouldn't necessarily use a student's name when writing a sensitive story. "When a student was saying [in the sex ed class], 'I don't know what the clitoris is,' I would just write, 'a student asked…'." But, she said she usually does name students as long as she's not embarrassing or harming them by doing so.

- **Talk to students as if you were one of them.** "I find that students are easy to talk to, especially since I am often mistaken for being a high school student. When you are a younger reporter you can relate to students better."

- **Get one teen to talk and others will jump in.** "If I ask one person [a question] then other people will come over and want to say something too."

- **Be patient and listen.**

"What do you do when you're upset or mad?"
"Sit in my room, listening to the stereo."
"What do you do when you're happy?"
"Sit in my room, listening to the stereo."
"What do you care about?"
"Nothing."
"What's important to you?"
He shakes his head, laughs. "Nothing."

St. Petersburg (Fla.) Times

Community Groups

Parents and taxpayers keep close watch on the schools. Irate parents have banded together to ban books, to promote prayer and to fight to keep sex education out of the school building. They are a major force in debates on everything from crossing guards to lunchroom rules. Their views should be monitored before they surface at board of education meetings. Virtually every school has an active Parent Teacher Association, and education writers should develop sources on all of them. Organizations as diverse as the Chamber of Commerce and the local Council of Churches also keep tabs on the schools, and taxpayer groups often lead battles to defeat school budgets they judge excessive.

Other Officials

Schools nationwide are relying more and more on state and federal funds to support special programs and fill budget gaps. They also face increasing federal and state mandates for performance under such measures as the federal No Child Left Behind law. Some states, such as California, have set limits on how much towns can raise taxes to pay for schools, and others have laws that monitor inequities in educational opportunity between poorer and wealthier districts. Education writers need to know which elected officials at the local, state and federal levels oversee education, and they must keep track of proposals coming before education committees in the various legislative bodies.

College and University Officials

"Higher education doesn't get nearly as much coverage but has just as much impact," says Jim Killackey of the *Daily Oklahoman*. College and university policy battles, especially at private schools, tend to be less public than those at the primary and secondary school level, but education writers are learning to uncover them. Their sources are administrators, teachers and students, along with the politicians who control funding for public universities and the alumni who help fund private universities.

While there may be fewer community groups battling for a say in higher education, disputes over financing, departmental expansion, accreditation, tenure, academic performance and admission standards can be just as heated and as newsworthy as battles for the minds of 8-year-olds. Here is an example:

> The California State University campuses at Los Angeles and Dominguez Hills have the dubious honor of being the only colleges or universities in the state where fewer than half of the graduates who took the new basic skills test for prospective teachers have passed.
> *Los Angeles Times*

DOCUMENTS

Important stories lie behind the dollar figures in school budgets and the statistics that fill reports on academic achievement. But to find these stories, reporters need to know where to look and what to look for.

Budgets

The school budget determines how much money the schools will spend in the next school year, gives some details about how this money will be spent and tells where the money will come from. The budget process can have as much to do with the caliber of local schools as can the district's teachers. If test scores have dropped, for example, the explanation might be that classes are bigger. And if classes are bigger, that might be because budgetary restrictions limited the number of teachers the school administration can hire.

New education writers *must* familiarize themselves with the intricacies of the local budget process. Who proposes budget items? Who evaluates these proposals? What time of year is the budget drafted? Who is responsible for approving it? Some school budgets are put up to popular vote. Others must be approved by the board of education or the city government.

Like most municipal budgets (see Chapter 19, Government and Politics), school budgets are compromises between attempts to improve programs by increasing revenues and attempts to hold down taxes, usually property taxes, by limiting expenditures. This basic struggle, however, can be obscured by technical terms and jargon.

"I was sitting in a press briefing going through a two-inch-thick school budget agenda, when I suddenly came to a paragraph saying federal (Title 1) funds in the district would be cut $1 million," recalls Saundra Keyes of *The Courier-Journal*. "The bottom line is that it's extra reading and math help for poor kids. I wrote a story saying that 2,500 low-income kids in the city wouldn't be getting special aid."

Statistics

All school districts compile statistics. These might range from the number of hot lunches served each day to the percentage of students skipping school. This process is often formalized by the federal and state governments, which require reports on the results of programs they fund, such as aid for handicapped and underprivileged children. Some of these statistics are routinely publicized, such as the scores of MCAS (Massachusetts Comprehensive Assessment System) performance tests mandated by the state at certain grade levels. But schools and districts often share their statistics only when they reflect academic excellence or improvement: Educators are no more anxious than anyone else to air their dirty laundry. However, any of these reports should be available to the public and, therefore, to reporters, if specifically requested. (See The Basics, Section F, Law.) Find out what reports your district is required to compile and when they are due. Each set of findings is a potential story.

In addition, the National Center for Education Statistics in Washington, D.C., publishes a vast array of statistics on American education from the number of students who have finished ninth grade to the average teacher's salary in each state.

> Students are likely to pay an average of 7 percent more to attend the United States' private colleges and universities in the fall, says the National Center for Education Statistics.
>
> *USA Today*

Comparisons of such numbers to local statistics can provide fertile ground for stories, too.

Laws and Regulations

Many of the activities of local schools today are dictated by federal and state governments. For reporters to be able to gauge how well schools are complying, reporters need to gain knowledge of the relevant laws and regulations, from the federal No Child Left Behind requirements to the changes governing bilingual education in Massachusetts that voters passed to force non–English speakers into "mainstream" classes more quickly. This background knowledge may be necessary simply to follow the conversation at a meeting or hearing in the principal's office.

"At a hearing there may be a quick reference to an amendment," notes Keyes. "If you know the amendment and you realize it could change funds to your district, you've got a front-page story. Some laws are referred to so commonly by educators they've become part of the jargon—like Public Law 94-142, which is a law funding programs for handicapped children."

When reporters don't understand a reference, they should always ask.

Specialized Publications

A variety of academic journals cover aspects of education. Many education reporters find that reading *Education Week* (www.edweek.org), which reports on elementary and secondary school education, and the *Chronicle of Higher Education* (www.chronicle.com), which covers college and university policy, helps keep them up to date on ideas and issues in the field, and can lead to story ideas.

Keyes was education writer for *The Tennessean* in Nashville when she read an interesting story in the *Chronicle of Higher Education* on what happened to Iranian students in the state after American hostages were taken in Iran. "That day I was on the phone to all the college campuses in Tennessee seeing if they had any Iranian students and how they were being treated," Keyes recalls.

BASIC STORIES

Reporters on the education beat will spend much of their time monitoring the intricate and ever-changing relationship among educational funding, educational programs and educational performance. These are the issues that tend to dominate school board, PTA and community group meetings, and these meetings tend to dominate the working days or evenings of many education reporters:

> The Boulder Valley School Board decided last night to ask voters on Oct. 18 to approve a $4.3 million tax hike that would protect threatened programs and add some new ones.
>
> *The Denver Post*

The trick is to leave the meeting with as detailed an idea as possible of how the decisions that have been reached or debated will actually affect readers through their taxes and through changes in the programs being offered their children. Good education reporters will ask, during or after the meeting, "How much will that cost the average property owner?" or "Will that have any effect on class size?" or "What programs will be cut if the increase is defeated?" The answers reporters get to these questions will form the backbone of their stories.

> If approved by the voters, the proposed tax hike would boost property taxes by $48 on a $120,000 house. That would increase the total assessment on such a home from $688 to $736.
>
> *The Denver Post*

These days, the news is just as likely to be of budget *cuts* as budget *increases*, and the budget process, instead of taking a few months, can make news throughout the year. As resources shrink and the pool of students swells, basic stories might cover anything from the elimination of band or sports to classrooms bulging at the seams, the top story in one issue of *The Denver Post*:

> More than 1,000 Jefferson County students will start their fall classes in cafeterias, libraries and even hallways because of a shortage of modular classrooms, district officials said yesterday.

Studies and reports on how students should be taught and graded, how they perform on standardized tests, and how the schools should be run also make basic education news. Often, especially if the news is good, these reports are released at public meetings:

> The number of failures in four basic courses taken by high school students in the South Colonie School District has dropped by almost 50 percent, the district Board of Education was told last night.
>
> (Albany, N.Y.) *Times Union*

Sometimes more embarrassing news also is aired in public:

> ALBEMARLE—Supt. Bryce Cummings said school staff members acted improperly last month when they ordered several students to remove their clothes to search for money stolen from a youth.
>
> "It shouldn't have happened, and it won't happen again," Cummings told a crowd of about 100 parents and students Wednesday night at North Albemarle Elementary School.
>
> The Charlotte (N.C.) *Observer*

Ultimately though, answers to questions about what and how students learn, and the quality of teaching and discipline in the schools, can be found only by visiting the schools themselves.

ENTERPRISE

The Dallas school board had decided to institute a competency test that elementary school students had to pass before they could be promoted. What would its effect be on students? To answer that question Dale Rice and Linda Austin of the *Dallas Times Herald* alternated spending one day a week in a third-grade classroom for an entire school year. With the help of school officials, the reporters followed the development of five kids who seemed likely to pass the test and five whose prospects were poor. The result was a series of articles with an unusual and important perspective.

"What impact does the school board have when it makes a decision?" asks Rice. "What really happens in school? We showed the outcome of a policy in very human terms."

> The last bell on the last day rang, and time ran out for third-graders in Sandra Warner's class.
>
> "Pull your chairs up around the table," she told the 10 students remaining in her room, after 15 of their classmates had been dismissed. "I want to talk to you."
>
> One of those left, a tiny girl, looked up with big, brown eyes. "We're gonna flunk," she said under her breath. . . .
>
> *Dallas Times Herald*

Dozens of enterprise stories can evolve by looking for the answers to Rice's question: What is the impact of school policy? Put another way: What goals does the school system set for itself? What goals do state and federal agencies set for it? How well are these goals met? Who benefits by these successes and failures? And who is hurt?

Aware of the high dropout rate nationally, Aleta Watson of the *San Jose Mercury News* set out to find out who hadn't made it through one middle-class high school and why. She also wanted to learn what had become of these young people.

Here is how her two-day series started:

> They're the children of high-school teachers, contractors and car salesmen, raised in large part in neat middle-class neighborhoods.

A second-grade teacher in her classroom at St. Casimir's Regional School in Albany, N.Y.
(Photo by Steve Jacobs, Albany *[N.Y.]* Times-Union)

But high school was boring, their grades were bad and paychecks were all they wanted.

So they quit.

It's a familiar story in any city in America. For dropouts are not just the castoffs of ghetto schools. They are the kids next door.

As Watson's series showed, questions about the education system's performance don't have to be reserved for occasions when new policy has been instituted or a new report released. A school's performance in teaching mathematics, for example, is newsworthy regardless of whether the curriculum has changed. Here are some examples of specific questions that might be asked about any school district at any time. Such questions are not asked often enough.

1. How equitably are funds distributed in the school district? Compare programs at schools in wealthier and poorer sections of town.

2. How much state and federal money does the school district receive? Do comparable districts get more or less? Has the district been as vigorous as it should be in seeking outside funds?

3. What kinds of programs does the school offer for students with special needs or abilities? What goals has it set for these programs? Have they been met?

4. How much does the school district pay each year to repair damage caused by vandals? Is vandalism increasing or decreasing? Are any comparative statistics available? Has the nature of vandalism changed? How does the system try to deal with it?

5. What efforts has the district made to integrate diverse populations into the district and to incorporate their cultures and backgrounds into the district's education? How is bilingual education handled in the district? What efforts are made to celebrate and teach about different cultures? How is this reflected in textbooks and other educational materials used in the schools?

6. Does the faculty reflect the ethnic and racial mix of the community? How strong an effort has the district made in affirmative-action hiring? Has that effort produced any resentment?

7. How much attention does the district pay to students who have no interest in attending college? Are their special needs for vocational training addressed? Are they met?

8. Is the district strict or liberal in its tenure decisions? Are good teachers being lost? Are poor teachers being retained?

9. How effective do the students believe their education to be? What suggestions do they have for improving programs?

10. How does the district's college placement record compare with that of similar districts? How well do students do when they reach college? Do they consider themselves well prepared?

11. How successful has the district been in attracting quality teachers? What are the educational and professional backgrounds of its teachers?

CHAPTER 24 SUMMARY: EDUCATION

What students learn in the classroom has much to do with how well the United States will compete in today's global environment. That's one reason for the marked growth in the importance of the education beat as the 20th century drew to a close. Covering education means attending meetings and tracking dollars and test scores. But it means much more. It means understanding how and what students learn, how they interact in an increasingly diverse world, and how vociferous national debates over issues ranging from learning measurements to sex education affect local school board policies.

To get started in covering the education beat, do the following:

- Check clip files to get a handle on important local issues, and read old budgets to understand how the school board has disbursed its money.

- Ask school administrators what statistics and what reports they must compile to comply with state and federal regulation. Then monitor these reports when they are written.

- Interview key people at all layers of the school district, from student leaders and the parent groups that support them to school principals and members of the board of education. Ask each what issues interest and concern them. Ask them their goals. Ask them what obstacles stand in the way of achieving those goals.

- Identify regulators who oversee programs mandated by state and federal law and experts at places such as universities, who can discuss the issues faced by a local district in the context of national debate.

- Spend time in the classroom so that you can get a sense of what students think of their own education and see what and how they learn instead of what administrators *say* they should be learning.

- Track national publications and websites that monitor changes in education philosophy and policy at a local, state and national levels.

ADDITIONAL READING

Condition of Education, review of education statistics published annually by the National Center for Education Statistics.

"Deconstruction and the Get-Real Press," Mitchell Stephens, *Columbia Journalism Review*, September/October 1991.

Directory of Education Associations, Annual listing of national, regional and state education organizations, U.S. Education Department.

The National Education Writers Association publishes tips on coverage and background material on important laws such as No Child Left Behind, www.ewa.org.

South of Heaven: Welcome to High School at the End of the Twentieth Century, Thomas French, Doubleday, 1993.

EXERCISE A
Research Assignments

ONE
Use research materials or interviews with people active in education to write explanations that could be used in a newspaper for the following terms:

1. Special education
2. Accountability
3. Tracking
4. Grade equivalent score
5. Open classroom
6. Tenure track
7. Gifted child
8. Percentile rank
9. Freshman-experience program
10. In-service training
11. Resource teacher
12. A criteria-referenced test

TWO
Visit a high school in your community and obtain the following information. Illustrate some of your answers with quotes.

1. **Attendance.** Find out what the school's policy is for class attendance and whether it has changed in the last five years.

   - Is class attendance up or down from the past? Why?
   - Are students free to leave the school grounds during unscheduled periods?
   - Are parents notified if students miss class?
   - Who is in charge of monitoring attendance?
   - How does the school deal with chronic or repeated absenteeism?
   - What efforts have been made to improve attendance?

2. **Enrollment.** Find out whether enrollment has declined or increased in the last five years and what the effects of the size of the student body have been on educational quality.

   - Have any teachers been laid off because of a loss of students? Has that meant a loss of young teachers?
   - Have class sizes changed?
   - Have any teachers been assigned to subjects for which they haven't been trained?
   - Does the school offer as many electives and extracurricular activities as it has in the past? Are facilities for these classes or activities overburdened?

- Have changes in enrollment affected student or faculty morale?
- What changes in the school-age population might be expected in future years?

3. **Standardized tests.** Find out what the standardized test scores for the school are for each grade in which such tests are given.

- Have these scores declined or increased in the last five years?
- How do test scores compare with those in neighboring schools and school districts?
- How do they compare with national statistics?
- Why do teachers think scores are increasing or declining? What do students think?
- What efforts have been made in the district to improve test scores?
- Is there any concern that too much stress on such scores interferes with rather than aids education?

EXERCISE B
Writing Assignments

Write stories based on each of the following collections of information. In each case you are writing for a newspaper dated tomorrow and read in the town where the events occurred.

ONE

The following press release was issued by the Uniondale School District:

> The winner of the annual Temple High School Outstanding Science Student Award was announced today. He is Mario Alvarez, a senior. The award—a bronze plaque—is given every year, on the basis of a vote by all the school's science teachers, to the student they consider the best science student at the school. Last year it was given to Susan George, who is now a freshman at Harvard University.
>
> Mario is now in Esther Sampson's advanced biology class. Last year he studied physics with Sam Victor. His hobby is botany, and he has compiled an album describing all the flowering plants grown in the Uniondale area.

From an interview with Sampson: "Yes, sure I'll talk about Mario. A fine, fine student. Did you know he was disabled? Mario's a paraplegic. Lost the use of his legs in an automobile accident four years ago. He was one of three students moved to Temple last year from Lakeview School for the Disabled as part of that new mainstreaming program—mixing disabled kids in with other students. Mainstreaming sure worked with Mario. He's gotten the highest scores on every test I've given this semester. And his botany project is great. He's got a half dozen friends scouring the neighborhood to find examples of flowering plants. He presses them and puts them dried in an album. Very impressive. One of the two or three best students I have had in 13 years of teaching."

An interview with Frederick Roland, assistant principal at Temple, and a check of the clips confirms Sampson's facts. Clips show that mainstreaming was quite controversial when first announced. It required the school board to spend $23,000 in ramps and other special facilities at Temple.

From an interview with Alvarez: "It was great news. All the kids were coming up to me in the halls today and patting my back and shaking my hand. And it has to help on my college applications. I still haven't been accepted anywhere. Schools? Well, I applied to Princeton, Stanford, Dartmouth and a couple of state universities. I think I sent out six applications in all.

"My disability, you mean? I prefer that word to 'handicap.' Well, I don't see how that had anything to do with it. But if this helps show people that disabled students belong in class with everyone else, that's great. Lakeview was a nice place, but it didn't have an advanced biology class. Botany? Well, I guess my disability did have something to do with that. When I first got my wheelchair, I was so excited to be independent again I'd go on these long walks. You don't exactly fly along in a wheelchair, and I noticed things I'd never noticed before. Then I just started keeping a record of things, that's all.

"No, I don't think I want to do research in botany. It's a little early, but I'm thinking pre-med. There's nothing like being sick to make you realize how important doctors are. My address: 666 First Street in Uniondale. I'm 17."

TWO

Press conference held at 10 p.m. tonight at Currier High School. Speaking: Charlotte Hall, president of the Clarkstown Education Association, union of Clarkstown's 187 teachers, and Charles Stewart, president of Clarkstown Board of Education.

Hall: "It's been too long coming, far too long, but tonight we can finally tell you that we've reached an agreement on a new contract for teachers in this district. For us it's not perfect, but in the end our students come first. The teachers in this district have been extremely concerned about ballooning class sizes. Classes of more than 30 were becoming quite common. Well, this contract sets a limit of 30. And I hope the parents realize that this will be as much a victory for their children as for the teachers. All the studies I have ever seen have noted that overenrollment slows learning. As for the money, I'll let Mr. Stewart speak to it. No one got exactly what they wanted, but I will strongly urge my members to support our agreement when it comes up for a vote a week from today. Remember, this is a tentative agreement until the majority of the 187 teachers in our rank and file vote for it."

Stewart: "Miss Hall has been a tough negotiator, no doubt about it, but I think I can come before the taxpayers tonight and say, 'We've held the line on excessive raises while improving the quality of your students' education.' Here are the terms: All the teachers in the district will get a 5 percent raise. For the district that comes out to an average of, let me see now, $1,625 a teacher. One of the stumbling blocks was how much new teachers will get, and we held the line there. Last year we started teachers at $19,200. We couldn't see a big hike here, and Miss Hall finally agreed tonight to $500 for a starting salary of $19,700. Frankly, that leaves us quite competitive with the rest of the state. Knowing the tax situation in this town, we did the best we could do. We in essence split the difference in our demands and added a sweetener, which is the guarantee that no classes will have more than 30 students. It's worth it. A strike in our town would have been ugly."

Stewart, in response to a reporter's question: "Yes, we have had classes with more than 30 students in the past. No, I don't think it was a detriment to the quality of education, but we fully support this new policy. I can say we have never had as many as 40 students in a class, but we may have had 35 once or twice."

Hall, in response to a reporter's question: "The average starting salary in this state last year, when we were at $19,200, was $19,350. I suspect a meager $500 increase will put us further behind. The key thing though was the class size and the fact that I can go to people already in the system and say, 'Hey, this is a decent raise.'"

Check of clips: Board and teachers have been negotiating for six months. Teachers originally demanded a 9 percent increase and class size no larger than 25. Pay scale in the district under the last contract ranged from $19,200 for a new teacher to $58,500 for a teacher with a master's degree and 12 or more years' experience. Teachers last week voted to strike "within a month" if a contract agreement could not be reached.

THREE

The Board of Education of Morrisville met tonight at Morrisville Elementary School.

1. Meeting began at 8 p.m. and ended at 11:30.
2. Board votes 9–0 to accept minutes of last meeting.
3. Communications: Dennis Allen's 6th-grade class raised $227 for the Muscular Dystrophy Foundation by organizing a car wash last week. Two students at Morrisville High School, Franca Stover and Gerald Loughlin, were Merit Scholarship semifinalists.
4. Report on Standard Reading Test scores by board president Charles Brown.

Brown: "As you can well see, this test is not good news. For the third straight year, the reading scores of sixth-graders in our system have declined. Three years ago the average reading score for sixth-graders was 79, which means that by the end of sixth grade they were right on track, reading at a late-sixth-grade/beginning-seventh-grade level. Two years ago the drop was to just 78 and last year 76; but this year our sixth graders got an average score of 73 at the end of the year. That means, ladies and gentlemen, that the average sixth-grader completing elementary school in this system has the reading skills equivalent on a national basis to a sixth-grader finishing his or her first semester. I find that appalling and think we've got to find a way to stop the slide. I've asked John Klein, who, as you know, is assistant superintendent for instruction, to come here tonight and give us his views on these test scores."

Klein: "No doubt this is discouraging, but I think the scores have to be seen in perspective. For one thing, these scores represent an average for *all* sixth-graders in this district. You may not know that we only had 57 this year. A few, frankly, are very slow learners and five have been retained. Some of these are reading at a second- and third-grade level, and these bring the average down. Still, this raises some grave questions about an educational experiment we tried last year. We decided to go to an *open classroom* approach—all 57 students were taught in one large open area by two teachers and a teacher's aide. The idea was for teachers to have more flexibility in their planning and teaching approach. But one, Ethel Rosegrant, missed a good part of the year … I think seven weeks this spring … with pneumonia, and we never did find a single substitute who could fit into that situation. One teacher can't keep track of what 57 students are doing, and instead of individualized instruction, I'm afraid there may have been too much wasted time. Personally, though, I would give the open classroom one more year to take hold. It hasn't really had a fair trial yet."

Trustee [board member] Jack Gantz: "I never liked all this experimental stuff anyway. Look, it is time we got back to basics—reading, writing and arithmetic. That's what I learned at school, and the kids today just aren't getting it. I move that we eliminate the open classroom at the elementary school next year so that this fiasco doesn't continue."

Trustee Alice Richardson: "I second."

Trustee Joan Dershowitz: "Isn't it a little extreme to be changing educational policy on the basis of a five-minute presentation? Mr. Gantz, I have friends with children in that open classroom. Those kids came home with beautiful work in arts and crafts. The brightest ones were able to meet in small groups to work on a wonderful social studies project that, as we bragged last month, was exhibited at City Hall. The slowest kids got individual attention that would have been impossible with just one teacher. Sure, all that went by the board when Ethel Rosegrant fell ill, but don't cure the patient by killing it. I propose that we ask Miss Rosegrant and the other teacher in the class, Paul Moore, to give us a report next meeting."

Board votes. First vote, 6–3 against Gantz's motion to eliminate open classroom in sixth grade. Gantz, Richardson and Bob Shaeffer vote to end open classroom. Second vote, 9–0 to ask teachers in open classroom to present a report.

5. Board votes 9–0 to spend $875 for a new tuba for the band.

FOUR

You hadn't remembered those chairs being so little, but the 15-year-olds do seem to fit in them just fine, and undoubtedly you did too at their age. But you're no longer 15, and you, like the principal and the superintendent, sat in one of those little chairs for about an hour today in Rodney Markham's 10th-grade biology class at Randall Regional High School as he quite deliberately got himself suspended.

Markham did exactly what he had told his principal he was going to do, exactly what he said he'd do when he called the newspaper. In a clear violation of district policy on sex education, he had shown his students, male and female, a series of large, full-color pictures of humans engaged in sexual acts. The district's regulations on sex education, you had learned, say: "Sex education should be conducted for boys and girls separately. Sketches of people may be employed briefly in the lessons, but under no circumstances are potentially pornographic photographs to be shown to these teen-agers."

The district's regulations say teachers may be suspended and, after full investigations, their contracts terminated, for "clear and willful violations of district policies." At 10:32 this morning, a couple of minutes after Markham's class had ended (it ran from 9:30 to 10:30 a.m.), District Supt. Max Whelan got out of his little chair, walked over to Markham and said: "You have clearly and willfully violated district regulations in teaching this lesson. I am therefore suspending you without pay effective immediately, and I will now institute procedures that I hope will lead to the termination of your contract. Please collect your belongings."

You didn't know whom to grab first, but you decided to go for the man himself: Rod Markham. He's a little guy, about 5-foot-6. He wears granny classes, he's prematurely bald and he says he's 28. Master's degree in education from University of Minnesota. ... He's been working here in Randall five years ... says he never taught anywhere else.

Your first question: "Well, you did it. How does it feel?"

Markham: "You can go over these things time and time again in your mind but still not be prepared for them when they finally happen. I would say the lesson was even more successful than I had imagined. You could see a look of real interest on those kids' faces as they learned from the pictures. You sensed that mysteries were being cleared up in their heads by getting a chance to see what these acts looked like. But I also have to say that Whelan's little speech hit me harder than I'd expected. It's no fun to lose your job, even temporarily. But the ACLU [American Civil Liberties Union] has gotten me a fine lawyer, and I think we're going to give them a hell of a fight."

You had written a story about this a week ago, when Markham first announced his plan. He said then: "In the years I've worked at this school I've grown increasingly frustrated and concerned by this policy. I do not believe any good can come from denying these young men and women full information on this crucial subject. I have decided to take a stand." This time you simply asked him whether it was worth it.

Markham: "I believe an important lesson was taught in this classroom today, both for these young men and women and for this community. I'm willing to pay whatever price is necessary to help take people out of the dark ages and to help the children of this area learn how to deal intelligently with the problems and joys of sex."

The students had been mostly quiet during Markham's lecture. They certainly seemed more interested in the five pictures of sex acts he showed them and in his lecture on love and caring than in the three adults sitting in the back of the classroom. Incidentally, those pictures were as explicit as could be—if they had been in a movie, it would have been rated X.

After the lecture was over, every one of the 23 students—13 girls, 10 boys—seemed to stand and clap or cheer. Some booed as Whelan walked over to Markham. You started interviewing some of the students before they filtered out into the hall. The other adults could wait.

Fong Lee, 15, ... lives in Westwood: "That was good. It was really fine. Look, no problem ... the poor guy."

Alan Jacobs, 14, ... lives in Westwood: "No, I wasn't at all embarrassed. The girls didn't bother me. The pictures didn't bother me. I learned something today from a great teacher. This is awful."

Katherine Emmers, 15, ... lives in Fort George: "Yeah, it made me feel a little uncomfortable, but we're not babies. We can handle it."

Steve Smith, 15, ... lives in Westwood: "The bastards. Hey, I've seen pornography. You think I can't buy *Hustler*? That wasn't pornography. It was graphic, but it was for good teaching. Just good teaching."

Grace Kim, 15, ... lives in Westwood: "No, of course I didn't mind having boys around. This wasn't giggle time. This was serious. Mr. Markham treated it seriously, and we took it that way." You could confirm that. There were no giggles or snickers.

The principal, Astrid Kane, had returned to her office. You found her there, but she said you'd better talk to Whelan. Whelan was in his office, and first you asked him about the students' applause and their comments.

Whelan: "We're not at the stage yet where we're going to let 15-year-olds make policy in this district."

You asked for the record why Markham was suspended.

Whelan: "This district draws a strict and important line between sex education and pornography; we have for ten years. You and your readers have to understand that. We do not believe that 15-year-olds should be exposed to material like what we saw today. Do you see the point? We believe that this type of instruction—and it should never be so graphic—should be done with boys and girls separately, so they won't be embarrassed and so it won't lead to anything. And we believe in the right to enforce the regulations that the board, the community and I believe in. Those pictures, let me tell you, were even worse than I expected. I really wish we could have stopped that teacher before he did what he did to those kids, but I'm glad at least that we can stop him before he does it again.

"He even waited until the last 10 minutes to show them just to spite us," Whelan adds.

As you were getting in your car, you saw Markham loading his car with papers and books and notebooks. He looked back at Randall High School and seemed to smile.

Back at the office, you called Joyce Jamison, Markham's ACLU lawyer.

Jamison: "Hi. I just got back from the high school. I told Whelan we're going to fight this thing all the way to the Supreme Court, if we have to. The state ACLU is clear on this: Students and teachers have the right to talk intelligently and openly about sex."

You recalled that Kane had said there were 28 students in Markham's biology class. Only 23 had attended. With Kane's help, you got the numbers for the other five students. Two parents just said their kids were "not feeling well." Two refused to talk. But Celia Zimmerman, of Westwood, the mother of Saundra Zimmerman, 15, said: "I'm just not that kind of a mother, and Sandy's just not that kind of a girl. Of course they were right to fire that man. We don't need pornography in our schools. No, you can't talk to Sandy, and yes, we had forbidden her to go to school today."

EXERCISE C
Story Assignments

1. Write a story on a meeting of a local school board. Before the meeting, stop by the school district's offices to get a copy of the agenda, and contact sources within the district to brief yourself on the issues that are scheduled for discussion.

2. Obtain a copy of the most recent budget for a local school district. Assume the budget has just been released. Based on interviews with sources in the district and research materials (such as the previous year's budget), write a story about that budget and its potential effect on the district.

3. Through interviews with faculty and students at a local public school, find a teacher who has a reputation for doing outstanding work in the classroom. Write a profile of that teacher that demonstrates why he or she is so successful. Try to obtain permission to sit in on some classes.

4. Write an article on facilities and programs for disabled students at a local public school or college. Find out how much the programs cost and whether the school receives state or federal funding to help pay for them. Spend some time with disabled students and ask them about the adequacy of the facilities and programs that are available. Contact the leaders of any on-campus organizations of disabled students. You might also talk with leaders of off-campus organizations that represent the disabled to get their views on what should be done.

5. Write an article on the writing skills of undergraduates at a local college or university. Interview teachers and students at the school. Do they believe writing skills have declined? Why? Look for test scores that might offer evidence of a change in writing skills.

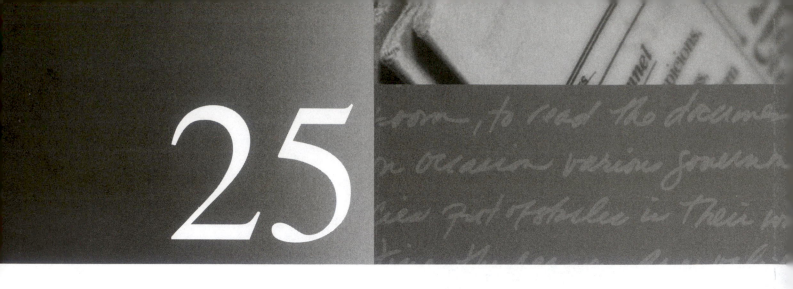

25

Business and Labor

Corporations determine what products will appear in our homes and how much of our income we will be able to devote to buying those products. The economic conditions under which those corporations operate—and how they respond to those conditions—help determine the environment in which we earn, spend, pay taxes, and get fired or hired.

Business is big news today, whether it is the story of the merger of two major banks and the impact of that merger on local services or the story of rising interest rates and their effect on home mortgages. Each day newspapers are filled with statistics on the rise or fall of retail sales, commercial occupancy rates, housing construction rates and the stocks on Wall Street.

Thick business sections also are allocating ample space to such stories as Ford Motor Co.'s latest quarterly earning report, JetBlue's new no-frills routes or fashion designer Ralph Lauren's decision to start a new business.

Newspapers devote generous pages to business and economic news in part for a *journalistic* reason: Editors realize the impact such news can have on many aspects of our lives. But business is also getting more attention for a *business* reason: The readers most interested in this news are the readers most attractive to advertisers—the well-off.

If business coverage is focused on the world of corporate executives, labor coverage looks at the situation of the less affluent but more numerous people who work under these executives—people who are, alas, less attractive to advertisers. "Many newspapers now have large business staffs," notes William Serrin, who covered labor for *The New York Times*. "But I know of no paper that has a large labor staff."

The labor beat—Serrin suggests it be called the "work beat"—offers a chance to report on some of the consequences of business and economic decisions. It looks at how people spend their eight or so hours each day on the job, at struggles to organize and protect workers, and at the periodic battles between employers and employees over wages and conditions:

> GRAND PRAIRIE—Members of United Auto Workers Local 276 made plans yesterday to continue their walkout at a General Motors plant in Arlington as negotiators worked to end the strike at 13 GM assembly plants nationwide.
>
> *The Dallas Morning News*

Labor reporters usually can find their way through the offers and counteroffers of contract negotiations without a course in accounting. Though a sense of labor history helps, many of the challenges of the beat involve dealing with people rather than poring over texts. It's essential, for example, for labor reporters to overcome any stereotypes they may have about people who work in clothes that get dirty. And in certain industries—building maintenance, for example—an ear for foreign languages and an understanding of the contentious national debate over immigration and immigration policies also can help reporters do a better job. Otherwise, it will be difficult to go beyond stories relaying the rhetoric of labor leaders to stories relating the reality of working conditions, attitudes on the job, and increasing divisions between newer and older generations of Americans in the work force, which today is as diverse a patchwork of ethnicities and races as ever in this country's history.

Business, on the other hand, is a difficult beat to walk onto without some training. Karen W. Arenson, who covers business and economics for *The New York Times*, majored in economics in college. When she got a business reporting job, however, she took additional night courses in accounting and in finance. Arenson wanted to be sure she understood all the numbers and terms through which businesses report on their performance and on which businesses and financiers base their decisions. "These courses tell you what a company is about and how to think about a company," she says.

Still, as much as an understanding of the numbers and the jargon can help, business and economic reporters, like all others, ultimately must turn to knowledgeable people for help. For example, Leon Wynter came to *The Wall Street Journal* with an MBA in economics, experience in banking and graduate training in journalism. But in struggling to understand the complicated workings of the banking regulatory system he was covering, he needed sources.

Two labor organizers fire up striking Verizon Yellow Pages workers as they demonstrate in front of the company's office building in Albany, N.Y.
(*Photo by Tom Killups of* The Troy [N.Y.] Record)

BUSINESS SOURCES

A reporter assigned to cover business in a city or town will want to start by figuring out what businesses the people in the area are engaged in. The local Chamber of Commerce can provide a basic list. There also are books that categorize and list businesses by something known as the *Standard Industrial Code.* Finally, the newspaper's library may have a separate, alphabetical file on businesses to help fill out the list and fill in the reporter on what's been written. (See Chapter 14, Research.)

Then it might be time to focus on a particular company. "You want to know: What is the company doing?" advises Arenson. "Who does it compete with? How successful is it? How profitable is it? What is its growth potential? What problems does it have or might it have in the future?" Business reporters also should be thinking about whom the company employs, where it releases its wastes, how it determines its price structure, what new products it might be introducing and, in general, what role the company plays in the economy and environment of the area. At the very least, the answers to these questions will give a reporter key background information to tuck away until the company finds its way into the news. Often, though, the answers can lead directly to an interesting story. Here are two paragraphs from the middle of a story about a fast-growing company in what its president perceives to be a growth industry:

> The firm, which has headquarters in Springfield, Ill., and employs more than 1,100 people in the St. Louis area, has become No. 1 or No. 2 nationally in five of its product markets. Sales zoomed 68 percent to $210.96 million last year, making Amedco one of Wall Street's darlings.
>
> The company began by offering consulting and accounting services to the funeral trade, and then moved into manufacturing and supplying items such as embalming liquids and biers for that industry.
>
> *St. Louis Post-Dispatch*

Analysts

It often makes sense to start reporting from the outside. Among the most knowledgeable sources a reporter interested in a company or industry can find are the securities analysts and investment bankers responsible for monitoring it. These are the people whose job it is to determine the attractiveness of companies or industries for potential investors. They can help make sense of the statistics a company releases and give a reasonably objective assessment of that company's strengths and weaknesses. Fortunately, they're usually happy to publicize their expertise by talking with reporters, as was the case in this excerpt from a *New York Times* article about wholesale changes at Aetna Life and Casualty Company:

> "It's been time for them to shake things up for years," said Donald E. Franz, an analyst at Smith Barney, Harris Upham & Company.

Securities analysts can be found with brokerage firms like Paine Webber and Merrill Lynch. They specialize in following specific industries.

Company Officials

In approaching a company itself, reporters can start either by contacting a public relations person and working their way up to the chief executive—getting smarter as they go along—or they can begin at the top and enlist the boss's help in leading them to other people with whom they should talk. Certainly, the person who runs the company should be somewhere on every reporter's list of sources. Here, the chairman of the board of Fotomat discusses efforts under way to turn around the company's financial problems:

"While the refinancing we seek is a prime ingredient in reshaping Fotomat, I believe we are making progress," he said. "Our current results indicate that our marketing and cost control programs are working."

St. Petersburg (Fla.) Times

Many men and women in business are wary of reporters, and it's often best to get to know them while working on a relatively noncontroversial story. Kathryn Harris' first assignment for the *Los Angeles Times* was to cover the semiconductor and computer industry. To get her feet wet in this unfamiliar area, she decided to "wade in" with a general story about the housing problems in Silicon Valley, the area in California where many of these firms are located. This story gave her a chance, she says, to meet the people in the industry in a "nonconfrontational" situation. Then Harris waded in a little deeper with a profile of a major corporation in the area—Tandem. "It's a good exercise," she says. "You talk to the competition, to the suppliers, to the customers, as well as company officials. If it's a company you're going to cover for awhile, it helps to get to know it inside out."

The Other Side

After spending much of their day talking with business people and then writing stories that in many cases will be read primarily by business people, reporters may be tempted to assume the perspective of the men and women they cover. That's dangerous. The suppliers, customers and competitors Harris suggests talking to provide a broader point of view on the operations of a company. But reporters must also seek out people from nonbusiness fields: union leaders, environmental groups, and public interest and consumer groups of the type spawned by Ralph Nader. And reporters should keep track of people who have left companies in their area; these sometimes disaffected employees can add balance to a story... if, that is, it's clear that they aren't just selling sour grapes.

"You want to cover as many bases as possible and get different points of view to the full extent that there are different points of view," says Arenson. She begins each story by jotting down what angles might be developed and what range of viewpoints might exist on each point. Then she decides what sources she might find to represent those viewpoints. "You can help define a story that way," Arenson says. You also can—if your selection is broad enough—ensure that your information won't be too one-sided.

Regulators

A month after joining *The Wall Street Journal* to cover bank regulation, Leon Wynter found himself embroiled in one of the hottest stories on his beat in years. The Continental Illinois National Bank, ninth largest in the country, was on the brink of failing. Wynter had to find out why and what might be done about it, a task he soon learned meant penetrating the bureaucracies of three federal regulatory agencies. "How much was the bank borrowing? How much were its deposits falling down?" These are among the questions Wynter needed answered. "I was calling a lot of people I didn't know to find out," he recalls.

The Federal Deposit Insurance Corporation was designing a package that would keep the troubled bank afloat. Wynter found himself in the unenviable position of having to get acquainted with the FDIC's chairman by calling him at home on a weekend. He also needed sources at the office of the comptroller of the currency, a division of the Treasury Department, that was keeping a watchful eye on the books of Continental Illinois, and at the Federal Reserve, which pumped in funds to rescue the bank.

All businesses are subject to some regulation by federal and state agencies. An airline, for example, might deal with the Securities and Exchange Commission when it is selling its stock, with the Federal Aviation Administration when it tries to schedule flights at busy airports, and with the National Transportation Safety Board should one of its planes crash. The owner of a funeral parlor might obtain a low-interest loan through the Small Business Association but might also be challenged by the Occupational Safety and Health Administration for exposing workers to unsafe conditions or by the Federal Trade Commission for misleading customers.

Business reporters should know who is keeping tabs on the businesses they cover. They also should keep in mind, as Wynter did, that the best information often doesn't come from the top regulators but from the lawyers who get the complaints, the investigators in the field and the middle-level bureaucrats who write the reports.

LABOR SOURCES

Labor reporters should start by tracking down the union leaders who are active in their towns, but it is important not to stop there. The head of a union of local clerical employees can discuss the workers' salary structure, their benefit packages, their organizing efforts and the union's likely demands in the next contract negotiations. He or she cannot give a firsthand account of what it is like to be a secretary in a firm in the process of installing new data retrieval software.

"You can't cover labor just by writing about John Doe, who is head of Local 33," says William Serrin. "If you want to cover work then you'll be in the offices and the department stores and the factories finding out what's really cooking." Serrin calls this "bottoms up" reporting.

For some reporters, interviewing workers means going to a local bar dressed in a faded pair of blue jeans. Serrin believes this is condescending: "You don't interview executives at their clubs, why always interview workers at bars? Like everybody else, some workers drink, but *x* times as many others just go home in the evening and mow the lawn."

When reporters are covering events in union headquarters or halls, they should keep an ear tuned to possible dissident groups. And, of course, management officials are crucial sources for the other side on labor stories.

Labor reporters also should be aware of union activities that are not related to formal negotiations: health plans, community involvement, legal and educational services, and political support for candidates. And additional stories about work can come from government agencies such as the federal Occupational Safety and Health Administration and its state equivalents. It's important to remember that the large majority of the workers in the United States, particularly service employees, are *not* unionized. Their problems with salary and working conditions should not be ignored.

When Jim Kadera of *The Oregonian* in Portland wrote a story on logging accidents, he interviewed a wide range of sources, including officials of the state Workers Compensation Department, a consultant to the state accident insurance fund, a vice president of a lumber company and the safety manager for an association of loggers. Here is Kadera's lead:

> When Delton Reich Jr., a 32-year-old choker setter, was crushed by a rolling log yesterday, he became the 15th logger to die in an accident in the state this year.

As unions continue to lose clout and membership, covering labor issues becomes more complex. The story of this country's immigrant workers, relied on heavily in industries as varied as agriculture and landscaping, can't be told from a union hall. It means building trust among men and women always fearful of being deported, making contacts among the social services workers and church workers who know them so that they won't mistake your reporting interest for law enforcement.

> Until five years ago, Rigoberto Ochoa of Charapan, Mexico, sneaked into California to work, picking peaches, prunes and grapes as an illegal migrant.
>
> But since 2002, he's been coming across the border each year by bus, carrying an H2B visa for temporary nonagricultural workers. As an employee of Amplex wholesale nursery off Ulmerton Road, the 39-year-old makes twice the $4.25 an hour he was paid as an undocumented worker.
>
> The three-day bus trip that he takes from Mexico each February and then back each December is tedious, but it's safe and inexpensive compared with what he went through as an illegal.
>
> *St. Petersburg* (Fla.) *Times*

The world of labor reporting has grown far more complex than it was in the era of powerful unions. But there's one other great equalizer for finding workers, unionized or nonunionized, particularly when times get tough: state unemployment offices.

DOCUMENTS

No matter how good they are with people, reporters haven't earned their pinstripes on the business beat until they've learned to make sense of all the numbers with which companies measure performance. Some are found in the reports and statements issued by *publicly held* corporations (companies in which the public can buy stock). Numbers hold the keys to an understanding of the company's profits, its debts, the cash it has on hand, its taxes and the payback investors can expect for their dollars. These numbers also may reveal a company's troubles: inventory that's piled up or has been depleted, capital investments in new plants that are being underused, profit margins that are lower than the competition's.

"There is no more fundamental skill required in doing well in this field than understanding corporate financial statements," says Chris Welles, a freelance business writer who was the director of the Walter Bagehot Fellowship Program in Economic and Business Journalism at Columbia University.

The federal government's securities and exchange laws require corporations that sell stock to the public to produce *annual reports* on how much they've earned, how much they've spent, how much they owe and how their performance compares with that of past years. These reports include a *balance sheet,* listing the company's assets (what it owns) and its liabilities (what it owes) at a specific time, as well as a *statement of income and retained earnings*, comparing the company's sales and operating profits for one year with those of past years. The charts on pages 431–433, drawn from a New York Stock Exchange publication, *Understanding Financial Statements*, provide an example and an explanation of typical versions of these reports.

"Some people look at balance sheets as dry," notes Arenson. "But they tell you how the company has used its money and where that money came from. If you don't get interested in that, perhaps you shouldn't be covering business."

Financial statements may supply reporters with straightforward stories, supported by quotes from company executives and outside analysts, about a company's performance. This story, based on a company report, must have been easy for the writer to find:

> The Tribune Co. reported profits of $21.6 million in its second fiscal quarter as gains from its newspaper and broadcasting groups more than offset losses in its Canadian newsprint and forest products operations.
>
> *Chicago Tribune*

In attempting to understand a business, however, reporters must often do more than simply report whether it is making a profit. Like potential investors, they will look for comparisons between the company's performance in this year or quarter of the economic year and past years or quarters:

> The beleaguered Fotomat Corp. said yesterday that it had its first profitable quarter in a year and a half during the accounting period ended July 31.
>   During the quarter, the St. Petersburg company earned $1.5 million, or 15 cents per share, on revenues of $50.8 million. During the same quarter last year, the company lost $2.6 million, or 30 cents per share.
>
> *St. Petersburg* (Fla.) *Times*

Like investors, reporters will often be interested in *ratios* within a financial report. Welles advises that business reporters investigate such things as *profit margin*—a company's profit as a percentage of sales (after taxes)—and *return on equity*—a company's net income as a percentage of all the money that has been invested in it. (The higher the return on equity, the more money investors are likely to make.) These methods of analysis won't always make it into a story, but they may be useful in acquiring a broader view of the company's performance.

The next step might be to look beyond the performance of one company to the performance of an industry as a whole. "Let's take a company whose earnings dropped 22 percent last year," suggests Welles. "If its major competitors dropped 10 percent, that's bad. But if its major competitors dropped 40 percent, that might not be such a bad performance."

While annual reports and quarterly financial statements include lots of information about a company, neither is as complete as the *10-K statement* publicly held companies must file with the federal Securities and Exchange Commission. These statements include information on everything from the legal proceedings that may be pending against a company to the salary of its top executives. They may be made available by a company; they will be made available by the nearest regional office of the Securities and Exchange Commission.

When a company wants to issue more shares of stock, it must provide potential buyers with an additional document called a *prospectus*. This will include information on the company's earnings, its major stockholders, its lines of business and its competition. The company is legally responsible for the accuracy of the information it includes in a prospectus. This document can be as valuable to a journalist trying to report on a company as it is to an investor thinking of buying a piece of it.

Often the most interesting stories are about trends in business, such as a sharp spike in the wage and compensation packages of CEOs (chief executive officers) at Fortune 500 companies. While single documents don't announce such trends, alert reporters who follow leading business publications such as the *Wall Street Journal,* the *Economist* and *Business Week* can spot them. And the mass of data compiled by government agencies such as the *Bureau of Labor Statistics* (www.bls.gov) can help reporters identify trend stories about everything from wage rates to inflation rates in different parts of the country.

Often the most passionate and interesting stories can be found in the personal challenges and achievements of those who build businesses. At a local level, these often are smaller businesses, privately held. State and county offices can help identify the businesses in your area. The state government, for example, registers businesses. It can provide basic information such as whether the company is publicly or privately owned and who its officers are. That's a starting point.

Reference books also can provide background information. Research publications such as *Business Information Sources* and the *Encyclopedia of Business and Information Sources* can help reporters find and sort through piles of paper generated by business. Others like Standard & Poor's *Register of Corporations, Directors and Executives* offer basic information on major corporations and a starting point for compiling a list of the top people in an industry nationally. And for reporters mired in the jargon of business, the *Modern American Business Dictionary* offers hope.

Labor reporters needn't worry as much about preferred stock or sinking-fund debentures, though they should become familiar with the wage scales, benefits and pension plans that might be discussed in a contract. A union's own newspaper can be a useful source of this and other labor information. While many union newspapers are little more than public relations sheets for union presidents, some are powerful voices for the political and economic interests of their members. One New York City union paper, the *Public Employee Press*, regularly provided the local dailies with leads to stories on subjects ranging from the deterioration of the city's bridges to generous real estate tax breaks being given local builders.

The Society of Business Editors and Writers (SABEW, http://www.sabew.org) runs workshops around the country on various aspects of business reporting.

BASIC STORIES

The business pages on a typical day will be filled with stories about new (and, if the company is to be believed, improved) products; plans to open or close branch offices or manufacturing plants; reports of higher or lower sales or profits; news of bankruptcies, acquisitions and mergers; stock, bond and commodities market reports, and the statistics that the government releases almost daily about the state of the economy. The most common labor stories discuss strikes, negotiations, layoffs and, on occasion, new hirings.

Here are some basic questions to keep in mind when reporting and writing these stories.

How Will It Affect Consumers?

Will the larger company created by the merger continue to offer the same services, and prices, to customers? What does the fall in the value of the dollar in relation to other currencies mean for American consumers? How are changes in the *prime interest rate*—a rate paid only by some favored corporations—likely to be felt by individual borrowers?

Not every story offers such an angle. Not every article has room for it. But business and labor reporters who want to interest a wide variety of readers in their stories must pay attention to the interests of this wide variety of readers. Here is a paragraph from a story on a possible strike by employees of Continental Airlines:

> A strike is not expected to present a major inconvenience to Los Angeles passengers because Continental operates only about 12 flights per day here.
>
> *Los Angeles Times*

How Will It Affect Investors?

> Fort Collins-based Centennial Bank of the West says it will be sold and plans a *"long-awaited announcement"* today about who will buy the bank.
>
> No further details were available late Wednesday, but *the news is no surprise* to local banking observers who've thought President Bill Farr has had his bank on the block for some time. ...
>
> *Rocky Mountain News*

Gulf and Western Industries, *in a widely expected streamlining move*, said yesterday that it would take a $470 million write-off in its just ended fiscal year to divest itself of several major lines of business. . . .

The New York Times

Both these leads raise the same question: Why did these reporters choose to emphasize the *predictability* of the announcements they are reporting on? The answer is that many of the people who turn to the business pages do so to gather information on which to base investment decisions—whether to sell their stock in Centennial Bank, for example—and the fortunes of such speculative investments may hinge on how events live up to expectations as much as on the events themselves. Bad news may be interpreted as good news by investors if they expected worse. The phrase *in a long-awaited announcement* tells investors and potential investors that Centennial Bank's move is not likely to jolt the stock market.

Often the information for investors is more direct:

The First Chicago-American National announcement drew positive reactions from bank stock analysts and from other bankers in Chicago. . . .

". . . It will be an exceptionally good deal for both parties," said Robert Wilmouth, chairman of LaSalle National. "First Chicago is making an excellent acquisition, and the price is very good also."

Chicago Tribune

How Will It Affect Workers?

The answer to this question will be of interest not only to a company's employees but to their family and friends, and to the merchants who sell to them. This story about the decline in the shoemaking business focuses on the fate of workers at one local plant:

. . . At the Gardena Shoe Factory, there are about 200 piecework employees—a third less than at peak operating capacity—all working four-day weeks. The plant made 3,000 pairs of shoes a day last year; it now turns out only 1,800.

"The Gardena plant could be gone in one or two years," says Arthur Hirshberg, who runs it for Desco Shoe Corp., its New York-based parent.

Los Angeles Times

How Will It Affect the Economy?

We may not use that product. We may not know anyone who works at one of those stores. We may prefer piggy banks to stock markets. But it is difficult to find anyone who can claim to be a disinterested observer of the waves of recovery and recession that raise and lower inflation, unemployment, profits, wages and interest rates. As a science, economics seems to be about at the stage medicine was 150 years ago. The predictions of economists often go awry. Their prescriptions often seem to be about as effective as leeches applied to cure a fever. But readers need clues to the future course of the national and local economy, and reporters—as humbly and as unpretentiously as possible—must try to provide those clues:

Balance Sheet

"Your Company"

Balance Sheet

Year ended December 31	Millions		The Company Owned
	2008	**2007**	
Assets			
Current Assets			
Cash	$9.0	$6.2	Generally bank deposits.
Marketable securities	—	2.0	Government or corporate bonds or stocks that can easily be sold.
Accounts and notes receivable	12.4	11.4	Amounts owed the company by its customers and others less amounts considered uncollectible.
Inventories	27.0	24.6	Raw materials, work in process and finished merchandise, stated at the lower of cost or realizable value.
Total current assets	$48.4	$44.2	
Property, Plant and Equipment			
Buildings, machinery and equipment, at cost	104.3	92.7	
Less accumulated depreciation	27.6	25.0	Loss of value through wear and tear.
	$76.7	$67.7	
Land, at cost	0.9	0.7	
Total property, plant and equipment	$77.6	$68.4	
Other Assets			
Receivables due after one year	4.7	3.9	Amount due to be owed the company, and likely to be collected, in the next year.
Surrender value of insurance	0.2	0.2	Value of insurance policy if cashed in.
Other	0.6	0.5	
Total other assets	$5.5	$4.6	
Total Assets	$131.5	$117.2	

Statement of Income and Retained Earnings

"Your Company"

Year ended December 31	Millions			
	2008	**2007**	**2006**	
Sales	$115.8	$110.0	$104.5	Amount received or receivable from customers.
Less				
Cost and Expenses				
Cost of goods sold	$76.4	$73.2	$70.2	Part of income used for wages, salaries, raw materials, fuel and supplies and certain taxes.
Selling, general and administrative expenses	14.2	13.0	12.1	Part of income used for salespeople's commissions, advertising, officers' salaries and other general expenses.
Depreciation	2.6	3.5	2.3	Provision from income for the reduction of the service life of machinery and buildings.
	$93.2	$89.7	$84.6	
Operation Profit	$22.6	$20.3	$19.9	The remainder after deducting the above expenses from sales, but before providing for interest charges and taxes.
Interest charges	1.3	1.0	1.3	Amount required for interest on borrowed funds.
Earnings before income taxes	$21.3	$19.3	$18.6	
Provision for taxes on income	11.4	9.8	9.5	Amount paid or payable for taxes.
Net income after preferred share dividend requirements (per common share: 2008—$5.24; 2007—$5.03; 2006—$4.97)	$9.9	$9.5	$9.1	This amount was earned for stockholders.
Retained earnings, beginning of year	42.2	37.6	33.1	
	$52.1	$47.1	$42.2	
Less dividends paid on				
Preferred stock ($5 per share)	(0.3)	(0.3)	—	
Common stock (per share: 2008—$3.00; 2007—$2.50; 2006—$2.50)	(5.4)	(4.6)	(4.6)	
Retained Earnings, End of Year	$46.4	$42.2	$37.6	Earnings reinvested in the business. Usually not all of the year's earnings are paid out in dividends; some are retained in the business for expansion or other purposes.

Liabilities and Stockholders' Equity

The Company Owned

Current Liabilities			
Accounts payable	$6.1	$5.0	Money owed for raw materials, supplies and services.
Accrued liabilities	3.6	3.3	Unpaid salaries, wages, interest and commissions.
Current maturity of long-term debt	1.0	0.8	Amount due in next year on money that has been borrowed.
Federal income and other taxes	9.6	8.4	
Dividends payable	1.3	1.1	Promised payments to stockholders.
Total current liabilities	$21.6	$18.6	
Other Liabilities	3.6	2.5	Other liabilities due after one year.
Long-term debt			
5% Sinking-fund debentures, due July 31, 2009	26.0	20.0	Long-term debt is the amount due next year on money borrowed.
Stockholders' Equity[2]			
5% Preferred stock[3] ($100 par: authorized and outstanding—60,000)	6.0	6.0	Amount originally invested in the company computed by multiplying the number of shares held, or outstanding, times the par value—an arbitrary stated value—of the shares.
Common stock[4] ($10 par: authorized—2,000,000; outstanding—1,830,000)	18.3	18.3	
Additional paid-in capital	9.6	9.6	Money received from the sale of stock at more than par value.
Retained Earnings	46.4	42.2	Earnings not paid out in dividends but reinvested in the business.
Total stockholders' equity	$80.3	$76.1	
Total Liabilities, and Stockholders' Equity	$131.5	$117.2	

[1] 5% *Sinking-fund debentures* are a type of *long-term debt*, or long-term borrowing, which must be repaid by setting aside a certain amount out of earnings at stated intervals. A debenture is a certificate of debt issued by a corporation—a corporate IOU. In this case, the company is paying 5 percent interest on that IOU.

[2] *Equity* is the amount of money that has been invested in a company.

[3] *Preferred stockholders* have first call on dividends, and their dividends are fixed—in this case, at 5 percent a year.

[4] *Common stockholders* are paid dividends only after preferred stockholders have been paid.

* *Source:* New York Stock Exchange.

WASHINGTON—The economy has slowed in the current quarter to a 3.6 percent annual rate of growth, substantially below the pace set during the first half of the year. ...

Although sharp drops in growth normally are cause for concern, some economists said the 3.6 percent growth rate for July through September was just what was needed to prolong the recovery.

Associated Press in *The Philadelphia Inquirer*

ENTERPRISE

The best business and labor stories seem to be written by reporters who can step back and provide some perspective on changes brought by new products, new markets and new technologies.

William Serrin persuaded his editors to allow him to wander around Pittsburgh for three or four weeks in "expanding circles," in search of stories about the effect on workers of the decline in smokestack industries. Few newspapers can give their staff such luxuries, but Serrin says his "serendipity expedition" eventually led to dozens of stories.

Kathryn Harris, in an effort to "be the first in the nation to report on trends" in a trendy field—video games—suspected that the entry of so many companies into the field would bankrupt some of them. She vowed that she would do a story on the field every six weeks just to keep up. Her close monitoring of the industry helped her write one of the first stories on sharp price cutting in the industry as the market for games softened.

Karen Arenson was reading through *The Wall Street Journal* when she came across an article reporting that Kraft had lost a lot of money and had taken an $18 million tax write-off on cheese. She investigated and came up with a good story—the national cheese industry was suffering because of a failure to plan properly for highs and lows in milk production.

Leads to enterprising business stories are all around us—on the shelves at the local supermarket, for example: Why did the brand name suddenly change on the milk cartons? How are these new sugar-free cereals selling? And leads to labor stories may be standing behind the counter at the supermarket: Will those new self-serve computerized checkout machines lead to wholesale layoffs of store employees? Do they result in fewer errors? Will they lead to any reduction in prices or only an increase in profits?

Many business stories will simply report on a company's earnings. Many labor stories will detail the progress of negotiations. But good reporters on either beat are too curious to restrict themselves to such routine coverage.

CHAPTER 25 SUMMARY: BUSINESS AND LABOR

The best business and labor stories are written by reporters who step back and provide perspective on the changes brought about by new products, new markets and new technologies. Many business stories will report on one company's quarterly earnings. Many labor stories will focus on worker-management negotiations. But business and labor reporters ask bigger questions to find better stories.

Always consider:

- **Who will be affected?** Whether writing about a merger, a layoff, a new product or a jump in gas prices, consider the consumers, workers and investors who will gain and lose ground as a result.

- **What and where is the data?** Business and labor news often is built around dollars and cents. Don't take the airline spokesman's word that the company restructured and laid off employees to "position itself as the strongest and best managed airline in the country." Look at the annual reports for the last few years and the more in-depth 10-K reports (filed with the SEC) to ascertain just how healthy the company is. Then get experts—market analysts of the airline industry—to help you evaluate this data.

- **Who is the competition?** One way of gauging the competitive health of an airline is to see how its performance measures up against competitors. Talk to the competitors as well. They may give you insights the company spokesman might studiously avoid.

- **What's the context?** If retail prices rose 0.3 percent last month, is that cause for alarm? It depends on the context. If it's a temporary spike fueled by sharply higher gas prices, it may not be. If inflation has been running at 6 percent a year, the 0.3 percent may represent an improvement. But if inflation has been below 2 percent for the last five years, a jump of 0.3 percent in a single month may be cause for alarm.

In covering local business and labor, find out what businesses drive the local economy and what services consumers rely on. Then spread a broad net in building your source files, talking to workers, labor leaders, state and federal regulators, competitors and analysts, as well as the business leaders. As with all good beat reporters, business reporters typically find out more when they rely less on the men and women at the top.

ADDITIONAL READING

How to Read a Financial Report: Wringing Vital Signs Out of the Numbers, John A. Tracy, John Wiley & Sons, 2004.

Keys to Reading an Annual Report (Barron's Business Keys), G. T. Friedland, Ph.D, and R. E. Welton, Ph.D, Barron's Education Series; 3rd edition, 2001.

Understanding American Business Jargon; A Dictionary, W. Davis Folsom, Greenwood Press; 2nd edition, 2005.

Understanding Business, McGraw-Hill/Irwin; 7th edition, 2004.

Webster's New World Business Writing Handbook, Richard Worth and Sharon Sorenson, Webster's New World; 1st edition, 2002.

Writing About Business; The New Knight–Bagehot Guide to Economics and Business Journalism, Terri Thompson, editor, Columbia University Press, 2000.

EXERCISE A
Research Assignments

ONE

Use research materials or interviews with people active in business and labor to write explanations that could be used in a newspaper article for the following terms.

1. Attrition
2. Annual percentage rate
3. Gross national product
4. Stopping the clock in negotiations
5. M1
6. Eurodollars
7. Market share
8. COLA
9. Tax shelter
10. The morning fixing of the price of gold
11. Shop steward
12. Fixed assets
13. Chapter 11
14. Liquidity ratio
15. Capitalization ratio

TWO

Choose a corporation active in your area. Obtain answers to the following questions about that corporation, and illustrate some of those answers with quotes:

1. Who is the chief executive officer?
2. Who is the chief operating officer?
3. Who is the treasurer?
4. Who is the marketing director?
5. Is the corporation publicly or privately owned?
6. In what business is the corporation involved?
7. What was its net income last year?
8. What was its operating profit last year?
9. Who are its major competitors?
10. What are its major challenges in the next year?
11. What waste products, if any, does it release into the area's environment?
12. If its employees are unionized, to what unions do they belong?
13. How many jobs does the company provide in the area?

THREE
Choose one of these groups of workers:

orderlies and nurses' assistants at a nearby hospital
interns at a nearby hospital
secretaries at a local college
professors at a local college
sanitation workers in a nearby town
police in a nearby town
workers at a nearby factory
teachers in a local school district
workers at a nearby fast-food restaurant
clerks at a nearby supermarket

Obtain answers to the following questions about these workers, and illustrate some of the answers with quotes:

1. What, if any, union do they belong to?
2. What is their average starting salary?
3. What benefits are they entitled to?
4. What percentage salary increase did they receive last year?
5. How does this compare with the increase in the cost of living in your area?
6. What educational background and training is required for their jobs?
7. How frequently are workers fired?
8. What chance for advancement is there?
9. Have there been any major layoffs in recent years?
10. If they were to leave their jobs, how difficult would it be for them to find comparable positions?

EXERCISE B
Writing Assignments

Write stories based on each of the following collections of information. In each case you are writing for a newspaper dated tomorrow and read in the town where the events occurred.

ONE
A press release issued by the McDermitt Industries Corporation today:

> McDermitt Industries Corporation, known for its leadership in the pest control business, was pleased to announce today that they have purchased the Get Em company, one of the nation's leading makers of rodent traps.
>
> MIC purchased 100 percent of Get Em, a privately owned company from its president, Harvey L. Mainsprig, for $2.6 million.
>
> MIC, with headquarters in Houston, Texas, is a publicly owned company with $60 million in assets. Their well-known products include Watch Out bug sprays and Oh No You Don't insect traps. MIC also sells agricultural pest controls under the MIC NIX label. MIC ranks number four among the nation's leading pest control companies.
>
> Get Em, which is exclusively in the rodent trap business, makes the popular Get Em mousetrap along with other rodent traps. The acquisition presents new challenges to MIC's aggressive management team because of Get Em's $27,000 loss last year and $12,000 loss in the previous year.

From interview with Mainsprig: "Yeah, I have a comment. Not a happy one. I've owned this company since its birth 31 years ago this month. Get Em has been my life. But we were losing money, and I just didn't have the capital to keep Get Em alive by myself. I owed it to our employees to find someone who did. MIC fits the bill, yes, they do. It's one fine, well-managed company."

Get Em's central office and its only factory are located here in Cedar Spring on South Main Street. Get Em employs 56 people.

From interview with Mayor Susan Apt: "Well, our goal is to save Get Em and the jobs it provides. McDermitt has the capital that Harvey apparently didn't have, but frankly we're a little worried about this. Harvey Mainsprig had a commitment to this town and its people. These new owners, some Houston corporation, could easily move the plant away from here. That's what we're going to have to make sure doesn't happen. I hope they didn't just buy Get Em for the brand name. I hope they bought the fine employees."

From an interview with George Gold, executive vice president of McDermitt, in Houston: "No, we have no plans to move Get Em. We are going to look very closely at their operations, but this is an exciting acquisition for us. We have great confidence in the company's future in the rodent trap field. Beyond that I wouldn't want to speculate."

TWO

1. DNA-Tec is a firm here in Watertown, working to develop commercial applications for gene-splicing techniques.
2. Three months ago, DNA-Tec introduced its first product, a widely publicized new bacteria that can increase the resistance of soybeans to certain types of insect damage.

3. Yesterday DNA-Tec's public relations director, Albert Devito, announced that the company had lost $3.2 million in the most recent quarter. Its sales were $5.1 million.

4. *Devito:* "Yesterday DNA-Tec's stock closed at 16 and a half."

5. *Devito:* "The company has lost money every quarter since it was founded three years ago: $5.2 million in the quarter before this; $10.2 million last year; $3.3 million in this quarter last year."

6. *Devito:* "We invested more than $10 million in a new laboratory to produce our soybean fortifier this year."

7. *Devito:* "We have sold a considerable amount of the product this month: there is no doubt that it is off to a fine start."

8. *DNA-Tec's president, Fred Strausberg:* "Let me emphasize that this is a fine, strong, promising company. We have expected some losses in these initial quarters as we begin to establish our product, but there is no doubt that this will soon be an extremely profitable company."

9. *Walter Kim, securities analyst with Andrews, Smith, Jones, specialists in the new biotechnology companies:* "To be honest, we expected a little more from DNA-Tec. So far, from what we have seen, their soy production just hasn't taken off like we had expected, but it is early in the game. Farmers may need more time to discover the product."

10. *Reynold Smith, who sells the DNA-Tec product at his chain of local farm stores, Seth Smith's Supplies:* "So far they haven't proven to our customers that this stuff works better than the pesticides we've been using for decades. It ain't cheap, and to be frank, some of our people are plain scared of it. We've sold some to folks who like to try something new. A lot of people will be waiting to see what they have to say."

11. *Devito, called for one final question:* "The product is not cheap. Yes, it may be more expensive than standard pesticides, but there is no doubt that farmers will save money on it in the long run, because it provides stronger protection against crop damage and is nontoxic."

12. Kim says the cost of treating an acre of soy with DNA-Tec's product is $14. The cost of using the organophosphate pesticide Parnagion is $12.50.

13. After announcement, DNA-Tec stock was down 1 point by closing time on the American Stock Exchange.

14. *Sharon Wolfer, securities analyst with Irving, Frank, specialists in biotechnology companies:* "Of course, I heard the news. No, it didn't surprise us. We knew they were having start-up troubles. But it's time for them to begin convincing investors that they will turn it around."

THREE

Paula Fortino is president of the National Office Workers union. Four months ago it won an election to represent 34 clerical employees at DNA-Tec here in Watertown. Fortino calls a press conference yesterday to explain that she will ask her DNA-Tec people for authorization to strike if she can't reach a contract settlement for them with DNA-Tec by next Friday.

"You can quote me on this," Fortino says. "These are some of the hardest working employees in this company. These are some of the hardest working employees I have ever seen. Yet here they keep roping in biology graduates who are still in diapers from every university in the country and paying them $100,000 a year, and my people, who are keeping the place running while they play with their test tubes, are making a lousy 18 Gs a year. Have you tried living in this community on that?"

Fortino is asked when the union might strike: "I will ask that my people call a strike Monday morning at 6. Let them try to run the place without us, that's what I say."

Fortino is asked if she knows that DNA-Tec lost $10.2 million last year and $3.2 million last quarter: "They keep saying that we should hang in there, that this thing is going to take off; well, my people can't pay rent with potential and promises. If they want to be a serious company, let them start paying like one. Strausberg hasn't exactly been suffering for the cause; he's bringing in 250 Gs a year, plus perks, during this so-called start-up time."

Fortino is asked what she is demanding: "Simple. Give us a 5 percent hike in wages this year; 5 percent again next year; and then when all the bean bugs are in their graves [three months ago, DNA-Tec introduced a new bacterial product designed to increase resistance of soybeans to certain types of insect damage], we can open this thing up and start again."

Papers filed with the Securities and Exchange Commission report that company president Fred Strausberg earned $246,000 last year. There are no records available on the salaries of scientists. Strausberg does not return phone calls to his office.

You interview DNA-Tec PR director Devito: "All I can say is that we have been negotiating in good faith; that we have made an offer of a 5 percent salary package over three years, that this is a company that is still in the starting stages and that with the losses we've suffered [confirms figures] we are in no position to pay more; and that we are outraged at Mrs. Fortino's attempt to hold a gun to our heads. That's it. No more questions."

In 20 interviews with DNA-Tec clerical workers in the cafeteria, none say they oppose the strike. Here are some representative quotes:

Ginnie Steward, secretary in the marketing department: "Look, most of us are here because this looked like an exciting place to be; but I support a kid, and on this salary I can't even buy him a bike. Nobody else around here is suffering. We're tired of being the heroes. We're ready to strike."

Ovidio Torres, secretary to the company president: "This is a good company. Mr. Strausberg's a fine man. But if he won't start paying us something approaching what we're worth, he's going to have to learn to do his word processing for himself. I say let's strike."

EXERCISE C
Story Assignments

1. Choose a publicly owned corporation and write a story on its performance last year based on the company's financial statements and interviews with people in and out of the company.

2. Write an article about the gardening and landscaping business in your area, focusing on one particularly successful company.

3. How difficult is it to start a restaurant in your area? Write about the obstacles that must be overcome and the chances of success based on interviews with a number of restaurant owners, workers and patrons. Focus on one restaurant.

4. Write an article on the unemployment situation in your town based on interviews with city officials, business leaders, labor leaders and unemployed workers.

5. Find a local union that is attempting to organize a new group of workers in your area and write an article on their efforts based on interviews with union leaders (there may be more than one union competing for the workers), workers and management.

26

Science, Medicine and the Environment

Those who equate science with sour memories of pop quizzes on the periodic table need to take another look. "It intrudes everywhere," wrote Henry Grunwald, then editor-in-chief of Time Inc., in the first issue of the general-interest science magazine *Discover*. "Airplanes crash and their designs are changed: science. The computer garbles your bank account: science. The atmosphere is polluted: science. It is cleaned up: science. Radiation hurts: science. Radiation heals: science."

If the issues addressed by science can be esoteric, they also can be central to progress and survival. It is science that has perfected nucleic acid testing to a point at which convicted murderers have been released from death row and prison, freed because their DNA did not—after all—match that of a killer. It is science that has tracked the spread of bird flu around the globe. And it is science that has led to that rarest of phenomena—near consensus among researchers that man-made climate change is indeed warming the globe at alarming rates. Reporters, buffeted by politicians, have not always gotten this story right, choosing instead to take the safe, but wrong, course of quoting in equal measure a diminishing handful of scientists who disagree with this evidence.

But if science is central to our lives, it is not always central to the pages of U.S. newspapers. In recent decades several major newspapers, including *The New York Times*, *The Washington Post*, the *Los Angeles Times, The Boston Globe* and Long Island's *Newsday*, have started weekly science or health sections. But on most medium- and small-sized papers—and on some large ones—science, medicine and the environment still are underreported terrain, in part perhaps because it is easier to draw advertisers to an arts or entertainment section than one examining the shrinking glaciers of the North Pole. Still, on any self-respecting newspaper, a lone science or environment or medical writer likely has staked out some portion of this territory. That means, however, that the remainder awaits exploration by enterprising reporters eager to separate themselves from the horde of journalism school graduates.

PREPARATION

Whether they have degrees in science or not, science writers can't afford to stop studying. "It can be fun to pick out a challenging story you know nothing about ... and learn," says

Jim Detjen, science writer for *The Philadelphia Inquirer*, who helped found the Society of Environmental Journalism (www.sej.org) in 1990. As an undergraduate at Rensselaer Polytechnic Institute in Troy, N.Y., Detjen took courses in physics, chemistry, biology and earth sciences. But, he says, "most of my expertise has been picked up along the way while researching stories."

Detjen notes that he spends about eight hours a week scanning two dozen popular and professional science journals ranging from *Physics Today* to *Science*. In the years before these publications were available on the Web, he would clip articles in areas he planned to write about or thought he might eventually write about. Today these and dozens of other magazines, including the Society of Environmental Journalism's own news service, EJToday, and its quarterly journal, *SEJournal*, are available online, often for a subscription fee.

Stuart Diamond, an English major in college, devoted two or three hours a *day* to sorting through the mail he got during his years as environment writer at *Newsday*. That mail included 50 to 75 letters and magazines a day, much of which ended in the voluminous file drawers Diamond stuffed full. "A story on solar energy eventually has to explain how solar energy works," says Diamond, adding that at times he has read hundreds of pages or more just to glean "a few crystal clear paragraphs on how something functions."

All this takes patience. "If you aren't interested in learning for learning's sake, you shouldn't be a science writer," Diamond counsels.

COMPLEXITY AND UNCERTAINTY

What scares reporters away from science stories is what scares students away from science courses: They seem so complicated, so abstract. That is a problem. Many scientists, for one thing, work in a language most of the rest of us don't understand—higher mathematics.

Science writer Jim Detjen of *The Philadelphia Inquirer* covering a story in Antarctica.
(Courtesy of The Philadelphia Inquirer)

There is no way a reporter without graduate-level training is going to be able fully to understand recent developments in subatomic particle physics.

Science news is also filled with a level of uncertainty that can trip up all but the most careful reporters. City councils, eventually, vote yes or no. Juries decide either to convict or acquit. Unemployment rates go up or down. Scientists, on the other hand, frequently get results that *if confirmed*, *suggest* a *relationship* between two things.

Science reporting presents more problems than most other kinds of reporting, There's no way around that. But good reporters who have mastered the skills outlined elsewhere in this book can succeed in helping the public understand how scientists are changing the world. Here are some suggestions on how that can be done.

Ask

The key to reporting and writing science is breaking codes. (See Chapter 3, The Language of News.) At some point reporters must force scientists to leave the equations and the statistics and try to explain in plain English what they've found and why it's important. Reporters may not be able to master the physics of subatomic particles. But, with work and help, they can understand something about the implications of their existence and properties.

To build understanding, science writers must be prepared to ask simple questions and to persist in pursuing those questions until scientists respond in language the reporter and, therefore, the reader, can understand. "If need be, I'll spend a half hour trying to get an understanding of a single phrase," says Stuart Diamond. If one source can't explain the point, Diamond will turn to another.

Explain

The next job is making sure readers will understand, too. Analogies can be invaluable for making sense out of the complex, as in a *New York Times* story that described a "magnetic gun" as so powerful that it was like "launching a bullet with a lightning bolt." (See The Basics, Section D, Analogies, Metaphors and Clichés.)

Specific examples, written in simple language, can help make the abstract or complex easier for readers to grasp. The following paragraphs from a *New York Times* story on the use of robots in brain surgery make clear just how delicate the procedure has to be:

> . . . he said it is important to secure any robot used in an operating room so that "some glitch does not injure the surgeon or patient."
>
> Such a glitch, which did not cause any damage, occurred in the second operation here, Dr. Ceverha said. A fleeting power surge while the computer was sending its instructions resulted in the robotic arm being off target by an inch. In the brain, Dr. Ceverha said, an inch is as good as a mile.
>
> The neurosurgeon working with the robotic arm that day recognized there was a problem before the drilling started, and the device was reprogrammed.

Qualify

No matter how significant a step forward they represent, few if any advances in scientific knowledge are reached without some lingering doubts remaining. Will the link between that virus and certain cancers prove merely coincidental? Can the work establishing the link be duplicated? If the connection stands up, will it lead to any progress toward a cure?

Reporters must make sure they are aware of what doubts the researchers, and their critics, hold. And in writing up those researchers' findings, they must be sure not to overstate their significance. That means using words like *suggests*, *indicates* and *points to an association*, rather than *proves*. And it means informing readers of the questions that remain to be answered.

Scientists in New Jersey *have reported progress* in developing an unorthodox form of nuclear power that they say avoids radiation hazards and does not depend on radioactive fuels.

However, the optimistic progress report by United Sciences Inc. of Princeton, N.J.,...*was greeted with some skepticism* by other physicists. They said while the process might eventually be useful, its success appeared technologically remote.

The New York Times

Bring Out the Significance

Without being oversold, the importance of scientific findings *does* have to be made evident—and right away. In a murder story, a reporter doesn't have to take time out to explain why death is important. But a science writer, dealing with esoteric and seemingly remote developments, almost always has to sell the story, to make clear why the reader should care. Sometimes this job is done in the lead itself, sometimes in the second paragraph.

The author of this piece devoted his lead to explaining what experts—his sources—considered to be the implications of research efforts with brain-dead lab animals rather than to detailing what scientists had accomplished:

Doctors who have been looking for ways to prevent the severe brain damage that follows stroke say they may be on the verge of success, offering some victims for the first time the hope of resuming normal lives.

The New York Times

Of course, interpreting significance entails risk. It forces reporters to sort out which "experts" really are expert and which are merely promoting their work.

Lessons from the Pros: Translating the Complex

Judy Foreman

Scientists and doctors have their own language. So when Judy Foreman, a nationally syndicated health columnist who worked for *The Boston Globe* for 23 years, goes to work on her latest column, it is her job to translate that jargon into language the public can understand.

"You ask doctors and scientists to use plain language," Foreman said. "If they say MI [myocardial infarction], you say, 'That means a heart attack right?' They say 'yes' or 'no' or 'not exactly.' It is a back and forth."

Foreman cautions, however, that reporters cannot sacrifice accuracy for simplicity. In one column, Foreman said she was trying to describe the different ways one can have a stroke. In the process of trying to write about strokes in comprehensible way, she wasn't specific enough about the different types one can have.

Judy Foreman, syndicated health columnist.

"I described this too generally, and several scientists wrote back saying, 'You have to describe the different clots starting in either the brain or the heart,'" Foreman said. "That kind of thing I deal with over and over and over again."

Here are her tips for writing an accurate and easy to understand health and science story:

- **Understand the basic ideas before you dive in.** "You can be too dumb. Scientists respect you more if you understand at least the principles of what they are doing. They don't want to spend an hour on the phone explaining basic molecular science."

Lessons From the Pros: Translating the Complex (continued)

- **Talk to the assistant first.** "For young science writers, try talking to graduate students or younger assistants. You tell them, 'I am not going to put your name down, but I just want to understand this, or if you could teach me the lingo so I don't sound quite as stupid when I talk to your boss.' You can use their help to explain the basics. It really helps. Then the big guys take you more seriously."

- **Keep verifying information until every detail is right.** "It is better to be wrong in a conversation with one scientist and to be embarrassed and feel stupid than be wrong in print where everyone can see it."

- **Ask many experts the same questions.** "You ask a lot of people the same question. In your own mind you put together what you think the combined answer is and then you go back to each of them and ask if your wording is right. It is a lot of back and forth. Sometimes I e-mail part of the story to every source and say, 'Have I got this right?' You keep testing your formulations over and over with different people to make sure you have got it right. The scientists don't have to agree on the judgment of a new finding but on what the facts are."

- **Ask scientists who have a competing viewpoint.** "It is totally fair to ask any scientists for the names of others who disagree with [them]. They will usually give names. Also, you can look at the clips and see what else was written on the topic and call those people."

- **Write for a general audience.** "Remember you are writing for your mom. . . . Basically, you are not writing for scientists. You have to make your story interesting and acceptable to regular people, but at same time you have to get the facts absolutely right or scientists won't talk to you again."

- **Never sacrifice accuracy.** "The older and more experienced I get, the more I keep rechecking my facts. When I was a young reporter, I felt embarrassed to check and thought that I had to get it right on the first try. But now I check all the time to make sure I get the facts right."

WHOM DO YOU TRUST?

Reporters usually are skeptical people, trained to doubt, to question, to see the other side. Yet some reporters seem to undergo a change of personality on the science beat. "A sort of spreading of the gospel theme has always been a part of science writing," laments Nicholas Wade, who writes editorials on science and technology for *The New York Times*. "A reporter in another field would be horrified if someone told him his primary responsibility was to get across his source's message clearly."

Part of the explanation for the lack of skepticism of some science writers is that science can seem so intimidating: It's difficult for a reporter who barely passed freshman chemistry to challenge the interpretation of a scientific issue just stated by a professor of chemistry. Another part of the explanation is that science can seem so pure. Aren't we taught from grade school onward that scientists are people who have devoted themselves to the rigorous and selfless pursuit of knowledge?

The best science writers, however, never forget that scientists, in fact, are far from infallible. Scientists can make errors in gathering the data on which they base their conclusions. They can make errors in interpreting their findings. And they frequently disagree among themselves, sometimes sharply, on subjects ranging from the origin of the universe to the impact of man-made environmental pollutants on the cancer rate.

Again, scientific findings are based on *evidence*—which is not the same as *proof*. Scientists interpret evidence differently, and different experiments can produce seemingly contradictory evidence. This is healthy. The history of science is the history of old theories being proven wrong.

It also helps to remember that scientists, like the rest of us, can have their blind spots caused by political, economic and professional interests. A scientist whose work is funded by tobacco companies, to pick an obvious example, may be extracautious about conceding a relationship between smoking and cancer. And scientists, no matter what degrees or prizes they have been awarded, are no more likely to make sense on political questions—the nuclear arms race, for example—than others of us who have thought deeply about these subjects.

This is not to say that science reporters must live in fear of charlatans and blowhards; it is only to say that they have to make the same judgments about the credibility of their sources that other reporters make. They must be cautious. Who is funding the research? What has the scientist accomplished before? How have other scientists reacted to the findings? What evidence does the scientist provide? Has the research been accepted for publication in a reputable journal or presented at a reputable conference? Who has competing theories?

The fact that a new theory is unpopular does not make it wrong. Ask Galileo! But the fact that an idea is not receiving support certainly must be considered and reported. In the end, the best means of gauging the credibility of sources is to talk to a lot of them—try to hear out the full spectrum of views. Careful and thorough reporting won't necessarily uncover who is right, but it will protect the reporter from being intimidated and the public from being misled.

SOURCES

The day news of a serious accident at the Three Mile Island nuclear plant made front-page headlines nationwide, *Newsday's* Stuart Diamond began telling his readers what had happened and why, in what was the worst accident ever at a nuclear plant in this country. Diamond's first article about the crippled plant said human error played a major part in causing the accident. It was an assertion the Nuclear Regulatory Commission, the agency in charge of regulating the industry and investigating the accident, denied and would continue denying for a week, Diamond recalls. But it was correct.

How did Diamond know more than the NRC and have the confidence to take on the experts? He had sources inside the plant. Diamond knew a scientist at Brookhaven National Laboratories who, according to the reporter, called a friend who was working for the utility, who in turn told the Three Mile Island employee that Diamond could be trusted.

A former investigative reporter, Diamond collects sources the way an entomologist collects insects. He keeps the name and phone number of every person he interviews; he adds to that file the names and numbers of experts in various fields drawn from the mail and the articles that cross his desk. In all, Diamond estimates he has amassed the names and phone numbers of 20,000 sources, enough to fill a modest-sized city telephone directory. As a result, he says, he never finds himself dependent on the availability of a single source at deadline time. "When I get a story at 3 in the afternoon, the first 10 people on my list may be unavailable," Diamond explains. "You need 15 names, just in case. You need depth."

Science reporters might begin building that depth with visits or calls to the following places and people.

Universities

University and college science departments, laboratories and research hospitals are full of one invaluable resource—experts. From the names of science faculty at a nearby university, new science writers can compile a first list of potential sources. Reporters should get to know these professors and be aware of their areas of expertise. "When I was working on a series on toxic wastes awhile ago," Jim Detjen recalls, "I approached a toxicologist at a local university and asked him to give me an impromptu lecture on basic toxicology and a list of what to read."

University scientists also make news in their own right:

> Scientists have discovered a tiny species of ancient human that lived 18,000 years ago on an isolated island east of the Java Sea—a prehistoric hunter in a "lost world" of giant lizards and miniature elephants.
>
> *The Washington Post*

When Detjen began as a science writer for *The Philadelphia Inquirer*, he spent two weeks meeting the public relations person for every major university and research center around Philadelphia. "Getting stories from PR people at major universities is one of the main ways of getting stories in science," he says.

Two directories put out by the American Association for the Advancement of Science (http://www.aaas.org) help reporters find out whom to contact. One, the *Public Information Contact Directory*, lists the addresses and phone numbers of public relations contacts at universities and public and private research centers. The other, the *Reporter's Guide to Key Research Activities in Science and Engineering*, summarizes research activities at 250 university, government and private research facilities.

Conferences

While science reporters obviously can't attend every major conference at which scientists meet to discuss their research, it is certainly useful to visit some. Conferences are good places

A discussion inside the clean room at the University of Albany Nanoscale Science and Engineering Center. *(Photo by Tom Killips of* The Troy [N.Y.] Record*)*

to learn about recent advances in a field and to meet some of the top experts. At times, a conference's list of participants can be as valuable—as a guide to sources—as the conference itself. (These lists are available to reporters whether or not they attend.)

Findings presented at a conference can be reported in a breaking news story, or they can lay the foundation for a broader look at a problem, as was the case with this story in *The New York Times*:

> The world's seas and oceans, already polluted with spilled oil, toxic chemicals and radio-active waste, are now being fouled by a new and insidious form of pollution—plastic waste.
>
> ...The problem has become so serious that 150 marine wildlife researchers from 10 countries met recently at the University of Hawaii in Honolulu for the *first international conference* on the issue.

Government Agencies

It's important that the science beat not be reduced to the "Gee! Wow! What'll they think of next?" beat. Science writers must remember that the rewards of science—superstrong plastics, genetically engineered plants, nuclear power—carry risks. One way to stay on top of the problems associated with science is to get in touch with the government agencies that are supposed to monitor and minimize many of those risks.

A reporter investigating a tip that workers in a local plastics plant are being exposed to toxic chemicals might turn to the federal Occupational Safety and Health Administration or the state department of health. An investigation of records at the local OSHA office, for example, would help determine whether the plant has been visited by federal regulators. Further information on that plastics plant might be obtained from OSHA's sister agency, the National Institute of Occupational Safety and Health, in Cincinnati, which puts out hundreds of documents that discuss the uses and potential abuses of various chemicals in the workplace.

Reporters sniffing around a local nuclear power plant would want to be in touch with people at the Nuclear Regulatory Commission. Reporters following a flu epidemic would contact the Centers for Disease Control and Prevention in Atlanta, which keep detailed information on epidemics nationwide and try to trace their cause. (Most federal and state agencies publish directories that define the responsibilities of their key personnel and provide phone numbers.)

Regulatory agencies should not be a reporter's last stop, however. The Nuclear Regulatory Commission proved a less than reliable source at the time of the accident at Three Mile Island; the Environmental Protection Agency moved slowly in cleaning up toxic wastes. Indeed, at times a regulatory agency's foot-dragging in enforcing its own rules becomes a major story in itself. A good place to start on such a story might be the General Accounting Office, which conducts investigations for Congress into how well certain federal programs are functioning.

Trade Groups and Professional Organizations

In contacting sources at trade organizations, it's important to find out who funds them and which economic and political interests they represent. Don't be fooled by independent-sounding names. During the debate in the 1970s over whether saccharin should be labeled a carcinogen, the Calorie Control Council was widely quoted attacking research that showed that the artificial sweetener caused cancer in laboratory animals. According to the *Columbia Journalism Review*, few such reports bothered to identify the Calorie Control Council as an organization representing the manufacturers of artificial sweeteners, including saccharin.

Representatives of trade organizations—the Atomic Industrial Forum and the Chemical Manufacturers Association are two of the most vocal—sometimes can be helpful sources as long as their views are carefully attributed and the other side is contacted. "Industry groups are more useful than people think," Diamond says. "People tend to distrust them, but they know more than anyone thinks because their livelihood is at stake." Certainly it's worth getting on the mailing lists of these organizations.

Professional organizations, such as the American Medical Association, are less likely to push a product the way the Atomic Industrial Forum pushes nuclear energy. But these organizations have their biases, too. Reporters shouldn't expect an unbiased response from the AMA on an issue affecting the income of doctors.

Public Interest Groups

Public interest groups—the Natural Resources Defense Council and the Environmental Defense Fund are two that are well known—also have an ax to grind. Nevertheless, they play an important role as watchdogs of government and industry. Reporters will want to be on the mailing list of a wide range of these groups. The scientific data behind their arguments is sometimes incomplete, but they can be quite useful in identifying potential stories. For example, environmental groups complained long and loudly about poor enforcement of toxic-waste laws under the Reagan administration before Congress began investigating. (The *Conservation Directory*, published annually by the National Wildlife Federation in Washington, D.C., provides an excellent list of public interest groups.)

Media Resource Service

One nonprofit organization, the Media Resource Service (MediaResource), has tried since 1980 to find responsible scientists in a range of fields who are willing to talk to reporters. MediaResource attempts to identify the areas in which scientists have expertise and the biases they might bring to an interview. When a reporter calls, the service, a program of Sigma Xi, the Scientific Research Society, acts as an intermediary, supplying the names and backgrounds of scientists who might be helpful on the story.

"If something comes up in the news and I need to write a story but don't know much about it, I'll call them," says Detjen. "Once a truck overturned and a beehive on it fell off. The bees went wild. They swarmed into a nearby development and stung enough people so badly that 25 or 30 went to the hospital. I needed a bee expert and I needed one quickly. ... They [Media Resource] helped me track one down and I was able to write a spot-news story explaining the bees' behavior."

MediaResource (http://www.mediaresource.org) can be reached by calling 800-223-1730 or by e-mailing mediaresource@sigmaxi.org.

The Hastings Center

If the story is not how terminally ill patients can be kept alive but whether it is *ethical* to prolong their lives artificially, reporters will want to give the Hastings Center a call. The center, located in Westchester County, N.Y., has a staff of philosophers, political scientists and sociologists who specialize in *bioethics*, the ethical ramifications of science.

JOURNALS

Too much science writing is really just the rewriting of articles that have appeared in science magazines and journals. Reporters seem to wait hungrily for the arrival of the latest issue of *Science* (www.sciencemag.org) or the *New England Journal of Medicine* (www.nejm.org), probably the two most prestigious American journals, in the hope that they will contain an article that can be popularized—perhaps a new development in the struggle to understand cancer, perhaps a new study on the relationship between alcohol and illness.

There is nothing wrong with using journal articles. In fact, reporters would be remiss if they failed to keep up with these important sources of information and ideas. But reporters who use a journal article as the basis for a story must be conscientious about making phone calls to its author and others in the field to verify, clarify and expand on the findings it reports.

This story by science writer Richard Knox, formerly of *The Boston Globe* and currently with National Public Radio, is based on a paper published in an issue of the *Proceedings of the National Academy of Sciences*:

> Scientists at Stanford University have gotten their hands on the elusive chemical "switch" that activates the machinery of cell division.
>
> The feat should make possible a long-sought goal of geneticists: To sort out the component parts of this crucial biochemical signal so they can understand how it works—or fails to work—in normal growth and in disease.
>
> In a scientific paper published yesterday, the researchers said. ...
>
> *The Boston Globe*

Knox's research began in a journal, but it didn't end there. In the paragraphs that followed, he went on to quote not only from a telephone interview with one of the paper's authors but from an interview with Dr. Gerald Selzer of the National Institutes of Health, whom he identified as a leading researcher in the field. Selzer called the findings "an important step in understanding the origin of replication in the bacterial cell."

One problem with covering science by reading journals is that journals are slow. Much of the news released in journals could have been available to the enterprising reporter months earlier. "By the time a story gets to *Science*, it's not fresh," says Stuart Diamond. "I've traced stories from a draft, to a research paper, to a technical journal to *The New York Times*. It usually takes six to eight months."

Diamond and other aggressive reporters try to learn the results of major studies and experiments *before* these findings are published in a journal. They hope their sources will lead them to potentially newsworthy research or that they themselves will spot interesting projects at their first public airing, such as papers presented at conferences. There is a danger in trying to beat the journals, however. The major scientific journals employ strict checks in an attempt to weed out sloppy research. Reporters working with unpublished findings assume more responsibility for evaluating the credibility of that work themselves.

REFERENCES

No science writer, no matter how well trained, can avoid stumbling on unfamiliar terms, names and designs. A science writer is sunk without quality reference material. Much good information is available online, but it's important to use credible sources, not "Dr. Bob's 10 Favorite Scientific Web Links." First of all, you'll have no idea who Dr. Bob is or who he represents. Second, his recommended sites, though easy to access, may well be as shady as Dr. Bob himself.

Here are some well-respected science and health reference websites:

1. SciCentral (www.scicentral.com) is an online resource for scientific research news. It presents the most recent news in scientific research, and access to topic searches. SciCentral contains links to other helpful research sites.

2. Questia Online Library (www.questia.com) is a database for scientific research with links to the full text of books, articles and tables on a broad range of science topics. The encyclopedia and the first section of most texts are free, but the full service requires a subscription.

3. Infomine (www.infomine.ucr.edu) is a free academic search engine connected to a range of full text articles, paid services, tools, tables and links to organizations with information. These resources cover the full range of life and physical sciences, and mathematics. They also cover business and economics, diversity, government topics and the humanities.

4. WebMD (www.webmd.com) provides information about disease, drugs and health, as well as data on clinical trials.

5. Technology Research News (www.trnmag.com) is a free technology research news website keeping up with the latest research developments. It also offers a glossary and search engine.

Even in this age of instant online access, every good science writer will want a few traditional reference books nearby.

1. *Van Nostrand's Scientific Encyclopedia.* What exactly is a *quark? Quark* (a subatomic particle) and more than 20,000 other scientific terms and concepts are discussed in this two-volume work. For more detailed explanation: McGraw-Hill publishes a 17-volume *Encyclopedia of Science and Technology.*

2. *The Way Things Work: An Illustrated Encyclopedia of Technology.* How are you going to explain to readers why the airplane crashed on takeoff if you don't really understand how any plane gets off the ground? This multivolume work is filled with explanations, for nonscientists, of how devices ranging from the artificial heart to airplanes work.

3. *McGraw-Hill Dictionary of Scientific and Technical Terms.* This can be the first step in translating scientific jargon into plain English. Among its 100,000-odd terms is *agitator body*, which is no more than a drum, mounted on a truck, for transporting freshly mixed concrete. *Black's Medical Dictionary* will aid in penetrating the vocabulary of medicine.

BASIC STORIES

Science seems to make news more and more frequently: An even smaller computer has an even larger memory; organs are being cloned and may someday provide transplants; radio astronomers think they can "hear" the Big Bang, generally believed to have given birth to the universe. This news usually falls into one of the following categories.

New Regulations

The federal government and state governments periodically revise regulations affecting the environment, energy pricing and exploration, and occupational health. Less frequently, they set standards for research in other areas of science, such as recombinant DNA (the replicating and rearranging of genes) and cryptography (the use and deciphering of secret codes). The most important regulations make news when they are announced and, if reporters are following their beat closely, some time after they are implemented, to determine whether they've worked.

> In an attempt to curtail the flow of chemical pollutants into New Jersey's rivers and underground reservoirs, the state Department of Environmental Protection next week will propose standards for disposing of hazardous wastes.
>
> *The* (Bergen County, N.J.) *Record*

Reports

Government agencies, congressional committees and private organizations periodically release reports or studies evaluating the latest scientific information available about a controversial subject:

> Acid rain could be reduced significantly with a 6 percent increase in consumer electric bills if utilities pursue the least costly pollution measures, *according to a new government study.*
>
> *The Providence* (R.I.) *Bulletin*

Stories on these reports should be discussed in the context of the ongoing debate to which they contribute. *The Bulletin* drew on an earlier study to provide context for its story:

> The National Academy of Sciences last month issued a report linking coal-burning boilers to acid rain in the Northeast and Canada.

Discoveries

Firsts always make news, whether in sports or in science:

> A satellite carrying an infrared telescope has discovered swarms of large particles around the star Vega, and scientists say they think the particles and the star make up a complete solar system like our sun and the...planets and thousands of asteroids and meteorites that surround it.
>
> *The Washington Post* News Service in *The Philadelphia Inquirer*

Understanding a first in sports—"the first woman to win three gold medals in cross country skiing"—is rarely difficult. But in science it may take considerable work to pin down just what makes the story significant:

> If true, it is the first evidence that the universe contains a second solar system like this one. Though scientists have speculated for years that the earth and its eight sister planets are not alone in the cosmos, they have never had evidence that their speculations were correct.

Advances in Knowledge

The news value of advances in knowledge, which may be reported in scientific journals, announced at conferences or uncovered by an enterprising reporter, often depends on their potential applications:

> SAN FRANCISCO—A new drug that was isolated from a fungus may significantly increase the success rate of organ transplants and enable surgeons to replace organs they couldn't transplant before, according to a panel of medical researchers.
>
> *Chicago Tribune*

Threats

And now the bad news:

> San Diego drinking water contains two to four times the levels allowed under new federal regulations of a group of suspected cancer-causing agents, according to chemical analysis performed for The San Diego Union.
>
> *The San Diego Union*

Chemicals pollute air and water; AIDS takes hundreds of thousands of lives; satellites tumble down from space; fallout from Chinese nuclear tests drifts down on the land where Pennsylvania cows graze. Science reporters owe readers the same thoroughness and the same care on these stories that they apply to scientific advances.

It is easy to alarm people. It is harder to help them evaluate just how dangerous those chemicals in their drinking water are. Science writers often must tread a thin line between a desire not to spread unwarranted panic and an equally strong obligation to give readers the whole truth. Some also must resist editors who, perhaps panicked themselves by the news of traces of a pesticide in food, aren't interested in the qualifying sentences explaining that the risks to humans are unknown and that the acceptable levels of consumption allowed by regulators are somewhat arbitrary.

ENTERPRISE

There are few, if any, beats on which reporters devote more time to stories that are not about breaking news. Science writers frequently step back from the rush of the new or the scary to give readers a more leisurely look at science at work or at the science that explains how the world works.

Explaining

The New York Times had a news story detailing the death and destruction unleashed by a major earthquake in Mexico, but it shared the front page with an article, by science writer Walter Sullivan, that tried to explain *why*:

> It was an earthquake that had to happen.
> The epicenter of the earthquake that devastated parts of Mexico yesterday lies along the front where the Pacific Ocean floor drives under the Mexican coast, tearing at the underpinnings of the continent.
> The relentless pressure has caused scores of earthquakes along the line, much like firecrackers on a string. It was just a matter of time before the next one struck. . . .
>
> *The New York Times*

A subject doesn't have to be as alarming as an earthquake to warrant an explanation. Scientists are working to understand aspects of the world as diverse as ice ages, human memory and honeybees. What they have learned can be fascinating.

Informing

The readers of science articles, whatever else they may have in common, all are consumers. They may want to know how to buy the latest and lightest laptop or how to find out how to guard against West Nile virus; whether to buy generic drugs and whether to feed their babies on demand. The answers to such questions, which often center on how to stay healthy and how to treat illness, are the basis of numerous articles, called *service articles* because they provide consumers with a service—information they may be able to use to improve their lives:

> The first prescription pill approved to fight genital herpes—Zovirax—reaches drug stores today, and already doctors are deluged with inquiries.

Doctors say the drug, known generically as acyclovir, will be a boon to many herpes sufferers. But it should be prescribed only for those who have at least six outbreaks of herpes sores a year.

USA Today

The pool of questions service articles might answer is deep: What can be done to reduce the pollution caused inside our homes by heating and cooking? What foods cause the lowest buildup of cholesterol? What's the most effective way of treating breast cancer?

Of course, in providing answers, reporters must take great care not to become inadvertent mouthpieces for those who profit by overselling a less-than-perfect remedy.

Research

Science writers don't always just sit back and wait for scientists to finish their research. Often the research itself is interesting, regardless of whether it has produced conclusions. What efforts are now being made to conquer AIDS? How are scientists studying the increasingly tiny particles they have found inside the atom? How do scientists investigate theories that brain chemistry can cause mental illness?

Jim Detjen decided to see what researchers were up to with the world's fastest laser:

HOLMDEL, N.J.—It's a slow day for the world's fastest laser at Bell Laboratories.

Tiny strings of glowing red and green light beams zigzag across the darkened room causing dust particles to dance in the air. A steady "Beep! Beep! Beep!" hums rhythmically in the background.

The researchers are firing their laser, a device that emits intense beams of focused light, at a relatively ho-hum pace. Since it is merely a demonstration, they have adjusted the laser to shoot out pulses of light that last for a leisurely 80 femtoseconds, or 80 millionths of a billionth of a second.

... A revolution is under way in the way people communicate. ...

The Philadelphia Inquirer

Public Policy

The intersection between science and society is always worthy of attention by reporters. Here is Robert Cooke of *Newsday* on the battle over the U.S. Endangered Species Act:

The rapid demise of species—and the genes that make them distinct—is spurring squads of ecologists and environmentalists to urge that the U.S. Endangered Species Act be protected from attack, or even strengthened, when it goes before Congress this year for reauthorization.

Many environmental issues raise questions of public policy:

Do high-technology toxic waste incinerators merely move pollution from the land to the air?

Can and should re-treated sewage water be recycled through our taps?

What is an acceptable rate for cutting our forests so that they can regenerate?

There are public policy issues lurking behind other areas of science too:

Could gene-splicing techniques accidentally produce dangerous organisms?

Might faster, more powerful computers pose a threat to privacy?

Is manned space flight a useful investment of the nation's resources?

Of course, the most serious of such questions are posed by weapons research.

Follow-Up

It's important in science, as in any area of reporting, to follow up. (See Chapter 13, Story Origination.) Solutions in science tend to come slowly. The public must be kept abreast of what progress is being made. Where does the search for an AIDS vaccine stand today? What are the chances of a catastrophic earthquake in Los Angeles, and can we learn enough to predict it? What is the latest evidence of global warming?

Sometimes the answer is simply no. Scientists, like other people, will trumpet their successes. They are a lot less likely to announce when they've failed. Following up then is no less important, though likely more difficult:

> Three hundred and fifteen physicists worked on the experiment. Their apparatus included the Tevatron, the world's most powerful particle accelerator, as well as a $65 million detector weighing as much as a warship, an advanced new computing system and a host of other innovative gadgets.
>
> But despite this arsenal of brains and technological brawn assembled at the Fermilab accelerator laboratory [in Batavia, Ill.], the participants have failed to find their quarry, a disagreeable reminder that as science gets harder, even Herculean efforts do not guarantee success.
>
> *The New York Times*

CHAPTER 26 SUMMARY: SCIENCE, MEDICINE AND THE ENVIRONMENT

Science writers need to be tuned in to the latest scientific developments and trends. And they need to be able to explain them to the general public. This is especially challenging for journalists reporting on hard-to-understand scientific developments. Above all, the science writer must be a translator, someone able to make the complex clear without oversimplifying, to explain advances in scientific understanding without exaggerating their scope or certainty, to get things right.

To succeed in writing about science:

- Read widely, but never fake knowledge you don't have.

- Establish a broad base of sources. Don't be afraid to ask a scientific source who in the field disagrees with him.

- Ask questions until you truly understand the answer. Some scientists are good at giving analogies that compare something esoteric to something everyone understands. Seek analogy and use it in writing. But be certain to test your own analogies to make sure they are accurate.

- Explain to your readers why they should care. In articles about science, that's not always obvious. And always: Write for consumers, not your sources.

- Maintain skepticism. Scientists, too, can get things wrong. Ask not just what they found but how. Then seek independent comment on both their methodology and results.

- Do your own reporting. Using journal articles for story ideas is fine, but make the calls needed to qualify the importance of the scientific advance.

- Don't go beyond the news. In science, it's sometimes the reporter who has to tell the editor that yet another journal article about good and bad cholesterol may not be worthy of good play.

ADDITIONAL READING

The Best American Science and Writing 2005, Alan Lightman and Jesse Cohen, editors, Harper Perennial, 2005.

The Craft of Scientific Writing, Michael Alley, Springer; 3rd edition, 1998.

A Field Guide for Science Writers: The Official Guide of the National Association of Science Writers, Deborah Blum, Mary Knudson and Robin Maranz Henig, editors, Oxford University Press, 2005.

Ideas into Words; Mastering the Craft of Science Writing, Robert Kanigel and Elise Hancock, Johns Hopkins University Press, 2003.

Science in Public: Communication, Culture and Credibility, Jane Gregory and Steve Miller, Perseus Publishing, 2000.

EXERCISE A
Research Assignments

ONE
Use research materials or interviews with scientists to write explanations that could be used in a newspaper article for the following terms.

1. White dwarf
2. Chemotherapy
3. Greenhouse effect
4. Local area network
5. Messenger RNA
6. Heavy water
7. Windows
8. ROM
9. Restriction enzyme
10. Halogenated organic compound

TWO
Write explanations for the following that might be used in a newspaper article on the subject. Draw on reference books and interviews with local scientists and science teachers.

1. How does an airplane get off the ground?
2. What causes sleet?
3. How do cats purr?
4. How does a breeder reactor work?
5. Why do stars appear to twinkle?
6. How does a battery produce energy?
7. How does photographic film work?
8. How do bats fly in the dark?
9. What causes a total solar eclipse?
10. What does an antihistamine do?

EXERCISE B
Writing Assignments

Write articles based on the following collections of information. In each case, you are writing for a newspaper dated tomorrow and read in the town where the events occurred.

ONE

Dr. Eric Vandenberg, a research orthopedist who has headed a team of six scientists at Wellfleet University Medical Center, a leading center in San Francisco in rehabilitative medicine, in a speech today:

"Ladies and gentlemen, friends. We are pleased to announce today that we have invented an artificial kneecap so flexible and durable that we think it will be possible, as soon as the federal Food and Drug Administration has reviewed our work, to implant it in growing children.

"We consider this a significant breakthrough for two reasons, really. The first is this: Nearly 2,000 children in the United States are born each year with a damaged kneecap. About 500 of these children have no kneecap at all and must walk stiff legged. The condition eventually leads to stunted growth in the impaired knee and life-long difficulties with walking. Secondly, about 1,200 children under 12 each year suffer serious and debilitating injury to one or both kneecaps. Through the demands of sports medicine, artificial kneecaps with the flexibility and movement of real kneecaps were invented about 15 years ago and have been used widely to replace the damaged kneecaps of athletes. Although these athletes can no longer compete professionally, they usually are spared a lifetime of pain and repeated operations. They recover about 85 to 90 percent of the mobility of a person with a sound kneecap. But until now, no artificial kneecap has been implanted in the knee of a growing child.

"There are, as you will see, a number of reasons for this. As we grow, our bones grow, and the ligaments attaching our bones grow. We get bigger, we get stronger. More pressure is placed on a natural kneecap as we get bigger, but of course the kneecap is growing as well. In the past we did not have a material flexible and adaptable enough to in a sense 'grow' at the same rate as the rest of our body. We also had to figure out what on average that growth was, how much the stress on a kneecap increases during natural growth and how we could construct a material that would respond to the expected increase in stress the same way a natural kneecap works."

"Five years ago we began experimenting with a material called Synflex-T. It is light, malleable and flexible when pressure is applied in certain ways over a period of time, but it also is durable and strong. Through four years of trials with chimpanzees we discovered ways to construct a kneecap that, we believe, will 'grow' at the same rate as the components of the leg attached to the kneecap grow. Two years ago the FDA gave us permission to operate on five toddlers at the hospital suffering from severe lesoitis, which is the name given the condition in which babies are born without a kneecap joining the upper and lower leg. We are now prepared to announce that all five of these children, who are now 4, are walking and running as well as their peers. Though they've grown an average of 8 inches, their ligaments and bones have not destroyed the kneecap because it has grown too, and at the right rate. ... The FDA has asked us to continue following the progress of these children for two more years. If, as we suspect, the Synflex-T kneecap continues to keep pace with their growth, we will ask to make this operation available to the 3,200 children each year who would benefit from it. The operation optimally should be done on children before age 2 so that bone structure and muscular development are not dwarfed by the birth disability. But it could also be done on older children who suffer a debilitating knee injury."

Call to Dr. Signor Vanderschmidt, who wrote a recent article on advances in artificial parts for the *Mid-Atlantic Medical Monthly*, a respected journal. Dr. Vanderschmidt is dean of the Medical School at Weibolt University in Boston:

"You know, I've been watching Eric's work eagerly for some months now. He is a brilliant young medical researcher who has already published widely in this field. This new kneecap should be a great step forward. It is even more important in my mind because it should give some children, born with serious disabilities, a chance to lead a normal life."

TWO

Alfred Gigli, director of environmental protection for the county health department, at a press conference today: "We've had some complaints of late from the families on Pawanett Road off of Western Highway here in Altoona. They've expressed concern for a few weeks now that their drinking water smells like gasoline. As you know, the homes along Pawanett used to be summer cottages and date back to before the time when the town started a central water system. All 17 homes draw their water from wells ranging from 50 to 125 feet deep. Anyway, we acted as quickly as possible and took samples of water at all the homes earlier this week. Our analysis at Tuckaboe Laboratories shows that the water had benzene in it. The house with the shallowest well belongs to Keith McBurney. That's number 14. We found 3 parts per million of benzene in his water sample. The other samples show a range from somewhere in the area of 850 parts per billion of benzene in the water to 2.5 parts per million.

"Just to be on the safe side, we've asked the fire department to take a pumper out to Pawanett to provide drinking water to residents until we can get to the bottom of this. We're also asking residents to boil their water before using it for cooking. ...

"How high is 3 parts per million? Well it means there are three parts of benzene for every 999,997 parts of water. That's not a whole lot. But it does mean that somehow benzene got into the underground water table, which is a cause for concern. We aren't sure where it got in, where it came from or how fast it's moving. There isn't any state regulation for benzene—it just isn't in water that much, but no one wants to drink water that smells like gasoline. Yes, the state does have a recommended level. It says no one should drink from a water supply with anything more than 5 parts per billion of benzene.

"Where did the benzene come from? We're looking into that now. We've asked the Arcon Gas Station on Faraquat Street to run a test on its underground gas tank. It's a good quarter-mile from Pawanett, but it's uphill and it's straight east. Another possibility is the Chemtron Industrial Products plant, which is no more than 100 yards to the north. The company makes dyes and plastics and synthetics, and it's our understanding a good bit of benzene is used in making these things. We've written to the company asking whether it uses benzene and in what quantities. ...

"One thing you really should understand though. Benzene is one of the most common chemicals around. Up until a few years ago it was in paint removers, rubber cement and artists' supplies, and you still get a pretty good hit anytime you gas up your car. ... You are likely to breathe a few parts per billion of the stuff just standing by a busy highway and breathing in. And workers are allowed to be exposed to up to 10 parts per million every day. ... Still, nobody wants to drink gasoline, and you always want to be careful with benzene. We know that it's been strongly linked to leukemia, or blood cancer, in workers exposed to levels slightly above that workplace limit. We don't know whether any amount of it is OK to smell or drink. It's always smart to be careful."

Call to McBurney: "Tell my wife this stuff is harmless. She's been getting headaches for a couple of months now, bad ones, right between the eyes, and the doctor don't know where they come from. It smells like we're standing in a gas station when we take a shower sometimes. I got two kids, 8 and 10, and you've got to wonder what this will mean for them in 20 or 30 years. Who knows? I've been asking around and no one seems to know. ... My wife's name? Naomi, she's 33. Kids are Douglas, he's the 8-year-old, and Sarah, she's 10. It's been roughest for Naomi though. The kids are at school and me, I work for the town Department of Public Works, but Naomi's home all day. Gigli may say this stuff is harmless, but then why does the state say 'Don't drink it'? And why does my wife get excruciating headaches she never got before?"

Call to Arcon Gas. Attendant says: "We have nothing to say. The boss has been called and we're looking into it. All I do is pump gas, friend. Talking to reporters isn't in my contract."

Call to Chemtron public affairs officer Dori Prentice: "Chemtron is a good neighbor. We've been at this site seven years. We hire people from the community. We contribute to charity. If there is a leak, and we certainly don't think we're responsible, it would come as a shock to us. Yes, we do have a benzene storage tank. It holds 2,000 gallons underground, but we doubt it leaks. Still, we'll do everything we can to cooperate with the investigation."

Call to Judy Goodman, professor of occupational health, Winston University: "Yes, we've done a lot of retrospective studies on benzene exposure. If the figures you're quoting me are right, I'd be a lot more concerned than Mr. Gigli. Benzene is like a lot of toxic chemicals; we know they're not good for us, be we can't be sure at what point they become dangerous. Still the state didn't set those standards for nothing. There's so much benzene in that water that a lot of it must be evaporating into the air. There may be danger not only in drinking that water but in breathing the air in those houses. They shouldn't even be running the water for any reason... if, again, those numbers are correct. I wouldn't even flush the toilet, or open it for that matter, with a couple of parts per million of benzene in the water. Is Gigli right about the state recommended levels? Yes."

Call to Raymond Barry, lab supervisor for Tuckahoe Laboratories: "Well, yes, we did those tests. Those are the numbers all right. And we ran three tests on each well just to make sure we didn't have sampling error."

EXERCISE C
Story Assignments

1. Assume that temperatures in your area have dropped to well below freezing and a severe cold wave is predicted for the next week. Write a sidebar on what causes frostbite and how to protect against it.

2. A drifter is charged with killing a local grocer. He is arrested after he fails to pass a lie-detector test. Write a sidebar on how lie-detector tests work and on how reliable they are.

3. An earthquake shakes buildings in your area but causes little damage. Write a sidebar explaining what causes earthquakes.

4. Try to find the latest article on scientific research at a nearby research center or university by using the local newspaper files and the help of the facility's public relations staff. After learning as much as possible about the research, set up an appointment with the scientist who supervised the work. Then write an article concentrating on one of the following:

   a. **The scientist.** Write a profile. How did the scientist become interested in that particular area of research, and what led him or her to the line of inquiry followed?

   b. **The process.** What steps were involved in achieving the scientific progress or discovery mentioned in previous articles? How long has the scientist been working in this specific area? Did the research team have any false starts? What inspired the team to design the experiments the way it did? What efforts were made to ensure against false results?

   c. **The future outlook.** What obstacles remain to be overcome in the particular line of research? What efforts will the research team make to overcome these obstacles?

5. Write a news story based on an article in the latest issue of the *New England Journal of Medicine*. At the end of the article, write down what questions you would have liked to have asked before writing the article and of whom you would have asked them.

Broadcast Journalism

For decades now, newspaper reporters have noticed that they have lots of company in their pursuit of news. Right at the front of the pack are always a couple of aggressive women or men pointing microphones at faces—microphones hooked up to small, high-quality digital recorders. One or two particularly neatly dressed reporters, meanwhile, are likely being trailed by high-tech video cameras as they jostle through the crowd.

Now, however, those newspaper reporters increasingly find themselves asked to bring along the microphones or appear in front of the cameras themselves. That audio or video might be placed on the newspaper's website or, perhaps, shared with local station or a network. In a digital age, the lines between various forms of journalism—various "platforms" for distributing news—are blurring. Interesting career opportunities might present themselves on different sides of those lines.

This book, of course, is primarily about news that is written to be read—not listened to or watched. However, to prepare our readers, should their careers take a different turn, we present this chapter on radio and television news. These discussions are borrowed from the fourth edition of *Broadcast News* (Thomson Wadsworth, 2005), which was written by one of the authors of this book, Mitchell Stephens (with Beth M. Olson). For a fuller discussion of radio and television, we suggest readers turn to that book. Still, journalists who do end up spending portions of their careers behind a microphone or on camera can rest assured that almost all the major principles of writing and reporting discussed in the other chapters of this book will be useful in broadcast newsrooms, too.

BROADCAST WRITING

In economic news today, a little to cheer about . . . but not much. The housing industry is one of the few areas where there are signs of life. And last month's new home sales were up two point two percent. Looking ahead, the government's index of future economic activity—the leading economic indicators—was almost flat last month . . . up just one-tenth of a percent.

ABC News

This report on the latest national economic statistics was read on ABC Television's "World News." Newspaper journalists should notice a number of differences between the way this report is written and the way newspaper stories are generally written. Those differences, outlined here, must be mastered by anyone attempting to make the switch to radio or television newswriting.

Conversational Language

Newspaper writing should never be *too* formal, but rarely does it get as informal as this: "… a little to cheer about … but not much." Radio and television news, on the other hand, since it is written to be read aloud, has to sound like something a reasonably friendly person might say aloud to us: It has to sound conversational.

Unacceptable:

The vice president of the New York City branch of the Red Cross stated in a press conference today that many Christmas toys can inflict injury upon unsuspecting youngsters.

Acceptable:

A Red Cross official warns that many Christmas toys can be dangerous for kids.

Write As It's Going to Be Read

Almost no abbreviations are used in broadcast newswriting: You write out the word *street*, unless you want the newscaster to make the sound *st*. Words like *point* and *percent* in the ABC story above are always spelled out—otherwise the newscaster might momentarily hesitate while trying to convert symbols to words. And graphic forms of punctuation like dashes (—) or ellipses (…) are used often, because they are so good at indicating where the newscaster should pause.

Short Sentences

The sentence is the main unit of organization in most broadcast stories, which are not long enough to have paragraphs. Those sentences must be kept short for two reasons. First, long sentences are hard for listeners or viewers to follow: Unlike newspaper readers, they can't go back and reread something they failed to understand the first time. Second, long sentences are difficult for newscasters to read out loud—without turning blue.

Unacceptable:

The Transport Workers Union agreed last night to "stop the clock" and continue negotiations in an effort to avert a strike, originally set for six this morning, which would have stranded two and a half million weekday bus and subway riders in the metropolitan area and disrupted the life of the city.

Sometimes in broadcast news details are sacrificed for the sake of conciseness.

Acceptable:

No subway and bus strike yet. The Transport Workers Union last night agreed to "stop the clock" and keep negotiating.

Long interjections or clauses in the middle of sentences create particular trouble. Often in these sentences the subject will be forgotten before the verb arrives.

Unacceptable:

In yesterday's Cherokee County election a measure *that would replace the five-person county commission with a one-man commission* was approved by voters.

Acceptable:

Voters in Cherokee County have ousted their five-person county commission. ... It'll be replaced by a ONE-person commission.

WSB, Atlanta

Few Numbers

Just think of all the numbers ABC could have included in that report on economic statistics: how many new homes were sold last month and this, the exact number for this month's and last's index of leading economic indicators, statistics from two months ago, statistics from last year. Instead, ABC made do with only two numbers. That's wise, because numbers, when read out loud, can easily confuse.

Unacceptable:

The proposed budget for the '08–'09 fiscal year calls for 2 point 5 million dollars in property tax relief for the state's 250-thousand property owners.

While viewers or listeners are figuring out when the 2008 fiscal year starts, they'll miss all the other numbers in this story.

Acceptable:

Next year's budget calls for 2 point 5 million dollars in property tax relief.

In broadcast news, extra numbers tend to produce confusion rather than add information.

Present Tense

Well, certainly not all the time.

Unacceptable:

Two people *are* being shot this morning.

But, like the Internet, radio and television, as Jim Farley of WTOP-AM in Washington explains, are the media of the "hear and now." Unlike newspapers, the news they present does not have to wait to be printed and distributed. Radio and television can report on what is happening *now*, so why not flaunt their timeliness by using the present tense?

The village of Hersey *is* still operating on emergency power.

KODY, Nebraska

A fire official *believes* there will be no more bodies found in the ruins of the Southgage, Kentucky, supper club that burned Saturday night.

NBC News

The news on radio or television is not that the secretary of state left for some destination *last night*; the news is that she *is* there *this morning*. On the air, old news spoils not in days but in hours.

Titles and Attribution First

Because the words in broadcast news will be heard once and only once, it's important to try to present information to viewers or listeners in a logical order. That means a person's title before that person's name.

Unacceptable:

Kofi Annan, the United Nations secretary general, says ...

Acceptable:

United Nations Secretary General Kofi Annan says....

Similarly, listeners or viewers should be told where information comes from *before* they are presented with that information. In broadcast news, attribution comes first.

Unacceptable:

Neither the cycle's driver nor his passenger was wearing a motorcycle helmet, *according to the investigating officer.*

Acceptable:

According to the investigating officer, neither the cycle's driver nor his passenger was wearing a motorcycle helmet.

WRKD, Maine

Nontraditional Leads

The lead to a radio or television story is generally considered to be its first sentence. Since this is broadcast, that's going to be a short sentence. There's certainly no room for the five Ws. This example of a story that tried to squeeze them all in was provided by Jerry Godby of WLOG, West Virginia:

Unacceptable:

A 17-year-old Logan resident was injured yesterday when he attempted to remove a baseball from a drain pipe while construction workers were moving the drain from the boy's front yard.

Acceptable:

A Logan teenager was injured yesterday after chasing a baseball ... into an unlikely place.

Broadcast leads are sometimes so short they are not even complete sentences:

In New York, one of the worst subway accidents in the city's history.

ABC News

Rather than suddenly rush out all the facts, newswriters often work to prepare listeners for those facts:

During a floor speech today, Senator Edward Kennedy will outline a tax reform proposal.

WBBM, Chicago

The details on the senator's plan can wait for later sentences. Here is another example of a lead that eases the audience into a story:

Another of those gigantic state lottery prizes comes up for grabs this weekend.

ABC News

Zingers (see Chapter 5, Other Leads) work particularly well:

> Abuse of the litter control program may result in the program itself being tossed out of the city budget.
>
> KGMI, Washington

The idea, as with newspaper leads, is to establish the angle of a story. The trick is to do that in a short, engaging sentence.

Short Stories

Here is a story from the news summary that begins the "NewsHour with Jim Lehrer":

> Los Angeles officials have cancelled a 122-million dollar contract with a Japanese company to build rail cars for the area's mass transit system. Public protest arose when the county's Transportation Commission awarded the contract to the Sumitomo Corporation—in spite of a lower bid by an American firm. Local citizens complained that county tax dollars should be used to create American jobs ... not Japanese ones.
>
> PBS

The next morning *The New York Times* devoted half a page to this story. Radio and television newswriters almost always have to make do with far, far fewer words. In fact, their stories are usually measured in seconds. This one took the NewsHour anchor 22 seconds to read—that's par for the course for a radio story, without tape or a television story without videotape. (You can determine how long a story is by reading it—aloud—at the pace the newscaster will read.)

Broadcast stories leave no room for the *inverted-pyramid* style of organization. (See Chapter 9, Organization.) Unlike a newspaper story, where readers can turn to another story when they get bored, radio and television audiences are expected to listen to the entire story. Therefore, there is no excuse for a story that peters out or ends with information of secondary importance. The news value in these short broadcast stories must remain high:

> One person was killed by the storms that hit Illinois yesterday. He was a construction worker in the Kankakee area—who was crushed when an unfinished house collapsed. Seven tornadoes struck the state yesterday.
>
> WSOY, Illinois

Snappers

The final sentence of a broadcast story may be used to help support the lead. It may add another fact, give the other side or mention what is likely to happen next, but often this sentence ends things with a little snap. (See Chapter 22, Features.)

> A magazine column in Washington recently labeled Senator John Melcher of Montana a vegetarian. Since he comes from cow country ... it brought some nasty mail from back home. Melcher also says he may no longer be invited to barbecues and weenie roasts. Melcher says he is NOT a vegetarian. *He IS a veterinarian.*
>
> WMAL, Washington, D.C.

RADIO REPORTING

What distinguishes the job of the radio reporter from that of the newspaper reporter is those small recorders the radio people lug around with them. In addition to getting all the basic information on a story, radio reporters have to make sure they record interesting audio to play in newscasts. That tape comes in two main varieties: actualities and voicers.

Actualities

Here the *actual* voice of newsmakers can be heard. They pass on expert knowledge, subjective comments or eyewitness reports:

> We had a state of extreme flooding ... vehicles were strewn over the area. ... It put your mind to somebody using a giant bowling ball and knocking cars and trucks around like there was no tomorrow. We had water on the highway in several places as high as four feet deep. Really and truly it was unbelievable.
>
> NBC

Actualities usually are between 10 and 25 seconds long. Radio reporters select them from interviews they have recorded with newsmakers, either in person or on the phone. (Those actualities are called *phoners*.) Actualities recorded in the field are often transmitted back to the studio through cellular phones. Then they are transferred to the newsroom's server so that they are ready to play in a newscast. (Sometimes these recordings are still called *carts*, after the tape cartridges onto which they once were dubbed.)

Before an actuality can be played in the newscast, someone will have to write a *lead-in* to introduce it: What are the basic facts of the story? Who is speaking? Is there anything else we have to know to understand this tape? A *write-out* is then needed to conclude the story. Usually it will make sure to mention again the name of the newsmaker who was speaking.

Here is an example of a complete radio news story with an actuality:

Lead-in: "T-V-A's generating plant at Brown's Ferry is out, and spokewoman Brenda Carnes says the agency is asking us to cut back on the use of electricity. ..."

Actuality: "The T-V-A today did issue an urgent appeal to all consumers to temporarily curtail their use of electric appliances during the peak hours of three p-m to nine p-m today. It's very unlikely that the emergency will deteriorate to the stages of a blackout, but we would like to point out that if you're not conserving electricity, it is costing us dearly because we're having to buy power to cover these peak periods."

Write-out: "Spokeswoman Carnes tells us the T-V-A doesn't know how long the problem will last."

Voicers

Here it's the reporter's own voice that's heard—from the scene of a news event. If the event was dramatic, the voicer might feature a detailed description:

> I'm sitting on the front lawn of a house. What remains of a single-story house is across the street from me. ... There's nothing but burned-out timbers. The house next door is gone. The house down the street is gone. The house on the corner—just a small portion of it is left standing. Directly across the street from me—about 50 feet away— appears to be the fuselage and one of the engines of the plane. There is a car across the street from me totally demolished and burned up.
>
> WINS, New York City

But the more typical voicer simply gives an analysis or explanation of an event:

> A reporter for the *Daily Mirror* newspaper put on a hardhat and an orange vest, walked into a train yard unchallenged and placed an electronic device—a dummy bomb—on a container of nuclear waste from a British power plant. The objective: to show how vulnerable the trains are that carry the deadly waste across Britain every week. Photographs document how easy it was to compromise the train. Politicians call it "shocking." An investigation is under way. Larry Miller, CBS News, London.

Voicers generally are from 20 to 50 seconds long. They may be recorded at the scene or recited, from notes, on the phone on the way back to the studio. They too will end up in the server for use in newscasts.

Voicers do require *lead-ins*, to introduce the story and the reporter, but in most cases do not require *write-outs*.

TELEVISION REPORTING

In television an important new element is added to the mix: visuals—generally in the form of moving images.

Television reporters at the larger stations are accompanied by at least one other person, whose job is to work the camera, the video recorder and the lights. The idea is to get *shots* on video that *cover*—illustrate—the subjects the reporter will want to discuss in the *narration*—the words that will be used with the video in a newscast. At a fire, for example, the camera operator will want to get shots of the firefighters, the survivors, any victims, the surrounding neighborhood and, if they got there early enough, the fire itself.

Video stories also require *sound bites*—short sections taken from interviews with newsmakers (the television equivalent of actualities). And they generally include *stand-ups*—sections, usually used at the end of the story, where the reporter is photographed speaking directly into the camera. (Stand-ups have much in common with radio voicers.)

Here's a typical videotape report, which gives an idea how long these elements generally run after the report has been edited:

Shots of burning building—6 seconds

Fire trucks—3 seconds

Burning building—4 seconds

Firefighters fighting the fire—6 seconds

Sound bite: Fire chief explains—7 seconds

Huddled survivors—6 seconds

Sound bite: Eyewitness—10 seconds

Covered bodies—4 seconds

Crying relative—3 seconds

Firefighters with fire almost out—4 seconds

Sound bite: Fire chief discusses deaths—8 seconds

Building smoking (no flames)—5 seconds

Stand-up—10 seconds

Writing to video is not easy. Visuals and narration must coordinate. (The visuals are usually indicated in the left-hand column of the page, leaving the right side for the narration.)

Unacceptable:

Crowds on sidewalk	*Few people* would be affected by the new city income tax. Its sponsors say only ten percent of the people who work here would even have to fill out the forms.

Acceptable:

Crowds on sidewalk	*Most people* would not be affected by the new city income tax. Its sponsors say 90 percent of the people who work here would not even have to fill out the forms.

In addition, the timing must be perfect. If those crying relatives are on for three seconds, the part of the narration that coordinates with that shot must also be exactly three seconds long. Still, when visuals and narrations are working together, television news can display a power that is difficult to match.

Here is an example of a short videotape report:

Street house is on 6 seconds	The Studwell family was asleep in their house on Woods Street in Alpine at three a.m.
Tree against house 7 seconds	when, police say, a gust of wind toppled this 75-foot-tall spruce tree. It landed on the Studwell's house.
Smashed front bedroom 6 seconds	Six-year-old Betsy Studwell was sleeping in the front bedroom on the second floor when the tree fell.
Parkin talking silently 6 seconds	Alpine Police Sergeant John Parkin says beams from the attic came crashing down on the girl's bed.
Sound bite: Parkin 8 seconds	"One beam hit her in the head. She was unconscious when we got there. Her mother was screaming. What a terrible accident."
Girl carried to ambulance 7 seconds	Betsy was taken to Englewood Hospital, where she is said to be in stable condition. Her parents and her sister were unhurt.
Leaves blowing on tree 5 seconds	Wind gusts of up to 60 miles per hour were reported in the area this morning.
Stand-up by roots of tree 12 seconds	"Sergeant Parkin says recent heavy rains may have loosened the ground around the tree's roots—making it vulnerable to one of those gusts. Steven Jones, WHVD News, Alpine."

CHAPTER 27 SUMMARY: BROADCAST JOURNALISM

The techniques introduced in this chapter are intended for writing for radio or television news:

- Don't get too formal.
- Avoid long sentences.
- Stick to the most important facts.
- Use the present tense when possible.
- Prepare listeners or viewers for what you are going to tell them.
- Coordinate writing with audio or visuals.

However, these techniques are worth learning for another reason: As our lives become more hectic and as information is hurled at us from more and more directions, we often need to be able to take things in quickly and easily. Newspaper-style writing has grown increasingly compact and conversational. And writing for the Web—where images, video and audio often are part of text stories—employs many techniques borrowed from broadcast journalism.

ADDITIONAL READING

Broadcast News, Mitchell Stephens and Beth M. Olson, Thomson Wadsworth; 4th edition, 2005.

Convergent Journalism: An Introduction—Writing and Producing Across Media, Stephen Quinn and Vincent Filak, Focal Press, 2005.

Modern Media Writing, Rick Wiber and Randy Miller, Wadsworth Publishing, 2002.

Telling the Story: Writing for Print, Broadcast and Online Media, Brian Brooks, George Kennedy, Daryl R. Moen and Don Ranly, Bedford/St. Martin's, 2001.

EXERCISE A

Rewrite the following broadcast leads to make them more effective. In each case you are writing for a newscast heard or watched today in the town in which the events occurred.

1. Robert Director, a convicted rapist, who has served his entire ten-year jail term but has reportedly told prison psychologists he will rape again, was released from jail today in Butlerville.

2. City school board president Jessica Small announced today that she will form a multicultural committee to consider complaints from Asian-American parents that their cultural traditions are being ignored in the city's schools.

3. A group calling itself the Anti-Car Brigade blocked traffic for one hour on Interstate 40 in Paoli today during rush hour, causing a three-mile-long backup, to protest what it called "this country's slavish subservience to the environmentally disastrous automobile."

4. After 14,500 city residents went up to six days without power following recent thunderstorms, Ardmore mayor Deborah Michelson demanded today that the local electric company, State Power and Light, give each household that lost power $750 and each business that lost power $3,500 to cover damages caused by the blackout.

5. Calling the board of trustees "shortsighted" and "out of touch with the information revolution," the president of Ripon Junior College resigned today after the board voted down his plan to phase out computers on campus for student use and require all new students to arrive on campus with their own laptops.

EXERCISE B

Write *broadcast* leads based on each of the collections of information in Exercise B in Chapter 4, Traditional Leads. In each case you are writing for a newscast heard or watched today in the town in which the events occurred.

EXERCISE C

Write *broadcast* stories based on each of the collections of information in Exercise C in Chapter 9, Organization. In each case you are writing for a newscast heard or watched today in the town in which the events occurred. Each story should be 25 seconds or less.

EXERCISE D

Select two actualities from this interview with the mayor of Haverford. Then write two voicers based on the interview, and write lead-ins and write-outs for the actualities and lead-ins for the voicers. All would be used in newscasts broadcast in Haverford today.

Q. "I'm with Mayor Susan O'Neill. Mayor O'Neill, we understand you have canceled the tree lighting ceremony before Christmas this year? Why?"

A. "Frankly, I'm fed up with this whole thing. It has been a real mess. Let me give you a little history on this: When I first became mayor two years ago, I noticed that the city organized this celebration of Christmas but did nothing to honor its many Jewish citizens as they celebrate Hanukkah. I got what I thought was a very simple idea: I decided to ask Harry Ashmead, the head of our fine Department of Public Works, to put up a large Hanukkah menorah next to the Christmas tree and to hold the tree lighting on the first night of Hanukkah—so we could light the menorah too and celebrate both holidays."

Q. "You did that last year, right?"

A. "Yes, we did. I thought it was quite nice really. We sang Christmas songs and Hanukkah songs, and everybody seemed to have a fine time, but then I started to get all these letters and petitions from a Christian group in the town. There was even a protest demonstration against me at Town Hall. They objected to the fact that the ceremony was held on Hanukkah, and they complained that there were too many Hanukkah songs. Since the city is no more than 20 percent Jewish, they said we shouldn't have more than one-fifth of the songs be Hanukkah songs."

Q. "How did you react to that?"

A. "I thought the protests were ridiculous. We're supposed to be encouraging broad-mindedness around here, not narrow-mindedness. We have to learn how to enjoy each other's traditions, not fight them. I'm not going to count the number of songs at a ceremony. I'm sure 99 percent of the Christians in this town agree with me."

Q. "So you made your decision?"

A. "Yes, I made my decision. I decided that if we can't have a holiday ceremony in a spirit of tolerance and understanding in this town then we shouldn't have any ceremony. I'm not going to stoop to the level of having to count songs. We can all now celebrate the holidays as we see fit with our friends and families."

Q. "Why didn't you just ignore the protests and have a holiday ceremony like you did last year?"

A. "Well, I just had enough, that's all. There are some people in this town who aren't mature enough to deserve a holiday ceremony, if you ask me. Maybe in a couple of years we can bring it back, when people have cooled off and grown up a bit."

Q. "Thank you, Mayor Susan O'Neill."

EXERCISE E

Write a videotape story for use in a television newscast in Amestown today based on the following information. Describe videotape you could realistically have expected to shoot at this event. You can use any sections from the interviews as sound bites, and you can make up your own stand-up.

Water main break on Spring Street in downtown Amestown this afternoon. Street is flooded. Water up to three feet high on Spring Street and on the nearest cross street, 23rd Avenue. Residential area.

From interview with Amestown Water Commissioner Peter Lane: "Well, you have to understand, there are a lot of old pipes under this city, and I guess one of them just broke. This is the worst water main break I've seen in my fifteen years on this job. It happened in a low part of town, a valley. We've got about three blocks covered with water, much of it too deep to walk through. We've got eleven houses on Spring Street and on 23rd with water coming in on their main floors, and a couple of dozen other houses with flooded basements. I can assure you that we've turned off the water into this old pipe. The leak has stopped. We have pumper trucks from the fire department here now, and we should get this whole thing cleaned up by tomorrow evening. Then we can fix the old water main. Won't have water service for most of the downtown area until tomorrow evening at the earliest, though. So, we're bringing in a few trucks with bottled water to help residents and the local businesses get by."

House of Georgia McFly, 2325 Spring Street. Water one foot high in living room. She has one daughter, Sue Anne Kelly. A doll floats across the living room floor.

From interview with Georgia McFly: "Look, I don't feel much like talking right now. This is the worst day of my life, OK? My living room is under water. My carpets, my furniture, some of my clothes, are ruined. I don't know who is going to pay for this. I don't know where me and my daughter are going to spend the night, OK?"

Rescue workers using rowboats to get people out of some of the homes on Spring Street. Jason Call is sitting in a rowboat after having been taken from his home at 2356 Spring Street.

From interview with Jason Call: "Well, you know, I happened to look outside this morning, and I saw the street begin filling with water. I called the police, and then I tried to keep the water from coming into my house. I closed the doors and everything, but it didn't work. The water just started pouring in through every hole and crack it could find. I must have a foot and a half on the first floor now. The basement I can't go near, and my front yard is a lake. I wanted to stay, but they said it would be safer to leave. So, you know, they came over in this boat and rowed me out."

Water is half-way up the windows of cars in the deepest parts. Fire department pumper trucks are working to pump it into storm sewers on other blocks. A few residents can be seen sitting, looking out the second-floor windows of their homes.

Visuals   *Narration*

THE BASICS

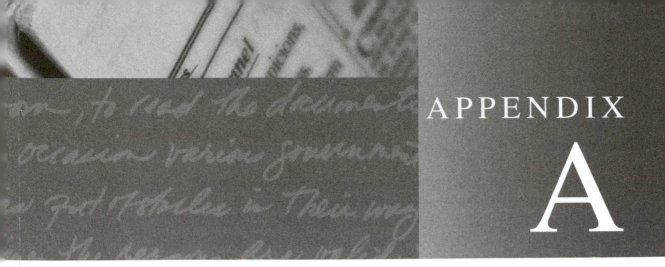

Format

Every newspaper has a set of rules for preparing and presenting stories on the page. These rules have only an indirect relationship to how a story will actually appear in print. They are a kind of newsroom shorthand, designed to enable different people in different parts of the paper to examine copy and work with it quickly and efficiently.

This is essential, since anything nonstandard in the look of the pages, or anything difficult to decipher, could lead to confusion, delay or, worse, a mistake in the product—the newspaper.

Since different newsrooms use different computers, from desktop systems linked by servers to internal mainframe networks, this chapter will keep its advice lean. Expect, on entering a newsroom today, to at minimum be asked to word process; to peruse the newspaper's library online; to navigate the World Wide Web by means of such search engines as the advanced *Google* search to quickly find information; and to gain mastery of newspaper's different *baskets,* or in-house filing system. Reporters with a command of *Excel,* a quick and effective way of making sense of patterns of numbers, will have a leg up. Depending on the size and expectations of the newsroom, reporters also might be asked to use *Photoshop* or a similar program to edit digital photos, and—in truly cross-media newsrooms—to contribute by filing web and/or audio versions of their stories.

The nature of news is changing fast. The reporter comfortable moving across the technologies of different media will have an advantage. But content remains—and always will remain—king. So build your reporting and writing skills before worrying about your technological dexterity.

That said, it's valuable to arrive in a new newsroom with a series of questions:

1. How and where are stories stored, edited and moved onto the page? Who *codes* these stories for layout, headline size and type, and column width (the answer typically will be the *copy desk,* where stories are edited for format and style).

2. How is the paper's *budget,* the list of story choices for the day or week, set up, and when does it "move"? Typically, moving happens in midafternoon on morning newspapers so that editors can begin the evening-long process of sorting what stories will run and where in the newspaper.

3. How often does the paper update its website, and what's the relationship between the Web operation and the news desk?

4. What, if any, skills are reporters expected to bring to the table other than reporting and writing stories? Are they asked to shoot their own photographs? Record audio? Build graphics? And, if not (still the case at the majority of newspapers), how do reporters, photographers and graphics reporters work together?

The first, and most important thing, for a reporter to learn is how a story moves from draft to the page.

FUNDAMENTALS

Use the Right Basket

No matter what its operating system, newsroom computers must be able to communicate among themselves so that stories can move from desk to desk and be stored electronically. Typically, every reporter is assigned a *basket*, where he or she keeps notes and writes stories. Other baskets are filled with stories in various stages of editing. Still others contain stories routed to certain *desks*—the *city desk* (which handles local news), the *national desk* or the *sports desk*. There are, therefore, baskets with city stories, baskets with national stories and baskets with sports stories, for example.

It is crucial that reporters know what *basket* a story should be *moved* to when they are finished writing. If a story goes to the wrong basket, only one thing protects it from being lost: the *slug*.

Select an Appropriate Slug

For formatting purposes, no single piece of information is more important on a story than the one or two words, usually totaling eight characters or less, used to identify it. This is called the *slug*. It is akin to the file names used with most computer software. A story on a bus accident, for example, might be slugged *BUSWRECK*. One on a city council action might be slugged *COUNCIL*.

Since the slug is the story's label, no two slugs on the same day can be the same. That's why *BUSWRECK* a better slug than *ACCIDENT*—there are too many stories that could go by that name. Similarly *MURDER* wouldn't work as a slug in a big city, where there are a couple of murders a day; but *MURDER* might be fine as a slug on a small-town paper, where stories on the subject are significantly less common. (Never use the slugs *KILL* or *SPIKE*: In newspaper jargon, these terms mean that the entire story will be deep-sixed, eliminated.)

Reporters also are always careful not to slug stories with obscene or derogatory words, because at times slugs are used as *jump lines*, the word at the end of a column announcing that the story it is being continued on, or jumping to, another page. It wouldn't do to use *JERK* to slug a story about the departing sheriff, only to have the jump line read, *See JERK, Page 6.*

Speed is critical in a newsroom as deadline approaches, and sloppy slugs regularly waste precious time. The best way to *retrieve*, or call up, a story is to search for it by slug using whatever proprietary system a given newsroom has set up. If the slug is misidentified or misspelled, the story will be hard to find. Whoever is looking for it either will have to scan basket after basket trying to find the story or will have to call up every story written by that author.

Editors use slugs to designate each story for a given day on the *story budget*. This is the list of proposed stories, by department and section of the paper, that editors evaluate in putting out the next day's newspaper. Editors often ask their reporters to "write a *budget line*." This is essentially a *focus statement* for a story. It consists of its slug, the writer's name, a sentence or two, an estimation of the story's length and a notation of whether *art*—photos or graphics—will accompany the story.

PROTEST (Smith)—City labor leaders have asked the workers to leave their jobs for 30 minutes at noon today in an effort to call attention to how much immigrants contribute to the city's well-being. (12 inches), w/photo.

Extend the Expiration Date

Once they've appeared in the newspaper, stories find their way to the electronic clip file. (See Chapter 14, Research.) However, stories that have not *run*—appeared in print—don't live forever in newspaper computers. If they did, even the sizable memory of these mainframes would reach overload. So in the *header*, the same area at the top of the screen where the basket and slug are identified, is a space to set an expiration date. At some newspapers, unpublished stories will expire, or be purged, from the system within a week unless the expiration date is extended. So the reporter working on an enterprise story about water pollution wants to do two things before writing a word: Decide on a slug, and extend the expiration date. There is no worse feeling than to try to call up a story only to find that everything you've written so far is now gone from the system.

EDITING THE OLD-FASHIONED WAY

There's something almost quaint in the 21st century, when laptop computers and the BlackBerry are almost an extension of our five fingers, in talking about the format of stories edited by hand and mailed as hard copy. That said, there remain occasions when freelancers, particularly in magazine work, do send information by snail mail and may even need to edit it on the fly.

Here are abbreviated instructions for dealing with such occasions.

Slugs

Typewritten slugs differ from electronic slugs in two important ways: First, each page needs the slug repeated with a page number following so that a story doesn't become jumbled or incomplete. For example, the first page of BUSWRECK would still have the slug BUSWRECK. But subsequent pages would be slugged BUSWRECK—2, BUSWRECK—3, and so on.

Second, reporters have to type their names directly below the slug on the first page. (In electronic newsrooms, computers automatically append the name of the person in whose basket the story is being written.)

Page preparation

1. Takes
   Pages on the printed page are often referred to as *takes*. Each take is numbered. Again, on that BUSWRECK story, take one will be slugged BUSWRECK, take two BUSWRECK-2, take three BUSWRECK-3, and so forth.

2. More
   At the bottom of each page of a story except the last page, type the word *more* and circle it. This tells anyone reading the story that there are *more* pages to read.

3. Endit
   Type one of the following symbols at the bottom of the last page—*endit*, the numeral *30* (a remnant of an old telegraph code) or the number sign, #. All three mark the end of the story.

4. Triple-space
   Some reporters double-space their copy, but it's wiser to use three space between lines. This leaves room for an editor's comments if another draft is requested.

5. Margins
   Copy should be centered on a page with room to type about 60 characters on each line. That will leave margins of almost an inch on either side of the page.

6. Dateline
   Stories that are written outside the town in which the newsroom is located should begin with the name of the city in which they are composed. The city's name should be typed in capital letters. If a story is from another state, the state name should be added, unless the city is well known. (See The Basics, Section B, Style, for rules on abbreviation.) Thus the *Houston Chronicle* would use *LOS ANGELES* for a story from one of California's best-known cities, but *MENDOCINO, Calif.*, for a story from that northern coastal town. In the *Los Angeles Times* and other in-state papers, however, the dateline would be simply MENDOCINO. Follow the dateline with a space, a dash and another space, and then start the story. Datelines should be indented, like any paragraph. Never use phony datelines. If the story is reported from the newsroom, it shouldn't have a dateline, no matter where it took place.

Copy Markings

Reporters rely on a set of symbols to make changes on the printed page neatly, clearly and economically.

A page that requires too many of these editing symbols may begin to resemble a work of abstract art. Try to send computer-clean copy to any editor. But a few editing changes on the page are acceptable.

Here are the symbols:

Punctuation

The period. ⊛   This *was* a short session⊛

The comma. ⋏   The man, who was tall, said . . .

The hyphen. =   The $40 million appropriation.

The colon. ⌃:   His firm had six clients, John Foster & Sons, . . .

The semicolon. ⋏;   Surviving are his wife, Margaret; two sons, John and Stephen, at home, a brother . . .

The apostrophe. ⌄   It's a new concept.

Quotations. ⌄ ⌄   "I can't believe it," he exclaimed.

The dash. —   She said quite loudly "balderdash."

Parentheses. ( )   The gauer (pronounced power) is found in Africa.

Deletion

A letter. ℓ   The bill was approved.

A letter in a word that
must then be *closed.* ⌒

Po͜lice.

A word. ➙

He ~~said~~ said that he was tired.

A line.

The survivors were taken to
Low Hospital. (Note: check on
their conditions) They were
identified as . . .

An entire paragraph
or block ("X" out
and draw lines to
where the story
picks up again)

~~Before the school was built the
land was occupied by Joe's
Pharmacy. Joe was a nice man,
still remembered for the lollipops
he would hand out to kids.~~

Addition

Insert space.   #

Frenchhorn

Let stand (after an accidental ⟨stet⟩
deletion).

The ~~man~~ said . . .

Insert letter.   ⋀

Tree blind mice . . .

Insert word or phrase. ⏝

It was the third time she had won . . .

Other

Paragraph.   ⎣

Sen. Bill Bradley yesterday
announced that a coalition of
senators from both parties would
propose . . .

Capitalize.   =

north Dakota

Lower case.   /

TEXAS

Italics.   ⸺

She ate 17 hot dogs.

Spell out.   ⬭

(Ind.)

Abbreviate.   ⬭

(General) William Westmoreland

Transpose letters.   ∾

hockey

Transpose words.   ⊓⌐

He briskly walked to school.

EXERCISE A

After each of the following story descriptions, write a slug that could be used to identify the story.

1. The local school board has decided to stop selling ice cream in the high school cafeteria.
2. Forty-thousand dollars worth of diamonds was stolen from a safe at a downtown jewelry store.
3. The coach of the local university's football team, Terence Howard, has been fired by the athletic director, Rand Dumont, after three straight losing seasons.
4. Local bakery workers have voted to strike tomorrow.
5. Three people, including an 11-year-old boy, were killed when the car in which they were riding smashed into a tree in Lakeville.
6. The mayor has announced a new plan to widen a two-mile stretch of Main Street in the downtown business district.
7. A local computer company, Micro Technology, has announced that it will soon be selling a laptop computer that can handle advanced engineering projects.
8. A group of mothers whose eligibility for child support payments has, the women say, been challenged by the city's Human Services Department, staged a demonstration in front of the department's offices.
9. Georgina Albert was found guilty of armed robbery following a two-month-long trial.
10. The city Board of Aldermen voted at the end of a long meeting last night to change its name to the Board of Alderpeople in deference to its newest member—Alderwoman Jane Piccalo.

EXERCISE B

Correct any errors in the following sentences using traditional copy-marking symbols.

1. Councilman Ewdards saidhe decid ed to support the bill after a discussion with mayor;
2. By the tme the firefighters were able to put out it the fire, it had destroyed two three story buildings.
3. Here is the list of contributors Thomas Belfry Robert Jones Sarah Humphrey and Elizabeth Hjersttrand.
4. Car skidded to a top about 40 feet from the edge off the cliff police said, but th boody was founded but the body was found at the bottom of the ravine.
5. "We will not bargain under the trheat of a strike, said Dr. Frank lombardi the school boards president
6. According to police the suspect was from Los Angeles, Calif., and hda never seen the Woman befre,
7. The returned jury with a verdict.
8. Janice madison alsso attended the meeting attended the meeting, but she did not speak on the ammendment.
9. Traffic will blocked be on Culpepper Ninth and Tenth streets for two weeks forcing cars to use hopkins Road of Eigth street when diving through business district
10. Lumpkin maintained he was not three when happened it he had never scene that woman before and he had know interest in the fortunes of Anderson Plumbing
11. There fire companies were called the scene one from the twon it self and one from each neighboring comunity.
12. The land was overgrown with weds, still it asw the towns and it wasa rsponable sight for a was a reasonable sight for a swimming pool.
13. The judge had bbeen been sceen with woman shortly before dey both disapeared. He known was for his antiabortion views
14. Each division of the cmpany was xsd considered a seperate entity with own management and sails staffs.
15. "It took alot of work on our paart," Howard said. "But man oh man did it ever But mnomn did it ever seem worthwhile on sunday when; we saw that kids face."

APPENDIX

B

Style

When newspaper editors talk about style, they usually don't mean the kind that distinguishes a Hemingway novel from one by Faulkner. They mean the basic rules that tell a reporter which words to abbreviate, which to capitalize, which spelling to choose or how to write numbers.

Without these rules to provide consistency, newspaper copy would be a mess.

Unacceptable:

Duke Power employs eighteen thousand in its 20-thousand-sq.-mile Carolinas SVC. area, down from an early 1980s peak of more than 20,000 employees. In '88, Duke power laid off 1.2 thou. workers.

These statistics are, in fact, correct. But the manner in which they are presented is as disconcerting to the eye as a businessman wearing one blue sock and one red sock. That businessman might have trouble gaining the trust of a potential client. A newspaper without a consistent style would have trouble gaining the trust of potential readers.

Acceptable:

Duke Power employs 18,000 in its 20,000-square-mile service area, down from an early-1980s peak of more than 20,000 employees. In 1988, Duke Power laid off 1,200 workers.

The Charlotte (N.C.) *Observer*

A consistent style makes stories more readable.

Unacceptable:

Senator Barbara Boxer, Sen. Kennedy and Ms. Feinstein supported the bill.

Acceptable:

Sen. Barbara Boxer, Sen. Edward Kennedy and Sen. Dianne Feinstein supported the bill.

And a consistent style helps the writer, too. A reporter on deadline who had to stop each time to puzzle out the best way to write *142 E. Ninth St.* would be lost.

All newspapers use a *stylebook*, which lays out the rules of style the paper will follow. That reporter on deadline simply has to turn to the section in the paper's stylebook on addresses to learn how *142 E. Ninth St.* should be written. After a while it will no longer be necessary to consult the stylebook—the rule will have been memorized.

The rules in these stylebooks are determined in part by tradition—newspapers have been abbreviating the word *Captain* as a title before someone's name (*Capt.*) for more than a hundred years. The rules are also based on taste: Some stylebooks call for *damn* to become *d—*. But, fortunately, the justifications for most style rules are efficiency and readability: *383,365* is easier to read and easier to write than *three-hundred, eighty-three thousand, three-hundred sixty-five*.

All newspaper styles certainly are not the same. More formal papers, such as *The New York Times*, use more capitalization and less abbreviation. They may also precede a man's last name with a courtesy title—*Mr.*

Most newspapers, however, have adopted style rules very similar to those set out in *The Associated Press Stylebook and Libel Manual* ... and with good reason: More than 1,400 newspapers in the United States run stories by AP, and it would be time-consuming indeed to make all those little style changes after these stories arrived in the newsroom.

Most larger papers have their own stylebooks—manuals with special rules on everything from the names of local institutions and neighborhoods to the preferred spelling of *Hanukkah*. Smaller papers often accept the AP's rules and stylebook wholesale.

Reporters will refer to their stylebooks frequently to check on more obscure matters, and they will memorize the rules that come into play regularly.

To avoid confusion, the examples in this book, including those from *The New York Times*, have been printed in accordance with the rules of *The Associated Press Stylebook*. (We do, however, use *yesterday* or *today* in place of the day of the week in discussing when an event occurred. We also add italics to many of our examples to clarify points.)

The exercises throughout are best completed with the help of a stylebook. (*The Associated Press Stylebook and Libel Manual* can be ordered through bookstores, online, or directly from the Associated Press, at 450 W. 33rd St., New York, NY 10001.) Some of the most commonly used style rules, in line with those set out by AP, are outlined in this section:

ABBREVIATIONS

1. Acronyms
   The first time an organization is mentioned, spell it out—*National Aeronautics and Space Administration, Organization of American States, Environmental Protection Agency*. The second time, its initials can be used—*NASA, OAS, EPA*. Unless the second reference follows closely upon the first, the initials (or acronym) should be followed, in parentheses, by the full name: the *OAS* (Organization of American States). The acronym of organizations widely known by their initials—*FBI, CIA, NATO, AFL-CIO*—can stand alone on first reference.

2. Addresses
   Abbreviate Boulevard (*Blvd.*), Avenue (*Ave.*) and Street (*St.*) *only* when giving a complete address. All other synonyms for road are always spelled out. It is 64 *W. 85th St.* (but she lives on *West 85th Street*) and 28 Amherst *Road*. (The numbers in a street address are always numerals; the street names below 10 are written out—*1 Fifth Ave., 8 12th St.*)

3. Dates
   Abbreviate *Jan., Feb., Aug., Sept., Oct., Nov.* and *Dec.* when used in a specific date. Always spell out all the other months: *Aug. 5, 1954, July 11, 1979, August 2006*.

4. States
The names of eight states—*Alaska, Hawaii, Idaho, Iowa, Maine, Ohio, Texas* and *Utah*—should never be abbreviated. The names of all other states should be abbreviated only when used after the name of a town or county. Spell out the names of states when they stand alone. Here is a list of proper abbreviations:

Ala.	Md.	N.D.
Ariz.	Mass.	Okla.
Ark.	Mich.	Ore.
Calif.	Minn.	Pa.
Colo.	Miss.	R.I.
Conn.	Mo.	S.C.
Del.	Mont.	S.D.
Fla.	Neb.	Tenn.
Ga.	Nev.	Vt.
Ill.	N.H.	Va.
Ind.	N.J.	Wash.
Kan.	N.M.	W. Va.
Ky.	N.Y.	Wis.
La.	N.C.	Wyo.

5. Proper names
In giving the formal name of a company, abbreviate *Co., Inc., Corp.,* and *Bros.* It is *St. Paul Fire and Marine Insurance Co.*, but the *insurance company*. Also abbreviate *Jr.* and *Sr.* when given as part of someone's name—*Harold M. Ickes Jr.*

6. Titles
Many titles are abbreviated when they appear directly before a name—*Gov. Deval Patrick.* Abbreviate *Dr., Gov., Lt. Gov., Rep., Sen., the Rev., Gen., Lt., Capt., Sgt., Cmdr.* and *Prof.* when they precede a name. But it is *President Bush.* And all titles are written out when they appear alone or after a name—it's *John Jones, a sergeant*, and *Deval Patrick, governor of Massachusetts* and the *California governor.*

CAPITALIZATION

1. Proper names
Use capitals to start each of the principal words in the formal name of a person, place, region, trademarked product, organization or company. Titles of books, plays and movies also are capitalized. So are the days of the week and the months of the year. It's *Army, China, Roseanne Arnold, Mideast, the South, Republican, Democrat, World War II, Yosemite National Park* and *Kiblin's Pharmacy.* It is *Coca-Cola* and *Coke* for the real thing, but *soda* for general references to the fizzy stuff we drink. And the book and movie by the same name are given as "*Silence of the Lambs.*"

2. Government bodies
Capitalize the full proper names of governmental entities—the *New Jersey Legislature*, the *Brockton City Council*, the *Denver Police Department.* Capitalization should be retained if the dateline or context of a story make clear *which* city council or police department is being referred to. It would be, "NYACK, N.Y.—The *City Council* last night. ..." Without such a clear reference, make it lowercase—the *legislature*, the *city council*, the *fire department.*

3. Titles

   Formal titles are capitalized before a name—*Republican State Chairman* Chet Upham, but not after a name—Chet Upham, *Republican state chairman*, or standing alone—*the Republican state chairman*. But this holds only for a person's formal title. It is *Republican leader* Chet Upham and *shortstop* Miguel Tejada, not *Shortstop* Miguel Tejada.

NAMES AND COURTESY TITLES

The first time a name is used in a story, use the full name, except for that handful of leaders famous enough so that their last name and their title alone will do—*Secretary of State Condoleeza Rice*, *Judge Lawrence N. Martin*, *Angelina Jolie*, but *President Bush*. For a New York City newspaper, *Mayor Bloomberg* would be sufficient; elsewhere it would be *New York Mayor Michael Bloomberg*. Subsequent references are by last name only, as in *Jolie*.

NUMBERS

In general, spell out numbers below 10 and use figures for 10 or above—*five* persons were killed, *23* injured. (Very large numbers use numerals and words—3 million people.) Here are some exceptions:

1. Ages

   Whether someone is *3* months old or *86* years, use a numeral.

2. Beginning a sentence

   Spell out a number when it begins a sentence—*Fourteen* people were injured yesterday. Years are an exception—*1985* was a very good year.

3. Dollars and cents

   Again, always use a numeral. It's *5* cents and *$1*. When amounts exceed $999,999, use the $ sign and combine a numeral and a word. It is *$3 million* and *$4.25 billion* (never carried beyond two decimal points).

4. Fractions

   Only fractions below one should be spelled out—*two-thirds*, but *1 1/2, 2.2*.

5. Percentages

   Always use numerals—*6 percent, 2.3 percent, 0.4 percent*. And it is percent, not per cent or %.

6. Time

   Use numerals except for noon and midnight. It is *4 a.m.* and *11:45 p.m.* (Use a colon to separate hours from minutes; a.m. and p.m. are lowercase.)

7. Weight and dimensions

   Use numerals (and spell out pounds, ounces, feet and inches). It is a *6-foot-5-inch* shark that weighed *350 pounds*, and it snowed *3 inches*.

PUNCTUATION

We will not attempt to address the many complexities of punctuation common to all writing here. For that, we recommend the AP Stylebook *and* one of the grammar books suggested in

The Basics, Section C, Spelling and Grammar. Here we will address three broad punctuation problems that trouble many journalists:

1. Commas

    AP style normally does *not* use a *serial comma*—no comma is placed before a conjunction that ends a series. It would be, "He bought carrots, milk and ice," *not*, "He bought carrots, milk, and ice." (The exception is in a series of long, complicated phrases. Then a comma before the conjunction ending the series may make things clearer.) Otherwise, the rules for the use of commas are standard. If there's no natural pause in a sentence, usually there is no need for a comma. Make sure, however, you remember the comma on *both* sides of an interjection or apposition—The movie's star, Sean Penn, was there.

2. Possessives

    In general, add an apostrophe and an *s* to the end of a singular or plural noun to form a possessive unless the noun ends in *s*. It is the *school's roof*, the *man's suit* and the *men's problem*. For plural nouns ending in *s* and singular proper nouns ending in *s*, simply add an apostrophe at the end to form a possessive—*John Jones' car*, the *Joneses' house*, the *United States' debt*. Common singular nouns ending in *s* take an extra *s* after the apostrophe—*the hostess's invitation*.

3. Quotation marks

    These should go around a speaker's exact words. (See Chapter 7, Quotations.) They are also around the titles of books, movies, plays, songs and articles—"*For Whom the Bell Tolls*"—and around nicknames introduced in a full name—*Karl "Mailman" Malone*. For quotes within quotes use, a single quotation mark before and after the material within the quote to be set apart—He said, "*Have you read 'The Kitchen God's Wife'?*" A comma or a period at the end of a quote belongs within the quotation marks—"*I couldn't believe the whole thing*," she said. The question mark, dash and exclamation point should be within quotation marks only when they apply to the quoted material; otherwise they belong outside. It is: "He asked, 'Why are you being so mean?'" But, "Why do you think he called you 'mean and callous'?"

SPELLING

A dictionary will answer almost all spelling questions. (See The Basics, Section C, Spelling and Grammar.) The AP recommends *Webster's New International Dictionary*. Here are some examples of the preferred spelling of words where two spellings are accepted by dictionaries: *goodbye, employee, whiskey, Vietnam, Taipei, Teheran, kidnapped*.

SEXISM

Some writers still persist in stereotyping. In a world in which women operate jackhammers on construction crews and men stay home with their children, this is not merely insulting, it's wrong. A doctor is not automatically *he*, nor is a nurse automatically *she*. One way of overcoming subconscious stereotyping is to use the plural rather than the singular.

Unacceptable:

A day-care *worker* is best prepared for the job if *she* ...

Acceptable:

Day-care workers are best prepared for the job if *they* …

ADDITIONAL READING

Associated Press Stylebook and Briefing on Media Law, Associated Press, Norm Goldstein, editor, Perseus Books, 2004.

"All the Obscenity That's Fit to Print," Mitchell Stephens and Eliot Frankel, *Washington Journalism Review*, April 1981.

EXERCISE A

Edit the following sentences to correct style errors.

1. The Gov. invited the 2 senators to visit the four Army bases scheduled to close January 15.
2. Twenty-three people, including a four-year-old girl, were on the bus when it skidded to a stop on Franklin Ave.
3. The Federal Bureau of Investigation is still investigating the kidnapping, but the Atty. Gen. announced that the family does not wish to press charges.
4. 40 percent of the county's population of forty-six thousand lives in redwood city.
5. The Reverend William Howard and Fred Neal, Chairman of the Church Finance Committee, were there, but Mr. Neal left early.
6. The injured included three employes of Franklin Locks: Mrs. Allison Hampton, thirty-two, of three Lakeview Road; Mr. Eliot Harms, twenty-three, of Seven Pinetree Street; and Ms. Julie Harrison, twenty-eight, who also lives with Mr. Harms on Pinetree Street.
7. Most Legislators in the state opposed the Equal Rights amendment.
8. Mrs. Norman's first child was born on Jan. 11, 1981, and her second child was born in Feb. of the next year.
9. The NAACP has scheduled 2 demonstrations for the month of Dec. in Atlanta, Georg. plus 13 demonstrations in March in other areas of the State.
10. John Marshall, President of the state's lottery, announced that 2 people would share the $3,700,000 pot.
11. The President of one local Computer Company said that 8 per cent of the settlers came from the East.
12. The House Ways and Means committee approved the Bill sponsored by Representative Clark.
13. He has played Bridge every friday night since he was sixty-two years old, and he ends each game with a can of sprite.
14. The Des Moines fire department fought the blaze for nineteen hours, calling in 120 firefighters, twelve pumpers, and 3 hook-and-ladder trucks.
15. Superintendent Rayoff said there was no doubt the schools roof needed repair but added that it might not need to be replaced.
16. Andrews, a captain in the police force, and lieutenant Richard Stole, were both seen in the Tavern.
17. Perhaps half the americans who served in viet nam never went near Saigon.
18. Haley's Canned Goods Company announced quarterly earnings of twenty-five million dollars, about 1/3 more than last year.
19. Nineteen eighty-four was the first year in which the mayor did not get a popularity rating of at least sixty percent.
20. According to Harry P. Swenson Junior, chairman of the communist party in the country, the conflict in the former Yugoslavia threatened to embroil much of Europe.

EXERCISE B

Edit this story to correct any style errors.

FLOOD RELIEF

perkins

Governor Arthur Montgomery toured flooded areas of Lewiston yesterday in the wake of the worst rainstorm in the city in more than fifty years.

"I've been in public office 25 years but I've never seen anything like it," the Governor said as he was paddled in a rowboat down Main St., which is still under four feet of water. "We will do everything possible to help the people here.

Junetta Diaz, Assistant Director of the state's Disaster Relief Agency, estimated that the damage to Lewiston alone would be two- to three million dollars. She added that the total damage to property in the county could surpass 10 million dollars.

Montgomery, a democrat was accompanied by Republican representative Carl Peters, who counted himself among the flood victims. "My house is on the hillside," he said, But I had 20 head of cattle grazing in a feedlot near the river. It rose so quickly that most of them drowned."

8 inches of rain fell in 3 hours friday, sending the Joscinta river over its banks and flooding areas that normally are bone dry. Geologists for the state already have identified the storm as a 100 year flood, or one that has one chance in 100 of occurring in any given year. Five people drowned when the storm hit at about 6:00 P.M. The water level rose to seven ft. on Elbow Rd., right next to the river before it began receding Sunday.

The flooding was compounded by the soggy Apr. weather which already has dumped 13 inches of rain in the area in the past twenty days. The last major flood in Lewiston occurred on August thirteen and fourteenth, 1926, when 6 people drowned and 13 were injured in a flood that followed eleven inches of rain over two days.

APPENDIX C

Spelling and Grammar

One major metropolitan newspaper reports accusations that a father and two sons sought "vengence" against two men they thought had attacked a family member; another newspaper refers to a man accused of murder as a "defendent."

The correct spellings of the words "vengeance" and "defendant" are facts that can be checked in any English dictionary. When such simple and universal facts are wrong, it is difficult to trust the other information in the story. In journalism, spelling always counts.

Sloppy grammar poses a similar threat to a writer's credibility and perhaps a larger threat to a reader's understanding. What's wrong with the following sentence?

> The councilman opposed the plan for the new sewage treatment plant, who had originally proposed the plant in the first place.

As written, this sentence makes it appear as if the treatment plant—made human—once proposed itself. The writer had meant to say that the *councilman*, who originally had proposed a new sewage treatment plant, now opposes the plan to build one. But in trying to say that, the reporter misplaced the modifying clause, the *who clause*. The lesson: Keep modifiers next to what they are modifying.

Correct use of the language is vital in journalism because it aids clear communication and because it provides evidence of the care and the intelligence of the reporter. Journalists must pay strict attention not only to the facts in their stories (see Chapter 12, Facts) but also to the sentences, words and punctuation marks used to convey those facts. When journalists fail to do so, they can destroy their ability to communicate. What was this reporter trying to tell us?

> After stealing second base, the catcher threw the ball into center field and he raced to third.

Perhaps:

> The base runner stole second base and raced on to third when the catcher's throw went into center field.

Newspapers have copy editors to double-check spelling and grammar, among other things. But good reporters always seek to save themselves embarrassment by double-checking their work before submitting it. The fact that a story will be seen by a copy editor is no excuse for errors.

Many reporters seem to have been bad spellers from birth, but they still manage to turn in clean copy simply by consulting frequently with a dictionary. It usually takes less than 30 seconds to look up a word. If it's necessary to look up every word containing more than five letters, do so!

Proper names present a different problem. The best solution is to ask—twice if necessary—while reporting the story: "Was that Stephens with a *v* or with a *ph?*" (See Chapter 12, Facts.)

Grammar can be harder to check; writers must develop an ear for it. Someone whose ear for words and their correct use proves unreliable can improve by studying. *The Elements of Style*, by William Strunk Jr. and E. B. White is a good place to start.

And, please, do NOT rely on computerized spelling and grammar checks to solve all your woes. The computer may not notice the difference between *their* suitcases, which is correct, and *there* suitcases, which is both wrong and confusing. Several students of Jerry Lanson, one of one of the authors of this book, repeatedly handed in articles with attribution set apart as its own sentence. For example, " 'I love to go fishing.' She said." This attribution should follow a comma, as in, " 'I love to go fishing,' she said." When Lanson investigated, he discovered the errors were put into the students' work by a grammar check program.

Here are a few of the errors that copy editors and writing coaches complain they see too often. (This discussion is not intended as a substitute for a good grammar book; several are listed in Additional Reading.)

WHO, WHICH AND THAT

> So there was only one number *which* really counted in the debate, and that number was 1984.
>
> *The Dallas Morning News*

"The worst and most common error I run into," says Paula LaRocque, writing coach for *the Morning News*, "is a misunderstanding of the words *that* and *which*." The sentence above, which LaRocque caught and displayed in her newsletter, *F.Y.I.*, uses *which* when it should have used *that*. *Which* is used in nonessential clauses—should they be omitted, the sentence would still make sense. *That* is used in essential clauses.

Unacceptable:

The rock *which* he grabbed . . .
The car, *that* had many other dents in it, was parked in the driveway.

Acceptable:

The rock *that* he grabbed . . .
The sign, *which* had been hit many times before, . . .

Who refers to individuals only. Legislatures, field hockey teams and Barbie dolls are *whiches* or *thats*, depending on the circumstances. (*Who* is used as a subject in a sentence; *whom* replaces it as an object.)

Unacceptable:

The City Council, *who* had opposed tax increases in the past, voted unanimously for the measure.

Acceptable:

The City Council, *which* had opposed tax increases ...

VERB TENSE

The tense of the verbs in a story should be consistent. Writers should switch from one tense to another only when communicating a change in time.

Unacceptable:

The snow fell steadily for four hours. Then, suddenly, the wind picks up.

Acceptable:

The snow fell steadily for four hours. Then, suddenly, the wind picked up.

Unacceptable:

Oliver said he had no difficulty adjusting to Florida's long, hot summers. He lived there before.

Acceptable:

Oliver said he had no difficulty adjusting to Florida's long, hot summers. He had lived there before.

AGREEMENT

Here's another *Dallas Morning News* sentence that was critiqued in LaRocque's *F.Y.I.*:

About all you can do to protect yourself is to thoroughly check out *the person* who is going to do the work before you hire *them*.

Singular nouns, such as *the person*, take singular verbs and singular pronouns, such as *him* or *her*. (Changing the sentence to read "the *people* who are going to do the work" would avoid the somewhat cumbersome *him* or *her*.)

Journalists violate the rule of agreement most frequently when dealing with collective nouns. These nouns—*group*, *team* and *council* are examples—take singular verbs and should be referred to by singular pronouns even though they refer to organizations of many.

Unacceptable:

The administration says *they* oppose the plan.

Acceptable:

The administration says *it* opposes the plan.

MISPLACED MODIFIERS

Modifying clauses or phrases are comfortable in a sentence only when placed near whatever they are modifying. This sentence refers to an agent, Kalafatis, and the baseball player he represents, Honeycutt:

> Once an excellent Class AAA hitter, Kalafatis says Honeycutt's record is deceptive. ...
> *The New York Times*

Presumably it was Honeycutt, not Kalafatis, who was the excellent minor league hitter, but the clause seems to be referring to Kalafatis because it is placed next to his name.

Dangling participles—exaggerated versions of this problem—are phrases that seem to modify nothing.

Unacceptable:

After climbing into the space capsule, his instructions crackled over the radio.

Acceptable:

His instructions crackled over the radio after he had climbed into the space capsule.

PARALLEL CONSTRUCTION

Phrases used in a series must be constructed in similar fashion.

Unacceptable:

The United States Constitution guarantees all citizens the right to bear arms, vote and freedom of speech.

Acceptable:

The United States Constitution guarantees all citizens the right to bear arms, vote and speak freely.

LaRocque noted a similar problem in this sentence from the sports pages of *the Morning News*:

> All week long, New York newspapers had reported that Martin would be fired for the *fifth* time in his volcanic career and *twice* as manager of the New York Yankees.

To be parallel with *fifth*, *twice* would have to be changed to *the second*.

ADDITIONAL READING

The Elements of Style, William Strunk Jr. and E. B. White, foreword by Roger Angell, Longman; 4th edition, 2000.

Harbrace College Handbook, Horner, Webb, and Miller, Harcourt Brace & Co.; 12th edition, 1994.

The Rinehart Guide to Grammar and Usage, Bonnie Carter and Craig Skates, Harcourt Brace Jovanovich; 3rd edition, 1993.

When Words Collide: A Media Writer's Guide to Grammar & Style, Lauren Kessler and Duncan McDonald, Wadsworth, 2003.

EXERCISE A

Correct any misspelled words in the following lists.

1. dicision	2. inferrence	3. fourty	4. restaurateur	5. judgement
refered	discreet	miniscule	accomodate	liason
definate	imposter	flourescent lamp	Columbia (the country)	Iridescent
defensable	cemetary	comissioner	publicly	stupefy
parallel	drunkeness	seige	correspondence	seize
knowlege	questionaire	transend	subpoena	desperate
neccessary	leisure	soley	alright	harass
predecessor	rehersal	maintainance	homocide	ammendment
circimstance	supercede	wooly	desert (sweets)	ecstacy
suceed	performance	attendance	licence	annoint
acheive	relevant	experience	mispell	alot (many)
dispensible	innoculate	stationary (paper goods)	extraterrestial	suprise
happenned	imminent	alledged	newstand	reknowned
wieght	fertalizer	detach	bookeeper	ommission
recommend	occurrence	sacreligious	Carribean	category
likeable	accidentally	withheld	similiar	agression
seperate	wierd	committment	tommorrow	aquit
occassionally	judgement	emigrate (move to)	tyrrany	excercise
cieling	publically	phaze (disconcert)	it's (possessive pronoun)	pasttime
precede	embarrased	alchoholic	ophthamologist	Moslim

EXERCISE B

Correct any grammatical errors in the following sentences.

1. The legislator that originally nominated her said nothing in her support.
2. These are a few among the many fine restaurants which France offers the gourmet.
3. Only the car in which he was riding was damaged.
4. He said he could quit the job, but only if he can be sure of getting another one quickly.
5. The series of home and away games are expected to attract the largest crowds of the year at either university.
6. The chief operating officer conceded that both his assistant and him received large bonuses.
7. The program is for workers who were employed in smokestack industries, are unclear how to fit into the 1980s and just lost their jobs.
8. Late for school four days in a row, the teacher forced the student to stay after school.
9. The county health department is searching for anyone whom, in the course of the day, may have seen the boy.
10. Each year the number of babies grow until soon there won't be enough food on the planet, he argued.
11. She throws the car into reverse and began to back out of the driveway.
12. The prime minister thanked the members of the crew of the plane that were so skillful in handling the sudden storm.
13. She finally saw a sculpture which interested her.
14. She was so attached to the dog who she had saved, that she mentioned it in her will.
15. The fire consumed four more houses on that block, quickly raging out of control.
16. He is one of eight men who is to be awarded a prize tonight.
17. Twice winner of the Blueberry Stakes, owner Sue Friedman decided to sell the horse for $500,000.
18. The council, who seemed tired after the long session, decided to adjourn.
19. The team decided they should return to fundamentals.
20. The stolen jewel was found by a local woman wrapped in a dirty rag.

EXERCISE C

Correct any spelling errors in the following article.

A former business coleague of Albert Spellman, the Delaware accountent accused of trying to swindel an elderly, wealthy woman, testafied yesterday that Spellman had recently been reciving alot of money from an anonamous source.

Philedelphia lawyer Fred Anderson says checks for hundreds of dollars arrived for Spellman in the mail. Anderson also said that Spellman, 46, who has been indited here on charges of fraud and conspirecy, had confieded a year ago that he, Spellman, was in "financially desparate straits," and was considering filing for bankrupcy.

Spellman alledgedly made threatening phone calls to Judy James, 76, a wealthy invalid. He then, it is charged, used his personal influence to convince her to pay him sizable "fees" to stop the calls, which James beleived came from mobsters.

At the end of an intence day of prosecution questioning, Anderson, a principle prosecution witness, conceeded, "In my judgement, it is not inconceivalbe that Spellman made those phone calls."

In seperate testimony on the preceeding day, Anderson—who had been supenaed by the court—said he had seen Spellman standing nervusly by a restaurant public telephone on June 4, around the same time one of the phone threats had been recieved by James.

If convicted, Spellman will face a sentance of up to 25 years.

EXERCISE D

Correct any grammatical errors in the following articles.

ONE

A driver, apparently intoxicated, dozed off momentarily at the wheel yesterday, causing an accident which critically injured he and his small son, according to police.

John Swados, 29, a Grand Lake auto mechanic, and son Mark, 10, was in critical condition at Lakeview Hospital, after Swados, returning home on Route 9W after an office party, apparently fell asleep at the wheel, causing him to lose control of the car, according to police.

Police say Swados's car leapt over a center divider, near Lake View Road, smashes through a rail fence, before it had crashed into a tree. Swados will be charged with speeding, negligence and under the influence of alcohol, police said.

Apparently dazed by the accident, highway patrol said they found Swados wandering several hundred yards away from where the car, a 1993 Volvo, who contained his son, lodged against a tree, who police freed from the wreckage. It occurred at 4 p.m.

TWO

The American Cancer Society has announced they will launch a massive, six-year study into the causes of cancer, a project involving nearly one million Americans.

The $2 billion study—similar in scope to an earlier American Medical Association cancer study—will examine a variety of factors, including lifestyle, how much you smoke, stress and environmental factors to determine which most contributes to the formation of the malignant disease, that yearly kills over 400,000 Americans.

The project will begin Oct. 1. The American Cancer Society has selected 915,000 applicants, none of whom have a previous history of cancer after a nationwide search.

In October, each person participating in the study will fill out a detailed questionnaire outlining their lifestyle and what habits they have. Computers would be used to analyze all data. The experimental group is monitored during the next six years by the 85,000 ACS researchers, and subsequent information—including causes of death—are submitted to computer analysis.

All persons in the study, according to the ACS, are over 30 years old. A majority of them live in urban areas. A minority has families with a history of cancer.

APPENDIX
D

Analogies, Metaphors and Clichés

> Drinking wine that has been stored in a metal drum or concrete tank is like spending a warm Sunday afternoon picnicking on plastic grass and sniffing paper flowers.
> That, at least, is the opinion of Vincent Nemeth.
>
> *The Wall Street Journal*

This sprightly opening to a feature story by William Burrows about a wine barrel maker does two things well: First, it leads with unusual verve into an explanation of how important a good, wood wine barrel is to Vincent Nemeth. Second, it engages readers through the cleverness of its images.

The emphasis on simplicity and precision in the previous chapters is not meant to scare reporters away from lively writing—especially in feature stories. (See Chapter 22, Features.) The words Burrows uses are simple, precise *and* lively.

This appendix promotes a device, used by Burrows, that can help reporters make their writing more vivid—the analogy. And it warns of two traps reporters often fall into while straining to enliven their writing—the mixed metaphor and the cliché.

ANALOGIES

Malcolm Browne, a science writer for *The New York Times*, had to explain a new, extremely powerful "magnetic gun." Browne struggled to paint an understandable picture of the "current" that "creates an electromagnetic field" that drives forward "the projectile" in the gun. But a sense of the gun's power did not really come across until he interrupted these descriptions and definitions with this analogy:

> It is like launching a bullet with a lightning bolt.

Analogies help reporters explain. By comparing relatively complex things to relatively familiar things—in this case a bullet and a lightning bolt—reporters can make difficult subjects comprehensible.

And well-chosen analogies can help enliven writing as well as help enlighten readers. This carefully constructed analogy helped brighten a piece on ocean life.

> If anemones are the flowers of the sea and jellyfish the dancers, then bacteria are the janitors and recyclers.
>
> *The Providence* (R.I.) *Journal*

A warning, though: The use of analogy is not without its pitfalls, even in the hands of experienced reporters. The comparison must be apt. For example, many of the reporters covering the nuclear accident at Three Mile Island in Pennsylvania, during which some radiation leaked out of the damaged plant, compared the radiation doses nearby residents were receiving to the radiation from dental or chest X-rays. But the radiation leaking from the crippled nuclear plant hit the whole body, including presumably more vulnerable areas, while medical X-rays are targeted to selected parts of the body. The analogy was misleading. (The levels of radiation escaping from the plant might more properly have been measured against the *whole-body* radiation airline passengers or residents of Denver are exposed to because there is less atmosphere to block radiation from the sun at higher elevations.)

Analogy can also tempt reporters into exaggeration, as in this sentence from the *Asbury Park* (N.J.) *Press:*

> Area rail commuters may need the speed of a world class sprinter or the agility of a pro football player if the state's transit agency decides to go through with a plan to eliminate direct train service between the Jersey Shore and New York City.

The article that follows this rather dramatic sentence demonstrates only that the new plan would force area commuters to spend at least an additional eight minutes rushing through a crowded station. Being Peyton Manning might help, but it hardly seems like a requirement for coping with the proposed change.

If inaccuracy is the most serious error that can result from improper use of analogy, overwriting is the most common. Journalists who fancy themselves fiction writers at heart cannot seem to resist inserting a "rosy-fingered dawn" or two at the first opportunity.

Weak:

He looks, getting out of the limousine, like an inelegant giraffe struggling to shift its huge body into the parentheses created by two stately trees.

Better:

He is big enough so that he doesn't so much get out of the limousine as he unfolds.
The Washington Post

MIXED METAPHORS

Many analogies employ metaphors—figures of speech in which something is spoken of as if it were something else. (Bacteria are not, in fact, janitors.) Metaphors create images. It is important to keep these images clear and consistent. *The New Yorker* magazine found this distasteful "mixed metaphor" in a column in the (Chicago) *Sun-Times:*

> [He] is using his tongue to paint himself into a corner. . . .

The problem is that, after we have been presented with the image of someone *using his tongue*, it is hard to swallow the image of him *painting himself into a corner*. The metaphors clash.

For another example, *The* (Cleveland) *Plain Dealer* began a story with this impossible metaphor:

> Cleveland Ukrainians know great strides are taken in little steps.

Strides *are* steps. You can't take big steps in little steps.

Try to work out the images in these sentences from *The* (Paterson, N.J.) *News*:

> According to Bologna, divorce is like dying. It often puts a man on the brink of suicide.

Some mixed metaphors can have the same effect.

CLICHÉS

When writing is full of *clichés*—tired expressions that have lost their originality through overuse—readers may begin to wonder whether the writer has anything fresh to say.

Here are some of the clichés found in one short *New York Times* opinion piece written by Richard Nixon after he left office.

the week that changed the world	over the long haul
hard-headed	height of folly
with open eyes	the bottom line
bitter enemy	

Expressions add liveliness to writing—if they are spontaneous. But when reporters grab the first expression that comes to mind, their writing is likely to make readers groan.

Unacceptable:

Boston School Committeeman John J. McDonough is thousands of dollars in debt and unprepared for the Nov. 3 election—but he's *feeling on top of the world*.

The Boston Globe

"Feeling on top of the world" is such an overused expression that any color in the picture it paints vanished long ago. The reporter should have discarded this washed-out phrase and searched further. Perhaps the candidate could have been described as "smiling like a man with a few million dollars in his campaign treasury." ("Grinning like a Cheshire cat" would not do.) Sometimes it's safer simply to fall back on a more prosaic wording. "He says he is quite happy" would have summed up his mood effectively without evoking groans.

Some clichés are just moldy old proverbs:

A penny saved is a penny earned.
A stitch in time saves nine.
The grass is always greener on the other side.
He who pays the piper calls the tune.
Variety is the spice of life.

Some are metaphors that have been overused:

the cream of the crop	raining cats and dogs
a slap in the face	burning the midnight oil
give the green light	hitting the nail on the head
no holds barred	a horse of a different color
dog tired	came out smelling like a rose

Some clichés are just words—neither sayings nor metaphors—that have been used together so often that they seem inseparable:

a sigh of relief	in no uncertain terms
the rules of the game	breathless anticipation
ups and downs	sure thing
in the final analysis	finishing touches
goes without saying	loud and clear
remains to be seen	long holiday weekend
nestled in the valley	financial circles
needless to say	tension is high
powers that be	speculation was rampant
leave in a huff	fueling speculation
more of the same	fond farewell

Unacceptable:

... the question remains whether there is a demand for four fashion magazines. *Only time will tell.*

The New York Times

When is a wording a cliché? Ask how readily it comes to mind. If the expression took no effort to find, it is often best to lose it.

Instead of doing the expected with the language, good writers play with our expectations. Sports fans are used to reading about the "ceremonial throwing out of the first ball." George Vecsey, writing about two well-publicized gentlemen—George Steinbrenner and Yogi Berra— on the first day of baseball's spring training, decided to have some fun with that phrase:

... two dozen fans applauded as the two men ambled out for the ceremonial *first click of the camera.*

The New York Times

ADDITIONAL READING

Edwin Newman, On Language, Edwin Newman, Gallahad Books, 1992.

I Must Say: Edwin Newman on English, the News & Other Matters, Edwin Newman, Warner Books, 1989.

EXERCISE A

Write an analogy that could be used in a newspaper story to describe:

1. A car smashed in from the front and from behind
2. An avalanche that flattened three houses
3. A dachshund
4. A humid, 90-degree day in April
5. Dwayne Wade's leaping ability
6. A surfer riding a big wave
7. The speed of the latest personal computers
8. Heavy-metal hairstyles
9. Jon Stewart's humor
10. Paris Hilton's singing ability

EXERCISE B

Rewrite the following sentences using analogies to make them clearer or livelier.

1. The stock market was up one day, down the next and then up again the day after that.
2. Fred Taylor was an extremely large man, who at 6 feet 5 inches and 260 pounds made his second-grade students look extremely small.
3. The baseball player had more success batting against that veteran pitcher than he had against any other pitcher in the league.
4. Since the drought began last year, getting a glass of water in a downtown restaurant has been almost impossible.
5. The computer terminal consists of a keyboard with all the letters of the alphabet, numbers and a few additional symbols laid out in rows, attached to a 12 inch by 9 inch screen on which words and pictures appear.

EXERCISE C

Edit the following sentences to remove any weak analogies, mixed metaphors or clichés.

1. The teenager was in critical condition, near death's door, her doctor said.
2. The sharp winds slapped against the oil rig like a fist.
3. The alderman's plan to nip the tax in the bud apparently fell on deaf ears as the council approved it by a 6–1 vote.
4. Only time will tell whether the rule will succeed in protecting the weaker sex from discrimination.
5. He ran the mile so fast that even a cheetah would have had trouble beating him.
6. Now that he is the one skating on thin ice, the shoe is on the other foot.
7. Signs that the economy is now on a firmer footing have the mayor's advisers thinking twice about the tax increase.
8. From time immemorial disaster has always seemed to loom on the horizon.
9. Without the state chairwoman's endorsement, his chances of winning the nomination were about as good as those of a tiny, wounded puppy trying to find a place in a world full of dog haters.
10. Mother Nature unleashed a hail storm of snow on the city, leaving the sanitation department with the Herculean task of cleaning up all the white stuff.
11. The fire licked at neighboring buildings like a huge yellow bulldozer.
12. The victim was at the ripe old age of 82.
13. Police said his attempt to beat a hasty retreat failed and he fell in a hail of bullets.
14. He said the new police cars, which are faster than a line drive hitting artificial turf, look like winners.
15. Exploding budget deficits could put a brake on the economy, clouding her chances.
16. Last but not least, Alfred Dodson threw his hat into the ring in the race for governor.
17. Demonstrating that it is never over until the last out, the team chalked up the victory with a three-run rally in the last half of the ninth inning.
18. Once the speaker warmed to her subject she minced few words.
19. He played with the idea like a cat playing with a ball of string.
20. Eating the potentially cancer-causing substance would be like swallowing a huge dose of cyanide.

EXERCISE D

Edit the following story to remove any weak analogies, mixed metaphors or clichés.

The crowd gathered at City Hall let out a roar of approval as one by one the members of New Milford High School's state championship football team stepped up to receive keys to the city from Mayor Frank Lodge yesterday.

Lightning-fast running back Roger Guianos received the loudest ovation, but the approximately 200 proud-as-peacocks spectators put their hands together for each one of the 47 hard-working players and the team's three razor-sharp coaches.

When, last but not least, New Milford's tough-as-nails head coach Rod Dokawitz made it to the makeshift platform on the steps of the historic old building, the crowd stood as one to applaud the entire squad. New Milford's loyal fans made more noise than the A bomb at Hiroshima.

"If only you could have beaten Fairfield, then maybe we'd have something to celebrate," a grinning Mayor Lodge quipped. New Milford suffered a heartbreaking defeat at the hands of Fairfield High School in the opening game of the season before chalking up 10 straight victories, including the wipe out of Lincoln Central in the state championship game Saturday.

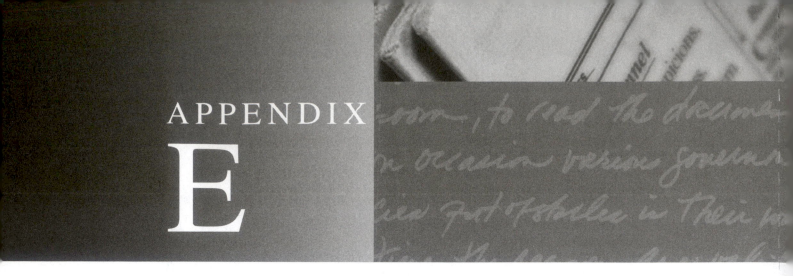

APPENDIX E

Ethics

Reporters, out on the town for a night together, often regale each other with tales of their adventures in gathering the news. But as the evening wears on, the bragging and joking may be replaced by soul searching: Was it wise to accept that free trip to Detroit to see that new car? Was the newspaper right to pay that prisoner a little something for an interview? Was I justified in getting the mayor's assistant to talk without identifying myself as a reporter? Was it fair to print that story about the mayor's drinking?

Unlike doctors, lawyers and certified public accountants, journalists do not have to pass licensing exams. The only rules they are bound by are their newspaper's policy, a handful of state and federal laws (See The Basics, Section F, Law) ... and their own consciences.

Some of the ethical decisions faced by journalists are straightforward: They should never pass off even a sentence of someone else's writing as their own. They must stick to the facts. They should never attack without solid proof. They should not distort the meaning of the quotes they use. They should struggle to be fair. They should honor their pledges to sources. Most of these principles of responsible journalism are outlined in previous chapters. (See Chapter 2, Fairness; Chapter 7, Quotations; Chapter 12, Facts; Chapter 15, Sources.) That does not mean the principles are always followed. But when trampled, as in the notorious case of former *New York Times* reporter Jayson Blair, the entire profession suffers.

Beyond these basic principles, however, the ethical calls get tougher. Many large newspapers and journalism associations have drawn up codes of ethics. Some have been around for the better part of a century. When closely scrutinized, however, these codes tend to dissolve into a pool of platitudes. Most, for example, speak reverently of the "public's right to know." But the right to know what? How? Does the public have the right to know that the governor frequents massage parlors? Does that right to know give journalists the right to pretend to be patrons of a massage parlor in an attempt to find out what the governor is doing there? These noble-sounding pronouncements, when applied to the real world, solve few ethical issues. They leave journalists disagreeing, sometimes vigorously.

What follows are some guidelines that we hope will help untangle, if not resolve, some of these arguments.

FREEBIES

Lunchtime and Christmas are two tempting occasions for reporters. At lunch they are vulnerable to check grabbers; before Christmas, to gift givers. Picking up a tab or dropping off a bottle of scotch are common and accepted practices in the business world. Reporters interviewing the health and safety officer of a chemical plant over lunch are likely to be greeted with "Don't be silly!" when they reach for the check. Reporters covering the courts may find a nicely wrapped bottle of Chivas Regal at their doorstep around December 18th with a little card saying, "Seasons Greetings from Flannery, Rivera and Blumenthal"—a local law firm.

Good meals and good scotch aren't cheap. Is there anything wrong with accepting these gifts? Many top editors say "Yes."

Few reporters are so hungry or thirsty that they can be bought by these relatively minor kindnesses. It is not that editors fear that their people will suddenly decide to leave out all quotes from the union about working conditions in that chemical plant or that someone will write a piece extolling the legal skills and good taste of Messieurs Flannery, Rivera and Blumenthal. Rather, many editors fear the subtle effects small favors may have on reporters—perhaps an inclination to give the gift giver a call on a story, when a number of other equally good sources would do. And these editors also fear even the hint that the news columns of their paper are for sale.

The safest strategy for any reporter, no matter what the paper's policy, is either to split the bill or to pick up the tab the first time and allow the source to return the favor the next time around. As for that Christmas gift, it should be returned with a gracious note: "Thanks for your thoughtfulness, but I'm sorry, I am not able to accept any gifts from a source."

Resisting the temptation becomes a bit tougher when the gift is an all-expense-paid trip to Palm Springs to preview the opening of the Sunswept Inn or to Mexico to observe filming of Movie Inc.'s latest feature. Reporters, particularly on smaller papers, ask, "How else can we afford to go to these places to write these stories?" The answer is that maybe there is no other way; but reporters who accept such *junkets* clearly are allowing the freebies to affect their decisions on what is news. These reporters are also leaving themselves vulnerable to a subtle pressure: They may feel a touch uncomfortable panning the resort or movie after being treated so kindly by its sponsors.

Readers deserve to be assured that the stories they are reading were selected because they were newsworthy, not because they came prepaid. And reporters must try to eliminate as many as possible of the slightly "uncomfortable" feelings that might slant, or give the appearance of slanting, their work.

Reporters are offered freebies for a reason, and that is exactly the reason they should be turned down.

CHECKBOOK JOURNALISM

Money, of course, can change hands in either direction. News organizations, striving for a competitive edge, have more than once paid for news. Some of the returning American hostages from Iran in 1981 were showered with gifts in the hope they would agree to exclusive interviews. Convicted mass murderer Charles Manson and H. R. Haldeman, who was convicted of Watergate-related crimes, both received five-figure payments from networks in exchange for interviews. Such propositions are made in local reporting as well, though the price tags will be lower. Police informants, for example, are just as happy to sell their information to reporters as to police. Is there anything wrong with slipping them a couple of twenties? We think plenty.

Money distorts both the news and the news judgment of reporters and editors. Sources who know they can hold out for cash before telling their stories will ignore all but the wealthiest news organizations and may be tempted to embellish their story a bit to up the ante. Editors and television producers who have paid for news may feel compelled to promote the story and to play it prominently—even if the story turns out to be a dud.

Perhaps there may come a time when the public's interest in learning something is so overwhelming that a news organization must decide to pay for it. But when someone asks journalists for money, their first inclination should always be to say "No."

CONFLICT OF INTEREST

A newspaper's reporter on consumer affairs writes an investigative series on local supermarkets. A leading supermarket, among the largest advertisers on the paper, rings the publisher and threatens to withdraw its advertising unless the series is stopped. The series is stopped.

A young reporter, on his first full day at work, is handed a press release from a major local retailer announcing that the company has filed for bankruptcy. But the release artfully avoids the uncomfortable word "bankruptcy." The reporter dutifully fills in the holes in the press release and clarifies what is going on. He is fired for not following orders to run the press release exactly as written—the newspaper had apparently agreed to do that as a favor to the retailer, one of its biggest advertisers.

These stories both are true. The supermarket investigation was killed in the *New York Post*. The young reporter was fired by the *Trenton* (N.J.) *Times*.

Newspapers are major local businesses, depending on advertising from other local businesses to survive at the same time that they report on issues that will affect those local businesses. Publishers who care to maintain the integrity and reputation of their papers learn early to say "No" politely but firmly when friends and advertisers ask them to tinker with the news. However, there are publishers, particularly on struggling newspapers, who will place their advertisers ahead of the integrity of the news columns. Reporters on such papers have little choice but to protest loudly and to move on if their protestations are ignored. Fortunately, many do take a stand. After the supermarket series was stopped in the *Post*, most of the paper's reporters went on a "byline strike"—they refused to allow their bylines to appear in the paper. After that *Trenton Times* reporter was fired, a quarter of the news staff quit.

Reporters also run the risk of getting entangled in their own webs of conflict. A reporter is a citizen with political and economic interests who will report on issues with political and economic impact. Like their publishers, reporters must be strong enough to resist the tug of any interest that might compromise their paper's commitment to unblinking coverage.

Reporters must resist the *appearance* of conflict as well. A police reporter should not be an honorary member of the PBA. A political reporter should not be helping to plan strategy for one of the candidates. A business reporter should not be moonlighting by writing press releases for a local corporation. And a city hall reporter should not be having an affair with the mayor's press secretary.

No matter how committed to fair and objective reporting these journalists may believe themselves to be, they owe it to their readers and to their papers to avoid—that phrase again—*even the appearance* of bias. *New York Times* editors demoted their wine critic when they learned that a book he had written was sponsored by a wine company. The critic had written nothing that compromised his integrity, but this business connection with a company he would have to write about gave the appearance of a conflict of interest. That was enough for *Times* editors.

MISREPRESENTATION

This is a classic "gray area," one in which the end is frequently held as justifying the means. The rule seems simple: Reporters should always introduce themselves as reporters *before* they begin an interview. But there are rare occasions when that rule will be violated.

The (Chicago) *Sun-Times* once had its reporters actually open a bar—The Mirage, they called it—to expose the under-the-table payments that saloon owners were asked to pay inspectors in Chicago. The reporters manning the bar certainly did not warn every corrupt inspector who walked into the place that the bartenders were journalists. Other reporters have posed as assembly-line workers, nurses in mental hospitals and college students.

So back to that simple rule: Reporters must introduce themselves as reporters before they begin interviewing someone except ... when? Many editors who have confronted this question have settled on this not entirely satisfactory answer: First, they say, it is rarely ethical to make believe you are someone else. But it may be justified if the story is of overriding interest and importance to the public and if there is *no* other way to get it. (Some editors wouldn't agree here; the *Sun-Times* missed out on one of journalism's top awards, reportedly because some members of the Pulitzer prize jury questioned the ethics of the whole "Mirage" operation.)

Certainly, it would have to be an awfully important story, and a carefully thought-out situation, before reporters allowed themselves to start playing make-believe. It might be acceptable to sidle up to an assistant to the mayor in a bar without revealing who you are if that seems the only way to check on reports that the mayor has been accepting kickbacks from contractors. It wouldn't be acceptable to pull that subterfuge in search of a mere scoop on the mayor's upcoming speech to the city council.

On the rare occasions when they are hiding their true identities, reporters must go out of their way to protect the innocent people they are duping into giving them information. Reporters should not print the admissions, confidings or tips of any person interviewed under false pretenses without, at a minimum, returning under their true identities as reporters to get the reaction and comments of the people they've tricked. And innocent people surreptitiously coaxed into participating—the honest nurse in a crooked abortion clinic, the inspector who doesn't take bribes but tells of those who do—should not be quoted without their agreement. It would not be fair to use their names, perhaps costing them their jobs, in passing on loose talk they had presumed was being shared with a coworker or bartender.

Television programs and movies might make it appear that "undercover" journalism is glamorous and commonplace. Occasionally such deception is necessary, but were it more common, the country would be facing, in effect, a secret police of undercover journalists waiting to trap people into mistakes. As a rule, people deserve to know when what they're saying could wind up on the front page of a newspaper. It requires truly extraordinary circumstances to warrant depriving potential sources of that basic right.

PRIVATE LIVES

Our personal secrets do not belong in the newspaper unless they somehow become newsworthy. The problem, again, is defining when that is. Should a reporter write that a congressman has a penchant for brunettes and martinis after work? The courts would probably protect the reporter's right to print that information. They accord public figures little right to privacy. (See The Basics, Section F, Law.) But most journalists would say that ethically the information should *not* be printed if the brunettes and martinis are not interfering with the congressman's work ... even if he's married. But if the women had no-show federal jobs or if the congressman's drinking began keeping him out of the office for days at a time, the answer would change. The private lives of public officials *should* be discussed in public *if* their outside activities affect how they are serving their constituents.

People who have *not* accepted positions of trust should get more protection. A profile of an up-and-coming young businesswoman should not mention the fact that she has a gambling problem. That aspect of her private life is not the public's business. However, should that businesswoman be arrested for embezzlement, her gambling becomes newsworthy and would, if it can be proven, be mentioned.

Rules such as these, of course, can be difficult to apply. What if that congressman just misses a few days of work a month and seems somewhat foggy but not clearly disoriented? What if that gambling businesswoman gets appointed head of the local Chamber of Commerce?

In this appendix we have presented some guidelines for journalistic behavior. We won't pretend that these guidelines will solve all the specific problems with which journalists will be confronted. When puzzling out individual problems, journalists should err, if they're going to err, on the side of the people about whom they are reporting. If it's unclear whether the public needs to know, it's better to lose the scoop and save a person's reputation. In all these ethical decisions, there is no substitute for a healthy conscience.

ADDITIONAL READING

Crises of Conscience: Journalism Ethics, Carl Hausman, HarperCollins, 1991.

The Mission: Journalism, Ethics and the World, Joseph B. Atkins, Iowa State Press, 2002.

The Press Effect: Politicians, Journalists, and the Stories That Shape the Political World, Kathleen Hall Jamieson and Paul Waldman, Oxford University Press, 2002.

The Elements of Journalism: What News People Should Know and the Public Should Expect, Bill Kovach and Tom Rosenstiel, Three Rivers Press, 2001.

Ethics and Media Culture, David Berry, Focal Press, 2000.

F

Law

If laws affecting the press make many journalists uncomfortable, it may be because journalists are aware that in too many countries, for too many centuries, such laws have been used to prevent the press from challenging or even disturbing the powerful. Reporters have only to examine some of the less liberal parts of the world today, or look into the early histories of their own countries, to see journalists operating in a legal straitjacket. The wording of the First Amendment—the guarantor of a free press in the United States—makes clear how concerned some of the country's first leaders were with protecting the press from legal restraints. It reads, in part: "Congress shall make no law … abridging the freedom … of the press."

The courts responsible for applying such 18th-century pronouncements to the modern world have usually interpreted the First Amendment as a shield against *prior restraint* of the news media. Recent arguments invoking national security have nudged the courts back a bit from this interpretation, but, in general, the first principle of our free press is that the government cannot *in advance* stop anyone from publishing.

However, the First Amendment has not been interpreted as preventing legislatures and courts from surrounding journalists with an intricate web of laws that both affect their ability to gather information and establish their liabilities *after* material has been published. The majority of journalists probably would agree that most—though not all—of these laws and interpretations of laws are consistent with the precepts of responsible journalism. Some help define those precepts.

Whether or not journalists agree with these laws, they must live with them. It is risky and foolish to try to function as an aggressive journalist in the United States without first gaining some familiarity with the laws affecting journalists. These statutes will rarely be in the foreground as reporters go about their business, but they will often be in the background.

This appendix provides a brief overview of the subject; we encourage you to turn to the Additional Readings for sources that will provide a more complete briefing. And local libraries and press associations should be approached for copies of relevant state and local laws.

LIBEL

The news can hurt. A front-page story reporting allegations that a doctor has had patients die because of negligence can cost that doctor her practice; a report that a teacher is a member of the Nazi Party can lead to the loss of his job; the printing of a charge that a local housewife is a prostitute can permanently damage her reputation. All these charges are "defamatory," to use the legal term. They may cause their subjects to be, again using legal terminology, "shunned or avoided" or "exposed to public hatred and contempt or ridicule" or "injured in their occupation."

Some words are almost automatically defamatory. Anyone who has been publicly labeled a burglar, drunkard, gangster or plagiarist presumably has been exposed to public contempt. Bigamist, crook, drug addict, fascist and Mafia member are but a few of the other words that would fall into this category.

Still other words may prove defamatory if leveled against certain people in certain circumstances. There would appear to be little sting in the charge that a minister was driving a car, but if that minister belongs to a religious group that does not believe in driving cars, the charge may in fact be defamatory.

Potentially defamatory stories must be handled with extreme care. People who believe that they have been injured in print may press for damages in a *libel* suit. Nonetheless, it is crucial to remember that there is nothing wrong with defaming somebody in a newspaper if proper care has been exercised in reporting and writing the story. If that doctor *has* had patients die because of negligence, if that teacher *is* an avowed member of the Nazi Party, if that homemaker *was* convicted of prostitution, then fine. As a reporter you can say, "I defamed you and I'm glad. What I wrote is true."

Truth is always the best defense in libel cases. If the story can be proven true, then the newspaper and reporter should win. Reporters should be aware, though, that the courts set particularly high standards of proof. With complex stories—a day-care worker accused of child abuse, perhaps—"truth" can be hard to prove, and the "proof" very much open to interpretation. Typically, editors try to minimize the risk of a libel suit by consulting lawyers before highly sensitive stories run.

Regrettably, even the most responsible and thorough reporting is not a guarantee against being sued. Anyone can sue for libel, and the cost of mounting a defense can be high, regardless of the outcome. Some legal experts fear that a recent spate of expensive libel judgments against the press has begun to inhibit sound investigative reporting. It can be hoped that the best newspapers, instead of being cowed by the number of libel cases and the size of some judgments, will redouble their efforts to establish truth.

But the point for beginning reporters to remember is that incomplete and sloppy reporting of stories can attract libel suits just as icy sidewalks attract negligence suits. And if someone's reputation *has* been hurt, and if the facts are *not* on the reporter's side, a newspaper may lose such a suit. It's not acceptable to ruin that doctor's reputation on the basis of just a few complaints by disgruntled patients. The reporter also had better not confuse Dr. Althea White with Dr. Doria White in writing the story. Such inaccuracy invites a libel suit and demands the printing of an immediate and prominent retraction.

However, if the reporter handles the facts carefully and bases the story on interviews with dozens of patients and colleagues and on death certificates and other hospital documents—in short, if the reporter has found proof—then the story has to be printed and the lawyers trusted, if necessary, to demonstrate its soundness in court.

Besides truth, there are three other, less noble, defenses against libel actions. The first is *privilege*. In general, reporters are responsible for the accuracy of everything in their stories, including direct quotations. Reporters can't base a libel defense on the fact that they merely quoted a colleague calling that teacher a Nazi. Careful attribution is little help here. But the law does give reporters the *privilege* of reporting on some events without fear of losing a libel action as long as the reporting is considered fair and accurate. Statements made in court or by public officials during official proceedings fall into this category.

Such a privilege exists because of the belief that people need to be able to talk freely in court or in other governmental proceedings and that the public has the right to know what was said.

If that teacher was accused of being a Nazi in court or by the mayor at a city council meeting, the allegations could be printed. (The charge in court will be scrutinized by the justice system; the reporter's obligation is only to keep up with the proceedings. The mayor's charge, even though it was privileged, still should be checked out and the teacher given a chance to respond. During the 1950s, reporters' failure to check out privileged charges made by Joseph McCarthy on the floor of the U.S. Senate helped spread the lawmaker's wild accusations about Communists in government.)

The courts also protect journalists who in the course of writing reviews or opinion pieces level what is called *fair comment and criticism* against the people they are discussing. This is another possible defense against libel. A critic can write that "a windup doll programmed to deliver lines on cue would have given a more satisfying performance," although such a statement obviously cannot be proved true. The courts have ruled, however, that placing yourself in the public eye as an actor does mean subjecting yourself to such criticism. Yet, it would not be defensible to charge that actor, without proof, with being drunk on stage. Such substantive allegations about the person's life go beyond fair criticism of a public performance.

The courts also have added a First Amendment defense intended to make sure journalists aren't prevented from criticizing anyone—particularly officials—by the threat of a libel judgment. Private citizens, they have ruled, must show that the journalist has been negligent—for example, that he or she failed to exercise reasonable care in reporting and writing. To win libel suits, public officials, along with some public figures, are required to demonstrate not only that they've been defamed and that the charge was false, but also either that the journalist knew the charge was false or that the journalist acted "in reckless disregard" of whether the charge was true or false.

This final libel defense was intended in particular to protect the press's right to investigate the powerful. Still, reporters do not want to have to fall back on the excuse that they were merely wrong, not negligent, deceitful or reckless in their reporting.

Libel, with the rarest of exceptions, falls under civil law. No one is likely to go to jail for libeling someone else. Nevertheless, successful libel suits can cost hundreds of thousands, even millions of dollars. Fear of litigation, however, is no excuse for timidity in digging up dirt. What the threat of libel should do is underline the need for care, accuracy and diligence in the excavation of that dirt.

PRIVACY

The courts have ruled that there is little privacy in news (though journalists might decide to keep some of the personal facts they dig up out of their stories for ethical reasons—see The Basics Section E, Ethics). Facts publicly obtained about a victim, suspect or witness that are pertinent to a breaking news story are, legally at least, fair game for reporters. Similarly, the courts have ruled that people who have injected themselves into the news—politicians, entertainers, athletes—have surrendered a fair degree of their right to privacy.

However, the courts draw the line at *intrusion* into people's homes in search of damaging information, at descriptions of people's private lives that portray them in a *false light*, and at stories that dredge up embarrassing facts about people whose actions are not considered newsworthy. A reporter, for example, might risk being judged liable for invasion of privacy for sneaking into a woman's living room in an attempt to find evidence that she is a bad mother, for misrepresenting the condition of her living room, or for poking into the private affairs of her family for no good, or newsworthy, reason in the first place.

Privacy law is rarely a concern in the daily reporting of news, but it may have to be considered in the course of working on an investigative piece or an unusually intimate profile.

PROTECTING SOURCES

You are working on an article about drug use at the local high school, and some students agree to discuss the situation with you on background. (See Chapter 15, Sources.) You agree not to use their names, but when the piece appears you find yourself asked to appear before a grand jury investigating drug sales in town. The prosecutor wants names. You explain that you can't violate your pledge to your sources. The judge responds that you have the same legal responsibility to testify about potential crimes as any other citizen and that you can be held in contempt of court if you refuse. Still, you won't break your word to your sources. Can the judge hold you in contempt of court?

Maybe. The Supreme Court has ruled that the First Amendment gives reporters *no* special right to avoid testifying in court. In response, more than 30 states have passed laws, called *shield laws*, bestowing on reporters the right to shield their sources in court. Sometimes, however, these laws turn out to provide less than perfect protection in the event of challenges in court, and they don't apply in federal courts. Then *New York Times* reporter Judith Miller spent 12 weeks in jail for refusing to name a source before a federal grant jury investigating allegations that the White House had leaked national security material. Even in states with shield laws, reporters have spent time in jail for protecting their sources.

Two basic needs of a democratic society are in conflict here. On one side is the need for a system of journalism in which reporters can investigate the underside of society without being used as surrogate police who will betray their sources at the drop of a subpoena. On the other side is the need for citizens to cooperate with the criminal justice system and the right of the accused to have a fair trial based on a full review of the evidence.

Without assurance of protection, journalists argue, sources aware of wrongdoing in government or in society would be less likely to come forward, inhibiting journalists in fulfilling their role as watchdogs on government. In support of their argument, journalists point to the First Amendment.

But how, counter lawyers, can prosecutors build a case or defense attorneys assure their clients a fair trial when journalists are allowed to withhold evidence that bears on the case? They cite the Sixth Amendment, guaranteeing everyone the right to a fair trial.

Judges, for the most part, have sided with those who believe the press has no special right to withhold potential evidence. And when forced to choose between their promises of anonymity to sources and the risk of going to jail, most reporters have chosen jail. This means that reporters investigating potentially criminal behavior may have to decide *before* they agree to accept information on background, deep background or off the record (see Chapter 15, Sources) whether they are prepared to risk a stay in jail to protect the anonymity of the source of that information.

Just to complicate matters, the Supreme Court has also ruled that reporters' pledges to their sources are like contracts—so reporters can be sued for violating them. If reporters feel they are caught in the middle here, they probably are right.

ACCESS

Reporters need to be at the meeting, to visit the scene, to sit in the courtroom, to read the documents. But on occasion government agencies put obstacles in their way. Sometimes the reasons are valid: the need to protect a reporter's safety, the need to protect a person's privacy, the need to prevent jeopardizing an investigation or a bidding process. The presence of numerous reporters, wielding bright television lights, as U.S. troops landed in camouflage gear on the beach in Somalia, certainly seemed to represent misuse of access by reporters. Sometimes, however, the reasons for denying reporters access are invalid: a desire to keep the public in the dark, to avoid the inconvenience of public debate or the heat of public anger.

Occasionally reporters get special privileges such as the right to cross police lines or to sit in special sections at meetings or trials. But usually they can attend or read only what the public can attend or read. In recent decades both public and press have been beneficiaries of new laws that expand the right of the public to monitor the activities of its leaders, laws that make some of the obstacles illegal.

Probably the most important of these laws is the federal Freedom of Information Act. This law sets up a process for obtaining access to documents of the federal executive branch and restricts the government's right to withhold documents from the public. The final say, when there's a dispute, rests with the courts. The FOI Act, as it is known, does not give reporters carte blanche to rifle the files of government, though its opponents like to say that it does. The law delineates nine categories of information the government can refuse to release, including properly classified documents, files from ongoing criminal investigations, personnel and medical files, and certain inter- and intra-agency memoranda. An appeals procedure is built into the act, but often reporters must be willing to hunker down for months to gain access to material with which a government agency is reluctant to part.

Still, the act has been used effectively as the basis for more than one investigative series. Jack Taylor, now with *The Denver Post*, filed nearly a thousand FOI requests while working on a series on the Bureau of Indian Affairs for *The Daily Oklahoman* in Oklahoma City in 1980. A thorough explanation of how the FOI Act can be used is contained in *The Reporter's Handbook*.

All 50 states now have their own public records laws, often called *sunshine laws*, designed to ensure the public access to a wide variety of the paperwork produced by state and local governments. The federal government and most states now also have laws requiring that most of the meetings of deliberative and decision-making bodies—city councils, school boards, committees—be open to the press. These laws generally allow the officials to close the door to the public and press *only* when they will be discussing personnel matters, business transactions, litigation or investigations of wrongdoing.

Though these laws can help reporters monitor government and uncover corruption or just plain incompetence, they are of little value unless reporters know them well enough to hold officials to them. That's why many reporters carry copies of these laws in their wallets.

The court system, meanwhile, has its own standards of access: trials, hearings and appellate proceedings are open to the press and public except in exceptional circumstances—perhaps the need to protect the identity of a secret witness. Grand jury hearings and judges' deliberations are closed to press and public.

Upon occasion judges, presumably concerned with protecting defendants from damaging pretrial publicity, have imposed *gag orders*, not only forbidding lawyers to talk, which is a judge's right, but forbidding reporters from reporting. These attempts—essentially efforts to impose prior restraint on the press—would seem to be violations of the First Amendment, and they have consistently been overturned on those grounds when appealed to higher courts. The Supreme Court has ruled that judges should shelter jurors or potential jurors either by denying them access to the news media during a trial or by changing the location of a trial, not by attempting to censor the news.

In combating gag orders, as in other areas in which the law touches their work, the best defense reporters have is a clear knowledge of their rights.

ADDITIONAL READING

The Associated Press Stylebook and Briefing on Media Law, The Associated Press, Norm Goldstein, editor, Perseus Books Group, 2002.

Communications Law, John D. Zelezny, Wadsworth Thomson, 2001.

The First Amendment, Daniel A. Farber, Foundation Press, 1998.

First Amendment Law, Gerald Gunter and Kathleen M. Sullivan, Foundation Press, 1999.

The Good Guys, the Bad Guys and the First Amendment, Fred Friendly, Random House, 1975.

Law of Mass Communications, Freedom and Control of Print and Broadcast Media, Bill Loving and Dwight L. Teeter Jr., Foundation Press, 2004.

Major Principles in Media Law, Wayne Overbeck, Harcourt Brace, 1998.

The News Media & the Law, published quarterly by the Reporters Committee for Freedom of the Press, Washington, D.C.

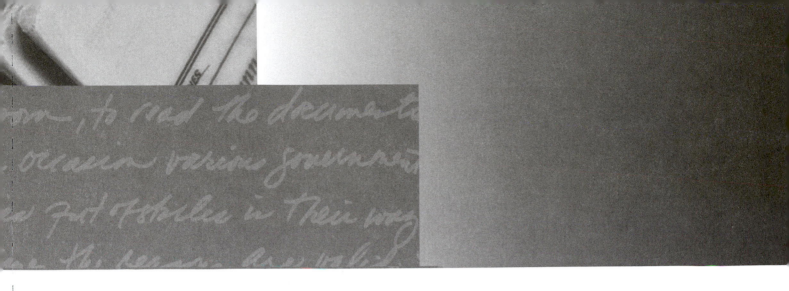

Index